Japanese Management in the Low Growth Era

Between External Shocks and Internal Evolution

Springer
Berlin
Heidelberg
New York
Barcelona
Hong Kong
London
Milan
Paris
Singapore
Tokyo

Daniel Dirks · Jean-François Huchet
Thierry Ribault (Eds.)

Japanese Management in the Low Growth Era

Between External Shocks and Internal Evolution

With 50 Figures
and 44 Tables

Springer

Dr. Daniel Dirks
Deutsches Institut für Japanstudien
Nissei Kōjimachi Bldg.
3-3-6 Kudan-Minami, Chiyoda-ku
Tōkyō 102-0074
Japan

Dr. Jean-François Huchet
Centre d'Etudes Français sur la Chine Contemporaine
Yu Yuet Lai Bldg., Room 304
43–55 Whyndham Street
Central, Hong Kong

Dr. Thierry Ribault
IFRESI-CNRS
2, rue des Cannoniers
F-59800 Lille
France

ISBN 3-540-64035-5 Springer-Verlag Berlin Heidelberg New York

Library of Congress Cataloging-in-Publication Data
Die Deutsche Bibliothek – CIP-Einheitsaufnahme
Japanese management in the low growth era: between external shocks and internal evolution / Daniel Dirks ... (ed.). – Berlin; Heidelberg; New York; Barcelona; Hong Kong; London; Milan; Paris; Singapore; Tokyo: Springer, 1999
ISBN 3-540-64035-5

Printed in Germany

Hardcover-Design: Erich Kirchner, Heidelberg

SPIN 10665030 42/2202-5 4 3 2 1 0 – Printed on acid-free paper

Preface

Ever since the abrupt end of the notorious *bubble economy* at the beginning of the 1990s, Japan's firms have been subjected to continuous pressures to reconsider their investment and market strategies, to restructure their organizations, and to overhaul their existing human resource management practices. What only a few years ago was hailed as one of the most advanced enterprise systems, is now being criticized as outdated, non-innovative, and too costly. Japan's business corporations clearly are in the midst of a search for new strategic opportunities and for re-creating the building blocks underlying their competitiveness, albeit arguably in different directions and at a varying speed depending on the industry concerned, individual firms' past experiences and current performance, and their degree of exposure to the global competition.

Just where the famous Japanese management or enterprise model will be heading from here must be of considerable concern both for researchers and practitioners alike; after all, one should not lose sight of the fact that we are dealing with the world's second largest national economy, and developments in Japan more likely than not will have a considerable impact on industries and firms elsewhere as well.

The future of the Japanese management system therefore was the focus of a conference (*Between external shocks and internal evolution: Towards a new phase in Japanese management practices*), bringing together for the first time three European research institutions located in Japan as co-organizers: the Deutsches Institut für Japanstudien (DIJ), the Maison Franco-Japonaise (MFJ), and the Istituto Italiano di Kyōto. Consequently, and as retraceable throughout the individual papers of this book, this event introduced a more European perspective to the discussion of corporate affairs in Japan, a debate that in the past has all too often been dominated by its reference to, and comparison with, the North American management model. Under the competent guidance of Daniel Dirks (DIJ), Jean François Huchet (MFJ) and Thierry Ribault (MFJ), the conference was specifically designed to bring together experts on the Japanese situation and commentators with no particular Japan expertise, who would relate current reorganization strategies and trends in Japanese firms to their own countries, mainly European, their firms often facing similar competitive challenges and environmental jolts.

The results of this insightful and, we believe, very fruitful exchange of academic analysis and practical orientation are reproduced in this volume. Daniel Dirks has undertaken the arduous task of organizing and managing the actual editing of the numerous papers. We would also wish to thank Mr. Horst Plambeck, Trier/Germany, for his professional support concerning the overall lay-out work, assuring that the book could be published within one year after the conference. Our gratitude goes to Mr. Haruo Hayashi (MFJ) and Ms. Michaela Lincke (DIJ) for their smooth coordination of the many organizational tasks surrounding such an event. Finally, we would like to acknowledge the generous support for this conference by the Japan Foundation, the EU-Japan Centre for Industrial Cooperation Tōkyō, the EU Commission (DG1), the CNRS, as well as the German and the French embassy in Tōkyō. The Friedrich-Ebert-Foundation contributed both to the conference as well as to the publication of this book.

Irmela Hijiya-Kirschnereit
Deutsches Institut für Japanstudien Tōkyō

Michael Ehrke
Friedrich-Ebert-Stiftung Tōkyō

Contents

Section 2
Corporate Governance and Control

Section 3
Industrial Organization

Section 4
Human Resource Management

Managing in a Low Growth Era—
The End of Managerial Idiosyncrasies?

Jean-François HUCHET, *Daniel* DIRKS *and Thierry* RIBAULT

The crisis in Japan lingers on. In the course of 1996, after five long years of uncertainty and flagging growth rates, a glimmer of hope was showing up on the horizon; but then, in October 1997, the Asian financial crisis plunged Japan into one of the most severe recessions that the country has experienced since the post-war period. Medium-term forecasts are almost unanimous in their pessimism. If there is any growth at all, it will be very weak; businesses are expected to be hit by low domestic demand and a slowdown in exports to the Asian market. As for the financial sector, even though a *big bang* has been decreed, it is likely still to be up against those old demons: bad debt, allegiance to politicians and bureaucrats, and outdated rules and regulations.

All added up, before any new, sustained period of growth begins, at least ten years will have gone by since the financial *bubble* burst. It is a long enough period of time for many people to come out with dire warnings about the end of the 'atypical' Japanese miracle, which has for so long defied the textbooks on neo-classic economics; long enough for many, more seriously, to speculate about Japan's definitive loss of economic hegemony in Asia, partly to the benefit of the United States and Europe, but above all to that of the Chinese giant with 'feet of clay'—the giant that carries on regardless, on its unswerving path towards modernization and growth.

However, set against Japan's contemporary economic history, this has also been a very short period. Japan, like all the other great industrial nations, has known periods of intense change in its social and economic structures. One has only to delve into the economic history textbooks to realize the almost ceaseless adaptation of management practices in Japanese firms since the Meiji restoration. Only Japan's spectacular success after the Second World War, and its rise to become the world's second strongest economic power, could have allowed us to assume that these firms were based on a stable and, in the past, unchangeable model.

In this context, what impact has this decade had on Japanese management methods? Is this a lost decade, or is it rather a period of creative adaptation? Does this decade promise deep and irreversible changes to the effect of what went on in 1860 or in the years following the Second World War, or are we witnessing only minor changes? Assuming that evolution is taking place, are we dealing here with convergence and with the alignment of Japanese management methods with Anglo-Saxon practices and, by that very fact, have we seen the end of Japan's idiosyncrasy in its management methods?

An international conference was jointly held in Tōkyō by the German Institute for Japanese Studies Tōkyō and the Maison Franco-Japonaise, in November 1997, at which Japanese, European and North American researchers were brought together in precisely this context and with regard to this generic order of questions. This book is based on the outcome of that conference. The analysis that is developed here sets out from a micro-economic point of view to focus on Japanese enterprises. However we did not want to hear only from managers or to restrict ourselves to analysing specific Japanese management recipes that have become known around the world, such as 'just-in-time' or quality control on the production line. Quite the opposite: specialists in industrial economics, finance, innovation as well as experts on Japan's pension system were also invited to present their views.

It seemed to us that through the Japanese enterprise could be discerned a range of interconnected questions: human resource management; relations between firms, leading on to an analysis of industrial groups, and particularly of multinationalization; subcontracting relationships; the evolving stance of small and medium-sized enterprises in their relations with the dominant companies; corporate strategies for their internal organization; the evolution of corporate governance and finance. We have therefore been able to widen the analysis to elements outside the individual firm, to incorporate the role of such institutions as banks, and to discuss the future of pension funds, or even the work ethic. Most of the contributions have thus maintained an approach that perceives the enterprise as an organization rooted in and influenced by the environment—political, institutional, social and international—within which it operates.

We also wished to decompartmentalize the studies carried out in the manufacturing area and those carried out in the service industries. After all, the service industries now occupy a more important place in Japan than manufacturing, with management methods developed in services that are sometimes different from *Toyotism*.

At the same time it is important to place the problems or adaptations identified within Japanese firms into an *international perspective*. In each of the areas examined (finance, organization, corporate governance etc.) we have asked European and North American specialists to provide a commentary on the chapters devoted to the situation in Japan. Of course, international comparisons can be made only with the greatest care, due to compatibility problems with the nomenclature, and with differing contexts, be they institutional, historical or political. However, such comparisons enable us to look outside Japan's too-often-promoted image, namely, of its being an exception. The results are the more convincing, in that our comparisons have mainly been made with various European countries, and not, as in most other cases, exclusively with the United States. In fact, the United States is used too often in comparisons with Japan, as a yardstick for companies' different ways of working and, by that very fact, for the adjustments to be made in a period of crisis. The comparison with various European countries has enabled us to transform Japan's status as an exception, acquired through comparisons with America, into one of *individuality:* the organization of Japanese firms is one model among others existing in different countries in Europe, who in turn see themselves differently from the model prevailing in the United States. This kind of comparison has also enabled us to stress the fact that Japanese firms are not the only ones to have carried out changes in their way of working so as to keep pace with evolution both at home and abroad.

Lastly, the contributions and commentaries presented at the conference have been revised and regrouped around certain themes and questions we thought important to deal with in this introduction.

The issues

Before getting into the analysis of the recent upheavals that Japanese enterprises have had to cope with, and their reactions to them, it seemed timely for us to ask each contributor for an 'inventory' accompanied by a brief historical review for each of the fields being studied. The exercise has proved interesting, in that it has given us a better understanding of the problems and also of the dynamics of those changes that are presently under way.

What emerges through these different inventories is a Japan that is much more *pluralist* than the traditional picture of 'Japan Inc.'. This pluralist Japan appears at once in the existing differences between manufacturing and services. Western references to the management methods of Japanese firms are almost exclusively devoted to analysing *Toyotism.* Yet whereas 60 % of the Japanese workforce was employed in services by the start of the 1990s, standard human resource management literature is based on rather different models derived from industrial firms—as Thierry Ribault makes clear in his analysis. Today, as in other industrialized countries, it is increasingly difficult to ignore these differences.

Pluralism is also evident in the various forms of *emancipation* to be observed in Japanese firms. By this is meant an emancipation with respect to Japan itself and, in a certain way, to the environment that traditionally governs firms' activities, such as financing, relations with the bureaucracy, or human resource management. Indeed, well since the 1980s, as is shown in the contributions by Yveline Lecler and Dennis Tachiki, certain Japanese enterprises have been making substantial progress concerning their relocating of corporate activities. This phenomenon now represents one of the most significant breaking points in the conduct of Japanese firms.

One may also perceive that firms operating as subcontractors to the big companies of the famous *keiretsu* have likewise begun to pursue their own emancipation, as Lecler shows. In direct relation to this phenomenon, the analysis undertaken by Susumu Watanabe of the evolution of small and medium-sized enterprises (SMEs) in Japan shows how, for the most part, they have actively been seeking to free themselves from the constrictions of subcontracting for the large enterprises, and also how they have been led to diversify their product and client portfolios. In some cases the effect has been to diversify the spatial organization of industries in Japanese regions. Some industrial districts, instead of being organized around a leading firm surrounded by its subcontracting SMEs, are now exclusively dominated by these smaller enterprises. They, in turn, maintain horizontal relationships that no longer correspond to the hierarchical structures that one finds in districts dominated by one or several *keiretsu*.

Of course, this pluralistic and more diversified Japan does not completely contradict the traditional analyses that have portrayed Japanese enterprises as conforming to a single norm. We have certainly gained a better understanding of Japan since the post-war period, based on numerous studies of the Japanese economy, though a tendency to present a too compact of a picture of Japanese firms could sometimes be observed. However, one must also acknowledge the result of ceaseless changes, either forced onto, or introduced by the enterprises themselves: changes that often pass unnoticed at the time, but that, after several years, end by having an important impact on the way in which firms operate.

Indeed, and contrary to certain established ideas, the opposition to progress that is casually imputed to Japanese enterprises is only partly true. The inventory forwarded here by the various authors from different fields concerning the organization of Japanese firms, indicates how far these firms have evolved, sought to adapt, and emancipated themselves from their relationship with the bureaucracy, for example—and all this sometimes well before the period of the 1990s that interests us here. Some firms have subjected their organizational structures to an almost constant revision so as to make them more effective, as is made clear by the studies of Yoshimura, Ueno and Kagono on Matsushita, or in Yoshiya Teramoto et al.'s contribution based on the Yokogawa example. Their conclusions, incidentally, support earlier work done on the history of Japanese firms (FRUIN 1994). In the same vein, methods of human resource management, as Daniel Dirks shows, or the organization of R&D activities, as examined by Martin Hemmert, have always existed in a certain state of fluctuation.

These findings are far from being without interest to the study of Japan's present difficulties. They enable us to identify more easily where the main problems, as identified today, have originated. Furthermore, this research enables us to locate starting points or first indications for solutions to the problems that the Japanese economy is now confronting. A convincing example is that provided by Shigeru Watanabe in his study of the evolution of corporate governance. The first half of the 1980s marked a turning point in the development of corporate finance. In effect, the large Japanese enterprises were recovering from a massive debt position that had been built up in the post-war period; from this turning point on they were able to achieve a relatively high degree of self-financing. This development modified considerably the control over corporate investments, as corporate governance switched from being external, and exercised by the banks, to being internal, and exercised mainly by the firms' own management. Watanabe relates his findings to the agency theory and in particular to its "free cash flow" argument (JENSEN 1986, KAPLAN 1997): In that light he identifies one of the main contributory causes, in the 1990s, of the creation of surplus productive capacity, and of the excessive ranges of products offered by Japanese companies, leading thus to grave investment errors and in general to a deterioration in profitability. These almost imperceptible trends over the course of the 1980s thus erupted into a serious problem during the 1990s, forcing the various stakeholders of Japanese enterprises to search for more profound solutions, such as improving internal control, while giving shareholders a greater influence over corporate governance.

Flexibility margins: are they exhausted?

The problems currently making the headlines of newspapers lead us to tackle directly the problem of *convergence* and, more precisely, that of a deliberate and ostensibly unstoppable evolution towards the Anglo-Saxon model. However, expressed in these terms, the convergence question implies that all means of cushioning the blows, both internal and external, have been exhausted. While there can be no doubt that the convergence question now represents a significant matter for examination, it would seem timely to proceed first of all by way of reflecting on the existence—and nature—of flexibility margins: potentially enabling a system to continue functioning effectively without completely altering the system's core elements. It appears, in fact, that Japanese enterprises have been able to effectively use these margins so as to absorb the internal and external shocks to which they have been subjected.

Obviously, when it comes to *shocks*, Japanese enterprises have suffered their share since the end of the 1980s: the bursting of the financial *bubble* and the severe fluctuations in the exchange rate have caused shock-waves that must not be underestimated. Very few other industrialized countries have had to suffer in so brief a period so many blows, or ones of such severity. All the more so when one adds, to these well-publicized reverses, others that are less known but that nevertheless amount to a long-term dynamic whose effects are hard to spot but are no less significant for enterprises. That applies across the board, from demographic changes, i. e., the phenomenon of an ageing population, to the younger generation's aspirations for a different life-style, particularly as concerns travel, leisure, social relations, consumption, and savings. Equally less conspicuous may be certain developments in the wake of changes of a geopolitical nature, associated with the end of the Cold War and with the growing power in Asia of China, South Korea and the Southeast Asian countries. Not all these changes have a negative impact on the enterprises, but they have a corrosive effect on firms' internal and external environment that obliges them to react and to adapt.

Bearing in mind the depth and diversity of these developments, it was impossible to ask the authors to provide a complete panorama of consequences for their own fields. Instead they have concentrated on businesses' reactions (or failure to react), and in particular on whether firms have had any margin for flexibility. And if they did, on what factors have these margins been based? Lastly, how have the margins been used to cushion the blows to which the enterprises were subjected?

From this perspective, the most representative contribution is made by Daniel Dirks. By studying the practice of *shukkō*[1], he has sought to analyse how Japan's manufacturing companies have used corporate groups' *internal labour markets*, so to speak, to try and reconcile the imperatives of cost reduction and the maintenance of employment security. One of his main conclusions, which is confirmed, incidentally, by other research (BOYER & JULLIARD 1996), is that so far the mechanisms for assuring job security within corporate groups have worked relatively well and have enabled enterprises to adapt without having to resort to massive lay-offs. The practice of *shukkō* clearly is one instrument of flexibility among others, the extent of their use varying according to the urgency of the crisis. However, the adjustments have so far not affected the labour market as much as the neo-classic textbooks would have us expect. This fact has, of course, largely prevented a major rise in the multiple costs of unemployment borne by society, and has given the corporate groups continued access to the technological and managerial competence of those involved in the *shukkō* practice.

Even so, there have also been cases where the shocks have been too violent for firms to avoid a fundamental challenge to some essential aspects of their working methods. As the chapters by Yveline Lecler, Dennis Tachiki and Susumu Watanabe show, using different analytical perspectives, the influence of exchange rates for example on manufacturing groups' exports has apparently created fractures and irreversibilities in their relations with subcontractors.

Generally speaking, groups' flexibility margins worked relatively well until the end of the 1980s, but thereafter have been insufficient to avoid massive relocations; this in itself has rendered questionable a fair number of variables in the way groups have been functioning. Even though it may still be too early for a final assessment, the present reversal in the rate of exchange, with a weaker level of the yen against the dollar, is unlikely to completely reverse these changes. Indeed the strength or weakness of the yen is not the only reason for the internationalization of Japanese firms. The rise in labour costs and property prices in Japan, the development of solvent markets in Asia, and the need to manufacture products locally rather than rely on exporting

---

[1] This practice corresponds to a temporary transfer of staff between firms.

(for demand and tariff barrier reasons): all of these factors have intensified the pressures driving large Japanese firms towards greater internationalization.

Similarly, Jean-François Estienne's contribution stresses the fact that a point of no return has certainly been reached regarding the question of the management of pension funds, taking account of the low rate of return for capital on the Tōkyō stock market since the bursting of the financial *bubble* at the beginning of the 1990s.

In summary it appears, in the course of examining the different fields analysed by the contributors, that the same problems have produced different effects according to firm and industry: some shocks have been easily absorbed, taking account of the firms' varying flexibility margins, others on the other hand have caused serious damage to previously established corporate practices.

Taking this context into account, we asked Takahiro Fujimoto to attempt to sum up the different positions and to provide us with at least some indication of a solution to this puzzling situation. Understandably, Fujimoto asserts that it is certainly wiser to approach this problem not from a global perspective, but at the level of each sector concerned. He suggests that one should try to analyse how change is reacted to and espoused in each sector, which he classifies according to international competitiveness and the type of structural change affecting the generic products offered. The most competitive industries by international standards, such as automobiles, appear not to have to undertake radical modifications of their production architecture as they enjoy sufficiently ample margins of flexibility to absorb shocks. All things considered, the adjustments to be made by Japanese firms operating in these sectors are minor; it is more a question of redistributing their assets and adjusting the range of their activities, rather than a complete overhaul of strategies and practices.

By contrast, sectors like banking, suffering from low international competitiveness, must face up to drastic changes in the type of products they offer. With their tight margins of flexibility to adapt to the impact of external shocks, all the more violent as international competition had traditionally been low, these sectors risk a much greater shake-up once they begin to adapt.

Fujimoto's ideas make a very useful reader's guide to understanding how Japanese enterprises have taken the punches, and how sharply they now must react. However they do not enable us to answer questions on a level that is less sector-based, but more 'societal': questions about the evolution of those practices used by all Japanese enterprises, ranging from human resource management to relationships with the banks; from subcontracting structures to corporate governance. From such a perspective we come up against a considerable difficulty in trying to understand the system's overall stability—and its serious breakdowns. In effect we need to place the various fields examined in this volume in their order of significance, in order to see whether breakdowns in certain fields have spread, or will spread, to others, and whether they have come to profoundly affect, or will do so in the future, the flexibility margins traditionally at firms' disposal.

Naturally, researchers tend to favour their own field, and therefore to evaluate change according to its impact within this field only. For example, those who work in the area of human resource management underline the effective working of flexibility margins and the basic continuity in the work structures of Japanese enterprises; others, mainly those engaged in the fields of finance, corporate governance and, to a lesser extent, those studying internationalization, have conversely placed their emphasis on the appearance of points of no return, on breakdowns, and on the effects of their spreading throughout the larger system. The studies by Shigeru Watanabe and Hideaki Miyajima, though far from adopting American positions, acknowledge that the reforms in the financial sector could lead to a greater role for shareholders in corporate control.

Nevertheless, the contributors do seem to agree on one point. The persistence of the slowdown in growth seems to be fundamental when it comes to the capacity of structures to resist. Growth eases the control of problems, and widens the margins of flexibility. In this context, the longer this period of slow growth continues, the more the margins of flexibility will be reduced and significant fault lines will emerge, affecting the inner workings of the entire enterprise system. To be sure, a lot depends less on individual firms but on the reactions of large sections of the Japanese economy in total: Cleaning up the balance sheets of the banks, reforming the financial sector and the supervising bureaucracy—especially the all-powerful Ministry of Finance—, bringing to an end the practices of state clientelism, particularly where it concerns construction and agriculture interest groups within the ranks of the Liberal-Democratic Party—practices that absorb most of the funds earmarked for boosting the economy; or, furthermore, restricting the transplanting of retired civil service chiefs onto the boards of Japan's larger companies. To sum up, all these reforms will be fundamental in restoring confidence to Japanese consumers, and thus in relaunching the economy into a new growth phase.

The question of flexibility margins leads on to the last of the themes that we had asked the contributors to address in their analyses, namely presenting an 'evolution scenario' and, in particular, touching on the question of convergence.

Convergence—or adaptation in divergence?

The question of convergence is certainly the one that most easily attracts clichés and unproven assumptions. Roughly speaking, the thesis of convergence declares that Japan, the atypical model, faced with the many-headed hydras of globalization, is on the edge of collapse, and that in order to overcome this impasse, it must copy the American model which, as is demonstrated by its economic performance over this last decade, serves as a reference point for all national economies.[2]

Just as it has seemed difficult to define any consensus on the question of flexibility margins, so it is for the question of convergence, though almost all of our contributors agree that present reforms will not necessarily lead to a convergence toward the Anglo-Saxon model. This does not mean, however, that Japan's enterprises and public authorities will not borrow certain methods and practices based on the Anglo-Saxon model. The reforms in the financial sector, for instance, emphasize greater financial transparency, a significant measure of deregulation and greater control by the financial markets over industry. However, these measures are far from turning Japanese companies into clones of American ones. In fact, as Dieter Ernst demonstrates in his commentary on the internationalization of firms, it is highly probable that "partial convergence may well coexist with persistent diversity".

Japanese structures, onto which these Anglo-Saxon methods will be grafted, are very different from the structures existing in American enterprises. Most authors here believe that this transplantation into a different environment—culturally, socially, institutionally and politically—ought to produce a very different structure from that which exists under the Anglo-Saxon model. The studies by Yveline Lecler and Dennis Tachiki, confirmed by Dieter Ernst in his commentary, demonstrate that the internationalization of Japanese firms takes on a very different form from that traditionally observed in American firms. We are not witnessing a "massive outsourcing" leading to the establishment of an open network composed of firms of several nationalities, as with American companies (BORRUS 1997). On the contrary, Japanese firms are internationalizing themselves while continuing to work with Japanese subcontractors, maintaining confidential relations with them, or re-creating abroad complete subcontracting networks modelled on past examples back in Japan. Foreign firms thereby manage to supply internationalized Japanese firms only at the lowest rungs of the quasi-closed network for low value-added activities. Similarly, if one accepts the analysis by Yoshimura, Ueno and Kagono, the internal structures of Japanese firms seem far from evolving from a "J" shape to an "M" shape. To the contrary, the organization continues to be refined according to criteria different from those prevailing in American enterprises.

In comparison, since the beginning of the 1980s, American enterprises have adopted various management methods developed by Japanese firms.

---

[2] See, as a representative example, the article by the American MIT economist Rudi DORNBUSCH in *Far Eastern Economic Review*, February 26th 1998: "Japan needs a vigorous market economy; the old model is dead (...) The right answer is a vast expansion of taxpayers and economic activity (...) That is what the US did in the early 1980s (...) Patently it has worked, since America enjoys both full employment and a balanced budget (...) Like sclerotic Europe, Japan must now adopt the US model. But since that is counter to Japanese culture, don't wait for it."

That does not mean, of course, that work practices of American businesses have been completely redesigned on the Japanese model.

In the debate over convergence, it would seem that those too eager to compare Japan only with America are in danger of adopting a one-sided perspective. Japanese enterprises are far from being the only ones in industrialized countries in need to adapt their work structures and practices. Firms in European countries, which are all marked in varying degrees by their national environment, have also embarked for some years now on major processes of adaptation and change. Robert Boyer's commentary on the evolving practices of human resource management emphasizes the fact that if one compares the state of evolution in two such countries as France and Japan—often considered those least in conformity with the American model—not only do their reforms tend to lead into different directions, but both systems are equally far from converging with the Anglo-Saxon model.

Finally, as the analysis of Professor Yui suggests, the history of Japanese firms illustrates that, in the past, the phenomenon of adaptation has not led to any real convergence, though Japanese firms have never stopped learning from American firms. Quality control methods were introduced just after the Second World War in order to improve standards of quality that in Japanese enterprises were badly lacking. Similarly, the multidivisional organization was adopted by some firms to improve their internal structure. Other examples could be easily provided. However, in each case these practices were digested, reinterpreted and adapted to better apply to local problems (SUZUKI 1991, FRUIN 1994, MORRIS-SUZUKI 1994). Herein lies perhaps one of Japan's greatest strengths. In the present delicate situation in which Japanese firms find themselves, history could well repeat itself once again if the elites succeed to restore overall confidence by importing and introducing into the system the right mix of reform elements. Just what these elements could be is the topic of the subsequent chapters.

References

BORRUS, M. (1997): Left for Dead: Asian Production Networks and the Revival of U.S. Electronics. In: NAUGHTON, B. (ed.): *The China Circle: Economics and Technology in the PRC, Taiwan and Hong Kong*. New York: Brookings Institution, pp. 139–163.

BOYER, R. and M. JULLIARD (1996): *Le rapport salarial japonais a-t'il atteint ses limites?* Paris (unpublished manuscript).

FRUIN, M. W. (1994): *The Japanese Enterprise System—Competitive Strategies and Cooperative Structures*. Oxford: Clarendon Press.

JENSEN, M. C. (1986): The Agency Costs of Free Cash Flow: Corporate Finance and Takeovers. In: *American Economic Review* 76, 2, pp. 323–329.

KAPLAN, S. N. (1997): Corporate Performance: A Comparison of Germany, Japan, and the U.S. In: CHEW, D. H. (ed.): *Studies in International Corporate*

Finance and Governance Systems. A Comparison of the US, Japan and Europe. Oxford: Oxford University Press, pp. 251–258.

MORRIS-SUZUKI, T. (1994): *The Technological Transformation of Japan—From the Seventeenth to the Twenty-first Century.* Cambridge: Cambridge University Press.

SUZUKI, Y. (1991): *Japanese Management Structures 1920–80.* London: MacMillan.

Japanese Management Practices in Historical Perspective

Tsunehiko Yui

1 Introduction

In the past, Japan was seen by Europeans as a geographically remote country, somewhere in the 'Far East'. By the same token, Japanese people had little awareness of most European countries—France, Germany, and Italy were perceived as being different from 'Western' countries. Furthermore, in contrast with attitudes toward the United Kingdom or the United States, Japanese knowledge and interest about business in the continental European countries was very limited. Before World War II, as far as Japan was concerned, Great Britain represented the pinnacle of achievement in commerce, industry, and finance; it was a model for Japan to try to catch up to. In the post-war period, the United States became the model whose business and management practices were emulated by Japan. Little attention was paid to developments in France, Germany, and Italy, despite their long histories of political and cultural eminence within Europe.

In recent years the phenomenal progress of transportation and information has rapidly shortened the effective distance between Japan and Europe. The international exchange of information and communication as well as international trade have expanded our knowledge and enhanced Japanese interest in business and management practices in these countries. Academic research has been stimulated by discovering that in spite of vast cultural differences, there are a number of features common to both sides. In this sense, this conference serves as a valuable opportunity to deepen our mutual understanding, and to consider what business methods will be best for both Japan and Europe in the twenty-first century.

2 American management and Japanese business: a historical perspective

Since this is the first paper of this conference, it is perhaps necessary to put Japanese management practices into historical perspective. It might also be useful to draw some comparisons with American practices, since the US has been the primary source of new management techniques in this century.

Japanese industrial enterprises began to import American management methods and practices from the second decade of the twentieth century.[1] In the inter-war period, the most successful fibre spinning companies (in both cotton and rayon) and the leading ship-building and electric machine companies in Japan successfully adopted the core principles of scientific management, represented especially by time and motion studies (SASAKI 1992). It should be noted that not only did the most successful industrial enterprises learn much about American management methods such as the Taylor system, but they almost simultaneously developed indigenous Japanese management practices, such as lifetime employment and promotion by seniority.

In the two decades after World War II, feeling that Japan's defeat had been the result not only of America's technological superiority but of superiority in management methods as well, Japan absorbed almost all the advanced management practices that were developed in the US. The establishment of the Japan Productivity Center (JPC) in 1954 reflected the growing interest in management and management education, and sparked a boom of interest in American management practices in Japan. In the 1950s and 1960s, almost all elements of American practices were eagerly absorbed. Some management practices, methods, and programmes were found to be very relevant and had important lasting effects.[2] Yet even those most influential practices proved useful only after considerable modification. Some essential aspects of the so-called 'advanced scientific managerial approaches', such as using linear programming, decision sciences, mathematical models, and others, were hardly adopted at all in Japan.

Quality control, the most successful management practice transplanted to Japan, is a good example of how American methods were modified. American statistical quality control techniques, which were usually imposed from the top, with workers being required to implement procedures on the basis of manuals provided by head office, were completely transformed in Japan during the 1960s, into the total production control (TQC) techniques that came to be recognized as a unique development of the Japanese management system. TQC was based on measures worked out through discussions between managers and shop-floor employees, with a strong emphasis on input from the workers who would be responsible for carrying out the procedures, and on widespread agreement among all concerned.

Nippon Denso had already introduced statistical control techniques in 1950 when it was designated as a parts supplier for the United States Army. These practices were reinforced and enhanced by Nippon Denso's contract with Bosch, which led to the standardization of production management and parts procurement. In 1957, the company embraced total quality control and rationalized its systems of production, distribution, and management.

---

[1] For an academic study on this topic, see the papers in DAITO & KAWABE (1983).

[2] The author has discussed this topic in YUI (1997).

In 1961, Nippon Denso won the Deming Prize for outstanding quality control performance (FRUIN 1995: 280).

Although the Japan Productivity Center advocated efforts to increase productivity and improve business management, it was not a blind adherent of American practices. After a visit to the US and Europe, Kōhei Gōshō, chairman of the JPC, proclaimed the aims and principles of the JPC, saying that "efforts to raise productivity should be made using Japan's own practices as the base, and incorporating American ideas (efficiency) and European attitudes (humanity)" (JAPAN PRODUCTIVITY CENTER 1985: 70–71).

In the postwar period, as in the pre-war era, institutions of higher education did not consider business management to be important enough for inclusion in their curricula. Only in the late 1970s were any faculties of business administration established at undergraduate level, after there had been a cooling-off of the earlier acute interest in management. In the 1960s, many large Japanese firms had sent their young college graduates to join MBA programmes in the US, but this experience was found to be almost useless, because sophisticated American management theory and practice could not be applied in their original forms to Japanese shop-floor oriented management.

Throughout the 1970s, Japanese industrial firms overcame the two oil crises that hit the Japanese economy severely (through their efforts to rationalize and develop energy- and labour-saving innovations). In the mid-1980s, the consistent growth of Japanese firms, and in particular the resilient improvement in their international competitiveness, drew the attention of the world business community to Japanese business and management. This culminated with the amazing success of Toyota Motors in global markets.

As these brief historical observations show, Japanese management practices are not based on culturally dogmatic attitudes, but have evolved over time to become institutional arrangements.

3 The basic characteristics of Japanese enterprises

Japanese management practices, together with labour management practices, which are well known and documented, are two of the basic elements of Japanese industrial enterprises. Looking at Japanese enterprises from a historical perspective, one can make the following observations that will point out the contrasts with what are generally considered to be the characteristic features of enterprises in the United States.[3]

First, as independent industrial firms, Japanese enterprises are not always large in size. They are less vertically integrated, less diversified, and less multinational in character than their American counterparts. Among the two

---

[3] For further details, see YUI (1988a).

hundred largest industrial enterprises in Japan, only paper, rayon fibre, and petrochemicals are highly integrated, and in terms of diversification (strictly double-digit, non-related diversification in different industrial categories), quite a few companies can be found. As is well known, Japanese enterprises are the least multinational in the world.

The size of Japanese firms is significantly smaller than the size of firms in the United States. For example, in 1992 Toyota, the largest company in Japan, had 65,000 employees, producing 4.5 million vehicles a year, while General Motors had 750,000 employees who produced almost 8 million vehicles per year. On the other hand, almost all Japanese firms have extensive inter-company networks that form enterprise groups. Typically, most major companies that produce items such as machinery, automobiles, electric appliances, or other complex products, have a string of subcontractors. These subcontractors are usually smaller in size, and in turn have their own subcontractors (YUI 1988a: 32–33).

Second, within the company the head office is relatively small, and neither greatly specialized nor stratified, though one result of the *bubble economy* has been a blurring of this aspect. Instead, Japanese companies have administrative offices at factory level, with their own distinct managerial organization and a complete set of managerial functions. At times the size and complexity of the organizational structure of main factories ("focal factories" according to FRUIN 1995) rivals or even surpasses that of head office.

Much of the reason for this focus may be found in the existence of multi-function manufacturing sites. A basic definition of such factories is a production site with appended planning, design, development, and process-engineering capabilities, plus an ambition to accumulate, combine, and concentrate experience for the propagation and improvement of products and processes. Focal factories exploit opportunities for *intrafirm* economies of scope by amassing and reshaping organizational capabilities in the midst of integrating product design, process development, and manufacturing. Factories with such capabilities were not at all common before World War I, increasingly so during the inter-war era, and widely present since the high-growth 1960s (FRUIN 1995: 24–25).

According to Mark Fruin, the Japanese enterprise as a system is based on "strategic interaction and alignment of three basic forms of organization—factory (shop floor), firm, and inter-firm network".[4]

Third, both in the head office and at the factory level, executives are salaried managers, promoted from within the company, and as a result the rate of turnover is extremely low. Almost all top executives are promoted from the ranks of middle managers who have had experience both at head office and the factory level. High levels of company-specific experience and know-how are coupled with in-house promotion and information exchange.

[4] For further details, see FRUIN (1995).

Fourth, demarcations between and within organizational boundaries are not rigidly fixed, so that a functional group at the factory (or laboratory) has the flexibility to perform the work of other groups. An engineer working in R&D at Factory A can take on work at the request of Factory B, without transfer payments or additional remuneration. It is not unusual for the head of production engineering at a major factory to be the factory manager at the same time.

From the logic of management theory, such flexibility and duplication of function may lead to confusion, but because turnover is low, the volume of communication among managers is high, and employees are trained in general rather than specialized tasks, such difficulties are largely avoided. In addition, coordination at each level and between departments is often facilitated by a General Affairs Department (*sōmu*), which frequently covers secretarial and legal affairs, and personnel functions—a seemingly unique Japanese solution.

Based on these fundamental organizational features, we can make the following observations about strategy and decision-making.

1. Japanese enterprises excel in manufacturing a full line of goods with 'fine-tuning' and in diversifying closely related products, but they are not always good at unrelated diversification.
2. Because of the emphasis on human resources at the factory or shop level, the momentum for decision-making comes from the middle or bottom, rather than from the top of the organization.
3. The high volume of communication and information within the company allows Japanese corporations to take full advantage of technological and market opportunities in their areas of specialization both in domestic and global markets.
4. The board of directors does not control management, but is rather controlled by management. The committee of senior executives (*jōmukai*), whose members are career managers, is the locus of de facto decision-making. However, this committee does not actually assume the responsibility of dealing with decisions of high uncertainty. Its function is usually to select from among the policy alternatives proposed by middle management. This may be part of the reason why the compensation of Japanese executives is remarkably low by American standards.

Many so-called Japanese management practices could thus be considered as being derived from these basic features of the organizational structure of Japanese business enterprises.

Based on these observations, the failure of Japanese enterprises in the late 1980s and the early 1990s—the era of the so-called *bubble economy*—cannot always be attributed to faults in the basic Japanese management system itself, but the 'mistaken approaches' of some firms as they confronted 'global standards' such as *growth in the size of the firms, strategies of unrelated diversification, overseas investment,* and *financial operations,* which had not been customary for Japanese industrial enterprises. In other words, during the *bubble economy* Japanese enterprises had attempted to emulate the very different American type of organizational capabilities rather than enhancing their own organizational strengths.

Actually, most Japanese enterprises are now beginning to recover their international competitiveness through rationalization, reducing the number of employees, and retrenching out of diversified businesses and speculative overseas operations. It is worth noting that quite a few companies, such as Toyota, Honda, Sony, Matsushita, Fuji Film, Bridgestone, and others, are now successfully regaining international organizational capability as well as competence. By contrast, many firms, including most of the financial corporations which over-expanded their operations under the umbrella of government protection, are now struggling to survive.

It is clear from what I have said that it is not easy for one country to adopt the organizational characteristics developed in another, even when there are clear advantages to doing so, but it is to be hoped that the discussion at this conference of the strengths and weaknesses of various systems may clarify how certain features of one system may be adapted in another to improve overall management practices.

References

DAITO, E. and N. KAWABE (eds.) (1983): *Education and Training in the Development of the Modern Corporation.* Tōkyō: University of Tokyo Press.

FRUIN, M. (1995): *The Japanese Enterprise System.* Oxford: Oxford University Press.

JAPAN PRODUCTIVITY CENTER (1985): *Seisansei undō 30 nenshi* [History of 30 Years of the Japan Productivity Center]. Tōkyō: Japan Productivity Center.

SASAKI, S. (1992): Scientific Management in Japan in the 1920s and 30s. In: *Business History* 34, 2, pp. 12–27.

YUI, T. (1988a): Development, Organization, and International Competitiveness of Industrial Enterprises in Japan, 1880–1915. In: *Business and Economic History* 17, pp. 31–48

YUI, T. (1988b): Development, Organization, and Business Strategy of Industrial Enterprises in Japan. In: *Japanese Yearbook of Business History* 5, pp. 56–87.

YUI, T. (1997): College Credentials and On-the-Job Skill Formation: Executive Managers in Industrial Japan. Paper presented at the *Franco-Japan Business History Conference,* Maison Suger, Paris.

STRUCTURE, STRATEGY AND INTERNATIONALIZATION

I Externalization of Organizations and the Dual Governance Structure

Norihisa YOSHIMURA, *Yasuhiro* UENO *and Tadao* KAGONO

Japanese corporations have developed organizational structures that differ from their Western counterparts. One important difference lies in the externalization of organizational units as legally independent firms, rendering the typical large Japanese firm a collection of inside divisions and outside subsidiaries (corporate group). This arrangement has a number of positive effects on firms' performance due to a blend of external and HQ evaluation, a reduction of governance costs and dysfunctional control functions, and the facilitation of organizational learning through the exchange of ('uncomfortable') information across companies. Based on an indepth case study (Matsushita Electric Industrial), the paper argues for the successful implementation of 'dual governance structures'.

1 Introduction

Large Japanese corporations have developed a unique multi-divisional structure which is slightly different from the European and American structure on organizational charts. Most researchers and businessmen in Japan have assumed that these slight differences are not in nature and the Japanese structure is only a variation of the Western multi-divisional structure. One of the differences is the externalization of organizational units as legally independent. These legal entities are called *bunsha, kogaisha* or *kanren kaisha* (affiliates or subsidiaries). In other words, Japanese divisionalized firms have at least two kinds of divisions, those inside and those outside. A typical large Japanese firm is a collection of inside divisions and outside subsidiaries, this collection being called a *kigyō gurūpu* (corporate group). The number of affiliates in major firms in the electronics and automobile industries is shown in Table 1.

US and European firms also have subsidiaries. The *unique characteristics* in Japan in this respect lies in the fact that the parent company performs the general HQ functions of the whole corporate group, while the control systems for divisions and subsidiaries are differentiated. The legal status of the subsidiaries are also manifold. Some affiliates are wholly-owned, some are majority-owned, and some are public enterprises. Some share employees (rotating employees among themselves and their parent) and have a com-

Table 1: Number of affiliates of major Japanese firms

	Sub-sidiary	Affiliate	Conso-lidated	Equity Method	Outline of Consolidated Firms
Hitachi	818	186	818	22	*Domestic43: Production 25 Sales 10 Others 8 Overseas 19: Production 14 Sales 4 Others 1
Tōshiba	532	157	134	86	*Domestic 34: Production 19 Sales 7 Others 1 Overseas 30: Production 16 Sales 10 Others 4
Mitsubishi Electric	145	92	98	35	Domestic 71: Production 23 Sales 26 Setting & Maintenance 10 Soft 8 Others 4 Overseas 27: Production 11 Sales 10 Others 6
NEC	438	93	365	33	Domestic Consolidated 118 Overseas Consolidated 245 (Subsidiaries: Development & Production 35 Development & Production & Sales 289 Sales & Soft-Development 114)
Matsushita Electric	706	N. A.	313	127	Domestic 76: Production 40 Sales 22 Credit 12 Credit 12 Overseas 237: Production 70 Sales 23 Others 144
Sharp	43	25	20	6	Domestic 9: Production 2 Sales 4 Others 3 Overseas 11: Production 6 Sales 4 Others 1
Sony	836	49	749	23	**Production 121 (Domestic 68 Overseas 53) Sales 37 (Domestic 3 Overseas 34) Sony Music 102 Sony Picture 513
Sanyo Electric	146	96	44	67	Domestic 28: Production 7 Sales 18 Others 3 Overseas 16: Production 16 Sales 6
Nissan Motor	550	146	100	26	Domestic 75: Production 7 Sales 58 Others 10 Overseas 25: Production 4 Sales 12 Others 9
Isuzu Motors	157	66	61	10	Domestic 58: Production 2 Sales 53 Others 3 Overseas 3: Sales 3
Toyota Motor	182	137	45	9	Domestic 8: Production 3 Sales 4 Others 1 Overseas 37: Production 7 Sales 8 Finance & Insurance 19 Others 3
Mitsubishi Motor	199	61	63	47	Domestic 47: Production 4 Sales 40 Others 3 Overseas 16: Production 2 Sales 5 Finance 5 Others 4
Mazda Motor	69	148	11	25	Domestic 7: Production 2 Sales 3 Others 2 Overseas 4: Sales 4
Daihatsu Motor	56	27	33	0	Domestic 31: Production 3 Sales 25 Others 3 Overseas 2: Sales 2
Honda Motor	281	93	214	160	Domestic 170: Production 8 Sales 156 Others 6 Overseas 44: Production 21 Sales 13 Finance 5 Others 5
Suzuki Motor	130	14	124	15	Domestic 111: Production 10 Sales 96 Others 5 Overseas 13: Production 4 Sales 9
Fuji Heavy Ind.	46	70	20	0	Domestic 3: Production 3 Overseas 17: Production 1 Sales 3 Finance & Insurance 6 Others 7

Source: TŌYŌ KEIZAI SHINPŌSHA (1994)

Notes: *Subsidiary*: parent's share of ownership > 50 %
Affiliate: parent's share of ownership 20–50 %
* figures for major consolidated firms only
** some overlap between affiliates

mon labour union with the parent, while others have an independent labour union, or no union at all.

We have discussed elsewhere how this organizational structure works (KAGONO & YOSHIMURA 1994). In this paper we will discuss its influence on the decision making and learning processes and the economic performance of Japanese firms.

2 Externalization of organization

A few examples will show the nature of the organizational structure of corporate groups and the diversity of subsidiaries within each group.

MEI group

Matsushita Electric Industrial (MEI) has developed a multi-divisional structure with distinctive features. The most distinctive is the complexity of its structure, where decision making processes are so complicated and chaotic that nobody in Matsushita could provide the entire picture of these processes inside the organization. This complexity is a result of certain design principles.

The *first* principle is the strict evaluation of the performance of organizational units, measured by return on sales. The *second* is the specialization of organizational units. Some divisions (*jigyōbu*) specialize in manufacturing and some (*hansha*) in sales. These divisions, however, are incomplete and depend on other divisions for doing business. Production divisions have manufacturing, research and development, and a few marketing functions while sales divisions cover sales, marketing and some product development functions. Some functions are shared between production and sales divisions. The production divisions, purchasing parts and components from specialized up-stream divisions, watch the global markets, develop new products, and sell products to the sales divisions. The complex transactions between divisions are coordinated by the invisible hands-principle of *internal* markets (KAGONO & CAMPBELL 1994).

These internal markets are open to outside market's, however, because transactions are based on (external) market prices. Purchasing divisions have the right to reject offers from internal suppliers, outsourcing them instead. Supplier divisions may sell their products to outside customers without any further permission, except when the product was developed jointly internally.

The *third* principle relates to externalization. MEI has 313 subsidiaries whose financial statements are consolidated with those of the parent for disclosure. Some subsidiaries of MEI are made public while others are kept private. MEI has legally separate subsidiaries which differ from each other with respect to their ownership relations with MEI, employment practices, historical contexts, and types of business they are in.

Degrees of independence in terms of subsidiary ownership are diverse. Wholly-owned subsidiaries, however, are in the majority. On the other hand, twelve large subsidiaries have been made public, including the following:

Kyūshū Matsushita Electric Co., Ltd.
Matsushita Kotobuki Electronics Industries, Ltd.
Matsushita Seikō Co., Ltd.
Matsushita Refrigeration Co.
Matsushita Communication Industrial Co., Ltd.

Victor Company of Japan, Ltd. (JVC) is an example of a majority-owned public subsidiary of MEI which has been managed almost independently. Recently, however, a director of MEI was dispatched to JVC as president in order to turn around JVC's flagging business. The company independently develops, manufactures, and distributes products.

Another example, Matsushita Electric Works (MEW), a minority-owned public corporation, is a sister company of MEI. While MEW distributes some products (electric shavers, lighting systems) through the marketing channels of MEI, it has its own distribution system for the majority of products. In fact, MEW competes with MEI with regard to products such as kitchen systems, housing materials, lighting systems, air-conditioning systems and so on. On the other hand, MEW procures parts, components, and products (microwave ovens for kitchen systems and air conditioners for air conditioning systems) from MEI. Despite these complex transactions between MEI and MEW, the two companies are managed independently and there are no personnel links between them except for a few interlocking directorships. Thus, JVC and MEW must both be considered independent firms rather than externalized subsidiaries.

Kyūshū Matsushita and Matsushita Kotobuki Electronics play a distinctive role within the MEI group, performing better than many of MEI's internal divisions. Both companies were originally established as suppliers of OEM products and components to MEI, using engineers and managers hired in rural, developing areas in Japan. As their original products began to mature, however, both diversified their product range with the help of technological staff from MEI and other subsidiaries.

Kotobuki's initial product were electric *kotatsu* (foot warmers). The company later diversified into VCR (video cassette recorders), directly competing with MEI's VCR division. Kotobuki then entered into an agreement with MEI to manufacture VCR only for the North American market. As VCRs became matured products, Kotobuki again diversified, this time into computer peripherals such as optical disk drives. The diversifications were made with the assistance of MEI's R&D centres and sales organizations. Developing the optical disc drive, Kotobuki thus enjoyed the cooperation of a research lab within MEI that had earlier developed optical devices based on the technology of CD players. This research lab had then promoted its ideas to various divisions and affiliates. Kotobuki was the fastest in responding, manufacturing and supplying optical disk drives to group-external customers on an

OEM basis, arranged through the sales force of MEI. Kotobuki's success in new product development was made possible due to its speedy reactions and its flexible capitalization on MEI's resources.

Kyūshū Matsushita Electric (KME) has also successfully diversified its product line. KME was established to supply products to the sales organization of MEI and parts and components to the various divisions inside the Matsushita Group as well as to outside customers through MEI's industrial sales force. As its original products matured, KME diversified product lines mainly into the office equipment area. Its speed in responding to the strategic initiatives of other divisions and affiliates proved a key in KME's successful product diversification.

However, KME has sometimes developed products that compete with the products of MEI or other subsidiaries. A typical example was the development of a low-price facsimile machine for the consumer market. The facsimile was originally manufactured by Matsushita Graphic Communication Systems (MG). MG had developed product and production technology for state-of-the-art, high performing machines for professional use. This technology, however was ill-suited for the growing low-price segments. MG thus gradually lost market share. KME then took the lead and quickly developed low-end products, distributed through MEI's consumer channels and helping the Matsushita brand to regain market share.

In summary, the two subsidiaries' strong performance can be attributed to their alertness to external and internal opportunities and their swift development of new products. Most of these 'new' products are not, strictly speaking, novel but had been supplied before by competing firms or divisions within the Matsushita Group. Both subsidiaries thus have played the role of a *sweeper* or *libero* in a football team. They have assumed a role that was not performed effectively by any other division or subsidiary and thus filled a *niche* not yet occupied by anyone else. It seems fair to suggest that both are thus in turn stimulating the alertness of other divisions and subsidiaries, as the latter's products may be taken over by these *sweepers*.

The degree of independence in terms of personnel also varies between subsidiaries. Most public subsidiaries hire workers, engineers, and managers by themselves. Key managers are dispatched from MEI to certain publicly owned subsidiaries, the extent of these dispatches varying as well. Kyūshū Matsushita and Matsushita Kotobuki must be considered the most independent as they do not accept the dispatching of any managers except during exceptional phases such as before these two subsidiaries were turned public. While two other public subsidiaries, Matsushita Refrigeration and Matsushita Seikō, do accept taking on a few key managers from MEI, Matsushita Communication is an example for a public subsidiary that shares most of its managerial personnel with MEI.

The large privately held production subsidiaries have received managerial personnel from MEI, under the same pay schemes and bonus standards as the parent company. Most sales companies, on the other hand, employ managers and sales personnel by themselves in local labour markets. Their presidents, however, are usually dispatched from MEI.

Historical reasons, underlying these conditions, are also diverse. Two major public corporations, Matsushita Seikō and Matsushita Refrigeration, for instance became subsidiaries of MEI when MEI acquired a majority of their stocks. Other major public subsidiaries are spin-offs from MEI, whereby a division or a set of divisions were legally separated from MEI and made public. Most of the private subsidiaries are spin-offs of divisions or were established as new companies. Some privately held subsidiaries (Matsushita Graphic Communication Systems, Inc.) were acquired by MEI. Sales companies, finally, became subsidiaries when independent wholesalers were merged and additional capital was infused from MEI.

The functions performed by the different subsidiaries also differ considerably. Most of the major public subsidiaries are engaged in product development and manufacturing. They are usually divisionalized and have their own production subsidiaries. Sales companies perform sales and marketing functions, while some (e. g., Matsushita Research Institute Tōkyō) specialize in R&D. Some affiliates (Matsushita Home Security, National Credit) perform after-sales or complementary service functions, while others again (Matsushita Logistic Service, Matsushita Real Estates) provide services to MEI and its subsidiaries.

The Hitachi Group

Hitachi, another diversified electronics giant, has developed a structure similar to MEI's. Hitachi has 818 consolidated subsidiaries, with twenty-nine public firms. Some minority-owned public affiliates (e. g., Horiba) do not share the Hitachi name and accept few personnel from the firm, but have close business relations with it. Most of the affiliates, in turn, have their own affiliates.

Some majority-owned public affiliates (e. g., Hitachi-Maxell) have presidents dispatched from Hitachi, while others (e. g., Hitachi Cable, Hitachi Metal, Hitachi Chemical, Nissei Sangyō) do not. Most of the privately held affiliates, such as overseas affiliates, are wholly-owned by Hitachi. Their presidents are (or had been) Hitachi employees. There are a few majority-owned private affiliates. The minority owners of these affiliates are usually other Hitachi affiliates except for joint-ventures with other independent corporations.

The affiliates' business relationships with Hitachi are manifold as well. Some are suppliers, some distributors and others again are manufacturers of products that are distributed through Hitachi's sales channels. As in the MEI case, there also exist suppliers of complementary products and services, firms performing R&D for Hitachi and its affiliates and finally those who do not have any significant business relations with any member of the Hitachi group.

Table 2: Listed affiliates of the Hitachi Group

Name of affiliates	Paid-in Capital (million ¥)	Parent's share of ownership	ROA	ROS 1	R0S 2
Hitachi	273,803		1.8	1.6	1.9
Hitachi Cable	25,891	51.4	3.0	2.8	3.0
Hitachi Construction Machinery	22,181	52.6	-1.6	-0.6	-1.3
Hitachi Software Engineering	21,640	62.5	3.8	3.0	5.3
Hitachi Metals	19,920	53.3	2.0	2.3	2.2
Hitachi Koki	17,812	21.7	3.3	4.3	4.6
Hitachi Transport System	15,955	55.4	3.6	2.1	2.8
Hitachi Chemical	15,022	56.0	3.0	3.5	2.3
Hitachi Medical	13,884	63.1	4.5	4.5	5.3
Hitachi Maxell	9,149	52.8	2.6	2.2	4.7
Hitachi Information System	9,059	63.6	0.7	-0.5	0.7
Kokusai Electric	8,304	20.9	2.8	2.5	2.1
Hitachi Sales	7,795	59.1	0.3	-0.6	0.2
Hitachi Plant Eng. & Construction	7,319	54.1	1.8	1.3	1.4
Hitachi Credit	7,098	52.5	2.3	5.9	3.2
Nissei Sangyō	5,437	56.5	2.4	0.6	1.1
Hitachi Electronics	5,019	61.8	4.6	3.8	3.8
Nippon Servo	2,547	51.0	-10.9	-6.5	-6.3
Hitachi Kiden Kōgyō	2,043	59.8	4.6	5.2	5.1
Kokusan Electric	747	19.8	2.9	1.9	2.2
Jidōsha Denki Kōgyō	2366	23.4	3.2	2.5	2.1
Shinmeiwa Industries	14,233	28.3	2.0	0.6	2.5
Seikō Electric	2,323	11.1	6.8	6.6	7.1
Tokico	8,162	21.0	2.4	1.1	1.8
Tōyō Machinery and Metal	1,100	23.4	-2.8	-3.1	-2.5
Nakayo Telecommunications	4,909	20.9	4.9	4.7	5.2
Horiba	6,569	13.2	2.9	5.3	4.8
Yagi Antenna	3,110	37.5	4.8	4.4	4.4
Nippon Columbia	6,783	13.2	0.2	-0.4	0.2

Source: cf. table 1

Notes: Fiscal year: April 1, 1993, to March 31, 1994
ROA: Ordinary Income/Assets
ROS 1: Operating Income/Sales
ROS 2: Ordinary Income/Sales

3 Hypotheses on externalization

Why have large Japanese firms externalized operations to this extent? While externalization certainly is an outcome of historical evolution, there may be some logic behind this development. Four major reasons have been proposed by various authors.

More autonomy
Some authors (MURAMATSU 1979) argue that organizational externalization is a means to give more autonomy to affiliates than to internal divisions. This is the most popular reason shared by many scholars and executives. ITO (1995) furthermore reasons that the autonomy of these subsidiaries encourages the development of a strategy and structure that better fits their specific environment and helps them to achieve higher performance.

Risk reduction
Another articulated reason is risk reduction. Some (AOKI 1984) have argued that the externalization is a means to reduce risk in new business development. It may be easier for parent companies to liquidate businesses when performed by affiliates.

Retention of capital gains
Externalization is sometimes thought of as a means to obtain and keep capital gains when affiliates are made public. Here, the profit derived from public offering of affiliates is retained by the parent.

Labour markets
Some authors argue that externalization is related to the labour markets. The wage levels of small firms are usually lower than those of large corporations. Externalization therefore is a means to capitalize on this wage difference (ODAGIRI 1992). Small firms are usually less constrained by the social norm that employees should not be fired. Externalization builds on this flexibility of small firms.

These reasons may explain some cases of externalization. For instance, NEC has established manufacturing affiliates in developing areas in Japan, a possible reaction to local labour market conditions (availability of labour, lower wage levels). Another example is Sony's recent move to turn Sony Music Entertainment (Japan) public. The purpose was to realize capital gains and to give the affiliate more autonomy in new business areas, differing from the existing manufacturing businesses. Many firms externalize their new business development projects, furthermore, when these are developed in a risky environment.

These articulated reasons thus cover some cases but do not explain why some *key operations* are externalized as well. For instance, it remains to be explained why many production and sales affiliates, whose employees have all been dispatched from the parent company, have been externalized, even though they are closely linked to the operations of their parent, need to be coordinated with internal units, and thus retain a risk level similar to that of these internal divisions. More persuasive reasons must be found.

4 Effective governance through the dual governance structure

The analysis of Matsushita's group management structure suggests that there is an important dimension of organizational design, i. e., externalization versus internalization (KAGONO and YOSHIMURA 1994). Many Japanese firms use this dimension as an organizational design parameter.

Some of the externalized subsidiaries of the Matsushita group are characterized by an alertness to external and internal opportunities and a swiftness in capitalizing on these opportunities. Kyūshū Matsushita and Matsushita Kotobuki Electronics are some of the more distinctive examples. This alertness may be the result of organizational decentralization. However, decentralization is only a necessary and not a sufficient condition. The fact that other subsidiaries and divisions, enjoying a similar degree of decentralization, are relatively less 'alert' and swift shows that organizational decentralization is not the key. The *key* here lies in what we call the *dual governance structure*. These affiliates are majority-owned by the parent while being made public. Both, the parent *and* the market govern these subsidiaries.

Graph 1: The structure of dual governance

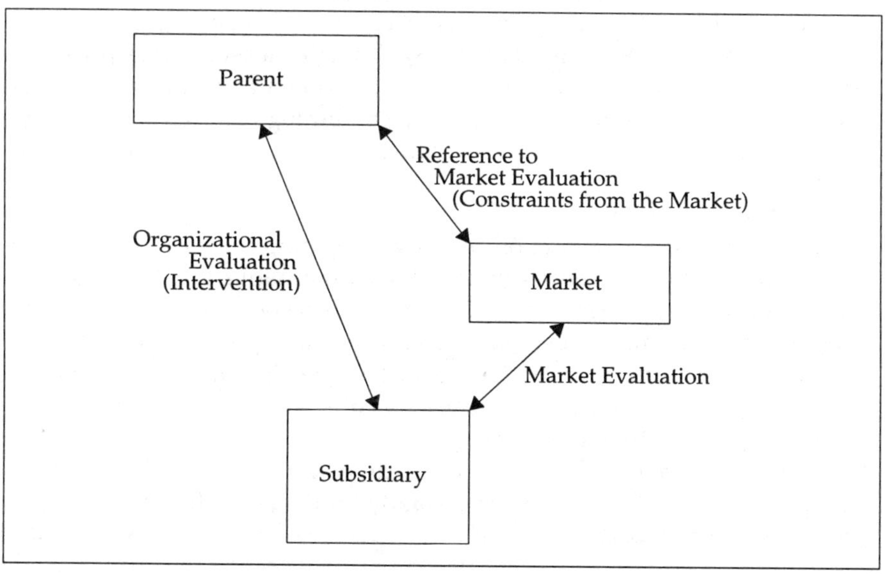

As public corporations, these subsidiaries are externally evaluated on the stock market, through the 'invisible hand' or numerous, anonymous evaluators and their selling and buying of equity. MEI cannot intervene in this evaluation process. If MEI decides to sell the stock, it may lose its majority. If the company buys the stock, insider trading may be suspected. Thus, the stock market's evaluation is independent from MEI.

While difficult to explain how exactly the market evaluates a company, numerous criteria are taken into consideration: profitability, market positions, top management leadership, technological resources, organizational culture, quality of human resources and so on. The multiplicity of criteria makes it difficult for the subsidiaries to improve their evaluation simply by temporary measures such as creating short-term profits while sacrificing long-term profit potentials.

At the same time, MEI internally evaluates these subsidiaries. MEI's evaluation is performed in two ways. First, through a direct evaluation. The subsidiaries are directly evaluated by MEI headquarters using the same criteria as applied to the other subsidiaries and divisions. Second, the indirect evaluation: assessing its subsidiaries, MEI takes the anonymous evaluation of the market into account.

The dual governance has several merits for parent firms and their subsidiaries:

1. More effective evaluations
   The combined evaluation is more reasonable than the purely internal or the purely external evaluation. The combined evaluation is more sound than the purely external evaluation because there is an internal evaluation performed by professional managers (at HQ) with profound knowledge of the affiliate's management and its business. The combined evaluation is more sound than the purely internal evaluation because the market evaluation combines the various criteria into a single measure, stock price, and because the market evaluation fuses various opinions of numerous investors into that same measure. Thus, by combining external with internal evaluations, the performance of subsidiaries is more reasonably appraised.
2. Reduction of governance costs
   The HQ can reduce evaluation costs by delegating some of its evaluation tasks to the market. The market evaluates the public subsidiaries daily, sending signals to the HQ whether it must intervene or not. If the HQ were to collect data daily to evaluate the divisions, huge costs would be incurred and the autonomy of the subsidiaries be discouraged. Externalization thus reduces the costs of subsidiary control.
3. Avoiding the dysfunctions of control
   Using an external evaluation, organizations can avoid control dysfunctions. The internal control system usually produces dysfunctions, such as when decentralized units pursue only those (few) goals that are evaluated

by the HQ and neglect other important tasks. When the HQ increases the number of criteria to avoid this dysfunction, another dysfunction emerges, i. e., HQ cannot effectively motivate the operating units as they feel that they are being overly controlled. When an external evaluation is used, the HQ can avoid this dysfunction while effectively controlling the units.

4. Quicker interventions
   HQ interventions are faster than market interventions. When the necessity of intervention in a subsidiary is felt, HQ can use strong and swift means of intervention, e. g., the replacement of top management. Such interventions by the market usually need a long time to be implemented. Investors must first gather majority proxies to replace top management. The anonymous investors can thus use the majority owner as their agent for quick intervention.
5. Restrained intervention
   Such strong interventions of the HQ in externalized subsidiaries are, however, more constrained than those in their internal divisions. The HQ can intervene in public subsidiaries but must disclose reasonable and legitimate reasons to the public for doing so. This constraint provides top management of these subsidiaries some security concerning their position.
6. Obtaining uncomfortable information
   The presidents of the public subsidiaries may have to refuse the HQ some of its requests and orders because these may hurt the interests of outside stockholders. This bargaining power of the presidents, which does not exist for divisional general managers, conveys uncomfortable information to the HQ, a final merit of dual governance. It facilitates organizational learning through the conveyance of uncomfortable information and the implementation of uncomfortable action.

The more appropriate evaluations and faster, yet more restrained interventions, made possible by the externalization of organization, put healthy pressures upon the top management of subsidiaries to improve performance. While these subsidiaries can thus increase their alertness and quickness, the HQ can reap these benefits without incurring extraordinary costs or dysfunctions of control.

These merits of externalization are the result of an effective governance of externalized units. They are most obvious when the operating units are made public while remaining majority-held by the HQ, though they exist to some degree for the other types of externalization as well. Here banks, especially the main bank, play the role of external evaluators even when the subsidiaries are kept private.

The dual governance structure has *demerits* as well. The strategic resource deployment capability of the parent is constrained by the outside stockholders who may have differing interests. The power of the HQ may thus be weaker when intervening in the management of subsidiaries. In addition, subsidiaries may seek more independence in a case where their parent loses its majority share.

5 Economic consequences of the dual governance structure

The effectiveness of the dual governance structure is most apparent, we have argued, when subsidiaries are made public. If our analysis is valid, it is predicted that the economic performance of public subsidiaries, where the dual governance is applied, is higher than that of purely public corporations, which are governed by the market (prediction 1). It is also predicted that the effectiveness of the dual governance structure is more apparent when the subsidiaries are majority-controlled by the parent (prediction 2).

To test these predictions, we classified the governance structures of public corporations in major industries in the manufacturing sector: chemicals including pharmaceuticals, iron and steel, general machinery, electric and electronics, and transportation equipment including automobiles.

Table 3 shows the distribution of the governance structure of public corporations in these five industries. The corporations are classified by the following criteria: Where a family and its associates hold 10 % or more of the stock, the corporation is classified as family-governed. If a parent and its affiliates own 20 percent or more and less than 50 % of its stock, the corporation is classified as a minority-governed subsidiary. It is a majority-owned subsidiary if the parent firm and other subsidiaries hold 50 % or more of total equity. The corporation, in which no dominant stockholder is identified, is classified as management-governed.

Table 3: Distribution of governance types in five industries

Type of Governance	Chemicals	Steel	Machinery	Elec. & Electro.	Transportation Eqp.	Total
Family	24 (13.19)	9 (15.52)	46 (23.59)	45 (22.50)	5 (5.62)	129 (17.82)
Management	107 (58.79)	23 (39.66)	95 (48.72)	79 (39.50)	34 (38.20)	338 (46.69)
Minority-owned	38 (20.88)	21 (36.21)	40 (20.51)	48 (24.00)	47 (52.81)	194 (26.80)
Majority-owned	13 (7.14)	5 (8.62)	14 (7.18)	28 (14.00)	3 (3.37)	63 (8.70)
Total	182	58	195	200	89	724

Source: cf. table 1

Table 3 shows that overall more than one third of public corporations are minority- or majority-governed subsidiaries. This number is larger than that of family-governed public corporations. The ratio of subsidiaries is highest in the transportation equipment industry, where the ratio reaches 56 %. It is lowest (about 28 %) in the chemical and general machinery industries. The table also shows that a significant number of corporations are dually governed.

Performance (the return on assets and the after-tax return on equity) of the governance structures are compared in table 4. The figures do *not* fully support our predictions. The ROE of the majority-owned subsidiaries is higher than that of the management-governed ones in chemicals, machinery, and electric industries and lower in steel and transportation equipment. The ROE of minority-governed firms is higher than that of management-governed only in the machinery industry. The ROE of the majority-owned subsidiaries is higher than that of the minority-owned and the ROA of majority-owned firms is higher than that of minority-owned firms except for the steel industry. While statistically significant at the 5 % level, the comparison does suggest that the dual governance structure works more effectively when the subsidiaries are majority-controlled by the parents.

The above analyses are limited because the other variables that influence performance are not controlled for and only one-year performance is compared. The comparison must thus be considered tentative. While not supporting our prediction 1, the analysis does, however, suggest that the dual governance structure works effectively under certain conditions where subsidiaries are majority-controlled by their parents (prediction 2).

Table 4: Comparison of performance across governance types

	N	ROA Return on Assets	N	ROE Return on Equity (after taxes)
Chemicals				
Family	23	5.05	22	3.92
Management	107	4.99	103	3.81
Minority	37	4.30	34	3.59
Majority	12	5.01	11	4.13
Total	179	4.85	170	3.80
Steel and Iron				
Family	9	-0.36	9	-6.84
Management	23	2.43	20	2.99
Minority	19	2.19	19	0.30
Majority	5	1.96	5	0.56
Total	56	1.86	53	0.13**

	N	ROA Return on Assets	N	ROE Return on Equity (after taxes)
Machinery				
Family	42	3.65	39	3.02
Management	95	2.54	88	1.53
Minority	40	1.85	35	1.75
Majority	14	2.51	14	2.00
Total	191	2.64	176	1.94
Electric Machinery and Electronics				
Family	40	4.11	37	3.18
Management	79	3.89	75	3.25
Minority	48	3.61	43	2.86
Majority	27	3.83	27	3.43
Total	194	3.85	182	3.17
Transportation Equipment				
Family	5	4.26	5	3.72
Management	34	2.99	33	4.83
Minority	47	2.77	45	3.18
Majority	3	3.65	2	4.41
Total	89	2.97	85	3.88

Note: ** Significant at 1 % level

6 Conclusion

We have analysed the effectiveness of the dual governance structure as developed by some Japanese corporate groups. The appropriate pressures for performance due to the externalization of evaluation and the faster but restrained interventions by the HQ are the sources of alertness and swift reactions as displayed by (certain) externalized subsidiaries. This externalization also facilitates organizational learning through the conveyance of uncomfortable information and the implementation of uncomfortable actions.

The classification of the governance structures of public corporations in major industries showed that one third of them work under the dual governance structure. The comparison of the governance structures' performance did not, however, support our prediction that the dual governance structure is always linked to higher performance. Nevertheless, the comparison does suggest that the dual governance structure may work effectively when a subsidiary is majority-controlled by the parent.

References

AOKI, M. (1984): Aspects of the Japanese Firm. In: AOKI, M. (ed.): *The Economic Analysis of the Japanese Firm.* Amsterdam: North-Holland.

ITO, K. (1995): Japanese Spin-offs: Unexplored Survival Strategies. In: *Strategic Management Journal* 16, 6, pp. 431–446.

ITAMI, H. and T. KAGONO (1994): *Keieigaku nyūmon* [Introduction to Management]. Tōkyō: Nihon Keizai Shinbunsha.

KAGONO, T., I. NONAKA, K. SAKAKIBARA and A. OKUMURA (1985): *Strategic vs. Evolutionary Management: A US-Japan Comparison of Strategy and Organization.* Amsterdam: North-Holland.

KAGONO, T. and N. CAMPBELL (1994): Organizational Prehistoric: Intra-Company Markets in Japanese Multinational Corporations. In: CAMPBELL, N. and F. BURTON (eds.): *Japanese Multinationals: Strategies and Management in the Global Kaisha.* London: Routledge, pp. 113–122.

KAGONO, T. and N. YOSHIMURA (1994): *Externalization of Organizations.* Working Paper, Graduate School of Business, Kōbe University.

MURAMATSU, S. (1979): *Takakka Kigyōron* [The Theory of Diversified Firms]. Tōkyō: Maki Shobō.

ODAGIRI, H. (1992): *Growth through Competition, Competition through Growth.* New York: Oxford University Press.

RUMELT, R. P. (1974): *Strategy, Structure and Economic Performance.* Boston: Harvard Business School.

SLOAN, A. P., Jr. (1964): *My Years with General Motors.* New York: Doubleday.

TŌYŌ KEIZAI SHINPŌSHA (ed.) (1994): *Nihon no kigyō gurūpu* [Corporate Groups in Japan]. Tōkyō: Tōyō Keizai Shinpōsha.

YOSHIHARA, H., A. SAKUMA, H. ITAMI and T. KAGONO (1981): *Nihon kigyō no takakka senryaku* [Diversification Strategies of Japanese Firms]. Tōkyō: Nihon Keizai Shinbunsha.

II Role of Inter-organizational Networks: The Case of Japanese Corporate Groups

Yoshiya TERAMOTO, *Naoto* IWASAKI *and Tōru* TAKAI

The existence and functioning of inter-organizational or corporate groups has long been a focus of economic research on Japan. Their specific features have been understood to differ substantially from a more market-oriented behaviour displayed by Western, especially US firms. However, in the wake of the collapse of the *bubble economy,* these networks have come under increasing criticism for their allegedly closed and non-innovative character. On the basis of a survey conducted among large Japanese manufacturers key restructuring issues for corporate groups are identified and explained. Strategies that support mutual learning, clearer performance criteria and greater decision autonomy for group members are given relatively more weight than before. An indepth case study reveals in more detail that in the future corporate group success in Japan will depend to an even greater extent than before on finding the crucial balance between the 'centrifugal' and 'centripetal' forces underlying the actual functioning of these networks.

1 Introduction

Inter-organizational networks are increasingly important in economic life because of their capacity for regulating complex transactional interdependence as well as cooperative interdependence among organizations. Inter-organizational networks are also interesting from a theoretical viewpoint because they can be studied under different disciplinary approaches, thereby offering a precious ground of common interest and potential dialogue among various branches of the social sciences.

As the term *network* is widely used, this article is interested in networks as modes of organizing economic activities through inter-organizational coordination and cooperation. In this sense, networks lie at the very core of organization theory.

Various studies have reported that the strategic network is an effective means for managing environmental turbulence and interdependence (e. g., RING & VAN DE VEN 1994). MILES & SNOW (1986) described inter-organizational networks as "a promising new organizational form to fit the fast approaching conditions of the 21st century" (1986: p. 62). It is a fact the inter-organizational network characterized by *keiretsu* groupings[1] has significantly contributed to the competitive strength of Japanese companies.

The defining characteristics of business developed through Japanese-style company group networks are their long-term, continuing nature, as opposed to the *ad hoc*, individualistic market trading of Western firms. American companies tend to choose between one of two routes, either internal trading or market trading, whereas Japanese companies prefer a mixture of the beneficial features of the market mechanism together with the positive aspects of negotiation within the organization, and have successfully constructed loosely constituted inter-company networks. In other words, as an amalgam of the market and the internal organization, by interweaving the market principle with the organizational principle, inter-firm transactions can be made similar in nature to external transactions, and the *keiretsu* company group network can be established as an intermediate form of organization.

This type of organization network, which may be described as *Japanese-style*, has attracted criticism as being prone to closed dealings, but on the other hand a trend can be seen for foreign car makers such as Ford and Chrysler to regard network efficiency highly enough to want to emulate its features in their business transactions. Observing that Japanese-style inter-company networks are at once criticized and at the same time actively imitated by some American companies (see FERGUSON 1990), it is clear that the *keiretsu* form an integral part of the competitive strength of Japanese companies.

However, since the collapse of the *bubble economy*, sudden environmental changes have made the transformation of the Japanese-style group network inevitable[2]. Accordingly, inter-organization networks have become as follows: They operate in highly complex and turbulent environments, making them more vulnerable to environmental changes than normal organizations (ANDERSON 1990, CONTRACTOR & LORANGE 1988). Environmental changes and uncertainties become a serious external threat in managing the networks. Moreover, there is a life cycle in network management, eventually leading to the demise of networks (D'AUNNO & ZUCKERMAN 1987, VAN DE VEN & WALKER 1984). That is, the existence and the growth of a network through a dynamic cyclical process contains the seeds of disintegration (VAN DE VEN & WALKER 1984). Because of reasons such as those described above, today's inter-organizational networks, including those of the Japanese cor-

---

[1] Japanese-style company groups are characterized by either *zaibatsu*-financial conglomerates with banks at their centre, forming a loosely knit horizontally grouped association of companies in widely differing sectors, or, within a single industry, large companies such as Toyota or Hitachi forming the centre of vertically connected *keiretsu* companies in a group network. This paper is focused on the analysis of the latter type of company group.

[2] For instance, in the automotive industry some companies are forced to expand their business transactions beyond the *keiretsu* manufacturers, while in the electrical appliances industry the restructuring and freedom of choice of formerly captive retail outlets are inevitable.

porate groups—subjects of this study—call for fresh thoughts and new perspectives.

The purposes of this article are twofold. First, it will present the general trend of today's Japanese corporate groups exemplified by empirical evidence; then, second, beyond the ideas of corporate restructuring and reengineering, it will attempt to offer a conceptual framework for *remanaging* Japanese corporate groups.

2 General trends of contemporary Japanese corporate groups

To gather a larger body of evidence about contemporary Japanese corporate groups, a postal questionnaire survey was conducted with a sample of 1,000 large companies listed on the Tokyo Stock Exchange (First Section). Financial institutions and life insurance companies were not included in the sample, since the Japanese commercial law prohibits them from investing more than 5 % and 10 %, respectively, in any given company. The total response rate to be analysed was about 25 %.

As an outline of the companies who responded to the survey, 85 non-manufacturing companies, 86 basic material manufacturers, and 69 assembly manufacturers took part. Ranked by capitalization, 22 companies were in the range 1–5 billion yen, 48 companies between 5–10 billion yen, 50 companies were from 10–20 billion yen, and 120 were capitalized at over 20 billion yen. In terms of staff number, 29 of the companies employed less than 1,000 people, 82 were in the range 1,000–3,000 staff, 41 between 3,000–5,000, 50 companies 5,000–10,000 staff, 29 companies 10,000–30,000 staff, and 9 companies employed over 30,000 staff.

2.1 Environmental changes and key issues

2.1.1 Recession's impact on business strategies

Many of the major Japanese companies engaged in aggressive equity financing during the period of Japan's *bubble economy.* These companies, however, abruptly abandoned such business practices in 1990, in the aftermath of several huge downturns in the Japanese stock market. The consequences were severe in the early 1990s for both Japanese banks and corporations. Large banks and insurance companies suffered as the hidden asset values on which they had relied heavily for expanding their businesses fell sharply. Most major companies' operational profits plunged dramatically during the serious economic recession that began in 1991. And since 1992, companies have been obsessed with redeeming convertible bonds that they had issued during the *bubble economy* and that have not been converted to stocks.

All this is further straining the corporate group system. Japanese companies and banks are far less willing than before to hold stock in corporate group-member companies, because they are no longer able to rely on the former certainty that stock prices would increase. The volatile state of the Japanese stock market has driven off most major buyers. Even if some companies wanted to issue new stocks, there are few to buy them. This situation, painful as it is for Japanese companies, may however offer foreign businesses and Japanese firms outside of a corporate group an important opening into the network.

2.1.2 Corporate groups' core business maturity

Graph 1 shows that 69.46 % of parent-companies in the sample declared that their core businesses are maturing. Though Japanese corporate groups have always been a focus of debate among academics and practitioners, observers' reactions concerning the corporate groups' core business maturity are actually becoming divergent. On the one hand, some company officials and researchers argue[3] that, driven by current trends in the competitive and political environments, corporate groups' present core businesses will wane sooner or later and firms will have to supplement them with newer pillars.

Graph 1: Life cycle stages of core businesses

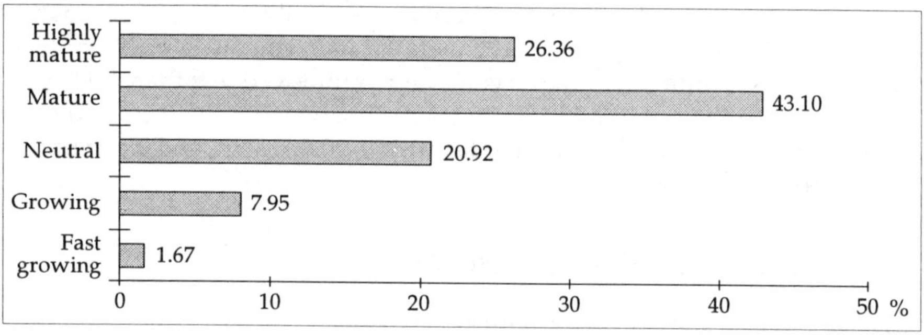

On the other hand, other experts suggest that corporate groups in general are better able to gain benefits through streamlining business processes and focusing on their core businesses. Kodak, for example, has been able to focus on its core business by outsourcing its data processing function to IBM. Kodak has achieved cost savings through reducing personnel, reducing assets, and so on.

In any case, Japanese corporate groups are increasingly entering into global strategic alliances and in the process restructuring the distinctive patterns of their overall industrial organization.

[3] On this subject, see 'Japan – The Long Climb Back to Health', *Chemical Week*, November 30, 1994, pp. 34–36.

Graph 2: Core businesses' product & market variety

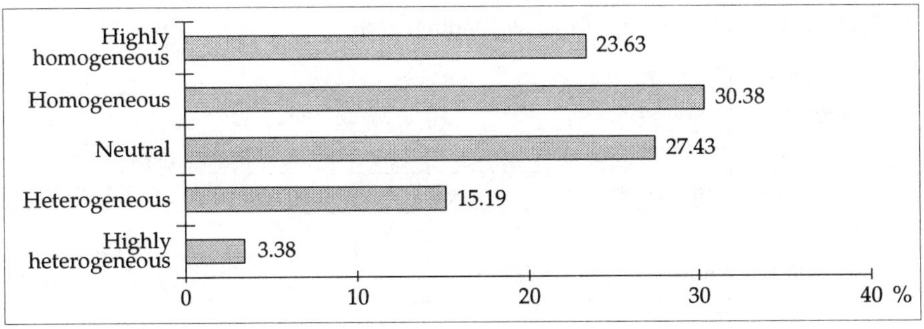

2.1.3 Corporate group restructuring

According to graphs 3 and 4, after the end of Japan's *bubble economy* corporate groups' consolidated sales growth (from 1992 to 1994) is lower than their consolidated net operating profits growth during this period. This means that many corporate groups (44.44 % in 1994) have been restructuring their organization, cutting costs, and reducing investments. Nevertheless, together, graphs 1 to 4 also show that the parent companies continue to focus most of their attention on their core businesses, whose products and markets are largely homogeneous. Parent companies could cut down on their management risks and stimulate and facilitate entrepreneurial behaviour by developing new businesses through the use of group members or subsidiaries. That is, in order to be more competitive and to diversify, companies could set up subsidiaries or autonomous business divisions within their present corporate structure.

2.1.4 Gradual financial deregulation

The Japanese economy has been experiencing a gradual process of financial deregulation, which has been associated with greater efficiency but accompanied by instability in the form of unsustainable increases in asset prices (OECD 1991).

The aim of financial deregulation is to increase competition, thus, raising efficiency of the financial system and with it overall welfare. The most obvious benefits of the reforms have been to widen portfolio choices, extend investment opportunities, and eliminate cross-subsidization among depositors. The result would be a more efficient allocation of scarce capital resources.

Moreover, financial deregulation and innovation has also made corporate liquidity reserves readily usable either for fixed or financial investment purposes. Deregulation and globalization have made market interest rates more flexible. In other words, deregulation is opening the door for corporate group outsiders to break into the networks.

Graph 3: Corporate groups' consolidated sales

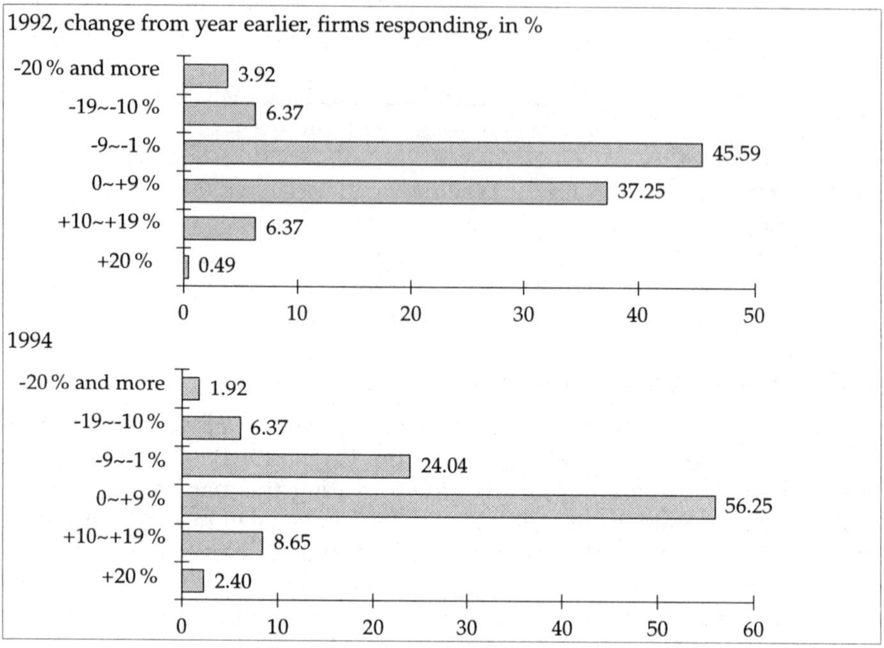

Graph 4: Corporate groups' consolidated net operating profits

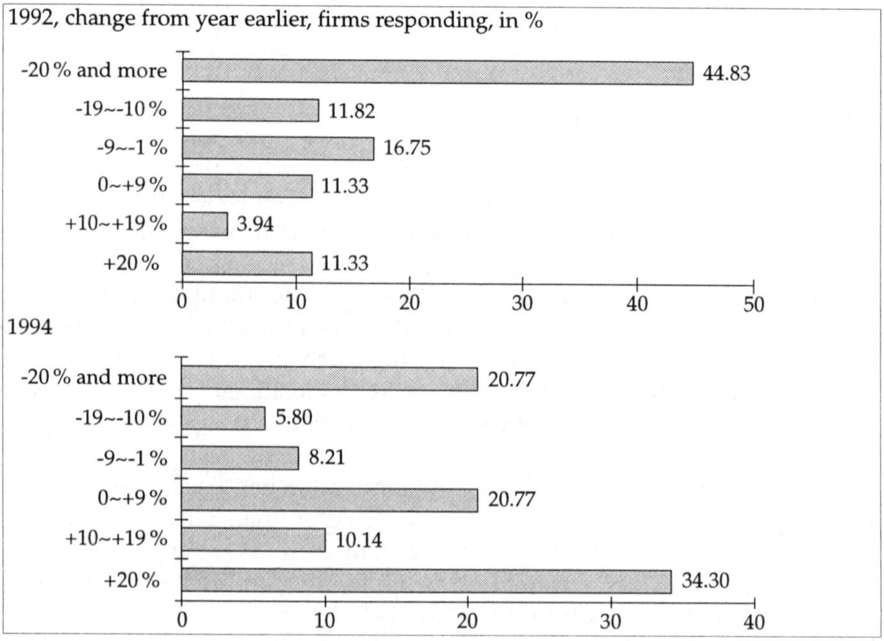

2.1.5 New accounting practices

Financial reporting reforms being considered by international regulators on a number of fronts would end the Japanese practice of buying and selling securities simultaneously for quick paper profits. They would also compel financial institutions to disclose larger amounts of bad loans than they do now.

While the prospect of stricter disclosure rules may not sit well with Japan's business community, it suits investors which have long sought to obtain more detailed information about companies. Moreover, in the past, corporate group members were asked to establish their financial statements separately and taxes were (and are still) deducted from each corporate group member's results. Parent companies therefore claimed that this regulation was unfair, so that actually consolidated financial statements are considered and officially practiced. The consolidation system has been and will be strengthened by other changes in the Japanese accounting systems (e. g., the range of consolidated subsidiaries being widely extended). The *keiretsu* are trying not only to improve the performance of parent companies, but also that of the corporate group as a whole.

2.2 Internal changes

Significant changes concerning Japanese corporate groups are much more likely to result from internal factors than from outside pressures. In other words, from a strategic standpoint many Japanese companies have made moves to reorganize their inter-company grouping, reorganizations which may in the past have arisen naturally. Next, we shall examine more specifically the changes in Japanese company group *strategy*.

2.2.1 Contemporary basic policy and change

According to graph 5, presently, corporate group-members are mainly subgrouped either by business area, by function and/or by ownership ratio. Though these subgrouping criteria will predominate in the future, it is apparent that the percentage of corporate group members subgrouped by function and by strategic focus will increase whereas those organized by other criteria will decrease. In other words, the group member subgrouping method actually becomes more strategy-oriented rather than operation-oriented, an indication of contemporary Japanese corporate groups' policy trends.

With the Japanese economy in recession, industry is no longer expanding and parent companies are unable to widely contribute to the traditional long-term relationships inside corporate groups. Thus, strategically, they are releasing their group members, promoting autonomous management in order to contribute to overall group growth (table 1). Once before, in 1986, when a sudden appreciation of the yen slowed the Japanese economy, even

Toyota advised its subcontractors to assume more autonomy and to develop business with other contractors (MORI 1994).

Graph 5: Present and future of Japanese corporate groups' organizing criteria

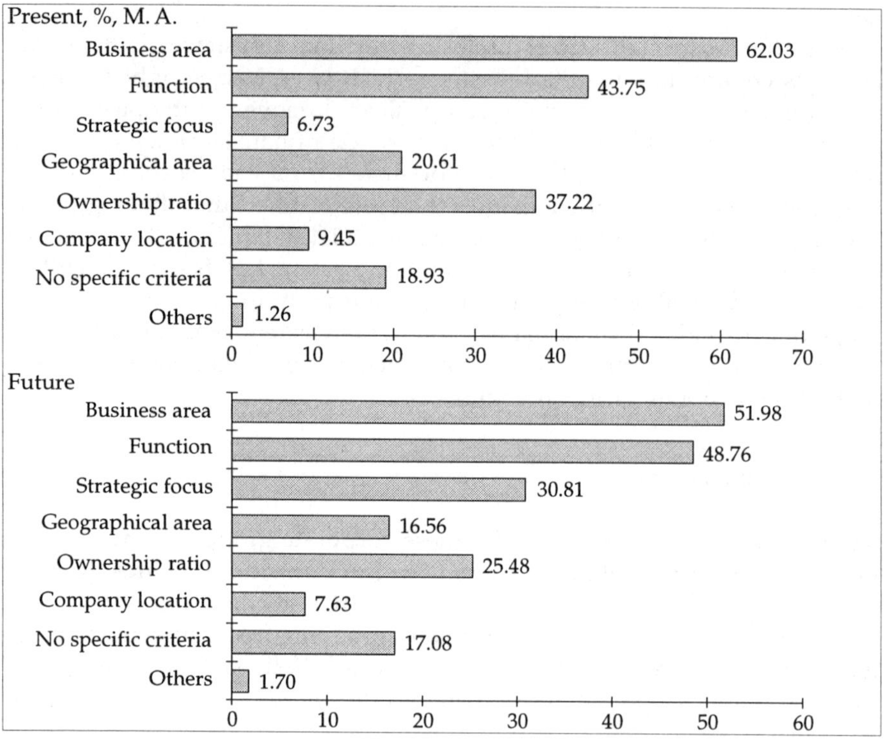

Table 1: Corporate Group Management Policy

Policy of Parent Companies	**Present (%)**	**Future (%)**
Group Members' Autonomous Management	53.42	78.64
Contribution to Parent Company	48.50	67.56
Co-existence & Co-prosperity With Other Group Members	58.01	71.23
Corporate Group's Total Power	64.11	89.24
Development of Group Business Strategy	40.87	74.09
Decentralized & Dynamic Group Operations	17.39	44.55
Merger, Buying Out, & Reorganization	17.40	63.18

Heretofore, the formation and development of Japanese corporate groups were not always undertaken strategically, following more of a 'natural' course of development and stressing operational over strategic purposes. In quite a few cases, the subsidiaries' major role was to provide a second career for parent companies' senior personnel as CEO or directors until their retirement.

Japanese corporate groups are becoming aware that it is also important to build up strong investment positions in order to compete globally. Strategically, the acquisition of firms has become another way of obtaining know-how.

In sum, Japanese corporate group policy is shifting to achieve a higher strategy orientation and group synergy.

2.2.2 Corporate group strategy

Japanese corporate groups' strategy change to 'total management' (table 2) is due to the changes in accounting practices (widened practice of consolidated financial statements) and the general trend to promote groups' business *strategy*. The strategy change from supporting and retaining less profitable group members to focusing on high-profit businesses is a logical consequence of the change in corporate groups' policy to confer management autonomy to group members and of the fact that parent companies want to focus their attention on their core businesses more than ever before.

Table 2: Directions of Corporate Group Strategy

Strategy	Parent Companies (%)
From Individual Management to Total Management	56.96
From Retaining Less Profitable Businesses to Focusing on High Profit Businesses	68.78
From a 360 Degree Approach to More Focused Areas of Products and Businesses	73.31
From Within-Group Trade to Group-External Trade	65.55
From Internal Resource Development to an Effective Utilization of External Resources	55.94
From Domestic Market-Centred to a Progressive Development of Overseas Markets	56.29
From Centralization of Strategy Formulation to Group Members' Participation in Strategy Formulation	72.04

As mentioned earlier, however, parent companies could reduce their management risks and stimulate and facilitate entrepreneurial behaviour by establishing new businesses through the use of group members or subsidiaries. That is, in order to be more competitive, companies could set up subsidiaries or autonomous business divisions within their present corporate structure.

Such strategy changes offer foreign businesses an important opening into the Japanese market, and are also indicative of the fact that Japanese corporate groups' are shifting from 'defensive' alliances[4] to strategic alliances. Furthermore, the progressive development of overseas markets demonstrates that Japanese corporate groups are on their way to enhanced globalization.

Finally, corporate groups' strategy change to allowing group members' participation in strategy formulation confirms their desire to foster general group business strategy, on the one hand, and decentralized and dynamic group operations, that is, their group synergy, on the other.

Graph 6: Corporate groups' core capabilities (%)

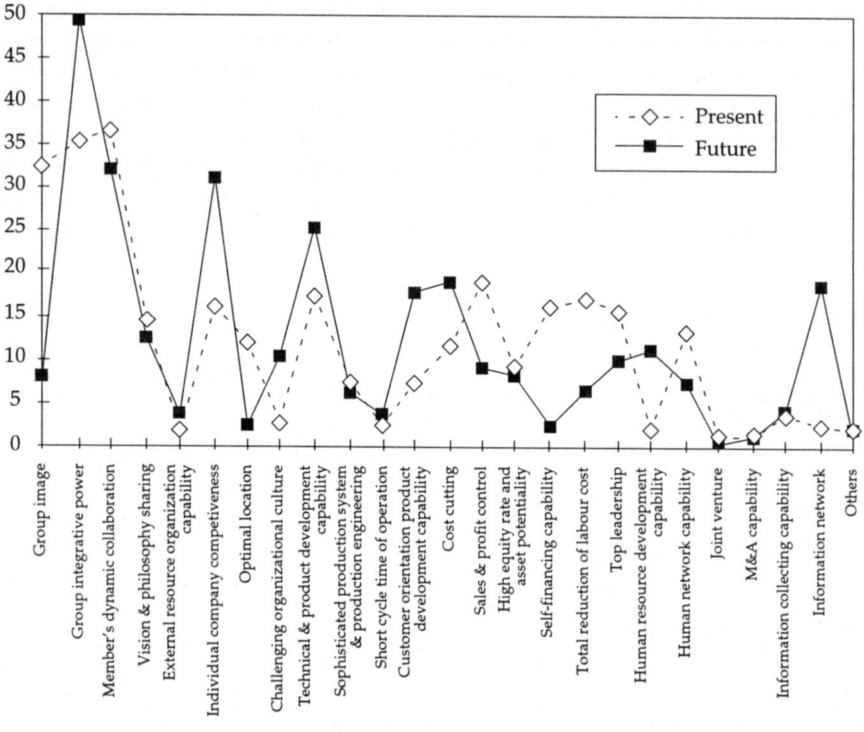

Graph 6 demonstrates that group integrative power, members' dynamic collaboration, individual company competitiveness, and technical and prod-

[4] The development of inter-company alliances within the Japanese domestic market has, in the past, emphasized alliances between group companies. Such alliances aimed aggressively at cost reduction, and are thus considered 'defensive'.

uct development capabilities will remain the main Japanese corporate groups' core capabilities in the future. Moreover, group members expect to be supported by sophisticated information and information network capabilities in the future.

Following the general trend of their policy and strategy, Japanese corporate groups' core capabilities are now oriented to greater group synergy and to developing better learning and strategic elements rather than merely pursuing operational aims.

2.2.3 Contemporary management

Corporate groups' management scheme

According to graph 7, the majority of Japanese corporate groups does not have regional headquarters or group general head-offices or even a corporate group recruitment policy. Most of them, however, feature a main bank, a personnel transfer system (*shukkō/tenseki*), a collaborative R&D system, group presidential meetings, collective sales networks, a corporate group trading system, technical advice and transfer systems, market and customer information sharing systems, collective information systems, lower-interest loan and debt guarantee systems, and downward expatriation (exchange of personnel between Japanese firms and their overseas subsidiaries) system.

Graph 7: Corporate groups' management scheme (%)

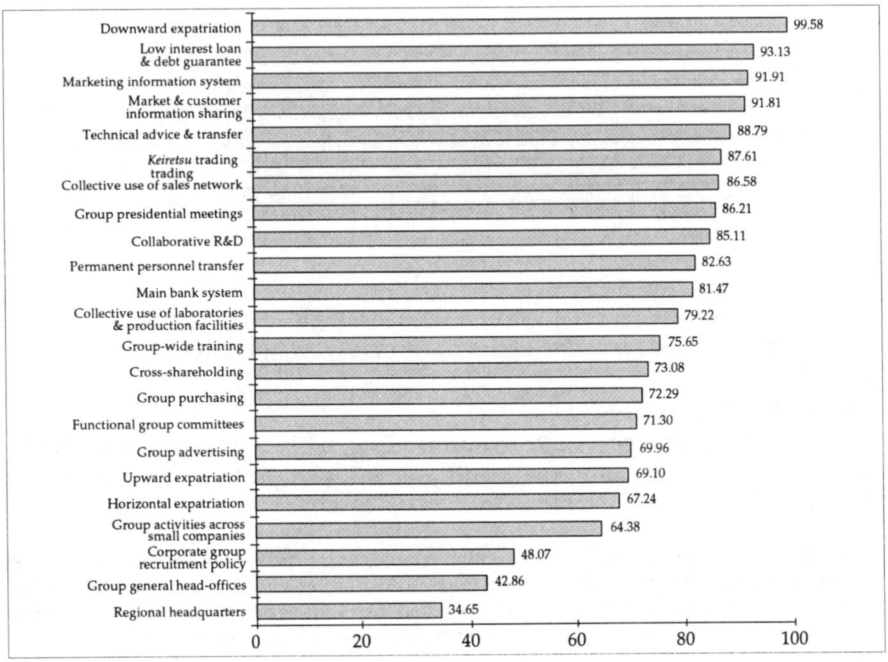

Graph 8, however, indicates that Japanese corporate groups will maintain or even strengthen their market and customer information sharing systems, their downward expatriation system, their collective information, technical advice and transfer systems, the collective sales network system, and the collaborative R&D system, that is, the *soft type scheme*, while loosening or weakening the others, namely the *hard type scheme*, such as the regional headquarter system, corporate group recruitment, horizontal expatriation, and so on[5]. This is a logical result of the corporate groups' policy and strategy choices.

Graph 8: The future of corporate groups' management scheme (%)

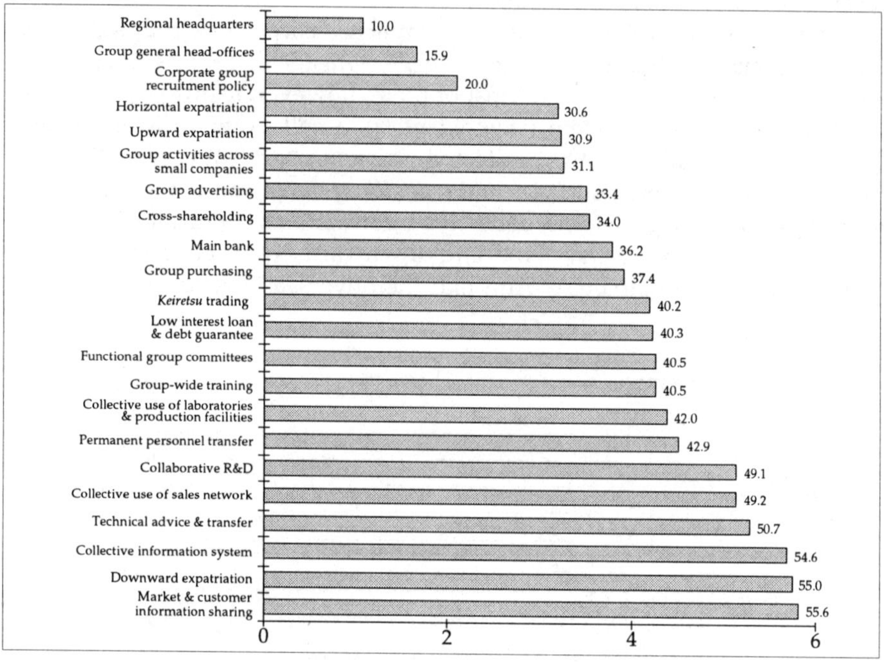

The *soft type* scheme is concerned with strategic learning and group synergy, while the *hard type* scheme is concerned with operational purposes.

Trading and financing principles

Concerning internal corporate group trading, table 3 shows that, in the future, Japanese corporate groups will give more importance to multiple or-

[5] A *soft scheme* is defined as a system which enables a group of companies to carry out its business smoothly through the transfer of information and know-how whilst a *hard scheme* is defined as a system which is based on the exchange of tangible resources (components, personnel) and 'objective' data (transfer prices, benchmarks etc.).

dering schemes, contribution and commitment to 'design-in' (close cooperation between parent firms and group members in the development process of products), and participation in information systems.

This suggests that Japanese corporate groups are becoming more learning-oriented, *the essence of this remanagement being to create a learning corporate group.*

Table 3: Principles of within-group trading

Principles	Present (%)	Future (%)
Market Price	75.00	73.51
Cost-plus Scheme	89.94	64.83
Multiple Ordering Scheme	9.74	13.94
Contribution & Commitment to Design-in	16.46	26.18
Participation in Information Systems	8.03	19.65
Others	0.88	1.50

Concerning the financing schemes of group members, table 4 suggests that most of corporate group members in our sample (44.64 %) will largely rely on self-financing in the future, rather than being financially supported by parent companies. In other words, group members are expected to be financially more independent, a consequence of corporate groups' policy to confer greater autonomous management to group members henceforward.

Table 4: Group members' financing schemes

Systems	Present (%)	Future (%)
Group-member Self-Financing	29.54	44.64
Major Part of Debts Guaranteed by Parent-companies	35.86	21.89
Loan With Lower Interest Rate by Parent-companies	21.10	19.31
Others	13.50	14.16

Performance evaluation

Though table 5 shows that Japanese corporate groups' present main performance evaluation standards are based on sales, contribution to parent-company, and profits, it also clearly indicates that, in the future, attainment of strategic mission, R&D, and product development capabilities will be emphasized more. This supports the aforementioned statement that Japanese corporate groups are becoming more strategy-oriented as well as learning-oriented.

Table 5: Performance evaluation criteria

Criteria	**Present (%)**	**Future (%)**
Sales	71.47	39.83
Profits	93.45	91.35
Security	15.52	15.85
Cash Flow	20.71	14.65
The Level of Contribution to The Parent Company	52.90	49.56
Strategic Mission Attainment	20.64	47.31
Acceptance of Staff and Its Level of Training	19.55	18.98
Information Gathering & Analysis	1.93	4.63
R&D and Product Development Capabilities	2.97	16.04
Others	0.85	1.79

According to table 6, almost all the firms in the sample (93.37 %) believe that performance evaluation will become more regular, evaluation standards will be communicated to the group member concerned (65.76 %), and parent companies will discuss the results of the evaluation (79.79 %) and the evaluation scheme itself (57.22 %) with group members.

This observation again supports corporate groups' avowed shift to a greater strategy and learning orientation as well as to a fostering of group synergy.

Table 6: Group members' performance evaluation scheme

Methods	**Present (%)**	**Future (%)**
Regular	76.55	93.37
Done by Parent Company Only	75.46	67.22
Disclosed to Group Members	26.92	65.76
Discuss the Results with Group Members	50.24	79.79
Discuss the Scheme with Group Members	23.67	57.22

Support and nurturing

Table 7 reflects the amount of management autonomy that parent companies are conferring to group members. Though decisions regarding top leadership, expatriation, and the transfer of personnel are still largely made by parent companies, middle management and other employees' recruitment and employment are usually initiated and decided by or together with group members.

Table 7: Personnel decisions by group members' organizational level

(Presently)

Level	Parent Companies	Group Members	Together
President	93.83	0.44	5.73
Directors	80.61	7.49	11.89
Middle Management	18.94	62.55	18.50
Staff	9.69	80.18	10.13
School and University Graduates' Recruitment & Employment	7.02	78.95	14.04
Mid-career Recruitment	4.82	82.90	12.28
Expatriate & Personnel Transfer	62.94	7.14	29.91

In the future, parent companies will gradually strenghten the involvement of group members (partially or totally) in decisions about personnel recruitment and/or employment to emphasize group synergy (table 8).

Table 8: Personnel decision—the future

Level	Parent Companies	Group Members	Together
President	92.77	0.60	6.63
Directors	69.28	7.83	22.89
Middle Management	13.85	68.67	17.47
Staff	7.19	80.24	12.57
Graduates' Recruitment & Employment	4.19	78.44	17.37
Mid-career Recruitment	4.22	80.73	15.06
Expatriate & Personnel Transfer	48.71	9.15	42.68

In sum, the *essence* of corporate group management is the dynamic balance between

1) the *centrifugal forces,* leading the corporate group, for example, to move from within-group trade to external trade, from internal resource orientation to the effective utilization of external resources, to developing overseas markets progressively, to moving toward multiple ordering schemes, thus, to moving toward a *learning orientation,* and
2) the *centripetal forces,* e. g., moving from a 360° approach to more focused areas of products and businesses, leaning toward group integrative power and members' dynamic collaboration, developing group business strate-

gy and the corporate group's total power and, thus, moving toward *strategy orientation.*

Graph 9: Centrifugal forces, centripetal forces and group synergy

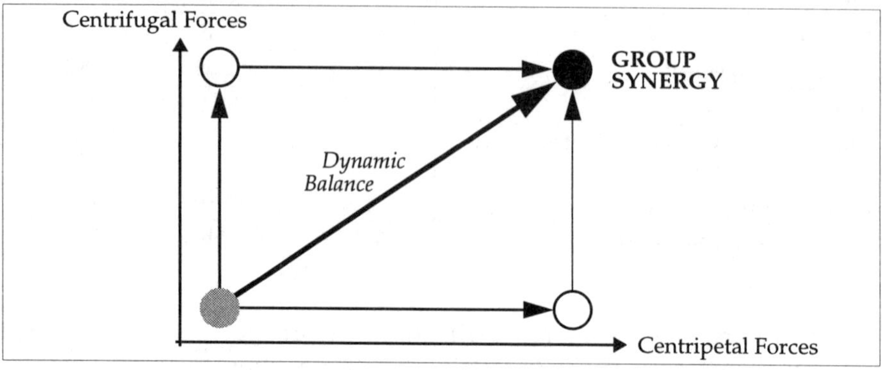

Table 9: Changing management principles in Japanese corporate groups

Elements	Present (%)	Future (%)
Management Philosophy	46.36	74.66
Management Mission & Business Plan	47.84	82.87
Top Leadership	58.37	71.43
Performance Evaluation & Rewards	30.47	68.94
Capital Investment & Loan	66.24	57.87
Technical Assistance & R&D Potential	36.79	59.26
Sales Channels	35.94	50.23
Human Resources	40.95	70.64
Organizational Culture	25.87	38.14
Information Sharing	23.94	67.75
Influence on Government & Industrial Society	18.54	41.12

Accordingly, most corporate groups will develop and strengthen their centripetal forces in order to use group members' management and financial autonomy, core business development, and institutional changes (e. g., due to deregulation) as powerful trumps in the new era of competition. Whilst also strengthening centrifugal forces binding group companies, emphasis is placed on common information systems, for example, in order to build opposing centripetal forces. In other words, group member firms' independent existence is strengthened with the ultimate aim of increasing synergy between inter-company group members.

The following section will use a case study of Yokogawa Electronic, to discuss in more detail some of the preceding findings. Concluding this paper will be a conceptual view on the evolution of corporate group management in Japan.

3 Corporate group management at Yokogawa Electronic

3.1 Overview

Yokogawa is a Japanese corporate group advocating "Global Group Management", composed of 61 affiliated companies in Japan and 39 overseas. Yokogawa Electronic, the head quarter (HQ) of this corporate group, has grown into a large company since 1915 in the business fields of measurement equipment and control devices. Consolidated group sales in 1996 amounted to 280 billion yen with 29,000 employees. The group has diversified its business into software, engineering, service, as well as manufacturing and selling personal computers through a group company, Japan Hewlett Packard, and medical systems by GE Yokogawa Medical Systems.

The basic policy of the Yokogawa group is as follows:

> "Our policy in terms of business diversification is to use and develop our accumulated technologies based on our main business, measurement equipment and control devices. When we have entered into a new business field like computer manufacturing and medical systems, we have allied with worldwide top-ranking companies disposing of excellent technologies in this business field" (Toshihiko AKAISHIZAWA, a director of Yokogawa Electronic).

Thus Yokogawa has developed two types of corporate group strategy: one is to enter into different business fields through joint ventures together with a world class company, the other is to establish subsidiaries related to its main business like software, engineering, staff functions and so on.

3.2 Establishing a global corporation through joint ventures

One of the corporate group strategies for Yokogawa is to enter into different business fields through joint ventures with leading global companies. One example is the founding of Yokogawa Hewlett Packard (YHP) in 1963. It goes without saying that HP is one of the largest PC manufactures. HP, however, had not been able to enter the Japanese market by way of a fully-owned subsidiary due to regulations in Japan at that time. As a result, at the first stage YHP was owned 51 % by Yokogawa and 49 % by HP, starting its business with Shōzō Yokogawa as CEO while key workers were transferred from Yokogawa. Today, Yokogawa maintains a 25 % stake in the venture.

Through this joint venture, HP could not only create a foothold in the Japanese market, but could also learn about management methodology in Japan. On the other hand, Yokogawa could gain know-how by allying with a foreign company, in addition to acquiring PC technologies. Since then YHP has changed its name into HP Japan (HPJ) and the relationship between Yokogawa and JHP has been basically based on the logic of capital, with Yokogawa being less influential on HPJ's business directly.

> "The relationship between Yokogawa and HPJ in business terms is actually weakening. However, we are now able to learn many things like business strategy, American rationality and management style. Adding to that, the relationship has been favourable in terms of entering new alliances with other foreign companies" (AKAISHIZAWA).

Alliances with leading companies have contributed to Yokogawa's growth. When General Electric (GE) selected a Japanese partner and founded Yokogawa Medical System (YMS) in 1982, one determining factor for GE, which had traditionally developed its overseas business through fully-owned subsidiaries, has been said to be the existence of YHP. Since then, GE's small-sized CTs that YMS originally developed have been supplied worldwide. In 1989, Yokogawa Johnson Controls (YJC) was established through a joint venture with Johnson Controls Inc. YJC has expanded its business in the building maintenance equipment business not only in Japan but also abroad, competing with Honeywell, the globally leading company in this market.

Moreover, Yokogawa has established a think tank specialized in human resource management in cooperation with Organization Resource Company (ORC). This joint venture has developed a new management system for employees posted overseas, and it is expanding into the consulting business. Arguably, Yokogawa's experience of partnering with top companies like HP and GE has led to the success of this particular business, as well.

Yokogawa can continue to enlarge its business domain in the future and progress its management logic, rather than only relying on technological information related to its main business, through alliances and close partnerships with leading companies, a crucial facet of Yokogawa's corporate group management:

> "It is very valuable and profitable that we can learn business philosophy and management methodology from international top-ranking companies. For example, our top management can meet and talk with Jack Welch, CEO of GE. Such an opportunity is very important and useful for considering our business strategy and management" (AKAISHIZAWA).

3.3 Building global group management through functional subsidiaries

The other facet of Yokogawa's corporate group strategy is to establish subsidiaries (group companies) related to its main business. This means to decentralize and transfer HQ's functions like production, financing, and R&D to the subsidiaries, which is a main pole of Yokogawa's corporate group strategy.

Historically speaking, the first period in the evolution of the company's group strategy was from the 1950s to the 60s when the company established many production subsidiaries. The second covers the 1970s to 1983, when these production companies were integrated. The third lasted from 1984 to 1992, when many new subsidiaries were created, e. g., engineering and software, in compliance with technological, economic and socio-environmental change. The fourth began in 1993, when the Japanese *bubble economy* had come to an end.

3.3.1 First period

The major characteristic of the first period was the establishment of many production-oriented subsidiaries. Their main purpose was to reduce production costs and attract cheaper labour. Top managers were dispatched from HQ. In other words, these companies were deeply related with Yokogawa HQ's business domain.

3.3.2 Second and third period

In the second period, Yokogawa endeavoured to integrate widely diffused subsidiaries, created in the previous period, in order to rein in rising expenses and to limit the perceived deviation from their original purpose.

During the third period, Yokogawa actively founded new subsidiaries (group companies) for enlarging its software and engineering business, on top of existing activities centred on 'hardware business'. In order to develop this strategy, the company established its New Business Planning Office.

At that time, these subsidiaries were not controlled by HQ, but by individual divisions. Although HQ made final decisions concerning the establishment of subsidiaries, each division independently planned and formulated that decision. Hence, each division managed, supported and took charge of these subsidiaries.

In the late 1980s, HQ as well as its group companies enjoyed growth supported by the generally strong economic environment.

3.3.3 Fourth period

Like other Japanese companies, Yokogawa and its group companies, however, faced a serious recession in the early 1990s. Under such economic conditions, most of the group members failed to achieve their original purpose, which was to attain over 30 % of their total sales through business with non-Yokogawa group companies. Most of them, in fact, achieved less than 10 %. Therefore managing and operating group companies *strategically* became a major issue for the Yokogawa corporate group. With its "*VE* (value engineering) *Plan*" drafted in 1992 as a turning point, Yokogawa started to implement thorough cost reductions, while at the same time reconstructing its previous corporate group-type management.

Adding to the integration and reinforcement of domestic group companies, Yokogawa has actively developed global strategies focused on the Southeast Asian region and on China in order to survive amidst the emerging mega-competition. Yokogawa now promotes to connect 39 overseas group companies with its domestic business for realizing its 'Global-Group Management'.

3.4 The Global-Group Management approach of Yokogawa

The basic policy of Yokogawa advocating "Global-Group Management" is to foster stronger and larger group companies independent from HQ. Through the empowerment of its group companies, Yokogawa seeks to realize the entire corporate group's advancement. In order to achieve that, Yokogawa pursues personnel transactions among group companies. Concerning the evaluation of an employee's performance, it has become an important factor for promotion whether he or she has had experience working for other group companies. Such an experience is considered useful not only for educating future managers, but also for creating a new overall management model by integrating and synthesizing external management styles.

In short, the establishment of group companies today is to enhance business opportunities and to create business synergy throughout the Yokogawa group by integrating group companies, adding to the reduction of total cost. In such a process, however, one *important problem* is how to enforce corporate *group identity.*

According to AKAISHIZAWA, "the relationship between HQ and group companies is changing, evolving from a 'HQ controls subsidiaries' type. Today, HQ's major role is to become a coordination centre for the business development of group companies. In other words, HQ searches for common denominators among HQ and group companies and promotes an effective and sophisticated use of business resources. Hence, in this year, we established the Affiliated Business Centre for the purpose of coordinating group companies' businesses and creating group synergy."

As mentioned above, Yokogawa is developing a multi-dimensional corporate group management; it is pursuing strategic management of joint ventures with top ranking companies, while at the same time fostering group companies related to its main business. It is difficult to integrate such a multi-dimensional structure into a single corporate vision. This problem will intensify when some of the group companies become listed on the stock exchange in the near future. Thus, Yokogawa group must consider its group management multi-dimensionally. In a way, Yokogawa's experience of concomitantly pursuing 'autonomy and integration' since the 1960s becomes useful for currently evolving its strategic corporate group management.

The driving force behind this evolving strategic corporate group management is to maximize both centrifugal and centripetal forces; the former is for expanding the existing business domain and the latter is for the integration of the diverse group strenghts. On this point, the deregulation concerning the law on holding companies in Japan in 1998 will greatly facilitate Yokogawa's task of enacting its new style of corporate group management.

4 Conceptual framework of Corporate Group Remanagement

Drawing on the results of our survey and the case study, we propose a model or framework for better understanding the new type of Japanese company group management (graph 10). In this framework, *Group Vision* is the starting point and, at the same time, the goal of corporate group management. Moreover, such an overall vision helps in determining the business strategies for the entire group. The creation of a vision is the result of an efficient planning process for designing the future of the corporate group. However, this should not be a one-sided affair, urged on by HQ; instead, each group member's expectations and goals should be adequately reflected in the process and then directed toward the realization of this group vision.

Graph 10: Framework of Corporate Group Remanagement

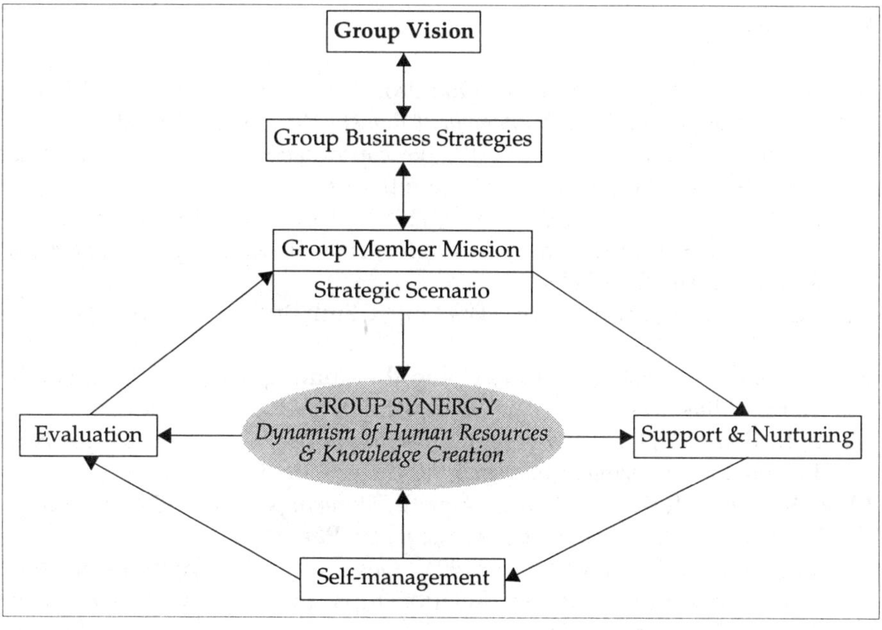

Next, *Group Business Strategies* are indispensable in realizing the group vision. However, it is noteworthy that individual group member's strategies alone are insufficient for this task. Hence, business strategies that encompass overlapping business areas are also of vital importance, thereby achieving a dynamic balance between centripetal forces and centrifugal forces governing a corporate group. As a principle, each group member can clearly decide its mission on the basis of the overall group vision and group business strategies. Again, this 'mission' must not be one-sided. It should rather be designed to foster information sharing and group member dialogue. The role of parent companies should therefore be *to evaluate* whether each group member's mission is accurately performed or not, and, if necessary, to *support and nurture* group members' business and human resources.

Finally and of central importance, the creation of *Group Synergy* lies at the heart of this modern Japanese corporate group management ('modern', thus 'remanagement'). Group synergy goes beyond the integration and coordination of each group member's resources and strengths. Personnel transfers and flows of information are the integrative forces to create group synergy, and corporate groups' present task is to move from "group member capabilities" to "corporate group capabilities", from "vertical transfer" to "horizontal transfer." In brief, today's reality dictates that 21st century corporate group management cannot be based on (1) parent company dependence nor on (2) a one-sided and upward/downward regulatory regime.

References

ANDERSON, E. (1990): Two Firms, One Frontier On Assessing Joint Venture Performance. In: *Sloan Management Review,* Winter, pp. 19–30.

CONTRACTOR, F. J. and P. LORANGE (1988): *Cooperative Strategies in International Joint Ventures.* Lexington: Lexington Books.

D'AUNNO, T. A. and H. S. ZUCKERMAN (1987): A Life-cycle Model of Organizational Federations: The Case of Hospitals. In: *Academy of Management Journal* 12, pp. 534–545.

The Chemical Week (1994): Japan – The Long Climb Back to Health. November 30, 1994, pp. 34–36.

FERGUSON, C. H. (1990): Computers and the Coming of the US Keiretsu. In: *Harvard Business Review,* July–August, pp. 55–70.

MILES, R. E. and C. C. SNOW (1986): Organizations: New Concepts for New Forms. In: *California Management Review* 28, pp. 62–73.

MORI, K. (1994): Industrial Sea Change. In: *Brookings Review* 12, 4, p. 20.

OECD (1991): *OECD Economic Surveys. Japan.* Paris: OECD.

RING, P. S. and A. H. VAN DE VEN (1994): Developmental Processes of Cooperative Interorganizational Relationships. In: *Academy of Management Review* 19, 1, pp. 90–118.

VAN DE VEN, A. H. and G. WALKER (1984): The Dynamics of Inter-organizational Coordination. In: *Administrative Science Quarterly* 29, pp. 598–621.

Commentary

Externalization and Inter-organizational Networks. How Globalization Transforms the Japanese Model

Dieter ERNST

1 A common theme: convergence versus diversity

The current crisis of the Japanese economy has forced large Japanese multinationals to reconsider their established modes of organization and corporate governance. Globalization has been the main driving force behind such changes. Its impact on corporate organization however does not necessarily conform to the popular convergence theory. Neo-liberals expect globalization to act as a powerful equalizer, both among nations and among firms. Among nations, globalization imposes new constraints on the policy-making of national governments, constraints that force a convergence towards economic liberalization, balanced budgets, and lower expenditures on welfare. Convergence is also expected among firms. Faced with similar constraints, firms are expected to converge in their organization and strategies, irrespective of their national origin.[1] BOYER has nicely summarized the underlying logic: "...everywhere firms facing the same optimizing problems find the same solution in terms of technology, markets and products, for there is one best way of organizing production—a single optimum among a possible multiplicity of local optima."[2]

The papers by Yoshimura, Ueno and Kagono and by Teramoto, Iwasaki and Takai convincingly demonstrate that the response of Japanese firms to globalization may not necessarily lead to a full-scale convergence with the Western model of the multi-divisional firm. Japanese firms do not blindly copy the U.S. model. Instead, partial convergence may well coexist with persistent diversity.[3] While both papers share a common message, each of them approaches it from a different angle. Yoshimura et al. argue that the 'externalization of organizations' may be messy, complicated and chaotic. Yet, as the case of Matsushita shows, externalization may well provide an appropriate solution to the complex requirements of global competition: a capacity to

---

[1] Prominent examples are VERNON (1977) and GRAHAM & KRUGMAN (1989).

[2] BOYER (1996), pages 47f. I agree with BOYER's conclusion: "This syllogism that equates globalization with convergence is logically flawed, and its premise may not correspond to the current state of the world economy" (ibid., p. 50).

[3] For similar findings, see ERNST & RAVENHILL (1997), and ERNST (1997a).

combine price leadership with product differentiation, speed-to-market and flexibility. Under certain conditions, externalization may be superior to the US model of outsourcing. Externalization may also have advantages relative to the idea that headquarters (HQ) is the only appropriate place for ensuring "corporate coherence" (TEECE, RUMELT, & DOSI 1994, and FOSS & CHRISTENSEN 1996).

Most contributions to the debate on *corporate coherence* underestimate the degree to which the dispersion of higher-end value-chain activities now cuts across the boundaries of the firm—hence the need for an analysis that covers such dispersion in the context of inter-firm networks (see ERNST 1997c).They are the focus of the paper by Teramoto et al. which analyses their role for the organizational restructuring of Japanese corporate groups. It is argued that the bursting of the *bubble economy* has led to a gradual disintegration of the *keiretsu*-type networks with far-reaching implications for corporate behaviour and industry structure. Outsiders to the *keiretsu,* both Japanese and foreign, may now for the first time have a realistic chance to enter such networks. Yet, this does not imply convergence to the U.S. model of the M-type firm. Building on existing strengths of the Japanese business system, Japanese firms will increasingly rely on inter-organizational (IO) networks in order to strengthen their learning efficiency and in order to improve their access to knowledge and capabilities. Based on a survey of leading Japanese manufacturing companies and two case studies (Yokogawa Electronics and Tōshiba), it is shown that far-reaching changes occur in the prevailing system of corporate governance. The main purpose of these changes is to combine decentralization and externalization of the value chain with an improvement of group-wide corporate coherence.

2 The hidden agenda of externalization

Based on a case study of the Matsushita group (MEI), Yoshimura and Kagono put forward two interesting propositions that nicely challenge established wisdom:

- "Large Japanese corporations have developed a unique multi-divisional structure which is slightly different from the European and American structure on organizational charts" (p. 21). The slight difference on the charts may hide some significant differences in nature. What looks like convergence on the surface, in reality is divergence.
- Even within the same group, i. e., Matsushita, there is a perplexing variety of externalization patterns: The organization structure of the Matsushita Group is complex and the "decision making processes are so complicated and chaotic that nobody in Matsushita could provide the entire picture of these processes inside the organization" (p. 23). It is due to this amorphous diversity that hierarchical control is out of the question. The frequent

changes suggest that it is difficult to coordinate the divisions and the affiliates through hierarchical means.

Why is there such a perplexing diversity of amorphous externalization arrangements? In the literature, one finds four explanations: i) The purpose is to give more autonomy to the affiliates than to the internal divisions. ii) Externalization helps to reduce risk in new business development. iii) The parent company can reap capital gains of public offerings, and iv) externalization is a means to capitalize on wage differences, with smaller companies paying lower wages and being less constrained in terms of long-term employment. None of these four explanations is satisfactory. A case study approach is necessary to uncover the hidden agenda of externalization.

The paper proceeds in three steps. It first describes some *major challenges* that currently confront the Matsushita group. It then highlights some important features of MEI's approach to the development of its multi-divisional structure, in terms of specialization, corporate governance, and externalization. The paper then concludes with some highly stimulating suggestions on what this case study implies for the theory of the firm and for management strategies.

2.1 How MEI develops its multi-divisional structure

MEI has had to cope with two major challenges: a rapid change in its product mix (including the pitfalls of malignant diversification), and quite drastic changes in its distribution system which traditionally has been its major strength. These challenges have defined the agenda for MEI's changes in corporate organization. The paper uses two *benchmarks* to identify some peculiar features of MEI's approach to organizational restructuring: the Western M-type firm, and the Japanese version of the M-type firm. Compared to these two benchmarks, the following peculiarities are highlighted:

a) Specialization

Apparently, MEI pursues a dual pattern of specialization: specialization by product and by function coexist.[4] How can one explain this dual pattern of specialization? An important finding is that the *principle of specialization is not pushed to the limit:* while the sales divisions specialize in sales and marketing,

[4] It is very difficult to understand the logic of some of these arrangements. Take the example of the production divisions (*jigyōbu*). They specialize in product development and production; they are usually small and organized around a single product. Limited marketing functions are normally attached. Their main tasks are to watch global markets for the product, develop new product ideas and test the ideas proposed by the division's development department. They closely interact with the specialized marketing divisions. The divisional sales activities are mostly directed toward the sales division. Yet for OEM sales, there are fairly close direct interactions with the customers. The same is true for the sales of parts and components which are directly shipped to the divisions

they have to share some responsibilities with production divisions. They also may have to deal with some additional functions, e. g., product development. Probably of greatest importance is the close interdependence between these different functional divisions. As both production divisions and sales divisions are not self-contained, each of them crucially depends on mutual cooperation. Such cooperation is not imposed by command from above: transactions are normally set on the basis of market price. For instance, buyer divisions have the right to reject the purchase from internal suppliers and outsource them. In turn, supplier divisions can "... sell their products to outside customers without any further permission, except when the product was developed jointly internally" (p. 23). This clearly invalidates some of the claims found in the literature that the Japanese production networks by necessity are closed to outsiders.[5]

b) Corporate governance

The focus is on the following features of MEI's governance structure: a) a rigorous evaluation of division performance; b) control is exercised by different actors, not just HQ; c) centralized control over financial transactions; and d) intra-firm transactions are based on market price. This set of features differs from the stereotype of the Japanese production system which raises the question of how typical MEI's approach is for Japanese firms. There are also important differences from typical Western governance structures. The paper thus apparently implies that *diversity continues to prevail, both among Japanese firms, and between Japanese and American firms.*

The paper could benefit from a clarification of the concept of corporate governance. For instance, as more and more stages of the value chain are dispersed beyond the boundaries of the firm and across national borders, this has added new dimensions. The issue today is the control and coordination of complex international production networks.[6] Corporate governance consists of common methods and procedures that shape the behaviour of network nodes, such as budgetary rules and procedures, evaluation proce-

---

of MEI. In turn, the sales divisions (*Hansha*) specialize in a certain distribution channel in a geographic area. They purchase products from various production divisions and affiliates and sell them to outside customers and distributors.

5 See for instance HATCH & YAMAMURA (1996), and PAULY & REICH (1997).

6 The concept of an 'international production network' (IPN) is an attempt to capture the spread of broader and more systemic forms of international production that cover all stages of the value chain and that may or may not involve equity ownership. This concept allows us to analyse the globalization strategies of a particular firm with regard to the following four questions: 1) Where does a firm locate which stages of the value chain? 2)To what degree does a firm rely on outsourcing? What is the importance of inter-firm production networks relative to the firm's internal production network? 3) To what degree is the control over these transactions exercised in a centralized or in a decentralized manner? And 4) how do the different elements of these networks hang together? This concept has been developed in studies prepared for the OECD (ERNST 1994), the Sloan Foundation (ERNST 1997c), and the Brookings Institution (ERNST 1997a).

dures, personnel management practices, database management, quality control norms, etc. (ERNST 1997c). Network nodes can be equity-owned affiliates and those legally independent firms that participate in the core company's inter-firm networks.[7]

A crucial aspect which has not been taken into account is the *dynamics of change* in MEI's corporate governance. Take the example of evaluation criteria of division performance. It is argued that divisions are ranked, in terms of their ROS (return-on-sales). But various sources have argued that evaluation criteria are now shifting to ROI (return-on-investment) (STOPFORD 1995, DOBSON 1995, KESTER 1996). This raises the question of whether there is not at least some limited convergence with US accounting practices.

A second example relates to the centralized control over financial transactions. It is argued that divisions deposit retained earnings with the HQ after paying overheads and receive interest on these retained earnings. If they are short of cash, they can borrow from HQ but have to pay interest, based on going market rates. But is this not changing? Since around 1994, there are apparently two important changes:[8] Subsidiaries have increased their reliance on reinvestment, thus reducing their financial dependence on the centre, i. e., HQ and the group's main bank. At the same time, MEI seeks to strengthen its control over its financial management network, trying to reestablish a certain degree of corporate coherence.

First, the decreasing dependence of subsidiaries on the centre for finance has increased their decision autonomy. Until the early 1990s, most of the funds required for the expansion of Japanese regional production activities in East Asia came from remittances from the parent company in Japan. Reinvestments by overseas affiliates and equity links with local investors played a very minor role.[9] This pattern is now beginning to change, especially in the ASEAN countries. Most of these investments are now locally funded and do not involve a transfer of capital from Japan.[10] Second, MEI is in the process of rationalizing its worldwide financial management network, linking regional centres in Singapore, Hong Kong, Malaysia, the U.S., and elsewhere, and placing them under the control of a global settlements centre to

---

[7] The following indicators have been used to establish whether a governance structure is centralized or decentralized: ownership patterns, the degree of local decision autonomy, local linkages, the role of regional headquarters, and the degree of local funding through reinvestments and a listing on local stock exchanges.

[8] For details, see ERNST & RAVENHILL (1997).

[9] During the peak of the recession, when most Japanese electronics firms faced a serious profit squeeze, Japanese parent companies actually used sophisticated transfer-pricing techniques to transfer back home any profits made in Asia (from an interview with a Japanese venture capital firm, November 1993).

[10] Between 1989 and 1992, the ratio of reinvestments of Japanese affiliates to Japan's total FDI increased from 35 % to 60 % for ASEAN affiliates, and from 54 % to 80 % for NIE affiliates. This is substantially above the ratios reported for affiliates in the U.S. and Europe (these increased from 15 % to 24 %, and from 10 % to 17 % respectively, see MITI 1994).

be set up in Japan (*Nikkei Daily* 1997a). This is a pre-emptive move ahead of the coming *big bang* deregulation of Japan's financial industry. The expectation is that this will help to improve the efficiency in the use of capital and to save transfer charges.

c) Amorphous externalization

The paper documents a great diversity of externalization patterns of what I would call *amorphous externalization*. They differ in terms of ownership relations with MEI, employment practices, product mix, stages of the value chain, and the original motivation for externalization. In order to highlight the root causes for amorphous externalization, the paper focuses on two extreme examples, Kyūshū Matsushita and Matsushita Kotobuki. Both are among the most profitable affiliates of MEI. Both come from humble origins, and were originally established as OEM suppliers to the MEI group for fairly low-end products. Both firms now have developed a reputation for quick and effective new product development; they also are both fiercely independent from HQ in terms of personnel as well as finance. Their main strength is their capacity to quickly target emerging market niches. They assume roles that are not performed effectively by any division or subsidiary and rapidly fill unexploited niches. They also force MEI's internal divisions to become more aggressive in order to avoid being overtaken by these 'outsiders'. Without amorphous externalization, both affiliates could not have played this role.

2.3 Implications for the theory of the firm and management strategies

Firstly, research on firm organization has focused primarily on the decentralization versus centralization dimension. This is a much too narrow focus. Decentralization is a necessary condition for competitive success, but not a sufficient one. The key is externalization: "The internal control system usually produces dysfunctions" (p. 30). Externalizing the control, organizations can avoid this dysfunction without incurring significant costs. The result is that HQ will not be overloaded with control and coordination functions: HQ can share them with other control agencies such as banks and capital markets. Both banks and the capital markets evaluate the performance of affiliates on a daily basis and are immune to the excuses and lobbying efforts of affiliate managers. This obviously is a different concept from the idea proposed by TEECE ET AL. (1994) that HQ is the only appropriate place for ensuring "corporate coherence".

Externalization of course also comes at a cost: it may lead to messy organizational charts, difficulties of coordination and lack of specialization (overlapping of activities). By designing suitable levels of externalization, organizations may maximize the benefits of externalization while minimizing its risks and costs (Kagono p. 31) Amorphous externalization may be the appropriate approach in the Japanese context, given the existing industry structure. This raises two important questions: i) To what degree does nationality of ownership matter, i. e. can externalization also work in an American or European institutional context? And ii) can amorphous externalization also work for overseas affiliates?

Secondly, amorphous externalization enables individual nodes of MEI's network to perform the function of "sweeper" organizations, thus addressing the niches and interstices left blank by MEI's internal divisions. It inserts some of the competitive pressures of the market into MEI's production network. More specifically, amorphous externalization has the following effects on individual members of MEI's production network: i) It exposes them to highly effective performance pressures. ii) Subsidiaries and affiliates have access to MEI's capability base. They can use them selectively, according to their needs.[11] iii) They are not burdened with a fixed product mix, but are free to develop and produce any product for which they have a competitive edge. And iv), they can avoid the disadvantages of excessive size, in terms of slow decision-making and rigidity.

Finally, externalization can mean many different things. There is not just one pattern of externalization as implied by much of the current literature on outsourcing. This paper shows that Matsushita's approach to externalization is fundamentally different from the US approach to outsourcing. It argues that this amorphous diversity of externalization patterns, while looking messy on the organizational charts, may have substantial advantages: it "... facilitates organizational learning through the conveyance of uncomfortable information and the implementation of uncomfortable action" (p. 31).

3 The dynamics of change of inter-organizational networks

3.1 Catalysts for the disintegration of *keiretsu*-type networks

During the 1980s, corporate growth in Japan has relied on aggressive equity financing within the *keiretsu*. This has led to a strengthening of *keiretsu*-type networks. Not anymore: the bursting of the *bubble economy* has forced Japanese companies and banks to reduce their equity shares in corporate group-member countries, as there is no longer any guarantee that stock prices will increase. The result is a gradual disintegration of *keiretsu*-type networks with far-reaching implications for corporate behaviour and industry structure.

The bursting of the *bubble economy* has acted as a catalyst for the gradual deregulation of the financial system. While this process remains painfully slow, there has probably been some improvement in terms of static allocation efficiency of investment. At the same time, there are attempts to tighten

---

[11] There are striking similarities with Acer's Client-Server organization model. See ERNST (1997b).

financial reporting procedures which is expected to end the Japanese practice of buying and selling securities simultaneously for quick paper profits. Together with more stringent tax declaration requirements, such stricter financial disclosure rules imply that corporate HQ is now under much greater pressure to improve consolidated results for the whole group rather than just for individual divisions. In other words, financial deregulation imposes greater pressure to increase efficiency. Inter-organizational networks are a peculiar form of organizational innovation to address this challenge. The paper by Teramoto et al. also claims that financial deregulation is likely to facilitate the opening-up of Japanese production networks: it may "...offer foreign businesses and Japanese firms outside of a corporate group an important opening into the network" (p. 40). However, no evidence is provided that this is happening.

3.2 A major challenge: Upgrading the product mix

Probably the greatest challenge for Japanese firms is to upgrade their product mix, according to the survey undertaken by Teramoto et al. In principle, there are two options to respond: concentrate on core competencies or diversify into newer, fast growing and non-homogeneous products. The first response is typical for many US companies and is the established gospel of strategic management gurus such as Michael Porter, Hamel and Pralahad etc., "focus on what you do best and outsource all the rest." This approach is driven primarily by a short-term financial logic: it improves static allocation efficiency and can also accelerate the speed of new product innovation. Yet, its long-term benefits remain in doubt, especially as long as outsourcing is not being balanced with an improvement of corporate coherence.

The immediate response of Japanese firms to the bursting of the *bubble economy*, not surprisingly, has been to cut costs wherever possible, and to consolidate their core businesses. Increasingly, however, they rely on the second option: they try to upgrade their product portfolio with the help of inter-organizational (IO) networks. "Diversify through externalization" appears to be the prevailing approach: "... in order to be more competitive and to diversify, companies ... set up subsidiaries or autonomous business divisions within their present corporate structure" (p. 41). The paper would be strengthened, if it would provide concrete evidence.

3.3 Changes in corporate strategy: From ad hoc to strategic management approaches

In response to the bursting of the *bubble economy*, Japanese firms experience a fundamental shift in their organization from an orientation toward operational requirements to a strategic focus (p. 43). Japanese corporate organization traditionally developed in an ad hoc manner. Primary determinants were the requirements of particular functions, such as human resource management, sales and distribution (in the case of Matsushita), and requirements that result from an industrial logic, i. e., production and logistics. For instance, in quite a few cases the purpose of establishing a particular subsidiary has been to provide a second career for senior managers as CEO or directors until their retirement (p. 45). Today, organizational change is driven primarily by a strategic purpose: to improve the organization's learning efficiency and to acquire, as quickly as possible, knowledge and complementary capabilities: "Japanese corporate groups are becoming more learning-oriented... (The main objective of organizational restructuring)... is to create a learning corporate group" (p. 49). Improving learning efficiency and capabilities, in turn, is an essential prerequisite for sustaining the companies' international market share. Does this not imply that NONAKA & TAKEUCHI (1995) have a normative focus, i. e., they discuss future perspectives and necessary changes rather than about what exists at present?

This shift from defensive to strategic restructuring however does not necessarily follow the US model of industrial outsourcing. While many Japanese firms have focused, during the early 1990s, most of their attention on a consolidation of their core businesses, they are now eager to combine this with a vigorous diversification of their product portfolio. However, diversification relies on a specific type of externalization, i. e., the creation of "...subsidiaries or autonomous business divisions *within* (DE) their present corporate structure" (p. 45). In other words, diversification relies heavily on some of the existing strengths of the Japanese corporate organization which differs quite substantially from the Western M-type organization. This does not support a pervasive convergence hypothesis. In the case of Japanese firms, organizational upgrading results in the spread of IO networks that are very different from the international production networks established by American firms.

3.4 Convergence coexists with diversity

One important finding of Teramoto et al. is that learning from the American experience is consistent with persistent diversity. Practically all the leading Japanese electronics firms have exposed themselves over the last few years to this learning. Yokogawa Electronic for instance has long-standing links with two American companies, each of which in its own field is widely regarded as a pace setter for organizational innovations. Yokogawa's management stresses the crucial importance of learning from US management practices." ... (W)e are... able to learn (from HP) many things like business strategy, American rationality and management style. ... It is very valuable and profitable that we can learn business philosophy and management methodology from international top-ranking companies. For example, our top management can meet and talk with Jack Welch, CEO of GE. Such an opportunity is very important and useful for considering our business strategy and management" (p. 54).

Does this imply that Yokogawa is transforming itself into a clone of HP or GE? And, furthermore, has such learning been a one-sided affair where Yokogawa adopts features of its American partners, while the latter remain unchanged? As for the first question, Yokogawa continues to differ from American firms in key features of its organization. For instance, one important objective of the company's "Global Corporate Management" doctrine is to balance increasing empowerment at every node of its IPN (international production network) with a sufficient degree of corporate coherence. The key mechanism for providing such coherence is an elaborate scheme of information-sharing through constant rotation of human resources. The focus is on the exchange of tacit knowledge embodied in skilled operators, technicians, engineers and managers. This peculiar approach to human resource management continues to distinguish Japanese firms from most of their American competitors.

As for the second question, take Yokogawa's joint venture with HP. It is important to note that learning has been a two-way process. Not only did Yokogawa gain knowledge about HP's organization and management practices, but also HP was able to learn.[12] Through this joint venture, HP was able to gain early on a foothold in the Japanese market, on which it could later build when it began to penetrate Japan's computer market. It also was able to learn about some peculiar features of Japanese management methodology. For instance, it was through this link with Yokogawa that HP became acutely aware of some organizational innovations in quality control, much earlier than many of its competitors. This knowledge of the existing far superior quality control procedures in Japanese firms is one of the reasons why HP, in the early 1980s, was able to criticize with full confidence the decline of quality levels in the U.S. semiconductor industry. HP was also able to reap similar learning effects in other areas where Japanese firms have a proven record of strength, such as inventory management, human resource development, and the acceleration of the design cycle for new products. All of this indicates that Yokogawa's links with foreign companies can certainly not be reduced to a one-way convergence to the US model. In the case of its link with HP, we are clearly talking about a case of mutual convergence or hybridization—both Yokogawa and HP have been able to learn from each other and to adapt elements of its partner's organization into its own organizational structure. There is simply no evidence that Yokogawa has converged to the HP model.

---

[12] See the discussion in ERNST (1997c) of HP's innovative approach to global chain management which arguably draws some of its inspirations from Japanese inventory management approaches.

4 Weaknesses and suggestions for future research

Both papers share one important weakness: they neglect or at least do not deal explicitly with changes in the organization of overseas operations. This is an important weakness: since the mid-1980s, most major Japanese firms have established increasingly complex international production networks that now cover almost all stages of the value chain, with the exception of hard-core R&D.[13] This raises a number of important questions that are central for both papers. As the value chain becomes dispersed across borders and the boundaries of the firm, what does this imply for key features of the Japanese corporate organization and its governance structures? What changes are necessary in order to reconcile such rapid dispersion with a sufficiently strong degree of corporate coherence? Can the approaches that work in Japan also be applied to different network nodes overseas? Or is it necessary to modify these approaches? And if such modifications occur in the organization of IPN, what feedback effects will that have on the organization and governance patterns back home in Japan?

Take for instance the case of MEI's current reorganization of its Asian production networks[14]. So far, MEI's subsidiaries in Malaysia, Thailand, Indonesia, the Philippines and Taiwan have each engaged in a wide range of businesses in each of these markets. This has prevented MEI from reaping the benefits of regional specialization. Due to recent progress in AFTA (ASEAN Free Trade Area), it is now possible to address the ASEAN market rather than individual national markets. This makes it possible to rationalize each individual affiliate's product mix, to establish an integrated regional production network where each network node now has greater decision autonomy over its more focused portfolio of activities. But decentralization is only part of the story. Of equal importance is externalization. For instance, MEI has already spun off National Thai Co.'s electronic parts, car audio equipment and fan divisions. Matsushita Communication Industrial Co. and other affiliated companies will run the new firms. In addition, MEI also plans to distribute the capital it injected into Matsushita Electric Co. (Malaysia) Bhd., Matsushita Electric Taiwan Co., and Matsushita Electric Philippines Corp. among these three firms' business divisions. This implies that these firms now have somewhat greater decision autonomy. At the same time, they will now have to raise capital independently in local and regional capital markets, with the result that they will be exposed to a variety of control mechanisms. This clearly implies that externalization is now also gradually being applied to MEI's overseas affiliates.

---

[13] For evidence, see STOPFORD (1995) and ERNST (1997a).

[14] See Nikkei Daily (1997b)

References

BOYER, R. (1996): The Convergence Hypothesis Revisited: Globalization but Still the Century of Nations? In: BERGER, S. and R. DORE (eds.): *National Diversity and Global Capitalism.* Ithaca and London: Cornell University Press, pp. 29–59.

DOBSON, W. (1995): *East Asian Integration: Synergies between Firm Strategies and Government Policy.* Toronto: Centre for International Studies/University of Toronto.

ERNST, D. (1994): Network Transactions, Market Structure and Technological Diffusion—Implications for South-South Cooperation. In: MYTELKA, L. (ed.): *South-South Cooperation in a Global Perspective.* Paris: OECD, pp. 5–45.

ERNST, D. (1997a): Partners in the China Circle? The Asian Production Networks of Japanese Electronics Firms. In: NAUGHTON, B. (ed.): *The China Circle.* Washington, D.C.: The Brookings Institution Press, pp. 210–253.

ERNST, D. (1997b): What Permits David to Defeat Goliath? Inter-Organizational Knowledge Creation in the Taiwanese Computer Industry. In: *Asia-Pacific Journal of Management* (forthcoming in 1999, Vol. 16, No.1).

ERNST, D. (1997c): *From Partial to Systemic Globalization. International Production Networks in the Electronics Industry.* Report prepared for the Sloan Foundation Project on the Globalization in the Data Storage Industry, Graduate School of International Relations and Pacific Studies, University of California at San Diego. (Jointly published as *The Data Storage Industry Globalization Project Report 97-02,* Graduate School of International Relations and Pacific Studies, University of California at San Diego, and *BRIE Working Paper # 98,* the Berkeley Roundtable on the International Economy (BRIE), University of California at Berkeley, April 1997.

ERNST, D. and J. RAVENHILL (1997): Globalization, Convergence, and the Transformation of International Production Networks in Electronics in East Asia. Forthcoming in: BORRUS, M., D. ERNST and S. HAGGARD (eds.): *Rivalry or Riches: International Production Networks in Asia.* Routledge: London.

FOSS, N. J. and J. F. CHRISTENSEN (1996): *A Process Approach to Corporate Coherence.* Danish Research Unit for Industrial Dynamics (DRUID) Working Paper 96-7. Copenhagen Business School.

GRAHAM, E. M. and P. R. KRUGMAN (1989): *Foreign Direct Investment in the United States.* Washington, D.C.: Institute for International Economics.

HATCH, W. and K. YAMAMURA (1996): *Asia in Japan's Embrace: Building a Regional Production Alliance.* New York: Cambridge University Press.

JETRO (1995): *JETRO White Paper on Foreign Direct Investment 1995.* Tōkyō: JETRO.

KESTER, W. C. (1996): American and Japanese Corporate Governance: Convergence to Best Practice? In: BERGER, S. and R. DORE (eds.): *National Di-*

versity and Global Capitalism. Ithaca, N.Y.: Cornell University Press, pp. 107–137.

MITI (1994): *Overseas Investment Statistics Overview.* Tōkyō: MITI.

Nikkei Daily (1997a): Matsushita Planning Global Financial Management Network. July 18, 1997.

Nikkei Daily (1997b): Matsushita to Restructure Six Asian Subsidiaries. July 3, 1997.

NONAKA, I. and H. TAKEUCHI (1995): *The Knowledge-Creating Company.* New York and Oxford: Oxford University Press.

PAULY, L. W. and S. REICH (1997): National Structures and Multinational Corporate Behavior: Enduring Differences in the Age of Globalization. In: *International Organization* 51, 1 (Winter), pp. 1–30.

STOPFORD, J. M. (1995): Regional Networks and Domestic Transformation: A New Challenge for Japanese Firms. Paper presented at the *Third Conference on Economic Cooperation in Asia-Pacific Community.* Institute of East and West Studies, Yonsei University Seoul, November 16–18.

TEECE, D., R. P. RUMELT and G. DOSI (1994): Understanding Corporate Coherence: Theory and Evidence. In: *Journal of Economic Behavior and Organization* 23, 1, pp. 1–30.

VERNON, R. (1977): *Storm over the Multinationals. The Real Issues.* Cambridge, Mass.: Harvard University Press.

III Modes of Corporate Internationalization: Japanese FDI Strategies in Asia-Pacific

Dennis S. TACHIKI

The conventional wisdom among large Japanese companies has been to import raw materials and components to produce value-added goods for the world market. In the face of global competition, this export-oriented strategy is giving way to a FDI-oriented approach. The internal evolution of Japanese companies means previously immobile production factors are now being located in the most efficient overseas production base: The closed corporate groupings (*keiretsu*) are giving way to strategic alliances. Economies of network are complementing economies of scale and scope. The internal evolution of Japanese companies is providing a partial answer to the business challenges they face in the 21st century.

1 Toward a FDI-oriented approach

In the postwar period, the conventional wisdom among Japanese companies has been to import raw materials and components to produce value-added goods for the world market. Despite a series of external oil and yen shocks over the past two decades, Japanese companies have sustained this competitive posture through the internal streamlining of operations and diversification of products. Their organizational innovations in human resource management, quality control, and lean production are some of the resulting legacies. What has evolved out of this post-war approach is an export-oriented strategy centred on growth industries, the re-emergence of corporate groupings, and the pursuit of economies of scale and scope (ODAGIRI 1992).

Now, in the face of increasing global competition and domestic deregulation, Japanese companies are finding an export-oriented strategy is no longer sufficient for maintaining their future competitive advantage. Companies from the developing countries are leveraging their own comparative advantages, intensifying competition in Japan's traditional export markets. Moreover, international and domestic pressures to deregulate the economy are strengthening the rights of consumers and foreign investors vis-à-vis domestic producers. Consequently, producers are making the difficult move up the learning curve into higher value-added goods while transferring selected low value-added operations to more efficient overseas production bases (YAMASHITA 1991).

The mobilization of personnel, machinery, and capital for overseas production presents Japanese managers with a new set of challenges. They are at a distinct disadvantage against local competitors in understanding local business practices, establishing reliable supplier networks, and learning the nuances of local consumer markets. To minimize their investment risks in a host country, many of them have sought strategic alliances with local companies. As Japanese companies link these partners to their global business plans, building regional logistics channels and reliable communication links increases in importance. In this connection, some Japanese companies are consolidating and coordinating their overseas operations to achieve economies of network (TOKUNAGA 1992).

Mobile production factors, strategic alliances, and economies of network are significant departures from an export-oriented strategy, suggesting this foreign direct investment approach is modifying the conventional wisdom among Japanese executives. A FDI-oriented approach is not a distinctively different management option. Japanese managers move back and forth across the export-oriented and FDI-oriented continuum depending on the availability of overseas business opportunities, the strength of the domestic economy, and the amount of corporate resources at their disposal. This has been the case during the recent recession in Japan, where FDI has declined from its peak in 1990 and value-added exports have increased (MINISTRY OF FINANCE 1995). What is significant about a FDI-oriented approach, then, is that it represents an expansion of firms' postwar repertoire of management options. Since Japanese companies are still at an early stage of implementing this approach, in this abridged paper I use an interpretative framework for discussing their (1) mobilization of production factors, (2) building of strategic alliances, and (3) pursuit of economies of network.

2 Mobile production factors

A key to a FDI-oriented approach is relocating popular but unprofitable domestic operations to low-cost overseas production bases. Scholars have documented how changes in the marginal utility of land, labour, and capital in Japan have shaped this strategy (e. g., URATA & NAKAKITA 1991). Thus, in this section, I focus on how Pacific economies are changing their trade and investment policies to attract FDI, and then present a profile of which Japanese companies are moving overseas.

2.1 Trade and investment environments

The Pacific economies vary widely in their levels of economic development. At one end of the gross domestic product spectrum are the Pacific OECD (Organization for Economic Cooperation and Development) member countries and at the other end are the developing Asian countries. Moreover, within the Pacific economies, there are noticeable disparities in economic development between urban and rural areas. Given this lumpy investment landscape, the flow of Japanese FDI in the Pacific region before the mid-1980s was mainly toward the Pacific OECD member countries and the urban areas of the developing Pacific economies (MINISTRY OF FINANCE 1995). The developing Pacific economies have been attempting to tilt the FDI investment field in their favour through the creation of subregional areas, fora for economic cooperation, and infrastructure.

Subregional areas
One factor in attracting Japanese FDI to the Pacific region is the emergence of three types of subregional areas: economic zones, growth triangles, and free trade areas. Graph 1 shows the conceptual connections between these different types of subregional areas.

Graph 1: Subregional areas

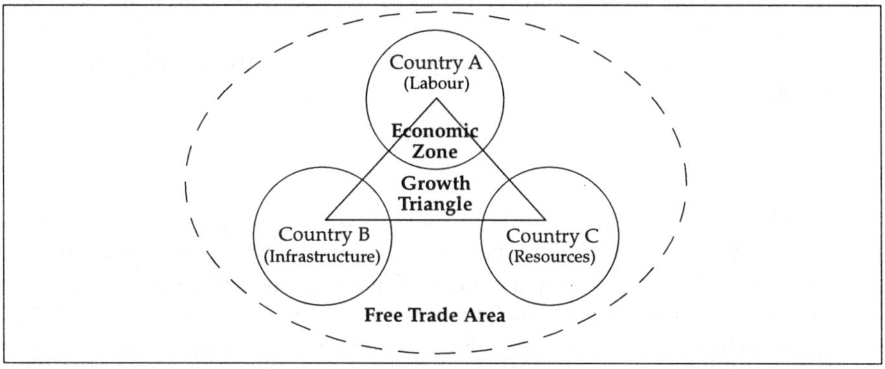

Bonded areas, foreign access zones, industrial estates, export processing zones, special economic zones, and economic and technical development zones are variations of economic zones (APO 1987). A common feature of these economic zones is the availability of fiscal incentives and infrastructure facilities unavailable in other parts of a country. On the fiscal policy side, companies are usually exempt from corporate taxes (tax holiday), import duties, excise taxes, import surcharges and value-added taxes. On the infrastructure side, most industrial estates provide improved land, utilities, roads and other support services (such as security and industrial waste disposal). Economic zones, then, simplify business practices and raise the infrastructure standards in one locale within a country to a level expected by transnational corporations.

A second subregional area is a growth triangle (THANT & KAKAZU 1994). Neighbouring countries, either informally or formally, agree to combine their respective comparative advantages in resources, labour, and socio-economic infrastructure. The Singapore-Riau Islands-Johore Growth Triangle is a notable example. Under this arrangement, Indonesia provides labour and raw materials, Malaysia manufacturing facilities, and Singapore the logistical support services. From an investor's perspective, this complementary relationship off-sets the comparative disadvantages of each country. From a government perspective, it allows them to leverage their fiscal budget in order to accelerate economic development in a particular region of their country.

A free trade agreement (FTA) is a third type of subregional area. Under this formal arrangement, signatory countries agree to ease restrictions on the flow of goods and, to some extent, on the flow of people, money, and information, for companies operating in the FTA. The coalescence of Pacific economies under such an arrangement includes the Australia-New Zealand Closer Economic Relations Trade Agreement, ASEAN Free Trade Area (Brunei, Indonesia, Laos, Myanmar, Malaysia, Philippines, Singapore, Thailand, Vietnam), the North America Free Trade Agreement (Canada, Mexico, the United States), the Central America Free Economic Area (Costa Rica, El Salvador, Guatemala, Honduras, Nicaragua), and the Andean Pact (Bolivia, Columbia, Ecuador, Peru, Venezuela). By creating a FTA across national borders, governments reduce a company's transaction costs and broaden its market access.

Economic cooperation

A second factor in attracting Japanese FDI is the growing economic cooperation among Pacific economies. Economic cooperation refers to government policies and schemes easing the flow of goods, people, information, and money across national borders. The main fora for promoting regional economic cooperation are the Pacific Basin Economic Council, the Pacific Free Trade and Development Conference, the Pacific Economic Cooperation Council, the Association of Southeast Asian Nations, and the Asia Pacific Economic Cooperation Forum (WOODS 1993). Graph 2 illustrates the extent to which countries have embraced this concept. The Northeast Asian, Southeast Asian, North American, and Oceania countries are members of the largest number of organizations. From a Japanese business perspective, they also define the economic boundaries of the Pacific region. The Latin American and South Asian countries are gradually joining the fold.

Local interaction between government agencies and business organizations (e. g., bilateral business councils, chambers of commerce and industry, and industry associations) is another important building block for institutionalizing economic cooperation. Private investors can express their opinions and requests concerning a host country's trade and investment policies through dialogues with the economic ministries, 'one-stop' investment boards, and quasi-government organizations. In turn, Pacific governments weigh whether responding to these business requests will contribute to their country's economic development. This iterative, and sometimes contentious, process has contributed to the fine-tuning of national economic policies. In some cases, this process leads to innovative regional initiatives. A good example is the brand-to-brand complementation (BBC) scheme. The BBC scheme harmonizes the individual tariff and local content rules across the member countries of ASEAN to attract larger direct investments from foreign automakers. Japanese automakers have found this scheme appealing; however, it has not been easy for them to implement a cross-border production strategy.

Graph 2: Fora for economic cooperation

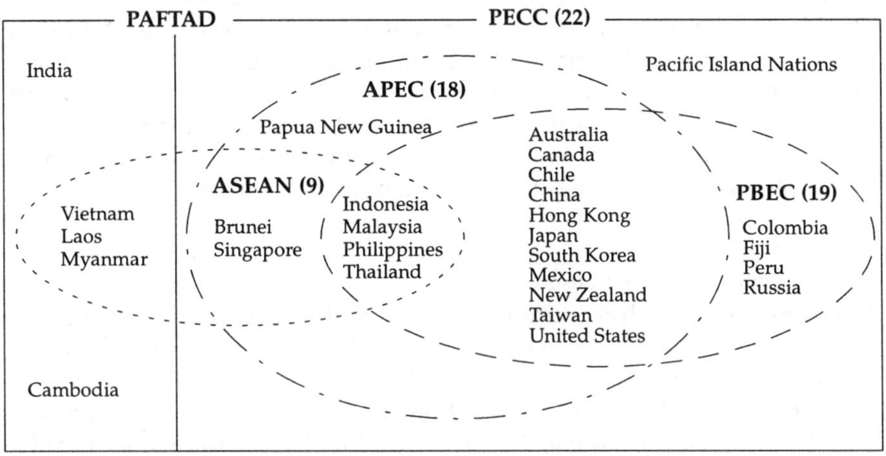

Notes: **PBEC** = Pacific Basin Economic Council; **PAFTAD** = Pacific Free Trade and Development Conference; **PECC** = Pacific Economic Cooperation Council; **ASEAN** = Association of Southeast Asian Nations; **APEC** = Asia Pacific Economic Cooperation Forum

Infrastructure

A third factor in attracting Japanese FDI are improvements in the regional infrastructure facilitating the flow of goods, people, money, and information. A JANCPEC (1992) study measures these flows by the volume of goods handled at container ports, the number of passenger arrivals at international airports, the volume of international telephone calls carried by submarine cables and communication satellites, and the volume of transactions in capital markets. The top hub cities in the Pacific on these measures are Los Angeles, Tokyo, Hong Kong, Singapore, and Sydney. None of the cities in South Asia or Latin America reaches the minimum threshold for any of the categories. A second flow extends from hub cities to domestic business centres. JANCPEC traces these secondary flows based on existing and planned communications links (satellite, submarine cable), shipping route schedules, and frequency of air cargo flights on established domestic routes. The overall flows from domestic business centres to hub cities and then to the global economy brings into relief the hub-and-spoke networks emerging in the Pacific region.

2.2 Japanese foreign direct investments

Subregional areas, economic cooperation, and infrastructure are shifting the FDI playing field toward the Asia-Pacific. Pacific economies account for eight of the top ten developing countries in the world receiving FDI from Japan and the developed countries (OECD 1996). It is premature to cite these trends as evidence for the blurring of national borders, however. Trade and investment bottlenecks remain, for example, due to limitations on landing rights, visa restrictions, incompatible communications hardware and software, and regulations on capital transactions. Japanese companies have factored these opportunities and obstacles into their business plans, leading to differences in their FDI by subregion and industry (TACHIKI 1996).

Trade and investment corridors

Taking into account the continuities and discontinuities in the flow of goods, people, information and money across national borders, graph 3 delineates four trade and investment corridors in the Pacific region. One corridor is located in Northeast Asia, anchored at one end by Tokyo, running down the coastal areas of South Korea, Taiwan, and China, and anchored at the other end by Hong Kong. Another corridor is located in Southeast Asia, extending from Chiang Mai (Thailand), through the western side of the Malay peninsula, and curves around through Jakarta to Surabaya (Indonesia). A third corridor runs between southern Canada (Great Lakes region), the United States, and northern Mexico (Monterey). The fourth investment corridor links Australia with New Zealand. Graph 3 shows that these corridors are where we find the greatest concentration of subregional groupings, economic cooperation, and infrastructure.

According to the TŌYŌ KEIZAI DATABOOK (1997) directory, nearly three-quarters of the overseas Japanese companies have chosen a location within the four trade and investment corridors. The remaining Japanese companies chose locations in the 'New Frontier' countries of the Pacific region. These are countries or regions that fall within two bands originating from the Kamchatka peninsula on the Russian Pacific. Both bands run through inland China, but one leg extends to Indo-China and the other leg to South Asia. When we exclude shipping and financial services companies, Japanese companies

Graph 3: Investment corridors in the Pacific region

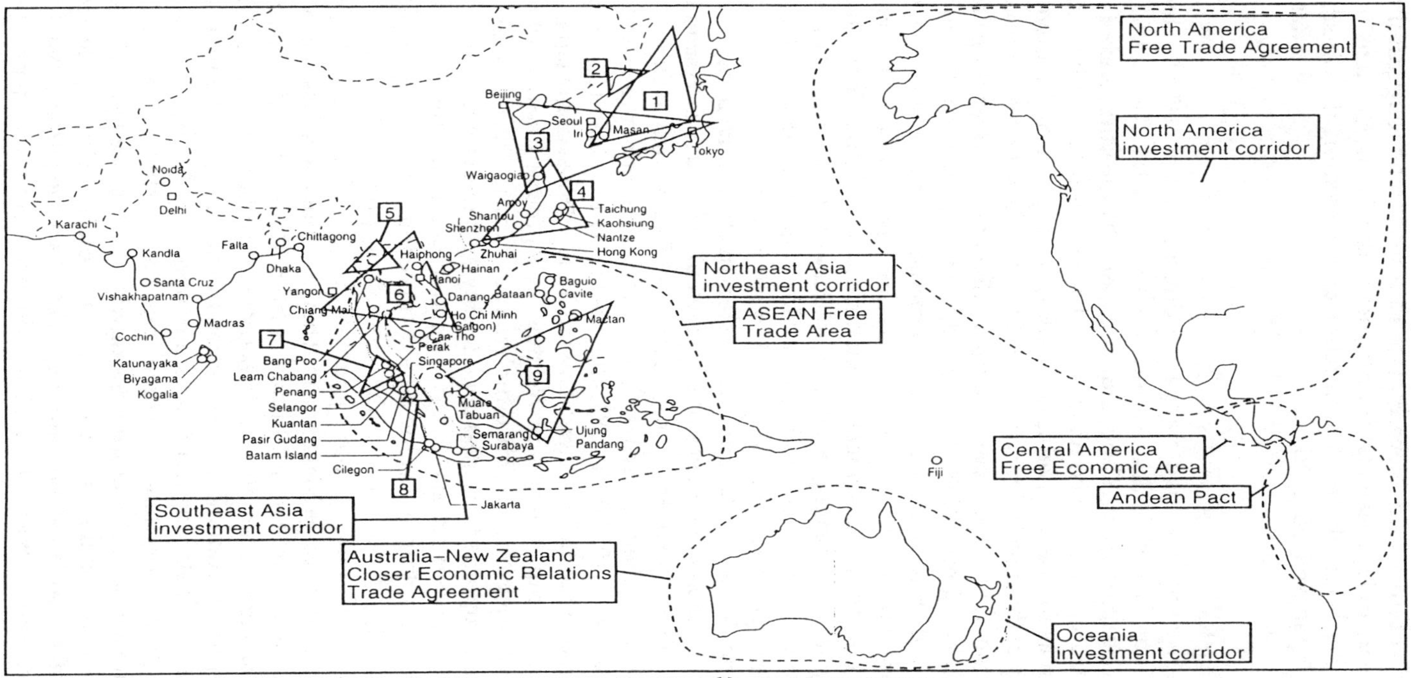

Note: ○ = Export processing zone ; □ = Capital ; △ = Growth triangle ; ( ) = Free trade agreement
Penang EPZs include Bayan Lepas, Prai, Pulan Jerejak; Selangor EPZs include Sungai Way/Subang, Ampang/Ulu Kelang, Telok Panglima Garang; Perak EPZs include Jalapang II, Kinta.
Singapore EPZs include Port of Singapore Authority, Keppel Wharf, Pasir Pangung Port, Jurong Port, Simbay Container Port, and Changi Airport.
Bangkok EPZs include Bangpa-In, Gateway City, Bo-Win, Laem Chabang.
Jakarta EPZs include MM2100 Industrial Town, Murunda, Modern Cikande, Tanjung Priok.
△1 Sea of Japan Economic Zone △2 Tumen Delta △3 Yellow Sea Economic Cooperation △4 South China Sea Economic Area
△5 Golden Quadrangle △6 Baht Economic Zone △7 Northern Growth Triangle △8 Growth Triangle △9 Eastern Growth Triangle

Source: Compiled by the Sakura Institute of Research

have made nominal direct investments in Latin America and the other developing regions of the world. Nevertheless, historical trends suggest these are the regions where Japanese FDI should move next. Thus, the density of cross-border linkages clearly is an important factor in shaping the direction and volume of Japanese FDI.

Core regional industries

By 1990, Japanese companies had made large direct investments in the tertiary sector (such as financial services and commerce) of the Pacific OECD member countries, plus Hong Kong and Singapore. At the other end of the economic spectrum, Japanese companies in the light and labour-intensive industries (such as food and beverages, textiles and apparel, and footwear) invest primarily in the developing countries. Between these two poles of economic development, the Asian newly industrializing economies (NIE) and dynamic Pacific economies (DPE—Thailand, Malaysia, Mexico, Chile) attract Japanese FDI from manufacturing companies. More specifically, the Asian NIEs maintain a comparative advantage in higher value-added manufacturing (such as computers, metal products, and chemicals). In contrast, the DPEs' comparative advantages are in resource-based industries (such as agri-products and non-metallic minerals) and low value-added manufacturing (such as electric and automotive parts and components).

This horizontal division of labour is not a static picture, but changes with the investment strategies of Japanese companies. One strategy is to segment product lines and relocate overseas popular products that are too expensive to produce in Japan. Take the cases of Sanyō and Sony in moving products, not factories. Between 1970 and 1984, they began video cassette recorder (VCR) production in South Korea and Taiwan. By 1985, most of the Japanese electric/electronic companies had moved their VCR production to Southeast Asia. In its place, they now produce higher value-added electronic goods (e. g., computer components, large-screen televisions) in the Asian NIEs. In 1993, China became a major site for VCR production, while the Southeast Asian countries moved up the value-added curve into computer peripherals. Another strategy is to segment the production process. For example, Mitsubishi Motors has entered into a joint venture with Proton Motor (Malaysia) for the assembly of passenger cars. They procure transmissions from the Philippines, wire harness and bumpers from Thailand, and electronic components through international procurement offices in Singapore. Changes in corporate strategy, then, have consequences for the volume and content of intra-regional trade (data not shown).

This cyclical process of domestic rationalization and diversification, and then overseas investment is characteristic of what I call a *core regional industry*. The early core regional industries include the textiles, electric/electronics and chemicals industries; the more recent ones are the automotive, food and beverages, and services (especially financial services, department stores, and transport and storage). It is in these particular industries that we find the greatest outflow of production factors from Japan to the trade and investment corridors.

3 Strategic alliances

As Japanese companies from these core regional industries relocate their low value-added production to an investment corridor, overseas business relations are neither exclusively based on market nor intra-firm transactions. Instead, the traditional Japanese *keiretsu* ties are giving way to a looser corporate structure based on strategic alliances. Between market and hierarchy, these relationships may take the form of licensing agreements, technological agreements, original equipment manufacturing agreements, and business agreements. Since FDI is becoming the favoured vehicle for overseas Japanese investments, I narrow my discussion to the issues of ownership and local partners in joint ventures.

3.1 Ownership

A common image of Japanese companies is that they prefer their FDI to be a wholly-owned subsidiary (WOS) in a 'greenfield' site. According to Japanese FDI data I have compiled in table 1, a slightly contrary picture emerges. Japanese companies rarely enter a market through merger and acquisition nor do we find a majority of cases are wholly-owned subsidiaries (TŌYŌ KEIZAI 1992, 1997). Instead, nearly two-thirds of the overseas Japanese subsidiaries began their operations through a joint venture. In half these cases, the Japanese partner is the majority owner (i. e., 50 % or more ownership) and in the other half the local partner is the majority owner (i. e., more than 50 % ownership). Between 1991 and 1996, Japanese companies have increased their share of ownership in overseas subsidiaries.

Underlying this shift is a change in the structuring of strategic alliances. In 1991, the typical joint venture was between a local partner and a Japanese company. By 1996, the Japanese trading companies, western TNCs, and other third party investors have become evident in overseas joint ventures. In short, there is a counter-intuitive logic at play here: Japanese companies are finding they must cooperate in order to compete in the Pacific economy.

Deviations from this norm for individual countries listed in table 1 reflect their trade and investment policies. In countries that have liberalized their policies—for example, the OECD countries and Hong Kong—FDI is more likely to be in the form of a wholly-owned-subsidiary. The reverse holds true where a country restricts foreign ownership of local companies (e. g., Indonesia, South Korea and the Philippines). This partially supports the notion that Japanese companies prefer WOS. Nevertheless, when we limit our discussion to the core regional industries, again we find Japanese companies are more likely to form overseas joint ventures. This suggests companies moving their product lines to different countries at some point must leverage their organizational resources through strategic alliances.

Table 1: Ownership of overseas Japanese subsidiaries by country

Form of ownership / region / country	1991 Joint Venture Local %	1991 Joint Venture Jpn[a] %	1991 WOS[b] %	1991 Number of companies surveyed	1996 Joint Venture Local %	1996 Joint Venture Jpn %	1996 WOS %	1996 Number of companies surveyed
Asia-Pacific								
Northeast Asia								
China	51	44	5	358	22	59	19	1,956
Hong Kong	13	30	57	827	6	34	60	1,113
South Korea	63	32	5	392	47	37	16	414
Taiwan	35	44	21	735	26	48	26	808
NEA ave./subtotal	*40*	*38*	*22*	*2,312*	*25*	*45*	*30*	*4,291*
South Pacific Forum								
Australia	14	26	60	468	6	34	60	540
New Zealand	15	43	42	79	7	25	68	138
Pacific Island Nations[c]	14	48	38	104	4	44	52	74
SPF ave./subtotal	*14*	*39*	*47*	*651*	*6*	*34*	*60*	*752*
ASEAN Free Trade Area								
Brunei	50	42	8	12	33	42	25	12
Indonesia	43	56	1	338	22	70	8	587
Laos					50	50	0	4
Malaysia	47	30	23	540	34	40	26	715
Myanmar					9	64	27	14
Philippines	65	25	10	183	43	32	25	331
Singapore	12	30	58	806	6	32	62	1,047
Thailand	65	27	8	820	44	48	8	1,135
Vietnam					9	72	19	114
AFTA ave./subtotal	*47*	*35*	*18*	*2,699*	*28*	*50*	*22*	*3,959*
Asia-Pacific ave.	**34**	**37**	**29**	**5,662**	**20**	**43**	**37**	**9,002**
North America								
North American Free Trade Agreement								
Canada	25	12	63	324	6	22	72	305
Mexico	39	24	37	114	16	35	49	165
United States	10	25	65	3,467	3	28	69	3,686
NAFTA ave.	**25**	**20**	**55**	**3,905**	**8**	**28**	**63**	**4,156**

Latin America								
Chile	14	43	43	35	8	52	40	48
Andean Pact								
Bolivia	33	67	0	3	0	67	33	3
Columbia	42	37	21	19	20	46	29	24
Peru	19	56	25	16	19	50	31	16
Ecuador	46	27	27	11	42	25	33	12
Venezuela	39	23	38	26	9	26	65	23
Andean Pact ave./subtotal	*36*	*42*	*22*	*75*	*18*	*43*	*38*	*78*
Country Ave./Totals	**30**	**36**	**34**	**13,010**	**16**	**42**	**44**	**22,401**

Notes: [a] Jpn = Japanese;
[b] WOS = wholly-owned subsidiary;
[c] Pacific Island Nations refers to West Samoa, Nauru, Tonga, Fiji, Papua New Guinea, Solomon Islands, Tuvalu, Kiribati, Vanuatu, Cook Islands, Niue, Micronesian Federation, Marshall Islands, Palau, New Caledonia, French Polynesia, Guam, American Samoa, North Marianas, Tokelau, Wallis Island, Pitcairn Island. N. A. = information is not available.

Source: Data tabulated by the Sakura Institute of Research from the Tōyō Keizai 1992, 1997

3.2 Local partners

Because over half of Japanese FDI was made after 1986, and because Japanese managers report it takes 10–15 years to unfold their full investment (paid-in capital), we are just beginning to discern how Japanese companies are attempting to integrate local partners into their overseas operations. According to the Japanese Ministry of International Trade and Industry's (1994) annual survey of overseas Japanese subsidiaries, a majority of the local partners are from the same industry as the parent company. The second largest category is with a local partner in the commerce (i. e., wholesale and retail) industry. These trends suggest Japanese companies are attempting to localize their marketing, sales, and manufacturing operations.

Among the core regional industries there are two approaches. The chemical industry seeks local partners in sales, while the textile, electric machinery and transport equipment firms seek local partners in supporting industries. There is less evidence for local partnerships in design and engineering, or research and development activities. The linkage between R&D and FDI is partially hidden, however, because small and medium-sized companies are more likely to develop new parts and components than large Japanese companies. To quantitatively reveal R&D and design and engineering functions in overseas operations, then, we would need to go to the four-digit Standard Industrial Classification categories specifying parts and component makers. At this level, during the past three years we find a growing number of Japanese companies have been moving their technical centres and R&D activities for certain product lines to their overseas subsidiaries. Denso, a major supplier to Toyota Motor, for example, has established an air conditioner R&D centre in Malaysia. From a comparative perspective, however, Japanese companies have not reached the level of R&D activities evident in the overseas subsidiaries of American companies (MITI 1996). In short, we are finding that the closed corporate groupings in Japan are giving way to a limited inter-firm, intra-network organizational form.

4 Economies of network

Attaining economies of scale and scope remain important management goals under a FDI-oriented approach. When a company spreads its production across not only the factory floor, but also national borders, however, it finds that logistics, expatriates, currency fluctuations, and communications become a greater share of its operating costs. Sustaining overseas operations, then, requires Japanese companies to consolidate and coordinate their overseas operations to achieve economies of network. Economies of network refers to producing goods and services across national borders in order to create greater value than could be realized producing domestically. At the centre of this process are regional headquarters (RHQ) and operational networks.

4.1 Regional headquarters

Most of the Japanese RHQs are in the core regional industries—that is, electric, electronics, and chemicals. In more recent years, Japanese companies in the automobile, general machinery, and services industries have begun to establish RHQs as well. Although a handful of the RHQs have been in existence for nearly two decades, three-quarters of them were established between 1988 and 1990 (TŌYŌ KEIZAI 1997). All of these RHQs are in industries that either have complex sequential operations or a long global reach. In a strategic sense, then, a RHQ is a corporate body for efficiently using managerial resources scattered throughout a region to promote the global business plan of the parent company. In this connection, the important dimensions of a RHQ are its strategic location, staffing and resources.

Location

Among the companies listed on the first section of the Tōkyō Stock Exchange, the parent company usually controls their overseas operations from a geographical division (e. g., Europe, Middle East, Africa, North and Latin

America, Asia and Oceania) or product division. When overseas production and sales grow in other regions of the world, however, geographical distance becomes a more pressing issue. As a rule of thumb, Japanese managers feel they can control their operations if they are located within a six hour flying time from Tōkyō. Outside this radius, around 500 TNCs have established a RHQ in Hong Kong, 254 in Singapore, and 63 in Sydney.

In keeping with my research focus, however, I am only interested in RHQs that have primary responsibility over the flow of goods, people, money, and information. When we use this simple criterion, there are only 16 cases of Japanese RHQs in the Asia-Pacific region: Singapore accounts for 80 % of the cases and Hong Kong for 15 % (Tōyō Keizai 1997). Since China is moving quickly towards a 'socialist market' and has re-acquired Hong Kong, some Japanese companies are moving their RHQs to other Chinese cities. Singapore may also eventually lose its locational attraction as the trade and investment corridors expand. This suggests Japanese companies locate their RHQs at strategic points in their production networks rather than anchor them in a particular geographical location.

Staffing and resources

Control over a RHQ depends on whether staff and resources are located in the parent company or in the RHQ. The average Japanese RHQ has 37 employees, of which eight are Japanese expatriates (Tōyō Keizai 1997). Among my select list of RHQs, an emerging trend is for the parent company to send one of its experienced managing directors, empowered with local decision-making authority, along with a few support staff. In these cases, overseas subsidiaries report directly to the RHQ rather than to a product manager or international department in the parent company. The overseas subsidiary makes local production decisions; however, RHQs handle cross-border transactions such as finance, distribution, inventory control and after-sales. In a small but growing number of cases, then, we are witnessing the decentralization of decision-making from the parent company to RHQs.

4.2 Operational networks

One of the notable features of the global production networks of Japanese companies is their patchwork character. In my interviews with overseas Japanese managers, I learned how they hope to integrate this patchwork in order to sustain the cross-border flows of goods, people, money, and information. Their comments gravitate around the importance of technological advances in telecommunications, transportation, and computers in stimulating the establishment of supporting services—that is, international value-added networks (IVAN). Graph 4 illustrates the key IVANs underlying the regional strategies of Japanese companies.

Between the telecommunications and computer axis, technological advances in global satellite and submarine cable communication systems facilitate the flow of decisions in real time. As the IVANs reduce cost and improve access, Japanese companies are using communications services for teleconferencing, financial transactions, and data transmission. Teleconferencing reduces the number of overseas trips and improves employee productivity. Inhouse Global Cash Management services allow once-a-month lump-sum cash transfers to settle export transactions, significantly reducing the cost and need for financial intermediaries (e. g., banks and trading companies). Data transmission services allow companies to manage the new product development process almost anywhere at anytime. Further advances in the multimedia industries promise greater integration of voice, visual, and data IVAN services.

Graph 4: Operational networks

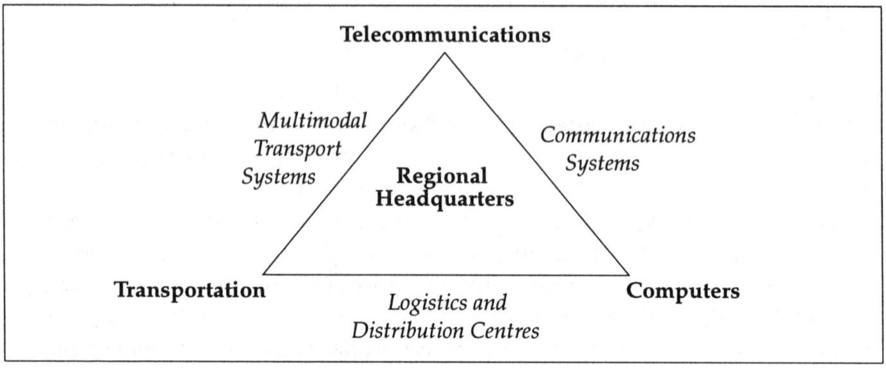

Between the computer and transportation axis, there are notable technological advances in the neglected area of logistics. In this phase of the production cycle, logistics companies are assuming greater responsibility for routing raw materials and components to factories. Using a strategic information system, they coordinate and collect raw materials and components from various suppliers and deliver just-in-time to the manufacturer. Logistics companies may even mix components in-transit from suppliers so that factories can flexibly make batch-runs. Moreover, suppliers and manufacturers in this closed computer system have access to information on the availability of components, in-route materials, expected delivery times, and invoicing. This IVAN service significantly reduces a company's coordination and inventory costs. An emerging innovation here is continuous acquisition logistic systems (CALS). CALS is an open computer protocol that promises a seamless process from the acquisition of raw materials to the distribution of finished products.

Between the transportation and telecommunications axis, technological advances in Multimodal Transport Systems (MTS) are integrating the movement of goods across land, sea, and air. MTS transport companies handle the door-to-door movement of goods, bonded warehousing, and customs clearance procedures for their customers. An illustrative example is the Mitsui Warehousing logistics and distribution operations in Southeast Asia. Mitsui Warehousing transports goods from Sony's Southeast Asian plants to a bonded warehouse in Johore (Malaysia). From Johore, it uses an electronic data interchange protocol called Tradenet to pre-clear goods through Singapore customs as well as at the destination port. As a result, they can quickly load and unload goods from container ships for shipment to consumer markets.

One must not confuse form from function, however. In form, many Japanese companies are experimenting and integrating these IVAN services into their regional strategies. In function, however, the lumpy trade and investment environment in the Pacific region leads to wide variations in the extent they are realizing cross-border economies of network.

5 Between shocks and internal evolution

The overseas investments of Japanese companies are part of the internal evolution occurring within Japan in response to the current external shocks. The FDI-oriented approach of Japanese companies is quite different from their response to the oil shocks and yen appreciation in the 1970s and 1980s. To highlight these differences, it is worth closing with five implications of this emerging approach.

First, a FDI-oriented approach is not a linear process, leading to the hollowing out of the domestic economy. Although companies in the core regional industries shift products to low-cost production bases, they still manufacture technologically advanced products in Japan. Moreover, when economic conditions dictate it, they sometime shift production back to Japan. The allocation of Japanese production factors in the Pacific contributes to fluctuations in the regional horizontal division of labour. Thus, Japanese FDI is leading to a regionalization of corporate activities, not a hollowing out of the domestic economy. The bigger issue, then, is the strain Japan's trade and investment imbalance places on its regional neighbours.

Second, under a FDI-oriented approach, the unit of investment for Japanese companies is no longer limited to a particular country but a subregional grouping. In this connection, Japanese companies tend to move popular but unprofitable products overseas. The assembly of a product takes place across national borders within subregional groupings. Overseas RHQs facilitate the implementation and coordination of these strategies. It is clear from my discussion, however, that this multi-track strategy emerges from trial-and-error rather than strategic intent. The business plans (e. g., *hōshin kanri*) of Japanese companies provide a window on how they organizationally balance their multi-track strategies (TACHIKI 1996).

Third, the institutional context is important in shaping the corporate governance of Japanese companies. Overseas Japanese subsidiaries have demonstrated a willingness to share ownership with foreign partners. Moreover, subregional groupings, fora for economic cooperation, and the local infrastructure expose Japanese companies to a new set of economic and non-economic stakeholders. Nevertheless, stockholders, local managers, labour unions, and other interest groups still do not have a strong presence in the corporate governance arena. As the political and financial institutions strengthen in the wake of the regional economic crisis, we should expect further internal evolution in the corporate governance of Japanese companies.

Fourth, a FDI-oriented approach brings into relief the systemic characteristic of Japanese business strategies. While outsiders proclaim Japanese lean production as the successor to mass production, Japanese companies are finding they can achieve greater value-added in the R&D and sales and marketing segments of the production cycle. Moreover, the internationalization of Japanese companies requires them to rationalize not only their internal business operations, but also the movement of goods, people, information, and money across national borders. Changes in any of these areas have consequences for the rest of the organization. Thus, the closed *keiretsu* system is giving way to an inter-firm, intra-network form of organization.

Fifth, production networks are where the action is at. The 'culturally unique' Japanese organizational innovations in human resource management, quality control, and lean production are becoming more universal. Career paths for Japanese expatriates take place not only within the company, but also across national borders. Quality control no longer refers to products, but also to managing processes. Lean production is giving way to production networks involving joint venture partners and IVAN providers. It is too early to pull their success stories together into a coherent analytical framework; but, clearly the lessons are from trial-and-error experiments within their production networks and not from the parent company.

To the extent Japanese companies can expand on their efforts in these five areas, economies of network may become a hallmark of their corporate strategies for the 21st century as lean production was in the 1990s and the 'Japanese management style' in the 1980s.

References

ASIAN PRODUCTIVITY ORGANISATION (1987): *Export Processing Zones and Science Parks in Asia.* Tōkyō: APO.

JAPAN NATIONAL COMMITTEE FOR PACIFIC ECONOMIC CO-OPERATION (1992): *Economic Development of the Pacific Region and Triple-T Networking.* Tōkyō: JANCPEC.

MINISTRY OF FINANCE (1995): *Ōkurashō kokusai kinyū-kyoku nenpō* [Annual Report of the International Finance Bureau]. Tōkyō: Ōkurashō (MOF).

MINISTRY OF INTERNATIONAL TRADE AND INDUSTRY (1995): *Kaigai tōshi tōkei sōran* [Statistics on Foreign Investments]. Vol. 5. Tōkyō: Tsūsanshō (MITI).

MINISTRY OF INTERNATIONAL TRADE AND INDUSTRY (1995): *Waga kuni kigyō no kaigai kigyō katsudō* [Overseas Business Activities of Japanese Companies]. Vol. 24. Tōkyō: Tsūsanshō (MITI).

ODAGIRI, H. (1992): *Growth Through Competition, Competition Through Growth: Strategic Management and the Economy in Japan.* Oxford: Oxford University Press.

ORGANISATION FOR ECONOMIC CO-OPERATION AND DEVELOPMENT (1996): *International Direct Investment Statistics Yearbook.* Paris: OECD.

TACHIKI, D. S. (1996): *Articulating FDI Strategies Through Business Plans: The Origins of Japanese Production Networks in the Asia-Pacific.* Boston: MIT Japan Program (Working Paper No. MITJP 96-31).

THANT, M., M. TANG and H. KAKAZU (eds.) (1994): *Growth Triangles in Asia: A New Approach to Regional Economic Cooperation.* Hong Kong: Oxford University Press.

TOKUNAGA, S. (ed.) (1992): *Japan's Foreign Investment and Asian Economic Interdependence: Production, Trade, and Financial Systems.* Tōkyō: University of Tokyo Press.

TŌYŌ KEIZAI (1992, 1997): *Kaigai shinshutsu kigyō sōran* [A General Survey of Japanese Companies in Overseas Markets]. Tōkyō: Tōyō Keizai Shinpōsha.

URATA, S. and T. NAKAKITA (1991): Industrial Adjustment in Japan and Its Implications for Developing Countries. In: YAMAZAWA, I. and A. HIRATA (eds.): *Industrial Adjustment in Developed Countries and Its Implications for Developing Countries.* Tōkyō: Institute of Developing Economies, pp. 13–142.

WOODS, L. T. (1993): *Asia Pacific Diplomacy: Nongovernmental Organizations and International Relations.* Vancouver: University of British Columbia Press.

YAMASHITA, S. (ed.) (1991): *Transfer of Japanese Technology and Management to ASEAN Countries.* Tōkyō: University of Tokyo Press.

IV Japanese Companies in Europe: Their Strategies and Management Practices

Corrado MOLTENI

Foreign direct investment (FDI) strategies of Japanese companies in Europe are undergoing major changes. The new phase is characterized by attempts to consolidate and rationalize corporate activities. At this point, an analysis of previous location and market strategies as well as of failures and successes in terms of a transfer of Japanese management practices to their European subsidiaries and joint ventures is necessary in order to better forecast future developments in this field. On the basis of three case studies exploring Italian-Japanese joint ventures, several success factors (and barriers) underlying the implementation of production, quality, and work practices are identified. While from a corporate point of view greenfield investments appear relatively more advantageous over other venture forms, existing constraints in the wider political and socio-economic environment will play an even larger role for FDI (location) decisions henceforward, given the overall reduced levels of Japanese investments abroad at the end of the 1990s.

1 Introduction[1]

According to statistics from the Ministry of Finance, Japanese corporations' direct investment in Asia in 1995 reached 1.19 trillion Yen (12.3 billion US$), exceeding the amount of investment in Europe for the second straight year (MITI 1997: 4). Then, on January 13th 1997, the Nikkei announced that "Japan's major electronic makers are poised to make big strides in Eastern Europe with the opening of new productions facilities" (*Nikkei* 1997). Taking advantage of rising purchasing power and lower labour costs in the former communist countries, these factories will supply finished products to the local market and parts for already established assembly plants in Western Europe. A few months later, in April 1997, the Nikkei reported Nissan's decision to integrate and rationalize its development units in Western Europe "as part of the efforts to prop up its European business, which saw huge losses in fiscal year 1996".

[1] Part of the findings of this paper have been presented at the International Research Seminar on East Asian Economies held at the Université Paul Valéry, Nimes (France) on June 19–20, 1997.

All these facts show that Japanese companies' strategies towards Europe, and the countries of the European Union in particular, are undergoing a major change. The first phase of Japanese direct investment is certainly over. What is occurring now is a process of consolidation and rationalization of corporate activities in most sectors. This has relevant implications on the size, the objectives, the location and the form of new investment as well as disinvestment. To analyse and discuss this change and the factors behind it is the first objective of this paper.

Moreover, at this stage, it is possible to more carefully assess the results of past investments not only in terms of production levels, profits and market shares, but also in the way Japanese management practices have been transferred and adjusted to the social and economic realities of Europe, or better, of each European country. Therefore, after an analysis of recent developments concerning direct investment abroad, our attention will be focused on the transfer of Japanese technology and production methods to the European subsidiaries. However, for research logistics and time constraint reasons, the study has been limited to subsidiaries set up in Italy in the form of joint ventures.

Japanese direct investments in Italy have in fact mostly taken the form of partnerships with Italian firms (in most cases with a minority stake), while only a limited number of firms have set up wholly-owned subsidiaries (MOLTENI 1996). However, while some of these ventures seem to perform well and to be developing as expected by the partners, others have failed to achieve their original objectives and have encountered all sorts of problems. This despite the fact that, on paper, all the prerequisites for a successful undertaking based on mutual advantages and the use of complementary assets were present.

Why does this happen? Why are some ventures successful while others are not? These are the questions I would like to address here by focusing on a few, selected case studies that can shed light on the factors preventing the partners to fully exploit the opportunities offered by a joint venture. Attention will be given to both strategic and managerial aspects, but in particular to the transfer of technology and Japanese production methods: a major goal for Italian companies but, obviously, also for the Japanese partners interested in raising the efficiency and the quality of production. In joint ventures, however, the transfer of foreign practices encounters more obstacles due to the need to integrate different corporate cultures, management styles and practices. As a result, such a transfer is not always a positive-sum game, but, instead, a rather long uphill path to satisfactory levels of production efficiency and return on investment. The cases examined below confirm the above, but do also illuminate how different arrangements can prevent or, for the better, support the process of integration and transfer of foreign (Japanese) managerial practices.

2 Recent developments in Japan's direct investment abroad

2.1 The drive to Asia

In the second half of the 1980s, Japanese companies entered the European market *en masse.* Direct investment (DI) in the manufacturing sector jumped from an annual average of 216 million dollars in the 1980–84 period, to more than 4.5 billion in 1990 alone (MITI 1996: 426). This impressive surge has been supported, first of all, by the accumulation of managerial, technological and financial resources inside Japanese firms that have made them particularly competitive in the international marketplace. However, the decision to invest was more directly influenced by a fear that increasing trade frictions and the process of European economic integration could result in trade and economic policies discriminating outsiders, and Japanese companies in particular. Many investments were thus undertaken to circumvent existing or potential entry barriers (export restrictions, antidumping duties, etc.), affecting industries such as consumer electronics and motor vehicles that enjoyed a strong competitive advantage (see BELDERBOS 1997). Moreover, many subcontracting firms in these sectors invested abroad in the wake of their parent companies, while a more limited number of Japanese firms moved their operations abroad in order to assure a quick response to the changing needs of their customers or, in some instances, to acquire additional and complementary resources.

The growth of Japanese DI abroad was financed with the resources accumulated in the past and additional funds that could be easily raised through the buoyant stock market of the late 1980s. As for the strong yen, this was an important, if not the most important, macroeconomic factor that induced companies to relocate their production facilities abroad and, at the same time, made direct investment a less costly and more attractive option. In fact, the rapid and steep yen appreciation (+ 37 percent between 1985 and 1988) supported Japanese DI abroad in two ways: through a 'relative price effect' and through a 'liquidity' or 'wealth' effect. As for the first aspect, the yen appreciation substantially reduced the international price competitiveness of Japanese exports and thus pushed Japanese manufacturers to move their production facilities abroad. With respect to the second effect, the yen appreciation rendered Japanese companies relatively more liquid and wealthy, and this new 'wealth' could be used to finance more cheaply their expansion abroad.

In the 1990s, however, with the collapse of the financial *bubble* in Japan, the completion of the Single Market in Europe, and the rapid economic growth of East and Southeast Asian countries, the picture has radically changed. As shown in graph 1, since 1991 the flow of Japan's DI to Europe has diminished both in value and relative terms. On the other hand, the share of Asian countries has increased considerably. Regarding DI in the manufacturing sector alone in 1995, the economies of Asia have attracted the largest amount (8.1 billion US$), well above the European share (2.0 billion) and even larger than the North American one (7.3 billion).

This drive to Asia is indeed the most conspicuous feature of this decade. It reflects the growth of the local market, but also the fact that the countries of Southeast Asia provide an excellent, cost effective export platform for Japanese multinationals and many medium-sized firms. Moreover, as argued by URATA (1992 and 1997), two types of strategy adopted by Japanese firms have led to this outcome. The first one is a strategy of 'product differentiation', the other of 'inter-process specialization'. Under the first strategy, companies undertake the production of low-tech or labour-intensive products in their Asian subsidiaries, while high value added, high-tech intensive products are manufactured in their plants in Japan. Following the second strategy, Japanese firms divide the production process into a certain number of sub-processes and assign each sub-process to the affiliated companies in the Asian country, where it can be performed efficiently and in a cost effective way. Under this arrangement, high-tech parts and components are produced in Japan, while less advanced parts and components are manufactured in different plants in Asia, according to the technological capabilities and the factor endowment of the countries. The final assembly is then carried out either in Japan or in the Asian subsidiaries.

Graph 1: The drive to Asia—Japan's direct investment in the manufacturing sector (Unit: 100 million US$)

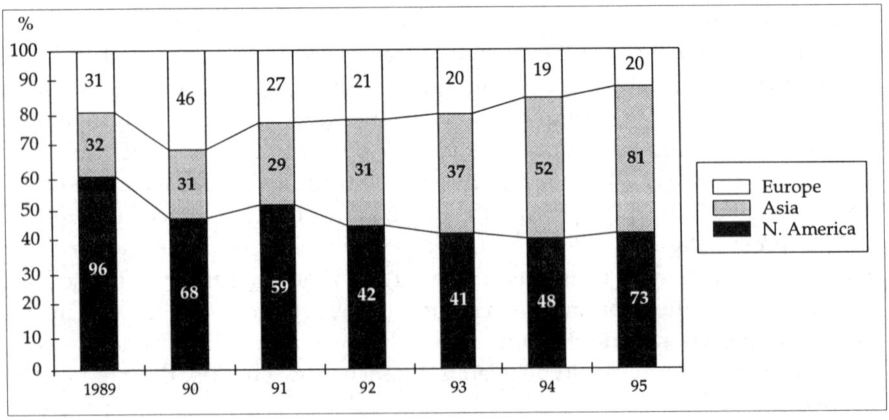

Source: MITI (1996: 422, 424, 426)

The higher attractiveness of the Asian region compared to Europe (EU) is indeed confirmed by the results of a MITI-commissioned world-wide survey carried out in 1994–95 on a sample of more than 3,600 companies in Japan and their 11,443 subsidiaries abroad (MITI 1996). According to this survey, 286 new subsidiaries were established in Asia in 1994, against 25 in Europe and 44 in North America, while only two years before, in 1992, Asia attracted 174 new investments, Europe 58 and North America 43. As a result, in 1995 the turnover of Asian subsidiaries had almost reached the level of those located in North America and was twice the level of the European ones (in 1989 the proportion was 5 for Asia, 12 for North America and 3 for Europe).The attractiveness of Asia also explains the higher level of reinvestment registered in the region, which in 1994 amounted to 7 billion dollars, a sum even larger than the 5.2 billion of new direct investments. In comparison, reinvestments in Europe accounted for only 1.4 billion dollars.

2.2 Features of Japanese investments in Europe and Italy

Regarding Europe, or better the European Union, Japanese multinationals have not significantly changed their investment pattern within the region as far as *geographical distribution* is concerned. As shown in graph 2, among the host countries that are most preferred are the UK, France, Germany, Spain and the Netherlands. The UK, however, is by far the most attractive location, whose share has been constantly rising. This is even more obvious if one looks at the size of investments undertaken in terms of capital and employment.

Graph 2: Japanese manufacturing units in Europe by location

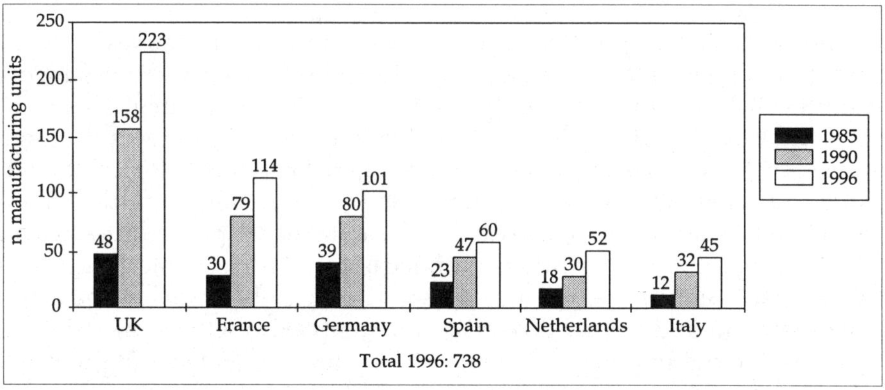

Source: JETRO (1997: 5)

In general, Japanese DI in Europe is concentrated at the *regional* level. As shown by THIRAN & YAMAWAKI (1996), the South East, Wales and the West Midlands in the United Kingdom, Bayern in Germany, the Île de France and

Este in Spain account for almost half of the employment of Japanese companies in the European Union. In the case of Italy, JDIs are concentrated in the northern part of the country and in particular in the regions of Piedmont and Lombardy, the industrial centre of the country. Only a few companies have chosen the south, despite the generous system of incentives provided, at least in the past, by the central government. Altogether only six manufacturing units are located in southern Italy, and of these two are the result of an acquisition by Bridgestone Corporation of existing facilities, and two are located in Abruzzo, the most advanced southern region (see MOLTENI 1996 for this and the following parts).

As in other countries, factors such as the quality of the labour force (an adequate supply of skilled workers) and the existence of an efficient transport infrastructure have influenced the location choice at the regional level. The concentration of Japanese activities itself is also a factor having a positive and significant effect. However, in the case of Italy, there is also the fact that many joint ventures have located their production activities in those areas where the Italian partner is already operating, i. e., northern Italy, in most of the cases, and the central regions in a few others.

The geographic distribution of Japanese investment in Europe also varies across industries. Investments in consumer electronics, motor vehicles and high-tech sectors are mostly located in the northern countries (the exception being car-manufacture investments in Spain, but these were undertaken before 1985). In Southern Europe, Japanese firms have invested in the so-called 'traditional sectors' (apparel and textile, in particular), the machinery industry and scale-intensive sectors such as chemicals. In Italy, for example, there have been no significant investments in the car and consumer electronic sectors.

This sectorial composition is associated with different modes of entry and forms of ownership. In general, wholly-owned, greenfield investments are prevailing in Northern Europe and in the UK in particular. This is, in fact, the best way to retain and fully exploit the competitive advantage owned by Japanese firms in terms of managerial and technological knowledge and capabilities. However, in the South and in Italy, in particular, investment has taken place mostly through capital participation, often with a minority stake, in joint ventures with local interests (see table 1). In some cases a joint venture seemed the best solution available to overcome external constraints and access barriers like the complexity of the legal and fiscal systems, the rigidities of the labour market, the fragmented and protected distribution system and, of course, the lack of linguistic skills. In many other instances, however, a more positive, assertive strategy has been observable that considers joint ventures as a tool to acquire new competitive advantages by pooling complementary resources and developing economies of scale.

These different approaches have also produced different results not only in terms of production efficiency and profitability, but also with regard to the transfer of Japanese management practices, as will be discussed in the next section, based on three case studies.

Table 1: Japanese direct investment in manufacturing by ownership form (1995 data)

	total	100 %	less than 100 %		
			≤ 50 %	> 50 %	total
EU	822	562 (68 %)	112	148	260 (32 %)
Italy	49	17 (35 %)	13	19	32 (65 %)

Source: MITI (1996: 130) for EU and JETRO (1996: 178–182) as well as author's own findings for Italy

3 The mode of entry and the 'Japanization' of management practices in Italy

3.1 The experience of Fiat-Hitachi Excavators S.p.A.[2]

Established in November 1986, Fiat-Hitachi Excavators is a major joint venture between a subsidiary of the Fiat Group (initially Fiatallis, now New Holland), Hitachi Construction Machinery (HCM), Sumitomo Corporation and, since 1995, Tōyō Umpanki Corporation, a specialized producer belonging to the Hitachi Group. With 1,650 employees, the company manufactures a full line of earth-moving machinery in two plants: San Mauro Torinese (near Turin) and Lecce in the south of Italy. The majority of the shares (54 %) are controlled by Fiat, with HCM owning 36 %, Sumitomo 5 % and Tōyō Umpanki the remaining 5 %. The Japanese partner (Hitachi), however, controls the key technology: the hydraulic system and components, developed and manufactured in Japan and from there exported to Italy.

Indeed, Fiat entered this joint venture in order to obtain access to Hitachi's technology, as the Italian company lacked the resources and above all the time to develop a product that could compete with the internationally recognized quality and performance of its Japanese partner. Moreover, by joining hands with Hitachi, Fiat hoped to gain an easier access to Japanese production methods and managerial practices. For HCM, on the other hand, the joint venture meant a faster entry into the European market and, more importantly, the possibility to overcome the anti-dumping duties imposed in

[2] This case study is based on several factory visits and meetings with Italian and Japanese managers in San Mauro Torinese throughout 1996 and 1997 and a visit to Hitachi Kenki's Tsuchiura Plant in September 1996.

July 1985 by the European Commission on imports from Japan (STRANGE 1993: 218).

Concerning these two aspects, Hitachi's strategy has been quite successful. Disregarding certain cyclical ups and downs, production volumes and sales have increased conspicuously since the start of operation, reaching a peak of 2,496 units in 1996 (against 1,132 in 1987). Moreover, due also to the depreciation of the Italian currency, the percentage of exports (sales outside Italy) has grown steadily and remarkably, from less than 30 % in 1987, to 55–60 % in the early nineties and more than 70 % in the last two years. This is a clear indicator that the company has succeeded in transforming itself from a domestic company to a truly European one, as expected by both partners.

For Fiat, the joint venture has enabled the company to rapidly solve its product problem in the largest and most demanding segment of the market: that of hydraulic excavators. HCM is in fact a specialized producer of hydraulic excavators, well known for their advanced technology and reliability. Moreover, HCM is also a research-oriented company, investing heavily in the development of innovative applications and technologies. Thus, by joining hands with HCM, Fiat not only obtained a state-of-the-art product, but could rely on its partner for future technological improvements. From this point of view, Fiat's reputation and image in the marketplace have been greatly enhanced by the joint venture.

As for the technology transfer and product upgrading, the Italian managers proudly refer to the improvements accomplished and the successful process of 'localization'. One reason for this is the fact that the plant in San Mauro is a type of 'greenfield investment', as it is placed in a building previously used by a company manufacturing rotary presses. The factory layout was newly designed, partly on the model of HCM's Tsuchiura plant. Equally new were the equipment and the machines installed. The local content ratio is also quite high (73 % in 1997, that is 62 % from Italy and 11 % from other European countries). The engines installed on the excavators are European (70 % Iveco/Fiat and the rest divided between Cunnings, Isuzu and other suppliers), as are most of the parts and components used as well as the production technology. The machine centres are Italian, the lathes and the boring machines German, and the friction welding machines British. The Japanese presence is particularly evident only in the welding section, where a set of gigantic Shinmeiwa robots operate.

However, as already mentioned, the core technology—the hydraulic components of the excavator, accounting for 20–25 % of the total value added—is entirely Japanese, imported from Japan and only assembled in San Mauro, irrespective of the dramatic appreciation of the Yen versus the Italian Lira. The cylinder technology, another key component of the hydraulic excavator, is also Japanese, from Kayaba. Therefore, technology transfer has occurred, but in a selected way so as not to affect the control of the key elements by the Japanese partner, whose contribution and cooperation remain essential for the success of the joint venture. Indeed, it could be argued that Fiat, notwithstanding its majority ownership, remains 'hostage' of the partner's technology. As for the changes in the organization of production and work processes, they are striking if the comparison is made with the past, though a wide gap continues to exist when compared with the present conditions at Hitachi's 'mother plant' at Tsuchiura in Japan.

The adoption and application of Japanese methods and practices is indeed a major goal of the company's managers. However, the adaptation to the distinctive characteristics of the Italian labour market, industrial relations system and, of course, management culture and style have produced *a hybrid model* with strong Italian traits. This is the first impression that a visitor gains when touring both plants. Managers and workers in San Mauro share a common canteen, but their dress codes remain quite different from Japan. There is no uniform like the one commonly used by employees at Tsuchiura. Furthermore, at the Italian plant there are very few posters providing information on production, workers and small group activities, while they can be found everywhere in Japan. The most striking difference, however, is the intensity of work. Although both plants were designed to operate at full capacity, during our visit the intensity and the dynamism noticed at Tsuchiura was much higher than at the Italian plant. This can be attributed to the size of the plant and the number of workers, though it is difficult to deny that this gap is also the result of a difference in workers' motivation and attitude towards work and 'company life'.

Regarding this last point, it is important to note that many of the workers at San Mauro are former employees of Fiat or other Italian companies, and not newly hired and trained young workers. In this respect, the company is not a greenfield undertaking. It is thus logical to assume that the workers' (and also managers') mentality and attitude are strongly influenced by their past experiences in the heavily unionized machinery industry. This is a sector in which adversarial rather than cooperative industrial relations have been prevailing for many years. It is therefore quite natural that many workers are at least sceptical about managers' introducing radical changes at the working place.

Moreover, in San Mauro all the workers are regular employees, while in Japan, especially when demand is surging, there is a conspicuous number of temporary workers (as many as one fourth of blue collars)[3]. The employment of temporary workers not only allows for a high degree of flexibility (numerical flexibility) concerning corporate human resource management but also essentially assures the long-term career of the 'core' employees. In contrast, at Fiat-Hitachi a contraction of business activities—as has happened in the past—can compel management to lay off employees, with all the negative consequences in terms of employee morale and commitment.

---

3 At Tsuchiura, many of the temporary workers are in fact foreigners of Japanese descent coming from South America and hired through manpower agencies.

This notwithstanding, the Italian management, with the support of a small number of Japanese managers/consultants, is sincerely attempting to improve the level of workforce participation and commitment. To this end, a system of individual performance evaluation (by the direct supervisor) and a correlated system of individual incentives have been introduced. This partly mitigates the rigid structure of wage and job classification fixed through labour agreements (nation-wide in case of the machinery sector). Moreover, an annual bonus is given to all employees on the basis of the overall corporate performance.

The company also relies more on internal promotion than external recruiting for filling positions of supervisors or higher responsibility. Training is another major concern of management. A large number of employees (about 200) have already been sent to Japan for short stays and training at HCM. Longer, intensive training schemes for selected individuals have also been organized. The problem, however, is that qualified, well-trained workers are the target of scouting by smaller but more flexible companies that can offer more attractive employment conditions; something that would not happen in Japan.

Workers furthermore are also invited to submit proposals for operation and working condition improvements. They are furthermore encouraged to participate in small-group activities, while particular attention is placed on quality. Each worker is responsible for the quality of his/her own task and every effort is made to improve the reliability and the integrity of the product. This has brought about a constant decrease in the number of defective products declared by dealers. The share of defective machines has decreased from an average of more than 3 % in the early nineties to less than 1.5 %, although these results are still below Japanese standards and, understandably, management's expectations. The same can be said for the level of absenteeism (around 3 %), which shows that years of efforts to raise workers' participation and commitment does not yet entirely offset the influence of past customs and habits. This, indeed, is the major drawback of the joint venture, as it has to adapt and adjust the innovative, advanced practices brought in from Japan to the constraints posed by the conditions inherited from the past. A problem that is even more evident in the case of P & D, the second joint venture discussed in this paper.

3.2 The experience of P & D S.p.A.[4]

P & D (Piaggio and Daihatsu) is a rather unique form of joint venture set up in February 1991 by Piaggio Veicoli Europei (a company particularly well

---

[4] Case study based on several factory visits and meetings with Italian and Japanese managers in Pontedera and a visit to Daihatsu Auto Body's Maebashi Plant in September 1996.

known for its production of scooters) and Daihatsu Motor. The company in fact is only in charge of the commercialization in Europe of minivans (small commercial vehicles) developed by Daihatsu, but assembled in Italy by Piaggio. In other words, the joint venture is the commercial arm and consultant of the Italian company, which is entirely responsible for the production of the motorvehicle. Piaggio, thus, is the first and only supplier of P & D. Production takes place in Pontedera, near Pisa, in a new building located within the historical works of Piaggio. Old and new thus coexist side by side and even inside the new structure, as next to the assembly line of the minivans, there is a line for three-wheeled vehicles, a traditional Piaggio product still manufactured and sold in Italy.

The case of Piaggio and Daihatsu is interesting because it is possible to observe how Japanese practices are transferred to Italy 1) through such a peculiar cooperative arrangement, 2) to a company with 5,000 employees and with more than seventy years of history and tradition, 3) to a social reality like that of Tuscany and the province of Pisa characterized by a strong political and cultural identity and 4) by the only Japanese car maker to directly invest in Italy. As in the case of Fiat-Hitachi, this joint venture was borne out of an exchange of product, technology and managerial knowledge (provided by Daihatsu) for production facilities and market access (provided by Piaggio). So far, however, the targets decided at the time of the establishment of the company have not been achieved. In particular, production has continuously remained below 20,000 vehicles per year, although it had been expected to reach a level of 35,000. The announced strategic reorientation of Piaggio activities (away from a mere manufacturer of motorcycles) has not taken place either, as the company today is only committed to maintaining a limited presence in the sector of minivans.

Two major factors explain this outcome: firstly, weaknesses in the commercial arm of Piaggio, due to not being used to dealing with cars and minivans; secondly, difficulties encountered at the plant level concerning the transfer of the Japanese production system. On this second point, no particular problems were posed by the technology transfer itself. The engines are imported from Japan, though in order to reduce costs, a diesel version manufactured in Italy has been added. Some of the equipment is Japanese (like the presses), but the dies, initially Japanese, are now Italian-made. The robots are Italian. Problems did occur, however, regarding the adaptation of the production process to the requirements of lean production. This is not so obvious if one looks at the organization chart only. As in other car plants that have adopted, or are adopting the lean production model, workers are organized in teams of 10–12 individuals and a team leader, a multiskilled senior worker with a wide experience. The leader is in charge of training, job rotation within the team and, in case of absentees, their substitution (as in Japan the team leader can work at the assembly line with his fellow workers). Wages, like in Fiat-Hitachi, are fixed by a nation-wide labour agreement according to the job and grade, though the company tries to attach more weight to individual evaluation, performed by the supervisors, and based on merit and performance. Five elements are normally considered: production volumes, productivity, quality, attitude to leadership and to organizational changes. These are also the main criteria for promotion. The company is furthermore committed to training and OJT in particular. In Piaggio as well, about 200 workers have been sent to Japan for training as future job leaders.

However, these efforts aimed at a radical change in both the work process and in workers' attitude, in reality have not produced the expected results. Firstly, the attempts to create a team of workers particularly committed to the new production unit was not successful. Over the last years, workers have had to be transferred to other departments because of overproduction problems or, as happened in the summer of 1995, to support the production of motorcycles. The result has been that young, dedicated workers specifically hired and trained for the new undertaking have been lost, while some old-guard workers had to be re-employed. This has made management's task to create a new environment conducive to workers' consensus and participation more difficult.

As mentioned by one of the Italian managers, "pre-existing conditions still greatly influence the mentality and behaviour", creating a major obstacle to diffuse a different attitude among workers. "Follow the directives, but do not take the initiative" is the attitude that seems to prevail, a passive attitude supported by the presence of a strong, militant union particularly determined to resist changes at the shopfloor. In other words, factors that do not foster mutual trust and workers' commitment seem to prevail on company attempts to promote worker participation and cooperative relations.

An evident sign of the difficulties encountered is the level of production efficiency, as measured by the high takt time, or the length of time that each worker is given to complete the job. While in the 'mother plant' at Maebashi, where an identical product is manufactured, takt time was 2'15" (at certain times even going down to less than two minutes), in Pontedera it was 4'50". A number that clearly shows how difficult the transfer of new practices is in an environment characterized by a strong, well-established industrial culture. The decision to stay within the boundaries of the old plant seems to have backfired. Instead of diffusing a new mentality to the entire plant, it is the old culture and way of thinking that is instead creeping into the new establishment.

3.3 The case of TMI Europe[5]

Quite a different situation was encountered at a newly set up company in Vercelli, a quiet town right in the middle of the rice producing district of Northern Italy. TMI Europe is a tripartite joint venture for the production of

[5] Case study based on a factory visit and meeting with managers of TMI.

dyed fabrics, set up in November 1993 by three companies: Teijin, one of Japan's leading firms in the sector of synthetic fibres; Mantero, an Italian firm renowned for the design and production of silk fabrics; and Itochū, the well-known *sōgō shōsha* (general trading firm). In this joint venture the majority of shares (55 %) is owned by Teijin, which also controls the technology, while Itochū and Mantero equally own 22.5 % of the capital.[6]

TMI's products are dyed fabrics made of so-called *shin-gōsen*, a high value-added synthetic yarn, that Teijin and other Japanese makers have been developing since the 1980s. Yarn (polyester filaments) is in fact produced in Japan, imported, and then twisted, woven, dyed and finished in Vercelli. Thus, the joint venture was not started with the simple aim of gaining Italian knowledge and expertise in the textile sector, but quite the opposite: to provide the European consumer with sophisticated products made available through Japanese advanced technology.

The Italian side's role, however, is important as Mantero is not only a major client of the joint venture, but also, together with Itochū, the main provider of information on market trends and developments. Indeed, it is the need to respond quickly and effectively to the rapidly and constantly changing demand that has prompted the Japanese maker to undertake a direct investment. On the other hand, for Mantero this project is important as it provides not only new fabrics and products that are highly appreciated by the European consumer. The fibres also represent an excellent substitute for natural silk, whose procurement is becoming a serious problem for Italian manufacturers. In fact, the supply of raw silk is practically a Chinese monopoly, strictly controlled by the Chinese authorities and, therefore, subject to quantitative restrictions and high price volatility. The possibility to reduce its dependence on a far-away, unpredictable supplier has therefore been another major factor inducing Mantero to participate in this joint venture.

As in the other two joint ventures discussed earlier, TMI Europe has thus been established with the aim to acquire a strong competitive advantage in the European market by pooling the complementary resources of the respective partners. However, differing from the other undertakings, this joint venture started as a totally new, greenfield investment. The buildings are modern, rational structures completed a few months before production started, all the equipment used in the different departments representing state-of-the-art technology developed in Europe and Japan. Some of the twisting and weaving machines are Italian, though the most advanced equipment (high-speed twisting machines and looms, as well as all the dyeing machines) have been imported from Japan. This fact shows that technology transfer has occurred on a large scale, but it also underscores that Japan's technology is well advanced and competitive even in the textile sector.

[6] In TMI Europe, the Managing Director is Japanese, while the President of the company is an Italian, Moritz Mantero, a member of the Mantero family.

Concerning TMI's labour force, experienced workers were employed only for the positions above section-chief. The large majority of the 300 employees are very young men and women (average age is 23), directly hired from high school or the vocational schools. They all work at the plant in their company uniforms, after taking both an on and off-the-job training that has taught them such essentials as the corporate philosophy and the basic tenets and principles of the Japanese management style. As mentioned by the company's managers, special attention was and is taken to hire young people that are particularly eager and inclined to work in a company where individual commitment and responsibility are particularly emphasized. This is possible as there is a strong competition for jobs available at TMI Europe in the rural areas near Vercelli, and managers can indeed choose the most suitable candidates. Moreover, many workers have been hired on a special, temporary contract[7] that allows the company to either dismiss individual workers or promote them to a lifetime job after a probational period that can last up to two years.

The availability of a young, 'non-contaminated' workforce, and the fact that seven section chiefs and several foremen were sent to Japan for training, has made the adoption of certain Japanese management practices easier. In particular, the company has introduced a particular system for the evaluation of individual performance through direct supervisors and has linked performance to salary increases. Efforts are being taken to increase job rotation, to train for multiskilled, multifunctional competencies, and to improve communication between management and employees. With the agreement of the trade union, the company has also been able to hire a limited number of temporary workers, who will guarantee a minimum of numerical flexibility.

Although it is premature to say if and how effective these attempts have been (full-scale operation only started in June 1996), it seems that in this case the adoption of new methods and practices has encountered less obstacles. The few indicators available so far show a clear improvement in the quality of products (the percentage of defects is remarkably decreasing), and concerning the development of a cooperative relationship between labour and management. Indeed, only seven employees participated in a recent textile sector strike. It seems, therefore, that in a greenfield undertaking like this one, the managers—those responsible for production, quality and the engineering department being Japanese—do not have to go to great lengths to adapt their ideas and attitudes to a workforce, ready and inclined to accept a different system of industrial relations and a different management style.

---

[7] Temporary training contracts (*Contratti di Formazione e Lavoro*) were introduced in Italy in 1984.

4 Conclusion

In the first part of the paper we have seen how Japanese firms' strategies concerning Europe have been changing in the 1990s, as a result of both the increased attractiveness of Asia and the adoption of new global perspectives that have considerably reduced the flow of Japanese direct investment into Europe.

We have also seen how Japanese companies investing in Europe have followed different strategies in different parts of the region. In Northern Europe and in the UK Japanese firms have invested heavily in those sectors in which they have a strong competitive advantage such as consumer electronics and motor vehicles. In Italy, on the other hand, there have been no significant investments in these sectors. Furthermore, wholly-owned, greenfield investments prevail in Northern Europe, while in the Southern countries and in Italy, in particular, DI has taken the form of joint ventures with local partners.

In the second part of the paper, we have seen how the implementation of the joint-venture strategy has affected the investment's performance and the transfer of Japanese technology and management practices. The findings based on the three case studies examined are summarized in table 2.

Table 2: Evaluation of three Japanese joint ventures in Italy

	P & D	F. H.	TIM
technology transfer	**yes** (but engine from Japan)	**yes**, except key-technology	**yes** (but yarn from Japan)
transfer of Japanese production and work practices	difficult	fairly successful (hybrid model with Italian elements)	successful
quality	?	increased, but still 1.5 % defects ratio	improving
production efficiency	takt time: 2′ 15″ vs. 4′50″ (Japan)	lower work intensity	?
worker commitment & participation	**low** ('follow the directives, but do not take the initiative')	high number of suggestions vs. 3 % absenteeism	**high**
production/sales	low production levels (20,000 vs. 35,000 planned)	strong sales performance	**rising**

Technology transfer has occurred relatively successfully in the three ventures. However, it is also true that such transfer proceeds more easily and to a greater extent where the receiving firm is majority-owned by the Japanese partner. In the other cases, technology transfer is mainly hampered by the Japanese side's determination to maintain control over the main source of its competitive advantage. In other words, there is a trade-off between ownership and technology transfer.

As to the transfer of Japanese organizational and managerial practices, it is evident that this occurs more smoothly for greenfield investments. In the case of already existing production facilities or new structures but with an older workforce, this process is much more complex and less likely to produce real, lasting change in employees' attitude towards work and the company in general. Here, the strength of tradition and of cultural factors becomes a serious obstacle to the introduction of both new ideas and practices. The result then often is a *hybrid model* that not necessarily represents the best integration of the various elements though, as we have seen, positive results are still possible when compared to the pre-joint venture situation at the local partner.

Lastly it has become clear from the cases examined that excessive rigidities and constraints in the labour market and regarding the industrial relations system can stand in the way of introducing innovative managerial practices and, therefore, represent a disincentive for foreign (Japanese) investment. In the current context, characterized by a reduced inflow of Japanese DI to Europe and an increased Japanese attention to Central-Eastern European countries, the removal of these rigidities becomes important in order to participate in the 'beauty contest' among European countries. Thus, even if Japanese DI in Europe is unlikely to grow substantially in the years ahead, its importance will continue to represent an incentive to reform the EU countries' social and economic institutions.

References

ABO, T. (1994): *Hybrid Factory. The Japanese Production System in the United States.* New York: Oxford University Press.

ACKROYD, S., G. BURRELL, M. HUGHES and A. WHITAKER (1988): The Japanization of British Industry? In: *Industrial Relations Journals* 19, 1, pp. 11–23.

BELDERBOS, R. A. (1997): *Japanese Electronic Multinationals and Strategic Trade Policies.* Oxford: Oxford University Press.

CONTRACTOR, F. J. and P. LORANGE (1988): *Cooperative Strategies in International Business.* Lexington: Lexington Books.

JETRO – Japan External Trade Organization (1996): *The 12th Survey of European Operations of Japanese Companies in the Manufacturing Sector.* Tōkyō: JETRO.

JETRO – Japan External Trade Organization (1997): *The 13th Survey of European Operations of Japanese Companies in the Manufacturing Sector.* Tōkyō: JETRO.

MITI – Ministry of International Trade and Industry (1996): *Kaigai jigyō katsudō* [Activities of Enterprises Abroad]. Tōkyō: Printing Office of the Ministry of Finance.

MOLTENI, C. (1993): Japanese Joint Venture in Italy: A Second Best Strategy? In: CAMPBELL, N. and F. BURTON (eds.): *Japanese Multinationals' Strategies and Management in the Global Kaisha.* London: Routledge, pp. 85–97.

MOLTENI, C. (1996): Japanese Manufacturing in Italy. In: DARBY, J. (ed.): *Japan and the European Periphery.* London: Macmillan, pp. 132–148.

Nikkei (1997): http://www.nikkei.co/enews/page/Auto-other.html, 01.13. 1997.

OLIVER, N. and B. WILKINSON (1992): *The Japanization of British Industry.* Oxford: Blackwell.

STRANGE, R. (1993): *Japanese Manufacturing Investment in Europe.* London: Routledge.

THIRAN, J.-M. and H. YAMAWAKI (1993): *Regional and Country Determinants of Locational Decisions: Japanese Multinationals in European Manufacturing.* IRES Discussion Paper 9517.

THIRAN, J.-M. and H. YAMAWAKI (1996): Patterns of Japanese Manufacturing Employment in the European Regions. In: DARBY, J. (ed.): *Japan and the European Periphery.* London: Macmillan, pp. 37–51.

URATA, S. (1992): *Japanese Foreign Direct Investment and its Impacts on Foreign Trade in Asia.* Mimeo. Tōkyō: Waseda University.

URATA, S. (1997): Japan's Foreign Trade and Direct Investment Relations with Southern Europe. Paper presented at the *Conference on "Japan and the Mediterranean World"*, Naples, October 16–18, 1997.

Commentary

Klaus GREFERMANN

In spite of regional differences, the general economic situation in most of the leading industrialized countries tends to be inundated with problems. This is especially true when it comes to labour markets. High unemployment is the core issue and also causes serious and negative consequences with respect to tax collection and social systems.

Internationalization—or as we now say 'globalization'—is blamed for this development. In a recently published book (MARTIN & SCHUMANN 1996) the authors point to high-tech communication, low freight rates and free trade without barriers and frontiers as factors which have led to a one-market world. Production capacities move to sites with the lowest tax rates, cheapest land prices, lowest standards in environmental legislation: in short, those places with the highest profits and above all the lowest labour costs. Thus, companies in Germany and other highly industrialized countries are blamed for creating new jobs only in countries which feature as many of these favourable factors as possible.

Particularly in Germany and Austria, workers are accused of working too little, receiving exaggerated incomes, spending too much of their time on holiday, and calling in sick too often. Because globalization sets free the forces of world markets and deprives nations of their economic power, the situation is said to be getting even worse. This process, originally begun and kept running by the economic and political elites in the United States, will transfer its effects to all countries worldwide. Consequently only a fifth of the total labour force will be needed in the future. The remaining four fifths will need to be entertained by medial bread and circuses to prevent them from turning revolutionary.

In contrast to this gloomy picture, the situation in Japan as well as Japanese companies' strategies and management practices are commonly painted in bright colours. Many studies and books have tried to demonstrate that the Japanese way, i. e., working hard, being 'married' to the firm, renouncing vacation time, companies' investing abroad and 'conquering' world markets, is the only successful path to be followed. For a long time Japan was considered the shining example to be emulated by the Europeans, but never to be matched. This gloomy message was most popular in Germany, but was not restricted to this country alone.

The situation has changed rapidly and fundamentally. When this conference began, turbulences had started to shake all of Asia. The seemingly irresistible economic rise of this growth region par excellence must now be seen in a new light, and the daily changing economic weather forecasts jeopardize many of the statements and assumptions of the papers this contribution is based on. Nevertheless, most of the experts presently seem to agree that the economic turbulences in Asia can be overcome and do not mark the beginning of a new trend.

This is the pessimistic essence of the 'Globalization Trap', typically written in Germany but based on many international papers and articles. It is certain that international linkages have grown considerably over the last few decades. By value, production in industrialized countries between 1964 and 1994 rose by some 9 % p. a., exports by 12 % p. a. and international bank credits by even 23 % (SHERMAN 1996: 3).

There are two main reasons for this international integration process. Firstly, technical, social and political changes have reduced the differences between nations. Secondly, many barriers which complicated or even prevented cross-border transactions have been torn down or, at least, lowered. Fast computers and a rapidly growing international network now enable deals to be made over huge distances in seconds.

Globalization has spurred on international competition. Transnational companies and their networks are rising and growing while seeking production and distribution sites worldwide with low costs and high profits. Faced with high unemployment, cities, regions, and countries compete in attracting investors. This competition tends to be unfair and to waste financial resources, thus EU officials have recently started to cease this un-economic race.

Structural changes characterize the growth of economies worldwide. The IMF has recently said that, taken together, Asia's economies will be half as large again by the year 2000 as they were in 1993 and that therefore in the year 2000 the Asia economies will already account for about 30 % of world output. This is very impressive, though TUGENDHAT (1996: 4) reminds us that in 1900 Asian economies accounted for about 32 % of world output. Nevertheless, the next century is expected to be—amongst other names—the 'Asian century'. The share of industrialized countries in world output declined from 88 % in 1970 to 80 % in 1995 and will continue to decline. Established companies and nations will have to fight for their economic lives.

This is what is forcing internationally active companies—but not only those—to reconsider their strategies. Firms in mature industrialized countries are no longer able to stay in their traditional home-markets with commonly low growth rates and profits, unless they occupy niche markets. But in a period when even niches in different countries can be linked and regrouped into considerable markets, this possibility will attract competitors.

Another option is trying to serve the growing regional markets in the world by means of classic export strategies. This could be an inferior method, however, when knowledge of trends and quick reactions are core issues in business. The third option is aiming at investments in growing markets which are new to the suppliers or have been covered hitherto by exports, thus relocating major but unprofitable domestic operations to relatively low-cost overseas production bases.

The comments on this subject then are arranged in the form of five theses:

1 The recent slowdown of FDI: A cyclical not a structural phenomenon

Foreign direct investments (FDI) are commonly considered to be the best indicators of internationalization. Since the beginning of the eighties, FDI have gained considerable importance. In 1980 stocks of foreign direct investments amounted to some 500 billion Dollars. The average growth rate of those investments was around 1 % per year. In the second half of the eighties growth accelerated to 34 % a year. This was a much more rapid growth than exports (13 %) and GNP (12 %). The following two years, 1991 and 1992, saw for the first time a reduction in these flows of investment. This slow-down is commonly attributed to the down-swing of business cycles in Japan and Western Europe. 1993 saw a recovery by 17 %, 1994 again a stagnation. Only a meagre growth rate was recorded in 1995, though results for 1996 show a considerable recovery by about 10 %. Currently there seems to be an upward trend again (UNCTAD 1991, 1993, 1995; see also Sherman 1996: 7–8).

Although these figures are not very reliable, since existing differences in methodology, definitions, and quality of national statistics prevent a clear picture, they are fully sufficient to show a tendency. It was only a cyclical downturn which temporarily stopped internationalization in the early nineties. The latest world investment report by UNCTAD (1997: XVI) forecasts, besides a considerable growth in export rates, a doubling of local production abroad by transnational companies within the next five years. Globalization will continue in whatever form.

2 A general shift between receiving countries of FDI

In the second half of the eighties, Japanese companies entered the European market in full force. Direct investments in the manufacturing sector alone rose from a yearly average of $ 216 million in the 1980–84 period to more than $ 4.5 billion in 1990 alone (see paper by Molteni, p. 93). Within Western Europe, Japanese multinationals did not change their investment pattern significantly. This is not only true for regional distribution but also for different industries. In Southern Europe, Japanese investments were mainly aimed at traditional sectors such as clothing and textiles, as well as machinery and scale-intensive sectors. Investments in northern regions of Europe were mainly in consumer electronics, motor vehicles and high-tech sectors. Molteni (p. 96) points to the fact that in Italy there have been no significant investments in the car and consumer electronic sectors. This sounds strange, because Italians are said to have a particularly close relation to these products and Italy should be a good production site and an interesting market.

There is another difference: In Southern Europe most Japanese investments have been carried out in the form of joint ventures, whereas in Northern Europe fully-owned greenfield mills are dominant. This difference was already pointed out by earlier research (ERNST & HILPERT 1990).

In the meantime, the flow of Japan's FDI to Europe has shrunk both in value and percentage terms. Asia is now the favoured area. But not only Japanese firms have increasingly discovered Asian economies for investments; other countries are also entering these promising markets. In 1996 a total of $ 42.5 billion went to China, $ 9.5 billion to Singapore, $ 8 billion to Indonesia and $ 5.3 billion to Malaysia. Molteni considers this drive to Asia to be the most conspicuous feature of this decade. It not only reflects the growth of the local markets but also the fact that Southeast Asian countries provide an excellent, cost-effective export platform for investing multinationals. As Japan is concentrating its efforts on its neighbour markets, it is thereby following a similar pattern as Germany, which has placed more than 55 % of its FDI in other EU countries (DEUTSCHE BUNDESBANK 1997: 10–11). The difference is that most production costs are much lower and potential profits are much higher on Asian markets. Recently, however, we have had to learn that risks are high, as well. It is not only pessimists who point to problems in Asia which remain to be solved in the future: environmental issues, growth of mega-cities, ethnic rivalries, discrepancies in income distribution and, last but not least, stability in governmental systems.

As for Germany (and for neighbouring European countries), this Asian predominance has two consequences. First, debates concerning the 'site Germany' have become fiercer as the inflow of foreign investments has declined. Pressure groups and lobbyists cite the negative attributes, discussed at the beginning of this paper, as the reasons for the withdrawal of foreign investors. This is especially delicate since most forecasters only a few years ago foresaw a rise of FDI in Germany as a consequence of unification and the outstanding geographical position of Eastern Germany for accessing Eastern European markets. Instead we now witness increasing German capital exports and falling foreign investments, the latter being down in 1996 to $ 3.8 billion which is much less than FDI to Poland and about the level of Norway (DEUTSCHE BUNDESBANK 1997: 10–11).

The second consequence is that German firms must follow the trend of 'Going Far-East' if they do not want to lose any opportunities in fast-growing markets. A recent survey by the Ifo Institute (KÖDDERMANN & WILHELM 1996) showed that China and other Southeast Asian countries gained importance as receivers of German FDI. Nevertheless, the stock of German investments in Japan, China, and developing economies in Asia and Oceania amounted to a meagre 5 % of all existing German FDI in 1995 according to the DEUTSCHE BUNDESBANK (1997).

Several reasons may be given for the hesitation of German firms to act as 'pioneers' on these markets: lack of 'colonial experiences', lack of knowledge about these markets and their socio-cultural backgrounds, and—last but not least—the dominance of small- and medium-sized companies content with their domestic or, uppermost, their West European markets. But change is inevitable. Take the European clothing industry, for instance, which has been moving away from regions with high labour costs to the more remote and 'cheaper' regions. When Europe became no longer viable, the industry moved via Cyprus, Malta and Turkey to Asia. The textile industry followed and so did the fibre industry after their production facilities had been fully depreciated. Now it seems to be the turn of respective machinery industries, with research facilities soon to follow. This leads us to the reasons why FDI are generally undertaken.

3 Motives for FDI are in a process of change

From the European point of view, the main reason for Japanese FDI originally was a 'conquering the world', flexing economic muscle, and being present in markets where 'the music was playing'. When in the eighties the process of establishing a Single Market was ostensibly leading to a potential 'fortress Europe', this spurred investors interested in being in that market of some 300 million consumers to act. This was not only true for Scandinavians and Americans, but for Japanese firms as well.

Meanwhile other motives for investing abroad are becoming more important for Japanese firms. Companies from developing countries are using their own comparative advantages, intensifying competition in Japan's traditional export markets. Moreover, international, but also domestic pressures to deregulate the economy are increasing (see Tachiki's paper, p. 73). Thus, it has become necessary for Japanese companies to transfer selected low value-added operations to new production bases.

This is the case for West European countries as well. The fall of the Iron Curtain has led to a slowdown of the foreign drain to Southeast Asia and, as it is commonly stated, presented production facilities with low labour costs just at their door, similar to those in some parts of Asia. There is a tradition of high-skilled labour forces in East European countries. Cultural similarities are manifold due to a long, common history.

The first wave of movement into these countries has, in the meantime, been completed. It turned out that a reengineered, lean production in Germany was often able to compensate higher labour costs and avoid disadvantages such as lower productivity, traffic jams, long customs procedures, or a high-crime environment in some of the FDI target countries (KÖDDERMANN & WILHELM 1996).

The approach of Japanese companies towards central Eastern Europe has been very cautious compared with German, American, Scandinavian, Austrian, and even Korean competitors. There are some signs that the approach of Japanese firms will change, at least with regard to Hungary, Poland, and the Czech Republic (Molteni, p. 91). But the question remains, why Japanese companies, whose products so brilliantly meet the demand of people with beginning purchasing power, are hesitant to invest in these emerging markets? We will come back to this question later.

According to the survey by the Ifo Institute quoted earlier (KÖDDERMANN & WILHELM 1996), in two thirds of all cases FDI is market oriented, be it to gain market share, or to safeguard it and participate in the general market growth. Only one fifth of all German investors considered labour costs to be of high importance when investing abroad, though putting more weight on that factor for the future. Most surprisingly, participants in this inquiry did not place much weight on subsidies and support programmes. This matches the findings of Molteni's research. He was told by the Japanese managers he interviewed that grants are an important factor in their decisions to invest in a specific country and region. However, more than the grant itself, the manifest support and the positive attitude of the local and central governments play an even larger role (p. 96).

4 M&A and strategic alliances gaining importance

Traditionally FDI has been executed as greenfield plants, fully owned by the investor. This is especially true for the established industrialized countries. According to Ifo studies (SHERMAN 1996) a dramatic shift towards mergers and acquisitions (M&A) has taken place since the mid-eighties. This is particularly true for transatlantic investments, though Japanese firms increasingly seem to prefer this form as well. Today about four-fifths of new capital investments are performed as M&As. The main reason for this is the emphasis put on the exchange of strategic parts of firms. M&As are an important means of avoiding excess capacity and, in addition, helping firms to enter existing networks of sales, supply and information. This is not only true for manufacturing but also for the financial sector, which in Europe in the past years has faced a wave of M&As.

Besides traditional greenfield investments, joint ventures and M&A strategic alliances without any capital linkage have gained importance (SHERMAN 1996: 12). Normally aimed at one defined target and designed only for a limited time, they can if successful be long-lasting and finally lead to an exchange of capital. In its recent world investment report, UNCTAD (1997: 135–136) has stated that given the strict policies of savings in many places, there will be less money for capital invasions in markets abroad. Instead, less capital intensive means would be used. This will increasingly favour mergers, strategic alliances and joint ventures instead of greenfield FDI in the future.

In addition, as Tachiki (p. 74) has emphasized in his paper, it is a fact that Japanese managers, suffering from distinct disadvantages against local competitors in understanding local business practices, in establishing reliable supplier networks, and in learning the nuances of local consumer markets, are increasingly trying to enter strategic alliances with local partners.

5 Social factors play an important role for the success of FDI

Three interesting case studies done by Molteni lead us to a very interesting question: What are—besides market forces and the political framework—the driving factors behind successful investments? Or, to put it in a more concrete way, to what extent can Japanese management practices and attitudes towards their labour force be transferred to different nations or, more exact, cultural spheres, and are there areas which meet these requirements better than others? Indeed, in the past we find a clear Japanese preference for certain regions within Europe (according to Molteni, the South-East, Wales and the Midlands of the United Kingdom, Bavaria in Germany and the East of Spain account for almost half of the employment of Japanese companies in the European Union) and this may be linked to these questions. And is perhaps the new accent on Asia a kind of 'back to the roots'? The case studies by Molteni refer to Italy only and, indeed, show different results, mainly depending on the mode of entry and the form of ownership chosen.

With regard to technology, transfers have shown to be quite successful in all three cases, though they were a little easier in the case of ventures with majority Japanese ownership. I believe this is normal: An ultimately successful technology developed under the pain of set-backs is something a team is more proud of than a technology bought. This point is not a typical Japanese-foreign problem.

Generally, as Molteni has concluded, the transfer of the Japanese organizational and managerial practices is much easier in the case of a greenfield investment. Again, in Europe this does not have too much to do with any specific Japanese pattern. A greenfield mill always means the creation of new jobs and is therefore highly appreciated by local authorities, which are proud of having won the competition of attracting an investor over other regions. This up-beat mood is transferred by media to the local people and contributes to the good performance of the FDI.

In contrast, mergers and acquisitions by Japanese or other investors are often consequences of a long-lasting decline of the local partner. The best and highest skilled workers might already have left the firm. Thus, the transfer of Japanese organizational and managerial practices to already existing production facilities or even to new structures with an old workforce is much more complex and less likely to be a success. "Strength of tradition and cultural factors in these cases becomes a serious obstacle to the introduction of both new ideas and practices" (Molteni, p. 106).

This leads us to the conclusion that a greenfield FDI with a workforce recruited from young people just out of school, training them on-the-job, led by several flexible and sensitive managers, is likely to promise best results.

The case studies by Molteni are clearly focused on work relationships only. They do not mention the Japanese 'specialities' such as quality circles, which must be difficult to implement in Italy not only because of language barriers. They do not refer to just-in-time deliveries and 'kaizen' and they do not touch the questions of cooperating with local authorities and acceptance by the local society, points which could be summarized by the question of 'How much do Japanese Managers want to stay in Italy?'

The preference of Japanese investors for the United Kingdom, in contrast, is well-known and, of course, the reasons behind it have been widely discussed especially among other regions competing for investments (see ERNST & HILPERT 1990). The following factors are seen as the main reasons for the Japanese preference to invest in the United Kingdom:

Similarities in socio-cultural environments

There is some correspondence between British and Japanese environments. Both are situated on islands which had long guaranteed them a 'splendid isolation'. Both still adhere to a monarchy full of history but without any real power. Nobility and traditions are highly appreciated. Last but not least, English is a worldwide language and more widespread in Japan than other Western languages.

Need for a change

In the United Kingdom there was a strong need for a change in the whole economic system especially for the revitalization of manufacturing industries. Any assistance was accepted and all parts of the society cooperated. In other parts of Europe the need for a change has not been as clearly felt, though presently the situation in East Germany is comparable to that of the UK earlier. More than grants and subsidies, the support and the attitude of the local authorities seem to have played an even larger role. Molteni even goes so far as to say that governments are so keen on attracting Japanese investors that they have changed their fiscal system, labour market and public administration's procedures and organization accordingly (Molteni, p. 96)

Investors from Japan are considered to be traditionally sceptical with respect to established European working regulations and traditions. Work structures seem to be too complex and, above all, too strictly regulated. Therefore, according to Ifo research (KÖDDERMANN & WILHELM 1996), takeovers of firms with an 'old' work force or in regions with strong labour unions will be avoided unless the situation calls for such a decision. This could be the case when a rapid market entrance is the most important strategic issue. It has taken a long time for governmental and union authorities to recognize this and to act more flexibly. Now it may be too late, since Japanese firms increasingly prefer Asian countries for their investments.

A certain 'we-too' behaviour
For many reasons (language, cultural links, etc.) American firms tend to invest in the UK. This automatically draws the attention of Japanese firms to this site. Japan is generally said to watch and to follow American patterns.

FDI structure
According to public opinion in Europe, Japanese investments abroad are connected with production sites. But it should not be forgotten that Japanese FDI concentrates mainly on sectors outside the manufacturing industry. Worldwide, only somewhat more than a quarter is placed here, whilst trade, banking, insurance and 'other sectors' are much more important. The United Kingdom is known for a dominance of banking and insurance investments, which command a 40 % share of all Japanese FDI when compared to the worldwide average of only 19 % (KÖDDERMANN & WILHELM). In Germany, trade-related investment is more important (35 % compared to 11 %), whereas manufacturing is below average.

Tachiki has shown that it was only relatively recently that Japan entered the Asia-Pacific region via FDI. Many limiting factors in the respective receiving countries had to be improved first. Meanwhile, however, there is a growing economic cooperation among countries in the region, and the modernized infrastructure has eased the flow of goods, people, money, and information (p. 77). Japanese investors have also become more familiar with the 'hidden networks'.

While previously Japanese firms preferred locating only manufacturing operations abroad in this region, Tachiki (p. 84) demonstrates that substantial change is taking place, including networks of regional headquarters which should ensure Japan's continuing success in the FDI field. This, of course, assumes that the Asian economies eventually manage to overcome the current crisis.

6 Summary

Internationalization and globalization of firms, markets and trade have led to major structural changes worldwide. These have forced firms, especially the larger ones, to intensify their activities in markets abroad. The contributions to the conference this paper is based on have dealt with these developments, problems and consequences. Some questions, however, remain:

1. Will globalization continue and what will be the main consequences for the countries concerned? Is the 20:80 ratio mentioned in MARTIN & SCHU-

MANN's publication likely to become reality (only 20 % of the current total labour force will be needed in the future—while 80 % will need to be entertained)?
2. Is the worldwide, and especially Japanese, FDI preference for Asia the correct strategy, particularly in the long term? Are the risks due to economic or political shocks not too high? Does this attitude towards Asia mean a withdrawal from Europe? What will the future of FDI activities in Eastern Europe be?
3. What is the reaction of investors when production costs continue to rise above average in a region after a stock of FDI has been built up? Will they withdraw these inefficient capacities and will the 'circus' of capacities around the world continue in the future? What will the most important cost factors in the future be, assuming continuous hikes in productivity?
4. Will this concentration on Asia involve the building of greenfield FDI, or are joint ventures if not strategic alliances the better way, particularly in capital intensive industries?
5. What importance will social factors such as cultural linkages, ethnic similarities or mutual understanding have in the future? Is there a tendency of internationalization or even globalization of people themselves? Will the 'world citizen', who feels at home anywhere, be the model of the future, or will a swing back to the roots, a return to native regions and their customs be more likely?

References

DEUTSCHE BUNDESBANK (1997): *Kapitalverflechtung mit dem Ausland.* Statistische Sonderveröffentlichung Nr. 10. Frankfurt: Deutsche Bundesbank.

ERNST, A. and H.-G. Hilpert (1990): *Japans Direktinvestitionen in Europa – Europas Direktinvestitionen in Japan.* Ifo Studien zur Japanforschung Nr. 4. Munich: Ifo Institute.

KÖDDERMANN, R. and M. WILHELM (1996): *Umfang und Bestimmungsgründe einfließender und ausfließender Direktinvestitionen ausgewählter Industrieländer – Entwicklungen und Perspektiven.* Ifo Studien zur Strukturforschung Nr. 24. Munich: Ifo Institute.

MARTIN, H. P. and H. SCHUMANN (1996): *Die Globalisierungsfalle.* Reinbek: Rowohlt.

SHERMAN, H. (1996): Globalisierung: Transnationale Unternehmen auf dem Vormarsch. In: *Ifo Schnelldienst* 49, 23, pp. 3–13.

TUGENDHAT, C. (1996): On the road to the 21st Century: Can Europe Meet the Challenge of Asia? In: *Ifo Digest* 19, 4, pp. 3–8.

UNCTAD (1991, 1993, 1995, 1997): *World Investment Report.* New York and Geneva: UNCTAD.

Corporate Governance and Control

V Presidential Turnover and Performance in the Japanese Firm: The Evolution and Change of the Contingent Governance Structure under the Main Bank System

Hideaki Miyajima

Recent theoretical and empirical research on the Japanese firm has highlighted characteristics of corporate governance of J-type firms compared to the Anglo-American type as a contingent structure where the controlling power of insiders systematically shifts to outsiders (main banks), once a firm faces financial distress. The purpose of this paper is to present some empirical evidence on the evolutionary process of this contingent governance structure and its recent changes, focusing mainly on the relationship between presidential turnover and corporate performance. Using a sample composed of one hundred large manufacturing companies, this paper tests the same specification of logit regression for five different time periods which include serious recessions during the postwar Japanese economic history (1956–1996).

1 Introduction

Recent theoretical and empirical research on the Japanese firm has highlighted a number of stylized facts as characteristics of corporate governance of J-type firms (Aoki 1988, Fukao 1995, Sheard 1994a). Along with the dominance of insiders on the corporate board and the mitigation of the pressure on the top management team from capital markets, the role of the main bank for disciplining top management has been emphasized. Given possible agency costs under the shareholder stabilization scheme, the main bank which is the largest debtholder as well as one of the largest shareholders has monitored client companies. The controlling power of the main bank is not any explicit one in the normal or favourable financial state. However, once a firm faces financial distress, governance shifts from insiders to the outsider (the main bank). In this sense, this system where the controlling power of both parties is contingent on the financial state of the firm is called by Aoki (1994a) a "contingent governance structure". It is supposedly different from the Anglo-American system which is based on takeovers and bankruptcy procedures. The purpose of this paper is to clarify the evolutionary process of this corporate governance structure and the recent changes in this structure, focusing mainly on the relationship between presidential turnover and corporate performance.

Let us explain our concerns in detail. A first issue of this paper is the historical process of governance structure in the Japanese firm. It has already been explained in the work of OKAZAKI (1993a, b), MIYAJIMA (1994, 1995) and YAFEH (1995) that the prototype J-type firm emerged during World War II and the postwar reform period.

However, it is important to note that by 1955 corporate governance still retained characteristics of a market for corporate control because the ownership structure of large firms was dispersed as a result of drastic reforms initiated by the US occupation army (GHQ). At the same time, the main bank relationship was not yet evident due to fierce competition among banks for potent clients (MIYAJIMA 1996). Therefore, it took a long evolutionary process for Japanese firms to establish the pattern of corporate governance stylized above. In this context, it is noteworthy that a necessary condition for sustaining contingent governance is that a rule concerning how to cope with financial distress needs to be shared among stakeholders (AOKI & OKUNO 1996: 204–5). Focusing on when and how this implicit rule concerning contingent governance was established, this paper attempts to analyse the evolutionary process of the corporate governance structure of Japanese firms.

Another concern of this paper is to provide empirical evidence on recent changes regarding corporate governance of the J-firm. Some researchers have pointed out that, as companies have become increasingly dependent on equity financing for new money due to financial deregulation since 1980, the monitoring capability of the main bank has declined. As a result, the budget constraints on which companies base their strategies has been much 'softer' than before, one reason for the emergence of the *bubble economy* in the late 1980s. This understanding has been suggested by AOKI (1994a) and IKEO (1995), and is now broadly shared among researchers and policy makers (ECONOMIC PLANNING AGENCY 1996).

On the other hand, however, empirical studies mainly discussing the 1980s have not produced any such evidence. For example, KAPLAN (1992, 1994) and subsequently KANG & SHIVSADANI (1995) have shown that CEO turnover is significantly correlated with company performance, especially stock performance, and income measures. MORCK & NAKAMURA (1992), KAPLAN & MINTON (1994) as well as SHEARD (1994b) report that the dispatching of a bank member to client companies has been closely correlated with corporate performance.

Although the sample size was different for each of these studies, they have all supported the view that the corporate governance of the Japanese firm is still effective in correcting moral hazard of top management, and that the city banks (main banks) play a central role in this disciplinary mechanism.

However, all these studies have been based on panel data of the 1980s. Therefore, even if their results have been confirmed by regression analyses, it is still possible that the disciplinary mechanisms of the 1980s were less functional than in previous periods.[1] Furthermore there is no empirical re-

[1] In fact, KAPLAN (1992) has pointed out that "the magnitude of these relations and the amount of turnover explained are arguably not overwhelming".

search concerning the change of governance structure which has occurred in the 1990s after the *bubble economy* collapsed. In order to clarify the recent changes in corporate governance in Japanese firms, we need to compare the estimation results of the 1980s with those of previous periods. Another purpose of this paper, therefore, is to offer empirical evidence for recent changes in corporate governance from a historical perspective by using the same sample companies to test the same specifications of regression for different time periods.

This paper proceeds as follows: the next section presents our periodization for Japan's postwar history. Section 3 explains the data and model behind our analysis. Section 4 is the core of this paper where the regressions results are abstracted. Based on the results of the previous section, together with some anecdotal accounts, section 5 gives our perspectives on the evolution and change of governance structures in large Japanese firms since 1955. Concluding remarks are presented in section 6.

2 Strategy for analysis: the periodization of postwar economic history

To clarify the evolution of the corporate governance structure since 1955, the basic strategy taken in this paper is to divide history into several sub-periods by focusing on corporate ownership and finance, and then to estimate the same specification of regressions for these sub-periods. First, let us briefly introduce our periodization and highlight the background facts for the following section.[2]

The first phase of the High Growth Era (HGE) (1955–1964)

The percentage of stock held by financial institutions and other business corporations relative to the total issued stock in Japan remained comparatively unchanged during this time, while the percentage of portfolio investors (individuals plus trust funds, i. e., the equivalent of mutual funds in the US) was relatively high. Large firms largely depended on bank loans for fresh money, while simultaneously raising a certain amount of their capital on the capital market. A main bank status was gradually established through severe competition among city banks for this designation.

The later phase of the HGE (1965–73)

The corporate ownership structure underwent a major change during the so-called 'Securities Recession' of the mid-1960s, when stock prices declined. Many companies faced a takeover crisis under new capital liberalization measures. In this context, they stabilized shareholding by relying on financial institutions and related companies. As the shares held by financial insti-

[2] See MIYAJIMA (1996, forthcoming) in detail.

tutions increased, main bank relationships became increasingly stable. Furthermore, large firms depended exclusively on borrowing as their external source for capital. According to my estimation, the growth rate of firms on an asset basis was positively correlated with the leverage (borrowing-asset) ratio in this period.

After the oil crisis (1974–1982)
The percentage of stock held by financial institutions and other business corporations relative to the total issued stock remained relatively constant during the 1970s. The dividend payout ratio was not sensitive to the *ROE* at all. The relationship often called 'stabilized shareholding' was completed around this period. On the other hand, as some have pointed out, main banks began to play an important role for rescuing companies facing financial distress (SHEARD 1989). However, it is also worth noting that from this period on, companies began to reduce their borrowing from banks, while the standard deviation on the leverage ratio of sample companies increases to a greater extent than before. This fact indicates that it was not possible for all companies to reduce their borrowing; rather, some companies continued to depend on the banks for their money.

Financial deregulation and the bubble (1983–1989)
It was in 1983 that financial deregulation began to influence corporate finance. From that year on, companies increasingly came to depend on equity financing for their capital needs, this trend becoming very clear in the late 1980s. While equity financing did not change the ownership structure, firms' capital composition improved dramatically. What should be noted here is that despite the fact that internal funds exceeded investment levels, companies raised money through equity financing and bond issuance as well as through borrowing. This money was then invested in land and securities.

After the bubble (1990–)
As investment levels decreased after the *bubble* collapsed, the share of internal funds to financing has increased, while external funding has depended largely on bonds. Although the ownership structure appears stable, there are signs that cross-shareholding has been relaxed due to the stock price decline. It is often pointed out that foreign investors and institutional investors such as life insurance companies have begun to exert an influence on the appropriation of income. Actually, the dividend payout ratio per value on the sample average has increased recently in spite of low corporate profitability, and thus has recovered its sensitivity to the *ROE* once again in the early 1990s.

In terms of corporate ownership and finance, Japan's postwar history can be divided into these five sub-periods. The question now is how the relationship between firms' turnover and corporate performance has changed over these periods. In order to clarify this point, we will determine the crucial phase for which the capability and effort level of top management can meaningfully be tested. Focusing on the profit rate trend among large companies as shown in graph 1, we have chosen the following five five-year intervals for each sub-period.

- the annual change of corporate presidents over the 1959–63 period, including the recession after the "Jimmu boom" (1956–57) and the "Iwato boom" (1959–61);
- the annual presidency changes over the 1965–69 period, including the "securities recession" (1965–66);
- the annual presidency changes over the 1974–78 period, including the recession following the oil crisis;
- the annual such changes over the 1984–88 period, including the recession after the yen appreciation following the Plaza Accord;
- the annual such changes between 1990 to 1994 including the post-*bubble* recession.

Graph 1: The development of *ROE* and *ROA* in the postwar period

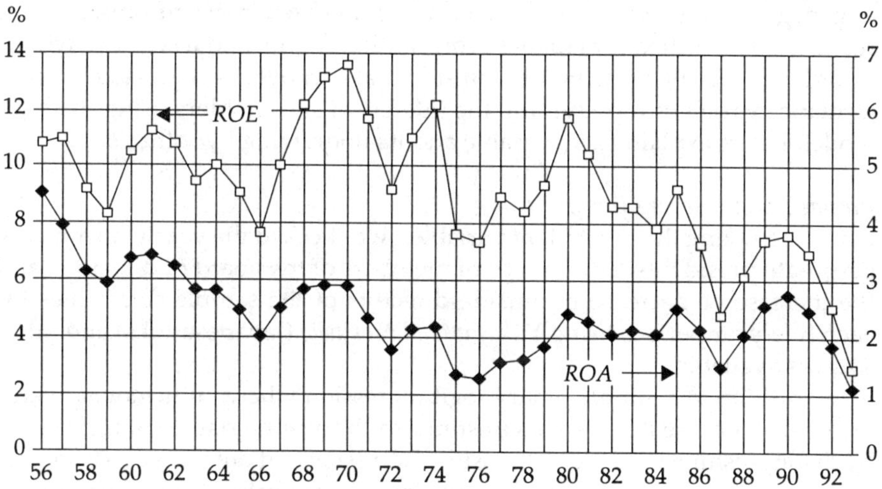

Source: JDB Corporate Finance Data Base

Note: Sample: 204 companies ranked as top 150 on an asset base in either 1957, 1964, or 1972

3 Data and model

3.1 The sample

To establish our sample, we first produced a data base composed of 204 large Japanese firms in the manufacturing sector, which were pooled from the top

150 firms in 1957, 1964, and 1972 respectively on the basis of total assets, using the JDB financial data bank. Then, we randomly picked 102 companies, considering the industrial distribution of companies in the original data base. 23 of these sample companies belong to labour intensive industries such as textiles, food and other miscellaneous industries, while 50 companies are located in materials-related industries such as chemical, iron and steel, and metals. The remaining 29 companies belong to machinery industries. It should be noted that the distribution of sample companies is slightly biased in terms of current industrial structure due to our focus on the high growth era. The basic information of the sample companies is summarized in table 1.

3.2 Construction of regression formula

The goal of this paper is to clarify which stakeholders have had the most influence on the turnover of company presidents, and whether the relation between presidential turnover and corporate performance has changed throughout the postwar period. More specifically, we ask whether the contingent governance structure which was summarized in the introduction can actually be identified for Japanese corporations or not and if so, since when? In order to clarify these points, presidential turnover is regressed on performance variables representing the interest of stakeholders using the logit model. Let us explain each variable and its underlying hypothesis.

Presidential turnover ($Turn_i$)
For constructing the dependent variables, we checked the yearly turnover of corporate presidents, any change of members of the board of directors, and the increase or decrease in outside directors of the sample companies for each five-year period, using *Yūkashoken hōkokusho* (Japanese 10ks) and other sources available.

In addition to a simple binary logit regression where all turnover events are one, otherwise zero, we have estimated the multivariate logit regression, by distinguishing turnover into inside succession and outside succession, assuming that the type of successor (insider or outsider) includes the information of the selection process. *Inside succession* is identified as the case where the president has been replaced by an insider (someone recruited from the ranks of the firm's existing board members). One possible expectation mainly raised by ABEGGLEN & STALK (1985) is that inside succession correlates with the interest of insiders, while the contingent governance hypothesis predicts that an inside succession does not show any correlation with the interest of outsiders.[3] *Outside succession* indicates that the president has been replaced by an outsider. In this case, it is assumed that an outsider has taken

[3] This hypothesis, which implies a dualistic control by insiders and outsiders, does not reject the possibility of a correlation of insider succession and the interest of insiders.

Table 1: Financial and governance characteristics of sample companies (no. of companies = 102)

(a) Financial Characteristics (million yen; %)

	the end of FY 1957		1967		1977		1987		1992	
	Average	Standard	Average	Standard	Average	Standard	Average	Standard	Average	Standard
Sales	20,734	18,203	67,122	58,896	207,194	195,043	356,794	432,489	464,296	567,861
Total asset	23,645	22,056	75,733	77,031	221,590	258,786	359,250	404,005	519,971	591,005
Number of employees	6,296	5,795	8,435	9,003	8,377	9,817	7,683	10,183	7,861	10,501
Debt	16,224	15,211	58,215	59,892	182,458	228,592	249,461	305,165	331,455	399,483
Equity	7,420	7,453	17,518	18,647	39,131	41,610	109,790	131,624	188,515	235,030
Debt-equity ratio	2.57	1.39	4.70	6.37	5.87	3.61	3.33	2.72	2.55	1.91

(b) Characteristics of President and Board

	1958		1968		1978		1988		1993	
	Average	Standard	Average	Standard	Average	Standard	Average	Standard	Average	Standard
"President; age"	61.5	6.7	63.7	6.8	64.6	5.1	63.2	4.4	63.1	8.1
Tenure as president	9.1	6.8	8.6	7.9	5.4	6.0	4.0	4.2	4.3	4.2
Tenure as board member	16.6	6.9	17.6	9.4	16.9	9.0	14.4	7.1	13.9	6.8
Length of time required to become president	7.4	6.6	9.0	6.9	11.5	6.8	10.3	6.0	9.3	5.4
Number of outside presidents among samples	12		15		13		11		10	
Number of board members	13.4	3.7	16.7	5.1	18.4	6.0	20.6	6.5	22.2	7.4
Number of outside directors	1.4	2.0	2.2	2.2	1.9	2.3	1.9	2.3	1.9	2.2
Number of outside auditors	1.2	0.8	0.6	0.8	0.6	0.8	0.6	0.8	0.7	0.9
Outside directors / No. of board members	10.0%	14.5%	14.4%	14.9%	10.5%	12.5%	9.9%	13.5%	9.3%	12.6%
No. of employees / No. of board members	462.4	355.7	492.5	406.7	302.7	171.4	326.9	348.9	303.2	298.4

Sources: Yūka Shōken Hōkokusho (Japanese 10ks), The Japan Development Bank (JDB), Corporate Financial Data Bank

the initiative to select the president. Therefore, this type of turnover would correlate with the interest of outsiders (debtholders, shareholders).

However, even if the control power is transferred from insider to outsider when a company faces financial distress, this fact would not be specific to the Japanese main bank system, instead being a general characteristic of any debt contract (AGHION & BOLTON 1992). According to AOKI (1994a), what is unique for the *main bank system* is that there is a particular area or 'main bank area' located between 1) where the output level exceeds a certain threshold point and the insiders of the firm will become residual claimants, and 2) where the output level is extremely low and the control right completely shifts to the debtholder. In this *main bank area,* the main bank is in charge for paying the same amount of returns to outsiders, while only a minimum wage is granted to insiders, the main bank receiving the residual, which may be negative in the lower trail of this region.[4]

Reinterpreting this view in the presidential turnover context, there is a unique area between 1) the performance level above which presidential turnover will be initiated by an insider and 2) the performance level below which turnover will be completely initiated by the outsiders. In this area, the insiders principally retain the control rights, though part of this control right shifts to the outsider parties. In fact, the transfer of control can take on various forms; for example, the incumbent president may be replaced by an outsider, an outsider may assume an influential position on the board despite the fact that the incumbent president is replaced by an insider, or an outsider takes over an influential position while the incumbent president keeps his/her position. In order to test this concept, this paper has estimated the multivariate logit regressions by allocating discrete numbers to the dependent variables according to the participation of outsiders to a company's board, defining an influential position as that of a senior director (*senmu*).[5] Turnover by death is excluded from the data where possible.[6] Table 2 reports the number of each type of turnover by period.

Performance variables (P_i)

The independent variables need to be selected so as to appropriately represent the interests of the various stakeholders of the firm. The proxy of the interests of the shareholders is the rate of return on stocks *(RRS)*. The variable for representing the interest of the *debtholder* is the interest coverage

---

4 AOKI (1994b) provides a more formal explanation.

5 We have constructed another set of dependent variables elsewhere which has been discussed in previous studies as "nonstandard turnover" (KAPLAN 1994) or "nonroutine turnover" (KANG & SHIVSADANI 1995), considering it an abnormal incident if the departing president is unable to assume the chairman position (table 2). See MIYAJIMA 1998 for more details.

6 However, turnover by illness is not excluded from the data unless a critical physical condition could be identified beyond doubt. Usually, it is impossible to verify that an 'illness' was not a pretence or official reason for a president's resignation.

Table 2: Presidency turnover in Japan (n = 102 x 5)

	definition	1959–63	1965–69	1974–78	1984–88	1991–95
All turn	number of $turn_i$	32	42	62	73	81
	frequency ($turn_i$/104)	30.8%	40.4%	59.6%	70.2%	77.9%
Insider	number of $turn_i$	20	32	53	61	69
	coposition ($turn_i$/all turn)	62.5%	76.2%	85.5%	83.6%	85.2%
Insider 2	Insider succession with accepting outsider	3	4	13	5	7
Outsider	number of $turn_i$	12	10	9	12	12
	coposition ($turn_i$/all turn)	37.5%	23.8%	14.5%	16.4%	14.8%
Outsider 1	insider–outsider	11	5	5	6	3
Outsider 2	outsider–outsider	1	5	4	6	10
Standard turnover	number of $turn_i$	19	24	43	56	67
	coposition ($turn_i$/all turn)	59.4%	57.1%	69.4%	76.7%	82.7%
Non-standard turnover	number of $turn_i$	13	18	19	17	14
	coposition ($turn_i$/all turn)	40.6%	42.9%	30.6%	23.3%	17.3%
Non-standard 1	successor = insider	9	9	13	14	11
Non-standard 2	successor = outsider	7	9	6	3	3
Out-exec	accepting outsider without presidential turnover	3	3	14	4	10

Source: Yūka Shōken Hōkokusho

Notes: The dependent variables are as follows:

Insider: Indicates instances in which the company president was replaced by an Insider (someone recruited from the ranks of the company's existing management)

Outsider: Indicates that the company president was replaced by an Outsider.
Outsider 1 = Insider president is replaced by an Outsider president.
Outsider 2 = Outsider president is replaced by an Outsider president.

Standard turnover: The former president assumes the post of chairman of the company.

Non-standard turnover: The former president does not take over as chairman of the company. For a more precise definition, see footnote 4, and KAPLAN (1994) and KANG & SHIVSADANI (1995).

Out-exec: Accepting Outsider director of influential position without presidential turnover. Here influential position denotes one above the position of Senior Director (*senmu*). An Outsider appointment is identified, when the incoming president has been employed by the firm for three years or less.

ratio (operating income / interest payment). In order to identify abnormally low returns, we also introduce a dummy variable *(NPD)* which is one if the two-year average pre-tax profit is negative. The percent change of employees *(ER)* is selected as a proxy of the interests of *insiders*. As a control variable, in addition to the age of the incumbent president, his tenure *(LS)* is introduced into the estimations. If the *LS* correlates significantly with the insider turnover, the insider turnover is assumed to be based on the seniority rule.

The variables defined above are all proxies of the interests of the *stakeholders*. However, to identify which stakeholders are the most influential for presidential turnover is not the same as to test whether the governance structure of Japanese firms really is efficient. In order to test this point explicitly, we have introduced the operating income to sales ratio *(ORR)* and the rate of return on equity *(ROE)* as proxies of the objective efficiency index. The former is to abstract from financial profits and losses, while the latter is selected as a commonly used major indicator for corporate efficiency.

It is a sensitive problem whether to use absolute performance or relative performance as performance variables, as MORCK, SHLEIFER and VISHNEY (1989) as well as KANG & SHIVSADANI (1995) have pointed out. It is reasonable to prefer the *relative performance*, calculated as the difference from the industry average, when we focus on the objective efficiency under a specific governance mechanism, as the issue is the ability or effort level of the incumbent president independent from exogenous factors (i. e., macro-economic fluctuations or industry-specific shocks). However, if we cannot accurately distinguish between endogenous and exogenous factors, and if corporate performance *per se* may influence the interests of stakeholders, it seems plausible that the stakeholders will be concerned with the absolute level of corporate performance. Since it cannot be ascertained *a priori* which is correct, an estimation should include both possibilities as independent variables. Thus, along with an estimation that the presidential turnover is regressed on corporate performance *per se*, this paper has regressed the turnover on industry-adjusted performance (NP_i) and the industry average (P_i) in order to control for industry-specific shocks. Considering that the president of a Japanese firm normally concludes a two-year contract, all performance variables are biannual averages calculated prior to the year when presidential turnover is checked.[7] Table 3 summarizes the detailed information of performance variables.

[7] Elsewhere, we have constructed governance variables which identify the extent of the main bank relationship and the role of large shareholders and introduced them into the regression as the intersection of performance variables. Regrettably, however, this paper had to omit their influence on presidential turnover. In detail, see MIYAJIMA 1998.

Table 3: Summary of performance variables (two-year average) (n = 102 x 5)

	1957–1962		1963–1967		1972–1977		1982–1987		1989–1994	
	Mean	Std.	Mean	Std.	Mean	Std.	Mean	Std.	Mean	Std.
RRS (%)	**17.0**	40.6	**7.9**	29.9	**12.8**	32.1	**25.2**	30.2	**-6.0**	36.7
NRRS (%)	**12.1**	39.5	**-2.0**	29.6	**5.6**	35.4	**2.5**	31.6	**2.2**	38.0
ICR	**3.4**	7.7	**2.1**	1.6	**1.7**	1.8	**4.0**	9.5	**7.3**	38.5
Number of *NPD*	**17**	–	**49**	–	**58**	–	**32**	–	**76**	–
ER (%)	**16.6**	6.2	**2.1**	6.6	**-3.1**	5.7	**-0.9**	6.5	**0.0**	6.0
NER (%)	**-1.4**	9.8	**-0.3**	6.3	**0.4**	5.4	**-0.4**	6.5	**-0.2**	5.5
ROE (%)	**17.0**	12.0	**8.6**	59.7	**4.0**	134.9	**12.5**	11.8	**7.3**	9.0
NROE (%)	**-1.0**	11.2	**-5.3**	59.7	**-10.6**	139.1	**-3.2**	11.8	**3.6**	11.5
ORR (%)	**10.8**	4.0	**8.4**	3.6	**5.9**	4.1	**4.8**	4.1	**3.4**	3.8
NORR (%)	**-0.5**	3.4	**0.3**	3.9	**0.0**	4.4	**-0.3**	3.9	**-0.5**	3.3
LS	**9.8**	6.7	**9.7**	7.7	**6.7**	6.4	**5.1**	4.6	**5.3**	4.4
Age	**60.9**	9.5	**62.8**	7.3	**64.1**	5.4	**63.3**	5.0	**63.8**	5.0

Source: JDB Financial Data Bank, Yūka Shōken Hōkokusho

Notes: 1. Definition is as follows:
RRS: rate of return on stocks
NRRS: the rate of return on stocks normalized by industry average
ICR: interest coverage ratio
NPD: abnormally low profitability
ER: change of employment level
NER: change of employment level normalized by industry average
ROE: rate of return on equity
NROE: ROE normalized by industry average
ORR: operational profit divided by sales (OR)
NORR: operational profit/sales ratio normalized by industry average
LS: the previous company president's length of service (LS)
AGE: the age of the previous company president
2. All performance variables are two-year averages.
3. Concerning details on the normalization of each performance variable, see Miyajima (1998).

4 The main results of estimation

Given the space limitations of this volume, we limited ourselves to reporting only the sign of performance variables to turnover, and the ratio of likelihood of our estimations (table 4). It is clear that the multivariate logit regression dividing the turnover events into inside and outside successions can explain the turnover much better than the binary logit regression using 'All turn', and the fit of the estimation employing the industry-adjusted performance is slightly better than the estimation using the raw performance according to the test of likelihood ratio. Therefore, hereafter we will focus on the estimation of the multivariate logit regression, using the industry-adjusted performance.

Table 4: Presidential turnover and firm performance

Panel A-1						
Model Logit; $Turn_i = c + a_1\, RRS + a_2\, ICR + a_3\, ER + a_4\, LS + a_5\, Age$						
type of turnover	independent variable	1959–63	65–69	74–78	84–88	91–95
N = 1		32	42	62	72	81
N = 0		470	443	435	433	423
	RRS	-	-			
	ICR		-b			-b
All turn	*ER*	-				-c
	LS	+d	+	+c	+b	+a
likelihood ratio		36.33*	28.68*	19.52*	44.54*	67.28*
Panel A-2						
Model Logit; $Turn_i = c + a_1\, NRRS + a_2\, ICR + a_3\, NER + a_4\, LS + a_5\, Age$						
likelihood ratio		40.74*	30.38*	25.62*	53.33*	69.73*
Panel B-1						
Model Logit; $Turn_i = c + a_1\, NRRS + a_2\, ICR + a_3\, NER + a_4\, LS + a_5\, Age$						
type of turnover	independent variable	1959–63	65–69	74–78	84–88	91–95
N = 0		468	438	427	430	416
N = 1		20	32	53	61	69
	RRS	-c	-			
	ICR		-			-
Insider	*ER*					-c
	LS	+		+c	+a	+a
N = 2		12	10	9	12	12
	RRS	-c				-
Outsider	*ICR*	-b	-a	-b	-c	-a
	ER	-	-a	-		
	LS					
likelihood ratio		23.90*	34.35*	19.46*	42.08*	63.78*
Panel B-2						
Model Logit; $Turn_i = c + a_1\, NRRS + a_2\, NPD + a_3\, NER + a_4\, LS + a_5\, Age$						
Outsider	*NPD*	+a	+a	+c	+	+
likelihood ratio		29.02*	37.56*	27.29*	49.08*	65.22*

Notes: 1. a = significantly different from zero at 1 % level, b = 5 %, c = 10 %
2. Sign of coefficient is added when significance level satisfied at 15 %.

3. The test of likelihood ratio at 1 % significance level is $\chi^2(5) = 15.086$.
4. Although all regressions include *Age*, this result is not reported.
5. The results of independent variables in Panel A-2 is almost the same as Panel A-1, and those of independent variables without *NPD* in Panel B-2 is almost the same as Panel B-1. The report of these results are omitted.
6. Dependent Variable (see table 2 in detail).
   All turn/All turn = 1, otherwise zero
   Insider/Outsider; Insider = 1, *Outsider* = 2, otherwise zero
7. Independent Variables (see table 3 in detail).
   RRS: rate of return on stocks
   NRRS: the rate of return on stocks normalized by industry average
   ICR: interest coverage ratio
   NPD: abnormally low profitability
   ER: change of employment level
   NER: change of employment level normalized by industry average
   LS: the previous company president's length of service (LS)
   AGE: the age of the previous company president

4.1 Inside succession

One hypothesis is that the likelihood of inside succession will increase if the incumbent president cannot guarantee certain employment levels. However, the inside successions do not show any significant correlation with the growth of employment *(ER)* or industry-adjusted growth of employment *(NER)* up to the 1980s. This observation is almost the same as KAPLAN'S (1992, 1994).[8] Remarkably, however, *NER* as well as *ER* have negatively correlated with inside succession in the 1990s. Although the coefficient on *NER* is not reported in table 4, the estimation result indicates that a one percent decrease of employment growth raises by five percent the likelihood of inside succession, which means that one standard deviation decrease of the *NER* raises such likelihood by roughly 31 %.

Another view on inside succession is that it does not correlate with the performance variables representing the outsiders' interests, since insiders can freely select their president unless performance were to be extremely low. This hypothesis is basically confirmed for all five sample periods except the later phase of the high growth era, when inside succession negatively correlated with *RRS* and *ICR*, although at a low significant level. It is after the oil crisis period that inside succession became sensitive to the tenure of incumbent presidents *(LS)*. An incumbent president retaining his position over a period of ten years was not so rare during the high growth era. However, the tenure average after the oil crisis period was 6.7 years compared to 9.7 years during the high growth era (table 3). It is noteworthy that the seniority rule of

[8] KAPLAN (1994) uses sales growth as a variable, while his working paper (KAPLAN 1992) reports no correlation between employment growth and nonstandard turnover.

presidential turnover or "conveyor belt" pattern of turnover (KAPLAN 1994: 524) was only established in the 1970s, and this rule has strengthened since.

4.2 Outside succession

The hypothesis that outside successions have a negative correlation with the rate of return on stocks *(RRS)* is not confirmed except for the first phase of the high growth era. Although not reported in this paper, the nonstandard turnover which KAPLAN (1994) and KANG & SHIVSADANI (1995) have employed as independent variables was neither sensitive to *RRS* nor to the industry-adjusted rate of return on stocks in the 1980s.[9]

Another premise concerning outside successions is that their likelihood to occur increases if a company faces financial distress. This view is basically supported throughout the five sample periods. However, there are several points to note in our historical perspective. First, not only the coefficient of the interest coverage ratio *(ICR)* but also the ratio of likelihood for the estimation decreased after the oil crisis period. This indicates that some kind of structural change happened during this time. Second, the coefficient of *ICR* as well as its significance level have decreased in the recession following the yen appreciation. The relation between outside succession and extremely low profits *(NPD)* is upheld. Although the significance level of both variables has improved for the 1990s, the coefficients of *ICR* and *NPD* are one fifth and one third respectively, compared to those of the high growth era. While the estimation result of our samples is consistent with that of KANG & SHIVSADANI (1995), it is worth noting that the coefficients for *ICR* and *NPD* and their significance levels in the 1980s became less distinct than before. Therefore, it can be inferred that the relationship between outside succession and default risks began to change in the 1970s; it was fairly weak in the mid-1980s and then was revived with some changes in the early 1990s.

4.3 Contingent governance

It is not a unique characteristic of the main bank system in Japan, when the control right moves from insiders to outsiders in case a company faces financial distress. What *is* unique, as pointed out in the previous section, is the 'area' where the insider is principally in control while accepting outside directors when the firm's performance falls below a certain threshold point. This hypothesis was tested using the multivariate logit regression where outside successions *(Outsider)* was given the discreet number '3', while the inside succession, accepting an outside director at a position higher than senior director, *senmu (Insider 2)*, is given '2', accepting an outside director at a posi-

[9] As for the definition of nonstandard turnover, see footnote 5.

tion higher than *senmu* without any turnover *(Out-exec)* is given '1', and all other cases 'zero'. The regression result is shown in table 5. While one of the three dependent variables *(Outsider)* is sensitive to the *ICR* in the later phase of the high growth era, two independent variables *(Outsider* and *Out-exec)* significantly correlate with the *ICR* at the 1 % level. This negative correlation became less clear in the 1980s and has partly been revived in the 1990s.

Table 5: Transfer of control rights and corporate performance

Model Logit; $Out_i = c + a_1\ ICR + a_2\ LS + a_3\ Age$				
	dependent variable	***Out-exec***	***Insider 2***	***Outsider***
1965–69	N = 0; 479	N = 1; 3	N = 2; 3	N = 3; 10
	ICR	-0.400	-0.026	-2.342a
		(-0.700)	(-0.053)	(-3.400)
	dp/dICR	-0.002	0.000	-0.043
	likelihood ratio		24.932*	
1974–78	N = 0; 461	N = 1; 14	N = 2; 13	N = 3; 9
	ICR	-0.901a	-0,392	-0.874b
		(-2.985)	(-1.425)	(-2.443)
	dp/dICR	-0.023	-0.009	-0.014
	likelihood ratio		23.355*	
1984–88	N = 0; 476	N = 1; 4	N = 2; 11	N = 3; 12
	ICR	-0.326	-0.012	-0.226
		(-1.043)	(-0.249)	(-1.330)
	dp/dICR	-0.003	0.000	-0.005
	likelihood ratio		15.137*	
1991–95	N = 0; 476	N = 1; 10	N = 2; 6	N = 3; 12
	ICR	-0.184	-0.004	-0.324a
		(-1.583)	(-0.179)	(-2.895)
	dp/dICR	-0.003	0.000	-0.007
	likelihood ratio		23.724*	

Notes: 1. Significantly different from zero at 1 % level, b = 5 %, c= 10 %.
2. Comparing the definition of dependent and independent variables, see tables 2, 3 and text.
$Out_i = 0$, no turnover
$Out_i = 1$, accepting outsider without presidential turnover
$Out_i = 2$, insider succession with accepting of outsider
$Out_i = 3$, the company president was replaced by an outsider
3. The test of likelihood ratio at 1 % significance level is $\chi^2(3) = 11.345$.

4.4 Presidential turnover and corporate efficiency

The last concern of this paper is whether presidential turnover in Japanese corporations correlates with firms' efficiency in the sense that the likelihood of presidential turnover increases if the company has performed badly in terms of objective efficiency indicators. As discussed in section 3, industry-adjusted performance should be used as an indicator because the point here is the ability or effort level of incumbent presidents independent from external factor shocks. The estimation result is summarized in table 6.

Table 6: Presidential turnover and corporate efficiency

Panel A:
Model Logit; $Turn_i = c + a_1\ NORR + a_2\ AORR + a_3\ LS + a_4\ Age$ **(Sign of** ***NORR*****)**

	1959–63	65–69	74–78	84–88	91–95
All turn	-3.783	-6.51b	1.662	-2.453	-5.488b
	(-1.259)	(-2.140)	(0.761)	(-1.269)	(-2.382)
dp/dNORR	-0.434	-0.919	0.330	-0.507	-1.174
likelihood ratio	21.71*	32.68*	22.91*	41.98*	63.15*
Insider		–			-c
Outsider	-a	-a	-c	-a	-a
likelihood ratio	22.47*	26.35*	18.79*	44.09*	58.04*
Out-exec	—		-a		-a
Insider	—				
Outsider	—	-a	-b	-a	-a
likelihood ratio	—	21.660*	21.922*	20.690*	30.209*

Panel B:
Model Logit; $Turn_i = c + a_1\ NROE + a_2\ AROE + a_3\ LS + a_4\ Age$ **(Sign of** ***NROE*****)**

	1959–63	65–69	74–78	84–88	91–95
All turn					
likelihood ratio	26.19*	16.81*	24.44*	42.89*	53.12*
Insider					
Outsider	-a	-a	+		-c
likelihood ratio	24.25*	21.22*	17.52*	44.20*	48.79*
Out-exec	—				-a
Insider	—				
Outsider	—	-a	+		-c
likelihood ratio		12.94	9.02	12.18	26.63*

Notes: 1. Only sign of coefficient is reported except "*All turn*".
2. Concerning notation and definition for dependent and independent variables, see tables 2, 3.
3. a = significantly different from zero at 1 % level, b = 5 %, c = 10 %.
4. Sign of coefficient is added when significance level satisfied at 15 %.
5. The test of likelihood ratio at 1 % significance level is $\chi^2(4) = 13.277$.

Apparently, the industry-adjusted operating profit/sales ratio *(NORR)* is correlated with outside succession throughout the five sample periods, and with 'all turnover' in the later phase of the high growth era, while the multivariate logit regression where the dependent variables are divided into three *(Outsider, Insider 2, Out-exec)* shows the same negative correlation after the oil crisis period as in this recent recession after the *bubble economy*. However, the result is slightly different, if the industry-adjusted rate of return on equity *(NROE)* is used. During the high growth era, the likelihood of a turnover increased if he or she could not maintain (at least) the average *ROE* level, whereas this relation became less likely after the oil crisis period. It is interesting to note that the results for *NORR* and *NROE* are different after the oil crisis. In general, presidential turnover clearly correlated with the objective efficiency indexes during the high growth era. However, this relation became less likely after the oil crisis when the seniority rule was established, and it was least likely in the 1980s. Thereafter, the relation between presidential turnover and objective performance recovered in the 1990s, when the inside succession was sensitive to the growth rate of employees.

Now, the question is how to interpret these results in terms of an evolution of the contingent governance structure in Japan.

5 Overview: Evolution and change in the contingent governance structure

5.1 The first phase of high growth era (HGE): the learning process for rules among stakeholders

The first phase of the HGE can be regarded as the period when the contingent governance structure gradually evolved. As long as the performance of companies was satisfactory, the pattern of the incumbent president appointing his/her successor from among members of the managing board was maintained. At that time, those who had ascended to the presidency in the 1950s in such leading industries as iron and steel, chemicals, and electronics handed down their position to their successors. This observation is consistent with our regression results whereby inside succession in this period has no negative correlation with the performance variables *(RRS, ICR)*. As long as the firm's finances were healthy, the top management team freely selected the new president without any intervention by outsiders.

On the other hand, the *early* phase of the HGE was characterized by a high frequency of outside succession, bearing a significant negative correlation with the interests of shareholders *(RRS)* as well as that of debtholders *(ICR)*. The former seems to be consistent with the fact that the top management team was facing potential takeover threats at that time as a legacy of postwar economic reforms. The latter fact suggests another feature of contingent governance in that the banks intervened if a company faced financial distress.

However, the main bank during this time tended to *over-intervene* in corporate management affairs because the bank excessively stressed the interests of the debtholders. This observation is partly derived from the fact that the frequency of outside succession was relatively high in this period (table 2). Anecdotally, it is worth mentioning that over-intervention by banks was socially criticized and, in extreme cases, the bank was prosecuted under the Anti-Trust Law (MIYAJIMA 1996). In this sense, city banks were still searching for an appropriate intervention strategy regarding client companies when the latter faced financial distress.

5.2 The later phase of HGE: Establishing the rules

It was after the securities recession that the rules concerning the contingent governance structure appear to have been established. Change in turnover showed two different characteristics from the previous period. First, cases of outside succession decreased, while inside successions with the accepting of outside directors increased. In addition, cases where banks dispatched personnel to fill positions above the level of managing director increased from 26 in the first phase of the HGE to 43 in the later period. Second, inside successions in this period were negatively correlated with the proxy of the debtholders' interests *(ICR)*, although the significance level is low (table 4). This fact indicates that insiders tended to voluntarily replace the incumbent top management when the possibility of an outsider intervention increased.

Moreover, the changing pattern of presidential turnover in the later phase of the HGE suggests that both the insiders and the main bank had learned a rule appropriate to the contingent governance structure. It can be assumed that the banks gradually preferred a more sophisticated form of intervention to that of direct involvement which often caused conflict, decreasing motivation of employees, and social criticism. On the other hand, as insiders observed that low profitability led to bank intervention, often involving drastic corporate restructuring, they gradually learned that in order to avoid such drastic bank intervention, the transfer of control rights, it was beneficial to assume the initiative to remedy a poor performance situation.[10] Thus, the contingent governance structure was institutionalized in the sense that rules concerning the transfer of control rights were established.

5.3 After the oil crisis: The typical functioning of contingent governance

After the oil crisis, Japanese firms faced a severe recession. The average interest coverage ratio of sample companies was around one, and 50 % of firms suffered negative recurring profits. In this phase, the frequency of turnover

---

[10] MIYAJIMA (1996) provides some anecdotal evidence concerning this point.

increased. The peak of presidential turnover was in 1977, with 15 cases in our sample. One characteristic of top management turnover in this period is that inside succession for the first time correlates with tenure *(LS)*, indicating that the seniority rule had been established. On the other hand, inside succession does not correlate with a change in employment *(ER)*, though this is a restructuring period with minus 3 % growth of employment in sample companies. While it is often (anecdotally) held that the top management team taking an initiative for restructuring tends to be penalized, this premise is not systematically supported.

Another characteristic of turnover in this period is that the frequency of inside succession, accepting an outside director for a position higher than senior director *(Insider 2)*, and the acceptance of outside directors for a position higher than senior director without any turnover *(Out-exec)* increased, and both are negatively correlated to the *ICR* (the significance level for the *Insider 2* being statistically not relevant). The ratio of likelihood of the multivariate regression is significantly different from zero at the 1 % level. Therefore, it is safe to say that the relationship, expressed as a contingent governance structure, played a significant role at this period.

Thirdly, the industry-adjusted rate of return on equity *(NROE)*, which formerly maintained a negative correlation with the outside succession as well as with the acceptance of outside directors *(Out-exec)*, lost such a relation. One possible reason for the lower sensitivity of turnover to *NROE* is that the sample companies had already accumulated a large amount of off-record assets (securities and land) by this time and, therefore, had the financial capability to cope with short-term financial distress. The ratio of gain on the sale and the valuation of securities and tangible assets to after-tax profit was over 70 % in 1975 when profitability was at its lowest for this period.[11] Companies implementing a shareholder stabilization policy in the later phase of the HGE unintentionally reserved disposable securities whose off-record value increased over the course of asset inflation.

In general, it is during this period that the characteristics of the governance structure of Japanese firms were typically established. On the one hand, the weight of insiders for control of top management increased. This aspect is reflected in the fact that inside succession began to be based on the seniority rule, a complementary element to the promotion system among white collar employees. One the other hand, the unique relationship whereby outsiders intervene according to the firms' financial situation was firmly incorporated under given high debt/equity ratios. One of the conditions of this structure is that the rules concerning the contingent governance structure were shared among stakeholders. The other condition can be seen in an increase in the value of off-record assets, providing the incumbent manage-

[11] SHEARD (1994a) has already pointed out this fact in a different context.

ment team with a certain amount of disposable funds which rendered firms more crisis-resistant.

5.4 The mid-1980s: a certain 'metamorphosis' in the contingent governance structure

Corporate performance decreased after the Plaza Accord of 1985. *ROE / ROA* declined steeply as is shown in graph 1, especially in the case of export-oriented firms such as electronics, automobile and shipbuilding manufacturers. There are two points to note. First, inside succession does not correlate with any dependent variables except tenure of the incumbent president *(LS)*, this coefficient increasing compared to the previous period. Second, the correlation between outside succession and the proxy of the interests of debtholders *(ICR)* decreased, and the inside succession with acceptance of an outsider director *(Insider 2)* and the acceptance of outsider directors without any turnover *(Out-exec)* became less sensitive to *ICR*. Although the outside succession still showed a negative correlation with *ICR*, its coefficient was one third lower than that during the high growth era. The extremely low profitability *(NPD)* does not show any negative correlation with the outside succession nor with *Insider 2* and *Out-exec*, which is, however, not reported in the base table. On the whole, our estimation is partially consistent with the result of KANG & SHIVSADANI (1995) for outside successions. However, it is more important to note that the relationship of presidential turnover to corporate performance in this period was not as sensitive as in the previous period and that the number of companies receiving directors from banks decreased in this period.[12]

One of the most likely reasons for this lower correlation is that firms increasingly improved their capital structures in the 1980s. After the oil crisis, companies attempted to reduce debt levels which is often referred to as *genryō keiei*. The average debt-equity ratio in 1987 was 3.33 compared to 5.87 in 1977. In addition, they were able to overcome their short-term difficulties by selling their off-record assets. For instance, several electronics companies such as Sony, Sanyō, and Sharp had a low or even negative operating income following the Plaza Accord but maintained about the same level of *ROE* and dividend payout ratio as before by selling securities and assets. In these cases, there was no change of corporate presidency. Thus, the free disposal of off-record assets by incumbent presidents obscured the control transfer point in this period.

The distribution of performance variables in this period differs from other sample periods because the recession caused by the yen appreciation mainly affected the export-oriented industries. Also, this recession was relatively

[12] We can base this conclusion on the regression estimation of nonstandard turnover and the dispatching of directors on performance variables.

short compared to the other crises on which we have focused. Therefore, although there is still room for further investigation and testing, it is tentatively safe to say that the disciplinary role played by debt or debtholders weakened for large firms, and in this sense the contingent governance structure 'metamorphosed' during this period.

5.5 After the *bubble:* diversification of governance structure

As the recession, originating in the stock price collapse beginning in 1990 and the land price collapse beginning in 1991, began to manifest itself in 1992, corporate performance declined sharply. The results of our investigation are still tentative because the data in this paper is limited to corporate turnover before 1995, and corporate performance in 1994. Given these constraints, there are three points to note.

First, the correlation between turnover and the proxy of shareholders' interests has not been reflected in outside successions. Nevertheless, the dividend payout ratio, which had a low correlation to the *ROE* since 1970, has recovered its position somewhat. This fact suggests that the general investor has still less influence over presidential turnover. Second, inside successions have shown a significantly negative correlation with changes in employment, despite the dismal employment situation. Third, the correlation between outside succession and *ICR* has recovered, i. e., there are still companies in which the discipline of debt continues to function.

These findings suggest that the governance structure of Japanese firms has diversified into two types; one, low-debt companies where insiders now play a significant disciplinary role for presidential turnover, and a second type, i. e., high-debt companies where the main bank plays an important role for disciplining the top management team, a fact supported by our regression results.

However, while insiders have partly freed themselves from the disciplining by the creditors or banks, this does not necessarily indicate a moral hazard problem. According to table 6, both outside succession and inside succession are significantly correlated with the proxy of firm efficiency *(NORR)*. An incumbent president unable to maintain corporate performance levels compared to the industry average is relatively likely to resign. One possible interpretation of this fact is that, given fierce competition in the product markets under globalization pressures since the late 1980s and the changing pattern of corporate finance from bank borrowing to equity finance in the open market, if companies perform poorly in terms of *NORR*, the president is compelled to restructure a firm by reducing employment levels. Thereafter, the incumbent president taking such an initiative to restructure is likely to resign. As far as sample companies are concerned, the discipline of product and capital markets is thus assumed to have worked well through this internal disciplining mechanism.

6 Concluding remarks

We have investigated the governance structure of Japanese firms through a quantitative analysis of presidential turnover and corporate performance in postwar Japan. Our main result is that the governance structure which has often been regarded as unique to Japanese firms, is not stable, but rather has evolved over time. This evolutionary process can be summarized as follows:

1. The contingent governance structure was fully established and has functioned after the oil crisis period in the sense that inside succession is based on seniority rule unless performance is extremely poor. Control rights systematically shift from insiders to outsiders conditional on the default risks.
2. The high growth era may be seen as the birth place of this structure in the sense that the rules concerning how to cope with financial distress were first shared among the stakeholders of Japanese firm.
3. The contingent governance structure based on the main bank system began to change in the 1980s, partly because firms decreasingly depended on debt, and partly because off-record assets made it possible for incumbent presidents to cope with short-term financial distress.
4. Entering the 1990s, the governance structure of the large firms in Japan has diversified into two types: companies under control of a main bank, and companies disciplined by product and capital markets. In both cases, the disciplinary mechanisms can be assumed to work comparatively well in the sense that the likelihood of presidential turnover increases if a company performs badly in terms of objective efficiency indicators.

References

ABEGGLEN, J. C. and G. STALK (1985): *Kaisha. The Japanese Corporation.* Tōkyō: Charles E. Tuttle.

AGHION, P. and P. BOLTON (1992): An Incomplete Contracts Approach to Financial Contracting. In: *Review of Economic Studies* 59, 3, pp. 473–94.

AOKI, M. (1988): *Information, Incentives, and Bargaining in the Japanese Economy.* Cambridge: Cambridge University Press.

AOKI, M. (1994a): Monitoring Characteristic of the Main Bank System: An Analytical and Developmental View. In: AOKI, M. and H. PATRICK (eds.): *The Japanese Main Bank System: Its Relevancy for Developing and Transforming Economies.* Oxford: Oxford University Press, pp. 109–141.

AOKI, M. (1994b): The Contingent Governance of Teams: An Analysis of Institutional Complementarity. In: *International Economic Review* 35, pp. 657–676.

AOKI, M. and M. OKUNO (1996): *Keizai shisutemu no hikaku seido bunseki* [Comparative Institutional Analysis of Economic Systems]. Tōkyō: Tōkyō University Press.

ECONOMIC PLANNING AGENCY (1996): *Keizai hakusho heisei 8 nen-do* [Economic White Paper 1996]. Tōkyō: EPA.

FUKAO, M. (1995): *Financial Integration, Corporate Governance, and the Performance of Multinational companies.* Washington, D. C.: Brookings Institution.

IKEO, K. (1995): *Kinyū sangyō e no keikoku: Kinyū shisutemu saikōchiku no tame ni* [Warning to the Financial Industries: For the Restructuring of Financial Systems]. Tōkyō: Tōyō Keizai Shinpōsha.

KANG, J. and A. SHIVSADANI (1995): Firm Performance, Corporate Governance, and Top Executive Turnover in Japan. In: *Journal of Financial Economics* 38, pp. 29–58.

KAPLAN, S. N. (1992): *Internal Corporate Governance in Japan and the USA: Difference in Activities and Horizons* (mimeo). Chicago: Chicago University.

KAPLAN, S. N. (1994): Top Executive Rewards and Firm Performance: A Comparison of Japan and the United States. In: *Journal of Political Economy* 102, 3, pp. 510–546.

KAPLAN, S. N. and B. A. MINTON (1994): Appointments of Outsiders to Japanese Boards. In: *Journal of Financial Economics* 36, pp. 225–258.

MIYAJIMA, H. (1994): The Transformation of Zaibatsu to Postwar Corporate Groups: From Hierarchical Integrated Group to Horizontally Integrated Group. In: *Journal of the Japanese and International Economies* 8, pp. 293–328.

MIYAJIMA, H. (1995): The Privatization of Ex-zaibatsu Holding Stocks and the Emergence of Bank Centered Corporate Groups. In: AOKI, M. (ed.): *The Corporate Governance Structure in a Transitional Economy.* Washington, D.C.: The World Bank, pp. 361–403.

MIYAJIMA, H. (1996): Zaikai chūihō to keieisha no senbatsu: jōtai izonteki gobanansu sutorakuchā no keisei [Financial Restructuring and Managerial Careers: The Formation of the Contingency Governance Structure]. In: HASHIMOTO, J. (ed.): *Nihon kigyō shisutemu no sengōshi* [Postwar History of the Japanese Firm System]. Tōkyō: Tōkyō University Press, pp. 43–108.

MIYAJIMA, H. (1998): Sengō Nihon ni okeru jōtai izonteki gabanansu no shinka to henyō [Development and Change in Post-war Japan's Contingency Governance Structure]. In: *Keizai Kenkyū* (Hitotsubashi University) 49, 2, pp. 97–112.

MIYAJIMA, H. (forthcoming): The Impact of Deregulation on Corporate Governance and Finance. In: CARLILE, L. and M. TILTON (eds.): *Is Japan Really Changing? Regulatory Reform and the Japanese Economy.* Washington, D.C.: Brookings Institution.

MORCK, R., A. SHREIFER and R. VISHNY (1989): Alternative Mechanisms for Corporate Control. In: *American Economic Review* 79, 4, pp. 842–852.

MORCK, R. and M. NAKAMURA (1992): *Banks and Corporate Control in Japan* (mimeo). University of Alberta.

OKAZAKI, T. (1993a): The Japanese Firm under the Wartime Planned Economy. In: *Journal of the Japanese and International Economies* 7, pp. 175–203.

OKAZAKI, T. (1993b): Kigyō shisutemu [The Corporate System]. In: OKAZAKI, T. and M. OKUNO (eds.): *Gendai Nihon keizai shisutemu no genryū* [The Origins of the Contemporary Japanese Economic System]. Tōkyō: Nihon Keizai Shinbunsha, pp. 97–144.

SHEARD, P. (1989): The Main Bank System and Corporate Monitoring and Control in Japan. In: *The Journal of Economic Behavior and Organization* 11, pp. 399–422.

SHEARD, P. (1994a): Interlocking Shareholdings and Corporate Governance. In: AOKI, M. and R. DORE (eds.): *The Japanese Firm: Sources of Competitive Strength.* Oxford: Oxford University Press, pp. 310–349.

SHEARD, P. (1994b): *Bank Executives on Japanese Corporate Boards* (mimeo). Tōkyō: Bank of Japan.

YAFEH, Y. (1995): Corporate Ownership, Profitability and Bank-Firm Ties: Evidence from American Occupation Reforms in Japan. In: *Journal of the Japanese and International Economies* 9, pp. 154–173.

The research for this paper was supported by a Grant from the Nomura Foundation for Social Science and a Waseda University Grant for Special Projects (97A-108).

VI Corporate Pension Schemes, Corporate Pension Governance, and State (De-) Regulation in Japan

Jean-François ESTIENNE

The worries concerning the several millions of US dollars that each of a number of Japan's biggest corporations has had to put into their pension funds should be moderated. These payments may just show the right stance of pro-active corporate pension governance, based on reliable assumptions and simulations. Japan's largest corporations will fully enjoy the benefits from the relaxation of the government rules that until now have provided very little leeway in the field of investment and technical assumptions. Indeed, deregulation of corporate pensions may be another, yet significant, stage of a long-term, government-initiated move toward a newly designed financial services market in Japan. A look at the economic and financial situation which prevailed at the time when the Japanese modern corporate pension schemes were created and how they evolved to their present state clearly helps to understand the need for change. Some may rightly stress that the promised *big bang* is still due, but the fact is that the *big burst* of the *bubble* is still occurring. The authorities may be willing to reach several goals at the same time: phasing out outdated rules and transmitting the urge for asset performance on sponsoring corporations, which in turn may aim for a better performance expected from the new providers of asset management services while putting pressure on their traditional financial partners. The latter, life insurance companies and trust bank are high on the target list of the deregulators.

But resistance to change may be rather strong and the free use of the newly granted freedom by the recipients may encounter limitations even tighter than previous Government regulations. The extension of benefits and duties of freedom to the majority of Japanese corporations implies the proper diffusion of corporate pension governance techniques, a competent choice of risk/return profiles and a maximization of performance, thus reducing each sponsoring company's operating costs.

1 Introduction

Financial newspapers around the world have reported numerous cases of Japan's biggest corporate names (for instance Hitachi, Toyota, Matsushita) unexpectedly allocating the equivalent of hundreds of millions of US dollars into their pension funds. At the same time, deregulation of State rules on investment of assets and technical assumptions were introduced and enhanced. It is impossible to deny the link between the current deregulation and the implosion of the financial *bubble*. The confidence of the Japanese 'salaryman' has been shattered as far as the State and its ability to regulate the financial systems are concerned.

The response from the Japanese State, after a certain amount of *gaiatsu* or foreign pressure, and due resistance to it in the first place, is the deregulation of the financial sector. This began several years ago with the licensing of new financial institutions and the provision of cross-access to segments of the financial services market which were formerly tightly off limits to each other (for instance: security firms were granted the permission to open bank subsidiaries and vice versa). Deregulation has now reached the long untouched corporate pension sector. This article deals with the content and context of deregulation of corporate pension schemes and its impact on corporate liability and corporate governance.

It may seem useful to define briefly what *corporate pension governance* is. In a nutshell, corporate governance is generally understood as the disposition, rules and mechanism which help a corporation to make the right decisions in order to adapt to changes in its environment and to improve its performance. Corporate pension governance is just the same, but especially focused on pensions systems handled and funded by corporations.

Pension commitments, which are a pillar of corporate welfare, can become a corporation's biggest liability in Anglo-Saxon countries, where pension funds are also an increasingly powerful counterforce that corporate top management has to face. For instance, US pension funds had a financial weight of USD 5 000 billion in 1996, were holding 22 % of all US equity and half the capital of the 25 largest US public corporations.[1]

In Bismarckian countries like Germany and Japan (not France where the State used to directly control the equity and management of many large corporations), pension funds can constitute the main feature for protecting capital stability of big industrial concerns against unfriendly takeovers which may originate from both national or foreign initiatives. These bodies may include some labour representation into their boards, implying the consensual understanding that capital stability also guarantees job security.

The first part of this article is a simple international comparison of pensions, more specifically corporate schemes, and provides a description of the existing pension schemes in Japan, with a particular focus on the corporate sector. The second part deals with the Japanese corporate pension schemes prior to deregulation, with respect to the economic and financial situation which prevailed in Japan when these schemes where designed and implemented. The third part features the content of the current deregulation and provides an analysis of the impact of deregulation on corporate liability and governance. In the conclusion, some of the major questions and considerations as regards the possible evolution of pension schemes in Japan and the next steps of deregulation are presented and analysed.

---

1 See Férone (1997: 9). With such a financial power, large US pension funds have access to the boards of the largest corporations and thus exert an influence on subjects like business ethics and higher dividends. This power is not limited to US corporations, pensions funds having an important influence on listed European big corporations as well.

2 The Japanese corporate pension schemes

In order to describe and characterize the Japanese pension schemes, it is necessary to refer to their usual definition and analytic tools commonly used in pension literature.

2.1 The three pillars

The most commonly used classification of pension systems is the 'three pillars' approach, used for instance by the World Bank, the Geneva Association and the International Social Security Association. The *first pillar* is usually a pay-as-you go, mandatory state-run scheme, with minimal contributions and benefits. The most frequent reference for this kind of scheme is Beveridge, who created such an universal scheme in the United Kingdom in 1942. The idea of the State playing a minimal role such as a first pillar strictly confined to redistribution is one of the main stances of the World Bank and is often found in its publications. The foreword of a 400-page report on pension systems states, "the study suggests that financial security for the old and economic growth would be better served if governments develop three systems, or 'pillars' of old age security: a publicly managed system with mandatory participation and the limited goal of reducing poverty among the old, a privately managed mandatory savings system, and voluntary savings" (WORLD BANK 1994: xiv). The first covers redistribution, the second and third cover savings, and all three co-insure against the various risks of old age.

The World Bank is very enthusiastic about pensions in Chile, where the target has been a total privatization and individualization of pensions. The actual success of the Chilean experience will take time to assess, and some critics underline that countries even more liberal such as the UK and the US still maintain a limited but nonetheless existing minimum social safety net in the form of a State pension scheme. France, with its social traditions of a Continental European country, shows a strong involvement of State in pensions and several Social Security, pay-as-you go, State-run schemes, with a separate first pillar scheme for salaried workers. Under this last scheme, lower paid workers can enjoy a State pension benefit that, together with the compulsory second pillar scheme for workers, may provide an amount of pension benefit close to the latest salary of the active duty period.

In Japan, the first pillar is a universal, state-run, pay-as-you go pension scheme called *kokumin nenkin*. This 70 million contributors-strong scheme is very close to Beveridge's ideals: all people aged between 20 and 60 are covered and must contribute. Both, contributions and benefits, are completely independent from revenue or estate, and are the same for everyone, provided the conditions concerning the length of the contribution period (minimum 25 years, maximum 40) are fulfilled. The financing of this scheme is split on an even basis between the State, the employers, and the contributing individual members.

The *second* pillar of pensions in most OECD countries covers full-time salaried workers. The schemes can be pay-as-you go (France, Japan), or funded (Anglo-Saxon countries, and to a certain extent, Germany) and are managed either at the country level (Japan), industry-wide (France), or at the company level (Anglo-Saxon countries, Japan, Germany). Defined contribution schemes (which are dealt with hereafter) in Anglo-Saxon countries allow individual members to select where their pension contributions are to be invested (including the portion paid by their employer).

The *third* pillar shall simply be mentioned here for the sake of completing this description, since this pillar rests entirely on individual initiative: according to ability, each individual is free to allocate some part of savings to cover part of his/her needs after retirement.

2.2 Defined benefit/defined contributions

When a pension scheme provides a *defined benefit*, the scheme's liability is to provide a pre-set performance. A benefit formula is used for this purpose which allows the calculation of the benefit when the contributing person leaves the scheme. A typical formula would take into account the salary (either the last salary, or the mean of all the salaries received during the whole career, or any intermediate formula), the number of service years and any other component that the scheme design may include (such as rank in corporate hierarchy, level of education, etc.).

In Japan (where all schemes are defined benefit), the trend for employers is to re-design their schemes in such a way as to avoid keeping both salary and seniority as full-weight factors in the benefit formula, instead moving towards a point system. But whatever the design may be, in case of a defined benefit scheme, the existence of this guarantee means that if the actual performance of the fund is below that level, the employer, as a last resort, is liable for any existing difference.

In the case of *defined contributions*,[2] the employer's liability is limited to the contribution level only, without any consideration for the performance of the investment made out of this contribution. The absence of any further commitment by the employer can easily and fairly be considered as a lack of se-

[2] A pension scheme is called a 'defined contribution scheme' when there is no benefit formula, and only the contribution level is known (for instance, x% of a salary goes to a trust for pension purpose). The benefit level thus is known only *ex post*, as a result of financial investments. Therefore the employee bears the financial risk (negative or positive), while the employer is not committed as regards the benefit level that the employee will receive (as opposed to the 'defined benefit' system where there is a formula to guarantee a certain level of benefit to the employee. In this case, the financial risk is borne by the employer).

curity for the contributing employee. However, any guarantees provided though defined benefit schemes could also easily be understood as a *cap*, since any performance above the guaranteed amount will be kept by the employer in exchange for his commitment to compensate for any underperformance of the fund.

Continental European countries (Japan included as far as pensions are concerned) usually provide defined benefit schemes, while defined contribution is more commonplace in Anglo-Saxon countries. However, France's *caisses de retraites* are in reality defined contribution schemes, when one considers the many amendments that were incurred by both the contribution and the benefit formulas. The benefit formula is expressed by a point system, and a new point value is set every year. Defined contribution systems, on the other hand, seem the only suitable arrangement for pay-as-you-go schemes, where the main assumption is that current benefits are paid out of the product of current contributions.

2.3 The liability dilemma in the case of corporate pensions

Corporate pensions are not a small part of total corporate liabilities, though possibly not recorded in their balance sheet. This is where corporate governance should interfere by demanding a thorough and accurate picture of both the fund's current and its future situation. The dilemma of corporate liability in the case of corporate pension schemes however can be put in a simple, straightforward way: while it seems normal that the employer provides (partial) pension arrangements for its staff, it is difficult to assume that the employer should take responsibility for a possible downturn in the financial markets. If a general financial crisis is such that the return from invested assets is significantly lower than the assumptions used for the plan, the pension funds obviously cannot fulfil their commitments (the case for most Japanese corporate pension funds at present).

Therefore, the plan needs additional income and assets which may come from three possible sources:

- increased return on assets
- an increase in contributions (with or without a burden-sharing by employees)
- an increase in the fund's capital to cover for a current and/or anticipated deficit.

The very existence of the defined benefit commitments under the present financial conditions in Japan is a costly liability. This was not the case in the past, notably during the 1980s when financial market performance was relatively strong. In such favourable conditions, the return on assets is such that defined benefit schemes turn into a real *bonanza* since no contributions from the employer may be needed who is then enjoying what in Anglo-Saxon countries is called a 'pension holiday'.

2.4 The Japanese corporate pension schemes

Japanese corporate pension schemes (for an overview of the entire system of pension schemes in Japan, see graph 1) can be grouped into two categories:

- severance payments (*taishokukin*)
- Employee Pension Funds (*kōsei nenkin kikin*)

Graph 1: A synthetic view of Japanese pension schemes

- first pillar: state run, compulsory, pay as you go
  - 1a universal pension
  - 1b employee pension scheme
- second pillar: corporate level, funded systems, defined benefit
  - 2a severance payments
  - 2b pension funds
- third pillar: individual savings for pension purpose

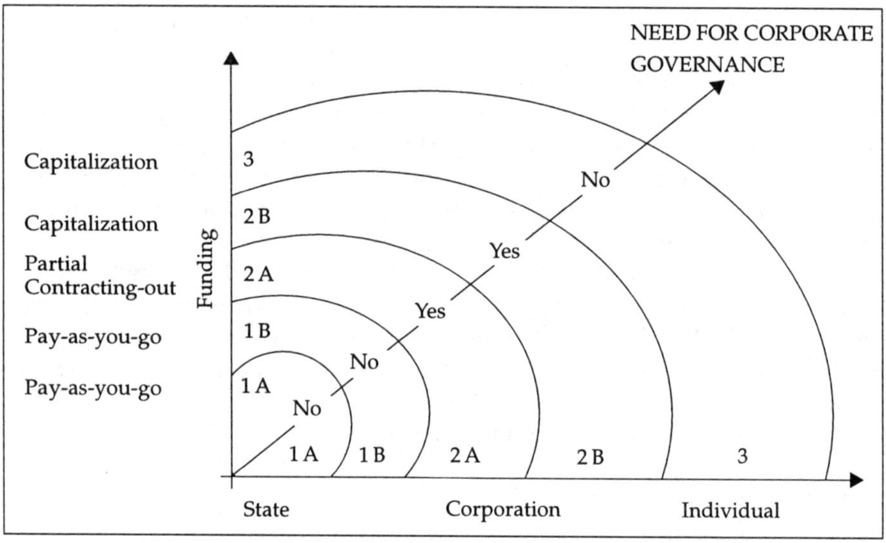

The first category is a traditional commitment for almost all Japanese employers, though not compulsory. The employer freely sets the rules and benefit formula which must be logged at the Labour Office. The only requisite is the prohibition of discrimination and the assurance that the rules are fair. Thus an extremely large range of arrangements does exist but the usual parameters, applied directly or through complex formulas, are the number of service years and the final salary. All of these schemes are defined benefits, which are most commonly paid in the form of a lump sum. Apart from rare exceptions, all contributions to severance pay are at the full expense of the employer only.

The funding methods of the severance payment liability are the following:

- in the company's balance sheet (in part or entirely). This is usually called the 'book reserve system' (*hikiate-kin*)
- in an especially designed vehicle (in part or entirely), the most commonly used being a Qualified Pension Plan (*tekikaku nenkin*).

The book reserve method is the most simple for the employer, since the level of reserve remains at its own discretion and there is no obligation concerning the quality or segregation of assets for the specific severance payment liability. There is no other requirement than the basic matching of the amount of assets and liabilities. No comprehensive data collection on severance payments (*taishokkin*) or book reserves (*hikiate-kin*) is available in Japan, apart from sample surveys (see, for example, CHŪŌ RŌDŌ INKAI JIMUKYOKU 1998).

The altogether 91,465 Qualified Pension Plans cover 10.78 million salaried workers in Japan, with reserves totalling ¥ 17.8 trillion (data as of March 31st 1996, see KŌSEISHŌ 1997: 389). Different in nature from book reserves, Qualified Pension Plans are a means of externalizing assets out of the company's balance sheet. Their implementation through a tax law of 1962 was aimed at securing the pension rights and assets of workers: contrary to the book reserve system, workers are the legitimate owners of assets in Qualified Pension Plans, and these assets will still be available in the event of their employer's liquidation. The existence of a Qualified Pension Plan allows the provision of an option to get the benefit not as a lump sum, but as a specified annuity. The beneficiary who meets the criteria (usually reaching the retirement age, having accumulated a set number of service years) and exercises his/her option, receives all or part of the benefit in fractions, over a set period, e. g., ten years, including interest paid until the period elapses.

The tax exemption on contributions is an advantage for the employer if the company is profitable. Japan's Tax Office is also quite an obvious winner since, apart from rare exceptions, a tax of 1.117 % is levied on the assets every year, irrespective of the profitability of the contributing employer nor of the performance of the assets. Considering the current average performance of funds entrusted to trust banks and life insurance companies, it becomes evident that almost half of the performance from assets goes to the Tax Office and as commissions (usually not performance-linked) paid to these trust banks and life insurers. In fiscal 1997/1998, the average performance of pension assets under management in Japan was 3.6 % (*Nihon Keizai Shinbun* 1998), the average commission paid for fund management 0.4 % (estimate) and the asset tax around 1.2 %. Thus the net fund performance, on average, hardly reached 1.5 %, compared to the benchmark 10-year Japanese Government Bond with its yield of around 1.6 % for the same period.

The second type of corporate pension schemes are Employee Pension Funds (EPF), which provide whole life annuities. These funds are under the supervision of the Ministry of Health and Welfare and do constitute a partial contracting-out arrangement. Under the EPF legislation, employers and employees (who share the contribution burden on an equal basis) benefit from a reduction of the contribution to the compulsory, pay-as-you-go State scheme for employees (*kōsei nenkin hoken*). The typical reduction, in 1997, is from 17.35 % to 13.85 %. The difference, 3.5 % in this example, is instead accumulated into the Employee Pension Fund and constitutes the partial contracting-out from a State pay-as-you go system to a funded Employee Pension Fund.

EPF provide two components of benefits. The first one is a substitution component (*daikō bubun*) which is designed to compensate for the reduction of the benefit provided by the State scheme. The second component is the additional one (*plus alpha*), at the cost only of the employer. The benefit formula may vary from one fund to another but is usually linked in a direct way to the average salary calculated for the whole period of service of the contributing employee, and to the number of service years. Both components can therefore be considered as defined benefit. As of March 31st 1998, there were 1,874 Employee Pension Funds in Japan (against 1,883 as of October 30th 1997), for a contributing population of 12.5 million and an amount of reserves of ¥ 47 trillion (March 31st 1998, see *Nihon Keizai Shinbun* 1998).

3 Before the deregulation: a tight environment

3.1 The economic context of postwar Japan

The 'Golden Sixties' is certainly a just expression with regard to Japan's economic expansion, and it is the decade when modern Japan's corporate pension schemes were established. The Qualified Pension Schemes[3] law was passed in 1962, while Employee Pension Funds were created in 1966. This period was of triple merit for the economy and for corporate pensions, in particular: growth of net labour revenue, positive demographic trends and financial markets providing a net positive performance. Inflation was then

[3] Qualified Pension Schemes (*Tekikaku nenkin*) are pension trusts linked to severance payment systems (*taishokkin*). *Taishokukin* is a traditional defined benefit pension system found in most Japanese corporations. With the usual exception of disciplinary dismissal, a benefit is paid when the employee leaves the company. The normal departure event is the reaching of pension age, but other reasons such as voluntary departure, non-disciplinary dismissal, or death are also covered. The benefit amount varies according to the reason for leaving (voluntary dismissal leading to the lowest payment) and the benefit formula may vary significantly from one employer to another, since the only limitations when setting such a system are acceptance by the employee and the approval of the Labour Office, which usually limits its role to preventing discriminatory treatment in the rules. The benefit is usually paid as a lump sum, while defined annuities (lump sum paid in fractions over a set number of years, plus interest), or life annuities may also be found.

part of the economic situation but was bearable as long as net growth was present.

Under such circumstances, certain categories of workers were able to request some kind of specific social treatment: employees of core sectors such as mining, steel, transportation, communications and most civil servants together with employees of nationalized companies. Thus, special schemes were created alongside the State compulsory schemes. For large private corporations, the Employee Pension Funds were created, while Qualified Pension Plans were available for small and large corporations. The idea behind the creation of Employee Pension Funds was to provide additional benefits for employees of large corporations at a low cost since the financial markets were expected to perform well above the then conservative 5.5 % compulsory assumption rate. In addition, employers would receive a rebate on their contribution to the State scheme.

The Tax Qualified Plans were designed mainly to help small and mid-size corporations to operate an externalization of reserves for their pension commitments in order to protect employee pension rights not included in companies' balance sheets. The tax authorities also encouraged all companies to accumulate assets granting a total tax exemption (later reduced to 40 %) for reserves accumulated in their balance sheets in order to hedge their *taishokukin* severance payment liabilities.

3.2 The implementation of a tight State-regulation package

The decade of the Sixties was a period of growth and the Japanese State's policy of economic guidance was a key for success. Strict government regulation was abundant and the field of corporate pensions was no exception. Two ministries were involved (the Ministry of Finance for the Qualified Pension Plans and the Ministry of Health and Welfare for the Employee Pension Funds), both providing the same set of rules:

a) a restriction of the type of financial institutions allowed to receive deposits from pension assets (trust banks and life insurance companies);
b) limitation of asset allocation, i. e., the '5 3 3 2'-rule whereby asset allocation should comply to the following: at least 50 % in fixed-income, Yen-denominated bonds with a sound rating (Japanese public entities at least), no more than 30 % in Japanese stocks, no more than 30 % in foreign securities, no more than 20 % in real estate;
c) a fixed assumption regarding the discount rate regarding net return of assets: 5.5 % p. a.;
d) mortality tables to be used as determined by the Ministry, with revision from time to time.

3.3 The progressive shift of the postwar equilibrium

The above listed regulations were not considered much of a burden as long as the economy and the stock market were growing. The asset allocation '5 3 3 2'-rule was tough but in line with what was then considered appropriate for corporate pension schemes. However, when the financial *bubble* burst, the equilibrium which had been resting on the growth of the economy and markets together with a tough set of regulations became too difficult to sustain. All alternatives were tried before the regulations concerning the 'war chest' of financial reserves of the corporate pension schemes were affected. Those who experienced the progressive collapse of the Japanese stock market in the late 1980s remember how strongly free market financiers from Japan and elsewhere expected the Japanese Government to intervene to 'help the market'.

The government has since provided some salvation such as the costly move to help the agricultural cooperatives recover from their accumulated losses. Another stance was the decrease of the discount rate to a minimum level, close to nil. This discount rate policy, made possible since inflationary pressure has disappeared, was intended to lead to a demand-led economic recovery. However, the drastic lowering of the discount rate has put the institutions whose mission is to provide a long-term and stable performance, such as life insurers and corporate pension schemes, in a difficult situation. This difficulty not only derives from a declining return on assets (depressed stock prices together with poor dividends, increase of non-repaid loans, and reduced interests earned from Japanese government- and other bonds), but also from the previous imposition of minimum levels of performance. These levels, 4.5 % for the guaranteed rate provided by life insurance companies and 5.5 % for the assumed return on financial assets for both the Employee Pension Funds and Qualified Pension Plans, were considered prudent when they were set in the 1960s. Thirty years later, they have actually become rather dangerous.

The guaranteed rate provided by life insurance companies has since been lowered from 4.5 % to 2.5 %, but some among the small and mid-size life insurers have been severely affected nevertheless. The failure of Nissan Mutual Life has demonstrated that the expectations, held by some, that the Japanese government would never resort to the liquidation of an insurance company proved to be wrong, as some pension funds have also had to experience.

3.4 Government regulation, deregulation and corporate governance

Since the burst of the financial *bubble* in 1990, the Japanese authorities have demonstrated that no financial sector would enjoy public protection from the consequences of disputable behaviour, i. e., assuming that financial markets were protected forever. Of course, the MoF (Ministry of Finance) itself has not been safe from blame, considering the 'quasi-organic' links between the civil servants of the regulatory authorities and the management of financial institutions under the scope of regulation.

Tight regulations have often been used as an excuse for ailing institutions. The decade of the 1990s is, in fact, a perfect demonstration that tight regulations are not always a safe precaution measure against financial corruption. Tight regulations have also been a barrier to the inevitable adaptation that a sizeable part of the Japanese financial sector has resisted for so long.

The next possible focus among Japanese financial circles may involve more life insurance companies and possibly some trust banks in bad financial shape. However, this government-managed Darwinian process of adaptation through failure of the unfit comes with a side effect: Japanese corporations who are sponsoring corporate Pension Funds and who are financing Qualified Pension Plans cannot fully rely anymore on the financial institutions they have been dealing with, usually for decades, nor on any government safety net. Simply paying contributions, premiums and fees will not suffice anymore. Japanese corporations will now have to manage their liabilities themselves, moving from a passive to a pro-active stance. Concerning corporate pension liabilities, this must be considered a historic (and often painful) discovery of the very existence and full meaning of corporate governance. The rise of the need for corporate governance is an almost symmetric consequence of the decline of Government regulations.

4 Deregulation of corporate pensions and corporate governance

The deregulation of pension funds is one step in the long process of the painful reform and adaptation process of the Japanese financial sector. However, this step is different from the previous ones since it is dealing not with purely financial institutions but with schemes and funds designed to finance the social welfare of the employees of Japanese corporations. This deregulation should thus be seen not only from the macro-perspective of the Japanese financial system, but also from the angle of each pension fund and sponsoring company.

4.1 The technical content of corporate pension deregulation

The first set of deregulation has been the progressive access to the services of asset management institutions, newcomers who are gradually allowed to compete with the heretofore privileged life insurance companies and trust banks. This deregulation process covering the type and proportion of assets accessible to these new institutions took several years. Even by 1997, not all pension assets could be entrusted to or at least be managed under the advice of these new asset management companies or investment management advisors. It is therefore remarkable that these new entrants have been able to secure an aggregated 5 % share of the asset management market. The trend of deregulation, however, is now firmly set and the time will come when Japanese pension funds and sponsor companies of Qualified Pension Plans will be able to freely select the institutions they are willing to entrust with their pension assets. The new features of pension deregulation, starting with the 1997 fiscal year, are dealing with the relaxation of the tightest rules: the discount rate and the asset allocation (or asset mix).

1. The *discount rate* which used to be set by the Ministries (Health and Welfare for Pension Funds, and Finance for the Qualified Pension Plans) at 5.5 % p. a. is now being relaxed within a bracket linked to the coupon of the 20-year Japanese Government Bond. The relaxation is a major feature since the economic balance of the fund implies that the discount rate equals the expected performance of the assets. Therefore, taking the more realistic stance of lowering the actual rate from 5.5 % to, for instance, 3 % per annum may seem quite logical by the current state of financial markets in Japan. While the actual performance of assets is the target, in a defined benefit environment assumptions matter too. Hence, if the plan was designed with a 5.5 % rate, and a set level of contribution was calculated on this assumption, the lowering of the rate triggers a premium increase since the new, lower assumptions mean that the previous goal will never be reached. Retaining the previous 5.5 % per annum anticipated revenue from assets does not seem realistic either, however, as the negative gap between the recorded performance and the anticipated one is creating a loss, accumulating into a recurring deficit for the fund.
2. The asset allocation ('5 3 3 2') rule is being abolished, thus fund managers will enjoy a much greater freedom in selecting their assets in order to maximize expected performance within an acceptable level of risk. This is also good news for foreign asset management companies and investment management advisors, since their (potential) Japanese clients will be able to allocate whatever share of their portfolio to foreign assets. Of course, the liability being in Japanese Yen, a relevant proportion of the assets must be of the same currency denomination. However, the advantages of using modern investment management techniques, such as Asset/Liability Management (ALM), will be made much more available, and if the recourse to ALM suggests an increase in foreign denominated assets, there will be no more limits to it.
3. The compulsory nomination of a Certified Pension Actuary (for Employee Pension Funds), especially licensed for computing pension figures: assets, liabilities, contributions, benefits. An actuary is able to assess the financial soundness of a pension scheme and inform the management schemes' sponsoring company about the possibility of a situation requiring correction measures to guarantee the future situation of the fund.

This compulsory feature is one of the important steps of corporate pension governance. Before the deregulation, most corporations were relying on the government and financial institutions to take care of the soundness and solvency of corporate pension schemes. Now fully in charge of their schemes, due to the deregulation, they have to face new responsibilities. Thus the advice and experience of an independent certified actuary is required.

4.2 The impact of deregulation on corporate governance

The deregulation set mentioned above is a clear sign from the state to corporations: they are now on their own. This is the true meaning of the current deregulations. There are almost no more guaranteed rates and sponsoring corporations themselves now have to make by the assumptions that used to be imposed by the State (see also graph 2). This is why the nomination of a Certified Pension Actuary has been made compulsory for Employee Pension Funds. For Qualified Pension Plans, which are under the supervision of the Ministry of Finance, no such requirement has been made, but a consultation with an actuary office seems rather advisable.

Graph 2: Deregulating pension fund schemes in Japan

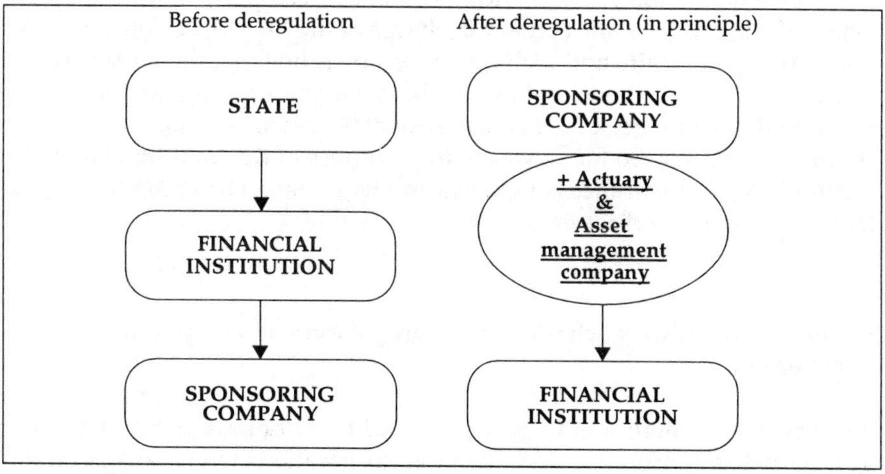

The setting of the actual rate and of the asset mix are decisions which will impact the pension schemes and affect their financial performance. Since a company's liability is set by the commitment of defined benefits, the underperformance of assets and the lowering of the expected rate of return mean that a deficit is created within the pension scheme which has to be compensated for by an increase in pension contributions. This increase of pension contributions has a direct impact on the level of corporate operating expenses. This in turn affects the company's profitability. Therefore corporate governance decisions, and their inevitable costs, are indirectly encouraged by the Japanese state.

4.3 Limits to the current deregulation

After existing for such a long time in a tightly regulated environment, many Japanese corporations, perhaps with the exception of the largest ones, may not be instantly ready for being fully pro-active concerning their investment management. The Japanese government is by no means unaware that for most Japanese corporations their loyalty to the corporate group, or *keiretsu*, is very important. Financial institutions which used to have the privilege of being entrusted with pension assets (life insurance companies and trust banks which are still holding an aggregate 95 % market share) are at the core of the financial ties that guarantee the cohesion of these groups. Therefore, the choice of financial institutions for the management of corporate pension schemes' assets may not have always been guided only by performance motives. There will be a fair proportion of corporations who feel they cannot take advantage from the new freedoms that pension deregulation provides if this would mean a conflict of loyalty with their traditional financial partners.

The best indication for which kind of stance a company is willing or able to take is the choice of the actuary in charge of the Employee Pension Fund. The Ministry of Health and Welfare is recommending that the actuary selected by the Employee Pension Fund be independent from the financial institution that is in charge of the management of the assets, in order to avoid any conflicts of interest. So far, however, the response of the traditional financial institutions (life insurance companies and trust banks) has been to promote their own internal actuaries.

5 Conclusion: the real challenge of deregulation and corporate governance

Henceforward, there will be three types of corporations as far as pension governance is concerned. First, the large corporations who managed to put in place their own corporate governance procedures and performed some asset/liability management even under the tight regulations previously in place. These corporations are in a position to impose a real commitment for performance on their financial partners.

The second type of corporation is of a smaller size and willing to enjoy the relaxation of rules to put in place their own corporate pension governance system. These corporations may be the actual target of deregulation as envisaged by the government in the first place. However, the proper corporate pension governance process must be initiated, and competent professionals need to trained or hired. As clients become more professional, a flight for quality of investment decisions may occur. This perspective should push traditional financial institutions to be more alert and competitive. If this truly happens, one of the main targets of the deregulators may have been reached.

Finally, of course, there may be a third type of corporation not yet ready for the challenging freedom brought about by these deregulation measures.

Postscript: a long-term perspective

The ultimate stage of deregulation may be the transfer of investment freedom (and risk) to the individual. This final stage is the equivalent to a defined contribution system, which is almost unheard of in Bismarckian, risk-adverse countries such as Japan, Germany, or France, but which is often encountered in Anglo-Saxon countries. There, the employer's only liability is to pay a certain amount of salary as a pension contribution. The beneficiary then adds his/her own contribution (which in some cases is allowed to be zero, hence the total amount of contribution coming from the employer only) and manages his/her account freely, the usual pattern being a range of products (with different risk/return profiles) offered by one or several providers selected by the employer. The most liberal formula would finally be the granting of total freedom to the employee, who would then be allowed to select any investment vehicle available on the market. This freedom given to the individual demands, however, that a wide range of investment alternatives and agents be available, with a proper set of prudential rules being effectively enforced. The average 'investment consumer' should then also be given access to proper independent information and advice. A minimum training in financial matters at school would further facilitate the upbringing of new generations of informed individual investors. All this, however, would imply a major change in Bismarckian countries, including Japan, and will therefore take a long time to ever implement.

References

CHŪŌ RŌDŌ IINKAI JIMUKYOKU (1998): *Taishokukin, nenkin oyobi teinen seiji chōsa* [Survey on Severance Payments, Pension Funding, and Retirement Policies]. Tōkyō, Rō'i Kyōkai Zaidan Hōjin.

ESTIENNE, J. F. (1996): *Vieillissement et retraites au Japon, une adaptation économique et sociale?* Paris: La Documentation Française.

FÉRONE, G. (1997): *Le système de retraite américain, les fonds de pension.* Paris: Montchrestien.

LOHMANN, L. J. (1995–1998): *LIA Facts* (Newsletter). Tōkyō: LIA

KŌSEISHŌ (1997): *Kōseishō hakusho. Heisei 9-nen* [Annual White Book of the Ministry of Health and Welfare]. Tōkyō: Kōseishō.

MURAKAMI, K. (1997): *Kigyō nenkin chishiki, shinban* [Knowledge about Corporate Pensions]. Tōkyō: Nikkei Bunko.

Nihon Keizai Shinbun (1998): Special Supplement on Pension Funds, 20 April 1998.

Nihon Kinyū Shinbun (1997): Kigyō nenkin saizensen. Shitamawari kikin sokushutsu ka [Recent News from the Corporate Pensions Front. Will the Number of Underfunded Funds Continue to Increase?], 28 July 1997, p. 7.

ROBERTS, L. and E. REYNAUD (1992): *Les systèmes de retraite à l'étranger: Etats-Unis, Allemagne, Royaume-Uni.* Paris: Institut de Recherches Economiques et Sociales.

SHALE, T. (1990): The Plot that Triggered Tokyo's Plunge. In: *Euromoney*, May 1990, pp. 32–36.

WORLD BANK (1994): *Averting the Old Age Crisis – Policies to Protect the Old and Promote Growth* (World Bank Policy Research Report). New York: Oxford University Press.

VII After Quasi-LBO Discipline: A Historical Reflection on Japanese Corporate Governance

Shigeru WATANABE

Free cash flow theory provides a more consistent explanation of the history of Japanese corporate governance than the main bank system hypothesis does. Sources of discipline on capital investment have been lost since constraints on available funds disappeared in the 1980s, and a market for corporate control is unlikely to emerge in Japan. Internal governance by management will be a major source of discipline as management undertakes reforms to improve return on investment. This voluntary restructuring by management is a move in the right direction, though it is apparently both weaker and slower than one forced by external shareholder pressures.

1 Internal governance and agency theory

> First, before the Second World War, a top manager was a shareholder of the company. On the contrary, very few top managers today are shareholders. Most of them are, so to speak, hired men.
> Second, pre-war companies were typically funded by paid-in capital. Almost every company now owes ten times as much debt as its paid-in capital.
> Third, pre-war managers had intensively examined a market before they invested and made business decisions based on profitability. Managers today rush to invest without paying any attention to market forecasts, being solely motivated by the idea of not falling behind in the game of rapid expansion.
>
> Tatsunosuke Takasaki
> "Managers today and yesterday"
> *Keidanren Monthly,* March 1954

In the late 19th century, huge modern corporations emerged in the United States, and the public corporation became the dominant business structure. Adolf BERLE and Gardiner MEANS voiced concern over the power of management in these big corporations with widely dispersed ownership: "[T]o Adam Smith, private enterprise meant an individual or few partners actively engaged and relying in large part on their own labour or their immediate direction. Today we have tens and hundreds of thousands of owners, of workers and of consumers combined in single enterprises" (BERLE & MEANS 1932:

349). With the separation of ownership and control in a modern dispersed-ownership corporation, shareholders may incur agency costs as managers find it easy to pursue their own interests rather than those of the shareholders.

In contrast, Alfred CHANDLER, Jr. saw the growing concentration of power among professional managers in a positive light: "In many modern business enterprises neither bankers nor families were in control. Ownership became scattered. The stockholders did not have the influence, knowledge, experience, or commitment to take part in the high command. Salaried managers determined long-term as well as short-term operating activities. They dominated top as well as lower and middle management" (CHANDLER 1977: 10). Modern corporations seem to have performed well with internal governance in the Berle/Means universe, where shareholders are powerless.

Even M. JENSEN and W. MECKLING wrote in 1976 in the conclusion of *Theory of the Firm*, now a classic paper on agency theory: "The growth in the use of the corporate form as well as the growth in market value of established corporations suggests that at least, up to the present, creditors and investors have by and large not been disappointed with the results, despite the agency costs inherent in the corporate form" (JENSEN & MECKLING 1976: 357).

American investors manifested their disappointment in the succeeding decade. Not only corporate raiders but also emerging active institutional investors proposed unfriendly takeovers and forced corporate break-ups, divisional spin-offs, and leveraged buy-outs. With the benefit of hindsight, a central issue was unrelated diversification. Until the 1970s, management sought diversification of business to secure the continuity and growth of a company. As Gordon DONALDSON wrote, "Perhaps the best example was the well-known Boston Consulting Group product portfolio two-by-two matrix of cash generation and use in which infant market positions were fed by mature market positions ('cash cows'). All this was changed in the 1980s" (DONALDSON 1994: 163). The dynamic nature of the matrix strategy is appealing. A problem associated with this strategy, however, is that it tends to create cross-subsidies within the company, and inefficient, non-core business lines find easy excuses for their low performance. Internal governance slackens with soft-budget constraints.

Borrowing from agency theory, Michael JENSEN reformulated the issue as a waste of free cash flows by managers. By his definition, "Free cash flow is cash flow in excess of that required to fund all projects that have positive net present values when discounted at the relevant cost of capital" (JENSEN 1986: 323). Free cash flow theory suggests that with free cash flow at their discretion, managers tend to waste it in negative present value investments because they seek the security and growth of the company for their own interests.

Steven KAPLAN's (1989) study on leveraged buy-outs (LBOs) provided the free-cash-flow theory with empirical evidence. According to agency theory, the essence of an LBO is that it creates a heavily debt-burdened capital structure, hence LBOs force an outward cash flow to service debt. They thus create incentives for managers to squeeze cash from their operations.

KAPLAN examined 76 large LBOs completed between 1980 and 1986. He found that these companies experienced an increase in operating income, a decrease in capital expenditures, an increase in net cash flow, and a mean increase in market value of 96 %. He concluded that these achievements were due to improved incentives rather than to layoffs (KAPLAN 1989: 217).

With the foregoing U.S. experiences in mind, I will use the concept of internal governance as well as the free-cash-flow theory to analyse Japanese corporate governance in the following sections.

2 Rapid expansion

Post-war Japanese top managers, who came to their posts after pre-war leaders had been purged, implemented significantly large-scale investments, with much emphasis on expansion speed and market share rather than on profitability forecasts (see, for instance, TAKASAKI 1954, HONDA 1963, NAKAMURA 1993). After that, they put their energy into controlling running costs. A prominent pre-war manager, Tatsunosuke Takasaki (cf. opening quote in section 1), the founder of Tōyō Can Company, saw the incredibly enthusiastic mindset of the post-war managers toward business expansion as too loose and too risky. Massive investment and rapid expansion, however, proved to be a successful business strategy in post-war Japan. The reason is that the realized market growth rate was much higher than what Takasaki had in mind when he commented on post-war management. The average real growth rate of the Japanese economy was 3 % over more than half a century until the Second World War. This growth rate meant a 50 % market expansion every ten years. In this modest and evidently ordinary economic environment, the success and survival of a firm depended on a careful examination of investment plans.

During the post-war high economic growth period, however, the economy grew by 10 % instead of 3 % annually. With a 10 % annual growth rate, the market expanded by a factor of 2.5 every ten years. Post-war managers' rapid expansion strategy became a success formula. This strategy's implicit assumption was that markets would grow enough to absorb fixed costs materialized. This strategy resembles that of Andrew Carnegie. In the expansive market environment of late 19th century America, Carnegie had invested more capital and had earned higher returns than any other steelmaker in the world before 1902: "[M]anagers of these capital-intensive giants often gave inadequate attention either to asset depreciation or to the forecasts and the return-on-investment data. ... Carnegie's success depended upon good information about direct operating costs. For that, accounting systems mattered. For the rest, faith and intuition sufficed" (JOHNSON & KAPLAN 1987: 34).

3 Quasi-LBO

The rapid expansion of a company puts a great strain on the balance sheet. From the mid-1950s to the early 1970s, Japanese manufacturing companies' balance sheets expanded by 17 % annually. During the same period, internal equity growth through retained earnings was 6 % (WATANABE 1994: 40). There was a strong need for external funds. Bank loans had to satisfy this need because of the tight regulations on capital markets.

Japanese manufacturing companies became more leveraged over the years through the mid-1970s, when the era of high economic growth ended. Equity ratios (equity over total assets) ended up at 14 %, which is as low as those of LBO companies in the United States. Japanese companies' over-leveraging was different from that of LBOs in the United States in the 1980s in such ways that it was unintentional, that it covered much broader industries than did the U.S. LBOs, including R&D-oriented ones, and that there was no concentrated ownership. Nevertheless, LBOs in Japan shared a major aspect of U.S. LBO, that is, a burden of debt service as a source of management discipline.

From the mid-1970s, Japanese economic growth slowed to an average growth rate of 3 %, which is close to the pre-war growth rate. In this low growth economy, balance sheet growth fell to around 5 %, which was within the range of internal equity growth. Net cash flow (internal cash flow after investment) changed from deficit to surplus. Graph 1, which compares changes in cash flow and capital spending for Japanese manufacturers from fiscal 1953 through fiscal 1995, clearly shows that the internal funding capabilities of these companies have improved substantially. Since the late 1970s, Japanese companies have been able to finance capital investment through cash flows (i. e., through retained earnings plus depreciation). Major corporations have thus had free cash flows.

Free cash flow was at first used to pay off bank borrowings, as the interest-rate hike during the oil crisis of the mid-1970s sent a clear signal to corporations about the financial vulnerability of a highly leveraged capital structure. These changes were clearly reflected in a shift in the capitalization structure of companies. Until the 1970s, the proportion of bank loans to total capitalization had been rising. In the 1980s, however, large increases occurred in the proportions represented by retained earnings, paid-in capital, and corporate bonds. Manufacturers' equity ratio had thus risen to 40 % by the early 1990s. Net interest expense, which previously ate up as much as 30 % of manufacturers' operating profits, has steadily dwindled, and in fact manufacturers actually enjoyed a net interest income in fiscal years 1989 and 1990, respectively (BANK OF JAPAN, respective annual editions). Debt service no longer is the important constraint on management that it once was.

As the overall growth rate decreased in the 1980s, corporations intensified their search for new growth opportunities. Diversification strategies had the attention of top managers. With abundant funds at hand and strengthened debt capacity, they could not only expand their overseas operations but also buy out spun-off U.S. companies. Increases in R&D budgets led many corporations to invest in biotechnology and electronics research projects, quite *en vogue* at the time, in search of new business seeds. Intra-company venture activities entered the business vocabulary (*Nikkei Business* 1986). Excessive product proliferation took place in an attempt to improve market penetration. Production facilities were renovated to become state-of-the-art factories. Abundant cash flow seemed to have been used effectively to sustain healthy growth; for instance, whereas a U.S. steelmaker used cash flow to buy an oil company, a Japanese steelmaker diversified into the high-technology semiconductor business (*Nikkei Business* 1991). Although many of these appeared to be smart moves by Japanese management, in the end most of them resulted in *over-investments*, which would not have taken place without free cash flows, increasing costs and yielding low returns, thereby resulting in net losses.

Graph 1: Cash flow as a proportion of capital spending

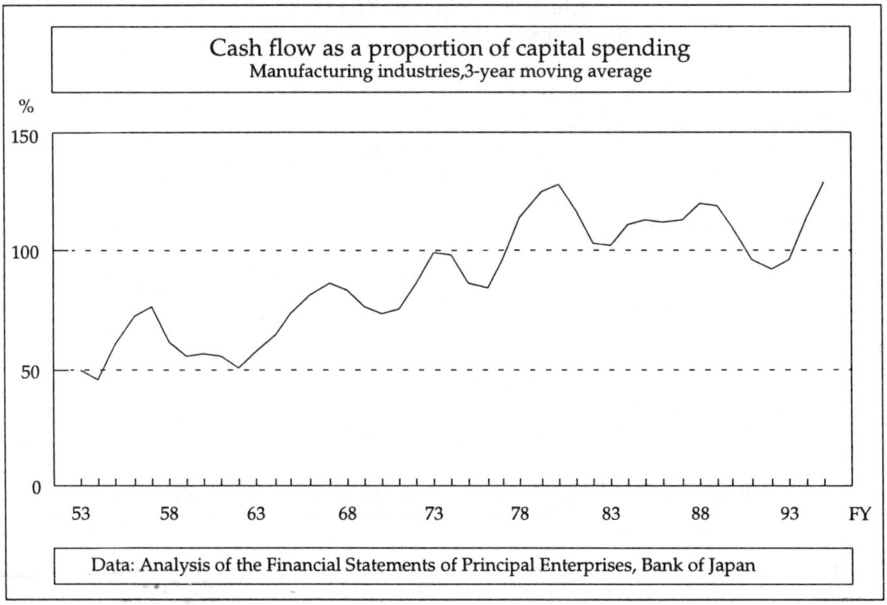

Source: BANK OF JAPAN (various annual editions)

Decreases in efficiency in the use of capital are reflected in changes in return on equity (ROE), which showed a cyclical fluctuation within a range of 10–15 % until the 1970s. In contrast, a significant declining trend in ROE beginning in the 1980s, to their lowest level of 2.4 % in FY 1993, is clearly shown in graph 2. The fall in ROE has been caused by declining returns on invested assets, not by changes in the corporate capital structure. From FY 1981 to FY 1991 decreases in return on investment contributed to a lowering of ROE by 6 percentage points, while the decrease in leverage's contribution to decreasing ROE was only 1 percentage point. This historical decline in ROE implies that Japanese corporate governance has been malfunctioning since the 1980s. Although economic factors other than governance certainly have affected ROE, a corporate governance structure inappropriately adapted to the new environment must share responsibility for the historically low ROE. Japanese companies underwent reverse LBO in the 1980s, when LBO made more sense than it had in previous decades. The significant fall of ROE concomitant with the emergence of free cash flow suggests that the debt-service burden played an important disciplinary role in Japanese corporate governance.

Graph 2: Historical changes in ROE

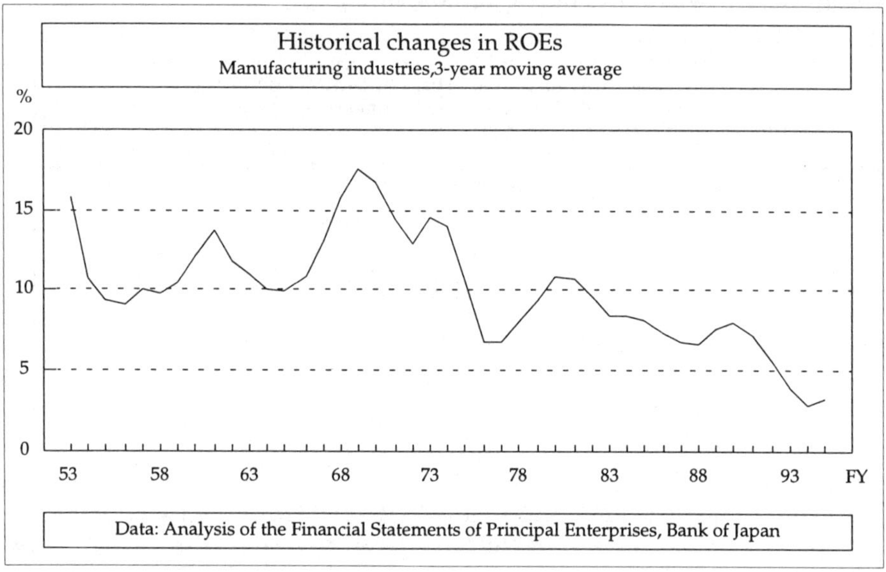

Source: cf. graph 1

4 The banking industry

During the high economic growth period, Japanese companies turned to banks for investment funds. In contrast, in the pre-war period Japanese companies depended on the securities market as their source of external funds. Banks at that time were largely independent from the central bank and the

Ministry of Finance (MOF). The Japanese government's wartime policies changed this financial system to ensure the allocation of funds to war-related industries. The government tightened the oversight of banks and facilitated indirect financing because this gave more discretionary control power over fund allocation to the government than under a securities-market system (BANK OF JAPAN 1984: 287–313).

This governmental financial control, which was kept intact to weather the economic crisis immediately after the war, became a unique feature of the post-war Japanese financial market. The Ministry of Finance protected banks by putting regulative constraints on interest rates, financial products, new entries to the industry, and the use of the securities market. As for the securities market, 40 years passed before the issuance of the first post-war unsecured corporate bond, issued by TDK Corp. in 1985, was allowed. The Bank of Japan also helped: it did not require reserve deposits from major banks. On the contrary, the Bank of Japan provided growth money only through low-rate lending to the major banks, which amounted to as much as 10 % of their funding during the high economic growth period (KURE 1981: 248–253). These policies resulted in high rents to the banking industry and perquisites to its overseers such as retiring to senior management positions in banks.

During the high economic growth period, when Japanese firms had strong capital needs, the domestic securities market was suffocated, and access to foreign financial markets was virtually prohibited. The firms waited in line for capital; Japanese banks were on the short side of non-clearing financial markets (capital shortage). Under these conditions, Japanese banks were in a position to exert influence over their borrowers. However, when financial environments experienced a 180-degree change in the 1980s, the banks found themselves on the long side of the markets.

5 The main-bank-system hypothesis

The term *main bank* as used in Japanese business society means the bank with which a company maintains the closest relationship. All else being equal, a company does financial transactions with its main bank. Business information will be transferred between them on a priority basis; information costs are reduced through the long-term relationship between a company and a bank. A main bank relationship is one type of 'relationship banking', which can be found elsewhere in other financial markets as well. Relationship banking prospers when prices and the quality of financial products are the same among banks. In this regard, the post-war period's strictly regulated financial markets facilitated the development of relationship banking. On the other hand, a main bank does not have priority over derivatives deals today because product differentiation is significant. With few exceptions, a city bank in a *zaibatsu* (corporate group) is a main bank to the group's companies.

Because of their common historical background, their relationships are stable. Since the end of the war, *zaibatsu* banks have extended their main bank relationships beyond traditional *zaibatsu* members, and other major banks also have formed main bank relationship webs (*Tōyō Keizai Weekly* 1996). Main bank relationships are generally concomitant with cross-shareholding.

Banks may monitor firms as creditors. The main-bank-system hypothesis goes beyond this point, insisting that the unique informal institution existing among Japanese banks works, or used to work, as *the* central and efficient corporate governance mechanism in Japan. The hypothesis posits that monitoring incentives and pay-offs are provided by the collection of rents from client borrower firms; thus it takes a positive view of the idiosyncratic postwar financial market regulations. Yet a prominent advocate of the hypothesis, Masahiko AOKI, suggests that the system also may work in a fully deregulated environment. AOKI writes, "[S]uccessive, yet partial, deregulations since the 1970s have impaired the coherence and integrity of the main bank's monitoring functions, facilitating the generation of the *bubble economy* in the late 1980s and shaking the foundations of the system. ... and I suggest a further deregulation that may make the main bank system adaptable to such an [increasingly securitized] environment" (AOKI 1994: 111). Two major claims of the hypothesis, unique rescue operation and unique monitoring role, deserve close examination.

5.1 Unique rescue operation

The main-bank-system hypothesis regards a rescue operation of client companies in financial distress by a main bank as a unique feature of the system by reasoning that the main bank provides implicit insurance to the client companies and, as a result of this insurance, implicitly guarantees loans originated by other banks (AOKI 1994: 119–121). However, these rescue operations are understood in the context of private restructuring, called a 'workout' in the United States. In general, it is to a creditor's benefit to make a concession *ex post* to rescue a company on the brink of bankruptcy in a case where a company has a higher value if it continues operation than if it were liquidated. In other words, 'lost investment opportunity' is always an issue for creditors to consider when a company is in financial distress.

GILSON, JOHN, and LANG examined 169 listed companies that defaulted on their debts between 1978 and 1987. They found that 80 of those companies successfully restructured their debts privately through the means of such a work-out. Furthermore, 70 % of the remaining 89 companies, which had filed for chapter 11 bankruptcy, attempted private restructuring before filing (GILSON, JOHN, and LANG 1990). In a work-out process, a rescue package (modifying interest rates, principal amount, maturity, and so forth) is negotiated among creditors. Bank lenders tend to be more sophisticated and are likely to recognize the benefits of a work-out: they are willing to make larger concessions to avoid hold-outs. For managers a work-out is tough: 60 % of senior managers leave the company, and it is difficult for them to find work with other listed companies (GILSON 1996: 317–318).

The bargaining to reach terms of concession mutually agreeable upon among creditors may suffer from hold-outs. In Japanese cases, a main bank may have incentives to make concessions larger than those of other banks because it can collect higher rents from the company. On the other hand, non-main banks may fail to renew their loans. There may also be other credible threats to negotiations. For instance, article 4 of the Japanese uniform-bank-loan agreements (*Gintori 4-jō*) stipulates that a bank can seize as collateral any of a borrower's properties at any time. This enables bank lenders with small stakes to unsettle the rescue deal and to induce concessions from the main bank seeking work-out. (*Gintori 4-jō* caused lower bond credit ratings for Japanese companies in the 1970s because this clause subordinates bonds to bank loans; however, it is not a major issue today, as the proportion of bank loans in corporate capitalization has diminished).

5.2 Unique monitoring role

Banks monitor firms, but only the firms in a low-return state because the banks' focus of attention is on the probability of default. Joseph STIGLITZ puts it this way: "They need not concern themselves with either how good the best prospects of the firm are or what the probability is that the firm will make off like a bandit" (STIGLITZ 1985: 143). Therefore, banks are not interested in monitoring the wasteful use of free cash flows. Having a free cash flow signifies that a company is in a high-return state in the creditor's view.

AOKI (1994) claims that a main bank monitors even firms in a high-return state through the contingent governance structure of the Japanese main bank (MB) system. He divides the range of output states into three regions: the high, or team-control, region; the low, or MB-control, region; and the critical, or bankrupt, region. In the *low* MB-control region, "the MB takes over control of output, pays only minimum wages to team members and fixed contractual payment to the general creditors, and receives the residual." In the *high* team-control region, team members are the residual claimants, and "the MB may receive a certain share of the contractual payment in the capacity of a creditor." Thus "the residual claimant status is to provide positive incentives for team members" (AOKI 1994: 125).

In this model, a main bank has strong incentives to degrade the client firm's internal governance discipline when the firm, or team, is approaching the *high* team-control region because high performance means the main bank loses rents. To function as a monitoring system under this model requires that the bank have its client's best interests at heart. If we can assume this integrity, the main bank system hypothesis becomes quite uncomplicated. If we stick to the widely held assumption that a bank is a self-interested business entity, it leads us to conclude that monitoring by the bank works only when companies are in the neighbourhood of financial distress; when they are not, the bank wants to encourage even wasteful over-investments.

From the viewpoint of the agency theory, a main bank is in the same position as a fractional owner-manager. As long as a main bank can exert some influence on the managerial decisions of a firm, the bank can benefit from preferential banking transactions with the firm at the cost of the entire shareholders, just as a fractional owner-manager can pursue perquisites without assuming their full cost. The agency theory seems a more straightforward and powerful explanation of the banks' behaviour in the late 1980s than the main-bank-system hypothesis. Back then, main banks encouraged client companies to invest and borrow funds for wasteful purposes: *Zaiteku* loans, to set up financial subsidiaries in Japan and in London to invest in stocks and junk bonds; acquisitions of foreign corporations; speculative land purchases. A well-known result of these main bank solicitations is the acquisition of the luxury Westin Hotel chain by a construction company, the latter ending up suffering huge losses (*Nikkei Business* 1988).

Among the so-called rescue-operation cases by Japanese main banks, few are documented and examined in depth because the participants are taciturn. The case of Ataka & Co., however, is exceptionally well documented, as some participants spoke out, and the CEO of one of the banks involved gave an account of the process in his book (IROBE 1982). Ataka, a large trading company, went bankrupt in 1977. Its main bank's retired officer was the company's executive vice president, and an ex-employee of another creditor bank had held the position of internal auditor at Ataka. For monitoring purposes, these were of no use. Ataka had never audited its subsidiaries, practiced 'creative accounting', and changed the articles of incorporation to allow an executive to spend company money for his hobby—collecting classic cars. In general, a retired bank officer sitting on the board of a company seems to have little incentive to be a 'spy' because the rest of his career depends on his reputation within the company, not at the main bank from which he retired.

Besides networking, another advantage is stressed in the literature regarding the main-bank-system hypothesis: "By observing the movement of payments into and out of those settlement accounts on a daily basis, ... [a main bank can enjoy] an extremely advantageous position in terms of information" (AOKI, PATRICK, and SHEARD 1994: 14). When Ataka collapsed, the losses from domestic business amounted to 120 billion yen. The main bank recognized the company's financial distress only when Ataka reported the liquidity problem caused by the failure of a petroleum refinery project in Canada; this caused an additional loss of 80 billion yen. With settlement accounts, a bank can recognize a liquidity problem only after a long period of poor management practices, often in the last stage of financial distress.

In Ataka's work-out case, the Ministry of Finance intervened in the negotiations concerning the sharing of losses among 16 Japanese banks in the final stage. Among the primary beneficiaries were foreign banks; their loans were guaranteed by the main bank in the early stage of the work-out. This implies that the main bank makes concessions to avoid hold-outs rather than to execute an implicit loan guarantee.

6 Voluntary restructuring

It seems that in good times, corporate governance structure does not particularly matter. When markets are growing, few resources are left to waste, and managers can take pride in their business achievement, any governance system may work fine. The real test of a specific governance system comes when this golden age has ended.

As a legacy of the quasi-LBO era, when clear financial discipline came from strong cash flow constraints, the internal financial control system of Japanese companies is underdeveloped. Among traditional divisionalized companies, only 10 % set a return on investment as a yardstick for performance measurement—and even then, in a limited and primitive way (WATANABE 1994: 72). Assets are not clearly allocated among divisions, and financial costs (interest cost and overhead) are charged to the divisions in a loose way; divisions with a low performance are typically waived charges. This control system causes internal governance to crumble when ample financial resources become available. The central issue may be described as a *soft-budget constraints problem.*

Overwhelming pressure from activated shareholders changed the landscape of corporate America in the 1980s and seems to contribute to its strong performance in the 1990s. Some insist that this be the course Japan should follow. A reference to history may support the possibility of change. The highly stable ownership structure is only a post-war phenomenon. In the pre-war capital market, it was not uncommon for hostile shareholders to interfere with the management of publicly held companies. Even at a prestigious company like Kanebo, the top executive, Sanji Muto, was fired by a corporate raider when he declined the raider's coercive requests (TAKAHASHI 1977: 248). However, a market for corporate control is not likely to re-emerge.

Stable and friendly shareholders control approximately 55 % of outstanding shares (NRI 1996). Banks and life insurance companies own listed companies' shares at the request of their client companies. They do so in the expectation of getting banking or insurance business from the company—a typical reciprocity transaction. Some nonfinancial companies also hold the shares of nonaffiliated companies. In this case, a company in a weaker position in business transactions, namely a supplier, owns shares of its client company. As in the financial institution's case, it is considered as a 'safe keeper'.

Banks and life insurance companies may consider whether the cost benefit and the amount of cross-shareholding need to be reviewed. Although there are no established formulas for assigning the costs and the benefits to each party, cash transfers in the form of interest, dividends, and fees between two parties provide a basis for analysis. Interestingly, capital gains are not taken into account in most cases; indeed, these shares are never supposed to be sold. If a financial institution succeeds in persuading its client company that the cost of stable shareholding exceeds the return from the accompanying business transactions, an adjustment may take place. In some cases, artificial transactions for this purpose might be engineered.

Financial distress on the part of the stable shareholder may be the most appealing reason to get permission to sell the shares. There have been many claims since the beginning of the recession in the early 1990s that cross-shareholdings are dissolving. In fact, some banks, insurance companies, and industrial companies have been liquidating a portion of stable stock holdings (NRI 1996). Most of these are corporations whose balance sheets have seriously deteriorated due to nonperforming assets. To date, however, the overall impact on the stable shareholding structure is negligible. In 1996 banks, insurance companies, and business corporations still owned 60 % of outstanding Japanese stocks (ZENKOKU SHŌKEN TORIHIKISHO KYŌKAI 1997). The decline of their share from the previous year was less than one half percentage point. Banks and insurance companies that are not in serious financial distress have been keeping the shares of their clients, as the selling of shares results in a shrinking or a termination of financial business. Banks are still competing with each other to be chosen as a main bank, a stable shareholder, at initial public offerings.

Japanese business leaders and lawmakers today recognize that some measures to take shareholders' interests into the management decision process are necessary to shape up corporate Japan. The commercial code and the tax code have been changed since 1994 to make stock repurchases possible. Stock options, which were first introduced in 1995 by Sony, are to be adopted in more general ways by the subsequent changes in the commercial code. Among approximately 2000 public companies, 32 have bought back own shares, and 94 adopted stock options in 1997. The numbers have been increasing but are still small. Neither in policy nor in practice is a creation of a market for corporate control considered as a viable option.

Japanese corporate governance has been and will continue to be modelled on the paradigm of Chandler's managerial capitalism, where salaried managers determine long-term as well as short-term operating activities. This system depends heavily on internal governance for success. The experience in the late 1980s alerted managers to the malfunctioning of their internal control system. There were few Japanese companies that were concerned with ROE as a financial goal until the early 1990s. Now, approximately 20 % of listed companies set ROE goals (TŌYŌ KEIZAI SHINPŌSHA 1997). This goal setting is motivated by the internal need for standards to measure performance of business lines. How good a job can internal governance perform without shareholder pressure? It is more likely that companies in a competitive market realize the importance of internal governance. Even with its triple-A credit rating, Toyota is frugal: "[S]ince 1995, the company has wrung nearly $ 2.5 billion in costs from the system, mostly figuring ways to use fewer parts and stripping waste out of production" (*Business Week* 1997: 107).

Restructuring of the internal governance system will be a slower process in Japanese companies because of the lack of shareholder pressures, though it is a step in the right direction. As a Japanese treasurer has commented to the author: "On some occasions, I feel a U.S. treasurer's job is much easier than ours, as the capital market is looking over his or her shoulder. We have nobody behind us to urge us to change." By observing the ongoing process we will have a chance to evaluate the effectiveness of the internal governance system of modern corporations.

References

AOKI, M. (1994): Monitoring Characteristics of the Main Bank System: An Analytical and Developmental View. In: AOKI, M. and H. PATRICK (eds.): *The Japanese Main Bank System*. New York: Oxford University Press, pp. 109–141.

AOKI, M., H. PATRICK and P. SHEARD (1994): The Japanese Main Bank System: An Introductory Overview. In: AOKI, M. and H. PATRICK (eds.): *The Japanese Main Bank System*. New York: Oxford University Press, pp. 3–50.

BANK OF JAPAN (annual editions): *Shuyō kigyō keiei bunseki* [Analysis of the Financial Statements of Principal Enterprises]. Tōkyō: Bank of Japan.

BANK OF JAPAN (1984): *Nihon Ginkō hyakunen-shi* [A 100 Year History of the Bank of Japan]. Vol. 4. Tōkyō: Bank of Japan.

BERLE, A. A. Jr. and G. C. MEANS (1932): *The Modern Corporation and Private Property*. New York: Commerce Clearing House.

Business Week (1997): Toyota's Crusade, April 7, 1997, pp. 104–114.

CHANDLER, A. D. Jr. (1977): *The Visible Hand*. Cambridge, Mass.: Harvard University Press.

DONALDSON, G. (1994): *Corporate Restructuring*. Boston: Harvard Business School Press.

GILSON, S. (1996): Managing Default: Some Evidence on How Firms Choose between Workouts and Chapter 11. In: BHANDARI, J. S and L. A WEISS (eds.): *Corporate Bankruptcy*. Cambridge: Cambridge University Press, pp. 308–321.

GILSON, S., K. JOHN and L. LANG (1990): Troubled Debt Restructuring: An Empirical Study of Private Reorganization of Firms in Default. In: *Journal of Financial Economics* 27, pp. 315–353.

HONDA, S. (1991): *Ore no kangae* [My Ideas and Opinions]. Tōkyō: Jitsugyō no Nihonsha (first published in 1963).

IROBE, Y. (1982): *Watashi no ayunda kinyū-shi* [My Experiences in the Japanese Financial System]. Tōkyō: Nihon Keizai Shinbunsha.

JENSEN, M. C. (1986): Agency Costs of Free Cash Flow, Corporate Finance, and Takeovers. In: *American Economic Review. Papers and Proceedings* 98, pp. 323–329.

JENSEN, M. C. and W. H. MECKLING (1976): Theory of the Firm: Managerial Behavior, Agency Costs and Ownership Structure. In: *Journal of Financial Economics* 3, pp. 305–360.

JOHNSON, T. H. and R. S. KAPLAN (1987): *Relevance Lost*. Boston: Harvard Business School Press.

KAPLAN, S. (1989): The Effects of Management Buyouts on Operating Performance and Value. In: *Journal of Financial Economics* 24, pp. 217–254.

KURE, B. (1981): *Nihon no kinyūkai* [The Japanese Financial Industry]. Tōkyō: Tōyō Keizai Shinpōsha.

NAKAMURA, T. (1993): *Nihon keizai. Sono seichō to kōzō*. 3rd ed. [The Japanese Economy. Its Development and Structure]. Tōkyō: Tōkyō Daigaku Shuppankai.

NHK SHŪZAI-HAN (1977): *Aru sōgō shōsha no zasetsu* [Collapse of a Trading Company]. Tōkyō: Nihon Hōsō Shuppan Kyōkai.

Nikkei Business (1986): Shinki jigyō [New businesses]. March 31, 1986, pp. 6–22.

Nikkei Business (1988): M&A Aoki Kensetsu [M&A Aoki Construction]. January 4, 1988, pp. 52–56.

Nikkei Business (1991): Shin-Nihon Seitetsu [Nippon Steel]. February 25, 1991, pp. 6–21.

NRI (1996): *NRI Corporate Finance Research Report. Vol. 11*. Tōkyō: Nomura Research Institute.

STIGLITZ, J. E. (1985): Credit Markets and the Control of Capital. In: *Journal of Money, Credit, and Banking* 23, 2, pp. 133–152.

SUMITOMO BANK (ed.) (1985): *Sumitomo Ginkō-shi: Shōwa 50-nendai no ayumi* [Corporate History of Sumitomo Bank, 1975–1984]. Ōsaka: Sumitomo Bank.

TAKAHASHI, K. (1977): *Nihon no kigyō keieisha hattatsu-shi* [A History of Japanese Corporations and Top Managers]. Tōkyō: Tōyō Keizai Shinpōsha.

TAKASAKI, T. (1954): Mukashi no keieisha to ima no keieisha [Managers Yesterday and Today]. In: *Keidanren Geppō* [Keidanren Monthly], March, pp. 14–15.

Tōyō Keizai Weekly (1996): Sumitomo kigyō shūdan [Sumitomo Corporate Group]. January 8, 1996, pp. 110–117.

TŌYŌ KEIZAI SHINPŌSHA (ed.) (1997): *Kaisha shikihō* [Japan Company Handbook]. Spring 1997. Tōkyō: Tōyō Keizai Shinpōsha.

WATANABE, S. (1994): *ROE kakumei* [ROE Revolution]. Tōkyō: Tōyō Keizai Shinpōsha.

ZENKOKU SHŌKEN TORIHIKISHŌ KYŌKAI (The National Conference of Stock Exchanges) (1997): *Kabunushi bunpu jōkyō chōsa* [Annual Survey of Shareownership Distribution]. Tōkyō: Zenkoku Shōken Torihikisho Kyōkai.

Commentary

From Voice to Exit? Corporate Finance Management and Corporate Governance

Xavier RICHET

1 Introduction

The three papers presented by J. F. Estienne, H. Miyajima and S. Watanabe on the evolution of the corporate governance and financial discipline of firms provide interesting analyses of the behaviour and the control of the J-firm; these presentations allow to draw comparisons with alternative forms of organization and control in other market and transition economies where there is some doubt about the possibility of implementing a real and efficient outside control model. Finally, the papers raise some fundamental questions on the future of corporate governance of Japanese firms whose recent low performance may signal the end of the dynamic industrial organization in this country.

I shall concentrate on two main points:

- How are the recent trends with respect to the corporate governance of Japanese firms to be understood in the context of globalization and economic change?
- What lessons can be drawn from the Japanese experience of corporate governance concerning alternative ways of controlling firms elsewhere, both in other developed market and in transforming economies?

For scholars not familiar with the literature on the corporate governance of Japanese firms, it is necessary to go back to some basic writings on the subject and particularly some of AOKI's seminal contributions whose methodology has inspired the two contributions on the evolution of corporate governance of Japanese companies in this volume.

In his paper *Toward an Economic Model of the J Firm,* AOKI (1990) coined several 'principles of duality'. Two of these principles, the second and third one, help to understand the nature of control of the Japanese firm:

- the *second principle* states that there exists a narrow symmetry between a firm's internal organization and the nature of financial control,
- the *third principle* states that managerial decisions in Japanese firms are under a twin control, i. e., the double influence of capital owners and labour instead of a unilateral control by shareholders only.

In a more recent paper (AOKI & DINC, 1997), he goes further and gives an interesting definition of what he calls 'relational financing', specifying the nature of the main bank in allocating resources among firms within the same industrial group. According to AOKI, this system is composed of three complementary elements:

- a type of relational contracting between banks and firms (see the second principle above),
- a specific inter-bank relationship (mutual delegation of monitoring),
- a particular set of regulatory measures such as entry regulation, financial restraint, deposit guarantees, and restriction on market financing.

Recalling these theoretical points allows us to better understand the framework within which Japanese enterprises are evolving, to assess the impact of globalization and deregulation on enterprise behaviour and to see, as Watanabe puts it, how these changes have been responsible for the historically low return on equity. Subsequently, suggestions can be derived as to how it would be possible to change the system into a more efficient one.

2 The control system in the J-firm

2.1 The rationale of internal control

Miyajima and Watanabe both analyse the extent of and the rationality behind internal control of firm behaviour as well as the division of labour between main banks and firms' managers, respectively main lenders and main stakeholders.

Implicitly, banks do not interfere in the day-to-day management of firms, nor in the setting of firms' strategy even when the level of financing allocated to companies is high. Apparently, therefore, the budget constraint on companies is 'soft'. While main banks are also important shareholders of their companies, this latter function appears to be more neutral as in a market economy with a strong external control of firms.

A *co-operative game*—the horizontal co-ordination mechanism—takes place among banks and firms as long as companies are able to achieve a certain level of profitability which is set *ex ante*. As a consequence, firms enjoy substantial autonomy concerning their decision-making but also concerning the appropriation of part of their profits which Watanabe calls the "free cash". This confirms an earlier assumption that the Japanese firm is partly controlled by its employees (*3rd duality principle* according to AOKI) who are in a position to secure a level of cash flow higher than necessary to conduct and finance their business.

We can draw interesting comparisons with well-known theories (RICHET 1994: 156pp.) on the discretionary power of managers (Williamson), the X-inefficiency theory (Liebenstein), the non-maximization behaviour of managers (Baumol) or the existence of organizational slack. According to the Western literature, the existence of such slack or inefficiencies can be overcome through the implementation of incentive tools in order to reduce the gap between agents and the principal. On the contrary, it seems that in the model of the Japanese firm, the existence of 'free cash' is a device to expand the company and to maximize employees' incomes as long as the firm is able to attain an expected, if not *ex-ante* planned, level of profit compatible with the rate of growth of the company.

2.2 Conflict resolution inside the model of the Japanese firm

In his seminal paper, Miyajima analyses how companies are controlled when they fail to match their profitability targets. The relational financing rules allow to anticipate bad results. In the co-operative game between banks and firms, the negative consequences of a failure both for management and the main bank act as a pre-threat to the partners. Tough measures that could be taken by the principal are not necessarily rewarding for either of the parties and can contribute to lowering the reputation of the firm and to destabilize the management's internal authority, jeopardizing the company's internal equilibrium.

Top managers in Japan are respected and symbolize authority and competence. An open questioning of their power can have a durable negative effect on the reputation of the company. In order to strengthen its power, on the other hand, the main bank tries to exert its control over the company more effectively by sending a representative onto the board of the company. Formally, however, he is not considered an official representative of the main bank but, instead, becomes a member of the company. The research undertaken by Miyajima shows an interesting correlation between the profitability of firms and the turn-over among top managers during the different stages of growth of the Japanese economy, providing a good illustration of this co-operative game between banks and companies. It would have been worthwhile to learn more about the profiles of newly appointed top managers in order to have a clearer view of their background and to see what kind of skills are preferred to conduct the restructuring of defaulting companies.

With the opening up and the deregulation of financial markets in Japan, the question is if, and how (long) the third principle of duality proposed by Aoki (employee-controlled firm) can survive. *Watanabe* ends his paper by stating that in Japan a market for control does not and will not exist, and that the internal governance structure is the most important source of discipline for companies without a cash flow constraint. However, as he writes earlier, profitability is declining and firms are no longer in a situation where they can reach the expected level of profitability to procure the amount of cash flow necessary to effectively perform the principle of dual control of the firm.

Another interesting question raised by Miyajima's contribution deals with the behaviour of ostensibly neutral shareholders. Could their behaviour be influenced by the opening up of financial markets and, if so, to what extent? In which way may their 'time horizon' be affected and what could be the trade-off between main bank financing and equity financing through the stock market?

2.3 Corporate governance and pension funds

Estienne's paper which concentrates on the opening up and the transformation of the pension system illustrates the impact of both deregulation measures and the implosion of the financial *bubble.* Given economic stagnation and the previous mode of calculating expected returns on capital invested to finance pensions, the present pension fund scheme is not able to raise the amount of capital necessary to provide for the pensions of workers and *salarymen* as expected. Another effect of this system's crisis is that companies will have to become more active in managing pension funds as the former, over-regulated system has definitely failed. They will now have to compete with new entrants to this market. Here again, interesting comparisons can be drawn with pension fund systems and their experiences in Europe, due on the one hand to the growth of its own aging population and continued under-employment, and the constraints of the repartition system on the other. Many specialists and policy-makers are thus advocating to adopt a more market-oriented pension system which would also play a major role in disciplining the control of firms through financial markets.

3 A comparison of the corporate government system and lessons for the Japanese firm

The corporate governance system in Japan stands on the opposite side of a control-oriented financial system in which agency problems are resolved essentially through a market for corporate control. The size and importance of pension funds have increased the high velocity of these markets, and there is a positive correlation between this market velocity (the level of sales of shares) and the turn-over of managers in firms when profitability is declining sharply as has been witnessed a few years ago in the U.S. In Japan, the deregulation of pension funds might contribute to create a stronger pressure by financial markets and to reduce the role of internal control of firms.

The Japanese type of corporate control is not the only 'heterodox' way of controlling firms. In France, the distribution of property rights among industrial and financial firms and the tradition of State interventionism in industry have also produced a specific model standing somewhere between the systems of internal control and market control, respectively. The recent move towards a privatization of State-owned French enterprises over the last decade has not paved the way to the development of a market-control model of corporate governance. Continued cross-shareholding among a few groups (the so-called '50 new families') leaves no room for external control, neither by shareholders nor banks. The banking system, ruled by the State for a long time, generally has not exercised strong budget constraint on firms which have relied on their own capacity to generate capital in order to finance corporate growth. Banks have, for the most part, remained neutral—if not passive—, limiting their power over debtors. In other cases, when they have exercised their discretionary power in the absence of stronger corporate control, banks' financial strategies have often failed. A more indepth study of the turn-over at the head of French firms would probably reveal that only a weak correlation exists between profitability and top management turnover, even for private corporations.

As far as French public companies operating on competitive markets are concerned (i. e., producing and selling goods at market prices), corporate governance has evolved since the middle of the 1980s when management was being 'privatized', that is, when it was no longer constrained by certain specific regulations (concerning employment, business strategies, financing). The main pressure exerted on management was to restructure companies and to make them profitable. In this respect, even State enterprises belonging to non-competitive sectors have begun to enjoy more freedom since and have been asked to concentrate on their financial results.

Although the Japanese model of corporate governance is now being reevaluated, both experiences suggest that in a growth-led market environment, business strategy matters more than the quality and effectiveness of control methods as long as the overall profits generated by these activities can satisfy managers, shareholders and debtors alike.

It is not surprising that the specific types of industrial organization and corporate control which have developed in Japan are seen as options to pursue in countries undergoing deep economic transformations in order to solve the problem of industrial and financial restructuring of firms, both privatized and not yet privatized ones. In Russia, for example, the historically evolved framework of financial and industrial groups allows, albeit in a different way, the complex relations that have developed between suppliers and clients firms to continue. Introducing banks into this complex organization enables these groups to bring in soft loans needed for restructuring. However, compared to the Japanese experience, self-discipline will not be on their agenda unless the central bank and other financial institutions are able to strengthen the 'budget constraints'. In China, on the other hand, industrial groups up to now have not been relying on banks while budget constraints were weak, and new shareholding companies have not yet developed sufficient tools to exercise their control over firms. Instead, the central bank continues to provide soft loans to partially loss-making companies.

References

AOKI, M. (1990): Toward an Economic Model of the Japanese Firm. In: *Journal of Economic Literature,* Vol. XXVII (March), pp. 1–27.

AOKI, M. and S. DINC (1997): *Relational Financing as an Institution and its Viability under Competition.* Stanford University: Center for Economic Policy Research Publication N° 488, May.

BERGLÖF, E. (1997): Reforming Corporate Governance: Redirecting the European Agenda. In: *Economic Policy. A European Forum,* N° 24, April, pp. 93–123.

Industrial and Corporate Change (1996): Special Issue on Firms, Markets and Organizations. Vol. 5, N° 2.

MAYER, C. (1996): *Corporate Governance, Competition and Performance.* University of Oxford: School of Management Studies (April, mimeo).

POHL, G. ET AL. (1997): *Privatization and Restructuring in Central and Eastern Europe.* World Bank Technical Paper N° 368. Washington, D. C.: The World Bank.

RICARTE, P. (1997): Le redressement laborieux des banques japonaises. In: *Lettre de conjoncture de la BNP,* September, pp. 1–4.

RICHET, X. (1994): *Economie de l'entreprise.* Paris: Hachette.

Industrial Organization

VIII Recession and Globalization: What Future for Japanese Industrial *Keiretsu?*

Yveline LECLER

Japanese industrial *keiretsu* (groups of firms with a strong interdependence in terms of turnover) which contributed to the Japanese economic performance over the past decades, have been facing internal as well as external constraints since the 1980s. The rise of the yen after 1985, the liberalization of Asian markets and the high growth pace in this region have all provoked an increase of foreign direct investment and a relocation of firms. This in turn has affected the volume of orders to suppliers in Japan, leading them to take measures to adapt to the new situation of globalized purchasing networks. An international division of labour in Asia is taking place, away from the former concentration on national structures, resulting in a structural evolution of the Japanese purchasing system and therefore the *keiretsu.* Based on these present changes, the constitution of Nippo-Asian *keiretsu* is proposed as a possible scenario for the future.

1 Introduction

The word *keiretsu* covers several realities of industrial organization in Japan. First, it refers to those groups which have created a close interrelation between their member firms through the practice of cross-shareholding. These groups are either multi-sectorial (jigyō shūdan) such as the ones resulting from the pre-war zaibatsu, or mono-sectorial, which does, however, not preclude a strong product diversification (as in the case of the Matsushita group, a large firm in which the *keiretsu* amalgamates several affiliates, all involved in electrical equipment and electronic appliances, but all specialized in hi-fi, computers, household electricals, etc., or product commercialization). These two types of *keiretsu* are based on financial links, including a main bank belonging to the group. Aoki (1988) has qualified them as 'financial *keiretsu*', as opposed to another type of *keiretsu,* namely 'industrial *keiretsu*' for which financial links might exist but are not the main basis on which their existence depends.

Industrial keiretsu are the main concern of this paper, that is to say networks of closely related firms but on the basis of the supply of manufactured goods as components of products destinated to be marketed under the name of the final assembler. In other words, we refer to the subcontracting system, even though this term in its Western usage often only covers the reality of the lowest level of the *keiretsu*. This Japanese extension of the term 'subcontracting' to the whole supply network as 'industrial *keiretsu*' is based on historical roots, that is to say groups of firms with intense, often non-financial interdependency links.

The origins of industrial *keiretsu* are to be found in the development of Japan in the inter-war period, during the war, and in the postwar era. These origins confirm the fact that there is no 'Japanese fate' (or in other words no purely cultural determinants) that can explain the creation of the industrial *keiretsu*. On the contrary, history and a given socio-economic context led the country to elaborate coherent forms of organizations to solve specific problems, under the influence of government incentives. This means that industrial *keiretsu* are constructed entities and that they can be progressively substituted by others (if the pivotal institutions are re-shaped). What is really of importance then is not why industrial *keiretsu* were formed in Japan, but why they kept existing, considering that the context into which they were born has disappeared a long time ago?

In fact, the position of small and medium-sized Japanese firms integrated in these *keiretsu* has changed over time. As shown by WATANABE (1996), the process of economic catching up is responsible for the fact that firms were hierarchized. This is linked to the period when the quasi-exclusive strong dependence relation between firms of industrial *keiretsu* was increasing. Later, during the high-growth period, some firms assumed more independence, and thus exclusive and relative-dependence relations co-existed. As Japan's economy advanced to become a leading industrial nation, an increasing number of firms started to design their own strategies while remaining in a position of relative dependence towards their principal buyer in terms of turnover. It is this period of increasing independence that is the starting point of the disintegration of industrial *keiretsu*, presently reinforced by the recession and the process of globalization.

The history of the subcontracting system and industrial *keiretsu*, already largely covered by the literature (LECLER 1993, NISHIGUCHI 1994), will first be briefly summarized (section 2). Their organizational principles, although rooted in this history, nevertheless explain why they have kept in existence over time. These principles that have been confronted with mutations resulting from recession and the globalization of the Japanese industry will then be discussed (section 3). Finally, the present dynamics of change will be explored in the light of future trends (section 4).

2 The basis of industrial organization

In 1868, when the Meiji government set in motion the process of industrialization of Japan, the country was an agricultural nation in which 80 % of the population was involved in the primary sector. A few large land owners coexisted with a multitude of small tenant farmers unable to survive solely on their farming income. These small tenants, seeking some additional income, became involved in the traditional industry sector. As the labour supply thus was high, wages were kept at a low level. This situation allowed small local firms to maintain low production costs, though the creation of a real national market was limited. Instead, foreign markets were targeted. Foreign currencies earned through export activities were entirely destined to finance the number one objective: supporting large-scale emerging modern industries through imports of raw materials, equipment, and foreign technologies.

Though these large-scale industries benefited from the flow of new capital provided by the newly established financial system, they still suffered from a lack of capital accumulation. In order to solve this problem, large firms resorted to the subcontracting of local suppliers. This process was motivated by the fact that larger firms could thus avoid additional investments in production equipment to meet growing demand, focusing instead on the acquisition of modern technologies. In order to master these imported technologies, however, firms needed skilled workers that the rural workforce was unable to provide at the time. Therefore they had to train workers, inaugurating the principles of training within firms, the lifetime employment system and the seniority wage system (LECLER 1993).

As the build-up of large-scale modern industries was given priority, access to capital and thus new technologies was relatively restricted for small firms. Instead, they had to base their competitive advantages on an abundant unskilled workforce and low wage levels. Dualism[1] hence became a structural component on which industrial organization in Japan was based. A division of labour was thus created, giving the large firms the opportunity to subcontract their most routine tasks to smaller firms, benefiting from their low production costs. These low costs were maintained over a long time by the intense competition between subcontracting firms. As a consequence, the subcontracting system proved an effective means to absorb shocks of economic fluctuations in the pre-war period.

Keiretsu appeared with the Second World War when the government used certain coercion measures to restructure the war economy which at the time was facing severe equipment, supply and quality problems, all in a context of low technological efficiency. The main purpose of these measures was to concentrate production capabilities on the military sector. In order to rationalize these capabilities, each part of the *keiretsu* was given a precise function and a specific role in the production process. This structure, born under government pressures, consolidated the existence of the *keiretsu* as a group of hierarchically organized firms, but also instituted a new division of labour (*bungyō*) in which the subcontractors:

1 There are different aspects to 'dualism' as recognized in the literature: dualism in the labour market, dualism in the products market, and dualism in the capital market.

- supplied a single and specified client (parent firm), which in turn would provide the necessary production technologies, and
- were organized in a pyramidal structure with different levels (parent company, grand-parent company, etc.)

Depending on the sector, and assuming slightly different forms, the subcontracting system was widely used again in post-war Japan. First, the objective was to meet the growing American demand for supplies during the Korean War. Later, the adoption of mass production facilities was requested. However, the accumulation of capital remained a major problem for large firms which needed to renew and enlarge their production facilities. The subcontracting firms could continue to survive, as they did in the pre-war time, with old equipment bought from their customers, performing the most routine tasks of the production process.

In the first years of the post-war period then, a subcontracting system linked to economic and social dualism was apparently revitalized in Japan. Subcontracting was used to benefit from low production costs and, as a buffer, to absorb the fluctuations of demand, but within an internal logic of the pyramidal structure created by the *keiretsu*. This meant that parent firms subcontracted to their affiliated companies, imposing a price that led those suppliers to subcontract to 'grand-children companies' the easiest parts of the production process, in some cases even involving a third or fourth level. In this framework, dualism made cost reductions possible at each level of the pyramid, through the use of less qualified workers and lower wages. The government actually had to adopt several laws to protect small firms, for instance from delays of payment.

Around 1960[2] the need to give more complex tasks to the subcontracting firms appeared as a consequence of technical progress. The subcontracting firms were technologically lagging behind, facing difficulties in supplying products or becoming involved in the more complex technological processes requested by their customers. These factors were slowing down the overall growth trend and constituted a problem for quality improvement on which corporate competitiveness was based.

Assistance to the subcontracting firms came from the large firms, taking on several forms and evolving over time.[3] It appears fair to say that it was precisely this assistance that constituted the key to the survival of industrial *keiretsu*.

---

2 The year 1960 is seen as a turning point for the Japanese economy, mainly because the rural workforce surplus had by then been more or less absorbed, consequently reducing the wage gaps between large and small firms somewhat.

3 Assistance through loaning or transfering machineries (often out of date for large firms but sufficiant for the tasks subcontractors were in charge of), acquisition of a minority capital interest in the supplier, training-consultancy-assistance.

2.1 Industrial *keiretsu:* a relational mode of organization

When the necessity to take charge of, or to contribute to the process of increasing the technological level of the subcontractors and their workforce becomes part of the subcontracting modality, large firms create or activate several mechanisms of competence transfer (e. g., supplier associations, workforce transfer consultancy assistance, see also LECLER 1993). In this framework, the main customer/principal gives assistance concerning both technological and organizational aspects, providing information even beyond the immediate transaction such as projections of market development, new organizational devices, training tools etc.

This competence transfer generates what can be called 'social flows', embodied in continuous communication flows, workforce exchanges facilitating the transfer of information across firms, training programs, etc. (LECLER 1993). These social flows are constitutive elements of relations within the *keiretsu,* complementing the 'industrial flows' composed of 'hard' supply factors, such as product specifications or delivery times.

As these principles of social flows are reproduced by corporate employment and training systems and the functional division in firms, they can be taken into account in the relation between a customer and its suppliers/subcontractors. Just like the overall industrial structure, the employment system was developed to face the problems which arose during the industrialization process of the country. Hence, a certain similarity can be observed between the explanatory factors of the operation of the industrial *keiretsu* and the characteristics of the employment system: lifetime commitment/guarantee of orders on a long-term basis; internal mobility of employees, continuous coming and going of staff, *shukkō* (loaning of staff), and guest engineers working within the firms; on-the-job training/informal know-how transfer; etc.

Comparing the employment and the subcontracting systems, respectively, reinforces the point of view that the relational network existing within the firm and facilitating communication between departments and plants does not stop at firms' borders. These systems are, on the contrary, extended to the industrial *keiretsu* members. We may consider this extension between the customers' and suppliers' factories as an illustration of the Japanese attachment to the notion of flows rather than stocks, as is suggested by TURCQ (1992: 94–95) when he writes, "... Japanese people prefer thinking in terms of flows rather than in terms of stocks; they do not consider the latter as a sum of possessions, but they regard it as an accumulation or a source of potential flow."

We could also consider, as DORE (1987: 170) did, that cultural values such as goodwill and benevolence favoured the Japanese entrepreneurs to cope with hierarchized relations. Whatever the full explanation may be, the intense dependence on the main parent-company remains a determining factor for these *keiretsu* networks.

Even when inter-firm assistance consisted at first mainly of leasing or selling machinery, and especially later when know-how transfers became more organizational than technical, the existence of relatively exclusive links between customers and their suppliers/subcontractors constituted a fundamental determinant in the development of competence transfers. Although it is true that the competence transfer would not have grown to such a large extent without the dependence relationship mentioned above, it is also evident that the former is responsible for the fact that the dependence relationship has continued to exist over time.

2.2 Interactions between dependence relationship and competence transfer processes

The dependence relationship allows the principal situated at the top of the pyramidal structure to focus on his own activities, i. e., the strategic tasks of design and assembly. All the intermediate activities, including sub-assembly—and increasingly the conception of some components and functions—can be delegated to other firms without any risk of losing control of the production line.

In effect, the supplier/subcontractor has created a production process entirely dedicated to its client's needs, through the assistance/dependence relationship.This process is so deeply integrated that the satisfaction of the client is a matter of survival (this refers to the notion of quasi-workshop). Hence it is not in the interest of the subcontractor to cut this link. At the same time, the customer has made substantial investments to assure that his subcontractor will provide him with services based on a technical, human, and organizational culture which is largely the reproduction of his own. The client can thus expect his investments to be profitable (only) in the long run. To switch his subcontractor would imply high disengagement costs and long and expensive investments to engage with another firm.

The consequence of this interactive circle between the two partners is that it is of a mutual interest to make the relationship last on a long-term basis. It is precisely because subcontractors are guaranteed that they will not be excluded if they cooperate that they can adapt their production processes to the needs and specifications of the customer. The guarantee of a long-term relationship leads to a reinforcement of the dependence relationship.

Furthermore, the numerous transfers of competence over time create an environment of trust leading to the permanence of the system. The perception of such a guaranteed relationship results in a strong interest for cooperating at each level to maintain overall efficiency. This efficiency is supported by a synergy of actions stemming exactly from this process of competence transfer and strong dependence relationship.

In summary, we can say that the link between a supplier/subcontractor and his client has exhibited a strong dependence, and has been built on capital of reciprocal trust accumulating over the duration of the relationship. This link has been further maintained through numerous exchanges of personnel, ample communication, and the frequent meetings that the various competence transfers have required. The concept of customer diversification, although suggested on different occasions, has never substantially threatened the concept of the main customer, partly because the advantages for the actors of the *keiretsu* have always outweighed any inconveniences. Hence, this dependence relationship must not be considered a disadvantage for the subcontractor; many subcontractors have been able to develop their activities further through this process, such as from the production of parts to the production of entire components, aided by client firm assistance and competence transfers.

3 Recession and globalization: a new order for Japanese industry

In the 1980s and 1990s, especially after 1985, Japan has faced several internal and external issues that seem to pave the way for a significant evolution of the *keiretsu* system.

3.1 Internal and external constraints: the breaking point of the 1990s

At the internal level, a shortage in workforce partly resulting from demographic problems has led to new aspirations for the younger generation. The just-in-time system appears to have suffered from its own success and has lost part of its efficiency (traffic problems, lack of drivers, etc., see LECLER 1993). Furthermore, excessive speculation during the *bubble economy* may have led to a change in attitude by Japanese shareholders. At the external level, Japan has had to cope with pressures, notably from the US, leading to voluntary self-limitation agreements, the re-appreciation of the Yen at the Plaza meeting, demands for higher local-content ratios in FDI target countries, etc. As a consequence of the appreciation of the Yen, of the increasing number of relocations, and of the growth of Asian countries, competition with imported and re-imported products manufactured in Asian countries (especially parts and components) has also begun to set in, albeit from a low level in the 1980s (table 1).

However, even though these constraints first appeared in the 1980s, it is the 1990s and their conjunction between recession and globalization that must be seen as the starting point of change becoming more concrete. After the end of the *bubble*, the Yen kept rising, reaching a level below 100 yen to the dollar, and resulting in a new wave of plant relocations abroad. Though this wave was less massive than the one that occurred in 1985–1990, whole segments of major industries nevertheless disappeared from Japan such as household equipment, television and video, while Asia supplanted North

America as investment location region. The Newly Industrialized Economies (NIE), becoming increasingly expensive themselves, were then themselves left behind somewhat by the ASEAN countries and China, who appeared increasingly favourable as far as industrial investments are concerned. More and more Japanese firms have thus turned to purchasing abroad as shown in graph 1.

Table 1: Substitution of parts previously ordered from suppliers in Japan by purchasing abroad

		(December 1988, firms percentage)
No substitution	**74.6 %**	
– No substitution yet and no projects for the future		56.3 %
– No substitution yet but projecting to do it in the future		18.3 %
Substitution	**25.4 %**	
– Substitution around 1 to 9 %		22.5 %
– Substitutions of more than 10 %		2.9 %

Source: CHŪSHŌ KIGYŌ HAKUSHO (1989: 103)

Graph 1: Evolution of international purchasing

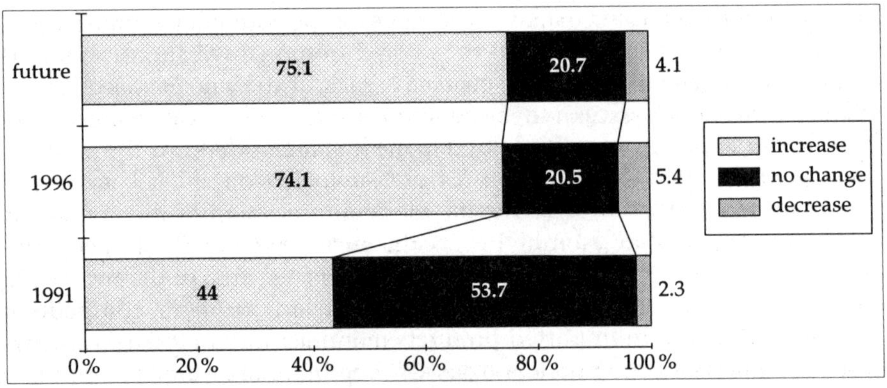

Note: Manufacturing industry, percentage of parent firms' purchases inside Japan, first rank and second rank subcontractors included

Source: CHŪSHŌ KIGYŌCHŌ (1997: 157)

3.2 Strategies to regain competitiveness: towards Asian networks

In the 1980s, product competitiveness in Japan slowly turned from production to design. The time needed to bring a new product to the market, and the number of options and variants available, were becoming more important than a simple focus on costs only. By contrast, in the 1990s, cost was taken again as the most significant strategic factor as confirmed by the development of evaluation/selection criteria of subcontractors (table 2).

Table 2: Evaluation criteria for subcontractors by parent firms

Ranking/ criteria	1987	1992	1996
1	reliability of delivery 42.0 %	cost down 31.6 %	cost down 55.2 %
2	enhancing product quality and complexity 26.8 %	reliability of delivery 30.1 %	shortening of delivery time 31.7 %
3	mass-production capabilities 26.4 %	shortening of delivery time 28.7 %	enhancing product quality and complexity 25.3 %
4	stability of payment for raw material and parts 20 %	quality control 25.1 %	quality control 22 %
5	quality control 19.9 %	enhancing product quality and complexity 25.1 %	broad variety, small-lot production 21 %
6	cost down 19 %	broad variety, small-lot production 18.8 %	reliability of delivery 14.7 %
7	shortening of delivery time 12.5 %	mass-production capabilities 13.2 %	capacity of adaptation to a sudden change of orders 11.3 %

Source: CHŪSHŌ KIGYŌCHŌ (1997: 160)

Important measures, some of them not entirely new, were undertaken. They did not all have a direct effect on the transformation of the *keiretsu*, however. Some of these measures were intended to revise the design methods which had led to what is called 'fat design' (FUJIMOTO 1994). This refers to waste caused by an excess of personnel in engineering departments, non-visible component quality aspects or an excessive number of components for every change in the product range.

The break with this strategy of fat design led to a policy of increasing component commonality, either by using the same components in several products or product generations, or by agreement with other customers (especially in the automobile industry) to jointly use product components that are produced on a larger scale and consequently at a lower cost.

Let us take as an example the case of a first-rank supplier within the automobile industry who managed 60 to 80 different varieties of one component, while 70 % of the whole volume supplied concerned only 7 to 8 of these.[4] In 1994 this supplier proposed to several car makers to study the possibility manufacturing only a limited number of standard components which could be jointly used, enabling them to concentrate orders and to cut cost.

The main consequence for the suppliers and subcontractors was a stronger concentration of orders for a small number of components, and thereby a higher concentration on a few suppliers or subcontractors. Other suppliers thus faced a decrease in their activities and had to look for new customers in order to compensate for the loss. A 1996 survey of the SME (small and medium-size enterprises) Agency shows that 22.4 % of the parent firms attributed the concentration of the number of their subcontractors at least partly to the cut in ordered components due to commonalization (CHŪSHŌ KIGYŌ HAKUSHO 1997:153).

Suppliers were also asked to reduce their own costs (as before whenever the Japanese economy went through a recession) not only at the production level, but also at the design level in which they are now increasingly involved. For instance, in the automobile industry in 1994, Toyota had to impose a 15 % reduction of costs on its suppliers over a three year time period. Nissan imposed a 10 % cost reduction and Honda 15 % (FOURIN 1995). This was obviously not a new practice, but it has encouraged the move abroad to Asian countries for suppliers, a decision facilitated in an environment of a strong Yen.

At the same time, most of the customers have revised their purchasing policy. The framework in which a supplier is selected has become international. The selection criteria now concentrate on a supplier's competitiveness more than on the long-term relationship or mutual trust. Firms who have recently selected new suppliers/subcontractors forward the following reasons: "the new supplier's prices are lower (46 % of sample firms)", "the supplier's specialized technology (45.2 %)", "the supplier is excellent in quality and precision (38 %)" (CHŪSHŌ KIGYŌ HAKUSHO 1997:163). Reasons such as "long-lasting relationship" or the like that used to be found before, have completely disappeared from the survey's answer. Thus the borders of the industrial *keiretsu* have begun to be crossed. For the suppliers, this has contributed to their customer diversification and to their search for greater competitiveness through relocating production activities to Asian countries where labour costs are lower.

Apart from incentives to be present in future growth markets (table 3), a major concern for firms opening or extending new plants in Asia clearly are these countries' low labour costs. However, some suppliers have also been requested by their clients to partake in this relocation process. While many of these investments must be considered as an export substitution from Japan to local production in these countries (graph 2), a growing number of com-

[4] This example is based on interviews conducted in 1994 by the author. The firm has requested anonymity.

ponents made in Asian countries have actually been re-imported to factories located in Japan. This shows that the purpose of FDI has not been limited to the servicing of local markets.

Table 3: Corporate objectives when investing abroad, manufacturing industries

	% of firms
Potential of market growth in host country	55.0
Reduce costs	50.0
Hire cheap labour	46.0
Counter the decrease in competitiveness due to high yen	21.7
The buyer requested that we follow him abroad	11.0

Source: ŌSAKA SHŌKŌ KAIGISHO (1993)

Graph 2: Origin of purchase by firms located in Asia in the electronic industry

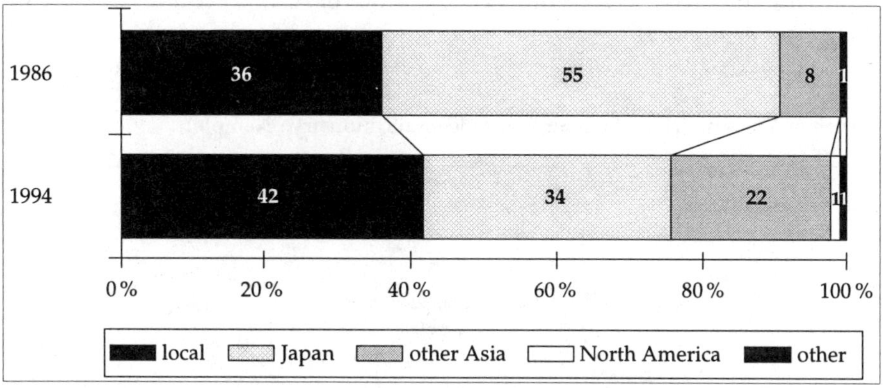

Note: Total amount of purchasing is 40 billion yen for 1986 and 2,400 billion for 1994.

Source: CHŪSHŌ KIGYŌCHŌ (1997: 133)

In some sectors, an Asian division of labour actually seems to be taking shape, leading to a growing amount of trade within Asia. Japanese imports and exports to and from Asian countries have significantly increased since the end of the 1980s, as well as cross-trade between Japanese plants located in Asia.

Let us consider the case of Matsushita.[5] The strategy originally developed by Matsushita had been to supply each market through local production, creating a 'mini-Matsushita' in each country that offered a sufficiently large market. In the 1990s, Matsushita changed its strategy to a country/product

[5] Interviews conducted by the author in September 1995.

specialization. In effect, the group has been transforming these 'mini-Matsushitas' for the production of one product in each country, which then would serve as a base for exportation to other countries in the region. This strategy aims to restructure the Matsushita group not only in Asia, but also in Europe and in the USA, with London and New Jersey as the respective network coordinator location.

As far as Asia is concerned, Singapore and, to a lesser extent, Hong Kong (for China) are nowadays the turntable for Matsushita's networks, notably for supplies of parts. It is from these two places that Matsushita makes its purchasing decisions of parts, components or products for the whole Asian region. From there, Matsushita then dispatches parts and components to its various plants. This regionalization of the division of labour is in fact easier to institute for electronics firms than for the automobile industry where the product is less complex and the weight of industrial *keiretsu* is not so strong. However, we may still conceive of this as a general trend that seems to be taking shape, aided by trade liberalization programmes such as BBC (Brand-to-Brand Complementation) or AICO (ASEAN Industrial Cooperation), and following the increase in technical capabilities of ASEAN countries and China (graph 3, 4 and 5).

Graph 3: Asian division of labour in the electronic industry (example)

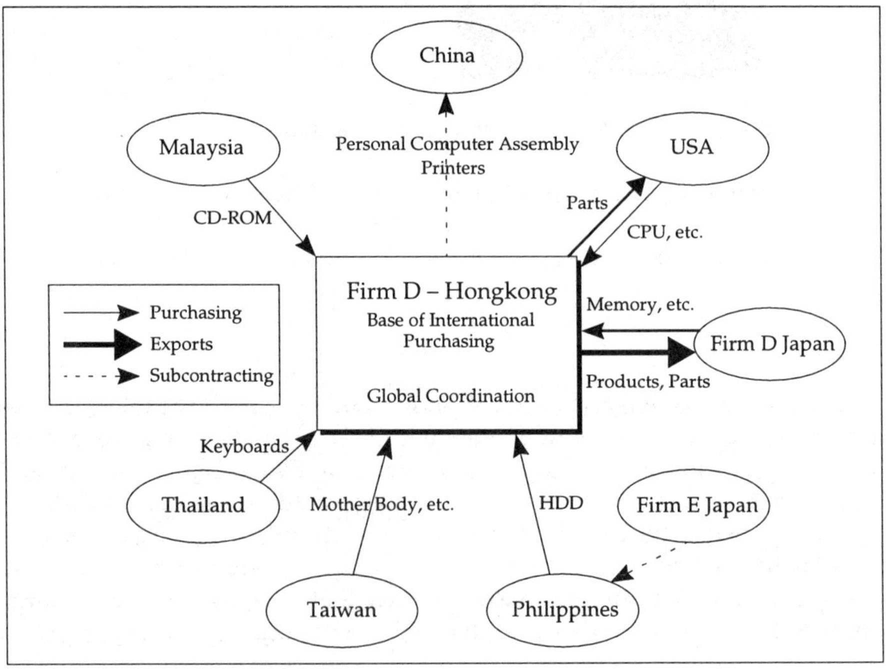

Source: CHŪSHŌ KIGYŌCHŌ (1997: 134)

Graph 4: Asian division of labour in the car parts industry (example)

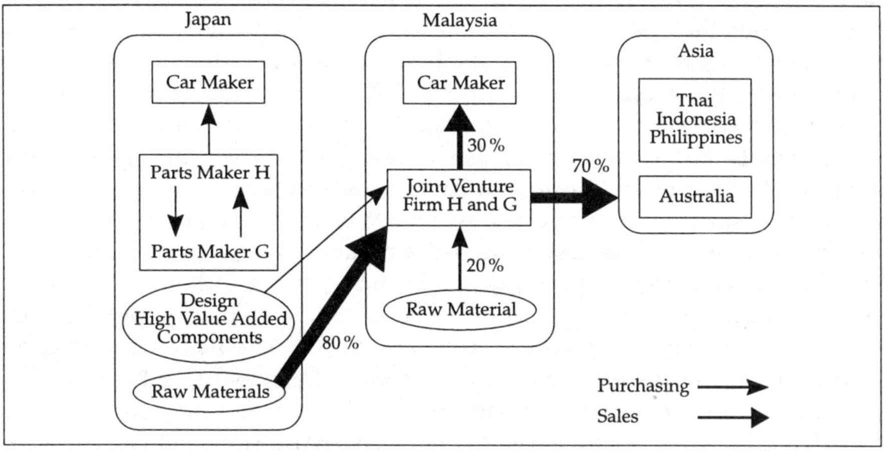

Source: CHŪSHŌ KIGYŌCHŌ (1997: 138)

Graph 5: Purchasing network of Toyota in ASEAN

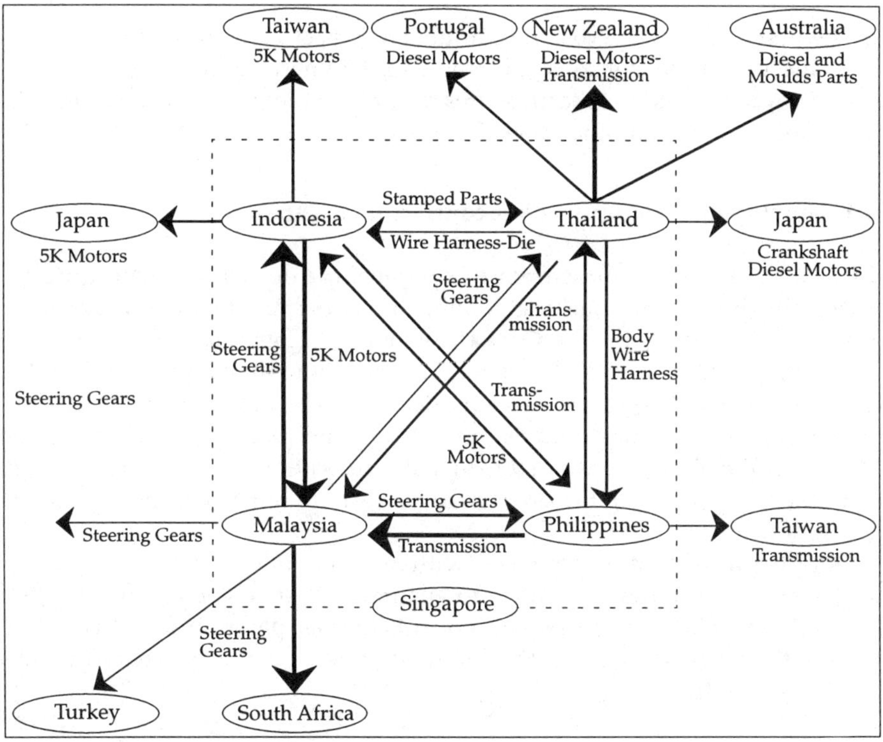

Source: FUKUDA, R. (1996)

This trend can only result in less orders for Japanese suppliers located in Japan, and can only create incentives for them to search for new customers, to re-evaluate their position in the network, or to also relocate to stay within the panel of suppliers selected on the basis of cheaper Asian production.

Of course, the present crisis within the Asian countries will affect these dynamics. Over the short term, foreign investments to ASEAN countries will probably slow down. Japan, also involved in the crisis, may have to cut back on its investment strategies. Even if comprehensive data is not yet available, some smaller firms are now seen to be withdrawing from the area. But in the long run, Japanese firms will probably have to continue sustaining their investments. Especially smaller firms, being rather flexible, may (re)open facilities if new opportunities arise. The devaluation of local currencies will enhance the competitiveness of ASEAN-made components. Taking these contrasting factors into account, the extent to which the dynamics of purchasing restructuring is affected will not necessarily be so broad and the previous trend of a growing Asian division of labour appears to remain intact.

4 What future for the Japanese industrial *keiretsu?*

In the first half of the 1990s, the cumulated impact of the recession, a strong yen, and relocation is thus considerable for Japanese suppliers/subcontractors. They are forced to take measures to adapt to the shift from a national division of labour to an Asian one.

4.1 The impact on suppliers/subcontractors in Japan

Most suppliers/subcontractors are experiencing a decrease in their turnover, especially due to a diminishing volume of orders from their main customers (graph 6). A survey by the Ōsaka Chamber of Commerce (ŌSAKA SHŌKŌ KAIGISHO SANGYŌBU 1993) shows that in 1993, more than half (54.5 %) of the 110 sample firms had recorded such a decrease. The slowdown of the national market can be considered as one of the main reasons for this situation (74.5 % of the above mentioned firms). But relocations and the procuring of components produced abroad at a lower cost are other reasons mentioned (30 % of firms).

Suppliers/subcontractors faced with such variations in the volumes of order are seeking new solutions to ensure their survival: enhancing their capabilities to introduce new components to their parent firms, diversification of their customer base, development of new products or entering new business activities (graph 7).

Graph 6: Reasons given by subcontractors to explain their decrease in sales (1996)

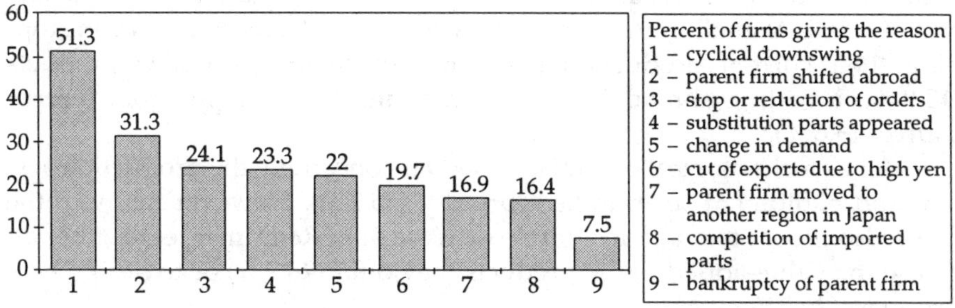

Source: CHŪSHŌ KIGYŌCHŌ (1997: 166)

Graph 7: Methods of adaptation by subcontracting SMEs

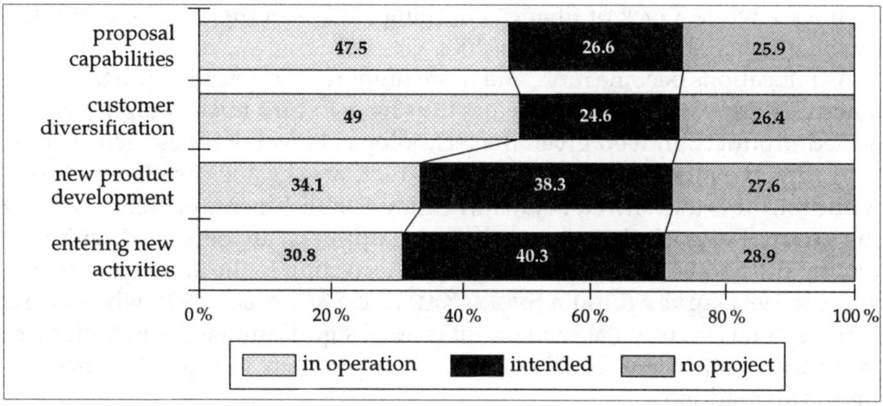

Source: CHŪSHŌ KIGYŌCHŌ (1997: 171)

Depending on their position within the division of labour and on the industries they belong to, different aspects are emphasized; nevertheless it appears that in most cases a single measure is not enough to secure the necessary adaptation. Therefore several actions are often simultaneously undertaken, as a survey of suppliers in the metal transforming industry, again undertaken by the Ōsaka Chamber of Commerce, shows (ŌSAKA SHŌKŌ KAIGISHO 1994). When asked about the measures they plan to implement, the sample firms answered that they intend to activate the three following elements (classified by decreasing order of importance):

- Increase technological control and R&D in order to sustain competitiveness owing to product quality and sophistication (50.8 %)
- Cut production costs to be able to compete on price (45.6 %),
- Specialize in small batches and very short delivery times—which units established abroad cannot easily do (43.6 %).

Given the percentage rates of the firms that answered in favour of each of the above three points, most are clearly intending to act simultaneously on several of them. A smaller number of firms considers decreasing or even stopping their current production lines and turning toward new products (12.8 %), investing abroad (9.2 %) or procuring their supply from foreign sources (5.6 %).

As far as technological control and R&D is concerned, the production system and equipment seem to be a priority (30.2 %). However many of the firms also choose to make an effort to increase their R&D in order to either increase the value-added of the products they offer (26.7 %) or to design new products (26.3 %).

The most frequent problem for firms intending to undertake prototype design and production is related to the availability of skilled labour (46.9 %). The larger firms of the sample are the ones that suffer most from this problem (86.7 % of the firms with 100–299 employees and 65 % of the firms with more than 300), while a lack of financial backing (34.7 % of the total) is rather felt by the very small firms (less than 100).

As relocations become more and more numerous, especially into the Asian countries, suppliers/subcontractors thus have to turn toward higher value-added products. Indeed given the technological level of investment in host countries, the more undifferentiated products are the ones produced abroad while the units that stayed in Japan, be they establishments or subsidiaries of the group that goes abroad or merely its suppliers, are entrusted with producing the goods at the top of the range. According to the above-mentioned August 1993 survey (ŌSAKA SHŌKŌ KAIGISHO SANGYŌBU 1993), whether the firm itself has invested abroad or not is not a significant factor. In both cases more than half of the firms[6] believed their products in Japan had become more value-added.

This trend, properly considered as the only means to face the recession, is not always easy to implement in different industrial sectors and for all types of suppliers (type of production, size of the firm). It is a trend very visible in the electrical/electronics sector, where it is simultaneously accompanied by a production transfer from one product range to another. However it seems to be more delicate in the automobile industry (LECLER 1995). In all cases, however, this process causes a recomposition of the supplier networks on a large scale which confirms, to a certain extent, a mutation from previous organizational and structural principles.

4.2 The relational basis threatened by network recomposition

Not all the suppliers are facing the new network definition and the changes occurring with regard to purchasing management principles in the same

[6] 50.4 % of the firms that have invested abroad and 53.4 % of those that have no foreign establishment.

way. The most efficient suppliers are not the problem, i. e., those situated at the first level, large firms that can supply both Japanese customers and foreign firms, competing with Western firms on international markets and developing strategies similar to those of their clients. For these firms, recession and globalization are elements which have been an incentive for relocation on one hand and the search for product innovation on the other hand.

The suppliers situated at the first level, but whose competitiveness ratio is below average and whose production is not strategic, together with suppliers situated at the second level, often very specialized but more technologically and financially fragile, have to face high competition from products made in Asia and cannot always relocalize. The local content requirements in industrialized countries, as well as in fast developing countries, have led to a revision in purchasing that is against these suppliers' interests. In third markets as well as in Japan, they now face competition from products made in Asia. The loss in their turnover (see table 4) can only be compensated by moving up the value-added chain and by diversifying their clients, an option again not open to all of them.

Table 4: Variation in the volume of orders to subcontracting SMEs over the last four years

%-change from the previous year

Evolution of turnover	Percent of firms
Increase	11.3
Uncertain	9.0
Decrease – less than 10%	14.1
Decrease – between 10% and 20%	22.7
Decrease – between 20% and 30%	23.5
Decrease – more than 30%	19.4

Source: CHŪSHŌ KIGYŌCHŌ (1993: 21)

At the bottom of the pyramid, the small subcontractors (third or fourth rank) engage in many simple and common processes. They can adapt somewhat more easily because there will always be simple jobs to do for closely located customers. This is confirmed by the percentage of firms targeting their activities on small-scale production for quick delivery. Other, less specialized firms, can survive by working for various sectors.

Although it is true that small subcontractors are fairly flexible, there are also firms in which managers/owners are old and where there is no successor, which choose to cease their activities in light of the difficult environment. Firms disappearing by 'natural death' are not rare. In sum, the traditional industrial organization shaped as a pyramid is undergoing major change (for more details see LECLER 1995).

Facing new and various constraints, the suppliers/subcontractors' first strategy is, as mentioned before, to search for new outlets and to increase the number of their customers. This is true whatever the position and the size of the firm is, and whether suppliers/subcontractors are establishing their activities abroad or not. Customer diversification seems to be an irreversible trend. Though customer diversification is not a new process for suppliers, already being on the agenda in the 1970s and 1980s, the present dynamics are happening on a larger scale. It is precisely because change happens on a larger scale that it constitutes a new issue.

In effect, the greater the number of customers increases, and especially the greater the rate of turnover realized through a single customer diminishes, the weaker the dependence towards that customer becomes. Furthermore, the necessity for suppliers to undertake more value-added production to sustain competition from Asian countries, instituting additional design capabilities, R&D etc., consolidates these dynamics. In fact, technological improvements, knowledge accumulation (design, prototypes), internationalization experience, etc. may even lead to a technological dependence of the customer on his suppliers. This situation, experienced in Europe, will thereby gradually constitute an *inversion* in the balance of power in Japan.

The strong dependence of the supplier towards its main customer, as we have seen, was a key element of the traditional system. It is because there was a quasi-exclusive dependence on a specific customer that the latter could transfer his competencies, and delegate more and more responsibilities to his suppliers without the risk of losing control over the production line. It is because of the competence transfer mechanisms that the 'social flows' became constitutive elements of the relation between customers and their suppliers/subcontractors. Today, however, the dependence and its side effect—the competence transfer—are apparently not perceived as necessary any longer, due to the discussed changes in the surrounding context.

On the other hand, it was because there were competence transfers and numerous exchanges, i. e. the 'social flows', that reciprocal trust was established and that the relationship was considered on a long-term basis. Those relational mechanisms have largely contributed to the performance of firms through the symbiosis and trust that they embodied. What kind of substitutes will be found to maintain this past high performance? The trust environment already has started suffering from the attitude of some customers, who, losing part of their competitiveness on international markets, are tempted to realize short-term economies. On the basis of a system rewarding the best offers, a main characteristic of Western practices, orders eventually go to firms which are not part of the *keiretsu* and especially to firms which are partly or totally foreign.

The basis of the relational system is also facing geographical problems caused by relocation. Production plants are further and further away from design departments, and the process of relational mechanisms, e. g., numerous visits on a quasi-daily basis, has become more complex, resulting in the transforming of exchange modalities between production units and their links with suppliers.

The constraints and determinants of globalization are certainly bringing deep changes that justify the debate on the disappearance of the *keiretsu* or their shrinking (SATO 1992). Nothing is yet definite, however, and instead of discussing the disappearance of *keiretsu*, it would be wiser to consider, at this stage, that the hierarchical pyramid structure of their division of labour is weakening, being replaced by networks which are globalized and more complex, centred around an Asian division of labour in which foreign firms play their part, and in which information circulates on a less personalized basis.

4.3 Towards Nippo-Asian industrial *keiretsu*?

At present, we can observe a convergence between Western and Japanese systems. Several relational principles have been introduced in Western countries following the Japanese success. Japanese transplants in the USA or in Europe (especially in the United Kingdom) have permitted us to test the adaptability of several Japanese principles of management of customers/supplier relations in a different social context (see, for example, ABO 1995). American or European suppliers that have benefited from competence transfers from their Japanese customers have restructured themselves and have made improvements in their technological and organizational capabilities. The Japanese system itself, however, particularly efficient as long as overall growth could be sustained, is presently at a turning point in its history. It is attempting to restructure itself through the adoption of practices often seen in conjunction with the process of corporate globalization (transplants, introduction of Japanese practices by Western firms, etc.). At the same time, Japanese firms are moving away from relational dynamics and becoming more transactional than they were in the past.

The present period is then an era of instability for *keiretsu*, and of a 'transactionalization' process of the relations between the various members of groups. This change can be viewed in terms of the non-adaptability of the relational model, at least in the main part, to a period of lower or fluctuating growth. It can be considered as a convergence phase or as a hybridization of Western and Japanese models, due to learning permitted by the globalization of firms. Nevertheless, recent developments can also be seen as a revitalization of pre-war and the immediate post-war Japanese practices, i. e., a country characterized by a growth jolt, linked to war episodes. In effect, are we going to see a resurgence of subcontracting as a means to absorb the macroeconomic fluctuations (buffer role) that the high economic growth period had made disappear, or that was confined to small firms? The context of Japanese society has naturally changed, and we can hardly imagine that Japanese suppliers could nowadays play the same part as the one played by small and medium-size firms in the past. Nevertheless, in the dynamics of globalization, small and medium-size firms from *other* countries of the Asian region could be playing this part. The Japanese firms' relentless pursuit of low labour costs in other countries in the early 1990s, when the Yen threatened to bring about a long-term drop in competitiveness, seems to be confirming this process.

Extrapolating from the various present trends, we can offer a possible scenario for the future, with all the possible errors that such an attempt includes. In Japan, firms belonging to industrial *keiretsu* in the past are becoming more autonomous from one another, searching for new customers, and increasing the sophistication of their products, leading to a break-down in the relational principles. If this trend continues, the Japanese purchasing system will resemble more closely a 'buying by catalogue' system, delivering to factories in Japan or abroad. This trend, however, is naturally confined to firms that have developed their own design or R&D capabilities.

In contrast, the past relational principles could be relevant again for the constitution of transnational networks in Asian countries. We could then imagine the constitution of *keiretsu* as:

- Japanese firms supplied by the world (or Japanese) market for strategic and highly sophisticated components, situated at the centre of a network in which
- upper levels would consist of firms in Thailand, Malaysia, etc. (Japanese transplants or firms linked to those originating from Japan), to which necessary competencies would be transferred, so that they could meet the need for sophistication, quality, etc., essential for Japanese product competitiveness. Those firms would be strongly, but not exclusively, dependent on a particular customer.
- Lower levels would include local firms and/or Japanese subsidiaries in Vietnam, Burma, etc., in charge of more simple processes, and absorbing the economic fluctuations caused by the Yen and by changes in demand.

Naturally, this may be one of the most uncertain parts of the scenario: Japan would need to fully integrate the concept of globalization in its mind-set in order to also transfer advanced technologies on a large basis as it has occurred within the former Nippo-Japanese *keiretsu*. The societies of host countries would also need to accept such structures and practices.[7]

In the electronics and electrical appliances industry, as well as in textiles, in which relocalization to Asian countries started before that in the automobile industry and where products are less complex, this type of structure is already appearing. Regional head offices, generally located in Singapore or Hong Kong, are selecting suppliers and subcontractors within the whole of the Asian region, on the basis of the best quality/price ratio but without competence transfer, are managing the supply system, and are dispatching

7 According to discussions with Tetsuo ABO, it seems that competence transfer practices are easier to establish in Taïwanese and Korean firms than in those from ASEAN.

parts to related factories as mentioned before. The generalization of such a scenario, thus, seems to be plausible, at least for some of the industries.

5 Conclusion: The changing Asian situation

The relevance of the proposed scenario and the strategies for an Asian division of labour, as well as the nature and forms of supply networks and exchange flows for the 21st century, strongly depend of the industries concerned. Between a rather horizontal division of labour as in the textile and the household appliances industries for example, and the very hierarchized or differentiated one of personal computers, or car manufacturing on the other side, the respective evolution will not, in most likelihood, tend towards the same network structuration (graph 3 and 4 above). Generally speaking, strategies will partly remain dependent on the measures taken by potential and present host countries to attract or constrain foreign investments and to structure their national industry (LECLER 1997). They will also be dictated by future directions of currency exchange rates and by the resulting changes in the comparative advantages of the nations concerned.

It seems that the tendency of internationalization of the division of labour in Asian countries is irreversible even if the present Asian crisis will leave some scars. What could be at stake in the area is a change in the position of investing countries mostly within the ASEAN area, but as far as the future of Japanese *keiretsu* is concerned, it seems that Japanese firms are already too deeply involved to have any interest to back off. Therefore, firms will probably continue to invest (even at a lower pace) to increase their integration rates and to cope with the national or regional regulations in terms of local content and so on. This will necessarily push *keiretsu* restructuring further.

References

ABO, T. (1995): A Comparison of Japanese 'Hybrid Factories' in the U.S., Europe and Asia. In: *Management International Review* 35, Special Issue 1/95, pp. 79–93.

AOKI, M. (1988): *Information, Incentives, and Bargaining in the Japanese Economy.* Cambridge/Mass.: Cambridge University Press.

CHŪSHŌ KIGYŌCHŌ (1989, 1993, 1997): *Chūshō kigyō hakusho* (White Paper on Small and Medium Sized Firms). Tōkyō: Chūshō Kigyōchō.

DORE, R. (1987): *Taking Japan Seriously.* Stanford: Stanford University Press.

FOURIN (1995): *1995 Nihon jidōsha buhin sangyō no Ajia jigyō tenkai: chōtatsu kōzō o kaeru Ajia de no jigyō kakudai* [The Shift to Asia of Car and Car-parts Industry: Increased Activities in Asia and the Changes in the Purchasing Structure]. Nagoya: Fourin Kabushiki Gaisha.

FUKUDA, R. (1996): *ASEAN ikinai-gai no kokusai bungyō taisei BBC/AICO/CEPT* [The International Division of Labour through the BBC/AICO/CEPT System in and outside the ASEAN Area], unpublished manuscript.

FUJIMOTO, T. (1994): *Nōryoku chikuseki no purōsesu to kajō tekiō: jidōsha sekkei no kēsu* [The Process of Knowledge Build-up and Excess Capability: The Case of Design in the Car Industry]. Discussion Papers Series n° 94-J-18 Faculty of Economics. Tōkyō: University of Tokyo.

HARADA, Y. (1995): Ajia to no kokusai bungyō no eikyō [Impact of the International Division of Labour with Asia]. In: *TBR Keiei Kankyō Rebyū*, n°2, pp. 9–12.

KAGEYAMA, K. (1996): Ajia ni okeru jidōsha sangyō no hatten: Toyota shisutemu o chūshin to suru kokusaiteki saihensei [The Development of the Car Industry in Asia: International Restructuring Centred on the Toyota Production System]. In: *Seikai Keizai Hyōron* 40, n° 1, January, pp. 59–68.

LECLER, Y. (1993): *Partenariat industriel: la référence Japonaise* [Industrial Partnership, Japan as a Reference]. Limonest: l'interdisciplinaire, collection technologies.

LECLER, Y. (1995): Délocalisations industrielles et restructuration du système de sous-traitance [Industrial Relocations and Restructuring of the Subcontracting System]. In: *Ebisu* n° 10, July/September (Tōkyō: Maison Franco-Japonaise), pp. 7–32.

LECLER, Y. (1997): Libéralisation des investissements étrangers: la surenchère entre les pays de l'ASEAN et la Chine [Liberalization of Foreign Direct Investment: the Competition between China and ASEAN]. In: *Informations et commentaires* n° 98, April/June, pp. 5–11.

NISHIGUCHI, T. (1994): *Strategic Industrial Sourcing: The Japanese Advantage.* Oxford: Oxford University Press.

ŌSAKA SHŌKŌ KAIGISHO SANGYŌBU (1993): Zaihan seizōgyō no kaigai shinshutsu dōkō [Foreign Penetration of Osaka's Manufacturing Industry]. Ōsaka: Ōsaka Shōkō Kaigisho.

ŌSAKA SHŌKŌ KAIGISHO (1994): Zaihan sokeizai sangyō no jittai ni kansuru chōsa [Results of Surveys on the Situation of the Primary Metal Processing Industries in the Ōsaka Region]. Ōsaka Shōkō Kaigisho.

SAKO, M. (1992): *Prices, Quality and Trust. Inter-firm Relations in Britain and Japan.* Oxford: Oxford University Press.

SATO, Y. (1992): Kokusaika no shinten to shitauke bungyō kōzō: – "gaikan": rekishi no naka de henbō suru Nihonkei shitauke bungyō seisan shisutemu [The Growth of Internationalization and the Structure of the Division of Labour in Subcontracting Activities – "A General Point of View": Lectures in History on the Changes in the Production System of the Division of Labour in the Subcontracting Activities in Japan]. In: *Shōkō Kinyū* 42, n° 6: pp. 4–21.

TSŪSHŌ SANGYŌCHŌ (1994): *Tsūshō hakusho* [White Paper on Trade]. Tōkyō: Tsūshō Sangyōchō.

TURCQ, D. (1992): *L'inévitable partenaire Japonais: repères dans un dédale* [The Inevitable Japanese Partner: Hints in a Daedalus]. Paris: Fayard.

WATANABE, Y. (1996): Shitauke chūshō kigyō to keiretsu, juchū seisangata chūshō kigyō no juzokuteki seichō kara jiritsuteki seichō e no michi [Subcontracting SMEs and Keiretsu, from Growth Based on Dependence to Growth based on Independence]. In: *Bijinesu Rebyū* 43, n°2, pp. 14–36.

IX A Changing Image of Japanese Small Entrepreneurs

Susumu WATANABE

Small enterprises played an important role in the development of the Japanese economy during its 'high growth period' of the 1960s and 1970s, but their number has recently begun to decline. Policy-makers and researchers interpret this to be a sign of declining industrial dynamism. This study examines the validity of such a view through a sectorial and sub-sectorial analysis of business demography over the period 1972–1994 and through a review of intertemporal changes in Japanese small entrepreneurs' profiles, motivation and modes of business launching. The spread of chain-stores in retail trade and elimination of petty manufacturers dependent on paternalistic subcontracting systems are identified among major causes of the decreasing number of small firms in these sectors, in addition to a range of macro-economic factors. The author suggests that changes in qualitative aspects of Japanese small entrepreneurship are more important than any quantitative trends. The rise of corporate entrepreneurship, emergence of high-tech-based small enterprises, and diversified entrepreneurial motivation are among the other topics discussed.

1 Introduction

Entrepreneurship is the driving force of economic development. Its effective supply in an economy depends on the size of potential entrepreneurial resources and on the degree of their effective manifestation. The former is governed largely by the socio-psychological climate of the society. The latter is partly determined by those economic, structural and technological factors which increase or decrease the height of their entry barriers: (i) the optimum scale of production, (ii) initial capital requirements, (iii) product differentiation, or buyers' special attachment to established enterprises, and (iv) cost differentials due to discrimination against new enterprises regarding their access to technology, capital, raw materials, etc. (BAIN 1965).

Nearly 30 years ago, towards the end of the 'high growth period' of the postwar Japanese economy, I discussed related subjects in the context of its manufacturing sector (WATANABE 1970). Broadly, my conclusion in that study was that small and petty entrepreneurs had contributed significantly to the rapid expansion of Japanese industries, although they were 'far removed from the lofty Schumpeterian model' of innovator-entrepreneurs

(SCHUMPETER 1961: ch. II). With the peculiarly Japanese paternalistic subcontracting system lowering their entry barriers, these low-grade entrepreneurs actively cooperated with a limited number of Schumpeterian genuine entrepreneurs such as Honda, Ibuka, Matsuda and Matsushita to maximize the latter's impact on the economy. Such an image of Japanese small entrepreneurs persisted until recently.

Nowadays, however, the situation appears to be changing rapidly. The larger companies' need for additional subcontractors disappeared with the end of the high growth period, while existing subcontractors are now threatened by their parent firms' overseas investment and procurement, as well as by their 'restructuring' efforts aimed at cost reduction. It is also true that the ever-continuing pressure for price cuts has made it increasingly difficult for small subcontractors to survive. Thus, small entrepreneurs are now forced to take rather drastic rationalization measures or to get out of the subcontracting system at least partially, if not entirely, by developing some original products. On the other hand, the advancement of information technology has opened up enormous opportunities for new types of small entrepreneurs, and a number of reforms in socio-economic institutions have lowered their entry barriers.

In brief, the profile of Japanese small entrepreneurs and the pattern of their business launching are changing rapidly. So is their motivation. This of course is not confined to the manufacturing sector.

These changes will be discussed below in some detail by way of updating the image of Japanese small entrepreneurs given in my 1970 paper. In doing so, I will examine how realistic the view is that small entrepreneurship is on the wane in Japanese industries—a concern fairly widely shared by Japanese policy-makers and experts on small enterprises. The Small and Medium Enterprise Agency (Chūshō Kigyōchō) has recently conducted a number of special surveys on related subjects, and their findings are reported in its annual *Chūshō Kigyō Hakusho* (White Paper on Small and Medium-sized Enterprises). People's Finance Corporation (KOKUMIN KIN'YŪ KŌKO = KKK hereafter) began to publish its *Shinki Kaigyō Hakusho* (White Paper on New Enterprises) in FY 1991. My analysis will be based primarily on information from these sources, which are referred to as "*White Paper*" and "*KKK White Paper*" respectively. I also gained some important insights through interviews with small business proprietors and local government officials in the Ōta District of Tōkyō, Sakaki Town of Nagano Prefecture, and Higashi Ōsaka City in autumn 1996 and spring 1997. My interpretation of these data is somewhat different from those of the institutions cited above.

2 Demographic trends in Japanese industries

The total number of non-agricultural private establishments—a rough proxy for enterprises in the absence of systematic firm-based data—in Japan continued to increase from 5,113,723 in 1972, at the end of the high growth period of the post-war Japanese economy, to a historical peak of 6,622,246 in 1989, in the middle of the *bubble economy* period. Then it began to decline, for the first time since the end of the Second World War. Since two-thirds of the establishments in Japan have 1–4 workers and another 30 % 5–29 workers, these changes are mostly attributable to the smallest establishment size groups.

Table 1: Changes in the number of non-agricultural private establishments, 1972–1994

Period	Initial no. of establishments	Birth per year	Death per year	Increment
1972–1975	5,113,723	313,627	211,875	101,752
1975–1978	5,389,300	333,043	183,847	149,196
1978–1981	5,849,321	358,530	220,530	138,000
1981–1986	6,269,071	294,293	249,239	45,054
1986–1989	6,494,341	275,574	232,939	42,635
1989–1991	6,622,246	271,318	311,571	-40,253
1991–1994	6,541,741	301,564	305,043	-3,479
1994	6,531,980	–	–	–

Note: The number of establishments at the beginning of each period is not always consistent with the annual increment figure, because the Censuses took place not always exactly at the same time of the year.

Source: *KKK White Paper* 1995, pp. 3 and 197, based on Census of Establishments for various years and related data bases.

In some sectors and trades, the number of establishments began to fall in earlier periods, as early as the first half of the 1980s in retail trade and in the second half in the manufacturing sector. Catering business (restaurants and bars) as well as wholesale trade joined them in the early 1990s. Losses have been particularly large in retail trade (-194,767 between 1981 and 1994) and in the manufacturing sector (-85,041 between 1986 and 1994). In fact, retail trade had fewer establishments in 1994 than in 1972. Wholesale and catering trades lost 14,379 and 7,176 establishments, respectively, between 1991 and 1994. In contrast, the number of establishments continues to grow in personal services (e. g., hair dressers, supplementary schools, cleaning shops, sport clubs, photo shops and hotels; +207,896 between 1986 and 1994) and construction industry (+36,113). Rising trends also persist in banking and insurance, real asset trade, and communication and transportation, which are not included in table 2 but jointly accounted for 8.6 % of the total non-agricultural private establishments in 1994. Gains in these trades, however, have failed to offset losses elsewhere since the beginning of the 1990s (tables 1 and 2).

Table 2: Changes in the average gross (net) annual birth rates of non-agricultural private establishments by sector or trade, 1966–1994

(%)

Period	Total	Manufacturing	Wholesale	Retail	Catering	Personal services	Construction
1972	5113723 (100)	793382 (15.5)	351492 (6.9)	1641490 (32.1)	514599 (10.1)	1066954 (20.9)	410203 (8.0)
1994	6531980 (100)	821430 (12.6)	470330 (7.2)	1584061 (24.3)	839122 (12.8)	1636920 (25.1)	612392 (9.4)
1966–69	6.5 (3.3)	6.0 (3.5)	6.6 (0.0)	5.0 (2.9)	15.8 (9.1)	6.3 (2.4)	5.4 (5.0)
1969–72	7.0 (3.2)	5.6 (2.4)	8.1 (4.3)	4.8 (1.4)	17.0 (8.4)	6.7 (2.7)	6.4 (5.9)
1972–75	6.1 (1.9)	4.3 (0.9)	8.1 (2.7)	4.3 (0.7)	13.3 (4.0)	6.1 (2.3)	5.4 (3.2)
1975–78	6.2 (2.8)	3.4 (1.1)	6.8 (3.0)	4.8 (1.6)	15.1 (6.5)	6.1 (2.8)	4.6 (3.5)
1978–81	6.1 (2.3)	3.7 (1.2)	6.4 (2.6)	4.4 (0.4)	14.1 (5.3)	6.4 (3.3)	4.7 (3.7)
1981–86	4.7 (0.7)	3.1 (0.0)	5.1 (1.4)	3.4 (-0.7)	9.0 (1.2)	5.3 (2.1)	3.2 (0.9)
1986–89	4.2 (0.6)	3.1 (0.2)	4.8 (0.7)	3.1 (-0.3)	6.4 (0.8)	4.9 (1.3)	3.6 (1.2)
1989–91	4.1 (-0.6)	2.8 (-1.2)	3.2 (0.0)	2.8 (-3.6)	7.7 (-1.0)	4.7 (1.8)	3.3 (0.6)
1991–94	4.6 (-0.1)	3.1 (-1.5)	5.2 (0.0)	3.9 (-0.4)	5.9 (-0.3)	5.0 (0.8)	4.8 (0.5)

Notes: (1) The average annual birth rate = the average annual number of establishments opened during the observation period ÷ the total number of establishments existing on the initial date x 100.

(2) The figures in parentheses are average annual rates of net increase in the number of establishments.

(3) The figures in the first two rows relate to numbers of establishments in the respective years, the figures in parentheses showing proportions in the total.

Sources: *KKK White Paper* 1995, pp. 5–6 & 177–178, and 1996, pp. 198–199, based on the same data bases mentioned in table 1.

Inter-sectoral differences in the demographic trends have naturally caused significant changes in the structure of the Japanese economy, as indicated in the second row of table 2. Rapid expansion of the manufacturing sector, as well as the 'high growth' of the overall economy, ended with the first oil crisis of 1973–74. This sector's share of the total number of establishments steadily declined thereafter, giving way to tertiary sector trades. Quantitatively, however, the decline in the manufacturing sector has remained modest—3 percentage points between 1972 and 1994. Far more spectacular have been developments within the tertiary sector: the share of retail trade fell by as much as 8 points while that of personal services rose by 5 points (table 2).

The decline in the overall number of establishments is a combined result of the reduced annual birth rate and the increased annual death rate: the former fell from a peak of 7 % around 1970 to 4.1 % before recovering to 4.6 % in 1991–94, while the latter rose from slightly more than 3 % to 4.7 % over the same period. The relative importance of the two factors varied depending on the sector or trade. In the manufacturing sector and in retail trade, the gross birth rate remained relatively stable since the beginning of the 1980s, while the death rate rose significantly. In contrast, in catering business the gross birth rate declined dramatically as the death rate remained more stable. The picture in wholesale trade is similar but less dramatic. Finally, in services and in construction industry both rates have remained rather stable although the gaps between the two have tended to narrow (table 2).

Obviously, it has become more difficult for a small entrepreneur not only to launch a new business but also to keep it going. The *15th Establishment Census* conducted in 1991 recorded 407,700 establishments set up within 18 months, as compared with 524,390 in the previous census in 1986. This means a decrease by 22 %. The six-year survival rate of new establishments declined from 74.1 % to 68.7 % between 1980–86 and 1985–91 (from 93.5 % to 85.9 % in the manufacturing sector) (*White Paper* 1997: 309–31).

According to table 1, one can see that the birth rate recorded a major dive in the first half of the 1980s, no doubt in connection with the slow-down of the macro-economic growth rate caused by the first oil crisis and by the appreciation of the yen. It touched the floor around 1990, when the death rate reached its peak jumping by 33 points compared with the previous period. Clearly, the mounting labour shortage and breathtaking price increases—especially wages and land prices—suffocated existing small enterprises and discouraged would-be small entrepreneurs from business launching. The problem was compounded by the collapse of the *bubble economy* in 1990 and by the increasing 'hollowing out' of industrial bases. The revival of active price competition in subsequent years—which led to *kakaku hakai* (or a general phenomenon of drastic price reduction)—has lowered entry barriers by reducing initial capital requirements, thus permitting a substantial increase in the annual birth rate in the early 1990s. The prolonged post-*bubble* stagnation had a similar effect by increasing labour supplies to the small business sectors and by reducing attractive wage employment opportunities elsewhere. The same factor, however, made survival of small businesses more difficult and kept the death rate at a peak.

In retail trade, and to a smaller extent in some other trades, the spread of supermarkets and other franchise chains is an important explanation for the decline in the number of establishments. Between 1985 and 1995, the number of franchise chains in Japan grew by 25 % from 588 to 734, and their member shops by 83 % from 86,908 to 158,736. According to the *KKK White Paper* 1996, 19.5 % of new businesses in retail trade, 9.6 % in catering businesses and 7.2 % in personal services started in this way. What is important is that multiple shops of conventional types are suppressed (either eliminated or discouraged from launching) for each of these chain stores. Indeed, Establishment Census data shows that between 1981 and 1994 nearly a quarter of a million single-site enterprises and head offices disappeared in commerce and catering businesses, while branches increased by a little more than half that number. Similarly, in manufacturing industries, the number of single-site enterprises and head offices decreased by more than 70,000 and that of branches rose by 30,000 between 1986 and 1994.

Financial entry barriers became higher for smaller entrepreneurs, as initial capital requirements grew enormously due to the appreciation of land prices and the use of high-tech equipment. Technological barriers rose with the complexity of technology, except for certain business areas based on information technology. Small entrepreneurs are also seriously handicapped in securing adequate manpower, because Japanese workers usually prefer jobs at larger companies.

As to the initial capital requirement, findings of KKK surveys in different years are revealing, although differences in the trade composition of the respondents limit inter-temporal comparability. Only 46 % of new entrepreneurs cooperating for the 1995 survey had started their businesses with a capital of less than 10 million yen, as compared with 76 % in 1985. The average varied considerably from one trade to another, however, ranging from 27.6 million yen for personal services and 19.4 million yen for catering businesses to less than 10 million yen for other services and the construction industry. The average for the manufacturing sector was 16.3 million yen. Across all trades, the average amount of initial capital of those who purchased real assets amounted to 45.8 million yen, against 12.6 million yen for those who did not (ibid., p. 329).

According to the Small and Medium Enterprise Agency's 1996 survey, 43 % of entrepreneurs who started their business before the mid-1950s were in possession of pieces of land initially, and 22 % purchased business sites. These percentages decreased steadily over time, down to 21 % and 7 %, respectively, by the early 1990s (Chūsho Kigyōchō 1997). The rapid urbanization that accompanied the high growth of the Japanese economy reduced the availability of personal property for business purposes, and the appreciation of land prices made it extremely difficult for new entrepreneurs to purchase land. Local governments' regulations on industrial locations and environmental protection have compounded the problem, partly by restricting the use of residential sites for business purposes.

The last factor is an important explanation for the decreasing number of manufacturing enterprises in the metropolitan areas of Tōkyō and Ōsaka, where local authorities' regulations on industrial location and environment often impede the replacement of old industrial sheds and machinery. Relatively dynamic enterprises and their plants are removed to other prefectures and less dynamic ones are discontinued. Another micro-level cause of the termination of manufacturing businesses relates to the problem of finding a business successor. Elderly proprietors I interviewed often mentioned that it would be difficult to persuade younger people to take over so low-paid businesses. Asked whether their attitude would change when the general business situation recovered, they replied affirmatively. In the meantime, small manufacturing establishments in municipal areas are increasingly displaced by apartment buildings, which are free of locational restrictions and easy for older people to manage. This is no doubt a factor contributing to the continuing multiplication of small establishments in the personal services sub-sector.

Japanese policy-makers are concerned about the reduced overall business birth rate for two reasons. First, given the active 'restructuring' efforts among the larger firms, the bulk of new employment opportunities needs to be created by new enterprises. Second, they interpret the low birth rate and especially the negative net birth rate to be a sign of diminishing industrial dynamism. This is particularly worrying because the corporate birth rate in Japan has always been lower than in the United States, where it has remained around 14 % against a death rate of about 12 % since the early 1980s, although the three-year observation period in Japan clearly causes a much greater understatement of the birth rate and overstatement of the death rate than the yearly observation in the United States (30 % of new enterprises disappear within a year and 60 % within 5 years in that country) (KKK 1990: 7).

Personally, however, I am more interested in qualitative changes in the Japanese small entrepreneurship. For one thing, it is still not clear to what extent the above-discussed trends are secular and to what extent cyclical. Not a few of the proprietors I interviewed (in manufacturing industries) were of the opinion that recovery of profitability could reverse the trends of business birth and death rates, e. g., by making it easier to step up investment in high-tech equipment and to find business successors. In fact, the birth rate bounced back in many sectors and trades between 1991 and 1994 (table 2). One may also question the meaningfulness of the comparison between the business birth rate in Japan and that in the United States. According to the 1972 Censuses of Manufacturing of the two countries, the numbers of establishments with fewer than 100 workers and those with fewer than 10 workers were 686,894 and 522,864 in Japan, and 278,240 and 158,985 in the United States. The Japanese figures were 2.5 and 3.4 times the American, when the Japanese population was about half the American. Considering the fact that the Japanese economy had passed its Lewisian "turning point" from a labour-surplus to a full-employment phase barely a decade ago (MINAMI 1994: ch. 9), there is little doubt that a large proportion of Japanese small business proprietors in 1972 had launched their businesses because they could not find satisfactory wage employment. The falling business birth rate might well be interpreted, at least partially, as a phenomenon of the transition from pseudo-entrepreneurship to more genuine Schumpeterian entrepreneurship. Recent survey results appear to be consistent with such interpretation, as will be discussed below.

3 New entrepreneurs' profiles

The mode of business launching has changed remarkably over the last few decades (table 3). Before the mid-1950s, during the postwar economic recovery period, most new businesses were set up by independent entrepreneurs (Type I). The actual proportion of such entrepreneurs must have been much higher than the table indicates because the information in this table concerns those who survived until the survey date. Also the death rate is bound to have been higher among Type I enterprises than among the other types of enterprises. That was a period when all sorts of daily consumption goods and services were short in supply, and small firms could easily find a market for whatever they produced with whatever means of production available. With the start of 'high growth' in the late 1950s, the 'spinning-off' of employees became a predominant form of business launching. With (Type III) or without (Type II) encouragement from ex-employers, who were trying to save capital and at the same time cut labour costs by using petty subcontractors, they often sought to improve their income by starting their own business (Watanabe 1970). In subsequent periods, when business conditions became more uncertain due to slower economic growth, quickly changing patterns of demand, accelerating technological progress and business globalization, employers encouraged employees to leave the company and work as their subcontractors for the purposes of maintaining business flexibility and securing labour supplies—petty subcontractors could mobilize their relatives and friends. More recently, the need for additional subcontractors of conventional types has become limited but larger firms have started to separate parts of their corporate systems by way of 'restructuring'. They have also begun to set up numerous subsidiaries with a view to diversifying their business and exploring promising new business lines (Type IV). In the meantime, developments on the supply side have made it increasingly difficult for petty entrepreneurs to launch their own business independently for reasons discussed above.

As one might easily surmise from such shifts in the mode of business launching, the proportion of former employees of large firms to total new entrepreneurs rose significantly over time, from 12.1 % in 1955–64 to 31.5 % in 1991–96. One-third of Type IV entrepreneurs are former employees of large enterprises, as compared with 21 % of Type II and 8 % of Type III (*White Paper* 1997: 322).

The average age of new entrepreneurs has risen considerably over time. In the mid-1960s, more than 60 % of new entrepreneurs among KKK's clients made their debut in their 20s or 30s, the highest concentration being between 25 and 35 years of age (WATANABE 1970: 539). The proportion of that age group accounted for just over 50 % of new entrepreneurs in KKK's surveys in 1992, 93 and 94, and for 44.6 % in 1995 when 20.8 % were 50 or more years old (KKK 1996: 9). In each survey, however, the average age varied depending on the trade. In the 1989 survey, for example, 54 % of new entrepreneurs in the manufacturing sector were more than 40 years old, while 72 % in services were under 40 (KKK 1990: 19).

Table 3: Changing modes of business launching

(%)

Period	I	II	III	IV	Total
Before 1955	47.3	30.0	18.2	4.5	100
1955–1964	36.7	38.3	13.9	11.1	100
1965–1974	21.6	50.2	14.0	14.2	100
1975–1984	15.5	54.8	14.0	15.7	100
1985–1990	10.0	52.7	16.2	21.1	100
1991–1996	8.7	46.7	20.1	24.5	100

Notes: I = Independent;
II = Spinning off without support from the previous employer;
III = Spinning off with support from the previous employer in the same business;
IV = The previous employer's subsidiary.

Source: *White Paper* 1997, p. 320, based on the Small and Medium Enterprise Agency's survey of December 1996.

The entrepreneur's age at the time of his or her debut obviously has something to do with the business experience and know-how required for the business venture. In KKK's 1989 survey, 83 % of the respondents had acquired such experience and know-how while employed by someone else. There were, however, considerable inter-trade differences, ranging from 93 % for the manufacturing sector and 90 % for wholesale trade to 64 % for catering business. On the average, across sectors and trades, they had 15.3 years' experience as regular employees at 2.4 firms. Two-thirds of this period (10.6 years) was spent in a trade related to their own. Some people intentionally changed their employers in order to search for a suitable line of business enterprise (ibid., pp. 92). As "more than 7 years experience as an employee" was very common among the new entrepreneurs in the 1960s, the length of experience required appears to have almost doubled over the last 30 years or so.

The increasing sophistication of technology and growing initial capital requirements must be among the main explanations for this change. The rising proportion of Type IV establishments (table 3) is another: companies usually entrust a new subsidiary, factory or branch office to an experienced staff member in his or her 40s or 50s. Quantitatively, however, the greatest contributing factor may be the prolonged average life span. The Japanese people's life expectancy at birth rose by more than 10 years between 1960 and 1990, and people at the age of 50 can now expect to live nearly 30 more years (Sōmuchō Tōkeikyoku 1996). Consequently, an increasing number of people look for an 'after-retirement job'. In many cases, they (or their wives) launch their own small business, often but not necessarily based on their experience and using their retirement bonus. Their intention is to supplement their household income accruing from pensions, and therefore they are rarely concerned about their business successor.

The last factor is a partial explanation for the rising proportion of new entrepreneurs without any experience in related business areas: they have grown from 14 % to 25 % of respondents in KKK surveys during the first half of the 1990s (KKK 1996: 13). Another explanation is related to those young entrepreneurs who start their business based on information technology, though these are not yet important in quantitative terms.

Female entrepreneurs have been increasing, now accounting for about 15 % of the total according to the Establishment Census data. They are heavily concentrated in catering businesses (42 %), retail trade (24 %) and personal services (23 %) (KKK 1990).

With a view to encouraging new entrepreneurship, the Japanese government introduced, in April 1995, a Temporary Law for Promoting Creative Business Activities by Small and Medium-sized Enterprises (*Sōzō-hō*). Defining "creative business activities" as the launching of a new firm or commercializing R&D results to create new products or services, the government provides tax concessions, financial incentives and special credit insurance to cover risk. By the end of February 1997, 1,883 cases had been approved, 33 % in manufacturing technology, 17 % in information and communication and 15 % in environmental businesses (*White Paper* 1997: 340).

4 Entrepreneurial motivation

In the 1970 paper I argued that economic development might bring about changes in the entrepreneurial motivation and suggested that around 1960, which is usually associated with the Lewisian turning point of the Japanese economy, a shift took place in small entrepreneurs' motivation from the pursuit of income or employment opportunities to Schumpeterian 'irrational' ones—that is, "pride and the desire for independence and power". Findings in more recent KKK surveys are in line with this interpretation.

In the 1969 survey where the respondents were asked to provide up to two replies, 64 % aspired for the status of business proprietor, 76 % of them mentioning that they wanted to give their abilities a free rein and 34 % that they did not want to take orders from other people (Category I). Only 26 % of the total replies were concerned with income or job opportunities: "income larger than wage earners", "need for supplementary income", "difficulty in finding a suitable wage employment" (Category II). In 1982 when up to three answers were permitted, these two categories of replies accounted for 52 % and 17 % of the total, while 27 % were related to life style: "want to live in my own way" and "want to use my time freely" (Category III). In 1989 when again up to three answers were permitted, 40 % of all replies were of Category I, 36 % Category III, and 24 % Category II (KKK 1990: 30).

The results of the three surveys are not quite comparable. Apart from the fact that the respondents in the 1969 survey were given two choices instead of three as was the case in the next two surveys, the items concerning the life style were not given as alternatives in the first survey. This was no doubt because these items were still almost unthinkable at that time. In other words, the entrepreneurial motivation has become more diversified, different people launching their own businesses in pursuit of different goals or ways of self-realization.

The 1989 survey found no great age-related differences in motivation. In each age group, Category I motives were dominant, followed by those of Category III. Category II motives were the lowest ranked. However, younger entrepreneurs tended to stress these (Category II) motives more than older entrepreneurs, the proportion of those who mentioned them steadily falling from 27 % in the age group below 30 down to 18 % in the age group 45 and above. In contrast, 40 % in the age group 45 and above referred to life style motives as compared with 34 % in the age group below 30. The percentage also declined with the age in the case of status motives, but only modestly from 41 % to 38 % (ibid., 37p.).

All this does not disprove the importance of income incentives, of course. In 1989, the average monthly income of the KKK respondents was 599,000 yen (incl. bonuses and other payments, as well as supplementary earnings, e. g., from housewives' part-time jobs). Their average age was 41.6 years. According to the Household Budget Census, the 40 to 44-year old wage-earners in that year had an average income of 478,000 yen per month. It follows that the respondents' average income was significantly higher than the national average of their age group. (It must be remembered, however, that since they had been screened for KKK loans, their situation must have been better than the average small entrepreneurs.) Their current income was 1.4 times as large as what they used to earn before launching their current businesses (435,000 yen). The proportion of those with monthly incomes 300,000 yen or less declined from 55.5 % to 30.8 %. The greatest increases were observed in the manufacturing sector, where the average income jumped by 72 %, from 362,000 yen to 620,000 yen, followed by construction industry (61 %, from 372,000 yen to 600,000 yen). In contrast, the average income actually fell from 357,000 yen to 354,000 yen in catering businesses, those with a monthly income of 200,000 yen or less increasing from 29 % to 38 % (ibid., 62p.). No wonder, then, that the corporate birth rate is declining so drastically in this line of business (table 2).

5 Subcontracting

The multiple-layered subcontracting system is one of the main characteristics of Japanese metal engineering industries. In this respect, too, remarkable changes have taken place in the last 10 years or so (*White Paper* 1997: 147).

First, according to surveys by the Small and Medium Enterprise Agency (Chūshō Kigyōchō 1997), the proportion of subcontractors in the total number of small and medium-sized manufacturing firms continued to rise from 53.3 % in 1966 to 65.5 % in 1981 and then fell to 51.6 % by 1996. The metal engineering industries—industries producing electrical and electronic machinery, transportation equipment and general machinery—are no exception: the proportion of subcontractors in these industries declined by about 10 points from 80–90 % to 70–80 % since the early 1980s. Obviously, the weeding out of weaker subcontractors is an important cause of the dwindling number of smaller enterprises in these industries.

Second, 'pure' subcontractors have become less common. Whereas in 1987, 81.5 % of subcontractors fully depended on subcontracted work, having no other (independent) sources of work, the proportion of such firms had declined to 48.4 % by 1996. At the same time, the proportion of subcontractors working for a single firm fell from 40.0 % to 31.7 % over the same period, while that of firms with 10 or more parent firms nearly doubled from 10.8 % to 20.3 %. Finally, partly for that reason, the average degree of dependence on a single firm has decreased: 71.3 % of all subcontractors relied on a single parent firm for 50 % or more of their business in 1987, as compared with 52.5 % of firms in 1996.

All these changes imply a need for greater efforts on the part of subcontractors. In order to survive, they invest in high technology, enhancing productivity as well as product quality, broaden their product range and increase flexibility of production facilities. Parent firms encourage their subcontractors to diversify clients through such efforts, partly because they now feel less certain of future work for subcontractors in view of increasing business uncertainty and partly because they want to stimulate more severe competition among their suppliers.

It is notable, however, that the Small and Medium Enterprise Agency's survey in 1996 discovered that 51.5 % of the responding subcontractors had been maintaining their business relationship with their primary parent firm for more than 20 years and another 30.1 % for 10–20 years (Chūshō Kigyōchō 1997). Obviously, subcontractors are trying to diversify their business partners, while keeping their relationship with their existing parent firms. The situation appears to be similar with these parent firms. Their degree of reliance on outsourcing or subcontracting has not changed much (table 4), though 76 % have started using new suppliers, in most cases without discontinuing business with their existing subcontractors.

In some cases, however, they do abandon existing subcontractors. One-fifth of the parent firms in this 1996 Survey had reduced the number of their subcontractors in the previous five years. Parent firms have become more selective, and they now use more capable subcontractors more intensively. Their efforts at cost reduction through a greater standardization of products and of parts and components add to this tendency, just as the expansion of in-house production and overseas procurement does. The in-house production ratio has risen at about one-third of the parent firms responding to the survey, in nearly two-thirds of cases because of the under-utilized facilities caused by the business recession and in the remaining cases because their own rationalization efforts had reduced production costs and enhanced product qualities beyond their subcontractors' levels. Regarding the procurement of parts and components abroad, slightly over two-thirds of parent firms has already secured overseas supply sources and three-quarters has been increasing overseas procurements. The trend was expected to continue in the future by about the same proportion of responding parent firms. Cuts in inhouse production and in overseas procurement were anticipated by no more than 18 % and 4 %, respectively.

Table 4: Parent firms' reliance on outsourcing and subcontracting

(% of respondents)

<table>
<tr><th rowspan="2">Degree of reliance*</th><th colspan="3">Outsourcing</th><th colspan="3">Subcontracting</th></tr>
<tr><th>1996</th><th>1991</th><th>1986</th><th>1996</th><th>1991</th><th>1986</th></tr>
<tr><td>nil</td><td>1.5</td><td>1.8</td><td>2.9</td><td>5.0</td><td>3.8</td><td>3.4</td></tr>
<tr><td>below 20</td><td>46.3</td><td>44.9</td><td>46.4</td><td>26.3</td><td>25.3</td><td>26.0</td></tr>
<tr><td>20–40</td><td>26.5</td><td>26.9</td><td>25.5</td><td>15.2</td><td>16.7</td><td>17.0</td></tr>
<tr><td>40–60</td><td>14.4</td><td>14.6</td><td>14.5</td><td>14.7</td><td>15.1</td><td>14.6</td></tr>
<tr><td>60–80</td><td>9.5</td><td>9.7</td><td>9.4</td><td>13.3</td><td>13.2</td><td>14.1</td></tr>
<tr><td>80 or more</td><td rowspan="2">1.8</td><td rowspan="2">2.1</td><td rowspan="2">1.3</td><td>20.2</td><td>20.8</td><td>20.4</td></tr>
<tr><td>100</td><td>5.3</td><td>5.1</td><td>4.5</td></tr>
</table>

Note: *Proportion of outsourcing values to total costs, and share of subcontracted work to total outsourcing value.

Source: *White Paper* 1997, p. 150, based on a special survey in November 1996.

Having said this, I need to add a few words of caution: these findings of the 1996 Survey must be interpreted carefully. The exchange rate of the yen in terms of the US dollar was at its historical high in 1995 (93.97 yen per dollar). It fell to 108.81 yen per dollar in 1996, but respondents in the Survey must have been under the spell of the dreadful experience in their recent past. The yen has weakened considerably since, and withdrawals of smaller firms from overseas production bases have increased. A similar survey may produce somewhat different results now. Nevertheless, the fact remains that parent firms have become stricter in evaluating their existing subcontractors and in selecting new ones.

From the subcontractors' viewpoint, major advantages of subcontracting arrangements accrue from the stability of business, from savings in their own marketing efforts and from low business risk, as indicated by 55 %, 42 % and 35 % of the respondents in the 1996 survey, respectively. However, rapidly advancing business globalization and technological progress have made their parent firms more dynamic, and consequently their own business conditions have become far from tranquil.

Table 5: Main reasons given by parent firms for subcontracting

(% of responding parent firms)

Reason	mid-1980s	1996
1. To save production capacity	39	28
2. To save labour cost	38	38
3. To utilize the subcontractor's specialized technology	29	37
4. To adapt to fluctuating demand	20	26
5. To save capital investment	20	17
6. To deal with small lots of diverse products	15	16

Source: *White Paper* 1997, p. 160.

For the parent firms, under the ever-increasing competitive pressures, labour cost saving remains one of the most important purposes of subcontracting (table 5). Items 1, 4 and 5 in the table obviously overlap to some extent. What is remarkable is the significantly increased emphasis on the benefits accruing from subcontractors' specialized technological know-how. The role of subcontracting as a buffer against fluctuating demand (item 4 and partly item l) appears to have increased during the serious business depression of the 1990s as compared to the starting period of the *bubble economy.* In this connection it needs to be noted that in a survey of subcontractors the Small and Medium Enterprise Agency conducted in 1969, fewer than 10 % of the respondents (mostly from metal engineering industries), and none in the automobile industry, mentioned this role of subcontracting as their motive (WATANABE 1971: 59). Clearly, it is wrong to say, as some authors do, that subcontracting in Japanese industries is primarily aimed at securing a buffer against business fluctuation. Indeed, the practice started and developed during the 1930s through the early 1960s as a means of maximizing production capacity under serious supply constraints, i. e., an extreme shortage of machinery and capital (WATANABE 1983: 27).

Needless to say, firms' motivation for subcontracting varies depending on the industry as well. In the above-cited 1968 survey, around 70 % of parent firms in metal engineering industries used subcontractors for the purpose of saving labour, capital and other factors of production, while 48 % (electronic parts manufacturers) to 82 % (automobile manufacturers) resorted to the practice in order to benefit from specialized technology owned by the subcontractor. Unfortunately, the data base cited in table 5 does not permit such an inter-industrial comparison.

6 Strategies for the future

6.1 Subcontractors' strategies

Larger firms' vigorous efforts at restructuring, as well as the growing globalization of their business operations, have been rendering their subcontractors' positions more uncertain and vulnerable. The rate of growth of annual sales tended to be lower among subcontractors, especially those at lower layers of the subcontracting hierarchy—i. e., sub-subcontractors, sub-sub-subcontractors, etc.—, than among independent firms (i. e., non-subcontractors), obviously due to more intense price competition. In coping with the situation, some subcontractors endeavour to strengthen their positions as subcontractor while others seek ways to leave the subcontracting system and become independent. Not a few resort to the first strategy for the immediate future and to the second for the more distant future. In the Small and Medium Enterprise Agency's 1996 survey, nearly half of responding subcontractors were trying to diversify parent firms and to enlarge their capacity to actively make business proposals to their parent firms rather than just waiting for instructions. Slightly over one-third were striving to develop new products, while 31 % were exploring new businesses. For the future, however, around 40 % of them opted for the third and fourth approaches and only one-fourth for the first and second (*White Paper* 1997: 164).

To reinforce their position as subcontractor, they invest in high technology in order to discourage their parent firms from overseas procurements by improving their own price and quality competitiveness and/or to attract on-the-spot orders and short-notice work of high value-added by increasing the flexibility of their production facilities. For example, a plastic-parts manufacturer I interviewed in Tōkyō had built a new plant with computerized production facilities, which helped more than double productivity and made it easier to recruit younger workers. A manufacturer of rubber auto-parts became specialized in high value-added small-lot items unsuitable for overseas procurement. With new equipment and technical personnel, he established himself as his parent firms' partner in new product development, thus paving the way for upgrading himself from a subcontractor to a 'cooperative firm', thereby enjoying a greater bargaining power.

More generally, rather than passively waiting for instructions as they used to, subcontractors are making efforts to acquire capacities to provide their parent firms with specialized technical know-how, e. g., for improving business systems and products and for a greater standardization of parts and components. Cooperating with other subcontractors, they also encourage their parent firms to place collective orders for a group of subcontractors producing related parts, rather than separate orders to each of them. This helps reduce the parent firms' purchasing costs and thereby raise profit margins for the subcontractors.

Those who find it difficult to improve their business prospects as subcontractor try to become independent. They are often prompted to do so by a realization that they are a main source of their parent firm's technological competitiveness.

6.2 Efforts towards independence

Independent small entrepreneurs stress the importance of efforts "to enlarge sales promotion capacity", "to develop original technology" and/or "to develop original products". In the above-cited 1996 Survey, 34 % of independent firms, as compared to 12 % of subcontractors, were in possession of industrial properties such as patents and utility models (*White Paper* 1997: 164).

A common approach is to develop their own original end-products while still working as subcontractor. Sometimes, firms specialized in different business areas cooperate in order to develop new clients as a group. Concerned about the 'hollowing out' of local industrial bases, local governments support such entrepreneurial efforts by promoting an exchange of marketing and technological information, and universities collaborate in their R&D. Since major companies are not interested in small markets of, say, below a billion yen, these efforts have a good chance of success (KANTŌ TSŪSHŌ SANGYŌKYOKU 1996: 31, 92).

For example, in Hamamatsu, 12 small firms from different trades have jointly organized a cooperative R&D association. Each firm has a one-room workshop in the same building, sharing a common business information base as well as a cafeteria, a meeting room and other service facilities. They have also contributed the same amount of capital to establish a marketing company. When this association receives an inquiry, its R&D committee discusses the project and makes a proposal to the client. When they succeed in developing an original product (e. g., an automatic curtaining system for hospitals), they jointly apply for a patent.

Another example is a group of 19 small and medium-sized enterprises in Nagano Prefecture, which formed an R&D cooperative for the development and production of specially-ordered ICs under the leadership of a local state university and the prefectural government. The university has made its work stations accessible for the firms, and its students collaborate in R&D. Sometimes technical guidance is provided by major electronics companies such as Seiko Epson.

Some small entrepreneurs are far more aggressive and aspire to what might be called a 'reversed subcontracting system'. Specialized in R&D and business planning, they contract out production and marketing of their products to major companies. For example, a former plumber developed a system for purifying waste water from restaurants and factories. As demand expanded quickly, he started using a number of major companies such as Yokokawa Electric Co. for marketing the equipment which bears his own brand. In the case of a housing company which developed low-cost steel-structured houses, construction work is contracted out to Mitsubishi Corporation, which mobilizes about 20 constructors in different parts of the country. A fully-customized IC company relies on Hitachi and Seiko groups for the production of its products, while an indicator company relies on Sharp and Ushio for the same.

Needless to say, these "fab-less" venture companies save large amounts of capital investment in production facilities. Their collaborators are enthusiastic because this arrangement permits them to make good use of those idle production capacities in the wake of the prolonged recession and shifts of production bases abroad. Another, probably even more important, explanation for their enthusiasm is that they can acquire the venture firms' technological know-how (ibid., pp. 19). Examples of similar arrangements on an international scale are not missing. For example, a portable liquid-tester company has its products fabricated by a German sensor-maker, because the latter's standard molds can be used to reduce capital investment. It is to be seen to what extent major companies will remain prepared to collaborate with smaller firms in this way, when the general business situation recovers and under-utilized production capacity disappears from their plants.

Another pattern of business development is the networking of a group of independent firms. For example, I know a family enterprise in Nagano owned by a former small-business counsellor of the local government. This firm plays the role of a marketing agent as well as that of a catalyst in connecting an engineer-entrepreneur specialized in R&D with a manufacturing firm. A former engineer at the prefectural research institute obtained a patent for a carbonic material which both purifies and holds water. A gardening firm has been brought in to take responsibility for the production of this material. The diffusion of computerized information systems has virtually eliminated geographical limitations, and firms located in different parts of the country can collaborate in such systems.

A number of recent developments seem to help activate small entrepreneurship. Initial capital requirements ceased to grow after 1993, as a result of the general phenomenon of *kakaku hakai* (drastic price cutting) which has resulted from intensified competition and related rationalization efforts by individual firms. Both the unit construction cost of business facilities and office rents in Tokyo fell by up to one-third during the first half of the 1990s (KKK 1996: 28–29). The spread of leasing services has also reduced initial capital requirements by making it unnecessary to purchase expensive high-tech equipment. Outsourcing of technical manpower and expertise is becoming easier even for small firms, as a result of the development of contract labour services and the networking of different types of small firms.

6.3 Impediments to venture businesses

While new types of small businesses are coming up in these ways, various institutional impediments to small venture businesses are currently discussed widely among policy makers (KANTŌ TSŪSHŌ SANGYŌKYOKU 1996: 26).

In Japan, all patents are disclosed to the public after three years. If major companies apply for all sorts of patents in related areas after the disclosure of a patent, the latter will become virtually ineffective. For this reason, small firms sometimes opt for keeping the know-how to themselves without applying for patents, despite the risk of losing the technology. Even with patented technology, there are loopholes in the Japanese intellectual property regulation, which sometimes makes it risky for small firms to collaborate with major companies. In order to avoid such risks, a venture firm specialized in opto-electronic product development has set up a paper company in California. When it sells its technology to a Japanese firm, the US company signs the contract so that California's stricter regulation can be applied to protect corporate interests.

Small venture firms without substantial assets tend to have difficulties in securing bank loans and therefore sell their technology or copy rights to major firms. Another cause of concern lies in official regulations for capital markets, such as the requirement of certain minimum scales of capitalization for listing on the stock market. Would-be venture entrepreneurs are discouraged and sometimes decide to launch their business abroad instead. Some industrial regulations have a similarly discouraging effect, as has been the case with minimum production scales required of beer breweries.

The government has not been inactive, of course. Apart from those policy measures already mentioned in connection with the *Sōzō-hō*, the Anti-Monopoly Law has been amended to enlarge the scope of activities by venture capital funds. At the time of writing (February 1998), a further amendment was being discussed to modify Article 11 of its law, which limits a financing company's capital participation in other firms to 5 %. The idea is to let the firm play a much more active role in supporting small venture businesses. Recent legalization of pure holding companies will certainly encourage non-financing companies' involvement in business ventures.

Venture businesses' access to the stock market and to bank loans has been made easier by lowering hurdles to the public sale of share and by strengthening official credit guarantee systems. Financing institutions such as banks and insurance companies have also started to change their policies in order to accommodate their needs. For example, they now accept intellectual properties as collateral, taking a greater risk in supporting venture businesses (NIKKEI SANGYŌ SHINBUN 1995: 44, 129).

While these problems of policy systems may be solved relatively easily and quickly, more time will be required to overcome some of the socio-psychological barriers to venture businesses. One such problem concerns young people's propensity for larger companies as their employer. This is indeed the primary cause of the serious recruitment problem among small businesses, and a number of venture firms have been established abroad—in China, Ireland, the United States, etc.—, for this very reason.

7 Conclusions

The Japanese economy has undergone a number of major shocks since the mid-1980s—the appreciation of the yen, the dramatic surge of overseas direct investment, and the rise and collapse of the *bubble economy.* It is still too early to isolate secular trends from shorter-term effects of these shocks. A recovery of the general business situation may reverse current trends. Indeed, in all the sectors and trades except catering, the gross business birth rate bounced back in the early 1990s. There are, however, a number of trends that seem to be well established by now.

The decline in the net birth rate of new enterprises is partly a cyclical phenomenon. From our earlier analysis, however, it is clear that it is more generally attributable to two longer-term trends: (1) the increasing importance of corporate entrepreneurship as manifested in the growing number of subsidiaries and chain-stores established by large companies, and (2) the decline of the petty pseudo-entrepreneurship dependent on the paternalistic subcontracting system related to manufacturers (metal engineering industries) or trading firms (garments and other light consumer goods industries). (1) is the explanation for the drastic shrinkage in the number of establishments in retail trade, and (2) for the downward trend in the number of manufacturing establishments.

The ascendance of corporate entrepreneurship ensues from enormously expanded R&D expenditures and requirements for more suitable human resources for innovative business ventures, from vastly increased prices of land and labour, and from major companies' efforts at adapting to the 'low growth economy'. In order to succeed in such efforts, these companies need not only innovative new technology, but also innovative management. They, therefore, often opt for a drastic reshuffling of top management, such as the replacement of a founder-chairman by an outsider. Although the rise of corporate entrepreneurship is something Schumpeter anticipated, his image of "routinized" innovations (SCHUMPETER 1954: ch. XII) is thus remote from the reality.

One may say, then, that the reduced number of establishments is not necessarily a negative phenomenon. It may be interpreted as one aspect of the Schumpeterian evolutionary process, that is, a reallocation of increasingly scarce production factors (i. e., land and labour) to better-paid new use. From another viewpoint, it is a reflection of diminished underemployment.

There is no denying, however, that a sufficient rate of supply of new industrial blood is desirable for the purpose of maintaining or enhancing industrial dynamism.

In this sense it is encouraging that new types of innovative entrepreneurs are appearing especially in information technology businesses. In order to encourage a much greater manifestation of genuine entrepreneurship in small business sectors, the deregulation of business activities and the rationalization of financing institutions will have to be accelerated. An important emerging issue here is the trade-off between industrial deregulation and environmental protection. For the purpose of discouraging the exodus of industries and encouraging new manufacturing investments, metropolitan governments have started to loosen those tight restrictions on industrial locations and activities they had introduced in earlier years. In theory, two solutions are possible. One is a more conventional approach of industrial estates or parks with adequate facilities for environmental protection. Another is environmentally acceptable industrial technology, which offers a most promising area of collaboration among high-tech-oriented small entrepreneurs, universities or other types of R&D institutes, and financing institutions. The scope for the first solution is quite limited in urban areas due to the shortage of land. Unless desired types of new technology come out at sufficient rates, therefore, there is a risk of environmental deterioration.

References

BAIN, J. S. (1965): *Barriers to New Competition.* Cambridge: Harvard University Press.

CHŪSHŌ KIGYŌCHŌ (1997): *Heisei 9-nen-ban chūshō kigyō hakusho* [1997 White Paper on Medium and Small Enterprises]. Tōkyō: Ōkurashō Insatsukyoku.

KKK – KOKUMIN KIN'YŪ KŌKO CHŌSA-BU (1990): *Shinki kaigyō no jittai* [A Survey on New Business Launching]. Tōkyō: Chūshō Kigyō Research Center.

KKK – (various years): *Shinki kaigyō hakusho* [White Paper on New Business Launching]. Tōkyō: Chūshō Kigyō Research Center.

NIKKEI SANGYŌ SHINBUN (1995): *Benchā shin-sedai* [A New Generation of Venture Businesses]. Tōkyō: Nihon Keizai Shinbunsha.

KANTŌ TSŪSHŌ SANGYŌKYOKU (1996): *Sangyō shūseki shin-jidai* [A New Era of Industrial Concentration Localities]. Tōkyō: Nikkan Kōgyō Shinbun.

MINAMI, R. (1994): *The Economic Development of Japan. A Quantitative Study.* 2nd Edition. London: Macmillan.

SCHUMPETER, J. A. (1954): *Capitalism, Socialism, and Democracy.* London: Unwin University Books.

SCHUMPETER, J. A. (1961): *The Theory of Economic Development.* New York: Oxford University Press.

SŌMUCHŌ TŌKEIKYOKU (1996): *Nihon tōkei nenkan 1997* [Japan Statistical Yearbook]. Tōkyō: Nihon Tōkei Kyōkai.

WATANABE, S. (1970): Entrepreneurship in Small Enterprises in Japanese Manufacturing. In: *International Labour Review* 102, 6, December, pp. 531–576.

WATANABE, S. (1971): Subcontracting, Industrialization and Employment Creation. In: *International Labour Review* 104, 1–2, July–August, pp. 51–76.

WATANABE, S. (1983): Inter-sectorial Linkages in Japanese Industries. A Historical Perspective. In: WATANABE, S. (ed.): *Technology, Marketing and Industrialization. Linkages between Large & Small Enterprises.* Delhi: Macmillan India, pp. 13–57.

Commentary

A New Step in the Evolution of Japanese Industrial Networks?

Yannick LUNG

1 Introduction

Many experts have tried to explain Japan's post-war economic growth by highlighting, amongst the various traits which have enhanced the competitiveness of Japanese industry, the essential role played by the specific supplying relationships. All of the interpretative grids being used (*Toyota Production System, Ohnoism, Toyotism, Lean Production*, etc.) emphasize the organization of sub-contracting, as an 'ideal-type' and a benchmark. This organization is often stylized in the form of a hierarchical pyramid with different levels (tiers-ranking). At the summit of the pyramid, the primary client maintains a direct relationship only with a limited number of first rank suppliers. These durable relationships are based on trust, and the suppliers are encouraged to improve their productive efficiency (productivity, quality, innovation) by increased coordination through a learning process—supplier clubs, sharing of productivity gains, the mutual exchange of engineers, joint product development, etc. Each level of the hierarchy tends to reproduce a weaker form of this type of relationship with the following, lower levels. These supplying relationships have been closely analysed and sometimes even translated into rules of management. Managers in North American and European companies have been trying to apply these methods so as to fully restructure their sourcing systems, adapting them all the while to local conditions.

Paradoxically, while many industries across the world are still converting to these rules of management, this type of relationship is now undergoing a thorough transformation in Japan. Supplying relationships are an integral component of the *Japanese industrial model.* Together, they comprise a coherent set of institutional arrangements (BOYER & FREYSSENET 1995, CHANARON & LUNG 1995). Yet, these supplier networks have been affected by the crisis concerning the very foundations of Japan's economic growth. This is the price of the country's former success:

- On one hand, the boom has run its course, and this will translate into a long-term period of low growth. This implies redefining the basis upon

which the fruits of growth have been distributed, since a system which is "lean on growth" is turning into one which is "lean on balance" (FUJIMOTO 1994: 7).
- On the other hand, the internationalization of Japanese firms, spurred by their competitiveness, has led to a weakening of their national base and thus a distortion of the local productive organization. The process of globalization encourages the creation of market relationships to the detriment of the previous system which had largely functioned according to the rules of partnership.

The papers written by Yveline Lecler and Susumu Watanabe both analyse this ongoing transformation of supplying relationships from a long-term, historical perspective. This allows for an identification of those characteristics of the current period which constitute a break with the past. However, the two authors do not use the same approaches:

- Watanabe's paper concentrates mostly on the development of small and medium-sized companies, covering broader topics than just the industrial sector, i. e., the issue of sub-contracting relationships. Rather, the paper refers to the importance of tertiary activities, especially household services. It focuses on the Japanese economy as a whole.
- By focusing to a large extent on the world-wide nature of these ongoing developments, Lecler's paper reviews the transformations of the industrial *keiretsu*—it concentrates purposefully on inter-company relationships, specifically within the manufacturing sector.

These different but complementary points of view shall be commented on in the following manner. Firstly, in section 2, the main aspects of these ongoing developments will be reviewed, including the characterizations which are common to both Watanabe and Lecler's contributions. To what extent do such transformations make it necessary to rethink the institutional arrangements which codified inter-company relationships during the Japanese economy's high-growth years? This will be the prime focus. Then, in section 3, an attempt will be made to delve into the authors' hypotheses about changes in Japanese industrial networks. Finally, in section 4, a brief conclusion will place the findings in a wider context.

2 A common diagnosis: Rethinking the institutional arrangements

Certain culture-based interpretations view the Japanese model of supplying relationships as a vestige of the feudal society—sub-contractors are relegated to a lesser status, one in which they are considered to be dominated and exploited. Watanabe and Lecler, on the contrary, argue that, with respect to its internal dynamics and the environment of which it is part (what can be called its contextual rationale), the Japanese model is a logical economic response to a given situation. This is shown by the way in which it has emerged, in its functioning, even in the manner in which it is being transformed. Above and beyond the issue of inter-company relationships, the whole set of the Japanese economy's institutional arrangements is therefore now being redefined.

2.1 The end of dualism?

For many observers (e.g., DORE 1987, CORIAT 1991, JACOT 1990, SAUTTER 1996), society in Japan, like its economy, is characterized by *dualism*. As opposed to under-developed countries where dualism leads to the de-connection of a modern, export-oriented sector from a more traditional sector and thus impeding development, dualism is one of the components which has helped regulate economic growth in Japan. The attributes of the Japanese company, as defined by AOKI (1995), have involved for the most part the large companies, i.e., those which made Japan into the world's second biggest trading nation.

Alongside several very competitive industrial sectors, great swathes of the Japanese productive system remain relatively inefficient from an economic standpoint. For example, the way in which many tertiary activities operate is deemed to be very traditional, as many small companies are family-run and productivity is low. It is even more meaningful that the competitiveness of certain sectors, such as the automobile industry, has been founded on a dualistic way of doing business; although the primary clients and the first and second rank suppliers all rely on highly efficient techniques and organizational methods, lower-level suppliers are often from this small, family-run business sector which still relies on traditional techniques. As the two authors point out, explanations for the genesis of this specifically Japanese model of supplier networks can be found in the high rate of growth during the post-war years and in the restrictions on resources (finance, equipment, labour, etc.) available at that time to satisfy the country's considerable investment requirements. Lecler also demonstrates a certain continuity with respect to the pre-war period, through the State's interventions aimed at the development of a war economy.

By sub-contracting a major part of their production, leading Japanese companies (primary clients and first rank suppliers) were able to focus on their core competencies (DOSI, TEECE and WINTER 1990), specifically on their ability to conceive and assemble systems and subsystems, taking advantage of the financial, technical, or human resources invested by their sub-contractors. In exchange, durable and special relationships were created, as the sub-contractors were also able to benefit from the technology transferred by their clients (techniques, quality management etc.). Moreover, due to their quasi-exclusive status, clients were guaranteed all of the profits which resulted from the improvements achieved by sub-contractors—this made it all the easier for the large customers to agree to transfer their technology.

The strict separation of Toyota and Nissan's supplying networks (CUSUMANO 1985) attests to the fact that the two rivals took great care to avoid leaks which would help their competitor. With such networks, it also became possible to create the conditions for a *partner-type* relationship between clients and suppliers (FRUIN 1992, LECLER 1993, SAKO 1992, SMITKA 1991). In this type of structure, complex methods like negotiation and cooperation underpinned mutual adjustments and coordination—this was very unlike a market which functions according to relationships of a relatively impersonal nature. To use the analytical framework presented by HIRSCHMAN (1970), and judiciously applied to relationships with suppliers by HELPER (1993), these methods corresponded to a "voice" strategy, rather than to an "exit" one. Of course, their implementation does not preclude applying other economic instruments in order to improve the mechanisms used to distribute the "relational quasi-rent" generated by this partner-like relationship (ASANUMA 1989: 30). Moreover, as HIRSCHMAN (1970) remarks, in order to privilege the "voice", the people involved have to find themselves in a situation of mutual dependence, albeit an asymmetrical one. However, this precondition is now starting to disappear, marking the end of the dualism which had typified the Japanese model.

There is now increased autonomy for sub-contractors, who, to a large extent, had previously relied on suppliers organized in a hierarchical network, a pyramid with the ultimate client at its top. On one hand, the learning process enabled sub-contractors to develop their own competencies, and thus to advance from the status of those who simply adopted their clients' technologies to that of becoming innovators themselves. As such, the system could make it possible for a company to upgrade itself. The ultimate clients (parent company or first-rank suppliers) were making greater demands, accentuating sub-contractors' efforts to achieve technological or organizational improvements, increasingly offering specific resources in order to secure orders. On the other hand, however, primary clients have been reducing their already limited number of suppliers.

The current economic environment in Japan seems to encourage support for people who are both entrepreneurs and innovators (an image first outlined by the economist Joseph Schumpeter). Hence, Watanabe considers it to be positive that the number of businesses in Japan has dropped since the early 1990s (matching a lower rate of birth and a high rate of mortality among firms). Far from being indicative of a weaker national economy, this trend shows that a necessary rationalization is taking place; the unavoidable decline of more traditional companies is expected to be compensated by a rise in innovative companies, the only ones deemed capable of leading the way to recovery.

Because of behavioural inertia, relationships with suppliers have been durable; in 1996, more than eight out of ten sub-contractors had been in a business relationship with their primary parent firm for more than ten years, and 50 % for more than twenty years (SMEA's survey cited by Watanabe, p. 218). However, many relationships have not been renewed, and those contracts which have tended to be drawn up more on a market basis. Sub-contractors were thus encouraged to diversify their client base so as to spread their own risks. This has been made possible by the fact that the services and products they offer have become both more specific and more generic; more specific, because the differentiation between their competitors and themselves has grown, and more generic, because they can satisfy a larger number of clients. Both authors go into great detail about these ongoing developments (Lecler, p. 188; Watanabe, p. 218), which they expect to accelerate as foreseen in a recent survey of sub-contractors. To a large extent, these changes have had the support of the primary clients themselves, encouraging their sub-contractors to turn to other customers, just like they themselves have turned to other suppliers. This offers several advantages to the primary client:

- there are fewer regrets in case the relationship ends;
- by increasing the short-term production volume, the sub-contractor can offer lower prices due to economies of scale and learning;
- the sub-contractor is encouraged to improve both product and process so as to find new business, and 'primary parent firm' benefiting indirectly from this.

2.2 Towards new institutional arrangements

The modus operandi which was prevalent during the period of high growth, and the methods which were highly efficient at the time, have tended to become a hindrance in this new environment, making it necessary to redefine the institutional arrangements. The rise of the Schumpeterian entrepreneur, i. e., the innovative entrepreneur as analysed by Watanabe, assumes that a different institutional framework now exists.

It is not that the image of the *innovator* is new in Japan—in many ways, the path followed by Honda can be identified as an industrial model based on a very different type of innovation than in the case of Toyota (BOYER & FREYSSENET 1998). However, if this ideal is to become the foundation for the Japanese economy's renewed dynamism, it then becomes necessary to rethink the entire institutional framework for there to be some kind of evolution in the social system of innovation (AMABLE, BARRÉ and BOYER 1997).

Watanabe focuses on what is required if the institutional environment within which companies operate is to be modified so that an 'innovative company' can be developed. He specifically brings up the issue of patents in Japan. From the point of view of small and medium-sized businesses, the system continues to exhibit many shortcomings (e. g., intellectual property rights protected only for a limited period of three years, or the asymmetry between large companies and SMEs). It becomes necessary therefore to undertake action in order to solve these problems (e. g., relying on technological advances in the hope that innovation can be kept in-house, or patenting in the USA so as to benefit from the greater protection there).

The issue of how innovation is funded (limited access to the financial markets, the role of venture capital) has also become a major problem, and not just anecdotally. Access to capital resources is particularly important in the analysis of the different forms of capitalism (CROUCH & STREECK 1996), especially in the opposition between Anglo-Saxon capitalism (the financial market) and corporative capitalism (with its greater links between banks and industry). These two dimensions are also studied in AOKI's (1988) economic analysis of the Japanese firm.

Finally, Watanabe briefly mentions the "socio-psychological barriers to venture businesses" (p. 224), especially as it pertains to young graduates' inclination towards working for a large company. Indeed, generalizing the figure of the Schumpeterian entrepreneur also assumes that there will be a thorough redefinition of values in favour of more individualistic attitudes, and, beyond this, an evolution of wage-earning relationships, encouraging the development of 'intra-preneurship' within organizations. Even if some ambitious transformations must occur before this type of behaviour can be generalized, the potential of the Japanese economy in this area is attested to by the success of the big-name companies (e. g., Honda and Sony), and by the fact that a large part of certain companies' competitiveness during the 1980s was due to the efficient ways in which their R&D activities were organized (CLARK & FUJIMOTO 1991).

Concerning the more meso-economic level of the *keiretsu* groups, advances in technological capabilities have reinforced sub-contractors' negotiating power through their mastery of technology and innovative development. These competencies have become complementary and indispensable for the primary client. At the same time, investment by suppliers in R&D has been increased so that these competencies can be further developed, accentuating the search for economies of scale and a reduction of fixed costs and, ultimately, prices, as requested by clients. Such attempts to rationalize and commonalize (that is, using the same components for several different products) have led top-tier customers to encourage sub-contractors to sell their products even to competitors (cf. above, and Lecler's text). This being the case, there can no longer be the same respect for the old rules, with their emphasis on the accumulation of a captive customer base ("loyalism" for HIRSCHMAN 1970) and on building trust.

Suppliers have always been forced to compete with each other—this was an essential method for encouraging them to improve competitiveness through lower prices or through innovation. However, such competition has now become more widespread, as other ways of coordinating business activities are diminishing. They may not yet have become quite as purely mercantile as is the catalogue purchase of components, subsystems, or modules (CHANARON 1995), but the nature of supplier networks has changed. This makes it necessary for other types of linkage to evolve, i. e., for the organization of networks.

3 Towards a new type of industrial networks?

Over the last few years, the concept of network has been widely used to emphasize the need to understand a company not on an individual level, but within the framework of a set of companies who, given their close interactions, need to cooperate. Using various methods, they are thereby trying to reinforce their 'systemic' competitiveness. What is interesting in this network concept is that it highlights the importance of inter-company relationships in creating industrial and competitive dynamics. Several authors have explicitly adopted this approach in the case of Japan (ODAKA, ONO and ADACHI 1988). From this point of view, it is possible to identify the ideal type in the Japanese system of supplying as a vertically hierarchized network which uses the tier-ranking of domestic companies, and wherein the ultimate client occupies a point at the centre of the network. This type of organization can also be called a 'company-network'. Thus, the current transformations of the Japanese economy may lead to changes in industrial networks, extending previous analyses (IMAI 1989) in two directions—horizontally for Watanabe, and towards a wider geographic base for Lecler.

3.1 From a company-network to a network of companies?

Watanabe, interested in the evolution of small and medium-sized Japanese businesses, insists that they need to reinforce their technological competencies in order to counteract their ultimate clients' temptation to find overseas suppliers. However, the development of new technologies requires ever increasing investments as well as a mastery of multiple competencies—it is difficult for a smaller company to achieve this. Moreover, the tendency towards a reduction of the number of firms who directly supply major companies contravenes the development of direct relationships based on cooperation, especially at the stage of joint development of products and processes. In this context, regrouping a number of smaller businesses in order to offer a common supply of products and services may constitute an efficient economic solution, in as much as it globalizes supply (through savings in administrative and in transaction costs) while allowing for the mutual abilities of the different parties to be strengthened. They are thus able to develop their specialities by acting in synergy/interactively with their partners.

In his paper, Watanabe evokes several examples of a 'network of companies' of this type, particularly involving cooperation in R&D. Such networks respond to a horizontal logic, in so far as there is no leader. In addition, they often rely on the scientific competencies of academic laboratories in order to successfully complete their projects. Such networks can be constituted on a territorial basis, though Watanabe apparently suggests that there is no geographic restriction to this type of network, and that it can include an international aspect. Yet analysis of local productive systems such as clusters

(PORTER 1990), or the Italian industrial districts and their modern version (technological districts), has proven that a dual proximity, both geographic and organizational (KIRAT & LUNG 1997), is necessary in order to ensure the network's institutional coherence. For the preservation of the horizontal character of inter-company relationships, a solid territorial basis is necessary.

Indeed, the problems of coordinating these networks are such that there needs to be a direct relationship enabling ongoing issues to be dealt with on a daily basis, and often face-to-face, this being the only way in many cases that indispensable mutual adjustments can occur. A wider geographic dimension assumes the preservation of a vertical logic.

3.2 Towards a wider geographic basis for industrial networks?

This is the solution which underlies Lecler's interest in her description of the formation of the Nippo-Asian industrial *keiretsu*. The scenario which she presents takes into account both the relocation of many sub-contracting activities throughout the countries of Southeast Asia over the last few years, and the changing nature of relationships within the industrial *keiretsu* (increasingly based on market relations rather than on personal factors). As opposed to Watanabe's paper, which studies small and medium-sized industries—who are often found at the furthest edges of the hierarchy—, her analysis of the industrial *keiretsu* focuses on all of the ranks, hence on a wider range of possible developments. The first rank firms are often companies that benefit from a high technological skill level, and who have long been involved in the processes of internationalization and market diversification.

As such, it can be hypothesized, as Lecler does, that the network transforms its structure through the constitution of 'transnational networks' which bring together different Asian countries. Due to the isomorphic relationships involved, network hierarchies can again be found in the regional division of labour which is the networks' geographic transposition:

- At the centre of the network, there are Japanese companies which concentrate their strategic activities, along with sophisticated, high value-added technologies.
- At an intermediary level, the newly industrialized countries phase in, with the competencies available to them, activities involving medium-type technologies. This could be achieved by local companies, by Japanese transplants, or by joint ventures.
- At the periphery, newcomers like Vietnam ensure the production of standardized and commonplace components, taking advantage of their much lower costs (salaries, weak currencies, etc.)

Thus, in the Lecler's study of Matsushita, as in other examples, there is evidence of a trend towards the development of a vertical regional division of labour throughout the Pacific Basin, with Japan at its centre, and with intermediary spaces and peripheral zones. Such a pattern is familiar to Western countries as well, who themselves have to a large degree been consolidated by the EU's integration and its extension towards the South (the Iberian Peninsula) and then towards the East. More recently, in North America, the United States has used NAFTA to stretch out towards Canada and Mexico. The generalization of such a pattern partially depends on the process of trade liberalization, encouraged by the WTO and further accelerated, at the behest of the IMF, in the wake of the Asian crisis. This generalization assumes above all that the networks' hierarchy remains relatively stable, despite the changes in its type of relationships and the widening of its geographic basis.

4 Conclusion

In conclusion, we shall first extrapolate the authors' interpretations before relativizing their analyses. In the interpretations proposed, rethinking the traditional hierarchical pattern of supplying relationships is deemed to mainly involve a journey towards forms which are newer, more horizontal or more internationalized. It is worthwhile taking into account the scenario in which dependency-based relationships become totally inverted, for this constitutes one possible outcome for components and subsystems suppliers who are progressing rapidly due to their full mastery of the latest high-performing technologies and their developing "organizational capabilities" (CHANDLER 1992), especially on an international scale.

Is it therefore possible to imagine that the client companies, those who design the entire architecture and who assemble the product systems, will over time lose their mastery of the value chain, to the benefit of suppliers who would then control the strategic points? Certain companies fear, amongst other things, the 'Intel Inside' syndrome, as well as the dominant position acquired by Microsoft in the computer industry—in both cases, this was detrimental to the computer makers, notably to IBM. In the automobile industry, there is a lesser concentration in assembly than in the production of certain sensitive components (pneumatics, transmissions, ABS etc.). In this latter area, a very small number of multinationals are the only suppliers worldwide. An example of this concern is the reticence of Japanese car makers to implement the principles of modular assembly already introduced by Europeans.

On the other hand, the patterns proposed by the authors for the analysis of supplying relationships are largely based on their indepth knowledge of developments which have been noticed in several industries (automobile, mechanics, electronics). These changes have been characterized by the large-scale production of product systems through the assembly of multiple components. Technological principles of this type, however, do not exhaust the full range of production systems which typify the manufacturing industries. Moreover, they do not correspond to the prevailing logic of the tertiary sector, especially in emerging fields such as new information and communication technologies. Though the restructuring of the Japanese economy may include the reorganization of its traditional activities, some new activities will also have to be developed. And with respect to these activities, it is important to be very careful before applying the conclusions of studies undertaken in other fields. The forms of inter-company relationships which are developing here are likely to be very original.

References

AMABLE, B., R. BARRÉ and R. BOYER (1997): *Les Systèmes Sociaux d'innovation à l'heure de la globalization.* Paris: Economica.

AOKI, M. (1988): *Information, Incentives and Bargaining in the Japanese Economy.* Cambridge: Cambridge University Press.

AOKI, M. (1995): The Japanese Firm as a System of Attributes: A Survey and Research Agenda. In: *Revue d'Economie Industrielle* 71, pp. 83–108.

ASANUMA, B. (1989): Manufacturer-Supplier Relationships in Japan and the Concept of Relation-Specific Skill. In: *Journal of the Japanese and International Economies* 3, pp. 1–30.

BOYER, R. and M. FREYSSENET (1995): The Emergence of New Industrial Models. In: *Actes du GERPISA*, n°15. Université d'Evry – Val d'Essonne, pp. 75–144.

BOYER, R. and M. FREYSSENET (1998): *The World that Changed the Machine.* Unpublished manuscript.

CHANARON, J. J. (1995): Constructeurs / Fournisseurs: spécificités et dynamique d'évolution des modes relationnels. In: *Actes du GERPISA*, n°14, Université d'Evry – Val d'Essonne, pp. 9–22.

CHANARON, J. J.and Y. LUNG (1995): *Economie de l'automobile.* Paris: La Découverte.

CHANDLER, A. D. Jr. (1992): Organizational Capabilities and the Economic History of the Industrial Enterprise. In: *Journal of Economic Perspectives* 6, 3, pp. 79–100.

CLARK, K. B. and T. FUJIMOTO (1991): *Product Development Performance. Strategy, Organization, and Management in the World Auto Industry.* Boston (Mass.): Harvard Business School.

CORIAT, B. (1991): *Penser à l'envers. Travail et organization dans l'entreprise japonaise.* Paris: Christian Bourgois.

CROUCH, C. and W. STREECK (eds.) (1996): *Les capitalismes en Europe.* Paris: Editions La Découverte.

CUSUMANO, M. A. (1985): *The Japanese Automobile Industry. Technology and Management at Nissan & Toyota.* Cambridge (Mass.): Harvard University Press.

DORE, R. (1987): *Taking Japan Seriously.* Stanford, CA: Stanford University Press.

DOSI, G., D. TEECE and S. WINTER (1990): Les frontières des entreprises: vers une théorie de la cohérence de la grande entreprise. In: *Revue d'économie industrielle* 51, pp. 238–254.

FRUIN, W. M. (1992): *The Japanese Enterprise System. Competitive Strategies and Cooperatives Structures.* Oxford: Clarendon.

FUJIMOTO, T. (1994): The Limits of Lean Production. In: *Politik und Gesellschaft*, January, pp. 40–46.

HELPER, S. (1993): An Exit – Voice Analysis of Supplier Relations: the Case of the U.S. Automobile Industry. In: GRAHBER, G. (ed.): *The Embedded Firm. On the Socio-Economics of Industrial Networks.* New York & London: Routledge, pp. 141–160.

HIRSCHMAN, A. O. (1970): *Exit and Voice.* Cambridge (Mass.): Harvard University Press.

IMAI, K. (1989): Evolution of Japan's Corporate and Industrial Networks. In: CARLSSON, B. (ed.): *Industrial Dynamics. Technological, Organizational, and Structural Changes in Industries and Firms.* Boston / Dordrecht / London: Kluwer Academic Publishers, pp. 123–155.

JACOT, H. ET AL. (1990): Du fordisme au toyotisme. Les voies de la modernisation du système automobile en France et au Japon. In: *Etudes et Recherches* 7–8. Paris: La Documentation Française.

KIRAT, T. and Y. LUNG (1997): Innovation and Proximity: Territories as Loci of Collective Learning Processes. Paper presented at the *93rd Annual Meeting of the Association of American Geographers.* 1–5 April, 1997, Fort Worth, Texas. (Revised version to be published in: *European Urban and Regional Science*, 1999).

LECLER, Y. (1993): *Partenariat industriel: la référence japonaise.* Limonest: L'interdisciplinaire.

NISHIGUCHI, T. (1994): *Strategic Industrial Sourcing: The Japanese Advantage.* Oxford: Oxford University Press.

ODAKA, K., K. ONO and F. ADACHI (1988): *The Automobile Industry in Japan. A Study of Ancillary Firm Development.* Tōkyō: Kinokuniya (Oxford University Press).

PORTER, M. (1990): *The Competitive Advantage of Nations.* London: Macmillan Press.

SAKO, M. (1992): *Prices, Quality and Trust. Inter-firm Relations in Britain and Japan.* Oxford: Oxford University Press.

SAUTTER, C. (1996): *La France au miroir du Japon. Croissance ou déclin.* Paris: Editions Odile Jacob.

SMITKA, M. J. (1991): *Competitive Ties. Subcontracting in the Japanese Automotive Industries.* New York and Oxford: Columbia University Press.

Human Resource Management

X Human Resource Management in Japanese Firms Undergoing Transition: A Hierarchical Approach

Hiroatsu NOHARA

This paper first aims at clarifying the so-called 'Japanese model of human resource management', by comparing it with the French model. This comparison also shows the 'exceptionalism' of these two models with regard to the American model. Secondly, it attempts to analyse the adjustment patterns of the Japanese model during the post-*bubble* recession using the typological tool of mechanical (peripheral), organic and structural change. The former two change types are based on the mobilization of existing 'social and labour conventions', while the latter type implies the creation of new rules by the actors for the adaptation of the system to radically different situations.

1 Introduction

The recession the Japanese economy is undergoing since the beginning of the 1990s has given rise to much questioning as to its nature. However, many analysts—irrespective of theoretical persuasion—seem to agree that it is structural rather than cyclical. In particular, they point to the increasingly glaring mismatch between the new conditions of competition in the international market and the institutional infrastructure which has grown up over the past fifty years, within the framework of the nation state, providing the foundation for Japan's rapid economic growth. In other words, the various institutional mechanisms hitherto regarded as the key to the country's economic success are falling into disuse and are even beginning to come into conflict with the current phase of economic globalization. In short, the foundations of yesterday's success have become the source of today's impasse.

Such diagnoses cannot fail but to call into question the *Japanese model of the firm*, a central plank of the institutional pacts that have constituted the engine of wealth production. The firm is indeed the site at which the various institutional forces converge in order to be transformed into productive capacity. Even if the macro- and micro-levels tend to be confused in the various debates, it is obvious that the fundamental issue for economists is to identify the limits of this model of the firm.

However, the main purpose of this paper is not to conduct an exhaustive analysis of the tensions that have become apparent in the Japanese model of the firm. Such a study is beyond the scope of this article. Rather, our aim is simply to investigate the nature of the changes that one of the elements of the model is undergoing, namely the *management of human resources* (HRM). However, anyone seeking to study the changes this model is undergoing will inevitably come up against two kinds of problems.

The *first problem* concerns the interpretation of the model. Although there is an extensive literature on human resource management in Japanese firms, there is still by no means any agreement on its general portrayal, or even on how the facts observed are to be interpreted (UJIHARA 1958, DORE 1973, KOIKE 1976, AOKI 1988). The various interpretations that have arisen as a result have created a sense of confusion.

The *second problem*, more methodological in nature, concerns our ability to evaluate. It might legitimately be asked how change can be evaluated or measured when every subject of analysis, at least in the social sciences, is constantly on the move? Are we sufficiently well equipped with analytical tools to be able to capture the changes taking place in complex realities?

Without claiming to be able to resolve all of these difficulties, we shall attempt in this paper to outline some possible responses to the problems raised. The starting point for this attempt will be the phenomenon of the *hierarchy.*

In the neo-classical literature, no real reference is made to organizations nor to hierarchies; neo-institutionalist approaches, on the other hand, seek to develop economic tools that make it possible to analyse the 'black box' that organizations constitute. Nevertheless, following WILLIAMSON (1975), who introduces the opposition between market and hierarchy, the hierarchical organization is regarded above all from the point of view of the allocation of informational resources, i. e., of the decision-making process; in contrast to the market, the hierarchy derives its efficiency from task specialization and centralized decision-making. Such approaches tend, therefore, to play down the economic role of the hierarchy in the management of human resources. It is true that some studies (see, for example, AKERLOF & YELLEN 1986) emphasize the economic rationalities of the 'internal labour market'—another term for the hierarchy—in terms of 'incentive theory', 'moral hazard', 'implicit contract', 'risk aversion' on the part of workers, etc.

However, most of these studies remain faithful to the principle of methodological individualism and adopt an analytical framework based on agency theory that reduces the employment contract to a simple bilateral relationship between principal and agent. From this perspective, the internal market is wholly devoid of any collective dimension and consists solely of innumerable individual contracts. Thus these neo-institutionalist approaches lead to a portrayal of the internal market that lacks the depth of the hierarchical organization, takes no account of the interaction between the actors and appears to be without structure.

In comparison with such a 'dematerialized' internal labour market, the early works published by labour economists (DOERINGER & PIORE 1971) seem to offer a richer analytical framework. These authors focus their analysis on the internal management practices firms adopt in order to stabilize the workers they select and then train. Their model of the organization usually includes a hierarchy of jobs, points of entry to that hierarchy and clearly marked routes along which employees move as they develop their skills. Structuring of this kind protects 'insiders' from the competitive forces that weaken the position of 'outsiders' in the external labour market. Thus they highlight the existence of an internal market that does not appear to operate in accordance with the principles of the Walrasien market. On the contrary, labour allocation and pay determination in this internal market take place in accordance with rules specific to each firm. Thus it is the hierarchy that plays the central organizational role, thereby giving rise to the segmentation of spaces between the external and internal markets.

Although they are not formalized to any great extent, these studies have opened up an interesting new path that has allowed economic analysis to take account of the hierarchy. Apart from the few neo-institutionalist endeavours already alluded to above, it would appear to be AOKI (1988) who managed to produce the most highly formalized account of the role of the hierarchy in HRM, while at the same time retaining the collective aspect of the production of skills. In particular, AOKI develops the notion of "rank hierarchy" (a set of incentives put in place within the internal market) by arguing that hierarchical principles can be used not only to resolve the problem of coordination (resource allocation, information flows) but also to address that of incentives (employee motivation). Without investigating the real core of his argument, we can follow AOKI to the extent of recognizing that the hierarchical organization—and the pay hierarchy that accompanies it—has three functions in the management of human resources:

1) It rationalizes the learning process, since employees' progression from the simplest to increasingly complicated tasks can reduce training costs through the effects of 'on-the-job training' and 'learning by doing'.
2) It encourages employees to maximize their efforts and to learn, not simply in the sense of resolving the 'moral hazard problem', which is implied in the 'shirking model', but also by making their progress up the hierarchy conditional upon their involvement in their work and the development of competencies over the long term.
3) It resolves the 'adverse selection problem'; career paths based on progression up the hierarchy allow individual employees' abilities to be tested at each level of responsibility, thereby avoiding any mismatch between individuals and jobs.

These three economic functions fall into a universal category of rationality that can be applied to all forms of hierarchical organization. We accept the validity of these statements and their general applicability, at least on a hypothetical level. However, our working hypothesis is that these functions, given their material form in various management tools, are mobilized very differently from one country to another, depending on the way in which the firm is integrated into the wider society. It seems especially important to take into consideration the interdependency between educational system and work organization in the firm. In this sense, what appears to be a universal rationality turns out to be mediated to a considerable extent through a specific "societal rationality" (MAURICE, SELLIER and SILVESTRE 1986). This interpretative approach, which is close to the notion of "embeddedness between economic action and social structure" as advanced by GRANOVETTER (1985), will serve as a starting point for our investigation.

In the first part of this paper, we will attempt to characterize the Japanese HRM model by conducting a comparison between France and Japan. The vast majority of comparative studies carried out in Japan take the Anglo-Saxon countries as their reference point, and a comparison with France may shed, it is hoped, new light on the Japanese model. In the second part of the paper, we will examine the changes of direction brought about by the current recession.

2 The construction of hierarchy in Japan

Our aim here is to synthesize, in the most stylized way possible, the various dimensions of the hierarchy in Japan, using the French hierarchy as a mirror in which to reflect and thereby form an image of its Japanese counterpart. We will begin by outlining the path taken by some categories of employees along the pay hierarchy before turning our attention to some of the HRM principles that underpin the construction of the hierarchy.

2.1 Wage scales

Table 1 below shows the progression of several categories of employees along the pay scale in accordance with age. Although they are very crude, these wage curves provide some interesting information, not only about the structure of the hierarchy at any given time but also about the career paths of dependent employees in the two countries.

France is characterized by the coexistence of several forms of wage curves corresponding to various types of incentive, or to the absence of any incentive. In other words, the various employee categories are treated in highly differentiated ways.

The wage curve of most manual workers in France reaches its peak very quickly. Whereas the pay of their Japanese counterparts continues to rise until the age of 45–49, that of French *manual workers* starts to stagnate after the age of 30. Moreover, the earnings of French manual workers rise only modestly in the course of their working lives. At the age of 40–44, earnings are only 29 % higher than at ages 20–24, compared with an increase of 80 % for engineers and managers (*cadres*).

This absence of a career structure for manual workers leads to several consequences. Firstly, pay does not seem to act as much of an incentive in the development of skills in this population. Secondly, promotion to a non-manual category, and particularly to the technician category, is a worthwhile prospect, but one that tends to diminish the status of the manual category, since many of the 'better' workers are able to leave this category altogether. Thirdly, the absence of promotion prospects for most manual workers increases the distance between them and other categories, does not aid the establishment of trust and obstructs the development of cooperative work relationships within the firm.

Table 1: Comparison of wage profiles by age (Manufacturing industry, male employees, 1986)

Age (years)	FRANCE (French Franc)			JAPAN (Yen)		
	Manual workers	Technicians	Engineers and managers	Manual workers	Technicians	Engineers and managers
18–19	5600	–	–	126000	–	–
20–24	5900 (100)	7300 (124)	11500 (195)	143000 (100)	147000 (103)	161000 (113)
25–29	6600 (100)	8500 (129)	13200 (200)	171000 (100)	183000 (107)	186000 (109)
30–34	7100 (100)	9600 (135)	16000 (229)	207000 (100)	24000 (116)	241000 (116)
35–39	7600 (100)	10300 (136)	18300 (241)	236000 (100)	297000 (126)	318000 (135)
40–44	7800 (100)	11000 (147)	20800 (267)	255000 (100)	345000 (135)	401000 (157)
45–49	7800 (100)	11500 (147)	21800 (279)	254000 (100)	392000 (154)	477000 (188)
50–54	7400 (100)	11500 (155)	22400 (303)	247000 (100)	401000 (162)	534000 (216)
55–59	7700 (100)	11500 (147)	22200 (288)	211000 (100)	458000 (217)	508000 (241)

Notes: • The 'Technicians' category corresponds to white collar workers with a college diploma (high school + 2 years of schooling), and the 'Engineers/managers' category to white collar workers with a university diploma (high school + 4 or more years of schooling)

• 'Wage' is the monthly amount of regular payment.

Source: The statistical sources are, for France, INSEE (1986), and for Japan MINISTRY OF LABOUR (1986).

As far as *technicians* are concerned, they constitute an intermediate category with a weak professional identity. This category is in fact made up of two heterogeneous populations, one of which consists of promoted manual workers and the other of holders of a qualification requiring two years of post-*baccalauréat* study. In the case of the former, promotion to the technician category represents a worthwhile extension of their wage curves. In the case of the latter, who have the status of 'senior technician', pay reaches a peak after only ten years in the labour market. For them, promotion to the engineer or *cadre* category is the only way of furthering their careers or increasing their pay. *Cadres* (managers) and *engineers*, in contrast, enjoy a high status as soon as they graduate from the *grandes écoles* (the most elitist engineering schools) which gives them both a great deal of professional autonomy and a high salary. The pay of *cadres* aged 20–24 at the beginning of their careers is twice that of manual workers of the same age and equal to that of the highest paid technicians. Moreover, their wage curve does not reach its peak until they are aged between 50 and 54. A pay scale of this kind constitutes a real incentive mechanism.

Compared with the French situation, dependent employees in *Japan* are organized and mobilized in a very different way. Here, the wage curves for the various categories of employees are similarly shaped, rising rapidly to a peak and then falling away gradually. The only differences between the categories are the end points reached and the rate of progression. Manual workers, for example, reach their peak pay level at the age of 45–49, when their pay is 78 % higher than at ages 20–24; managers and engineers, on the other hand, reach their peak pay level at the age of 50–54, by which time their starting pay has almost tripled.

These differences, essentially homothetic in nature, do not reveal any great split between the various categories of employees, unlike in France. In fact manual workers, technicians and engineers are all covered by a single status clause and, in many cases, by the same payment system. However, this overall homogeneity at the category level does not exclude pay individualization based on the annual evaluation of each employee carried out by his superior. This individual evaluation of competencies (*satei*) applies to all categories, including manual workers, a practice that seems to set Japan apart from European countries (KOIKE 1981). In effect, therefore, firms very subtly differentiate employees' pay within the limits of the career paths laid down *ex ante* for each category.

In any event, pay tends to be a uniting factor for Japanese employees, at least at the beginning of their careers, unlike in France, where it has a divisive effect from the outset. It is only as they advance along their career paths that the narrow pay differentials in Japan begin to widen gradually. Thus graduate engineers (with degrees requiring four or more years of higher education) and technicians with diplomas requiring a two-years higher or further education begin their careers on salaries that differ little from those of manual workers of the same age (20–24). Their starting salaries constitute the minimum level of pay in the labour market.

This dissociation between formal qualifications and pay, a phenomenon specific to Japan, runs counter to the teachings of the 'signalling' and 'adverse selection' theories. Furthermore, their pay levels remain lower than those of very experienced manual workers, at least until they are around 35 years of age. This slow rate of progress along the pay scale, which from a European point of view seems to offer little in the way of motivation, is accepted by young graduates, even though they are aware that it does not always encourage risk-taking or creativity. Nevertheless, the wage curve for non-manual workers does diverge from that for manual workers. From the age of 35–40 onwards, it begins to accelerate, eventually reaching a peak that is more than double the pay of manual workers. As a result, managers and engineers at the end of their careers acquire professional recognition and legitimation through their elevated position in the hierarchy.

2.2 The construction of hierarchy

After this analysis of pay, we shall turn our attention to the construction of the hierarchy. The diagrams reproduced below are intended to summarize some of the basic principles underlying the organization of hierarchy specific to each country. Although they are extremely simplified, they do have the merit of presenting, in condensed form, a number of stylized facts, which will make it easier to outline our interpretative system.

Graph 1: A comparison of corporate hierarchies in Japan and France

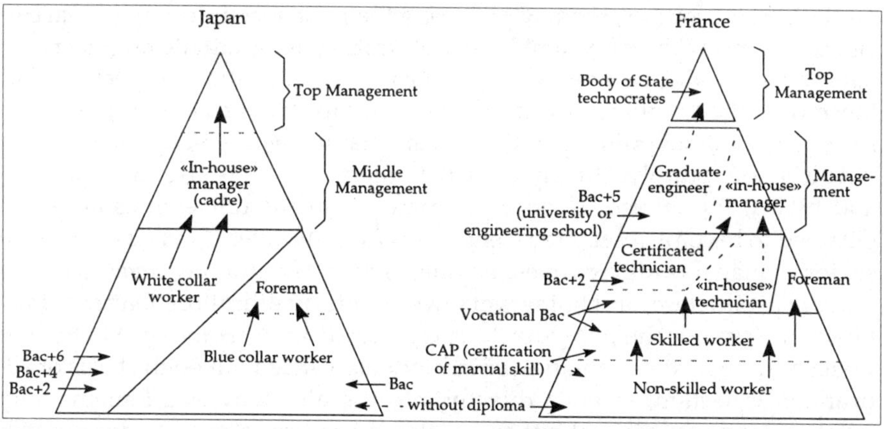

Note: The level of education corresponds to a number of schooling years after the baccalauréat (high school graduate)

Source: NOHARA (1995)

2.2.1 The case of France

The strategies adopted by actors in order to gain access to the hierarchy are very complex in France, in the sense that they combine formal qualifications, professional experience and seniority. This complexity is closely linked to the organizational structures of French firms, which have put in place a system of work organization dominated technically and organizationally by the notion of *job*. This notion is the key factor in both the technical management of production and the social management of jobs (job classification). The hierarchy in French firms is based essentially on this job classification system, to which employees gain access through a variety of routes and by adopting a range of different strategies.

In other words, the hierarchy is sustained by both external and internal mobility. Thus at all levels of the hierarchy, including the highest ones, employees holding the formal qualifications stipulated for that particular level and self-taught people promoted from the lower levels exist alongside each other. It is as if these two categories of actors are constantly competing with each other for vacant jobs by enhancing, in their own particular ways, the human capital they possess. A struggle of this kind tends to encourage actors to adopt their own independent, and sometimes highly creative strategies, but there can be no doubt that such a design also tends to weaken the identity of each category and, ultimately, to undermine the legitimacy of the hierarchy.

These two modes of access to the hierarchy naturally have their own internal logics: The match between formal qualifications and jobs is based on the collective agreement negotiated between the social partners and legitimated by the state. These rules are external givens to which French firms have to acquiesce. At the same time, the educational system selects pupils for its various levels and courses, thereby preparing them for specific occupational categories: those with five years' higher education are graduate engineers (or *cadres*), those with two years' higher or further education are technicians, those with the vocational *baccalauréat* or CAP (*certificat d'aptitude professionnelle,* or vocational training certificate) are manual workers, and so on.

This labour supply, already extremely hierarchized, is also finely graded and highly specialized. Science graduates from the universities are often destined to become researchers, engineers from the major *grandes écoles* to be senior managers or executives, engineers from the minor *grandes écoles* to work in production, and holders of lower-grade qualifications (*brevet de technician supérieur* or the two-year *diplome universitaire de technologie*) to be senior technicians. This evaluation of individuals, carried out on the basis of educational selection, extends directly into the hierarchy and remains very much in evidence throughout an employee's entire career. The importance attached to educational qualifications gives rise to various occupational identities that are used to legitimate the existence of hierarchically arranged 'territories' and the strategy of external mobility in the labour market.

This segmented situation results in a certain imbalance of power in the organization of creativity in manufacturing industry: those engaged directly in production (i. e., technicians and manual workers) are not allowed to play as full a role as possible in the technical aspects of product design and manufacturing, since engineers tend to 'parachute' their ideas on to the shop floor without consultation. In other words, the existence of hierarchized territories hinders the development of a wide-ranging dialogue between the design and production functions and of sufficiently rigorous compromises between technical 'inventiveness' and manufacturing feasibility. Faithful to the doctrine of Taylorism, *France* thus tends to produce a hierarchy characterized by a clear split between design and production (BOYER 1990). The former function is overvalued, while the latter is not given sufficient consideration.

Over and above the influence over organizational structures exerted by educational qualifications, firms also have some scope to take the initiative in constructing the hierarchy. In doing so, they are explicitly recognizing the allegiance that employees without formal qualifications develop through the stabilization of their position within the firm. This interaction between the firm and employees is based on highly personal strategies. The ambition of semi-skilled manual workers is to be promoted to the skilled worker category, while that of technicians is to become engineers or *cadres*. The system of internal promotion between the various categories serves as an incentive mechanism for those wishing to become involved in their work, to invest in continued training or simply to escape from the status of manual worker and the unfavourable conditions associated with it. Thus this mechanism creates groups of self-taught employees, such as the so-called 'in-house' technicians or *cadres*, who coexist with their formally qualified colleagues but are unable to transfer the standing they have acquired within the firm to the external labour market.

2.2.2 The case of Japan

In comparison with France, the hierarchy in Japan is based simultaneously on continuity and discontinuity. As far as *discontinuity* is concerned, three different dimensions should be highlighted.

The first is the more or less complete closure of the organization to its external environment. The hierarchy in Japanese firms is constructed almost exclusively on the basis of career paths that are internal to the organization. As a result, any links with the external labour market are confined to a certain number of low-status jobs, while access to the higher levels or to managerial or supervisory positions cannot be gained through external mobility.

This detachment from the external labour market tends to channel actors towards internal strategies (promotion) and to create a 'balkanized' labour market. This fragmentation is fairly consistent with the system of educational qualifications, which is not intended to 'qualify' the labour force but simply to guarantee its 'potential'. Thus educational qualifications, even the best (awarded by one of the best universities), are unable to acquire any measure of transferability and thus be recognized in different organizations.

The second dimension concerns the gender segregation in the labour market. The division between male and female wage-earners, which reflects a powerful social norm governing the differentiation of gender roles, is proving to be very resilient in Japan. While the educational certification relatively protects the female workers against job and wage discrimination in France, a lack of socially recognized skill-standards weakens their position in Japan. Irrespective of status or the nature of their employment contract, female employees are seldom allowed to develop their careers to the full. They are, to a greater extent, excluded from the mechanisms governing progress up the hierarchical ladder, because they do not have the same training opportunities as men and are often obliged to abandon their careers for family reasons.

The third dimension refers to the split between the manual space ('blue collar' category) and the non-manual space ('white collar' category). This split manifests itself in the absence of any link between these two categories. In other words, manual workers, who very often are high-school graduates, are first allocated simple tasks and then acquire experience by rotating between different jobs, thereby becoming 'functionally flexible'. However, they remain confined to their own particular career path, which advances within a relatively closed space from which the only exit is promotion to a supervisory job (position of foreman). Nevertheless, this compartmentalization of the various categories, which is not necessarily status-enhancing in Japan as it is in France, does not seem to sap the motivation of manual workers when it comes to skill development. The manual career path, whose separateness is compensated for with a wide wage curve, creates its own logic of incentive, involvement and integration into the organization. This logic is further strengthened by the high degree of continuity between the manual category and supervisory positions, in the sense that promotion to such a post represents the natural and legitimate culmination of the manual career path.

As far as *continuity* is concerned, mention should be made of the importance of the 'melting pot' in which new recruits are immersed in transcending the various divisions between statuses and categories, particularly in the 'white collar' category. Whether they have received two, four or six or more years of higher education, university graduates constitute a more or less undifferentiated population of recruits from which, after a period of between ten and fifteen years, the new generation of senior managers will be selected. In other words, the entire population of new recruits is treated as a single reservoir of human resources from which specific resources are gradually extracted.

Thus the process of differentiation takes place over time and is based more on what the new recruits learn than on the status or category to which they belong at the beginning of their careers. Moreover, the 'technician' category has neither a place in the classification system nor any real equivalent in Japan. This is why the technician category is not included in the Japanese diagram (graph 1). The tasks performed by technicians in France are allocated to experienced manual workers at the end of their careers and to foremen, as well as to university graduates with six years' higher education at the beginning of their careers. This break-up of the technicians' role may well explain why the boundary between design and production in the Japanese hierarchy is somewhat ill-defined. The separation of tasks that is one of the guiding principles of Taylorism is certainly not eliminated, but it is attenuated to a certain extent, if not modified (NOHARA 1987). This phenomenon reveals the extent to which occupational categories and the division of labour are *social constructs* that depend on national contexts.

Not having any immediately useful skills, all these new recruits undergo the same occupational and organizational apprenticeship. Their skills develop during a long process of socialization: the new recruits begin by exploring technically limited tasks carrying little responsibility, gradually extending their sphere of competence by moving on to related tasks. The hierarchy of educational levels and university degrees is of little importance during this period of apprenticeship.

However, its effects make themselves felt as individuals advance along their career path, and particularly when it comes to promotion within the hierarchy. In fact, although the majority of university graduates advance at more or less similar rates for almost ten years, the principle of selection and competition begins to emerge at this point. Thus 35–40 is a pivotal age, since it is then that selection to the first rung of the management ladder takes place. This selection is based not on a shot in the dark or on a gamble on any particular individual, but rather on the system of assessment that constantly evaluates, on an annual basis, each individual's progress in the learning process and his/her ability to cooperate and contribute to the collective effort. This encourages employees to incorporate long-term considerations into their career strategies. Nevertheless, sustained and exacting competition of this kind finishes by producing the hierarchy at around age 40 and leads to the differentiation of university graduates into managers and non-managers. This competition continues subsequently, in an extremely selective way, as employees progress towards the upper echelons of the hierarchy.

This structuring of internal career paths, which combines collective cooperation and individual selection, might well correspond to the principle of "tournament competition" outlined by Rosenbom (ROSENBAUM 1984). However, the question remains as to why and how Japanese firms manage to organize such a slow selection process that seems in some respects to be demotivating and in others to be one element in the production of cooperation. Thus the management team, including senior executives, is produced over time as each generation succeeds the previous one. As a result, a high degree of continuity is maintained as the base of the pyramid. In this way, the hierarchy acquires a dynamic, temporal element rather than being simply vertical.

3 The transformation of the Japanese HRM model

We shall now turn our attention to the examination of the type of change the Japanese HRM model is undergoing in this period of a long recession. This model, outlined above, contains a set of rules and practices capable of structuring the organization of the internal market. These rules and practices are not immune to external shocks. On the contrary, they react either by encouraging certain patterns of behaviour or certain kinds of social relationships, or by obstructing the emergence of new behaviour patterns that are inconsistent with the principles underlying them.

In some instances, they are also capable of renewing themselves by laying a new foundation for the social infrastructure on which the interplay between the actors is based. In this case, the new elements emerge sometimes at the heart of the central regulatory mechanisms and sometimes on the periphery, although it is difficult to distinguish what is merely an extension of the existing model from what might be considered a radical alteration of it.

Faced with the complexity of these real shifts, there is a need to equip ourselves with a methodology capable of dealing adequately with the question of change. An interesting path has already been opened up by SILVESTRE (1986) who put forward a typology of mechanical, organic and structural change:

- *Mechanical change* denotes a change in the social behaviour of actors or institutions that takes place only at the margins of the system without affecting the central core of trade-offs that enable the system as a whole to adapt. Such a change is, therefore, a mechanical effect produced by the absorption of external shocks.
- *Organic change* denotes a certain plasticity in the most widely legitimated and accepted rules that constitute the heart of the system. Although the central principles of the system are mobilized in order to absorb tensions and conflicts, that mobilization is achieved through an extension of the sphere in which those principles can be applied rather than through any fundamental change in their nature.
- *Structural change* finally denotes a response that seeks to modify the fundamental principles of the system when the shocks disturb its centre of gravity. This triggers a process of change affecting social behaviour and requiring new trade-offs. Institutional change of this magnitude cannot take place without the actors engaging in a collective learning process or the emergence of new actors.

Like so many others, this typology is not perfect. In particular, it is static and takes no account of the fact that events take place in time. For example, it may be that a change that seems to be mechanical at one point could end up by changing over the long term into a structural change, as a result of the threshold effect or for other reasons. Or, conversely, apparently 'radical' changes can become commonplace as they are worn away by routine and time. Despite this problem, which remains unresolved, the typology outlined above does make it possible to identify more clearly the responses of Japanese firms to the current crisis and to understand the consequences of those responses for the Japanese model of HRM.

According to the composite index compiled by the Economic Planning Agency, the recession that began to take hold in 1991 bottomed out in the last quarter of 1993, but in the absence of any clear sign of an upturn it has remained dormant until today. Many firms, having built up surplus capacity by over-investing at the end of the 1980s, have had to face a crisis of profitability. The continuing rise of the yen against the dollar worsened the situation by weakening firms' international competitiveness.

During this recession—the longest Japan has ever experienced—many firms have had to embark on a restructuring of their activities, which has been accompanied by job losses. Nevertheless, the extent of these losses, although considerable, does not appear to be any greater than those that followed the first oil shock. On the other hand, they have been spread over a longer period. This slowness in adjusting the size of the workforce is undoubtedly linked to the nature of corporate governance in Japan, which is less subject to short-term financial discipline and tends to put off radical restructuring of industrial activities and to avoid taking drastic measures if at all possible. This is consistent with what various studies have already revealed of firms' behaviour when faced with the need to adjust the size of their workforce to demand (see also the contribution by DIRKS to this volume).

Their first reaction is to reduce the volume of overtime, while at the same time freezing recruitment. Secondly, firms do not rehire those employees on fixed-term contracts, while at the same time reallocating workers among the various establishments within the group to which they belong. Finally, if they fail to make a profit for two consecutive years, they negotiate 'voluntary' retirement for older members of the workforce, who tend to be more expensive than their younger colleagues. The bargaining often focuses on an increase in the lump sum allowance, which in theory is proportional to seniority. As a result, redundancies are rather rare, except in the case of bankruptcy. The same pattern of behaviour has been observable in the current recession, albeit with a few modifications, which confirms the existence of a routine behaviour pattern among firms.

Over and above this general outline of labour market trends, which requires specific statistical studies, we shall try to discover how the whole set of rules and practices has reacted to the economic situation and whether those reactions have led to changes in the Japanese model of HRM.

3.1 Mechanical change

This crisis has, once again, weakened the position of female wage-earners, most of whom exist on the periphery of the central employment regulation system. The weak position of women has three dimensions:

Firstly, because of the reduction in recruitment levels, it has now become more difficult than in the past for young people leaving the educational system, when it was normal for school-leavers and new graduates to go straight into firms, to gain access to the internal labour market. This increased selectiveness disadvantages female graduates in particular, since the office jobs that have been their traditional destinations are now much reduced in number as a result of computerization. This situation has led them to either accept the various atypical types of employment contract or to delay their entry into the labour market.

Secondly, the relationship between young women and firms is one of mutual mistrust, in that their 'temporary' presence in the firm and the lack of investment devoted to young female employees creates a vicious circle. This so-called 'statistical' discrimination is based on a principle that is diametrically opposed to that of the mutual commitment to long-term investment in human capital that applies to male employees. Although they are integrated into the internal labour market, and despite the introduction of equal opportunity legislation in the employment sphere, women do not have the same opportunities to make a career for themselves like men do. In fact, most women abandon their careers, not so much nowadays when they marry as when their first child is born, but in any event before they have placed their feet on the first rung of the management ladder. Thus women still account for only 3 % of the total population of 'supervisors'. Similarly, it is significant that the quit rate for women aged between 20 and 29 has remained around 25 % per year during the recession (RŌDŌ DAIJIN KANBŌ 1994).

Finally, the recession has led to an increase in the number of married women in precarious employment relationships and accelerated their move into the external labour market. In 1995, more than 20 % of the wage-earning population (10 million out of a total of 47.8 million), 75 % of them women, were on part-time, temporary or other types of precarious employment contracts (SŌMUCHŌ TŌKEIKYOKU 1996). Thus the number of outsiders has increased.

All in all, firms' initial response to the recession has been to marginalize an increasing share of female wage-earners, who exist on the periphery of the wage/employment trade-off. This change is essentially quantitative in nature. However, it may well be asked whether the further continuation of such a trend will not, in the long term, begin to undermine the interests of firms themselves. In the light of the forecast shortage of young workers in the near future and of rising qualification levels among young women, Japanese firms will be forced to integrate women more closely into their organizational structures, a move that will lead to profound changes in their model of HRM.

3.2 Organic change

The most widely respected wage/employment trade-off is the mutual, long-term commitment between firms and their (male) employees that is symbolized by the notion of 'lifetime employment'. Firms undertake to guarantee employees a job and a minimum level of career advancement at each stage of the life cycle; for their part, employees constantly undertake to improve their skills, which is the best guarantee for the firm's long-term development and survival, while waiting for their efforts to be rewarded. It is this system of mutual expectations, fashioned in the course of Japanese social history, that provides the basis for the production of the hierarchy (NOHARA 1993). Although this system is based on an ethnological notion of trust, such a collective cognitive system (FAVEREAU 1989) nevertheless has to permanently demonstrate its legitimacy while at the same time confronting the harsh laws of the market economy. To this end, two additional, interacting mechanisms have developed in order to ensure that the system survives in the face of economic vicissitudes.

Firstly, Japanese firms tend to favour a mode of development based on endogenous growth, which is achieved through diversification of their activities. This phenomenon is particularly evident in 'mature' industries such as iron and steel, textiles and basic chemicals (NITTA 1991), but is by no means confined to them. Some firms try to convert declining industries into industries of the future, by making maximum use of their internal resources, and particularly their human resources. Others harness to their own ends a generic technology, such as micro-electronics or materials science, in order to create new products and enter new areas.

In contrast to European countries, where restructuring is synonymous with mergers, take-overs and concentration, often leading to job losses, the process of industrial reorganization in Japan tends to be accompanied by the creation of subsidiaries and thus of 'pyramid-shaped' groups of firms. Such a strategy, based on long-term considerations and the exploitation of internal resources, is not, of course, unrelated to the prevailing form of corporate governance. Characterized as it is by a relative lack of stockholder control and pressure to generate short-term profits, corporate strategies in Japan allow planning over the long term, which entails risks that are more difficult to control than if a purely financial strategy was adopted.

Secondly, this trend towards internal diversification goes hand in hand with the mechanism of internal labour mobility. The Japanese system of work organization already has a certain degree of flexibility, based on job rotation (KOIKE 1976). Since pay is not directly linked to any particular job or task, the definition of which tends in any case to be vague, employees are less likely to resist switching between functions. On the contrary, their notion of a career tends to include a number of changes, whether it be allocation to a new job, a period of learning or even a transfer to a different establishment. Although there is some resistance to internal mobility, and local disputes certainly occur, firms are able to mobilize this mechanism, often giving joint control to the trade union, in order to adapt to fluctuations in output, the introduction of new technologies or industrial restructuring. For example in 1993, 804,000 male employees moved between establishments within the same company; this was equivalent to one-third of the total exit flows (i. e., 2,360,000 male employees left their employer in that year, see RŌDŌ DAIJIN KANBŌ SEISAKU CHŌSABU 1994). Internal fluidity of this kind gives firms a high degree of organizational flexibility. There is no doubt that this kind of regulation was spontaneously adopted in response to the destabilization of the productive system caused by the current recession.

However, this mode of regulation, confined as it is within the firm, has its limits, as well as a certain tendency to break out beyond the confines of the firm, making it necessary to extend its field of application. In an economic situation in which the number of surplus workers 'hoarded' by manufacturing firms is put at more than one million, firms are transferring part of their workforce, mainly to subsidiaries, but also to subcontractors or client companies. It is mainly employees aged 45 and over who are being offered a transfer to subsidiaries. Most seem to accept the transfer as a second-best option, while in some cases mobility has been enforced, even if the employees concerned retain their original employment contract. This practice of transferring workers for longer or shorter periods, which is known as *shukkō*, existed before the recession, but seems to have become more prevalent and now affects between 350,000 and 400,000 people (RŌDŌ DAIJIN KANBŌ SEISAKU CHŌSABU 1994; see also DIRKS in this volume).

This reflects an extension of the boundary of the internal market towards the firm's corporate group. This phenomenon may be interpreted as an extension of the rules of the existing trade-off which, despite local tensions, makes it possible to reconcile the principle of 'lifetime employment', reductions in employment levels and the diffusion of innovative capacity within the group. We shall use the term *organic* to denote such a change, since here the fundamental rules of the trade-off, based on complex social transactions, demonstrate their plasticity in adapting to new situations.

Nevertheless, as the recession persists, the limits of such plasticity are constantly being pushed back. *Shukkō,* in which the main employment conditions of transferred workers are retained because the original employment contract remains in force, is increasingly being replaced by *tenseki,* which denotes a permanent transfer and the rescinding of the original contract. Most of those transferred permanently experience a deterioration in their employment conditions. This transfer has much in common with the 'reclassification' that is a feature of many of the social plans drawn up by French firms. In Japan, however, this 'reclassification' mainly concerns white-collar workers aged 50 and over, including managers. Taken in conjunction with the accelerated ageing of the wage-earning population, an excess of supervisory staff weighs heavily both on the organization of the firm and on its wage bill.

From the point of view of the hierarchical approach, mobility of this type does not simply reflect increased selectiveness in promotion decisions, nor a 'funnel' effect caused by the filtering out of the least effective members of the supervisory category. Rather, it may well call into question the validity of the existing incentive mechanisms, by undermining the trust on which the mutual commitment is based and destabilizing to some extent the key category of employees that embodies the most entrenched employment norm. If it continues to gain ground, this phenomenon may well result in an opening up of cracks within the construction of the hierarchy, which would be an indication of a shift towards structural change.

3.3 Structural change

A long period of stagnation is conducive to a questioning of management practices that have become routinized. HRM practices are not immune to this tendency and many firms are trying, in a voluntarist way, to experiment with their long-established practices. Over and above the influence of the recession itself, these trends also underlie the changes taking place in the productive paradigms, as a regime based on the technological cycle of imitation/assimilation/development gives way to one in which the emphasis is on the creation of new technological resources. As a recent report by the Japanese employers' association shows (NIKKEIREN 1995), HRM in that country is currently experiencing a proliferation of institutional innovations.

One of the most prominent characteristics of these innovations is the trend towards a reconfiguration of the various components of the work process in such a way that they become both more autonomous and more interactive. This reorganization is leading to a reduction in the (overall) size of the organization (downsizing), a flattening of hierarchies and a simplification of the horizontal and vertical channels of communication. In concrete terms, it manifests itself in the elimination of jobs and hierarchical levels through the adoption of project-based organizational structures and the abolition of the distinction between managers and those engaged directly in production tasks.

In effect, hierarchical organizational structures are being replaced by networks of autonomous but interconnected 'cells'. This trend is blurring the boundaries of the organization, and stands in sharp contrast to the organizational principles that structure internal labour markets in general and the production of the hierarchy in Japan in particular.

The *second* aspect concerns the various attempts to renew incentive mechanisms, particularly the wage system, long considered excessively rigid and ill-suited to the new competitive conditions. Attempts are being made to put in place a new system, albeit one that takes a wide range of different forms, that combines greater flexibility with increased competition. Some firms have already introduced *nenpōsei*, a lump-sum salary which is renegotiated annually and depends to a large extent on individual performance. Performance-related pay has the advantage of fluctuating, both upwards and downwards, in accordance with individual results, and of individualizing to a large extent the remuneration of each employee.

Such strengthening of incentive mechanisms is intended to encourage autonomy and individual creativity, particularly among white-collar workers, whose productivity is considered rather mediocre, even if this development means sacrificing some of the benefits of cooperation. However, this new mechanism would seem to leave unresolved the question of agreement on the criteria for assessment of individual performance and of frequently coming into conflict with the feelings of equity that employees have hitherto shared.

The *third* aspect concerns the increasingly heterogeneous nature of the wage-earning population. Many firms are seeking to create a certain degree of heterogeneity in their workforces, which runs counter to the traditional emphasis on company culture, regarded as an integrative and homogenizing influence on the workforce. The relative homogeneity and compactness of the male wage-earning population, which were conducive to the diffusion of information and to the development of collective learning at a time when Japan was striving to catch up technologically with the industrialized West, are becoming one of the factors blocking creative initiatives that depart from the norm.

As a result, new practices are being introduced. Some firms are hiring high-level specialists on fixed-term contracts and, as a compensation, paying them high salaries well in excess of the normal pay scale. Others are establishing 'fast tracks' for promotion to management positions by selecting young employees at a very early stage, and yet others are diversifying the channels through which young graduates are recruited by changing their traditional relationships with the universities.

The *fourth* aspect concerns firms' initial attempts to externalize parts of the HRM function, such as recruitment, training or even employee evaluation. Since HRM has traditionally been a strictly internal and confidential matter, firms have built up large departments to deal with this area of their activities and have seldom had recourse to outside services. The standardization of management tools that will result from this externalization will undoubtedly have an effect on external mobility.

Some of these institutional innovations constitute a direct assault on the most widely legitimated rules on which the Japanese model of HRM is based and are intended to create new patterns of behaviour among employees. Indeed, close observation of what is happening on the ground shows that the creation of new rules is being accompanied by innumerable attempts at mobilization involving the social partners or interactions between individual actors. In this sense, what might be called *structural change* already exists in an embryo-type form although, taken as a whole, the micro-innovations that are taking place are not yet coming together to form a clearly defined, coherent whole, in other words a new model of HRM.

These micro-innovations may remain in a latent state for a long time, or they may fail to survive transplantation into the existing structure and eventually wither away. Nevertheless, the possibility of a radical change in HRM practices is not excluded either. Certain actors are already engaged in—contradictory—collective learning processes. Even though they seem to have little room for manoeuvring at the moment, the space in which the social partners interact is less confined than in the past. Those interactions may become very extensive, particularly if financial globalization ended by changing the Japanese form of corporate governance, which to date has been responsible for ensuring a compatibility between the slow rate of return on equity and the mutual, long-term commitment on employment.

References

AKERLOF, G. and J. YELLEN (1986): *Efficiency Wage Model of the Labor Market.* Cambridge: Cambridge University Press.

AOKI, M. (1988): *Information, Incentives and Bargaining in the Japanese Economy.* Cambridge: Cambridge University Press.

BOYER, R. (1990): *New Directions in Management Practices and Work Organization, General Principles and National Trajectories.* Working Paper N° 9130. Paris: CEPREMAP.

DOERINGER, P. and M. PIORE (1971): *Internal Labor Markets and Manpower Analysis.* Lexington, Mass.: Heath Books.

DORE, R. (1973): *British Factory—Japanese Factory. The Origins of National Diversity in Industrial Relations.* Berkeley: University of California Press.

FAVEREAU, O. (1989): Marchés internes, marchés externes. In: *Revue Economique* N° 40, pp. 273–328.

GRANOVETTER, M. (1985): Economic Action and Social Structure: The Problem of Embeddedness. In: *American Journal of Sociology* 91, 3, pp. 481–510.

INSEE (1986): *L'enquête sur la structure des salaires 1986.* Paris: INSEE (L'Institut National des Statistiques et des Etudes Economiques).

KOIKE, K. (1976): *Shokuba no rōdō kumiai to sanka* [Trade-Unions and Participation at the Workplace Level]. Tōkyō: Tōyō Keizai Shinpōsha.

KOIKE, K. (1981): *Nihon no jukuren* [Skill Formation in Japan]. Tōkyō: Yuhikaku.

MAURICE, M., F. SELLIER and J. J. SILVESTRE (1986): *The Social Foundations of Industrial Power: A Comparison of France and Germany.* Cambridge, Mass., and London: The MIT Press.

MINISTRY OF LABOUR (1986): *A Basic Survey on Wage Structure.* Tōkyō: Ministry of Labour.

NIKKEIREN (1995): *New Japanese-Style Management System.*Tōkyō: Nikkeiren.

NITTA, M. (1991): Diversification industrielle et strategie de gestion des ressources humaines dans l'industrie japonaise du textile synthétique. In: *Sociologie du Travail* XXXIII, 1/91, pp. 119–134.

NOHARA, H. (1987): *Les acteurs de la dynamique industrielle au Japon. Rapport de recherche du LEST.* Laboratoire d'Economie et Sociologie du Travail. Aix-en-Provence.

NOHARA, H. (1993): Le syndicat d'entreprise et le micro-corporatisme au Japon; acteurs, compromis et dynamique temporelle. In: GAZIER, B. (ed.): *Emploi, Nouvelles Donnes*. Paris: Economica, pp. 39–54.

NOHARA, H. (1995): Diversité nationale dans le mode d'articulation entre le système éducatif et le système productif: comparaison France-Japon. Paper presented at the *25th Symposium of 'La Société Franco-Japonaise de Gestion'*, 13 May 1995, Tōkyō: Waseda University.

RŌDŌ DAIJIN KANBŌ SEISAKU CHŌSABU (1994): *Koyō dōkō chōsa hōkoku. Heisei 6-nen* [Report on the Survey on Employment Trends 1994]. Tōkyō: Rōdō Daijin Kanbō Seisaku Chōsabu.

ROSENBAUM, J. (1984): *Career Mobility in a Corporate Hierarchy*. New York: Academic Press.

SILVESTRE, J. J. (1986): Marchés du travail et crise economique: de la mobilité à la flexibilité. In: *Formation – Emploi* N° 14, pp. 54–61.

SŌMUCHŌ TŌKEIKYOKU (1996): *Rōdōryoku chōsa nenpō* [Annual Report on the Labour Force Survey]. Tōkyō: Sōmuchō Tōkeikyoku.

UJIHARA, S. (1958): *Nihonteki rōdō shijō no mokei* [A Model of the Japanese Labour Market]. Tōkyō: Tokyo University Press.

WEITZMAN, M. L. (1984): *The Share Economy*. Boston: Harvard University Press.

WILLIAMSON, O. E. (1975): *Markets and Hierarchies*. New York: Free Press.

Commentary

Jacques JAUSSAUD

The contribution by Hiroatsu Nohara addresses the issue of human resource management (HRM) in Japan, whose mechanisms are under strong pressure in the context of sluggish economic growth and globalization of industries in the 1990s.

Although HRM in Japan as a model is still a matter of discussion among academics, Nohara argues that AOKI's contribution gives a satisfactory insight with respect to the concept of 'rank hierarchy'. Hierarchical principles as developed by AOKI (1988) address both coordination and incentive questions (moral hazard and adverse selection risks). However, general principles are implemented in very different ways in Japan and elsewhere, according to their institutional context.

In the first part of this paper, Nohara attempts to specify HRM mechanisms in Japan, taking France as a comparison. In the second part, the author considers the directions of change under the current recession.

1 HRM mechanisms in Japan, as compared to France

Where a significant number of scholars take Anglo-Saxon countries as a reference, this paper compares HRM in Japan and in France, in order to shed new light on the Japanese model. Wage systems are first considered, followed by the way hierarchy is constructed in both countries.

Regarding wage systems and, more precisely, pay scales, Nohara compares wage profiles for three types of employees in France and Japan, respectively: manual workers, technicians, and managers (including engineers). His main conclusion is that increases in wages for manual workers are very limited in the French case, and occur mainly during the first years of a worker's career, before the age of 40–45. Wage increases do not appear to be used as an incentive for manual workers in France. On the contrary, wage increases are much higher in the Japanese case, and may occur during the whole working life. This suggests that wage increases are regarded as an incentive mechanism in Japan for manual workers, technicians, engineers, and managers.

COLE (1971), DORE (1973) and KOIKE (1994) have all emphasized this difference when comparing Japan with Anglo-Saxon countries. Nohara finds that, compared to France, Japan still appears as a specific case. One wonders, however, whether table 1 is fully satisfactory for such a comparison. Does the category *manual worker*, in the case of Japan, include non-regular workers? A large part of manual workers without career perspectives in Japan are employed as non-regular workers (JAUSSAUD 1996). Looking at France, at least until the 1980s, non-regular employment was much more limited in extent than was the case in Japan. As a result, more information is needed before one can fully appreciate the validity of the comparison based on table 1.

Nohara goes on to explain how wages are linked to qualification as provided by the education system in France, whereas in Japan, it is mainly linked to experience acquired over the course of the entire work career. Education systems differ in their objectives: providing qualification and expertise in France, improving and assessing potential in Japan. Here again, HRM mechanisms are related to the institutional context. As a result, wages are much more widely spread in France than in Japan at the beginning of workers' careers.

The construction of the hierarchy also differs significantly between the two countries. In France, as Nohara notes, the "system of work organization ... [is] ... dominated technically and organizationally by the notion of *job*. This notion is the key factor in both the technical management of production and the social management of jobs (job classification)" (p. 250).The author underlines how academic background determines the point of entry for young workers in the hierarchy. Such specialization based on academic background strengthens the partition between production and design, inherited from Taylorism.

This said, it should be added that academic background does not prevent internal promotion in French firms often based on professional training, further education, and a strong commitment to one's work. This is supposed to lessen the negative effects of excessive specialization based on academic *cursus*. In Nohara's view, however, self-taught promoted staff and their formally qualified colleagues still constitute two different categories of workers within French firms.

In the case of Japan, the hierarchy of firms reveals both *discontinuity* in some dimensions, and *continuity* in others. Regarding discontinuity, the author underlines three distinct features:

- a complete closure of the organization to its external environment, the hierarchy being "constructed almost exclusively on the basis of career paths that are internal to the organization" (p. 251). This, again, is consistent with the Japanese education system, improving and assessing potential, rather than providing functional qualifications;
- gender segregation. In France, women benefit from formal qualifications as a means of lessening the extent of gender segregation. The situation is markedly different in Japan;

- a split between the blue collar and white collar categories. Promotion for manual workers in Japan is a life-long process. It is not so in France or in the Anglo-Saxon countries. KOIKE (1994) underlines the positive effects of the Japanese case. However, the consequences of a strict separation between blue collar and white collar workers as underlined by Nohara is, to the best of our knowledge, yet to be studied. There may, in fact, exist a wide range of consequences in terms of communication and cooperation between blue and white collars. Further research on this issue is needed.

Regarding the issue of continuity as underlined by the author, it is our opinion that a lot of questions still remain to be solved. According to the paper, particularly in the white collar category, "whether they have received two, four or six or more years of higher education, university graduates constitute a more or less undifferentiated population of recruits from which, after a period of between ten and fifteen years, the new generation of senior managers will be selected" (p. 252).This is not consistent with a few cases we personally know in which four-year graduates from prestigious universities employed in big Japanese companies were offered at the very start of their careers training abroad with bright international career advancement prospects. This would not be the case with two-year graduates. Furthermore, the paper does not provide precise information on this "more or less undifferentiated population of recruits": Is there a significant proportion of two-year higher education graduates, or are they very few? Is higher education *cursus* not taken into account at all when designing career paths during the first 10 to 15 years? Or is it only taken into account for recruitment itself? Case studies might be one way to shed light on these questions.

2 The transformation of the Japanese HRM model in the context of low growth and globalization in the 1990s

Designed in the context of high-speed growth, HRM mechanisms in Japan now need to be adapted to low growth, an aging population, and fierce competition both in Japan and abroad.

However, do adjustment mechanisms simply have to work to an extent previously not needed, or do they need to be modified, or even completely changed? These three steps may be found within the process of change. As a consequence, Nohara refers to SILVESTRE's (1986) distinction between *mechanical, organic,* and *structural* change, relating to these three dimensions of change.

Regarding mechanical change, the paper mentions a higher pressure on female wage earners, as job offers for this category decrease and as women suffer job reductions first. Nohara emphasizes that strengthening gender segregation may not be consistent with structural change in the Japanese context, in particular the shortage of younger workers in the future as forecast. Dramatic change in the HRM of female workers may be needed.

As to organic change, the diversification of firms' activities and *shukkō* (transfer of workers to outside companies) are presented. *Shukkō* is increasingly of the *tenseki* type, which means that the worker is definitely transferred to a new employer, enduring a loss in income and status. This is a clear manifestation of change as *organic* rather than merely *mechanical*.

Regarding structural change, the paper simply mentions a few innovations in the field of HRM in Japan as listed in a recent NIKKEIREN report: reconfiguration (downsizing, flattening of hierarchies), various attempts at renewing incentive mechanisms, hiring high-level specialists on fixed-term contracts with high salaries, and externalizing some of the HRM functions. The paper underlines the extent to which such innovations question the cohesiveness of HRM practices in Japan. No information is, however, given as to what extent such innovations have been implemented or not.

3 Concluding remarks HRM Resource Management in Japan

A comparison with the French situation is scarce in the literature and the paper cautions us not to adopt any simplistic view regarding ongoing changes involving *adaptation* and *structural* reforms. However, in our view, many questions raised by the paper still need to be investigated. At this stage, one is still not able to appreciate to what extent structural changes are required in HRM in Japan, or in which direction these changes might be implemented.

References

AOKI, M. (1988): *Information, Incentives, and Bargaining in the Japanese Economy.* New York: Cambridge University Press.

COLE, R. (1971): *Japanese Blue Collar: The Changing Tradition.* Berkeley: University of California Press.

DORE, R. (1973): *British Factory – Japanese Factory. The Origins of National Diversity in Industrial Relations.*Berkeley: University of California Press.

JAUSSAUD, J. (1996): Gestion des ressources humaines: l'adaptation des effectifs dans la grande entreprise japonaise. In: *Ebisu* 12, pp. 7–41.

KOIKE, K. (1994): Learning and Incentive Systems in Japanese Industry. In: AOKI, M. and R. DORE (eds.): *The Japanese Firm. The Sources of Competitive Strength.* New York and Oxford: Oxford University Press, pp. 41–65.

SILVESTRE, J. J. (1986): Marchés du travail et crise économique: de la mobilité à la flexibilité. In: *Formation – Emploi* N° 14, pp. 54–61.

XI Limits and Latitude of Labour Adjustment Strategies in Japanese Companies

Daniel DIRKS

Personnel management policies, one of the hallmarks of the Japanese enterprise system, have come under increasing pressure in the wake of the collapse of the *bubble economy*. Notably, employment guarantees and seniority principles are regarded by critics as too costly and outdated. An analysis of current personnel adaptation measures reveals, however, that adjustments undertaken are less dramatic than expected. Nevertheless, it is argued that the specific strategies pursued are potentially conducive to organizational restructuring and the development of competitive competencies. Hence, any convergence toward more 'Western' methods of large-scale dismissals is not to be expected any time soon.

1 Introduction

With the demise of the *bubble economy*, Japan's industry has entered one of the severest and most protracted recessions in its post-war history. For one, deflationary trends in capital and real estate markets, coupled with substantial overcapacities and weak demand conditions, have negatively affected corporate profits and capital returns. Despite some signs of renewed strength regarding firms' investment behaviour and a clear improvement of their overall profit situation over the past two years (OECD 1996), domestic sales remain depressed in most industries. At best, one can speak of a "very moderate recovery" (KEIZAI KIKAKUCHŌ 1996: 11) of the Japanese economy.

At the same time, this recession's repercussions extend well into the general labour market where, for the first time since 1953, the number of officially registered unemployed has surpassed the mark of two million persons (December 1995: 2.1 mio.). Correspondingly, the unemployment rate reached 3.2 % at the end of 1995 and remains, for Japanese standards, persistently high (RŌDŌSHŌ 1996).

More than any other recession-related indicator, the worsening of the conditions in the Japanese labour market appears to herald the end of an entire era during which Japanese firms came to be known as work time-, rather than head count-adaptors in times of economic adversity (ABRAHAM & HOUSEMAN 1989, DORE, BOUNINE-CABALÉ and TAPIOLA 1989). In the past, companies refrained from resorting to lay-offs affecting their core workforce in larger numbers due to several factors, ranging from the specificities of their personnel policies to a generally labour-friendly jurisdiction and the threat of public ostracism by the mass media (DORE, BOUNINE-CABALÉ and TAPIOLA 1989, AOKI 1990, SCHREGLE 1993, ITOH 1994).

This is not to say, of course, that cyclical downturns and rising costs have not at times resulted in the dismissal of employees in Japan as well. However, these actions have almost unilaterally affected those at the periphery of the firms' workforce, viz. so-called temporary employees, day labourers, and very often female workers. They, just as all those employed in small and medium-sized enterprises (SME), do not usually enjoy the same employment security privileges as their (male) colleagues on the regular career tracks in the larger firms of Japan's economy (NAGANO 1992, RŌDŌSHŌ 1996).

Overall, however, it is an empirical fact that the rate of job switchers has always remained within a relatively low and narrow range (7.9 % – 9.6 % p. a. with respect to the total workforce), and that the number of those leaving their company for any given reason actually *decreased* during recessions as recorded since 1975 (RŌDŌ DAIJIN KANBŌ 1995a: 12). An "increasing commitment by management to the practice of long-term employment" (OECD 1996: 100) is reflected in the fact that Japan's employees are enjoying the longest average and median length of service and the highest retention rate, i. e., the probability that a person is still employed at the same company after a given period, among all leading OECD member countries (OECD 1996: 96).

In this recession, on the other hand, that apparent job security is coming under substantial pressure. It is telling that the public debate on this issue identifies exactly those as the main targets of current and future restructuring activities that heretofore have benefited most from corporate career systems, seniority-based pay schemes, and lifetime employment practices: white-collar employees in administrative and managerial positions (ECONOMISTO 1995).

While in the West, corporate restructuring and the improvement of overall productivity are usually associated with *downsizing activities* (= reduction of headcount) in response to diminished revenue growth expectations, technological innovations, and so forth (NOLAN & CROSON 1995: 66–67), Japan's firms have by and large eschewed that option. Instead, firms' initial strategic responses to the worsening of their business environment have been focusing on a concentration on core product categories and services and a more selective diversification (investment) behaviour than in the past and on a quantitative and qualitative broadening of their international activities. Regarding inevitable cost-reduction measures, these are primarily aimed at improving organizational processes and at raising the profile of individual business units in terms of their own decision autonomy and accountability (DIRKS 1997).

It is increasingly becoming clear, however, that the current crisis is not simply a cyclical economic downturn but instead that a number of structural factors (e. g., growing international competition, a possibly reduced long-term potential growth rate, an aging workforce) are coming into play. Japan's firms, too, are now facing a difficult choice: should they hold on to their idiosyncratic human resource employment practices and guarantees, potentially jeopardizing productivity and profitability rates, or should they alter their policies towards a more Western standard? And if they decide in favour of the former, will there be options available to substantially improve capital returns while maintaining a *Japanese approach* to the general labour problem?

This paper will proceed by, firstly, presenting data on Japanese firms' responses to the recession of the 1990s with regard to their labour situation and relating these figures to earlier periods of economic distress. Secondly, a unique Japanese approach towards corporate downsizing via the growing use of interfirm personnel transfers will be discussed. Then, the long-term economic viability of these practices is analysed with respect to transaction cost, informational, and innovation theory-related arguments. Finally, some of the more salient institutional factors capable of explaining this peculiar approach are presented, arguing that systematic changes of any major type will need to take into account the delicate balance between flexibility and stability factors, respectively. The *central hypothesis* underlying the following sections is that the unique character of Japanese firms' employment adjustment reactions carries the potential of achieving two seemingly contradictory goals simultaneously—maintaining overall employment stability and guarantees while improving corporate competitiveness.

2 Reacting to rising labour costs

In the past, Japanese firms have responded to economic crises with a variety of personnel-cost related adaptation measures. A reduction of overtime work, hiring freezes, or the transfer of personnel to other, less affected departments feature among the more prominent cost reduction instruments. In each case (e. g., the two oil shocks, the 'yen shock' of 1985), actual lay-offs of regular employees apparently were avoided as far as possible (DORE, BOUNINE-CABALÉ and TAPIOLA 1989, ITAMI ET AL. 1995).

It can be argued, however, that the current slump is markedly different and substantially more severe than its predecessors. Hence, it would follow that in the 1990s Japanese firms are forced by necessity to discontinue their adherence to the principle of employment security and to rid themselves accordingly of surplus labour believed to exist widely within companies after the hiring excesses of the *bubble economy*.

As graph 1 depicts, however, the present situation is much less dramatic than critics of past behaviours would have it. Here, personnel adaptation measures taken by Japanese companies during three different recessions are juxtaposed, with each of the three quarters given indicating that period during which a maximum number of respondents reported to have pursued any cost reduction activity at all.

Graph 1: Personnel cost reduction measures in three different recessions

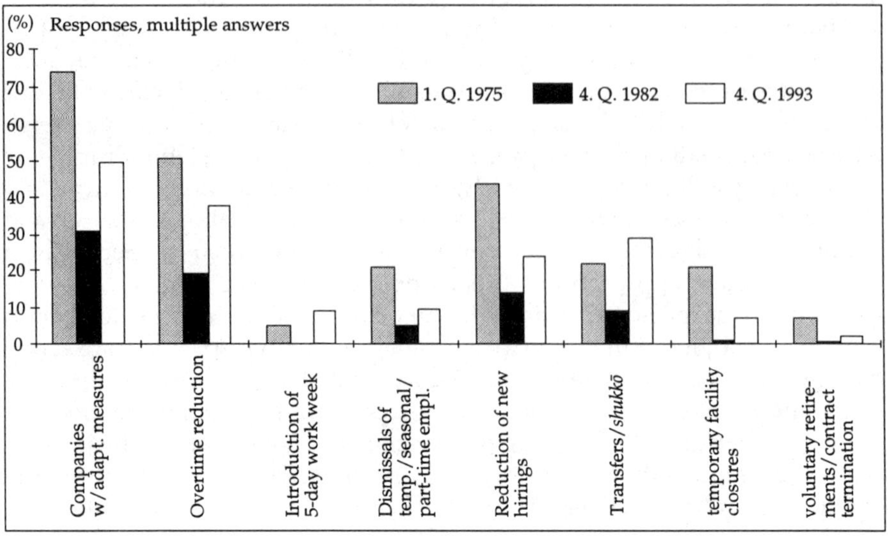

Note: Q = Quarter; data from approx. 5,400 establishments with >30 employees (response rates: 55–60 % per survey); all industries excl. financial services, real estate.

Source: RŌDŌ DAIJIN KANBŌ (1996b: 268)

It immediately becomes clear that, as before, actual large-scale dismissals of employees remain the exception. Even reducing the number of non-regular workers (temporary etc.) plays less of a role than in the past.

It must be stressed, however, that non-regular workers bear the brunt of the job losses that do occur. For instance, while the so-called *part-timers*, who make up about 2/3 of the entire non-regular category (RŌDŌ DAIJIN KANBŌ 1996a: 39), occupied a share of 13 % against the regularly employed workforce as registered in a Labour Ministry study for 1994, 22.4 % and thus a disproportionately higher percentage of all job losses recorded in that year affected these *part-timers* (RŌDŌ DAIJIN KANBŌ 1995: 35).[1]

On the other hand, a decrease in the amount of paid overtime worked and in the hiring of new staff, respectively, continue to be major sources for cost reduction activities. Conspicuously, and for the following discussion of main importance, personnel transfers have gained momentum in the 1990s, becoming the second most important labour adjustment instrument for companies in Japan.

[1] Relatively higher fluctuation rates for temporary workers have a long history in Japan, as NISHIGUCHI (1994: 25–28) demonstrates.

A longitudinal analysis over the course of this most recent recession (graph 2) reveals that, firstly and expectedly, the use of transfers increases progressively over time. Secondly, however, and of comparable importance is the fact that at the beginning of this downturn personnel transfers are already not entirely uncommon. This is an indication for the existence of a certain level of experience related to this instrument that permits companies to aptly apply it in times of economic distress.

Graph 2: Personnel adaptation measures 1990–1996

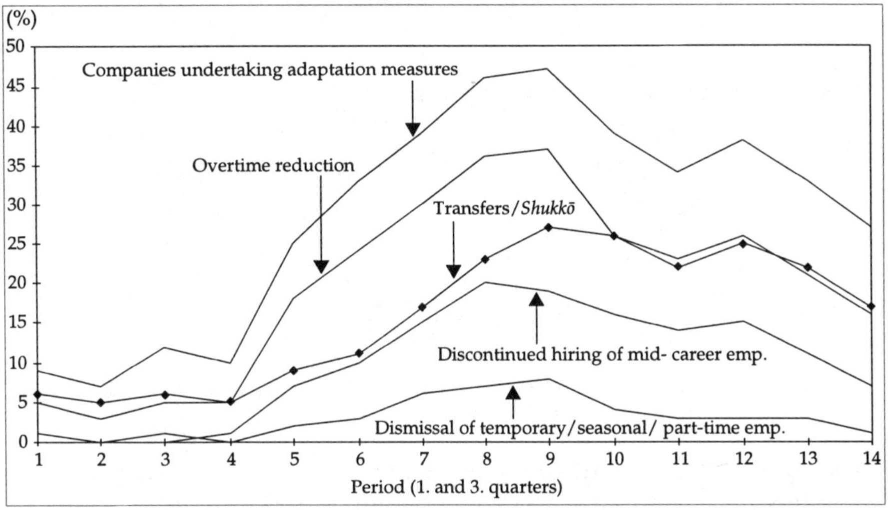

Source: cf. graph 1

This conspicuous emergence of personnel transfers between companies as a means to adjust a firm's workforce and to spread overall labour costs, while searching for more effective employment opportunities for their employees, will be the focus of the following sections.

3 The importance of 'quasi-internal' labour markets

3.1 Empirical significance

While job rotation, i. e., the principle of moving personnel among departments within the same company, has long been known as one of the standard human resource development policies in Japanese firms, transfers of people *between* companies have found relatively less attention in the relevant literature. Principally distinguishing between two major types of such transfers, *shukkō* as a temporary and *tenseki* as an irreversible 'loaning' of personnel (OGIHARA 1994: 4, 112), their basic characteristic lies in the fact that labour is being redeployed not through regular market mechanisms but instead through intermediary or 'quasi-internal labour markets' (INAGAMI 1995: 27).

Under a *shukkō* agreement between a sending and a receiving company, the respective employee is temporarily lent out to the latter firm (graph 3). Legally, the original employment contract remains intact while a second contract, stipulating his or her duties towards the new (temporary) employer, enters into force (OGIHARA 1994). A transfer or loaning agreement between the two firms regulates such details as work conditions, remuneration, and social security and pension insurance payments.

Graph 3: Elements of a transfer (*shukkō*) arrangement

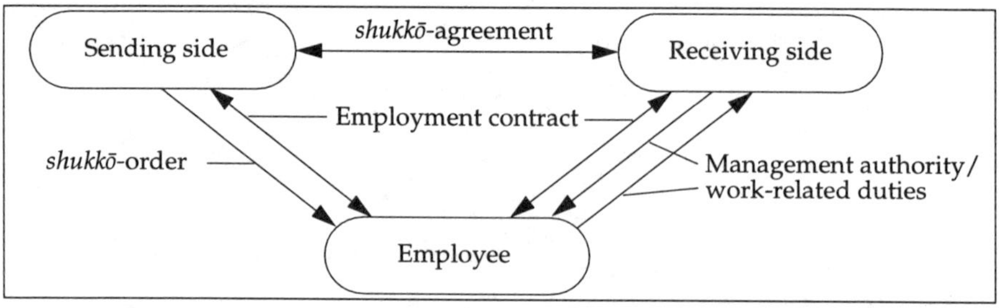

In many cases, any income gaps arising from different (lower) wage levels on the receiving side are covered by the sending firm. As a principle, thus, the given wage and work condition standard is to be guaranteed to the affected employee, possibly by offering additional wage benefits, an issue closely monitored by the unions (RENGŌ SŌGŌ SEIKATSU KAIHATSU KENKYŪJO 1992).

Regarding the *tenseki* regime, the original contract is severed, thus resulting in a new, and exclusive, employment relation with the receiving firm. Often, the candidate has already worked for his new employer under a *shukkō* arrangement and is then directly changed to a *tenseki*-type transfer. In a *tenseki* case, all the work and remuneration conditions at the new company apply while any special benefits or subsidies supplied by the former employer cease to exist.

How important are personnel transfers within the Japanese economy? The available data is somewhat inconclusive due to the relative paucity of research on this subject to date. Throughout the 1980s, individual studies have suggested a growing use of these transfers. A more comprehensive analysis (KOYŌ SHOKUGYŌ SŌGŌ KENKYŪJO 1987: 14–17) revealed that by 1986, 97 % of all larger companies (>5,000 employees) were making active use of *shukkō*. By then, 8.2 % of their officially registered workforce was in reality being employed elsewhere. For the entire manufacturing sector, this rate stood at

7.2 %, meaning that even in more than half of all smaller companies (less than 300 employees), the practice of *shukkō* was common. A later report establishes a total number of 5.6 mio. persons across the entire economy working under some type of transfer regime (ITŌ 1995: 83).

Table 1: Importance of personnel transfers by age group

	Total	<40 years	40 years	40–44 years	45–49 years	50–54 years	over 55
a) regular employees (total)	2,179,190	1,188,781	990,409	297,172	292,301	260,138	140,798
b) at original location	1,951,804	1,095,522	856,282	273,231	262,741	215,362	104,948
c) *shukkō* (a-b)	227,386	93,259	134,127	23,941	29,560	44,776	35,850
(ratio of *shukkō*, %)	(10.4)	(7.8)	(13.5)	(8.1)	(11.3)	(17.2)	(25.5)
d) *tenseki*	8,872	1,823	7,049	341	341	1,370	4,997
(ratio of *tenseki*, %)	(0.5)	(0.2)	(0.8)	(0.1)	(0.1)	(0.6)	(4.8)

Notes: 'regular employees' = all employees excl. temporary and seasonal workers; 'ratio of *shukkō*' = (c÷a) x 100; 'ratio of *tenseki*' = (d÷b) x 100.

Source: MINISTRY OF LABOUR (1995), *Monitā chōsa*. Quoted in: ITŌ (1995: 15).

There are no recent comprehensive surveys on the transfer situation within the entire Japanese economy. However, an unpublished report by the Ministry of Labour suggests that the use of such transfers has risen further, and about one out of every ten Japanese employees across all sectors is now working beyond the borders of his or her official employer (table 1).[2]

These figures also demonstrate that *shukkō* is the more widespread type of transfer mode, *tenseki* being applied mainly to older employees. Also, the implementation of the *shukkō* mechanism is correlated with the age of the transferees, though younger workers are also affected to a substantial degree.

Graphs 4 and 5 finally show that a typical transfer is one initiated by a large manufacturing company, with a smaller to medium-sized enterprise in the service sector on the receiving end. It should be noted, however, that manufacturing firms still account for around 30 % of all transfer receivers,

[2] This figure, however, must be treated with caution, as it intuitively appears too high when extended to the overall Japanese economy. The quoted survey is biased in that it probably over-represents larger companies, though no such information was given in the available source. At the other extreme, the OECD (1996: 101) puts the share of transferees to the total labour force at 0.5 % without bothering to divulge its data source. The truth, thus, lies somewhere within that range, though the importance of transfers in large companies (up to 10 % of their total employee force) has been consistently confirmed.

thus adding a note of caution to any overly simplistic claims denoting a swift structural change of the Japanese industry towards a service-oriented economy.

Graph 4: Personnel transfers by economic sector

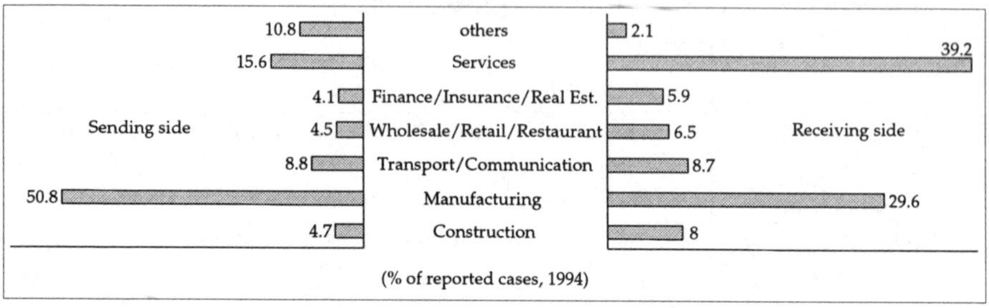

Note: *shukkō* only
Source: RŌDŌ DAIJIN KANBŌ (1995: 37).

Graph 5: Personnel transfers by firm size

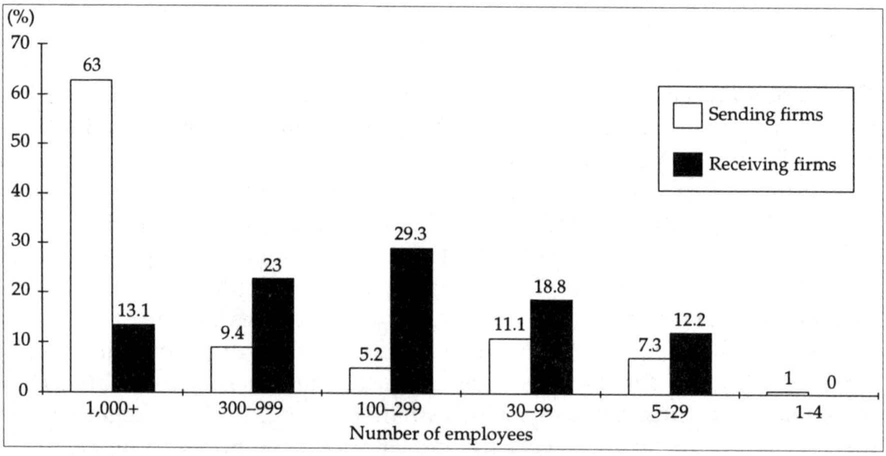

Note: figures for 1994, % of reported cases
Source: cf. Graph 4

In summary, it is appropriate to conclude that the use of employee transfer between companies in the Japanese economy has grown into a phenomenon of sizable proportions. Such transfers have become even more dominant in sectors troubled by structural problems such as the steel industry. There, more than 28 % of all employees are currently sent out under 'loaning' arrangements (Kokusai Sangyō-Rōdō Kenkyū Sentā 1996: 52). Other sectors still are a long way from such a situation. However, labour transfers have evolved into a standard instrument for adapting to structurally and cyclically difficult economic times.

3.2 Types of transfers

The legal difference between the *shukkō* and *tenseki* type of personnel transfers has been briefly discussed above. Classifying a specific transfer according to the purpose or strategy attached to it, a set of four different types or models can be distinguished whereby graph 6 concentrates, for convenience's sake, on the relatively more prevalent *shukkō* transfer:

Graph 6: *Shukkō* types

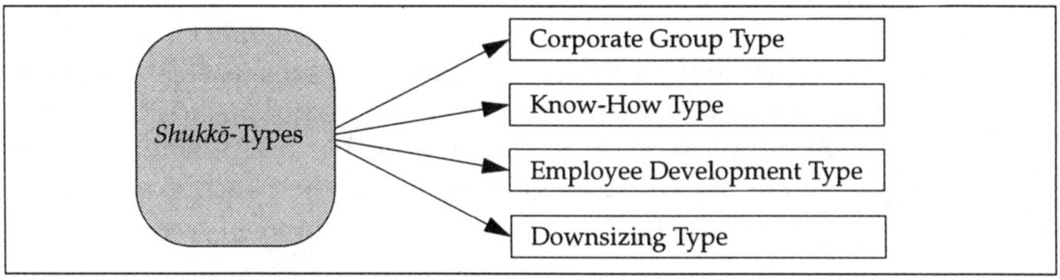

Source: Nagano (1992: 61–65)

The corporate group type denotes the transfer of personnel to strengthen and deepen inter-firm relations, typically between companies that maintain supplier/customer links or, for instance, entertain joint research and development activities. A capital relationship may exist, though is not mandatory. In recent years, substantial spin-offs and diversification efforts have increased the necessity for firms to provide human resources to these new entities as an asset provision-cum-control instrument (Nagano 1992).

The latter form is related to the second transfer type, the know-how model, whereby usually small and medium-sized companies in need of technical or managerial qualifications are offered this kind of expertise via the transfer of experienced personnel. It is difficult to substantiate the empirical relevance of this type. However, recent research (Toray Keiei Kenkyūjo 1995: 22) exemplifies that the vast majority of transferees (approx. 87 %) sent by those companies studied came from higher echelons of management (kachō, buchō, and kakarichō) and were installed in similarly high -in many cases even higher, nominally at least- positions at the receiving firms. This observation suggests that a transfer of crucial know-how does take place, although no formal proof can be given on this general level.

The third, employee development type relates to the educational and career promises that a (temporary) dispatchment to a different work and task environment principally incorporates. Whether or not such a prospect will materialize in the end depends, of course, on the conditions of the individual case. It must be assumed that the likelihood of such an expectation is positively correlated with a lowering of the age of those sent.

Conversely, older age groups are more likely to be subject to the last type of downsizing-oriented employee transfers. It has long been customary to release workers upon reaching official retirement (often 55 years), re-employing them at the same or a different firm at reduced income and benefit levels. Here, however, the downsizing type includes those transferees sent out specifically to adjust to a situation of overcapacity and demand slumps. Older employees are typical targets of such policies to allow for a bigger reduction of seniority-induced overall labour costs.

3.3 Case examples

With regard to the paucity of available studies on the reality of employee transfer regimes and given the reluctance on the corporate side to disclose any such relevant information on a broader scale, the analysis of individual cases becomes an alternative research approach. Three such examples are given below.

NKK[3]

For NKK, as for the rest of the Japanese steel industry, this present recession is principally a deterioration of an already difficult situation, following two decades of restructuring and the curtailing of production facilities (DIRKS 1995). In the most recent years, the company has experienced a decrease in total sales of almost 12 % between 1991 and 1995 (budget period ending March 31 of the following year, non-consolidated data) and dwindling ordinary profits that resulted in outright losses in both 1993 and 1994.

Thus, in 1993 NKK embarked on a new, 'medium-term business plan' based on the overarching goal of rationalizing all business activities, trimming overall costs, and reducing staff functions (non-direct operations). This plan included a downsizing of the total number of employees by 3,200 people, a figure that was later (1995) revised upward to around 5,000 in response to the protracted economic difficulties facing Japan. Originally, this (earlier) figure was to be exclusively achieved through the use of *shukkō*, apportioned in a one-third/two-third distribution among administrative/managerial (*white collar*) and production (*blue collar*) workers.

[3] The following account is based on interviews with the Corporate Planning and Human Resources Departments at NKK in July and December 1996 and on publicly available data (various editions of the *Nihon Keizai Shinbun* 1993–1996, YŪKA SHŌKEN HŌKOKUSHO SŌRAN HEISEI 8NEN (Annual report 1996)).

All transferees were given a return guarantee to the parent company and were sent to 'related firms' (*kankei gaisha*). By 1996, the downsizing target had been met almost to the point; currently 6,466 *shukkō* transferees are registered against 17,692 people inside NKK. Hence, roughly a quarter of all 'official' employees are actually today working elsewhere.

Preceding this recession, NKK had already enjoyed a long-time experience with the use of *shukkō*. For example, in 1985 the electronics division was spun-off, with almost 700 employees sent to the new company as its initial core workforce. More typically, NKK has always seen the provision of qualified personnel (=know-how transfer type) to related firms and the opening up of new career prospects for individual employees via transfers as the two most important tasks of its *shukkō* policy. However, due to the severity of this crisis, worker transfers have come to resemble more of a downsizing type image. Around 20 % of all transferred white collars, for instance, have been sent to non-group firms, a growing number of transferees' status is being changed from *shukkō* to *tenseki*, thus precluding any return option, and NKK has had to set up a special task force within its human resources department charged specifically with finding additional firms willing and able to receive labour transfers.

Despite this apparent trend toward a more cost-oriented, workforce downsizing policy with its inherent danger of suffering from a lack of a more proactive, innovative approach to corporate renewal, there are also some bright signs. Firstly, the proportion of younger personnel (<45 years) sent out has increased from 10 % to about 35 %, suggesting a possibility of actually improving the personnel development function of these transfers, irrespective of any additional downsizing value this policy also carries. Younger people, this contention holds, are more likely to profit from a broadening of their individual experience basis than someone much closer to retirement.

Secondly, NKK has begun to offer regular training courses to those sent out to other firms (*kishukkōsha kenshū*). This move implies an attempt to systematically nurture and support individual career development programmes in connection with a transfer.

Finally, the organization of a special *shukkō* monitoring and development group demonstrates a growing ability on the firm's side to manage and employ this instrument under various circumstances. Hence, as business conditions improve it may be expected that employee transfers are (once again) focused more on the first three types of *shukkō* and considerably less so on their simple downsizing potential.

Automaker A[4]

In contrast to the steel industry, the experience of a long and deep recession is a relatively novel one for the Japanese automobile makers. Three decades

[4] This account is based on similar documents as the NKK case, cf. the previous footnote. Two interviews were conducted in addition in July 1996 and January 1997. However, as

of sales and income growth had obviated any need for drastic personnel restructuring measures before the beginning of the 1990s.

Nevertheless, about 5 % of A's workforce had on average been working inside related firms throughout the previous decade, often in product development or other, technology-related projects (know-how type), or to manage and control firms that A held a major capital share in (corporate group type).

Today, however, this figure has doubled to around 10 % of the entire workforce. Of that number, around 60 % are employed in sales (dealerships) and distribution outlets operating as legally and financially separate firms. Here, the typical transferee is between 20 and 40 years old; their deployment as a sales force is seen as a means for developing individual experience and capabilities. After 2-3 years, they are scheduled to return to A-company. Obviously, however, the timing of this substantial increase in *shukkō* activities coincides with a need for revamping domestic sales and for curtailing labour costs. Thus, it is analytically difficult to distinguish between different transfer types in recessionary periods, as this case also exemplifies.

Again, there are indications that, while serving a downsizing purpose as well, the use of *shukkō* has additional economic value beyond a mere cost reduction instrument for the sending firm. In A's case, about 75 % of all transferees are lent out on request of the receiving side. Even discounting for likely situations in which individual firms have been 'convinced' to accept such transfers by the sender, the large number of firms soliciting additional personnel suggests that there is a demand for labour that is then reallocated via these quasi-internal markets. Secondly, the original department's head within firm A often functions as counsellor for the individual transferee, systematically assisting in the solving of any adjustment and career development problems. Finally, there are examples of transfers from the automobile sector into seemingly unrelated, yet technologically close areas such as food manufacturing, textile, or construction, thereby enabling a lateral transfer of technical know-how across industries as a type of diversification or cross-fertilization.

NTT[5]

NTT's *shukkō* practice started well before the current recession. The company faced its very own crisis in 1985 when its monopoly position over the Japanese telecommunications market was finally loosened in the wake of substantial deregulation legislature passed for that year. The issue of personnel transfers in this connection is particularly illuminating since it combines two crucial aspects related to this measure: on the one hand, a strategic attempt

---

in the case of other automakers interviewed, this company has requested strict anonymity. Hence, the use of corporate data here is scarce at best and is simply to demonstrate the peculiarities of the automobile industry in general with regard to *shukkō*.

[5] This case is reported in TAKITA (1994: 25–30). This volume, incidentally, features a set of insightful *shukkō* accounts from the point of view of individual transferees.

to develop new business activities and to diversify into a more balanced product and services portfolio using transfers as a means to enact these strategies. On the other hand, the firm faced considerable difficulties in terms of (passive) resistance ("*shukkō* allergy", TAKITA 1994: 28) on the employees' side, accustomed to decades of job security and membership in a large and well-established company.

Diversifications by their very nature are often institutionalized through the setting up of relatively small business units and require a substantial amount of entrepreneurial acumen. In the years following the privatization acts, NTT has invested considerable resources into fostering a cultural change among its rank and file workers and managers towards an acceptance of *shukkō* as a viable strategic means of restructuring while maintaining the benefits of overall employment guarantees. On the basis of a corporate-wide employee survey, a campaign was initiated to propagate '*shukkō*' as an indispensable way for the firm to rejuvenate itself while, at the same time, offering the opportunity for the individual transferee to broaden his or her scope of experience and thus improve personal career prospects.

By the company's own account, these efforts have proven successful, as not only the increase in the *shukkō*-to-total employee rate shows (10 % in 1993 vs. 2 % 1989) but also the fact that today possibilities for being sent out are actively sought after by a growing number of employees.

4 Economic rationality behind employee transfers

In the Japan-related literature, extant management strategies and tools such as the inter-firm transfer of employees are often explained by linking these measures to the surrounding institutional framework comprising legal, political, and socio-cultural elements and their respective historical evolution. In order to make any predictions about the future of the Japanese corporate model, however, the economic *viability* over the longer term of such employment-securing practices as described above also needs to be considered. It is suggested that, given the condition of an increasingly globalized competitive environment in major industries and thus a (partial and probably gradual) decrease in the relative influence that domestic environmental factors exert on firms, the practice of safeguarding employment for workers and managers will only be sustainable if there is a clear link to creating economic value, and thus recognizing capital-linked stakeholder claims as well.

From a macro-economic standpoint, furthermore, the *shukkō* instrument as a simple cost-reduction method only must be expected to undermine that viability once the receiving end reaches its labour accumulation limits. Such *value-creation* should, however, be defined in sufficiently broad terms to incorporate the wider range of possibly positive transfer effects. These can be observed on three levels: the individual employee, the firm or organizational level, and the general market or industrial arena.

4.1 The individual level

A first and non-negligible effect of the use of *shukkō* as an alternative to the more drastic measure of lay-offs in times of economic distress relates to a rather obvious motivational factor. Despite the fact that for many a transfer is only a second-best alternative to a continued employment with the original firm, the real threat of being made redundant is thereby eschewed. The methods are changing, yet the principle of employment guarantee is maintained.

A second motivational factor is connected to income and work environment issues. While a change in working conditions can often not be avoided, especially when a transfer involves moving to a smaller firm or unit, in 80 % of all cases (*shukkō*) the previous salary level is guaranteed and pension plans are continued as originally devised (RŌDŌSHŌ 1996: 277).

Finally, and from a standpoint of human resource development perhaps most importantly, a transfer can positively affect the improvement of technical, conceptual, and social skills, provided that new tasks and responsibilities are offered to the transferee at the new work place (NAGANO 1992). The interesting point here is that such a skill upgrade can principally proceed even under the conditions of a downsizing-type transfer, underscoring the argument that the transfer option can be superior to a lay-off policy.

4.2 Organizational development and inter-firm transactions

Earlier, the know-how transfer type had been specifically noted as a mechanism for conveying technical and managerial expertise across companies, typically from larger to smaller firms. The importance and successful implementation of this task has been confirmed in surveys of personnel-receiving firms (TORAY KEIEI KENKYŪJO 1995).

The second transfer type, pertaining to the strengthening of corporate group links, can be explained and argued for under a transaction cost perspective (WILLIAMSON 1987). The importance of inter-corporate relationships in the emergence and functioning of the Japanese enterprise system has, of course, been argued sufficiently elsewhere (see, e. g., FRUIN 1992). Here, it is maintained that these ties are further strengthened at relatively lower transaction costs through the use of employee transfers. It can be expected that such a type of *personalized linkage* allows for a more effective transfer of information across corporate boundaries, raises mutual trust levels, and lowers cooperation and control costs arising between, for example, a parent company and its legally separate subsidiary.

At the same time, the option of decentralizing formerly large and potentially bureaucratic organizations can be more fully exploited if qualified personnel can thus be supplied to the new units. The network functions often pursued within such corporate groups are facilitated by the transfer of implicit or 'tacit knowledge', expertise known to be crucial to innovation and product development processes yet difficult to codify or standardize and therefore inextricably linked to the bearer of such knowledge, the individual expert employee (NONAKA & TAKEUCHI 1995). Hence, the *shukkō* instrument can prove highly supportive of such a know-how transfer.

Another information cost-related advantage accrues from the guarantee function the sending company takes on in terms of the quality of the personnel lent out. Receiving firms can principally rely on this guarantee, as repeated breaches of this -implicit- contract would result in severely defensive behaviour regarding transfer requests in the future. Such a guarantee, in turn, lowers personnel search and hiring costs for the receiver.

Finally, under an organizational development (OD) perspective, personnel transfers related to a restructuring and/or diversification of a firm potentially decrease bureaucratic sclerosis in organizations, instill new momentum into traditional corporate cultures, and foster entrepreneurial thinking. Obviously, none of these principal advantages will be easily corroborated by 'hard facts', i. e., measurable data. However, it is certain that in the absence of personnel transfers these same advantages will not simply occur by themselves but will instead have to be instigated by alternative means, a difficult task especially under recessionary conditions.

4.3 Structural change

The role of small and medium-sized enterprises (SME) has repeatedly been underscored in the debate on identifying innovative sources for the restructuring of national economies. In Japan, these firms have consistently been disadvantaged by the lack of a functioning labour market. Often, it has proven difficult for them to acquire qualified personnel, an impediment to their potential function as restructuring catalysts (KEIZAI KIKAKUCHŌ 1996: 381, RŌDŌSHŌ 1996: 278).

Both existing SME and newly created firms spun off from larger companies benefit from the use of quasi-internal labour markets as long as an ideal (textbook) market remains underdeveloped in Japan. Through employee transfers, it becomes thus possible to achieve a better allocation of labour resources. Slack, in other words, is being reintegrated into the productive process.

5 Flexibility demands and stability requirements

5.1 Fundamental paradoxes

As indicated earlier, it has become customary to focus on the *explanation* of certain (nationally bounded) business practices by relating to their 'embeddedness' into a specific socio-economic environment (GRANOVETTER & SWED-

BERG 1992). This has also been a common approach in the study of the Japanese firm, where the specificities of its stakeholder arrangements and the role of the state in economic affairs have been typical topics of discussion (see, for example, AOKI 1989). The recent upheavals in the course of the Japanese economy after the demise of the *bubble economy* are, however, necessitating a renewed assessment of the importance and impact of at least some of these factors. For example, the role of the so-called 'main banks' as financier and firms' central governance control institution has been highlighted as one of corporate Japan's more salient contextual elements (AOKI 1989). Current changes in the capital structures of many corporations, such as a more frequent switching of main banks or a restructuring of financial sourcing at the expense of bank loans (OECD 1996), will have effects on the prevailing corporate governance system.

Similarly, existing practices and policies prevalent in the Japanese labour market such as the employee transfer issue discussed here can be -and have been- explained with reference to a range of institutional factors. Most of these have evolved during the high-growth era of post-war Japan, though some authors have attempted to establish the 'roots of modern management' in Japan with reference to the ethical and legal codes of the warrior and merchant classes of some 200 to 300 years ago (WHITEHILL 1991).

Circumventing here the substantial and largely unresolved problems of *culturalist* explanations for social phenomena in Japan, a reference to the development of postwar industrial relations and the concomitant public, legal, and political measures to support the status quo is an alternative and sufficiently satisfactory path to explaining Japanese firms' principle of guaranteeing employment security, thus maintaining a relatively high degree of stability in their labour relations.

Such a reference must, however, deal with a number of rather fundamental *paradoxes* in the development of postwar industrial relations in Japan, an approach that has begun to gain currency in non-Japanese publications on the subject over the past few years. This more recent development must be understood as a timely reaction to what has, over the past decades, often been a relatively one-sided, ahistorical and as such naively confirmatory repetition of the thrust of an early (English language) book by ABEGGLEN (1958) who had praised the fundamentally 'harmonious' labour relations in Japanese firms. This 'harmony' was assumed by him to be embodied, and continuously reinforced or reproduced, in the three 'pillars of Japanese management', i.e. job tenure or 'lifetime employment', seniority-induced wage schemes, and company unionism.

More recent research does not refute the existence of these principles *per se*, but the intention of these more critically-minded authors is rather to explain the existence of management policies such as a relatively higher concern for employment guarantees (the topic of this paper) with reference to the historical *fact* of intense labour conflicts especially over the first three postwar decades (KUMAZAWA 1996, PRICE 1997), a point often neglected by those who prefer to evoke the image of some kind of fundamental penchant for social harmony at the core of the Japanese (collective) psyche, however elusive that may be.

Such critico-historical analysis must, then, confront a number of basic paradoxes that are not easily 'explained away' and may be one reason why the Japanese situation appears somewhat enigmatic to many outsiders. Prime examples for such contradictions are the observation of fierce and protracted labour (union-)-management disputes over the first decades of postwar Japan, with the employers' or management side eventually emerging as 'winner'. Yet this victory has not led to any type of despotic regime reminiscent of earlier stages of (Western) capitalism (PRICE 1997: 6). Instead, the strong control that management exerts over internal work conditions has, at the same time, seen a clear commitment by employers not to resolve to lay-offs in times of economic difficulty regarding their (usually male) core workforce.

A second such paradox can be seen in the fact that while the labour movement has lost its role as a politically and socially independent or autonomous force, management has shown an increasing willingness to engage in bargaining and consensus-seeking activities with employee representatives (usually in-house) concerning wage negotiations and, an important task in the context of this paper, restructuring measures such as personnel transfers (PRICE 1997: 271). A final example of paradox is the observation of the continuous process of social 'standardization', i. e. the nurturing of a commonly shared ideology that (virtually) all Japanese are 'middle-class', hence somewhat homogenous in achievement, taste, aspirations, etc., and the fact that inside Japanese corporations there has always existed a strong tendency for interpersonal, career, and status-related competition (AOKI 1990). This observation is further supported by the fact that, contrary to an often-held belief, companies have actively pursued and implemented remuneration schemes that relied, to some extent at least, less on seniority principles and more on merit-based pay, thereby exposing the *differences* between (Japanese) individuals (KUMAZAWA 1996: 13).[6]

In facing these various contradictions inherent in Japan's postwar economic development and, more specifically, that of its industrial relations since 1945, these works arrive, on the surface, at somewhat similar conclusions as earlier research, namely that the system's current elements or institutions tend to support and mutually reinforce each other. Two aspects are especially noteworthy: the management or 'capital' side, while enjoying considerable latitude in its organization and control of the workplace and the production

---

[6] 'Merit' in the traditional sense of employee evaluation by Japanese firms is, however, also assessed under a long-term perspective, i. e., including such aspects as 'potential for development', 'experience build-up', etc. I am grateful to Jacques Jaussaud for having pointed out this peculiarity of merit-assessment in Japan during the conference's discussions.

process is well aware of the dangers arising out of overstepping its managerial prerogatives. One such mistake could be the denouncing or termination of the basic (though informal) contract with its core workforce related to the latter's job security. Corporate memories may not be made for eternity, but the postwar historical lessons that have taught the firms' upper echelons how acrimonious labour conflicts could become even in Japan have apparently not been forgotten. And lest companies should *forget* these lessons, the judicial system has over the course of this period developed a pronounced bias in favour of employee job security, making it rather difficult for a firm to dismiss workers, not to mention larger scale lay-offs (SCHREGLE 1993).

The second element acting as a reinforcement to this implicit labour contract is related to the former argument, yet extends into the wider society. As the Japanese system of management-employee practices has evolved over the past few decades, the growing reliance on consensus-oriented mechanisms and the basic guarantee of employment security have come to be taken as *given*, almost as a social right or title by those who have benefited from this system, i. e., primarily (male) workers and employees in large companies, though job tenure has also been a prominent feature in many small and medium sized companies (KOIKE 1988).

Hence while unskilled labour, part-timers, and most women have at best only marginally profited from this arrangement (PRICE 1997), the *working elite* that has enjoyed these benefits has been sufficiently large numerically to convert practices that have evolved only relatively recently in something close to an official *ideology* or moral belief. Any company overstepping these boundaries faces the very tangible danger of public ostracism, exemplified and in most cases also voiced by the mass media that swiftly exposes and attacks even cases of relatively modest 'restructuring' (= lay-offs) when compared to Western examples (USUI & COLIGNON 1996). At the same time, this strong public sentiment pertaining to labour market stability has led to a number of public support programs that offer financial assistance to those companies seeking alternative work opportunities for their employees (OECD 1996: 124–127).

5.2 Balancing stability and flexibility

Where the more recent, historically informed analyses differ from their predecessors on the Japanese enterprise system and their labour relations, respectively, is in the awareness that any institutional arrangement may change, as in fact these practices and institutions have *evolved* into their present-day structure in the first place. While some might discern a likely change catalyst in a rise of employee dissatisfaction with given work conditions (PRICE 1997), within the scope of the analysis as presented here it is argued that while employee transfers are not unproblematic for the parties involved, they at least strive to maintain the traditional management-labour contract.

Table 2 contrasts some of the major variables comprising the personnel management system. For each variable or element, regulations can vary between the two extreme points of complete flexibility or rigidity, respectively. In practice, corporate employment systems will vary with regard to their concrete mix of flexible and more stable regulatory aspects. However, in terms of *changing* a given personnel regime, it is important to realize that not all factors can be rendered flexible simultaneously without maintaining some basic stability lest the outcome will deviate substantially from the envisaged change path—and most likely in an undesired fashion.

Table 2: Stability and flexibility factors in employment relations

flexible ◄——	elements of personnel management	——► stable
performance-based	reward system	results-independent
decoupling of individual worktime/ operational time	working schedules	operational and individual work time identical
temporary work, overtime regimes	length of work	fixed work hours
frequent lay-offs	employment security	no-lay-off guarantee
personnel transfers, job rotation	work location	fixed work location

Source: based on WALWEI (1996: 219)

Hence, *shukkō* and related practices can be seen as an attempt to balance the demands for a flexible accommodation to environmental change and a revamping of internal cost structures with the need for maintaining a sufficiently high level of stability, in this case the basic guarantee of employment security. Other attempts to adapt the overall employment system to cyclical and structural pressures while adhering to this *minimum stability postulate* include the growing use of non-regular employees and the increased hiring of "mid-career specialists" (NIKKEIREN 1996: 14–15, RŌDŌ DAIJIN KANBŌ 1996a: 25) at the same time as the position of a core, permanently employed (elite) workforce of generalists is further cemented, albeit at a numerically somewhat lower level than before (NIKKEIREN 1996: 13–14).

In fact, Japanese companies appear to be rather wary concerning a complete overhaul of previously relatively stable regulations such as their reward systems. A recent study reveals that even regarding the introduction of currently widely discussed (annual) performance-based pay schemes (*nenpōsei*), more than 84 % of firms had not yet (1995) implemented such a system and, remarkably, not even 40 % of those who had not done so were considering an implementation in the future at all (NIHON JINJI GYŌSEI KENKYŪJO 1996: 13). Such conservative behaviour regarding a comparatively low relative wage flexibility has naturally drawn criticism, voicing a need for reform

(OECD 1996: 112). On the other hand, there is plenty of (anecdotal) evidence that Japan's firms are, in fact, experimenting with a wide range of changes related to their hiring, remuneration, and promotion practices and a restructuring of their work organizations (ECONOMISTO 1996). Under the surface, thus, adaptations of and within the system are taking place, though not in any uniform or one-sided fashion.

Hence, a reinterpretation of the apparent reluctance of Japanese companies to swiftly and completely revamp their existing employment practices will need to take into account the ongoing search for a new balance between stability and flexibility accorded to the system's elements. As the discussion of the growing reliance on personnel transfers has demonstrated, such a search is best understood as a continuous quest for adaptability, building on previous experiences and commitments but not without ample room for new and innovative solutions (*limited path dependency*).

6 Conclusion

None of the potentially beneficial effects of the employee transfer practice in Japanese firms can be considered a guaranteed fact, particularly in times of economic depression. In addition, a number of problems must be associated with this instrument, such as the difficulties of adjusting to a new work environment for the individual employee, the risk of not finding an adequate post upon returning to one's former company, or the possibility of being switched to a permanent transfer status (*tenseki*) altogether (NAGANO 1992, ITŌ 1995).

Similarly, receiving firms do occasionally report cases of inferior quality and low motivation among transferees, though these reports are conspicuously rare (RŌDŌSHO 1996: 278). Also, there are limits as to the number of workers an individual firm can absorb, especially in terms of older employees thus received (NAGANO 1992).

On the other, more positive side these problems must be contrasted with the alternative of laying off workers in larger quantities to achieve cost reductions in economically difficult times. This may result in short-term improvements of capital returns, though it will potentially prove detrimental to the longer term development of such a company. So far, Japanese firms have been able to restructure and adjust to difficult environments without endangering the basic social contract with their workforce, according the latter a considerably strong sense of employment security. Hence, the growing use of *shukkō* (labour transfers) is testimony to these firms' flexibility in reorganizing themselves while keeping stable some of the pillars of their underlying management model.

Hence in more general terms, if a nationally bounded management model is an answer to balancing the various extant stakeholder interests under the environmental conditions specific to a historic period, and if the Japanese model is adequately characterized as one relatively stronger committed to maintaining 'harmonious' or consensus-oriented industrial relations than, for example, enhancing 'shareholder value', then such a model can only claim a longer term viability if it succeeds in finding intelligent solutions to increasingly conflicting interests: preserving employment guarantees while at the same time competing for increasingly mobile, globally oriented, and return-conscious capital. Any successful solution that assists in reconciling these conflicts must be considered a true *trailblazer.* The use of measures such as personnel transfers appears to offer one suitable tool regarding this task.

References

ABEGGLEN, J. (1958): *The Japanese Factory: Aspects of Its Social Organization.* Glencoe, Ill.: Free Press.

ABRAHAM, K. and S. HOUSEMAN (1989): Job Security and Workforce Adjustment: How Different are U.S. and Japanese Practices? In: *Journal of the Japanese and International Economies* 3, pp. 500–521.

AOKI, M. (1989): *Information, Incentives, and Bargaining in the Japanese Economy.* Cambridge: Cambridge University Press.

AOKI, M. (1990): Toward an Economic Model of the Japanese Firm. In: *Journal of Economic Literature* 28, March, pp. 1–27.

DIRKS, D. (1995): *Recession Management in Japan: The Case of Nippon Steel Corporation.* Working paper 95/3. Tōkyō: German Institute for Japanese Studies (DIJ).

DIRKS, D. (1997): Out of Recession and Beyond: Indications for a New Type of Japanese Management? In: *Euro Asia Journal of Management* 12, January, pp. 5–23.

DORE, R., J. BOUNINE-CABALÉ and K. TAPIOLA (1989): *Japan at Work: Markets, Management and Flexibility.* Paris: OECD.

Economisto (1995): Howaito karā tsukaisute [White collars—Used and Discarded]. 23.5.1995, pp. 26–37.

Economisto (1996): Soko made yaru no ka. Nihon kigyō no shinjinji seido jitsureishū [Are They Going That Far? A Compilation of Examples Regarding New Employment Systems in Japanese Companies]. 20.8.1996, pp. 84–89.

FRUIN, M. (1992): *The Japanese Enterprise System.* Oxford: Clarendon Press.

GRANOVETTER, M. and R. *Swedberg* (1992): *The Sociology of Economic Life.* San Francisco: Westview.

INAGAMI, T. (1995): Chōki antei koyō to jun naibu rōdō shijō [Long-Term Employment and Quasi-Internal Labour Markets]. In: TORAY KEIEI KENKYŪJO (ed.): *Chūken kigyō ga okareru kankyō no henka to koyō seido no arikata ni kansuru chōsa. Chōsa kenkyū hōkokusho.* Tōkyō: Toray Keiei Kenkyūjo, pp. 27–79.

ITAMI, H. ET AL. (eds.) (1995): *Nihon kigyō no tekiōryoku* [Adaptive Capabilities of Japanese Companies]. Tōkyō: Nihon Keizai Shinbunsha.

ITŌ, M. (1995): Shukkō/tensekisha no shokugyō hendō [Employment Changes for Transferees]. In: TORAY KEIEI KENKYŪJO (ed.): *Chūken kigyō ga okareru kankyō no henka to koyō seido no arikata ni kansuru chōsa. Chōsa kenkyū hōkokusho.* Tōkyō: Toray Keiei Kenkyūjo, pp. 81–93.

ITOH, H. (1994): Japanese Human Resource Management from the Viewpoint of Incentive Theory. In: AOKI, M. and R. DORE (eds.): *The Japanese Firm. The Sources of Competitive Strength.* Oxford: Oxford University Press, pp. 233–264.

KEIZAI KIKAKUCHŌ (ed.) (1996): *Keizai hakusho. Heisei 8-nenpan* [Whitebook on the Economy 1996]. Tōkyō: Keizai Kikakuchō/ Economic Planning Agency.

KOIKE, K. (1988): *Understanding Industrial Relations in Modern Japan.* New York: St. Martin's Press.

KOKUSAI SANGYŌ-RŌDŌ KENKYŪ SENTĀ (ed.) (1996): *Risutorakuchāringu to koyō* [Restructuring and Employment]. Tōkyō: Kokusai Sangyō-Rōdō Kenkyū Sentā.

KOYŌ SHOKUGYŌ SŌGŌ KENKYŪJO (ed.) (1987): *Kigyō gurūpunai jinzai katsuyō ni kansuru chōsa kenkyū hōkokusho* [Report on Human Resource Deployment within Corporate Groups]. Tōkyō: Koyō Shokugyō Sōgō Kenkyūjo (today: Japan Institute of Labour).

KUMAZAWA, M. (1996): *Portraits of the Japanese Workplace. Labour Movements, Workers, and Managers.* Boulder: Westview Press.

NAGANO, H. (1992): *Kigyō gurūpunai jinzai idō no kenkyū* [A Study of Interfirm Personnel Transfers]. Tōkyō: Taga.

NIHON JINJI GYŌSEI KENKYŪJO (ed.) (1996): *Shōrai aru beki jinji kanri o kangaeru tame no kiso chōsa* [Basic Survey Regarding Future Personnel Management]. Tōkyō: Nihon Jinji Gyōsei Kenkyūjo.

NIKKEIREN (Nihon Keieisha Dantai Renmei) (ed.) (1996): *'Shinjidai no Nihonteki keiei' ni tsuite no foroappu chōsa hōkoku* [Follow-up Report to "Japanese Management of the New Era"]. Tōkyō: Nikkeiren.

NISHIGUCHI, T. (1994): *Strategic Industrial Sourcing. The Japanese Advantage.* New York and Oxford: Oxford University Press.

NONAKA, I. and H. TAKEUCHI (1995): *The Knowledge-Creating Company.* New York and Oxford: Oxford University Press.

NOLAN, R. and D. CROSON (1995): *Creative Destruction. A Six-Stage Process for Transforming the Organization.* Boston: Harvard Business School Press.

OECD (ed.) (1996): *OECD Economic Surveys. Japan.* Paris: OECD.

OGIHARA, M. (1994): *Shukkō/tenseki/shokutaku no jinji no taigu* [Personnel Management of Transfers and Temporary Workers]. Tōkyō: Chūō Keizaisha.

PRICE, J. (1997): *Japan Works. Power and Paradox in Postwar Industrial Relations.* Ithaca/London: Cornell University Press.

RENGŌ SŌGŌ SEIKATSU KAIHATSU KENKYŪJO (1992): Shuyō kigyō ni okeru shukkō no jittai to rōshi kyōgisei no dōkō [Present Conditions Related to

Shukkō in Large Companies and Trends in the Consultation System between Labour and Management]. In: *Rōsei Jihō*, No. 3109, pp. 31–42.

RŌDŌ DAIJIN KANBŌ (Seisaku Chōsabu) (ed.) (1995): *Sūji de miru koyō no ugoki. Koyō dōkō chōsa hōkoku* [Data on Labour Trends. A Report]. Tōkyō: Rōdō Daijin Kanbō/Policy Planning and Research Department, Ministry of Labour Secretariat.

RŌDŌ DAIJIN KANBŌ (Seisaku Chōsabu) (ed.) (1996a): *Shūgyō keitai no tayōka ni kansuru sōgō jittai chōsa hōkoku* [General Report on the Growing Diversity of the Labour Structure]. Tōkyō: Rōdō Daijin Kanbō/Policy Planning and Research Department, Ministry of Labour Secretariat.

RŌDŌ DAIJIN KANBŌ (Seisaku Chōsabu) (ed.) (1996b): *Rōdō keizai dōkō chōsa hōkoku* [Report on Trends in the Labour Economy]. Tōkyō: Rōdō Daijin Kanbō/Policy Planning and Research Department, Ministry of Labour Secretariat.

RŌDŌSHŌ (ed.) (1996): *Rōdō hakusho. Heisei 8-nenpan* [Whitebook on Labour 1996]. Tōkyō: Rōdōshō/Ministry of Labour.

SCHREGLE, J. (1993): Dismissal protection in Japan. In: *International Labour Review* 132, 4, pp. 507–520.

TAKITA, S. (1994): *Shukkō – howaito karātachi no shishūki* [Shukkō—White Collars' Mid-Life Crisis]. Tōkyō: Kōdansha.

TORAY KEIEI KENKYŪJO (ed.) (1995): *Chūken kigyō ga okareru kankyō no henka to koyō seido no arikata ni kansuru chōsa. Chōsa kenkyū hōkokusho* [Survey on Changes in the Business Environment Related to Medium-Sized Enterprises and the Current State of the Employment System. A Report]. Tōkyō: Toray Keiei Kenkyūjo.

USUI, C. and R. COLIGNON (1996): Corporate Restructuring: Converging World Pattern or Societally Specific Embeddedness? In: *The Sociological Quarterly* 37, 4, pp. 551–578.

WALWEI, U. (1996): Flexibilisierung und Regulierung des Beschäftigungssystems: Optionen und Effekte. In: *Mitteilungen aus der Arbeitsmarkt- und Berufsforschung* 29, 2, pp. 219–227.

WHITEHILL, A. (1991): *Japanese Management. Tradition and Transition.* London: Routledge.

WILLIAMSON, O. (1987): *The Economic Institutions of Capitalism. Firms, Markets, Relational Contracting.* New York: Free Press.

Commentary

Jacques JAUSSAUD

Daniel Dirks analyses labour adjustment strategies in Japanese companies and pays particular attention to *shukkō* or transfers of employees to other companies. *Shukkō* is very often mentioned as a Japanese particularity in the Human Resource Management (HRM) literature, but has not been sufficiently studied. Dirks' paper is thus a very welcomed contribution in the field.

The author reminds us of the difference between *shukkō*, which is a temporary transfer of workers to another company, and *tenseki*, also known as *tenseki shukkō*, which is an irreversible transfer. In the former case, the worker is still employed by the company that has initiated the transfer, and does not suffer any loss in wages, pension scheme, or career opportunities. The latter case of transfer does not confer on the worker similar privileges.

There is a lack of reliable data in studying *shukkō*. Dirks was able to secure some useful information from the Ministry of Labour. In order to provide a more correct explanation of the problem, he attempts an alternative approach based on case studies; he studies three different companies, in the steel, automobile, and telecom industries. The author also questions the economic rationality of *shukkō* and other specific Japanese practices in the field of HRM at a time when Japan faces increasing problems with the globalization of markets.

In the present comment, we would like to develop two sets of remarks: on data provided in the paper, and on the way *shukkō* implementation is analysed. The reader is asked not to consider these remarks as criticisms, as *shukkō* and, more broadly, HRM practices in Japan are a difficult subject to study. Our intention is simply to point out some questions in order to contribute to the enhancement of knowledge in the field of HRM in Japan.

1 Some remarks on the data used

Dirks raises questions regarding the way Japanese companies have handled the problem of rising labour costs in recession periods over the last two decades. Graph 1 (p. 270) is derived from a report by the Japanese Ministry of

Labour, translated in English as *Report on Trends in the Labour Economy* (RŌDŌ DAIJIN KANBŌ 1996b; see the references in DIRKS). The graph compares personnel adjustment measures taken by Japanese companies during three different periods of recession. Dirks draws two important conclusions from the graph in which he asserts that "actual large-scale dismissals of employees remain the exception", and that "reducing the number of non-regular workers (temporary etc.) plays less of a role than in the past" (p. 270). He may well be right, but in our view more accurate data is needed before a conclusion of this nature can be reached.

Graph 1 shows a number of companies which have indicated an implementation of such adjustment measures. We have, however, no information on the *number* of workers involved in each case. We may find useful additional data in the *Report on the Special Survey of the Labour Force Survey* (SŌMUCHŌ TŌKEIKYOKU 1997): Table 15 in the February 1997 edition, for example, provides us with "unemployed persons who quit their previous job, by reason for leaving the previous job ... and status in employment". This source, and possibly others as well, would provide a clearer picture of the extent of dismissals in recession periods, for both *seishain* (or regular workers) and others. Statistics from the *Annual Report on the Labour Force Survey* (SŌMUCHŌ TŌKEIKYOKU 1996) also provide information regarding, for example, the reduction in working time. However, regarding *shukkō*, which is what we are mainly concerned about here, Graph 1 provides useful data, as there does not exist, to the best of our knowledge, any systematic investigation on this issue.

Even though precarious employment is not the main topic of this paper, we would like to take this opportunity to mention how difficult it is to identify the population involved. On the basis of data from the Ministry of Labour (RŌDŌ DAIJIN KANBŌ 1995), the author writes, "it must be stressed, however, that non-regular workers bear the brunt of the job losses that do occur. For instance, while the so-called *part-timers*, who make up about 2/3 of the entire non-regular category (RŌDŌ DAIJIN KANBŌ 1996a: 39) occupied a share of 13 % against the regularly employed work force as of 1994, 22.4 % and thus a disproportionately higher percentage of all job losses recorded in that year affected these part-timers (RŌDŌ DAIJIN KANBŌ 1995)".

In fact, in our opinion, *part-timers* make up more than 13 % of the work force. We have attempted an investigation of this issue and the results are reported in *Ebisu*, the research publication of the *Maison Franco-Japonaise* (JAUSSAUD 1996). There, we have underlined differences in definition between the *Labour Force Survey* and the *Report on the Special Survey on the Labour Force Survey*, which are both publications of the Management and Coordination Agency (Government of Japan). We argued that only the latter gives a clear picture of precarious employment in Japan (23.35 % of salaried workers in 1994, excluding agriculture). Dirks is right to mention data based on a more restrictive definition, as there are only few studies based on the definition used in the *Report on the Special Survey on the Labour Force Survey*. However, we would recommend that researchers consult this *Report* more often when studying precarious employment in Japan.

Let us now consider how *shukkō* implementation has been analysed in Dirks' contribution.

2 On the manner in which *shukkō* is implemented

The paper contains useful information on the way *shukkō* is implemented. On the basis of Graph 4 (p. 274) for instance, Dirks tells us that "a typical transfer is one initiated by a large manufacturing company, with a smaller to medium-size enterprise in the service sector on the receiving end. It should be noted, however, that manufacturing firms still account for around 30 % of all transfer receivers, thus adding a note of caution to any over-simplistic claims denoting a swift structural change of the Japanese industry towards a service-oriented economy" (pp. 273). Furthermore, it appears that in some cases (possibly several cases) the sending firm is a large manufacturer, the receiving firm being one of its subsidiaries in service activities oriented towards manufacturers, with the mother company its big(gest) client. In other words, quite often large manufacturing companies set up service subsidiaries by 'spinning off' departments and then transferring personnel. More specific research on this issue would be very useful.

Dirks also indicates that "diversification efforts have increased the necessity for firms to provide human resources to these new entities as an asset provision-cum-control instrument" (p. 275). We face here the traditional question of 'hen and egg'! Japanese companies, as suggested in the NKK and NTT case studies, quite often pursue diversification strategies in order to provide jobs to *seishain*. Again, we feel that further research is needed: to what extent do HRM motivations determine diversification strategies?

Regarding the Automaker A case study, Dirks writes that "three decades of sales and income growth had obviated any need for drastic personnel restructuring measures before the beginning of the 1990s" (pp. 277). This is true for the car industry as a whole, but not for all its manufacturers. In the case of Mazda, for example, it should be noted that this company already had significant experience in job adjustment practices, including *shukkō*, before the depression of the 1990s. Furthermore, even though the recession of 1985–1986was rather short, car manufacturing companies had to implement drastic restructuring measures, including the dismissal of 9000 'part-timers' between October 1985 and October 1986 (JAUSSAUD 1996).

In the end, one is not fully convinced of the hypothesis that HRM practices in Japan are economically rational. We are, however, in complete agreement with Dirks' proposition that it is this issue which is crucial in the context of globalization. Such practices have to be based on economic rationality in order to last and develop. *Shukkō* within the context of intercorporate relationships may be a way to lower transaction costs, as mentioned in the paper, but to what extent? Japanese human resource management practices are deeply rooted in 'official ideology or moral belief', or more precisely, one could say, in regular workers' expectations. However, our experience from Europe demonstrates how rapidly such expectations may change under the pressure of environmental factors. In our opinion, the question of these HRM practices as economically rational has to be reassessed more precisely, which is in no way an easy task to accomplish.

3 Concluding remarks

Dirks' paper undoubtfully provides useful insights into the question of *shukkō*, and more widely on the specificities of HRM in Japan. The organizers of the seminar have asked whether practices such as *shukkō* exist in France or other European countries. This is a very interesting question. We are, in fact, reminded of some cases of *shukkō*, for instance the Leroy Somer electrical engines manufacturer sending specialists in automation to the Saft storage battery manufacturer in the 1980s. However, *tenseki*, more than *shukkō*, might be identified as a *French* practice, as companies who need to dismiss workers have the legal obligation to set up what is called a *plan social* (social plan) in order to help these employees find other jobs. In such situations, companies resort to identifying firms that could possibly employ workers made redundant as a way of fulfilling their obligations deriving from this social plan.

References

JAUSSAUD, J. (1996): Gestion des ressources humaines: l'adaptation des effectifs dans la grande entreprise japonaise. In: *Ebisu* 12, pp. 7–41.

SŌMUCHŌ TŌKEIKYOKU (1996): *Rōdōryoku chōsa nenpō* [Annual Report on the Labour Force Survey]. Tōkyō: Sōmuchō Tōkeikyoku.

SŌMUCHŌ TŌKEIKYOKU (1997): Rōdōryoku chōsa tokubetsu chōsa hōkoku [Report on the Special Survey of the Labour Force Survey]. Tōkyō: Sōmuchō Tōkeikyoku.

XII Flexible Employment in Japanese Retailing: Toward a Just-in-time Employment Management

Thierry RIBAULT

The emergence and development of hyperflexible employment structures and mechanisms in the Japanese retailing sector are analysed, based on indepth case studies of four different retail formats: a food supermarket, a General Merchandise Store, a department store, and a Convenience Store. The sophisticated differentiation into flexible job categories and their management is linked to specific integration factors emanating from the institutionalized Japanese wage-labour nexus. In addition, a number of non-market complementarities (statutory, gender, socio-cultural) between the supply of and the demand for these flexible jobs are identified. Recent developments in Japan are found to be only insufficiently explained by traditional segmentation theories.

1 Introduction

Since the 1980s one can see a generalization of flexible employment practices in Japanese retailing whatever the formats, the most recent ones tending to rely more than before on particular types of employment. Linked to this phenomenon, if the different levels of the *peripheral workforce* (i. e., labour contracts apart from the 'core' or *seishain*), have been developing differently depending on different retailing formats, employers' behaviour since the early 1990s might augur a general trend towards a relative growth of these types of employments. The most striking differences between formats are linked to the (non-)existence of a *core* of employees. Some formats use this core as a means to improve labour productivity, while others have a recourse to a peripheral workforce as a means to reduce their labour costs and increase market share.

What are the implications of such new management practices for the Japanese employment and human resource management models? To answer this question we will first present some case studies done on four retailing formats. Following an interpretation of the results, the notion of a *hyperflexible integrated segmentation* of the labour force will be developed to try to better understand the present situation and the future of human resource management in Japanese retailing.[1]

---

[1] We will refer in this contribution to a comparative study done for the French Commis-

2 Job segmentation in four retail formats

We will depict the segmentation of employment systems by using a theoretical system that distinguishes between 'core' and 'periphery' employees (fixed term contracts vs. a more precarious status). The lack of macroeconomic data for the various sectors means that, instead, the analysis here is based on four large retailing firms, each representative for the evolutions that have taken place in their respective sectors.

2.1 Food supermarkets

In the food supermarket chain we interviewed (180 stores, 70 % of sales are food-related products), the core workforce, mainly male employees in their 35–40s, can be further classified into an 'inner core' of *seishain*, full-time employees on an established career path and with high average seniority (see graph 1). Of the part-timers, some (*pāto 1*) work long hours[2] and have a good deal of experience. They are on permanent contracts, or on one-year contracts, renewable—and in practice renewed—every year and thus quasi-permanent or belonging to the 'core workforce'. This segment is made up mainly of women who have returned to work after having married and had children. They are often aged between 40 and 50. The quality of direct customer service depends largely on them.

Another, much larger group of part-timers (*pāto 2*) are employed to work short hours (fewer than 30 hours per week) and are paid less than 1.2 million yen annually, a tax threshold level in Japan. This group is part of the peripheral workforce; its members often work as assistants to the *pāto 1* and are usually recruited on short-term (renewable) contracts of between 6 months and one year. These employees are usually 'housewives', and their work is generally regarded as providing a second family income, although there are differences within this group.

Finally, the 'outer periphery' is made up largely of *arubaito*, casual jobs performed by students, trainees and others on fixed-term contracts of between 2 and 6 months, renewable indefinitely. They are working around 20 hours per week and filling precise slots in the store's work schedule. In practice, this category is not made up solely of university and high school students but also contains a larger proportion of 'housewives'.[3]

---

sariat Général du Plan (1997): *France-Japon: l'emploi en détail – Essai de socio-économie comparative*, January 1997. The co-authors are Jean GADREY (Univ. Lille I), Florence JANY (Univ. Lille I) and Thierry RIBAULT (CLERSE-IFRESI-CNRS). Special thanks should be given to Camal Gallouj, Christophe Baret, Hiroatsu Nohara and Kazunari Honda for their precious participation and help during this two year research project.

2 More than 30 hours, sometimes even more than 40 hours per week: these are 'full-time part-timers'.

3 In the supermarket we surveyed, 25 % of these workers were students while 75 % of

Graph 1: Employment segmentation in a food supermarket chain in Japan

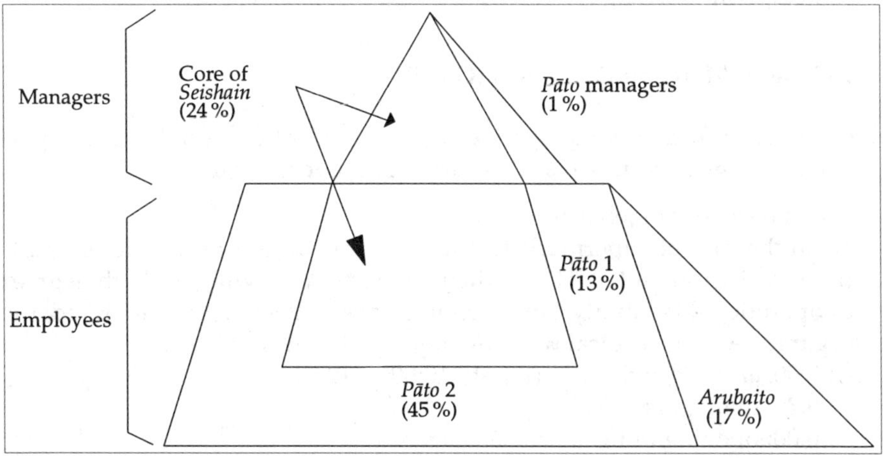

Source: GADREY, J., F. JANY and T. RIBAULT (1998a), in % of total workforce

In summary, the following observations were made for this retail format:

- On a quantitative level, the peripheral categories are large: *arubaito* account for 17 % of the total workforce, and altogether 45 % of the workforce in the company studied were in the *pāto 2* category (part-timers working fewer than 30 hours). In the non-food retail trade, the overall proportion of *pāto* is lower (about 18 % in 1992, excluding unincorporated establishments). In the retail food trade as a whole (excl. unincorporated establishments) it is 26 %[4]. Thus supermarkets appear to make a relatively high use of *pāto*.
- On a qualitative level, there is an 'inner core' and an 'outer periphery' (*arubaito*, fixed-term contracts), but workers between these two extremes (part-timers, *pāto*) are not managed in the same way. For example, what we have called *pāto 1* for the sake of simplicity is a category that is often further divided into two to four sub-categories.There are some very significant differences in terms of wages and social benefits between full-timers and the different categories of part-timers: some *pāto* work a full-time schedule (40 hours per week or more) and have considerable seniority and experience. However, they are paid markedly less (basic pay excluding bonuses is lower, annual bonuses are low or non-existent, the level of so-

them were 'housewives' or young people, working in the shop while waiting for something better to turn up or not wishing to put a lot of effort into a full-time, permanent career.

[4] See SŌMUCHŌ TŌKEIKYOKU (1992).

cial benefits is lower)[5], since it is their contractual status that is lower, rather than their working hours or the functions they perform.

2.2 General Merchandise Stores (GMS)

This retailing format is the approximate equivalent of a qualitative hypermarket in France[6], with 40 % of its turnover made in food.

a) Broad diversity of job status

As in the case of supermarkets, the work schedules of the different part-time workers are inter-related, their connection allowing for high degrees of operational flexibility. For example in one of the GMS we analysed, the organization of a typical working day is as follows:

- 08:00: *arubaito* arrive (work until 10:00 or 12:00)
- 09:30: managers arrive
- 10:00: opening of the store; *pāto* arrive
- 11:30: *seishain* arrive
- 16:00–17:00: *pāto* leave; *arubaito* arrive
- evening until 21:00 (closing time) or 21:30: remain *seishain* and *arubaito.*

The time schedule of part-timers does not seem to be an important point of discussion in the negotiations between employers and employees, at least not as much as it is, for example, in France. The contracts' renewability and their variability certainly offer an explanation for this fact. The minimum working time of 'house-wives' is between three and four hours in the morning. When they are employed, the company determines their working days and hours together with them, giving them ample autonomy to decide which days and at what hours they wish to work.

In the case of GMS, there is also a distinction between core and peripheral workforce in terms of human resource management, but as in the supermarkets, this distinction does not seem to be considered as a social fracture. As in the supermarket case, the division of labour in the GMS does not correspond to any strict dichotomy between a 'core' and a 'periphery'. Instead, polyvalence is dominant in GMS as well.

b) Internal market / external market

In the GMS format, there is a kind of internal labour market for part-timers. This market is relatively sophisticated, varying from company to com-

---

5 Broadly speaking (for there are differences between the various sectors of the retail trade, as well as from firm to firm), the annual pay (incl. bonuses) of an experienced *pāto 1* is about 40 % of that of a full-time employee, although the average working time is about two thirds of that of a full-timer (30-35 hours, compared with 45-50 hours). The hourly rate is therefore about two thirds that of a full-timer. This situation would be unthinkable in France, since the two categories of employees do virtually the same work and have the same experience.

6 Qualitative hypermarkets reintroduce different aspects of service quality (such as full-service cheese or meat counters) while retaining a high level of quantitative productivity.

pany, and it is very selective. In one of the GMS we analysed, only 1.5 % of part-timers are at the highest level, while 5 % are at an intermediate and 14 % at the basic level of *pāto 1*. 79 % of part-timers are of the *pāto 2* type including *arubaito*. Average seniority and age of the different categories of part-timers are 14 and 48 years respectively for *pāto 1*, 4 and 43 years for *pāto 2*.

Internal markets for part-timers have been introduced to ensure a minimum of motivation and to gradually allow a predomination of flexible jobs inside firms.

c) Flexibility schemes

Another big GMS chain (150 stores) we analysed showed the following flexibility scheme. Contracts in this chain are mainly fixed and short-term (see graph 2). 80 % of part-timers are recruited under contracts of less than 6 months duration. External flexibility, based on short term contracts, is a basic element of the human resource management in GMS. A second pillar is its use of external personnel: 25 % of employees are either *arubaito* on short-term or part-time contracts or 'demonstrators', i. e., personnel sent by wholesalers, producers or other retailers to sell products inside the stores.

The weight of part-timers (*pāto 1* and *pāto 2*) in the GMS we studied is relatively important: 15 % and 39 %, respectively, of employees (twice the figure compared to a typical French hypermarket for example). The 'core part-timers' represent almost one third of total part-timers. The previous remarks concerning wage and social benefits aspects of *pāto* in supermarkets apply here as well.

Graph 2: Employment segmentation in a General Merchandise Store chain in Japan

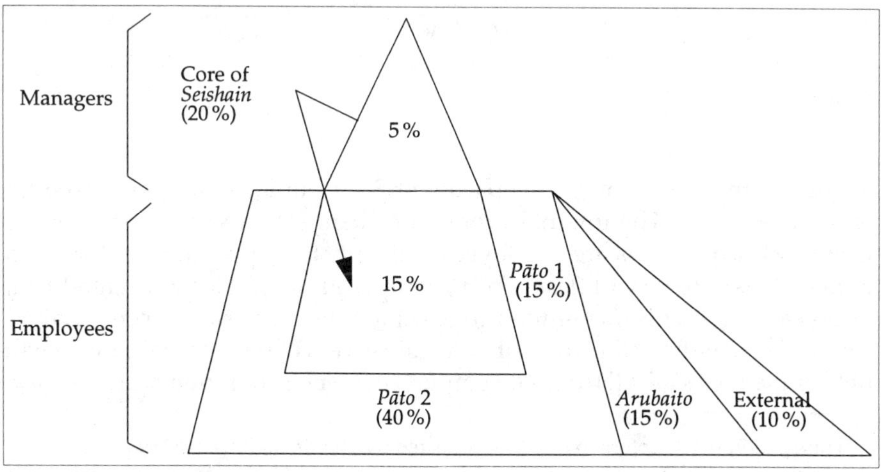

Source: cf. fig. 1, in % of total workforce

In summary, here again we face a job segmentation with a very limited core and a finely stratified periphery. This stratification is organized around two poles: an external flexibility pole (*arubaito*, external personnel) and an internal flexibility pole (*pāto 1* and 2).

2.3 Department Stores[7]

Job segmentation in Japanese Department Stores differs from that we found in the previous retailing formats (see graph 3):

- the core of *seishain* (full-timers) is larger: 36 % of all jobs;
- part-timers are in a minority: 12 % of jobs;
- the external workforce (*haken tenin*) comprises 50 % of total jobs[8].

Graph 3: Employment segmentation in a Department Store in Japan

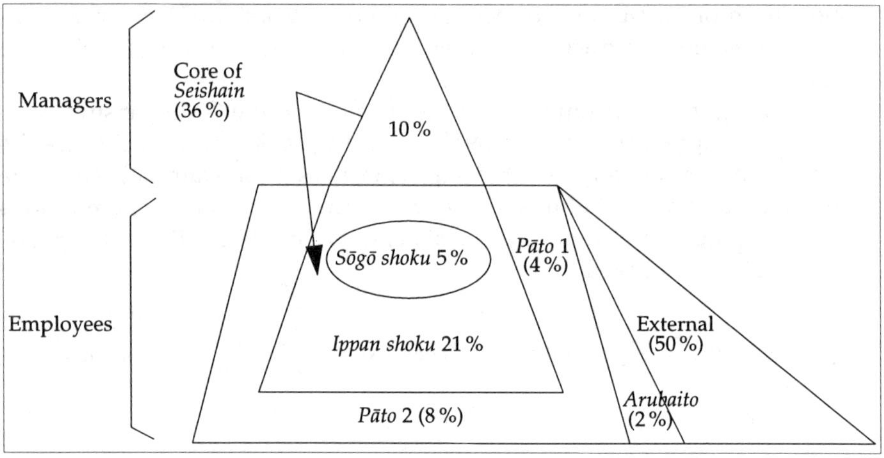

Source: cf. fig. 1

This segmentation makes Department Stores unique compared to other retailing formats. The internal promotion channels for *seishain* are very selective. 21 % of *seishain* are employees with only few opportunities to be promoted. This category of *ippan shoku*, composed of females graduated from two-year universities, is limited to specific functions (sales, secretarial, receptionists), without the possibility to gain access to the internal career channels of the *sōgō shoku* (70 % male employees). The promotion scales of *ippan*

[7] This section partly refers to material collected by Hiroatsu NOHARA (1996).

[8] Mostly found in Department Stores, *haken tenin* are employees sent by suppliers or by wholesalers to promote the sales of specific products or to supplement the workforce.

shoku are thus short and there is little chance they can achieve a management position. In other words, even though their official status is that of a *seishain*, *ippan shoku* employees must be considered to be *pāto 1* or even *pāto 2*, from the perspective of their career-track. However, their remuneration and their social benefits systems are not the same as the one applied to *pāto*, and *ippan shoku* are actually younger than *pāto* in other retailing formats (32 years old on average in the firm interviewed).

Note also the low level of *arubaito* in the Department Stores: they are mainly seasonal workers employed during peak periods (summer time and at Christmas).

2.4 Convenience Stores

This format is assuming a growing importance in the Japanese retailing landscape. Since it has very specific characteristics concerning human resource management, a deeper analysis based on RIBAULT (1998 and 1999) is merited here.

a) External and internal flexibility

We have seen earlier that Department Stores have an average of 50 % of their workforce seconded by external companies (wholesalers or producers), while the GMS and the supermarket analysed were using more *pāto*-type part-timers. In the case of Convenience Stores, the employment structure is heavily made up of *arubaito* workers. It seems to be nearer to the fast food industry structure, except that the latter has an even more limited core of full-timers.

In the company studied, full-timers made up 17 % of total workers (see graph 4). The main external flexibility factor are *arubaito*, namely students and 'housewives'. 64 % of all workers fall into this flexibility category. The duration of their labour contracts ranges from two months to less than one year, and they usually work less than 8 hours per day for less than 3 days a week.

Internal flexibility, i. e., *pāto* employees, concerns 19 % of employees. 'Core part-timers' (*pāto 1*) (namely part-timers working more than 30 hours a week) comprise 23 % of total part-timers, the rest (77 %) being 'peripheral part-timers' (*pāto* 2). This proportion is higher than what we found in other retailing formats, meaning that in the case of Convenience Stores jobs of inferior status (*pāto* 2 and *arubaito*) predominate the employment structure.

Convenience Stores employ *arubaito* mainly to facilitate adjustment of working hours to a fixed activity while supermarkets insist more on finding full-timers to meet their time schedules[9]. Just-in-time employment is

[9] See also JAPAN INSTITUTE OF LABOUR (1990: 260)

the main characteristic of this employment structure in the Convenience Store format. It is a format which appears like small traditional retailing where family employees have been replaced by flexible wage earners. The past family-type hyperflexibility has thus been supplanted by a salary-type hyperflexibility, with very few employees having a full-time position in this new structure.

Graph 4: Employment segmentation in a Convenience Store chain in Japan

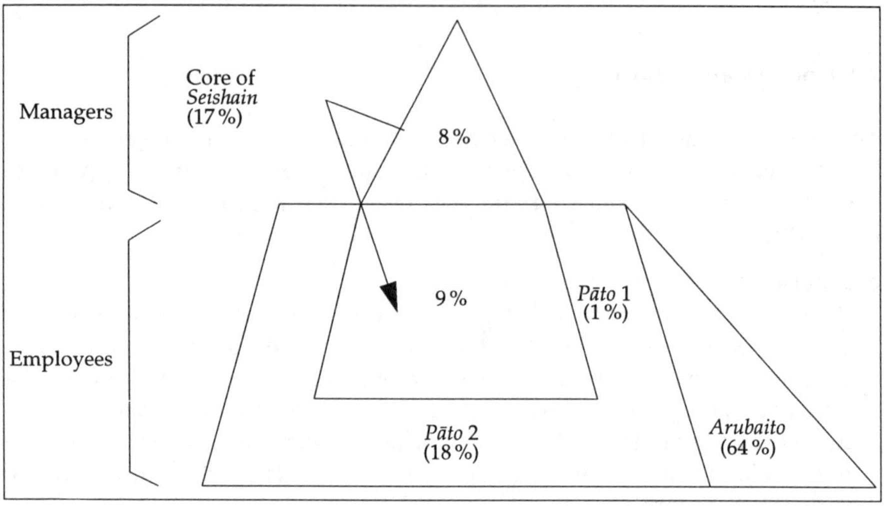

Source: cf. fig. 1

b) An integrated management of segmentation

Why can Convenience Store's flexible employment management be considered as integrated? We will distinguish two factors: the division of labour and the promotion and remuneration systems.

Unlike one would imagine, flexible jobs in Convenience Stores are not empty or without task responsibilities. Let us give two illustrations of the relative valorization of these jobs through the division of labour.

The first example is the system of functional equivalence between levels of grade classification. For example, in the firm we studied an *arubaito* could replace a store manager when he was absent, or accomplish the tasks which were theoretically under the responsibility of a full-timer (*seishain*). Moreover the tasks attributed to the *arubaito* could be the same as for the store manager: budget and benefits management, personnel management in the store, interviews with applicants and training. This system of functional equivalence exists at each level of the hierarchy and has a strong effect on the polyvalence of workers at the store level.

The second illustration of the valorization of flexible jobs through a division of labour concerns ordering tasks, a particularly strategic issue for Convenience Stores. Here again, there is no strict relationship between the hierarchy of status in the store and the actual degree of responsibility attributed to each. For example, the chief of the *arubaito's* team, whose status was that of a part-timer, could process orders which were as important or even more important than orders processed by full-timers. Also, *arubaito* could process orders in the same category of goods as full-timers with much shorter experience.

In other words, this structure is one with a very segmented job hierarchy but at the same time giving every employee the possibility to assume responsibilities in their work, though this relative valorization of flexible employment is hardly reflected in the promotion and remuneration systems. Even though we can observe some sophistication of these systems, remuneration and promotion are still very different for core workers (full-timers) and for peripheral workers (part-timers). As a whole, in the company we studied, the annual labour cost of a full-time employee (including bonus and social costs for employer) is about three times higher than for part-timers, and there is still a two-fold gap in terms of labour cost per hour.

Based on these case studies, what, if any, are the new features of human resource management practices in Japanese retailing?

3 What is the future of the Japanese model of human resource management?

3.1 Diversity of flexible jobs

Regarding flexible jobs, there is no single type of employee or of employment relationship. The different categories of flexible jobs are not rigid and can vary in relative scope. Furthermore, employees can move from one category to another during the course of their working life.

This result brings some nuances to the analysis of labour markets in terms of dualism, which is often based on an exclusive observation of employment systems in the *manufacturing* sector. According to the *dualistic approaches* (see for example EBIZUKA, ISAGAI and UEMURA 1994), the labour market can be roughly divided into two parts: a core of regular employees, enjoying good employment conditions, and a second part made up of non-regular employees, excluded from those conditions. However, our observations of employment structures in the retailing sector lead us to conclude that labour force preferences appear to be much more diverse as time availability patterns of workers are also manifold. Instead of a 'polarization of working hours' between regular employees with a heavy (time-) work load and non-regular employees with fewer working hours, one should rather consider the diversification of working hour patterns in relation to individual preferences and socio-economic constraints specific to each of the employee populations, without pre-judging the quality of jobs with no reference to their perception by their holders.

Table 1 shows the diversity of flexible jobs and their characteristics in the case of Convenience Stores: one can distinguish *autonomization* objectives, *socialization* objectives and *subsistence* or *expectation* objectives. These different objectives reflect differences between individual employees in correspondence with differing supply profiles[10]. Convenience Stores take particular advantage of this diversity even though other retailing formats do so as well.

Table 1: Who are the part-timers in Convenience Stores?

	Students	'Housewives'	'Others'
Working hours Working days per week	18.0 3.5	28.3 5.2	34.0 5.1
Age	90 % < 24	60 % > 40	70 % < 24
Working period	*Males* 50 to 70 % evening 20 to 30 % night *Females* 20 to 40 % afternoon 30 to 60 % evening	53 % morning 45 % from morning to evening 2 % evening	*Males* 25 % evening 44 % night *Females* 50 % from morning to evening 20 % evening
Seniority	15 to 20 months	50 months	23 months
Average monthly salary	*Males* 60,000 yen *Females* 45,000 yen	81,000 yen	*Males* 140,000 yen *Females* 95,000 yen
Socio-economic constraints on employment	Studies and out-of-school activities	Fiscal system Family	Fiscal system Desire of autonomy from the company
Satisfaction	Degree: ++ Dissatisfaction with wage, interesting work, valorization of competencies	Degree: + Dissatisfaction with wage, human relations and work atmosphere	Degree: 0 Dissatisfaction with wage, working hours, length of work and working atmosphere
Job characterization	*Autonomization employment* Precarious short term job, mainly motivated by a complementary financial need	*Socialization employment* Precarious long-term job, mainly motivated by a complementary financial and activity need	*Subsistence and expectation employment* Precarious job, time variable, mainly considered as a main activity, a subsistence, an expectation, or a full-time employment

Sources: based on author's case studies of 1996 and NIHON RŌDŌ KENKYŪ KIKŌ (1995)

[10] The category 'others' in table 1 is mainly composed of freeters (50 %). This expression

A survey conducted on part-time workers in supermarkets confirms this fact. When employees were asked why they chose their job, answers differed between 'full-time part-timers' (working more than 7 hours a day), 'long-hours part-timers' (working between 5 and 7 hours a day), and 'short-hours part-timers' (working less than 5 hours). While the first group was concerned that they increase the household's income and that they gain social contacts through their work, these incentives were of lesser importance as working hours become shorter, and other goals such as "to have enough to live on" and "to make the most of competencies" predominated [11].

Socio-economic constraints which partly govern job selection are very different for each of the employment categories. Similarly, the management and organization of the diversity of flexible jobs, employees' relation to their job, the compatibilities between working time and non-working time, and finally respect of social and family conventions are all factors which contribute to the *integrated aspects* of job segmentation (theory).

3.2 Integration of working time and non-working time

The organization of working time and its relationship with non-working time are essential to the social compromises enabling the given flexibility in Japanese retailing. There are different types of related *complementarities* between the different categories of jobs. An integrative management of job segmentation is based on those related categories of differentiated jobs and status. Convenience Stores are particularly good at exploiting this kind of management, even though they are not the only ones to do so. Whatever the format, we notice several complementarity levels of employees depending on time segments. Table 2 summarizes different forms of complementarity found in the Convenience Stores chain discussed earlier.

- First we can distinguish a *statutory* or *hierarchical complementarity* based on a fundamental division between, on the one side, a minority of full-time employees (mainly male) and, on the other, a non-homogeneous body of non-regular workers, where female employees are in the majority.
- The second kind of complementarity is a structural one: one could call it *gender complementarity*, i. e., female employees working during day time, men during mornings and evenings.

---

means 'free arubaiters' and is applied to young employees who decide to have a 'free life' before joining a large firm under a long-term commitment. They have generally not passed the university entrance examination and are still living together with their parents. 20 % of the category 'others' are females holding several jobs at the same time. This shows that the Convenience Store format is particularly able to take advantage of behaviours considered as 'marginal' in the Japanese society.

[11] See KOYŌ SOKUSHIN JIGYŌDAN SANGYŌ RŌDŌ KENKYŪ SENTĀ (1993).

- The third complementarity is based on the social status in each one of the male and female populations, a *socio-cultural* or *socio-professional complementarity*:
  - for female employees there is a first level of complementarity between 'housewives', 'others' and students. 'Housewives' and 'others' are mainly at work during morning hours while students work in the afternoons and evenings;
  - for male employees, there is a first level of complementarity between junior college students and university students and the category 'others': the former work in the evenings while the latter work evenings and at night. There is a second level of complementarity between male students (college and university) and the 'others' employees: students mainly work on limited time segments (morning, afternoon, evening, night) while freeters (free-lancer) mainly work on full day schedules.

Table 2: Types of complementarities of flexible jobs in Convenience Stores

	Statutory complementarity or hierarchical complementarity	*Gender complementarity*	*Socio-cultural or socio- professional complementarity*
Female empl.	Non-regular employees 80 to 90% of total workforce Mainly female employees ↔ ↕	Daytime: high proportion of female employees ↕	– 'Housewives' and ↕ 'Others': all day and morning ↔ – Students: afternoon and evening ↕
Male empl.	Full time regular employees 10 to 20% of total workforce Working mainly during daytime Mainly male employees ↔	Nocturnal (evening and night): high proportion of male employees	Complementarity A – college students: evening – univ. students and 'Others': evening and night ↕ *Complementarity B* ↔ – univ. students: limited segments of time – 'Others': all day

Sources: cf. table 1

GADREY, JANY and RIBAULT (1998a, 1998b) show that one of the most important consequences of such links between the different levels of complementarity is that Japanese part-timers work in a foreseeable time schedule environment. Employees are recruited on the basis of contracts explicitly specifying their working time both in terms of length of time and in terms of time schedule. Regularity of working hours and a relatively low level of overtime work are two other features of the working conditions of part-timers in Japanese retailing. While the ability of employees to foresee their time organization is a crucial negotiation point with employers, usage conventions of employment are respectful of the family division of roles and tasks, organizing a time flexibility compatible with those conventions.

3.3 A challenge for existing segmentation theories

This section will draw heavily on the results of recent work by GADREY, JANY and RIBAULT (1998a, 1998b). Earlier, we have used the notions of 'core' and 'peripheral' which both belong to the traditional segmentation theories. One of the major issues, however, concerning the integration of *pāto* into job classifications is that in terms of these theories this group contains characteristics of both core and peripheral jobs.

In the pioneering work by DOERINGER & PIORE (1971), and later in the approach by GORDON, EDWARDS and REICH (1982), the opposition between core and periphery (or between primary and secondary segments in DOERINGER and PIORE's terms) is based on the concept of internal labour markets. Workers inside these internal markets benefit from several advantages: high employment security related to seniority, promoting rules reserving employees internal jobs without being in competition with outsiders, and internal rules for the determination of wages linked only marginally to the external economic environment. These jobs (and employees) are associated with the core qualifications of the firm. Peripheral jobs are conversely characterized by a high instability or insecurity, no career perspective and lower wages, depending much more on the prevailing general economic situation.

Considering the way *pāto* are managed and their present development, peripheral jobs appear not to fit in either of these two categories. Instead, *pāto* are characterized by:

- good security and stability, and the possibility to remain inside one company until the end of one's career, which is generally a characteristic of core jobs. The average length of service is usually high;
- *pāto* jobs require competencies central to the company in terms of service to customers and, increasingly, in terms of technical skills (for example food preparation) which is another feature of core jobs. More recently, some Japanese researchers have thus begun to qualify these jobs as being a "key labour force" in the food retailing (HONDA 1996);
- perspectives of career promotion are almost non-existent: the fact that we can encounter internal hierarchical ranks does not contradict the quasi-impossibility to become *seishain*;
- hourly wages (including bonuses) are 30 % to 50 % lower than those for *seishain* for similar tasks;
- social benefits are extremely limited.

While the first two points are characteristics of core jobs, the last three are typical for a peripheral or secondary status. We may overcome this categorization difficulty by using a three-level segmentation, referring to GORDON, EDWARDS and REICH (1982). This approach distinguishes an independent primary segment (re-grouping professional and technical activities with a relative autonomy of work), a primary subordinated segment (with semi-skilled jobs for more routinized and controlled tasks) and a secondary segment (the same as in the dualistic approach by DOERINGER and PIORE). The *pāto* status would fall approximately into the primary subordinated segment.

This solution does not solve the problem, though, because it is still difficult to understand why employees having the same tasks, with approximately the same experience and seniority, and exercising functions at the core of the firm are managed in such markedly different ways. In the theory of GORDON, EDWARDS and REICH (1982), primary subordinated segment employees have functions, qualifications and responsibilities which are inferior to, and basically different from independent primary segment employees, who are the only professionals inside the firm. This is not quite the case of *pāto*, however, and even less so over the course of the past few years in Japan.

As FREATHY & SPARKS (1995) argue, one of the main weaknesses of the traditional theoretical framework of labour segmentation lies in "its focus upon individual firms without reference to the wider structural issues operative within the labour market" (p.192). Namely in terms of responsibility of employees and managers, we are facing important shifts which cannot easily be taken into account by these theories. As demonstrated above, part-time workers in Japanese retailing can access to a relatively high level of responsibility while their job conditions continue to retain 'secondary' features. Another point not developed any further here, but worth mentioning at this stage, is the trend of a relative 'de-skilling' of senior managers, with a growing centralization of decision-making at head offices. A similar growing need for "a good implementation staff rather than strategic decision-making staff at store level", reducing the autonomy of senior managers, has been identified in British retailing by FREATHY & SPARKS (1995: 192).

This inability of traditional segmentation theories to provide an adequate explanation of employment systems in Japanese retailing is not only due to a 'Japanese specificity'. Segmentation theories are influenced by their American origins and by the particular types of dualism in that society. But they are also influenced by *industrialism* and by their orientation on the American *industrial* employment model of the 1960s and1970s, a model which later spread to Europe as well. Other researchers have shown how this segmentation model was not adaptable to European and American tertiary employment systems of the 1980s (see, for instance, GADREY 1991). One could argue that it is even more difficult to apply traditional segmentation theory to Japanese retailing and service activities.

For each period, for each national context and for each activity sector then there is a need for re-conceptualizing relevant segments, giving a full role to 'socio-economic spaces' which determine these segments (e. g., the family division of roles). Only with a 'societal' approach is there an opportunity to identify the main factors and actors of the social construction of employment segmentation.

3.4 Toward a hyperflexible integrated segmentation

A very sophisticated differentiation in flexible jobs and in their management in the various retailing formats studied was found. The distinct working rhythms of these jobs demonstrate a diversity of complementarities between groups of employees with different motivations and time availabilities. This differentiation constitutes the central element of the hyperflexible integrated segmentation of employment.

While we encounter this segmentation in all the formats, Convenience Stores seem to develop a specific ability to take advantage of it on a 24-hour basis. Convenience Stores thus become the model of a hyperflexible integrated segmentation of employment. The weight of the core full-time workers is much reduced and external flexibility based on *arubaito* is the main way of adjustment to the local economic conditions. It is a model which does not exactly square with the general model of retailing activities in Japan (40 % of all employees in this sector belonging to the 'core' work force), nor with the existing industrial models, be they Fordist, post-Fordist or Toyotist, where 80 % of workers are part of the core (Sōmuchō Tōkeikyoku 1992: 42–43). Convenience Stores, thus, are facing a retailing format characterized by 'hyperservice', requiring 'hyperflexibility' of employment and of its management, to work under high-rationalization conditions. This hyperflexibility means a massive use of relatively precarious jobs. Just-in-time employment (see CLEMENT 1991) underlies the employment structure and management of Convenience Stores.

GADREY (1991) has developed a model of "flexible segmentation" characterized by, among others, two points directly related to our discussion here:

- a growing share of external recruitment to the detriment of internal promotions, and
- a sharp reduction of primary subordinated segments (with semi-skilled jobs but high length of service), and an increase of part-time employment, or fixed-term contracts, under a relatively 'secondary' status, filled by external employees.

Our interpretation in terms of hyperflexible integrated segmentation is close to GADREY's model, except that we insist more on the fundamental role of the diversity of employment status (especially of flexible jobs), and on the integrated aspects of this subtle segmentation. Besides other things, this integration means the re-introduction of internal labour market aspects into job categories which have been mainly developed on the external labour market. Even for relatively high responsibility tasks, for instance, we found that status and remuneration conditions were lower than those for full-timers.

Carl MOCK (1995) has also proposed the notion of "integrated segmentation" but in a different accentuation. His analysis in terms of categories of labour relates to 'submarkets', namely family-type enterprises, small and medium-size commercial enterprises and big firms, giving a central role to the fluidity between those markets through personnel transfers between the different entities of the same 'industrial territory'.

However, among the adaptation capacities of Japanese companies to the economic environment, the weight of personnel transfers should not be overestimated. Analyses of employment flexibility based on personnel transfers are usually concentrated on manufacturing sectors (see the paper by DIRKS in this volume; see also KOIKE 1994, 1996). This transfer practice, however, is not necessarily practical for all industries and, in any case, remains a minor adjustment tool in retailing firms. Instead, the internal segmentation of employment status as a flexibility tool should not be underestimated.

In the case of Japanese retailing, stratifications linked to social profiles of employees are crucial to this labour segmentation. In other words, the integrative dimension of hyperflexible segmentation consists more of a matching of the finely stratified supply of status, on the one hand, and a demand, again finely stratified, for working hours and time availability, on the other, than in a firm's ability to organize personnel transfers between itself and its subcontractors inside its 'territory'.

Employment segmentation in Japan is a much more refined exercise than generally presented by labour market analysts, reflecting a much more complex interaction between 'institutions'. For example, gender is a fundamental factor of the segmentation of supply and demand which is often cited but never really analysed.

4 Conclusion

Our analysis of the employment situation in Japanese retailing has demonstrated that it is not so much a structural dualism of the labour market, nor the industrial dualism with big firms on one side and a myriad of subcontractors on the other side, which are the corner stones of the 'shock absorbing' mechanisms inside retailing firms. Instead, the emergence and development of hyperflexible employment structures and mechanisms enable firms whenever necessary to re-introduce internal market features and to take advantage of 'national forms of institutionalization of the wage-labour nexus' (GADREY 1991). Such forms lie, for example, in the rules governing part-time labour, fiscal regulations-based preference structures, a social insurance system based on the household unit, low social charges for flexible jobs, a family division of tasks and roles, and the relatively high cost of school and university education (see OSAWA 1996).

If complementarities are crucial to jobs and status segmentations, this is so because they are in a relative coherence with these national forms of an institutionalization of the wage-labour nexus. When institutional factors of integration gradually lose their regulating power, we can expect that new internal integration factors will develop in their place: the introduction of internal labour market features for employees recruited under fixed short-term contracts with a high turnover can be interpreted in this way. It is this ability to balance between market and non-market forms of integration which has until now contributed to the relative stability of employment segmentation in Japanese retailing.

References

CLEMENT, R. (1991): Une organisation flexible du temps de travail dans la grande distribution. In: GADREY, J. and N. GADREY (eds.): *La gestion des ressources humaines dans les services et le commerce*. Paris: L'Harmattan, pp. 51–70.

DOERINGER, P. and M. PIORE (1971): *Internal Labor Market and Manpower Analysis*. Lexington, Mass.: D. C. Heath.

EBIZUKA, A., A. ISAGAI and H. UEMURA (1994): *Reconsidering 'Hierarchical Market-firm Nexus'*. Hitotsubashi University Seminar Paper. Tōkyō: Hitotsubashi University (unpubl.).

FREATHY, J. P. and L. SPARKS (1995): Understanding Retail Employment Relations. In: WRIGLEY, N. and M. LOWE (eds.): *Retailing, Consumption and Capital*. Harlow: Longman, pp. 178–195.

GADREY, J. (1991): Les systèmes d'emploi tertiaires: de la segmentation flexible aux approches typologiques: In: GADREY, J. and N. GADREY (eds.): *La gestion des ressources humaines dans les services et le commerce*. Paris: L'Harmattan, pp. 137–163.

GADREY, J., F. JANY and T. RIBAULT (1998a): *France – Japon – Etats-Unis: L'emploi en détail – Essai de socio-économie comparative*. Paris: Les Presses Universitaires de France, Collection Economie en Liberté (forthcoming).

GADREY, J., F. JANY and T. RIBAULT (1998b): Niveaux et systèmes d'emploi dans le commerce de détail japonais: une comparaison avec la France. In: *Revue Formation Emploi*, n° 61, pp. 3–17.

GORDON, D., R. EDWARDS and M. REICH (1982): *Segmented Work, Divided Workers*. Cambridge, Mass.: Cambridge University Press.

HONDA, K. (1996): Human Resources Management in Japanese Food Chain Stores. Paper presented at the *Conference on Employment Structures in European and Japanese Retailing*, Maison Franco-Japonaise, Tōkyō, 22-23 October 1996.

JAPAN INSTITUTE OF LABOUR (1990): *Survey on Arubaito in Commerce and Food Service Sectors*. Tōkyō: Japan Institute of Labour.

KOIKE, K. (1994): Learning and Incentive Systems in Japanese Industry. In: AOKI, M. and R. DORE (eds.): *The Japanese Firm. The Sources of Competitive Strength*. New York: Oxford University Press, pp. 41–65.

KOIKE, K. (1996): *The Economics of Work in Japan*. Tōkyō: LTCB International Library Foundation.

KOYŌ SOKUSHIN JIGYŌDAN SANGYŌ RŌDŌ KENKYŪ SENTĀ (1993): *Sūpā de hataraku pātotaimu no koyō no kadai ni kansuru chōsa kenkyū* [Survey on Employment Management of Part-timers in Supermarkets]. Tōkyō: Ministry of Labour.

MOCK, C. (1995): *Competition and Cooperation in Japanese Labour Markets*. London: Macmillan Press.

NIHON RŌDŌ KENKYŪ KIKŌ (Japanese Institute of Labour) (1995): *Conbiniansu stoa no keiei to rōdō ni kansuru chōsa kenkyū* [Survey on Employment Management in Convenience]. Tōkyō: Nihon Rōdō Kenkyū Kikō.

NOHARA, H. (1996): *Monographie 'Grands Magasins'*. Tōkyō: Maison Franco-Japonaise (unpublished manuscript).

OSAWA, M. (1996): Politiques publiques et emplois féminins au Japon. In: HIRATA, H. and D. SENOTIER (eds.): *Femmes et partage du travail*. Paris: Syros, pp. 199–216.

RIBAULT, T. (1998): L'emploi juste-à-temps dans la distribution au Japon: le cas des convenience stores. In: *Revue Formation Emploi*, n° 61, pp. 19–33.

RIBAULT, T. (1999): Working Time in Japanese Large Food Retailing. In: BARET, C., L. SPARKS and S. LEHNDORFF (eds.): *Managing Working Time in Large Food Retail Organizations: a Comparison between France, Germany, Great Britain and Japan*. London: Routledge (forthcoming).

SŌMUCHŌ TŌKEIKYOKU (Management and Coordination Agency) (1992): *Shōgyō kōzō kihon chōsa* [Employment Status Survey]. Tōkyō: Sōmuchō Tōkeikyoku.

Commentary

Flexible Employment in Japanese Retailing: Comparisons with Canada and Questions Concerning the Segmentation Theory

Diane-Gabrielle TREMBLAY

1 Introduction

Thierry Ribault's paper first develops along some case studies related to job segmentation in four retail formats. The author then asks what is the future of the Japanese model of human resource management? This question is asked in the perspective of traditional theories of job segmentation. The author highlights the diversity of flexible jobs observed in terms of working time and of social status of jobs, and defends the hypothesis that these observations present a challenge for existing segmentation theories, particularly the theory developed by Doeringer and Piore (1971). The author refers to another model of segmentation by Gadrey (1991), which he considers to be closer to his observations made in the retail sector in Japan. Gadrey's original paper refers to flexible segmentation as characteristic of the service sector (or tertiary sector) employment systems, and Ribault defends his idea of a hyperflexible integrated segmentation.

The first question of interest, in my opinion, is what are the implications of such new management practices on the Japanese employment and human resource management models? Secondly, and more theoretical, I am interested in the concept of the *hyperflexible integrated segmentation* of the labour force, which the author considers to be more appropriate to understand the characteristics of human resource management in Japanese retailing at present and in the future.

My presentation is composed of four parts. After this short introduction, I will relate the findings on Japan to the situation in Canada (or North America), in comparison with that of France, to which Ribault refers. I will then comment on the proposition of "hyperflexible integrated segmentation", with regards to other theories on segmentation and employment systems. A few specific questions will be addressed to the author on this issue, particularly concerning the categories of employment status established and demarcations between them. Finally, I will comment on the general applicability or specificity of the author's proposition, as well as on the general question of convergence or divergence of employment systems, referring here to my own research on Japanese transplants in Canada and other research on North American employment systems (see the various references under Tremblay).

2 Comparison with Canadian Retail firms

In this first section, I will relate the observations on the Japanese retail sector to the Canadian situation in general, and also to Japanese transplants in Canada, on which I have done a survey (TREMBLAY & ROLLAND 1997a, 1997b). The latter comparison, of course, is only partially conclusive as these studies do not cover retail stores but manufacturing firms instead, as most research done on Japanese transplants in Canada (ROBERTSON ET AL. 1992, MORRIS 1994, BOYER 1992).

One question that needs to be asked concerning the distinction between "core" and "periphery" in the segmentation of employment systems, mainly along the lines of fixed-term contracts versus more precarious forms. The author refers to different categories of part-timers, amongst which *pāto 1*, working long hours and having a good deal of experience, are on permanent contracts or one-year contracts; these seem to resemble more what would be referred to as "occasional" or "temporary" workers in Canada and North America. In recent years, contingent work has increased considerably in Canada and the US, as have short-term or contract work of different forms (that is, temporary, independent or autonomous work, as referred to in Canadian statistical classifications; see TREMBLAY 1997a).

Another observation of interest is the GMS format with its kind of internal labour market for part-timers. The author mentions that this market is relatively sophisticated and, depending on the companies, also very selective. As in Japan's retail sector, internal labour markets for part-timers in Canada are designed to ensure a minimum of motivation and to gradually allow step by step flexible jobs to predominate in the firms. The majority of part-timers in Canada are, however, seen as contingent, replaceable workers, for whom the firm has no career plans, using them as a short-term, cost minimizing strategy only.

In Canada, it is mainly youth between 15–24 years that are affected by temporary or contractual work (17 % of women and 16 % of men of that age group in 1994, see *Statistics Canada Survey*, in TREMBLAY 1997b). These figures continue to be quite high both for men and women aged 25 to 34, diminishing thereafter somewhat though increasing again for older age-groups. Here, as in Japan, social and institutional factors related to the family organization are clearly at play. Social services and the public administration traditionally seen as sectors dominated by stable, core-type jobs present a fair percentage of temporary work (13 % and 11 % respectively). Retail services, however, have the highest percentage of part-timers (29 %). In this perspective, there is certainly a similarity with the Japanese situation, in terms of the use of part-time and of women and young people, who in Canada are often students as well. Other forms of non-standard employment, such as temporary (4 %) and independent forms (6 %), are less frequent in the retail sector. We do observe however, that a fair percentage of retail workers hold two or more jobs (10 %), a percentage which is higher than the average on the labour market (7 %).

Data indicates that contingent work today makes up about one third of the Canadian labour market, although some estimates have been much higher, indicating that as many as 50 % of Canadian workers have not worked "regularly, full time, all year round" in the year preceding this Census (see, again, TREMBLAY 1997b). While macro-data on forms of employment always contains the difficulty of correct estimation and we might thus be better off with more conservative assessment, there has nevertheless been a clear increase in non-standard work for all employment groups, with the exception of men between 45 and 54 years where the situation is stable. Whereas young people are most affected by non-standard work forms, some 40 % of women are as well. As in Japan, women form the bulk of workers used in non-standard or peripheral forms of work in retail and in services in general. Retail has a very high percentage of such non-standard work, rising further from 40 % in 1989 to 42 % in 1994 (TREMBLAY 1997a: 117). This fact reflects an increase in all sectors, except for services to consumers, which already had a very high rate. This leads to a question concerning the Japanese case and the lack of macro-data in Ribault's paper: Is the use of non-standard or flexible forms of employment in retail a 'new' form of human resource management or is this not a traditional form of a gendered division of labour observable in Canada and North America in general (TREMBLAY 1996, 1997b, 1997c)?

In terms of social and institutional explanations, many elements relating to family responsibilities, still predominantly assumed by women in Canada as well, contribute to explaining the strong percentage of women in these types of peripheral forms of work. Participation rates of women in Canada have considerably increased over the last few decades (57 % on average), including those age-groups with children to take care of (25–45), where the rate is the highest (77 %). In the future, women in Canada will continue to participate in the labour market almost as regularly as men, as they are having less children per woman and returning to the workforce after shorter periods of time. However, firms' HRM strategies as well as remaining difficulties to balance work/family obligations (TREMBLAY & VILLENEUVE 1997a, 1997b) continue to contribute to the fact that many women face peripheral forms of work, principally part-time. Part-time employment for women is thus often considered a 'choice under constraint'.

Incidentally, over the recent years the high and stable participation rate of women in conjunction with the rising levels of specialization in some retail stores (computer, music, sports, etc.) have led to the development of a stronger career perspective for some, including women. However, this is not true for all retail formats.

3 Questions concerning the employment system and segmentation theories

On the basis of the case studies presented, Ribault defends the idea of an integrated management of segmentation, on the basis of the division of labour and the promotion and wage systems observed. Ribault indicates that unlike what one might expect, flexible jobs in Convenience Stores do not lack content nor responsibility and have some form of relative valorization through the division of labour. He mentions for example that an *arubaito* can replace a store manager in his absence, or he can accomplish the tasks which are normally under the responsibility of a full-timer (*seishain*). Ribault adds that the tasks attributed to the *arubaito* can be the same as for the store manager: budget and benefits management, personnel management in the store, interviews with applicants, training administration. In his view, this system of functional equivalence exists at each level of the hierarchy and has a strong effect on the polyvalence of workers in the stores. The second example of the valorization of flexible jobs through division of labour is related to ordering tasks, which the author considers as strategic. Here again, he considers that there is no strict relation between the hierarchy of status in the store and the actual degree of responsibility attributed to each status.

The author concludes that given a very segmented job hierarchy, every employee has the possibility to assume task responsibilities, though this relative valorization of flexible employment is not actually reflected in the promotion and wage systems which, despite some degree of sophistication as noted by Ribault, are still very different for core workers (full-timers) and for peripheral workers (part-timers).

Three comments or questions arise from these observations, two comparing with the situation in North America, and a third related to the theoretical dimension of segmentation and employment systems (see also TREMBLAY 1997b). First, has the service sector in general not always been characterized by a less precise division of labour, and more flexibility and polyvalence in task distribution and job descriptions. Is this so-called "valorization" or task flexibility therefore anything new for the retail and service sector in Japan? While perhaps different in France, where hierarchies tend to be stronger as indicated by Ribault, these characteristics appear to be rather traditional ones in Canada and, probably, in the US as well. The differences observed between Japan and France may thus be indicative of Japan's convergence with North American labour market practices and forms of flexibility. Not knowing the Japanese service sector very well, I cannot say whether this is something new, and therefore indicative of convergence, or whether the Japanese service sector has not always been rather different from the ideal-type, J-firm characteristics of the large Japanese automobile firms. I tend to think the latter, all the more so since some Japanese transplants in Canada are also farther away from the typical "J model" than some of their (purely) Canadian counterparts. For a full discussion, see TREMBLAY & ROLLAND 1996a.

Secondly, as concerns the same task allocation regardless of status (full-time or part-time), can this not be related to a general move towards a flexibilization of tasks and a reduction of the division of labour in many industrial and service sectors? Comparative research on Japanese transplants and domestic ('quality-oriented') firms in Canada (TREMBLAY & ROLLAND 1996b, 1996c) has revealed, for example, a development of various elements indicative of a reduced division of labour, of a sharing of responsibilities at different levels of the hierarchy, even in manufacturing sectors. In terms of employment systems defined by OSTERMAN (1987, 1984, see also TREMBLAY 1997a), industrial sectors appear to be moving towards salaried systems, whereas some service sectors traditionally characterized by salaried systems now tend to be moving towards a stronger division of labour and therefore a more industrial type of employment systems. 'Salaried systems' imply a diffuse division of labour, relatively high job autonomy, some horizontal as well as vertical mobility, and in general good working conditions. 'Industrial systems', on the contrary, have very precise job definitions, little autonomy, vertical mobility and a relatively good job security based on the 'last in – first out' principle. They are generally found in blue collar jobs (traditional industrial environments), but also in certain, Taylorized jobs, e. g., the insurance industry.

Thirdly, there is not one, unique type of employee and of employment relations; the different categories of flexible jobs are not rigid and can vary in relative scope, this probably being more the case in the service than in the industrial sector. In relation to this, Ribault mentions that following tensions in the labour market and in family structures, employees may move from one category to another during the course of their working life. In Canada, men may switch from one to the other (generally from non-standard to standard forms of employment), while women over 25 who are in non-standard employment tend to be 'trapped' there and do not have the possibility of crossing the 'bridge' that men and some younger women cross to enter regular or standard employment. It must be added that an increasing number of both men and women are now moving from standard forms of employment to non-standard work in the context of downsizing in North America in general and, additionally, of high unemployment in Canada.

I agree with Ribault that the apparent diversity of employment systems forces us to better differentiate the analysis of labour markets in terms of *dualism,* as in fact previous analyses have largely been founded on observations of North American manufacturing employment systems in the 1960s and 1970s. According to these dualistic approaches (e. g., DOERINGER & PIORE 1971), the labour market is roughly divided into two parts: a core of regular employees, enjoying good employment conditions, and another part composed of non-regular employees, excluded from those conditions.

We have argued earlier that industrial manufacturing systems themselves have tended to move closer to forms of salaried employment (as described by OSTERMAN 1984, 1987), while certain service sectors (such as insurance and some parts of banking) have come to resemble more the industrial type, and it is clear that employment systems have diversified. However, I find it difficult to conclude from this "that labour force preferences appear to be much more diverse as time availability patterns of workers are also manifold" (Ribault, p. 303). While "the organization of working time and its relationship with non-working time are essential to the social compromises enabling the given flexibility in Japanese retailing" (p. 305), this also being the case for many service sectors in Canada (TREMBLAY & VILLENEUVE 1997b, TREMBLAY 1997a), I am not convinced that the labour supply characteristics determine work employment systems in the sense that they are a more important force than labour *demand* characteristics, i. e., firms' HRM strategies.

While Ribault's paper does not stress this factor for Japan, Canadian research has shown that demand factors are important determinants for work patterns, and particularly for the flexibilization of employment status and work hours (TREMBLAY 1997b, 1997c for Canada, NEGREY 1993 for the US). It is preferable to assume that corporate HRM strategies are "socially constructed" and indeed partly built upon the difficult work/family balancing problem, leading many women to exercise a 'choice under constraint' and to 'choose' part-time work as a form of work/family balancing solution. This is a hypothesis currently further developed (TREMBLAY & VILLENEUVE 1997a), following earlier research on similar subjects in Canada (LEE, DUXBURY and HIGGINS 1994).

Nevertheless, Ribault's proposition of flexible segmentation appears appropriate not only for the Japanese retail sector, but for many service sector employment systems in Canada and the US as well. Moreover, Ribault introduces some interesting analytical categories to refine the segmentation analysis, particularly a structural *gender complementarity* (female employees working during day time, male employees working during mornings and evenings) and a *socio-cultural or socio-professional complementarity.*

According to Ribault, given the way they are managed and their present development, *pāto* jobs however do not fit in to any of these categories. In certain ways they are similar to the characteristics of core jobs, while in others they are more of a peripheral or secondary status. Very obviously then, the three-level segmentation introduced by Osterman (1987) following Gordon, Edwards and Reich (1982) is often more appropriate in explaining present-day labour markets, especially if service sectors are taken into account. This approach distinguishes an independent primary segment (professional and technical activities with relative autonomy in their work), a primary subordinated segment (semi-skilled jobs for more routinized and controlled tasks) and a secondary segment. The *pāto* status, like many service sector jobs in Canada (TREMBLAY 1997a), would then fall into the primary subordinated segment.

Ribault considers this typology to be insufficient. However, a delimitation in the *number of segments* probably is no solution either, lest we arrive at the impossibility of establishing a typology, and achieving a *random distribution* of jobs only. In such a case, the *empirical application* of segmentation analysis would run into the difficulty of finding the adequate variable allowing a discrimination of jobs into exclusive categories. Some earlier work done in Québec in the 1980s has tentatively highlighted this difficulty (TREMBLAY 1997a), with different variables leading to different dividing lines between segments.

Ribault's analysis of the retail sector and the gendered division of labour also highlights the fact that one of the main weaknesses of the traditional framework of labour market segmentation lies in its focus on individual firms rather than on the wider structural issues within labour markets. Beyond the devolution of responsibilities by managers to employees, as discussed by Ribault, I believe the social construction of employee profiles and particularly of gendered profiles must also be taken into account.

4 Convergence or divergence?

The first question related to this issue has to do with defining whether the HRM practices described concerning the Japanese retail sector are in fact 'new' practices, or whether they are typical of the Japanese employment system in the service sector, which clearly differs from the typical J-firm described for the automobile and other industrial sectors as well as of many J-firms abroad (TREMBLAY & ROLLAND 1996a, 1997a). If indeed this is a new HRM system for the Japanese retail sector, then clearly there *is* a convergence with the North American employment system of the service sector, while some divergence with French HRM practices may persist, as Ribault explains.

Secondly, traditional segmentation theories fail to give us an adequate explanation of employment systems in Japanese retailing and this is not only due to a 'Japanese specificity'. It is true that segmentation theories have been influenced by their American origins and by the particular types of dualism characteristic of the US in the 1960s and 1970s. Recent research has highlighted the diversification of the employment system even in the US, the introduction to the new edition of Doeringer and Piore's book (1985) taking these developments into account, as does other research in Canada and the US (amongst others, BETCHERMAN ET AL. 1994, MELTZ & VERMA 1993, and TREMBLAY 1997a for Canada; NEGREY 1993, and APPELBAUM & BATT 1994 for the US). No appropriate employment system classification has, however, been sufficiently developed to date.

Thirdly, and finally, Ribault is correct in saying that "For each period, for each national context and for each activity sector then there is a need for reconceptualizing relevant segments, giving a full role to 'socio-economic spaces' which determine these segments" (p. 308). In my view, the gendered division of labour is one of the key determinants in this perspective, although it has often been neglected. Even the 'societal' approach does not always give adequate weight to the gendered division of labour within the family as an important aspect in identifying the main factors and actors related to the social construction of employment segmentation. Ribault's paper goes a long way in this perspective, but needs to be complemented by more detailed information on the gendered division of labour within the Japanese family.

As OSAWA (1996) mentions for Japan, and TREMBLAY & VILLENEUVE (1997a, 1997b) do so for Canada, work and non-work are very much intertwined. As countries vary in the specific configuration of this relationship, this probably constitutes a Japanese specificity which has some influence on the labour market situation for men and women. Many things are implicitly presumed concerning Japanese women's labour market participation and the gendered division of labour within the family, these factors certainly influencing HRM strategies of Japanese firms. However, we need more information on the evolution and present conditions regarding these two issues, key determinants of HRM strategies and labour market segmentation, in order to determine whether there is true convergence or divergence between Japan and other countries.

References

APPELBAUM, E. and R. BATT (1994): *The New American Workplace. Transforming Work Systems in the United States.* New York: ILR Press.

BETCHERMAN, G., N. LECKIE and A. VERMA (1994): *HRM Innovations in Canada: Evidence from Establishment Surveys.* School of Industrial Relations, Industrial Relations Centre, Queen's University at Kingston.

BOYER, R. (1992): *La surprenante capacité d'hybridation du modèle japonais: l'exemple de la CAMI* (mimeo). Paris: Gerpisa.

DOERINGER, P. and M. PIORE (1971): *Internal Labor Market and Manpower Analysis.* Lexington Mass.: D. C. Heath (new edition: 1985).

GORDON, D., R. EDWARDS and M. REICH (1982): *Segmented Work, Divided Workers.* Cambridge, Mass.: Cambridge University Press.

LEE, C., L. DUXBURY and C. HIGGINS (1994): *Les mères au travail; concilier la vie professionnelle et la vie familiale.* Rapport de recherche no. 15. Québec: Centre Canadien de Gestion.

MELTZ, N. and A. VERMA (1993): *Developments in Industrial Relations and Human Resource Practices in Canada: an Update from the 1980s.* Industrial Relations Centre, Queen's University at Kingston.

MORRIS, J. (1994): The Japanization of Industry: A Review of Developments in the UK and Canada. In: NIOSI, J. (ed.): *New Technology Policy and Social Innovations in the Firm.* New York: Pinter Publishers, pp. 173–186.

NEGREY, C. (1993): *Gender, Time and Reduced Work.* SUNY Series in Sociology of Work. New York: State University of New York Press.

OSAWA, M. (1996): Division sexuelle du travail et du temps au Japon. In: HIRATA, H. and D. SENOTIER (eds.): *Femmes et partage du travail.* Paris: Syros, pp. 99–216.

OSTERMAN, P. (1987): Choice of Employment Systems in Internal Labour Markets. In: *Industrial Relations* 26, 1, Winter, pp. 46–67.

OSTERMAN, P. (1984): Introduction: The Nature and Importance of Internal Labor Markets. In: OSTERMAN, P. (ed.): *Internal Labor Markets.* Cambridge: MIT Press, pp. 1–22.

ROBERTSON, D., J. RINEHART and C. HUXLEY (1992): Team Concept and Kaizen: Japanese Production Management in a Unionized Canadian Auto Plant. In: *Studies in Political Economy,* N° 39, pp. 77–107.

SUGITA, K. (1996): Temps et travail au Japon: partage ou complémentarité? In: HIRATA, H. and D. SENOTIER (eds.): *Femmes et partage du travail.* Paris: Syros, pp. 217–230.

TREMBLAY, D.-G. (1997a): *Economie du travail. Les réalités et les approches théoriques.* Montréal: Editions Saint-Martin/Télé-Université (new edition from 1990).

TREMBLAY, D.-G. (1997b): The 'New Division of Labour' Debate and Women's Jobs: Results from a Survey Conducted in Canada from a Gendered Perspective. In: OECHTERING, V. (ed.): *Spinning a Web from Past to Future: Women, Work and Computerization.* New York/Berlin: Springer-Verlag, pp. 293–303.

TREMBLAY, D.-G. (1997c): Change and Continuity: Transformations in the Gendered Division of Labour in a Context of Technological and Organizational Change. In: *Proceedings of the International Industrial Relations Association European Conference.* Dublin: Oak Tree Press House, pp. 31–57.

TREMBLAY, D.-G. (1996): Innovation, Employment Systems and Division of Labour: An Analysis of the Canadian Banking Sector. In: LITTEK, W. and T. CHARLES (eds.): *The New Division of Labour: Emerging Forms of Work Organization in International Perspective.* Berlin/New York: Walter De Gruyter, pp. 397–418.

TREMBLAY, D.-G. and D. ROLLAND (1998): Employment, Qualification and Innovation in a Knowledge Economy; The Case of Japanese Transplants in Canada. In: SALES, A. (ed.): *Knowledge, Economy and Society.* Forthcoming.

TREMBLAY, D.-G. and D. ROLLAND (1997a): Le modèle japonais de gestion des ressources humaines. In: CHANLAT, J.-F. (ed.): *Entreprise et Société.* CD-ROM. Montréal: HEC.

TREMBLAY, D.-G. and D. ROLLAND (1997b): Le modèle japonais de gestion au Canada: vers une hypothèse d'hybridation. In: *Japon in Extenso,* no. 46, September (Poitiers: Éditions Corpus), pp. 15–26.

TREMBLAY, D.-G. and D. ROLLAND (1996a): *The Japanese Model of Management in Canada. Towards a Theory of Hybridization.* Research Note 96-2. Montréal: Télé-université, Direction de la recherche.

TREMBLAY, D.-G. and D. ROLLAND (1996b): The Japanese Employment System and Evolutionist Economics. Results from a Survey on Japanese Transplants in Canada. In: *Proceedings of the 1996 Conference of the European Association of Evolutionary Economics*, on the Web Site of the European Association of Evolutionary Economics.

TREMBLAY, D.-G. and D. ROLLAND (1996c): Le système d'emploi japonais et sa contribution à l'innovation et à la qualification des salariés. In: TREMBLAY, D.-G. (ed.): *Innovation, technologie et qualification; multidimension et complexité du processus d'innovation.* Québec: Presses de l'université du Québec. Collection Études d'Économie Politique, pp. 83–104.

TREMBLAY, D.-G. and D. VILLENEUVE (1997a): Aménagement et réduction du temps de travail; réconcilier emploi, famille et vie personnelle. In: *Loisir et Société* 20, 1, July (Québec: Presses de l'université du Québec), pp. 107–157.

TREMBLAY, D.-G. and D. VILLENEUVE (1997b): *Aménagement et réduction du temps de travail; défis et perspectives.* Québec: Télé-université.

Innovation and Technology Management

XIII Japanese Corporate R&D in the 1990s: Change and Continuity

Martin HEMMERT

In the recent discussion about R&D management practices in Japanese manufacturing firms, a number of managerial features have been described as typical for Japanese firms, in contrast to firms in Western countries. The empirical base for this discussion was the 1980s, a time when Japanese management was commonly regarded as superior to that of Western firms. In the 1990s, however, the environment for Japanese business R&D has drastically changed, pressing firms for cost reduction and a strengthening of their technological base at the same time. In response to these environmental changes, Japanese manufacturing firms have applied rationalization, focus, and globalization strategies concerning their R&D activities. The most significant managerial differences to Western firms, however, appear to persist for the time being, at least on the average. On the other hand, the differences among Japanese firms in the field of R&D management are widening.

1 Introduction

In the last decades, as a consequence of the accelerated proliferation of technological innovations in industrial products and processes, R&D management has become a central part of the corporate management system in industrial firms. Concerning this tendency, Japan is no exception. Consequently, the field of R&D management has drawn more and more attention in the context of the Japanese corporate management system.

Therefore, this paper addresses the peculiarities of R&D management as it is applied by Japanese firms in the context of the firms' overall management system. Section 2 gives an overview of what might be regarded as the Japanese corporate R&D system. This review mainly refers to the 1980s, the period when Japanese management practices were regarded by many observers as a success model. In particular, it will discuss in what fields of R&D management significant differences between Japanese firms and their counterparts in other countries appear to exist, and the impact of these differences on managerial performance is assessed.

Thereafter in Section 3, recent tendencies in the R&D management of Japanese firms will be analysed. Based on the observation that the business environment Japanese manufacturers are operating in has largely changed in the 1990s, firms' managerial responses in the field of R&D are scrutinized and evaluated. Finally, in Section 4, some implications for the overall Japanese management system are drawn from the perspective of R&D management.

2 Review: Profile of Japanese corporate R&D

2.1 Preliminary remarks

From a viewpoint of research methodology, it appears to be problematic to analyse and discuss certain management tools applied by *some* companies in a given country and then qualify these features as typical by assuming that the analysed companies are representative of *all* companies in that country. Apparently, because of the vast number of firms that are operating in Japan (presently around 3 million incorporated companies), their totality can neither be expected to have the same, or even similar, management systems, nor will they have clear-cut structural and managerial features distinguishing them from all firms located in different countries.

However, since the recent rise of institutional economics, researchers have widely recognized the strong impact national environments exercise on the formation and evolution of firms' management systems. Whereas this does not mean that these institutional factors totally determine, directly or indirectly, all firms' management systems, it can be fairly assumed that *as a tendency*, wide international differences in the firms' environment will result in different management systems in certain respects.

In the case of Japan, the reference frame for international comparisons of firms' management systems are mostly the firms in other highly developed countries in North America and Western Europe. Therefore, the subsequent analysis will focus on certain management features related to R&D that appear to occur more frequently in Japanese firms than in North American and Western European ones. Consequently, the discussion of their implications for firms' performance is centered on a comparison between Japanese and Western firms as well.

2.2 Analysis by managerial field

Subsequently, a number of behavioural and structural features that have been identified in earlier research as typical for or predominantly found in Japanese manufacturing firms are discussed. Some of these features apply not only to R&D, but also to other managerial activities, or even the corporate management system as a whole. Nevertheless, these more general aspects are also explicitly listed as far as they are essential for the functioning of corporate R&D management in Japanese firms.

Another fact to be noted is that the discussion about R&D management focuses, sometimes implicitly, on large firms. Consequently, the following characteristics may not be representative of Japanese manufacturing firms as a whole, but only of large corporations that indeed account for the bulk of industrial R&D performed in Japan. In fiscal year 1995, firms with a capital of more than 10 billion Yen accounted for 73.8 % of all intramural R&D expenditures in manufacturing (SŌMUCHŌ TŌKEIKYOKU 1997: 82–83). While large firms are the most important performers of industrial R&D in other countries as well, the concentration of R&D appears to be higher in Japan than in Western countries.[1] This structural feature interferes with some of the R&D management tools applied by Japanese firms and can be interpreted at the same time as an outcome of the institutional surroundings in Japan, as will be argued later.

Strategic behaviour concerning technology choice

Little is known about the actual decision-making processes concerning strategic technology choices in Japanese firms. However, at least to some degree, their behaviour seems to differ from that of their Western counterparts. OKIMOTO and NISHI illustrate for the case of the semiconductor industry that Japanese firms showed, when they had to decide whether to stick with a given technology or to switch to a new one, a strong preference for the former, whereas American firms tended to pursue the latter (OKIMOTO & NISHI 1994: 200–202). In general, top Japanese firms have frequently succeeded in creating competitive strength by pursuing incremental improvements in a given field of technology (IMAI 1991; MONDEN 1991: 340–371). Only a few of them have become known for breakthrough innovations.

This is not to say that Japanese firms are unable to advance into new fields of products or apply new manufacturing processes. On the contrary, econometric evidence strongly suggests that many of them succeeded in almost entirely switching their main lines of business through internal technology-driven growth, not M&As (GOTŌ 1993: 61–67). The driving force behind these strategies, however, was the exploitation of new opportunities for a *given* technology or technological path from the firms' point of view. Therefore, the strategic behaviour of many Japanese firms concerning technology choices may be classified as conservative, as they tend to stick with a given, familiar field of technology when pursuing technological advances.

R&D organization structure

It goes without saying that the organizational structure of R&D activities in manufacturing firms is primarily determined by factors such as the size of the firm or the characteristics of the R&D activities in the industries it is en-

[1] According to national R&D statistics, there is a strong positive correlation between R&D intensity of business firms and firm size in Japan, whereas in the United States and Germany, to the contrary, there is no such clear interrelation between R&D intensity and firm size (SŌMUCHŌ TŌKEIKYOKU 1997: 84–85; NATIONAL SCIENCE BOARD 1996: 120; BMBF 1996: 562–563).

gaged in, not by its country location. Comparisons of Japanese and Western firms have shown, however, that even for firms in the same industry that have a comparable size, significant international differences exist (OKIMOTO & NISHI 1994: 190–194). In large Japanese companies that operate in R&D-intensive industries, a three-layered organization structure with corporate labs, divisional R&D units and development units attached to single production sites is frequently seen. On the other hand, the R&D organization structure appears to be more centralized in large American firms. In these firms, only a two-layered R&D structure with corporate and divisional labs can be typically found, with no R&D units on the production site level. As a consequence, the number of organizational units concerned with R&D is comparatively large in Japanese firms, indicating a high degree of decentralization or fragmentation of R&D activities.

Employment practices for R&D staff

The employment practices applied for R&D workers in Japanese manufacturing firms strongly interrelate with the Japanese employment system as a whole. Concerning large firms, its basic characteristics are observed as (ERNST & WIESNER 1994: 103–133; WAKASUGI 1994: 168–171; WESTNEY 1994: 166–169):

- predominant recruitment of new university graduates;
- long-term employment;
- seniority-based compensation systems;
- institutionalized transfer of R&D workers among R&D units as well as between R&D and other departments.

There has been some dispute about the question of whether employment practices for R&D workers really differ that much between Japanese, American and European firms. An international comparative study showed that the R&D staff in Japanese firms was not much more frequently transferred between units and departments than in the case of their U.S. and European counterparts (SHAPIRA 1995: 123–125). However, various empirical work has confirmed that the remaining features listed above largely apply to the R&D staff in Japanese firms, whereas they are less typical in manufacturing firms of Western countries (SAKAKIBARA & WESTNEY 1985; ERNST & WIESNER 1994; SATO 1995). As a result, the skills acquired by R&D workers in Japanese manufacturing firms are more firm-specific and less profession-specific than in Western firms.

R&D budgeting

A common feature of R&D budgeting in Japanese manufacturing companies appears to be its high degree of project orientation, in contrast to European and American companies that seem to budget on the basis of organizational units to a higher degree. Besides the R&D operational expenses that are allocated to each organizational unit concerned with R&D, a substantial part of the R&D expenses in Japanese firms is budgeted according to R&D

projects in progress. These expenses are decided on outside the regular budgeting process (WAKASUGI 1994: 166–168; WESTNEY 1994: 186–188). Empirical evidence on this issue, however, is very limited, and does not permit a general conclusion on international differences.

Cooperation between R&D and other activities

A feature often stressed when analysing R&D management in Japanese manufacturing firms is the close cooperation between R&D and other corporate activities, namely production and marketing. In particular, it is pointed out that in the course of development projects, production and marketing managers are involved from an early stage on (ODAGIRI & GOTŌ 1993: 107–108; WAKASUGI 1994: 165–166). A comparative study of Japanese and U.S. manufacturing firms conducted in 1985 revealed that in electronics, more than half of the R&D projects conducted by the Japanese firms were suggested by departments other than R&D or by customers. In U.S. electronic firms, the corresponding figure was only 10 % (MANSFIELD 1988). Notably, however, in the other surveyed industries (chemicals, general machinery, autos, instruments), there was no large difference in the percentage of externally proposed R&D projects between Japanese and U.S. firms. While on average interdepartmental links between R&D and other corporate functions appear to be stronger in Japanese manufacturing firms than in Western ones, significant inter-industry differences appear to exist concerning this aspect.

R&D project management

This area strongly interferes with the previous one, the cooperation between R&D and other corporate activities. The way R&D and other corporate departments cooperate strongly determines the way R&D projects in a firm are evolving. Concerning R&D projects in Japanese manufacturing firms, the frequent use of cross-functional project teams is emphasized. In a comparative study of Japanese, American and European automobile makers, the Japanese companies turned out to give comparatively more competence to product managers who are responsible for development projects, whereas in U.S. firms, the position of functional managers was stronger (CLARK & FUJIMOTO 1991: 247–285). Moreover, particularly in the area of product development, phase-overlapping project management appears to be implemented in a number of large Japanese firms (NONAKA 1994: 211–219). This means that one development phase is started before the previous one is finished, aimed at a reduction in the overall development time for a given product. In Western firms, to the contrary, there appears to be less time overlap between the phases of such projects.

External and international linkages

A final area often discussed in the context of international differences in R&D management is the frequency and mode of external R&D cooperation in general and international R&D linkages in particular. Some observers have noted that Japanese firms are frequently and closely cooperating with their suppliers in their R&D activities. Empirical evidence confirms this view insofar as the vast majority of external R&D cooperations Japanese manufacturing firms maintain are vertical ones (GOTŌ 1993: 88). When interpreting these results, however, differences in industrial organization between Japan and Western countries must not be overlooked. In general, the final producers in Japanese manufacturing are less vertically integrated than their American and European counterparts (HEMMERT 1996a: 19–21). This means that at least some of the suppliers Japanese firms are closely cooperating with would be in-house departments in the case of Western firms. Therefore, it cannot be generally stated that vertical R&D ties in Japanese manufacturing are stronger than in the U.S. or in Europe.

Another topic often stressed in this context is the importance of government-initiated research cooperation for Japanese firms. For sure, there are a number of cases, such as the famous VLSI project, in which this cooperation apparently worked, contributing to the international competitiveness of the participating firms (SAKAKIBARA 1995: 79–100). An overall analysis of the cooperation projects that have taken place since the 1960s, however, reveals that in the majority of cases the institutional linkages between the participating firms have been rather weak, indicating a low degree of cooperative involvement (GOTŌ 1993: 90–100). A comparative study of the structure of Japanese and U.S. research cooperation showed that institutional links between the participants appear to be, at least on average, higher in the U.S. than in Japan (ALDRICH & SASAKI 1995: 86–88). Altogether, empirical evidence does not justify the view that external R&D links of Japanese manufacturing firms are strong by international standards. To the contrast, it might be argued that there is relatively little inter-firm cooperation among Japanese firms.

Finally, the field of international linkages of R&D activities shall be briefly addressed. Empirical research has revealed that Japanese manufacturing firms have, at least in certain fields, been more active in entering strategic alliances with foreign firms than Western ones (OKIMOTO & NISHI 1994: 202–205). This observation provokes the conclusion that international linkages of Japanese firms are stronger than those of American or European firms. Another important aspect, however, is the internationalization of *intra-firm* activities. In this respect, U.S. as well as European firms are far more strongly internationally committed than Japanese ones (BELDERBOS 1995). The high number of international strategic alliances Japanese firms are involved in may therefore, at least partially, be interpreted as a substitute for the internationalization of their intra-firm organization.

2.3 Synthesis and managerial evaluation

The analysis in the previous section has shown that in almost every managerial field related to R&D, there is a discussion about differences between

Japanese and Western firms. In some areas such as strategic planning and R&D budgeting, however, the empirical base for such arguments is very limited, while in others, e. g., R&D personnel management, the evidence of different studies is not always consistent. Finally, in the fields related to external and international R&D linkages, international differences in industrial organization create a bias when comparing Japanese with American and European companies. It could even be argued that because of the high project orientation of R&D in Japanese firms and its seemingly less clear separation from other functions than in Western firms, the scope of R&D activities might be defined differently in Japanese and Western firms. These factors altogether make a general comparison of Japanese-, American-, and European-style corporate R&D somewhat questionable.

Nevertheless, there is good reason to believe that to a certain extent, systematic differences in the R&D management of Japanese and Western companies *do* exist, as the institutional environment Japanese firms are embedded in differs from those in Western countries. In the context of R&D, three such institutional settings can be particularly addressed (HEMMERT 1996b: 253–269): Firstly, Japanese science and technology policy hitherto has been focusing more on the fostering of technology diffusion than on creating incentives for innovations. This has encouraged firms to pursue 'follower' rather than 'leader' strategies in technology management. Secondly, the education and university system in Japan has provided firms with a generally well-educated workforce. It failed, however, to produce a high number of graduates with specialized skills. This has forced manufacturing firms to heavily invest in skill formation for their employees, resulting in skill profiles that are, in contrast to many R&D employees in Western firms, rather firm-specific than profession-specific. Thirdly, and strongly related to the previous point, the external markets for highly skilled workers as well as for venture capital are less developed in Japan than in many Western countries. This has reinforced the practice of Japanese firms to recruit almost all employees immediately after their graduation from university as well as the formation of firm-internal labour markets, and also contributed to the concentration of industrial R&D in large firms.

Because of these differences in the institutional environment of firms,[2] a reasoning about international differences in corporate R&D management appears to be justified. The R&D management in an 'ideal' large Japanese manufacturing firm of the 1980s may be altogether described like this: The firm hires its R&D personnel almost exclusively from universities and trains

---

[2] A further argument could be made with reference to the structure of the Japanese capital market. As the market for venture capital is underdeveloped in Japan, the concentration of R&D activities in large firms is further supported. Comparative research on different countries' capital markets shows, however, that Japan is not necessarily the only major country to which this argument applies. An OECD study reveals that Japan may be grouped in this respect together with Germany and France, in contrast to the United States and the United Kingdom (OECD 1995: 67–90).

them in-house. Most spend their whole professional life in the same firm. R&D activities are divided into long-term projects that are worked on in the corporate lab, and short- and medium-term development projects that are pursued by divisional labs and engineering units at the firm's production sites. In general, product development projects are given high priority in the field of R&D, since these activities are strongly related to the corporate market performance. In the course of such projects, staff from different R&D units as well as from the production and marketing departments closely work together. This is fundamentally supported by the generalistic professional background of most employees, since they are familiar with a wide scope of corporate activities. In order to speed up product development, the stages of development projects are planned and conducted concurrently. R&D activities are strongly oriented on incremental improvements of familiar processes and products. The firm closely cooperates in some of its R&D projects with its first-tier suppliers that are located next to the firm's production sites. R&D core activities are entirely concentrated in the domestic locations.

When R&D management is practiced in the form as explained in this somewhat stylized description, certain advantages can be expected in terms of business performance. Because of the high priority given to product development, the number of new models delivered to the market will be high. Moreover, as a result of the close coordination between R&D and marketing units, the newly developed products will mostly fit to market needs. When such market demands are changing, the relevant information is quickly transmitted to R&D managers. As a result of concurrent processes, the new products that are suited to the changed market needs will be developed in a relatively short time. Well-organized routines in development projects assure high product quality standards.

However, there are also a number of disadvantages to be considered when such R&D management is implemented. As a result of the comparatively low professional specialization of most R&D workers and the strong market orientation of R&D activities, long-term orientated research projects receive relatively little attention. This decreases the firms' ability for implementing breakthrough innovations. Moreover, as a consequence of the large number of products that are developed and marketed, firms are vulnerable to recessions and shrinking market volumes, as unit costs are rapidly increasing. This is furthermore related to the fact that as a consequence of the firms' employment practices, their workforce cannot be reduced substantially in the short to medium term.

It goes without saying that the relative importance of these aspects, both positive and negative, largely depends on the technological and market environment a firm is operating in. When its activities are concentrated in business lines with mostly familiar, mature technologies and demand is expanding or at least stable, the type of R&D management outlined above can principally be expected to work well. When breakthrough innovations occur or cutting-edge technology in unknown territories must be developed internally and demand is volatile or shrinking, however, the corporate business performance will be vulnerable to these environmental changes.

These arguments can be linked to the R&D performance of Japanese manufacturers in the 1980s. The predominant observation in this period was that Japanese corporate R&D, as well as other managerial activities, was superior to that of their Western rivals. In particular, product development performance of Japanese automobile firms was found to be significantly better than that of American and European firms not only in terms of speed, but also in cost efficiency and quality (WOMACK, JONES & ROOS 1990: 104–137; CLARK & FUJIMOTO 1991: 67–91). However, the R&D performance and competitive strength of Japanese firms appeared to be overwhelming as well in many other industries, including such technology-intensive ones as electronics, communication equipment, and instruments. Japan's global market share in high-technology industries steadily increased throughout the 1980s (NATIONAL SCIENCE BOARD 1993: 440–446). Moreover, between 1980 and 1990 the number of patent applications in Japan (which are predominantly undertaken by Japanese firms) almost doubled (NIHONKOKU TOKKYOCHŌ 1996: 203).

This outstandingly good performance was based on a wide range of factors and cannot be explained by any single reason. Concerning R&D, however, the conditions for the kind of management described above in stylized form were quite favourable. Japanese firms were facing expanding markets, and they were mostly operating on the basis of familiar technologies. As they were catching up to first-rate Western firms hitherto leading in technological terms, there was still mostly only a limited need to work on the technological forefront.

The catching-up process was, to be sure, in itself a remarkable achievement performed by Japanese manufacturers, as it required high capabilities to acquire and develop further technological knowledge. The remaining question, however, is how Japanese firms have responded to the drastically changed business environment in the 1990s? This is the issue to be discussed in the next section.

3 R&D strategies of Japanese manufacturing firms in the 1990s

3.1 Environmental changes

The generally favourable business environment most Japanese manufacturing firms were operating in during the 1980s has changed drastically to their disadvantage after 1990. In particular, demand conditions for manufactured goods have rapidly deteriorated. This applies to the domestic as well as to the international market.

Inside Japan, the economic situation has worsened since 1991 as a consequence of the burst of the *bubble economy.* Stock and real estate prices that had been extremely overvalued plummeted, resulting not only in severe problems for the financial system, but also in a stagnation of the Japanese economy as a whole, since many investors have been running out of liquidity. Whereas no recession occurred in the sense of negative growth rates, the Japanese economy experienced only minimal growth between 1992 and 1994 (KEIZAI KIKAKUCHŌ 1996: 131). Moreover, the Yen sharply strengthened against the US-Dollar and other major currencies from 1992 onward (NIHON GINKŌ KOKUSAIKYOKU 1996: 177), leading to a suppression of Japanese manufacturing exports in the subsequent years.

Beside these changes concerning demand conditions, the technological setting has also changed for many Japanese manufacturing firms in recent years. As was mentioned above, they continuously gained strength on international markets throughout the 1980s, while at the same time advancing their technological position against their Western competitors. As a result, they have reached a world level in an increasing number of industries and product lines, resulting in a growing need to strengthen their internal base of long-term technology development.

Admittedly, the picture concerning the relative technological level of Japanese manufacturers is very diverse. In some industries such as steel, Japanese companies had been regarded as the world's technology leaders since long before. In others like pharmacy, they are still lagging behind some first-rated American and European companies in the 1990s. *As a tendency*, however, it can be assumed that as a result of the advances in the 1980s and before, the number of Japanese firms that are now challenged to make technological advancements at the global forefront has significantly grown. One indicator for this is the balance of technology trade in which fees for technology imports are compared with revenues from technology exports. In the case of Japan, this balance had been deficitary until quite recently, but has been showing surpluses in the 1990s (SŌMUCHŌ TŌKEIKYOKU 1997: 25).

This set of environmental changes can be expected to present Japanese manufacturers a complex managerial challenge. For one reason, the market and technology factors mentioned above are basically contradictory in their impact, as the former calls for cost reduction, the latter for expansion. Even when taking into account that the market factors may be regarded as somewhat more short-term in their nature than the technology factors, a managerial dilemma in the field of R&D may arise. Moreover, under the assumptions made in the previous section, the environmental changes should result in a mismatch between the R&D management as it was practiced by many Japanese firms hitherto and new strategic requirements.

3.2 Responses in the R&D management of Japanese manufacturing firms

Subsequently, the managerial strategies Japanese manufacturing firms have developed in the 1990s in the field of R&D in response to the drastically changed environment are discussed. Three such strategies are identified:

rationalization, focus, and globalization. The findings are based on an analysis of statistical and survey data as well as on information directly gained from firms. Between the summer of 1996 and the spring of 1997, the author conducted exploratory interviews with senior R&D managers of five medium- and large-sized companies in the machinery, electronic, and automobile industries concerning their strategic reorientation in the 1990s.

Rationalization

First insights into firms' strategic orientation can be gained from national R&D statistics (graph 1). After a long period of strongly increasing R&D expenditures, Japanese manufacturers' R&D spending began to shrink slightly in fiscal year 1992, a tendency that prevailed throughout 1993 and 1994 and was accompanied by a decrease in the percentage of sales spent on R&D (R&D intensity) as well. Thereafter, nominal R&D expenditures increased again. The R&D intensity, however, has remained below its pre-recession peak.

Graph 1: R&D expenditure and R&D intensity of sales of Japanese industrial companies, 1970–1996

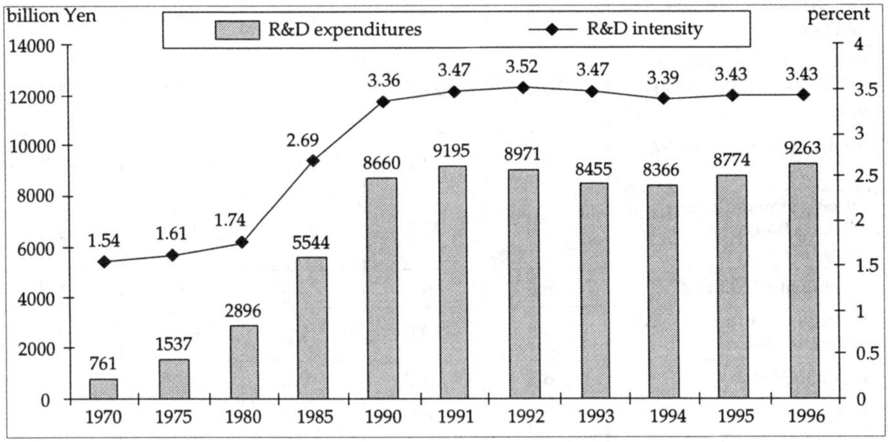

Source: SŌMUCHŌ TŌKEIKYOKU: *Kagaku gijutsu kenkyū chōsa hōkoku*, various editions

Admittedly, the reduction in corporate R&D spending in the first half of the 1990s can hardly be described as a dramatic one, neither in absolute nor in relative terms. It does indicate, however, a remarkable development, as this was the first time since the introduction of national R&D statistics in 1960 that industrial R&D expenditures in Japan actually shrank. Moreover, the decrease in R&D spending was not concentrated on a few industries, but spread throughout the whole manufacturing sector.

The national statistics therefore strongly suggest that in many Japanese manufacturing firms, a strategic reorientation in R&D from expansion to rationalization has occurred. Because of their high aggregation level, however, the data does not permit insights into managerial attitudes and strategic decisions made by firms. This gap can be filled by the analysis of survey results. In a questionnaire from late 1993, data from around 600 large and medium-sized companies in 20 industries was collected by the Economic Research Institute of the Japan Society for the Promotion of Machine Industry (KSKKK 1994a). Table 1 lists the results for the whole sample and for four major manufacturing industries.

Table 1: R&D reorganization measures carried out or considered by Japanese industrial firms, 1993 (percentage of firms who indicated the items among all responding firms)

	Chemicals	General machinery	Electronics	Vehicles	All industries
Strengthening of communication between R&D and business units	48.8	52.3	61.8	46.7	43.7
Concentration and fusion of R&D units	35.4	34.1	40.0	28.9	29.9
Promotion of mobility of researchers; flattening of R&D organization structure	30.5	22.7	40.0	31.1	23.7
Establishment of new R&D units	11.0	18.2	20.0	13.3	12.3
Introduction of flexible working hours *(sairyō rōdōsei)*	11.0	22.7	27.2	17.8	9.0
Closing of R&D units	9.8	4.5	3.6	4.4	4.8
Introduction of annual salary system *(nenpōsei)*	0.0	0.0	1.8	2.2	4.8
Internationalization	6.1	2.3	3.6	15.6	3.4
Other	3.7	6.8	0.0	6.7	3.4
Sample size	$n = 82$	$n = 44$	$n = 55$	$n = 45$	$n = 586$

Source: KSKKK (1994a)

The survey results indicate that many Japanese manufacturing firms have been relatively active concerning the reorganization of their R&D management in the early 1990s, a finding that is in accordance with the results of other empirical research (KAGAKU GIJUTSUCHŌ 1995: 14–15). The items listed in table 1 reflect a variety of managerial measures that will regain our attention in the next subsections. In the context of rationalization that is addressed here, however, only the measures that are related to an expansion or retrenchment of R&D activities are discussed.

At a first glance, few firms appear to have restricted their R&D activities, as less than 5 % of them were explicitly closing R&D units. The 'concentration and fusion of R&D units', however, what can by and large be regarded as a euphemism for such closings, was the item indicated second most often and far outnumbered the 'establishment of new R&D units'. Moreover, this tendency applies to all major R&D-intensive manufacturing industries, indicating a trend that is not limited to particular sectors or product lines.

Therefore, the survey data confirms other statistical findings that the continuous expansion of R&D activities, dominant in Japanese manufacturing throughout the 1980s, was in many firms replaced by a rationalization strategy in the first half of the 1990s. In fact, all R&D managers interviewed by the author with only one exception affirmed the application of this strategy at their firms.

Focus

Referring again to the survey data listed in table 1, another remarkable finding is that two of the three most frequently indicated items address the strengthening of communication between R&D and other departments and the promotion of mobility of researchers. This is somewhat surprising when considering the fact that Japanese manufacturers are commonly regarded to have a relatively good record here, as was discussed in detail in the previous section. However, the management of many Japanese firms apparently believed that there was still room for improvement, and they have placed high priority on reorganization measures in this area.

Further insights can be gained from the analysis of R&D reorganization moves conducted by large Japanese electronic companies. This industry is the biggest R&D performer in Japan, comprising about one third of the overall industrial R&D spending. Furthermore, it is dominated by a relatively small number of firms. Therefore, the measures taken by these firms determine to a certain degree the strategic orientation of Japanese industrial R&D as a whole. Table 2 summarizes their R&D reorganization measures undertaken between 1992 and 1996.

Notably, in almost all of the large Japanese electronic firms some major R&D reshuffling occurred over this period, indicating a high intensity of organizational change. A thorough look reveals, furthermore, that there are significant differences between firms concerning the strategic direction of their reorganization measures. However, the majority of them were apparently transferring resources from the corporate labs to the R&D units on the business line level and, namely, to the development and engineering units at the factory level. Under the assumption that the task of the corporate labs primarily lies in long-term oriented research, whereas the units at the factory level are mostly concerned with product development and other activities closely related to production, this means that in most of the large Japanese electronic firms managerial attention has shifted from the former to the latter. This is remarkable, since the field of product development had also been hitherto regarded as a stronghold of Japanese manufacturers.

Table 2: R&D reorganization measures of Japanese electronic firms, 1992–1996

Hitachi	amalgamation of 2 corporate R&D centres; establishment of new development centres in each business unit (8/1993) shift of 30 % of the personnel working at corporate R&D labs to development centres at the business units (4/1995)
Tōshiba	reorganization of 12 research institutes into 6 new units; fusion of 2 central research institutes into 1 R&D centre (10/1992) establishment of 3 new R&D units in the microelectronics division; shift of 200 R&D workers from the corporate laboratory to division level units (4/1996)
Matsushita Electric	reorganization of central research institute into technology support units for each business line (11/1993) reorganization of central technology department into a basic research and an applied research department; fusion of 27 research institutes into 9 new institutes (2/1994)
NEC	establishment of 7 new development institutes and 1 technology institute that are attached to the development and the business groups; replacement of R&D workers from the central R&D institute to the new units (8/1992)
Fujitsū	reorganization of 3 regional and 5 functional research institutes into 4 new project units (6/1993)
Sony	establishment of a new central development centre (1/1993) establishment of a R&D planning office to coordinate R&D activities on the business line level (12/1993)
Mitsubishi Electric	reorganization of 4 central research institutes into a business operation unit; focus on product development (6/1993)
Sharp	reorganization of 3 research institutes and 2 development centres at business units into 1 technology research institute and 4 product development institutes (4/1993)
Oki Electric	establishment of a multimedia business promotion unit that is jointly staffed with business planning, engineering and research personnel (3/1994)
Sanyō Electric	reorganization of 7 central research institutes into 4 new units; upgrading of 7 research centres and 1 technology centre at business units to research institutes (12/1993)

Source: KSKKK (1994b); Nikkei database; interviews with corporate R&D managers

Empirical evidence altogether shows that many Japanese manufacturing firms in the 1990s appear to focus their attention in R&D on activities where they previously had been regarded to already hold a competitive advantage over their counterparts in Western countries. This tendency could also be observed in the cases of some of the directly surveyed firms. Tōshiba, one of Japan's largest electronic manufacturers, for instance, has made persistent efforts to concentrate its vast R&D resources on improvements in product and process development and to diminish the segregation among its many R&D units by regrouping them.

In the course of the 1970s and the 1980s, a considerable number of new research labs and other R&D units was established at Tōshiba, resulting in a total number of 11 research units at the corporate level and 12 more at the divisional level, alongside with numerous engineering units at the factory level at the beginning of the 1990s. This resulted in a vast technological potential, as Tōshiba had a R&D unit in almost every field related to its business activities, but also in an increasing segregation among these units, as each of them was restricted to the field it was assigned to.

Then, in October 1992, a major restructuring of Tōshiba's R&D organization occurred, the first in 23 years (*Nihon Sangyō Shinbun*, 25.11.92). A large number of R&D units on the corporate as well as on the divisional level were regrouped, and 2,000 of the 12,000 R&D employees were assigned to new tasks. The strategic aim behind these measures was an increase in operational flexibility, as the new R&D subunits have no defined field of work and are simply named unit 1, unit 2, and so forth.

Another managerial tool introduced at Tōshiba's R&D in recent years is the internal funding system of corporate R&D units by the business divisions (LAAGE-HELLMAN 1997: 70–71). The corporate R&D centre and its subunits are only partially funded by the headquarters, the remainder of their budget being provided by the divisions. This results in a strong influence of the divisions on the activities of the corporate R&D centre, and may also lead to a strengthening of communication between corporate and divisional R&D managers.

Finally, in April 1996 another reorganization of the R&D organization structure in the field of microelectronics occurred (*Semiconductor World*, July 1996). Again, several units were regrouped in order to concentrate R&D resources on the development of new multimedia products, among others regarded as crucial for the technological future of the company. This move was accompanied by the reassignment of 200 R&D employees from the corporate to the divisional level in an effort to strengthen the company's competitiveness by a shortening of development lead times.

Altogether, the company is aiming at a strengthening of the competitiveness of its business divisions by concentrating its efforts on improvements in product and process development, areas where it previously (already) had a good performance record.

However, there are also some new tools in the field of personnel management currently discussed in Japan that are strongly related to R&D. Two frequently mentioned buzzwords here are *sairyō rōdōsei* and *nenpōsei*. The first essentially means that employees are only required to fulfil the task they are assigned to, with no enforcement of full-time presence at the office. In practice this implies the loosening of working hours and the abolishing of overtime pay. The second term translates literally into 'annual salary system'. What is meant in most cases are measures to increase the performance-based component in salary schemes, which in large Japanese firms has traditionally been mainly based on seniority. Both instruments are discussed in the context of increasing the creativeness and personal motivation of R&D workers, fields that have been hitherto regarded as relatively weak in Japanese firms.

The survey results in Table 1 indicate that these instruments have been implemented by only a small minority of firms. Still, the introduction rate of flexible working hours has been relatively high in the machinery, electronic, and vehicle industries. What cannot be determined by such survey data, however, is the actual scale of the measures that have been applied inside the firms. Firm-specific research has shown that those companies that have introduced one or both measures have done so mostly on a small scale only (KSKKK 1994b: 87–88). Typically, these were applied to a few dozen senior researchers in central R&D units, as confirmed also by R&D managers interviewed by the author. The overwhelming majority of employees have not been, or only marginally, affected by it.

Altogether, a majority of Japanese manufacturing firms seem to have reinforced the managerial tools that had been their traditional stronghold in R&D and product development. On the other hand, the introduction of new management techniques has been slow, and in most cases on a limited, experimental basis only. These measures may be interpreted as supporting moves to further endorse a *focus strategy.* Empirical evidence indicates that the R&D staff in Japanese firms were widely frustrated in the 1980s about their working conditions. In particular, there were frequent complaints about too long working hours, too low salaries, and too little freedom of work (ERNST & WIESNER 1994: 150; SHAPIRA 1995: 137). Through a gradual alignment of their incentive structures and promotion systems, without changing their fundamental structure, a number of firms apparently aims at increasing the motivation of their most gifted R&D staff members by giving them better incentives for individual working efforts. However, in most cases these steps seem only to apply to researchers and engineers in the corporate labs, and not to those R&D units at the divisional and production site level.

Globalization

Finally, the globalization strategy conducted by Japanese manufacturing firms shall be discussed from a R&D perspective. In graph 2, the trend in R&D expenditure of Japanese manufacturing firms' foreign affiliates since the 1980s is depicted. The increase here has been very rapid, as R&D expenditure in foreign countries has risen by more than fifteen-fold compared with its 1983 level.

Graph 2: R&D expenditure by foreign affiliates of Japanese manufacturing firms (in billion Yen)

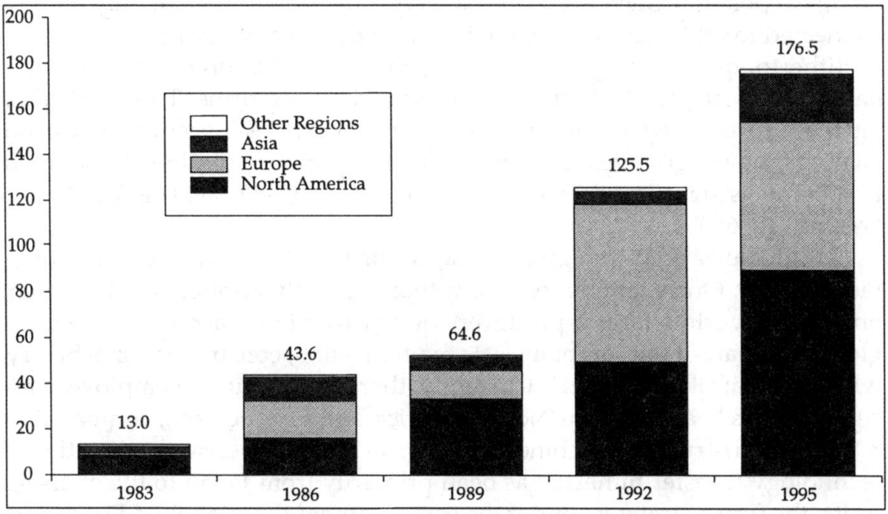

Source: TSSS: *Kaigai tōshi tōkei sōran*, various editions

A different picture evolves, however, when the relative importance of the R&D investments made by Japanese firms abroad is taken into account and compared with the corresponding figures for other industrialized countries. The ratio of Japanese manufacturing firms' R&D expenditure in foreign countries in relation to their domestic R&D investment was 2 % in 1995, up from 0.8 % in 1986 (TSSS 1998). The corresponding figures for the manufacturing industries of the United States and Germany in the first half of the 1990s are roughly 10 % and 15 % respectively (NATIONAL SCIENCE BOARD 1996: 161; BMBF 1997: 54). These numbers starkly illustrate the relative backwardness of Japanese manufacturing firms concerning the globalization of their R&D activities.

Nevertheless, the pace of progress in the globalization of Japanese industrial R&D has been quite high since the second half of the 1980s. Recent empirical research confirms that large Japanese manufacturers, particularly in high-tech industries such as electronics and chemicals, have been actively pursuing the globalization of their R&D activities in recent years (KIBA 1996; TAKAHASHI 1996; KEIZAI KIKAKUCHŌ CHŌSAKYOKU 1997).

Another central issue is the *quality* of R&D activities conducted at foreign subsidiaries. Firms' motives for the globalization of R&D activities can be roughly classified into two subgroups. The first group of motives is oriented towards the setting-up of foreign R&D activities in the course of the general progress of the corporate globalization. R&D units established in this context are typically concerned with the support of local production or marketing activities. The second class of R&D-oriented globalization motives focuses on the use of local R&D resources in order to strengthen a firm's global technological position. Such R&D units are typically stand-alone or only loosely connected to other activities of the firm in the respective country.

Hitherto, the former group of locally oriented R&D units was predominant in the foreign R&D activities of manufacturing firms. This applied to Japanese firms as well as to firms from other countries. Recent surveys and analyses, however, reveal that the relative importance of globally oriented R&D units is significantly increasing (KIBA 1996: 15–17; PEARCE & PAPANASTASSIOU 1996: 95).

This globalization strategy was also confirmed during the author's interview survey. One example for a firm that evidently applied it is Komatsu, one of the world's largest producers of construction machinery. The most globalized part of the company is its main division, construction machinery, which also applies for R&D. Currently, there are about 200 employees assigned to R&D activities in North America and Europe each, compared to 800 in the construction machinery division in Japan. Whereas the direction of technology transfer hitherto has been primarily from Japan to the overseas units, the firm's strategy aims at the establishment of a global R&D network with mutual know-how transfers between units in different countries. An example for the company's globalization efforts is the development and production of large-scale trucks that have been transferred from a plant inside Japan to a North American joint venture plant in Illinois (*Nihon Keizai Shinbun*, 22.7.93: 11). Komatsu has since taken over the stock majority of that joint venture.

Altogether, empirical evidence indicates that the recent increase in foreign R&D of Japanese firms is not solely a consequence of these firms' globalization strategies in other activities such as production and marketing, but is at least partially rooted in firms' efforts to globalize their technological base as well.

3.3 Managerial evaluation

The previous discussion has revealed that Japanese manufacturing firms have responded with a variety of R&D strategies to the environmental challenges they have been facing in the 1990s. Statistics as well as survey results and case studies have shown that there has been a high degree of activity in R&D restructuring, particularly during the recession years from 1992 to 1994.

How do Japanese firms' R&D strategies appear from the perspective of strategic management theory? Cost reduction and rationalization efforts are regarded as a typical managerial response when facing a recession, although this strategy is neither always the right one, nor free of risk (GHEMAWAT 1993). The focus on a firm's managerial strengths in the face of constrained business conditions can be interpreted as a materialization of the concept of core competencies that has been widely discussed in recent years (HAMEL & PRALAHAD 1994). Furthermore, the globalization strategy is now commonly regarded as an appropriate response to the intensifying market competition for manufactured goods (DUNNING 1993).

Altogether, Japanese manufacturing firms' responses to the environmental changes in the 1990s appear to be in accordance with the recommendations forwarded by managerial theory. Their recent R&D performance record confirms this view, as Japanese firms have done remarkably well under the constrained conditions of the 1990s. Patent output has been stabilized on a high level (NIHONKOKU TOKKYOCHŌ 1996: 203). Moreover, many large firms have succeeded in further shortening their lead times in product development and thereby have maintained their competitive advantage against their Western competitors which themselves have significantly improved their performance in this field (HEMMERT 1997).

Therefore, it seems fair to conclude that Japanese manufacturing firms have been, at least on an aggregated level, quite successful regarding their managerial responses in the field of R&D to the changed business environment. What do these strategies mean, however, in the context of the Japanese system of corporate management? Has it, from the viewpoint of R&D, essentially changed? Is there any convergence with Western firms? These are the issues that will be briefly discussed in the final part of this paper.

4 Implications for the Japanese corporate management system

The analysis of Japanese firms' managerial responses to the altered environmental conditions in the 1990s has shown that there has been a high intensity of reorganization in Japanese manufacturing firms' R&D management, and at present it seems that these measures have been successful in many cases. Japanese firms essentially proved to possess the flexibility to adapt their management to changes in their business environment. Interestingly, however, German manufacturing firms, confronted with a similarly grave recession and increased competition in the early 1990s, have adopted similar strategies (SCHRÖDER 1997: 135–140). Does this indicate, after all, that Japanese manufacturing firms' R&D management is converging internationally?

The analysis on the level of specific managerial responses leads to a different picture. As has been pointed out, most Japanese firms are very cautious concerning modifications of their employment practices, which is one of the areas where they differ most from their Western counterparts. Moreover, the focus strategy analysed above mainly implies a reinforcement of managerial tools that are believed to have previously been typical for Japanese firms' R&D, including the high priority placed on development projects and a close cooperation between R&D and other activities.

Therefore, although certain changes definitely have occurred in some areas such as the increased globalization of R&D, it seems that there is a high degree of continuity in Japanese corporate R&D management. Notably, Japanese manufacturers have shown a strong ability to adapt to a largely changed environmental situation without much altering the basic structure of their management practices. This casts doubt on the view that the characteristics of Japanese-style R&D management are simply an outcome of a historical latecomer situation that is due to disappear together with this latecomer position itself.

The analysis in this paper, moreover, has revealed another aspect that may become central to the evolution of Japanese corporate management in the future. Differences between individual firms seem to widen. This has become very clear in the case of the firms that have been surveyed by the author. The observation of increasing differences between Japanese firms' R&D strategies and management styles, however, is not restricted to only a few cases, but seems to apply more generally (METHÉ 1995).

In summary, even in the past it was only partially justifiable to distinguish a Japanese-style corporate R&D management in contrast to a R&D management practiced by American and European firms. The differences that *do* exist, however, namely in the fields of personnel management, organizational structure, and project management seem to largely prevail over time, even when firms are confronted with changed environmental conditions. On the other hand, the diversity among Japanese firms' R&D management strategies appears to be increasing, making it less and less appropriate to generalize findings based on only one or a few cases of Japanese manufacturers. Thus, the concept of a *Japanese-style* R&D management itself may also become gradually obsolete.

References

ALDRICH, H. E. and T. SASAKI (1995): Governance Structure and Technology Transfer Management in R&D Consortia in the United States and Japan. In: LIKER, J. K., J. E. ETTLIE and J. C. CAMPBELL (eds.): *Engineered in Japan. Japanese Technology-Management Practices.* New York and Oxford: Oxford University Press, pp. 70–92.

BELDERBOS, R. (1995): *Overseas R&D by Japanese Electronics Multinationals. Evidence From the Basic Survey 1992.* Mimeo, Institute for Economic Research, Hitotsubashi University (unpublished).

BMBF – BUNDESMINISTERIUM FÜR BILDUNG, WISSENSCHAFT, FORSCHUNG UND TECHNOLOGIE (ed.) (1996): *Bundesbericht Forschung 1996.* Bonn: Bundesministerium für Bildung, Wissenschaft, Forschung und Technologie.

BMBF – BUNDESMINISTERIUM FÜR BILDUNG, WISSENSCHAFT, FORSCHUNG UND TECHNOLOGIE (ed.) (1997): *Zur technologischen Leistungsfähigkeit Deutschlands.* Bonn: Bundesministerium für Bildung, Wissenschaft, Forschung und Technologie.

CLARK, K. B. and T. FUJIMOTO (1991): *Product Development Performance. Strategy, Organization, and Management in the World Auto Industry.* Boston: Harvard Business School Press.

DUNNING, J. H. (1993): Multinational Enterprises and the Globalization of Innovatory Capacity. In: GRANSTRAND, O., L. HÅKANSON and S. SJÖLANDER (eds.): *Technology Management and International Business.* Chichester: Wiley, pp. 19–51.

ERNST, A. and G. WIESNER (1994): *Japans technische Intelligenz. Personalstrukturen und Personalmanagement in Forschung und Entwicklung.* Munich: ifo Institut für Wirtschaftsforschung (= ifo studien zur japanforschung 7).

GHEMAWAT, P. (1993): The Risk of *Not* Investing in a Recession. In: *Sloan Management Review* 34, 2, pp. 51–58.

GOTŌ, A. (1993): *Nihon no gijutsu kakushin to sangyō soshiki* [Innovation and Industrial Organization in Japan]. Tōkyō: Tōkyō Daigaku Shuppankai.

HAMEL, G. and C. K. PRALAHAD (1994): *Competing for the Future.* Boston: Harvard Business School Press.

HEMMERT, M. (1996a): *'Intermediate Organization' Revisited. A Framework for the Vertical Division of Labour in Manufacturing and the Case of the Japanese Assembly Industries.* Tōkyō: German Institute for Japanese Studies (= Arbeitspapier 96/5).

HEMMERT, M. (1996b): Technologieführer Japan? Die Umstrukturierung der japanischen Forschungslandschaft. In: *Japanstudien* 7, pp. 239–278.

HEMMERT, M. (1997): Back to Being Lean: The Streamlining of Japanese Industrial R&D in the 1990s. In: *Proceedings of the 4th International Product Development Conference,* Stockholm, May 26–27, 1997, pp. 331–345.

IMAI, M. (1991): *Kaizen. The Key to Japan's Competitive Success.* Singapore: McGraw-Hill.

KAGAKU GIJUTSUCHŌ (ed.) (1995): *Minkan kigyō no kenkyū katsudō ni kansuru chōsa hōkoku* [Report on the Research Activities of Private Enterprises]. Tōkyō: Ōkurashō Insatsukyoku.

KEIZAI KIKAKUCHŌ (ed.) (1996): *Heisei 8-nenpan kokumin keizai keisan nenpō* [Annual Report on National Accounts]. Tōkyō: Ōkurashō Insatsukyoku.

KEIZAI KIKAKUCHŌ CHŌSAKYOKU (ed.) (1997): *Kōzō kaikakuka ni aru kigyō kōdō. Kigyō kōdō ni kansuru ankēto chōsa hōkokusho* [Enterprise Behaviour under Structural Reform. Report on a Questionnaire Survey about Enterprise Behaviour]. Tōkyō: Keizai Kikakuchō Chōsakyoku.

KIBA, T. (1996): *Nihon kigyō no kaigai ni okeru kenkyū kaihatsu no pafōmansu ni kansuru chōsa* [Survey of the Performance of Japanese Company R&D Abroad]. Tōkyō: Kagaku Gijutsu Seisaku Kenkyūsho (= NISTEP Report No. 43).

KSKKK – KIKAI SHINKŌ KYŌKAI KEIZAI KENKYŪSHO (ed.) (1994a): *Kenkyū kaihatsu no keizaiteki kōka ni kansuru chōsa* [Investigation of the Economic Effects of R&D]. Tōkyō: Kikai Shinkō Kyōkai Keizai Kenkyūsho (unpublished).

KSKKK – KIKAI SHINKŌ KYŌKAI KEIZAI KENKYŪSHO (ed.) (1994b): *Minkan kigyō no kenkyū kaihatsu katsudō ni kansuru kiso chōsa* [Basic Investigation of the R&D Activities of Private Enterprises]. Tōkyō: Kikai Shinkō Kyōkai Keizai Kenkyūsho (unpublished).

LAAGE-HELLMAN, J. (1997): *Business Networks in Japan. Supplier-Customer Interaction in Product Development.* London and New York: Routledge.

MANSFIELD, E. (1988): Industrial R&D in Japan and the United States: A Comparative Study. In: *American Economic Review* 78, pp. 223–228.

METHÉ, David T. (1995): Basic Research in Japanese Electronic Companies: An Attempt at Establishing New Organizational Routines. In: LIKER, J. K., J. E. ETTLIE and J. C. CAMPBELL (eds.): *Engineered in Japan. Japanese Technology-Management Practices.* New York and Oxford: Oxford University Press, pp. 17–39.

MONDEN, Y. (1991): *Shin Toyota Shisutemu* [The New Toyota System). Tōkyō: Kōdansha.

NATIONAL SCIENCE BOARD (ed.) (1993): *Science & Engineering Indicators 1993.* Washington, D.C.: U.S. Government Printing Office.

NATIONAL SCIENCE BOARD (ed.) (1996): *Science & Engineering Indicators 1996.* Washington, D.C.: U.S. Government Printing Office.

NIHON GINKŌ KOKUSAIKYOKU (ed.) (1996): *Kokusai hikaku tōkei 1996* [Comparative Economic and Financial Statistics 1996]. Tōkyō: Nihon Ginkō.

Nihon Keizai Shinbun (22.7.93): Komatsu, yūshutsu kenki o kaigai seisan. Endaka taiō, mazu beigōben de ōgata danpu [Komatsu to Substitute Construction Machinery Exports by Foreign Production. Reacting to the Yen, Firstly for Large-Scale Damps at US Joint Venture], p. 11.

Nihon Sangyō Shinbun (25.11.92): Tōshiba kenyū kaihatsu sentā: kenkyū kaihatsu bumon o saihen [Tōshiba's R&D Centre: Reorganization of the R&D Activities], p. 5.

NIHONKOKU TOKKYOCHŌ (ed.) (1996): *Tokkyochō nenpō. Dai 87-kan. Heisei 7-nenpan* [Annual Report of the Patent Office. 48th Edition, 1995]. Tōkyō: Nihonkoku Tokkyochō.

NONAKA, I. (1994): Product Development and Innovation. In: IMAI, K. and R. KOMIYA (eds.): *Business Enterprise in Japan.* Cambridge and London: MIT Press, pp. 209–221.

ODAGIRI, H. and A. GOTŌ (1993): The Japanese System of Innovation: Past, Present, and Future. In: NELSON, R. R. (ed.): *National Innovation Systems. A Comparative Analysis.* New York and London: Oxford University Press, pp. 76–114.

OECD – ORGANIZATION FOR ECONOMIC CO-OPERATION AND DEVELOPMENT (ed.) (1995): *National Systems for Financing Innovation.* Paris: OECD.

OKIMOTO, D. and Y. NISHI (1994): R&D Organization in Japanese and American Semiconductor Firms. In: AOKI, M. and R. DORE (eds.): *The Japanese Firm. Sources of Competitive Strength.* Oxford: Oxford University Press, pp. 178–208.

PEARCE, R. and M. PAPANASTASSIOU (1996): *The Technological Competitiveness of Japanese Multinationals. The European Dimension.* Ann Arbor: University of Michigan Press.

SAKAKIBARA, K. and D. E. WESTNEY (1985): Comparative Study of the Training, Careers, and Organization of Engineers in the Computer Industry in the United States and Japan. In: *Hitotsubashi Journal of Commerce & Management* 20, no. 1, pp. 1–20.

SAKAKIBARA, K. (1995): *Nihon kigyō no kenkyū kaihatsu manejimento* [R&D Management in Japanese Enterprises]. Tōkyō: Chikura Shobō.

SATO, H. (1995): Corporate Careers of R&D Personnel. In: SHAPIRA, P. (ed.): *The R&D Workers. Managing Innovation in Britain, Germany, Japan, and the United States.* Westport and London: Quorum, pp. 45–58.

SCHRÖDER, H.-H. (1997): Innovationsstrategien und Technologiepolitik in Deutschland. In: LICHTBLAU, K. und F. WALDENBERGER (eds.): *Planung, Wettbewerb und wirtschaftlicher Wandel. Ein japanisch-deutscher Vergleich.* Cologne: Deutscher-Instituts-Verlag, pp. 107–152.

Semiconductor World (July 1996): Tōshiba: Kenkyū, kaihatsu taisei o saihen. ADI sakusen ga chakuchaku to susumu [Reorganization of R&D at Tōshiba. ADI Strategy Progressing Smoothly], pp. 12–13.

SHAPIRA, P. (1995): Comparisons and Contrasts in R&D Management in the United States and Japan. In: SHAPIRA, P. (ed.): *The R&D Workers. Managing Innovation in Britain, Germany, Japan, and the United States.* Westport and London: Quorum, pp. 121–142.

SŌMUCHŌ TŌKEIKYOKU (ed.) (1997): *Heisei 8-nen kagaku gijutsu kenkyū chōsa hōkoku* [Report on the Survey of Research and Development 1996]. Tōkyō: Nihon Tōkei Kyōkai (published annually).

TAKAHASHI, H. (1996): *Kenkyū kaihatsu kokusaika no jissai* [The Reality of R&D Internationalization]. Tōkyō: Chūō Keizaisha.

TSSS – TSŪSHŌ SANGYŌSHŌ SANGYŌ SEISAKUKYOKU (ed.) (1998): *Dai 6-kai kaigai tōshi tōkei sōran* [6th Statistical Overview of Foreign Direct Investment]. Tōkyō: Ōkurashō Insatsukyoku (published triennially).

WAKASUGI, R. (1994): Organizational Structure and Behaviour in Research and Development. In: IMAI, K. and R. KOMIYA (eds.): *Business Enterprise in Japan.* Cambridge and London: MIT Press, pp. 159–177.

WESTNEY, D. E. (1994): The Evolution of Japan's Industrial Research and Development. In: AOKI, M. and R. DORE (eds.): *The Japanese Firm. Sources of Competitive Strength.* Oxford: Oxford University Press, pp. 154–177.

WOMACK, J. P., D. T. JONES and D. ROOS (1990): *The Machine that Changed the World.* New York: Rawson Associates.

Commentary

Japanese R&D Management Practices: The Globalization Challenge

Marc HUMBERT

1 Introduction

The aim of this paper is to briefly comment on a very rich and interesting text, by comparing both Japanese and Western R&D management practices in order to assess whether there has been any kind of convergence of these practices during recent years. It seems that both Western and Japanese firms, as far as technology creation is concerned, are facing a common globalization challenge (see also Humbert 1995, 1996). Before elaborating this point a little further, however, I had first better present the pieces of knowledge about Japanese practices I have learned from the paper presented by Martin Hemmert.

According to his paper, strong differences between Japanese and Western firms due to different institutional settings have existed and continue to do so, as recent developments have not changed much of the basic structure. My comments will be organized into two sections. Firstly, I will address what I have felt to be the basic message of this paper, while in section 3, I will attempt to focus on what to me seem to be the most important points that need to be discussed.

2 Change and continuity in Japanese practices

Hemmert discusses a list of managerial fields where R&D management could present clear-cut differences between Japanese manufacturing firms and their Western counterparts. He thus starts out with a series of differences derived from the existing literature, these managerial fields and the alleged Japanese-specific behaviour being the following:

(i) *strategic technology choices*
Japanese firms, when they innovate, generally tend to stick to familiar fields of technology and to make incremental improvements rather than switching to a new technology and thus pursuing radical change.

(ii) *organization structure of R&D activities*
Firms often have a three-layered organization with 1) corporate labs, 2) divisional labs, and 3) R&D units attached to production facilities. Es-

pecially in R&D intensive industries, large Japanese firms (and not American ones) do have this third level which indicates a high degree of R&D decentralisation or fragmentation.

(iii) employment practices

Employment practices concerning the regular staff of large companies that are considered as Japanese-specific seem to apply to R&D employees as well, except for the fourth one: 1) a predominant recruitment of new university graduates, 2) long-term employment, 3) seniority-based compensation schemes, and 4) frequent transfers of R+D employees between R+D units and to other departments within the firm. According to Hemmert, the latter has been overstated in some reports with regard to R+D employees.

(iv) R&D funding

Japanese firms seem to budget a larger part of total R&D expenses according to R&D projects (in progress or to be launched) than to allocate funds to individual units or divisions.

(v) R&D links with other departments

Japanese firms have been seen as organizing a closer cooperation between departments, especially between R&D, production and marketing, than their Western counterparts; the commented paper expresses clear doubts concerning this contention.

(vi) R&D project management

During the lifetime of an R&D project, Japanese management seems rather different from Western management on two points: 1) the leading role is usually played by product managers and not by functional managers, and 2) the phasing is a step-by-step one, but step '(n+1)' may be launched before step 'n' is completed. Therefore Japanese firms are said to have implemented a 'phase-overlapping' project management.

(vii) External linkages

Concerning external linkages for R&D, the paper differs from previous positions on three points: 1) vertical R&D links in Japanese manufacturing should not be considered stronger than in Western countries, since Western firms simply are more vertically integrated, 2) despite government promotion of cooperation projects, there are rather weak institutional linkages between participating firms and, in any case, comparatively little inter-firm cooperation among Japanese firms, and 3) the substantial number of international alliances by Japanese firms may be interpreted as a substitute for the low level of internationalization of firms' internal organizations.

The starting point for the discussion is that, however questionable some of the items of the above list may be, institutions in Japan are different from their counterparts in Western countries. As firms thus are embedded into different institutional settings, there is good reason to suggest that systematic differences do exist with regard to corporate R&D management. Furthermore, one may assume that the Japanese characteristics deliver both advantages and disadvantages.

Three institutional settings are stressed in this paper: Firstly, Japanese science and technology policy has focused more on *technology diffusion;* this could explain point (i) and, to some extent, points (ii) and (v) above. Secondly, the education and university systems provide firms with very well educated graduates lacking, however, high professionally specialized skills. This is consistent with the prevailing style of recruitment as firms must organize skill formation in-house, while employees acquire firm-specific skill profiles and thus tend to stay employed within the same firm on a long-term basis (see (iii) above).

Finally, the Japanese external market for highly skilled professionals (and for venture capital as well) clearly is underdeveloped, as a consequence of the preceding argument and leading to the same implications.

During the 1980s, Japanese firms achieved good performance records resulting from certain specific advantages: a quick responsiveness to an expanding market, requiring new models (products) with incremental improvements only to adapt rapidly to minor changes in customer needs. On the other hand, firms suffered little from given disadvantages: little attention paid to, and low ability to conduct, long-term (basic) research projects orientated towards breakthrough innovations were not a problem as firms first and foremost had to catch-up and carefully adapt to the general market evolution. Moreover, overall growth offset any difficulties stemming from their high market dependence and thus their (potential) vulnerability to a recession.

However, in the 1990s, Japanese firms have had to endure challenging environmental changes: 1) a stagnating or shrinking demand, resulting from a domestic economic stagnation and, externally, from a revaluation of the yen against Western currencies, and 2) catching-up being more or less achieved, firms have had to strengthen their internal base of long-term technology development.

Hemmert examines the most frequent responses, further illustrated by two cases, namely Tōshiba and Komatsu, that confirm the general view of a three-pronged strategic response by firms, the first one being combined with one or both of the latter two:

1) *Rationalization* refers, at the national level, to a *stagnation of R&D expenses* and of the ratio *R&D-to-sales* in Japanese industrial companies since 1991. This rationalization has led many companies (30 % in a survey of 600 companies in 20 industries) to opt for a *concentration and fusion of R&D units,* rather than closing them altogether, and (especially in high-tech industries) to transfer redundant R&D workers to other departments or to units within production facilities. Tōshiba's strategic re-orientation is along these lines, following the motto "concentration and selection" (shūchū to sentaku) and transferring a substantial part of the funding of R&D units

from headquarters to the business divisions (this is also Komatsu's practice).

2) *Focus* seems to mean a reinforcement of the main tool that has underlaid the effectiveness of R&D: the strengthening of the communication between R&D and business units is by far the leading step taken by Japanese firms (44 % in the quoted survey). This decision is consistent with the reallocation of R&D workers from central to divisional labs and from there on to R&D and engineering units at the business level. It is also consistent with attempts to reorganize the entire corporate structure (beyond a simple cutting of costs) in order to enhance overall efficiency. A small minority of firms have furthermore implemented two new management tools aimed at increasing the creativity and personal motivation of R&D workers: *sairyō rōdōsei* and *nenpōsei*. The former refers to the introduction of flexible working hours without overtime pay for researchers who are simply required to fulfil their given *task*, while the latter is an annual salary system to increase the performance- or merit-based component of the salary to the detriment of the previously dominant seniority component (this is a change Komatsu introduced).
3) *Globalization* has, in the past, been relatively underdeveloped when measured by the ratio of R&D expenditures abroad to domestic investments: while standing at 0.8 % in 1986 for Japanese manufacturers, this figure rose to 1.8 % in 1994, still far below Western standards (10 % and more), though showing a significant increase especially since 1992. Moreover large firms in high-tech industries have been much more active in this respect since about 1985. They have been establishing abroad two types of R&D units, i. e., some in support of local production and marketing and others as basic R&D units (typically 'stand-alone'), tapping into local expertise and strengthening the technological competence of the firm as a whole.

In the past, Japanese R&D management typically seemed different from Western R&D management; do these changes that have been implemented now show a convergence between the two styles? Initially, it appears that the three response strategies are consistent with the 'Western' management theory: facing a recession, it is usual to rationalize, reorganize and reduce costs, and to focus on the firm's strengths and core competencies. In this context, this would mean to focus on given advantages of the R&D units at the business level and to make use of firms' abilities to transfer workers between units and departments, all under the premise to enhance globalization as the necessary response to increasing global competition. Thus, *the Japanese style of response has not been Japanese-specific*. Furthermore, according to Hemmert, this response by Japanese firms has been relatively successful as firms have been able to reinforce their competitive position in world markets.

However, the use of the same methodology for adaptation does not necessarily mean a convergence of R&D management practices. On the contrary, a focus on traditional strengths, specific to the Japanese system, appears to further deepen the existing differences. Hemmert thus supports the idea that Japanese firms have adapted their R&D management practices "without changing their fundamental structure" (p. 340).

Among the changes related to R&D management practices in Japanese firms as pointed out by Hemmert, only three moves can, as a matter of fact, be considered completely new: 1) the funding of R&D projects by business divisions themselves, 2) the introduction of a merit-based salary system, and 3) the increase of R&D globalization and the growth of investment into basic R&D performed abroad. Here, only the latter two are elements that are clearly converging with Western practices.

In sum, however, I do not completely agree with all assertions made by Hemmert about Japanese and Western practices, and I also believe there remain open questions concerning some important practices still to be examined. We will turn to this issue in the next section.

3 R&D crisis, Japanese culture, and globalization

There is no serious doubt concerning Hemmert's assertions about what differences continue to exist between Japanese and Western management practices in R&D. However, I would like to ask for a more complete diagnosis of the current Japanese situation in order to facilitate a better understanding of past and future differences. Thus my first point is that the present diagnosis of the Japanese situation in general, and concerning some of the more detailed aspects, is not perfectly clear to me. I am interested in how much the institutional settings considered in the paper are of relevance, in what way they are linked to the Japanese culture, and how they are related to processes of globalization. However, answering these questions would require an in-depth exploration, not confined to an economic analysis in the strictly orthodox meaning, in order to arrive at a clearer understanding of this reality which governs much of the Japanese R&D management style and, more broadly, of the relation between technology and culture in Japan (see also Humbert 1991).

3.1 About the diagnosis

There is no room here to go into all the details of such a diagnosis. Thus, I would simply like to make some remarks to facilitate a discussion on four series of points:

A) I do not completely agree with simplified comparisons with Western countries. Instead, I believe that we would need more information about, for instance, the ostensibly greater vertical integration of Western companies as assumed by Hemmert. The past ten years in the PC industry, for example, provide a puzzling picture when one compares firms like Intel,

Compaq, Dell, or Microsoft on the one hand, to others such as NEC, Fujitsū, Tōshiba on the other. Certainly, there is a wide variety of developments that would have to be taken into account here.

Furthermore, Hemmert writes that venture capital is scarce in Japan compared to the USA. That may be true; however, what about the relative size of savings and investments? Can we simply say that it is easier to fund new projects in the USA than in Japan? Thirdly, the way money is allocated to R&D units, and how projects are proposed and selected, seems to be at least partly firm-specific. Centralization (e. g., of R&D decisions) can take different ways in Japan and Western countries, respectively, thus we need more research to better understand these matters.

B) I wonder whether the concepts of 'R&D units' and perhaps even 'R& D expenditure' have exactly the same meaning in Japanese firms and in Japanese statistics as in Western countries. In Japanese firms, research and development functions are usually clearly separated. For example, Mitsubishi has a European branch of one of its central research institutes in Rennes (located inside the science park *Rennes Atalante*) where research on cellular phones is undertaken. On the other hand, separated by only a few kilometres, Mitsubishi's production facility (in Etrelles) produces GSM terminals, collaborating for its latest innovations with the relevant business unit's development centre, in charge of information and communication systems and located thousands of miles away. Is it possible that in many cases, inside a Japanese firm's production facilities, (certain) engineering and even maintenance departments simply have not been labelled 'R&D units', something that appears to be impossible in Western enterprises? Thus, are we sure that we are always referring to the same thing here?

C) Much current research focuses on the R&D *crisis* in Japan. However, I am not convinced about the dimension and the timing of this Japanese R&D 'crisis'. Japan's overall R&D expenditures compared to its GDP were close to 3 % in 1995, while the USA reached 2.5 % and the European Union a mere 1.9 %. That does not reflect any comparative weakness in R&D *per se,* though we are probably best advised to choose a middle-range position, located somewhere between the pessimistic view of certain observers and the optimistic one adopted by Hemmert who writes that, after all, Japanese firms have competed very well globally in recent years.

The pessimistic view is usually supported by empirical data. When did this decline set in? In 1987 (the beginning of the *bubble economy*), the ratio of R&D to total investment began to decline, and since 1991 the Japanese manufacturing industry has been enduring a stagnation of its R&D expenditures and intensity. However, are these the relevant ratios to observe? Between 1955 and 1978, the Japanese rate of return on R&D investment progressively declined, followed by an increase from 1978 to 1991, though not returning to the high 1967 level. Again, after 1991 there was a decline, though by 1995 its lowest recorded level to date had been surpassed and a slight increase was again recorded. What is the reason for this development, and what are its consequences, if any? Could *rationalization* of R&D expenditures mean something different than a mere reduction of R&D? In Europe, for example, we have learned that "the EU R&D policy should include mechanisms which provide for an overall rationalization" (Hüber 1997). Are there not better indications concerning the *productivity* of R&D and its recent evolution, e. g., the number of patents, the number of scientific publications, etc.? To my knowledge, Japan has been doing relatively well with respect to both criteria.

3.2 Japanese-ness facing globalization?

One can agree with Hemmert's emphasis on the "institutional settings" (p. 331) as the basis of international differences in firms' behaviours.[1] Any actual convergence between Japanese and Western firms' practices would mean some changes in the characteristics of these 'institutions' and a growing 'globalization flavour' inside firms in both regions. However, Japanese culture or Japanese-ness have been said to be able to accommodate with many imports from abroad, sticking to a 'basso ostinato' according to the social analyst and philosopher Maruyama Masao. As I am not qualified to make any strong assertions about this contention, I will simply allow myself some remarks that may open a future discussion.

1) Is there any convergence of *Science and Technology Policies*? Some puzzling facts remain such as how (the efficiency of) such a low level of government funding of industrial R&D compared to Western countries can be explained? In the West, the usual stance is that there is no use of government spending in R&D unless it comes in large quantities. Will prevailing policies be challenged by the end of the catching-up phase for Japan (when diffusion of existing technologies is no longer the main task) and by the rise of globalization?
2) Emphasis is often put on the *Education and University System*. Japanese are considered among the best-educated people in the world, with highly qualified workers as an acknowledged source of competitive advantage. However, as Hemmert points out there are no 'professionals' and (thus) only low levels of basic R&D. The former leads to the absence of any external labour market as professional skills are learned and acquired within a firm and are thus to a certain extent firm-specific. As to the latter, while diligence and commitment of workers and managers are taken for grant-

[1] This is preferable to the restrictive concept of 'national system of innovation' where what is called 'system' is clearly not a system, i. e., an entity that would have in itself the main resources for reproduction and evolution. Instead, we are better off thinking in terms of a set of not precisely defined entities which are embedded within a societal system (see, for example, HUMBERT 1997).

ed, are these the qualities which are necessary for an innovative R&D? While some new practices in the management of researchers are now being considered to enhance individuals' personal creativity, is the gap between Japanese and Western innovation styles thus narrowing? Perhaps some hybridization is worth seriously contemplating as an opportunity for the future?

3) *Globalization* regarding technology and innovation certainly is an important theme. Technology by essence is universal as the laws of physics are the same everywhere, even if aesthetics and culture can modulate some shapes and shades. However, is globalization seriously challenging the homogeneity or the Japanese-ness of Japan's *industrial* fabric, especially its way of doing R&D? Or will the *basso ostinato* continue its gentle song?

References

HÜBER, R. (1997): EU R&D Policy, Evolution or Revolution. In: FOUNDATION IDATE (ed.): *Research and Development Policies. New Industrial Deal and European Challenges.* Montpellier: Idate, pp. 173–223.

HUMBERT, M. (1991): Perdre pour gagner? Technique ou culture, technique et culture. In: *Espaces Temps* 45/46, pp. 53–61.

HUMBERT, M. (1995): *Globalization and Innovation.* Working Paper No. 2, Birmingham: EUNIP (European Network on Industrial Policy).

HUMBERT, M. (ed.) (1996): *The Impact of Globalization on Europe's Firms and Industries.* 2nd edition. London: Pinter.

HUMBERT, M. (1997): *Emerging Globalization of Production and Technology. From National Systems to Technico-Industrial Systems.* Working Paper No. 7, Kalmar: Institute of Social Sciences, University of Kalmar.

XIV The Phase Variety of Product Systems and System-Based Differentiation: An Alternative View on Organizational Capabilities of the Japanese Firm for Product Innovation

Ken KUSUNOKI

Literature on the Japanese organizational capabilities for product innovation emphasizes that the management of linkages and interfaces of different bodies of functional knowledge composing a particular product system lies at the heart of organizational capabilities. Therefore, such studies have assumed that Japanese firms have advantages in industries where a product shapes a complicated system composed of many subsystems with high interdependencies. However, this paper proposes that such understanding of the Japanese organizational capabilities for product innovation may be potentially misleading because it premises that a product can be grasped as a uni-phase system and an organization can be functionally differentiated and then integrated for approaching product innovation. Instead, this paper emphasizes two important concepts underlying organizational capabilities for product innovation: the *phase variety* of a product system and *system-based differentiation* of a product development organization. The aim of this paper is to develop an alternative view of the Japanese organizational capabilities for a better understanding of the Japanese model of product innovation.

1 Introduction

This paper presents a conceptual model to provide an alternative understanding of organizational capabilities of the Japanese firm for product innovation. Since the 1980s, the Japanese model of approaching product innovation has attracted substantial interest in the field of innovation management since it has been recognized to include some unique organizational capabilities as well as limits. Existing studies exploring the Japanese capabilities for product innovation have consistently argued that the Japanese model possesses advantages in introducing product innovations by efficiently and effectively improving product quality while it encounters certain limits in realizing radical innovations including discontinuous changes in product concept and functionality. Such studies on the Japanese capabilities emphasize that the careful management of linkages and interfaces of components and functional knowledge composing a particular product system lies at the heart of organizational capabilities. Therefore, existing studies have assumed that Japanese firms possess competitiveness in product innovations in industries where a product shapes a complicated system composed of many subsystems with high interdependencies.

However, this paper proposes that such an understanding of the Japanese organizational capabilities for product innovation may be potentially misleading, because it premises that a product can be grasped as a uni-phase system and an organization can be functionally differentiated and then integrated for approaching product innovation. Instead, this paper emphasizes two important concepts underlying organizational capabilities for product innovation: the *phase variety* of a product system and *system-based differentiation* of a product development organization. The aim of this paper is to present an alternative conceptualization of the Japanese organizational capabilities for a better understanding of the Japanese model of product innovation. Rather than being a definitive statement, I regard this paper as one that raises new conceptual perspectives and issues that are in need of further research and consideration in practice. I would like to encourage readers to treat all the statements in the paper as tentative hypotheses open to discussion and verification. To begin with, I briefly review studies in innovation management that have provided a conventional understanding of organizational capabilities for product innovation of the Japanese manufacturing firm.

2 Integration capabilities and system complexity

Every product is a 'system'. Substantial literature on the management of innovation has consistently emphasized that core capabilities of the Japanese firm consist in 'integration capabilities'. Integration capabilities can be defined as capabilities to integrate subsystems into a whole product system by coordinating interfaces and linkages between subsystems.

Let us take a facsimile machine for example. Developing a fax machine requires a number of different elements since a fax machine is a complex system consisting of many subsystems. Looking at physically distinctive elements, a fax machine can be understood as a system of 'components' such as a scanner, modem, printer, data-compressing software and so forth. At the same time, a fax machine can be regarded as a system consisting of different disciplines of functional knowledge. Fax machine development depends on different disciplines of engineering knowledge such as electronics, mechanics, optics, software programming, process engineering and so on. Besides these kinds of engineering knowledge, other types of functional knowledge such as manufacturing and marketing are also required for developing a fax machine. Studies on innovation management so far have demonstrated that the capabilities of integrating these different subsystems efficiently and effectively into a whole product system lie at the heart of the Japanese strength in product innovation.

CLARK & FUJIMOTO (1991) conducted comparative research on product development projects in Japanese, US and European firms in the world automobile industry to reveal that one of the crucial organizational capabilities of Japanese auto firms consists in the heavyweight product manager (HWPM) structure used in development projects. The HWPM structure is an organizational design that delegates a wide range of influence including concept creation to a product manager (PM) who is responsible for coordinating various engineering groups as well as manufacturing and marketing departments involved in the product development projects. In order to facilitate cross-functional integration, a PM with a strong influence over each functional activity enhances communication across functional groups, keeping frequent face-to-face contacts with project members at the working level. This organizational design is a good example of the Japanese organizational capabilities that intensify integration of different functional disciplines into a product as a whole system. CLARK & FUJIMOTO demonstrate that such integration capabilities strengthen product integrity which shapes competitive advantages of product development in Japanese auto firms in terms of development productivity, lead time and product quality.

HENDERSON & CLARK (1990) and HENDERSON (1991) explored the Japanese organizational capabilities for product innovation based on their case study into the photolithographic alignment equipment industry, focusing on the 'architectural innovation' which represents a complex and subtle type of product innovation. In the architectural innovation, much of the functional knowledge within each subsystem remains unchanged, but some of the ways such subsystems are integrated change substantially. Since architectural knowledge of the linkages of subsystems tends to become embedded in the communication channels and problem-solving strategies of a product development organization, architectural innovations are often screened out by information filters and existing patterns of communication unless a firm possesses particular organizational capabilities of deliberately making architectural knowledge an active focus of attention. Japanese firms' competitiveness in the industry reflects such capabilities. At Canon, many engineers were moved across disciplines to ensure that at least some members of a product development team have cross-functional or cross-disciplinary experience. For instance, the optical designers were encouraged to learn about the mechanical and electronic aspects of the product, and engineers moved frequently between the design and manufacturing groups. Canon mastered the explicit management of architectural knowledge to encourage high levels of interdisciplinary or interfunctional argument within the context of a tightly knit and highly committed design team. Leadership from a HWPM also enhanced this process. HENDERSON illustrates that these integration capabilities of Japanese firms play a vital role in outperforming competitors because they may realize subtle but competitively important product changes.

The organizational capabilities of facilitating product integrity can be considered as capabilities to cope with the complexity of a product system. Existing studies have explicitly and implicitly considered a product system as a boxes-and-lines configuration. Here the system complexity of a product is a function of the number of subsystems (boxes) and the degree of interdependencies between subsystems (lines). The greater the number of boxes and lines included in the whole product system, the greater the system complexity becomes. The Japanese model of integration capabilities represents capabilities for product innovation at the whole system level by creating interfaces and linkages of subsystems within the product system consisting of complicated boxes and lines.

In this line of research, Japanese competitiveness in product innovation can be regarded as being contingent upon the product system complexity. Japanese firms are generally competitive in automobile, machinery and many electronics industries, most of which are characterized by high levels of system complexity. On the other hand, they are less competitive in product innovation in such industries as pharmaceuticals and general chemicals where the boxes-and-lines configuration of the product system is less complicated. These tendencies seem consistent with the argument that their strengths lie in integration capabilities.

2.1 Limits of integration capabilities

The studies on integration capabilities of Japanese firms shed light on the limits of the Japanese model of innovation as well as its strengths. First, the concept of integration capability cannot help but involve some trade-offs between parts and the whole. Since there are interdependencies between subsystems (components; disciplines; bodies of functional knowledge), it becomes difficult for a firm to concentrate on pursuing innovation within each subsystem if its goal is to maximize the integrity of the whole product system. The Japanese model forces a firm to pay strong attention to the interdependencies of subsystems even in deepening functional knowledge at the subsystem level. In this case, developing a product by making the best of integration capabilities may mean a sacrifice of possible innovation at the subsystem level at least to some degree.

The typical case is the HWPM structure, which is a sort of matrix organization to handle the trade-offs. The functional structure which is organized around functional disciplines has advantages in continuously pursuing frontiers of functional knowledge though it becomes difficult to reach a higher level of product integrity. Compared to the functional structure, the HWPM structure is a mechanism to make a 'better compromise' at the cost of potential innovations within subsystems. For example, in the auto industry Japanese manufacturers still tend to lag behind their competitors in Europe in terms of componentry innovations, which would be closely related to the profile of Japanese capabilities.

Second, similar limits can be found in the Japanese capabilities for architectural innovation. As mentioned, architectural innovation depicts changes in linkages of different functional knowledge while each functional knowledge remains unchanged. Changing linkages or combinations of an existing set of subsystems leads to an iteration of 'fine-tuning' of the product system within a specific frame. Hence architectural innovation may sooner or later reach a deadlock where a firm should be in need of a totally new set of functional knowledge. However, the Japanese model of approaching product innovation may not be able to cope with such radical innovation since it depends on integration capabilities for a given set of subsystems. These limits of integration capabilities of the Japanese firm are consistent with our conventional understanding that the Japanese model does not work for creating a breakthrough while it displays strengths for incremental improvement.

Third, Japanese firms encounter a challenge that some organizational mechanisms underlying the integration capabilities are becoming exposed to learning by western competitors. Even if the Japanese model itself can remain effective for product innovation, it would lose its competitive edge when the underlying organizational mechanisms are transferred to western competitors.

Fourth, the recent use of advanced information technologies for product innovation challenges the meaning of organizational capabilities for coping with system complexity. For example, in the aircraft industry which is characterized by a high system complexity, Boeing used advanced information technologies such as 3-D CAD for developing its B777, which dramatically improved development efficiency (AOSHIMA 1997). Such use of advanced information technologies threatens the Japanese model because architectural knowledge can be packaged into a 'portable module' which is independent of organizational contexts. If such use of information technologies can substitute for the organization-specific knowledge regarding linkages of product subsystems, integration capabilities of the Japanese firm could be totally meaningless. This challenge to the Japanese model would become serious especially in industries with high system complexity where Japanese firms have built competitiveness through their integration capabilities.

In sum, the Japanese model of product innovation is vulnerable to challenges by recent changes in competitive environments for innovation as well as to limits inherent in integration capabilities, assuming that the essence of the Japanese organizational capabilities lies in these integration capabilities.

2.2 What precedes integration: functional differentiation

A product development organization needs integration obviously because 'differentiation' comes before integration. Subsystems emerge only as a result of differentiating the whole product system into a specific set of parts. That is the reason why firms need integration (LAWRENCE & LORSCH 1967). Interestingly, however, previous studies on innovation management have not paid much attention to the notion of differentiation while providing rich and wide understanding of integration-related issues. Most studies consciously or unconsciously postulate the traditional concept of differentiation as a common perspective to view organizations. The traditional concept of differentiation is *functional differentiation* as found in the concepts of "the nearly decomposable system" (SIMON 1969) and "task partitioning" (VON HIPPEL 1988). Most studies have shared this basic conceptualization of differentiation in considering integration capabilities. The definition of product subsystems such as disciplines, bodies of functional knowledge and components presupposes the conventional concept of functional differentiation.

However, the ways in which Japanese organizations approach product innovation consistently suggest that the Japanese model is based on a totally different logic of differentiation. If the Japanese way of differentiating a product development organization substantially differs from functional differentiation, previous literature assuming that the Japanese strength lies in its integration capabilities such as cross-functional integration would by definition become somewhat misleading since the nature of integration depends on that of differentiation.

For instance, it is widely found that Japanese engineers tend to frequently move across functional disciplines throughout their careers (KUSUNOKI & NUMAGAMI 1997). Furthermore, they often move seamlessly across development stages from concept creation to product design, process design and even pilot runs at a factory in the course of developing a specific product, which is known as a 'no-hands-off style'. If the Japanese firm is truly based on the functional differentiation, one should address the question: why do engineers perform such various activities in the process of a product innovation process in spite of being under functionally differentiated organizational design? One possible explanation to this would be the concept of "task redundancy" (NONAKA & TAKEUCHI 1995). In other words, functional subsystems of the Japanese organization are less differentiated, and each function is defined only in a vague fashion, which eventually results in substantial overlapping between functions. However, a more straightforward explanation would be that the Japanese organization still holds a particular level of differentiation, but it is much different from the conventional concept of functional differentiation.

Taking another example from the facsimile machine industry, Japanese firms played a dominant role in developing small-sized, low-priced machines in the 1980s, which drastically expanded the market. These product innovations enabled Japanese firms to establish dominant positions in the global competition (KUSUNOKI 1995). In these cases of product innovation, the integration of design and manufacturing functions was a critical issue since the key to such innovations was 'design for manufacturing'. At Matsushita (Panasonic), however, the coordination between the two functional departments, design and manufacturing, was not so intensive, and the manufacturing department itself developed these new products almost independently of design and other R&D groups, though its formal function is to concentrate on manufacturing. The Matsushita approach does not fit the traditional understanding of functional differentiation and integration, which assumes that the design department concentrates on performing design functions while the manufacturing department focuses on its manufacturing function, and the results from the two functions are integrated afterwards.

Integration capabilities such as cross-functional ones are required when functional differentiation underlies the organization. However, the above anecdotes imply that the traditional model of functional differentiation and integration do not fully work in the Japanese firm from the beginning. If that is so, we are in need of an alternative understanding of organizational capabilities of the Japanese firm and an alternative concept of differentiation that better fits the Japanese model of product innovation.

3 Phase variety: the third dimension of product system

As mentioned, existing literature has regarded a product system as a boxes-and-lines configuration. Thus a product system can be characterized along two dimensions: the number of subsystems and the degree of interdependencies between them. However, there is a third dimension which has been overlooked: the phase variety of a product system. The concept of 'phase variety' indicates that there are various aspects simultaneously within a single product system and therefore a product system can be seen from a variety of perspectives. Given the system-phase variety, there can always be a range of views regarding 'what the product system is' within a particular product. Any product system by nature possesses system-phase variety, though the traditional understanding has presupposed a product as a uni-phase system. Our alternative conceptualization of the differentiation is founded on the idea of treating a product as a *multi-phase system.*

For example, a fax machine is a product with system-phase variety. If engineers view a fax machine as a 'business telecommunication tool' that substitutes for conventional telex machines, they would put priority on speed and cost of transmission as well as terminal compatibility in evaluating the product to be developed. If it is viewed as a 'copier with a transmission function', one would think of picture density and the printing method employed in the machine as the most important criteria for evaluating the product system rather than the transmission speed. Others could view the machine as a 'telephone with a memo pad'. Given this system view, manufacturability of the product system matters because a firm must reduce the product cost on a mass production basis in order to spread fax machines as commodities suitable for home use. Likewise, a watch can be interpreted as a device for indicating the time, as a tool for scheduling, as a piece of jewellery, as a possibility to express a specific life style and so on. Thus a particular product system potentially encompasses a variety of views or perspectives on the system. This refers to the system-phase variety.

Most previous studies on innovation management have attributed system complexity to the number of boxes and lines included in the product system because they have looked at complexity only during a specific phase of the product system, implicitly ignoring the multi-phase nature of a product system. If the system-phase could be fixed to a particular one, the pattern of differentiating subsystems should be determined automatically and rationally by given interdependencies within the product system. The traditional concept of functional differentiation appears to premise this logic of differentiating subsystems on a given specific phase of the product system.

If we distinguish types of knowledge required for product innovation between know-why, know-how and know-what (GARUD 1996), the notion of functional differentiation focuses on the former two types of knowledge. Functional differentiation provides a focusing device for continual problem-solving and learning within each functional subsystem, which deepens know-why on particular principles and theories underlying the functioning of the subsystem in a 'learning-by-studying' or 'learning-before-doing' fashion. At the same time, knowledge on how to link the functional subsystems represents know-how which is created by a process of 'learning-by-doing'. If we pay attention to the phase variety of a product system, the understanding of what exactly the product is becomes critical knowledge in addition to know-why and know-how. This is the know-what representing an understanding of the specific system configuration that different customers may want and the different uses they may put these systems to.

More specifically, such know-what under the phase variety of a product system can be defined as an evaluation criteria for the product. The respective perspectives on the product system determine the way of thinking about the product's value for the customer. As typically seen in the case of automobiles, an evaluation criterion for the whole product system is related to many components or functional subsystems, rather than having one-to-one correspondences to a specific subsystem. Furthermore, an automobile as a product system encompasses many evaluation criteria simultaneously such as driving performance, NVH (noise, vibration and harshness), comfortability of packing, fuel economy and so forth. This co-existence of many different criteria shows that the automobile is a system with a high degree of phase variety. Phase variety depends on the profile of know-what possessed by the organization as well as on objective characteristics of the product.

4 System-based differentiation

Given the phase variety of a product system, an organization can be differentiated into subsystems with different system perspectives which focus on different phases or aspects of the product system. A group of people with a specific system perspective can be a differentiated unit to continuously learn about a specific phase of the product system by conceiving a unique configuration upon the system phase. This logic of differentiation is labelled *system-based differentiation* which is different from functional differentiation. The system-based differentiation institutionalizes the concept of system-phase variety. Graph 1 contrasts functional differentiation and system-based differentiation.

Graph 1: Functional Differentiation and System-Based Differentiation

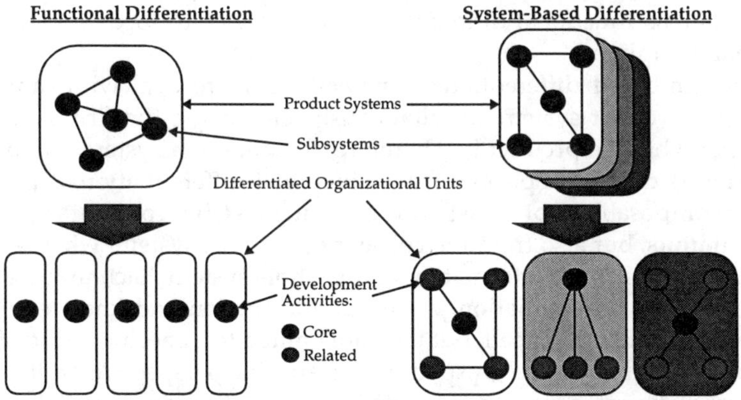

- Coping with system complexity
- Uni-phase product system
- Each differentiated unit focuses on a specific set of functional activities and learning of specific functional knowledge
- Ex ante division of labour determined by organizational structure
- Emphasis on know-why (differentiation) and know-how (integration)
- Cross-functional integration through coordination and communication at a project

- Coping with phase variety of a product system
- Multi-phase product system
- Different system-phases encompass different configurations including multiple sets of functional activities
- Each differentiated unit focuses on learning of system-level knowledge on a specific system phase
- Ex post division of labour through interaction of units with different system perspective
- Emphasis on know-what
- Synchronization of differentiated system perspectives through bounded cohabitation at a project

The logic of functional differentiation-integration assumes that organizational learning about the knowledge for product development should proceed at the levels of each of functionally differentiated subsystems and of their linkage on the given configuration of functional differentiation with a single specific phase of the product system. The logic of system-based differentiation, however, presumes that learning proceeds at the level of product system itself since the product system configuration is not fixed to a specific one. In other words, there can be several patterns of partitioning subsystems simultaneously. Hence, 'what the product system should be' can itself become an object of learning in the process of product development.

System-based differentiation is a mechanism to enable an organization to learn the know-what of the product system, reducing the system-phase variety which a product system by nature possesses. Given the system-phase variety, it is almost impossible for a firm to directly pursue learning at the subsystem level by using functional differentiation as a focusing device, since the way of differentiating the product system into functional subsystems is truly uncertain. Instead, it is first necessary to differentiate the whole product system with phase variety into different perspectives, each of which corresponds to a particular important phase of the system. Though the product as it is cannot be an object of learning due to the phase variety, system configuration of the product can be unified upon each differentiated perspective on the product system. In short, system-based differentiation is a device to make an organizational unit focus on a single phase of a product system whereas functional differentiation is a device to focus on a single functional discipline.

The system-based differentiation enables a firm to deal with multiple phases of a product system simultaneously, enhancing the firm's understanding of what the product is. Therefore, the notion of system-based differentiation is different not only from functional differentiation which assumes decomposability of a system with a single stable configuration into functional units, but also from the concept of 'holonic system' where every unit preserves the entire information of the whole system. Each unit created by system-based differentiation possesses information and knowledge on the whole system within itself, but they are limited to a specific phase of the product system that can be grasped from a specific perspective on the system. Thus, each unit is *specialized-holistic*, i. e., specialized in a particular system phase but pursuing the phase for a whole product.

If we assume that the Japanese model of product innovation is founded on the system-based differentiation, we also assume that organizational units in the Japanese model which are seemingly organized around functional disciplines are virtually dealing with different system configurations upon different system phases. For instance, suppose a fax development project includes 'functional' groups such as 'scanner development', 'printer development', 'packaging', 'manufacturing' and 'marketing'. Given the notion of system-based differentiation, these groups are not organized primarily to pursue functional activities. The printer group should pursue the progress of the whole product system that is viewed as a 'printing system', the packaging group pursues effective and efficient combinations of components from the system perspective of viewing a fax as a physical construction composed of many components, while the manufacturing group performs development activities seeking for manufacturability at the level of the whole product system, viewing a fax as a system suitable to a high-volume production process.

As mentioned earlier, people often move across different functional groups and work on several tasks with different functional disciplines simultaneously in the course of developing a product. At Matsushita's fax machine development projects, for example, engineers of the manufacturing group are occasionally involved in the design process of printing components, while those who belong to component design groups often go to factories to join the floorshop-level activities for the manufacturing of fax machines to be developed. Such interfunctional transfers or concurrent assignments of engineers beyond functional disciplines would be due neither to task overlapping nor to redundancy of work definition given a particular pattern of functional differentiation. Under the notion of system-based differentiation, such behaviour of engineers is more or less 'natural', since each organizational unit can be assumed to encompass problem-solving and learning activities at the whole system level from the specific system perspective. Therefore it would be a quite natural consequence for engineers at component design groups to be involved in the floorshop-level activities at manufacturing plants if such seemingly 'manufacturing' activities are on the system phase on which they concentrate. Such characteristics of Japanese product development organizations, i.e., that respective organizational units perform a variety of functional activities in an almost self-sufficient fashion, would be regarded as substantial 'redundancy' of functional activities from the notion of functional differentiation.

Of course, respective units cannot afford to perform all functional activities for the product development due to resource limitation. If they could, system-based differentiation would result in developing many final products simultaneously for one product market. Instead, each unit performs a limited number of core activities that play a major role in the particular system-phase on which it concentrates as well as other related activities having strong interdependencies with the core activities (see graph 1). In this sense, system-based differentiation creates quasi-self-sufficient units in terms of development activities.

The conventional model of functional differentiation assumes an *ex ante* division of labour, because prior design of the organizational structure should sharply control behaviour and activities within functional units. Thus, the model supposes a hierarchical distinction between structure and activities. In the system-based differentiation, however, structure by itself does not determine the details of activities within each unit, though organizational units are apparently designed so as to correspond to particular functional activities such as scanner design, printer design, manufacturing, marketing and so forth. Activities included in respective units are determined only in the process of interaction between units which focus on different perspectives on the product system. In other words, the division of labour in the system-based differentiation is settled in an *ex post* fashion, and its pattern can be flexibly changed in the course of product development.

NEC's strategic approach of substituting CMOS for conventional bipolar semiconductors for its supercomputers is a good illustration of the system-based differentiation.[1] Using the CMOS technology for a supercomputer CPU is an innovation that drastically improves the cost-to-performance of a

[1] The description of NEC supercomputer development is based on author's interviews with managers of the Computer Division, NEC.

supercomputer since it possesses substantial advantages in cost reduction over the bipolar technology that has been used for high-speed CPUs. In this case of product innovation, NEC assigned the task of developing the CMOS-based CPU for supercomputers to those who had been responsible for the development of bipolar-based CPUs at the supercomputer division.

This decision appears somewhat irrational for two reasons. First, as a technological discipline, CMOS semiconductor technology differs substantially from bipolar semiconductor technology. Hence those who had been involved in the bipolar-based CPU development at the supercomputer division of NEC needed to learn a very new body of knowledge concerning CMOS technology, which would take much time and effort. Second, though the supercomputer division included few CMOS engineers, there were a number of engineers in other divisions such as semiconductors within NEC who specialized in CMOS technology as technical disciplines. It would have been more rational for NEC to put these engineers knowledgeable in the CMOS discipline into the supercomputer division for developing a CMOS-based CPU for its supercomputers. Why did NEC choose this approach of placing bipolar engineers at the supercomputer division? In NEC's strategic intent, it was far more important for the innovation of the CMOS-based supercomputer to have engineers with knowledge and experience concerning the whole product system of supercomputers, rather than the technical knowledge of CMOS itself. As the engineering group of bipolar-based CPU was to work on the development of CMOS-based ones at the division, engineers could make the best of their accumulation of knowledge and experience with regard to high-speed processing of the product system. NEC's strategic idea was to attach importance to their particular perspective or view on the product system of supercomputers, rather than to their profile of technical knowledge at the discipline level. In sum, the engineers at the CPU design group did not specialize in designing bipolar-based CPUs for supercomputers but actually in the specific phase of the product system (high-speed processing) on which they focused.

Another good example of system-based differentiation can be found in the Japanese interfirm networks known as *keiretsu* systems. The Japanese model of *keiretsu* represents a *real* network with stable, long-term relationships of organizations while the western model is oriented more toward *virtual* interfirm networks, often described as 'virtual corporations'. Such a difference is due to the fact that the Japanese model of *keiretsu* network includes the mechanism of system-based differentiation among firms while the western model is based on the network of functionally differentiated firms. For instance, firms in Toyota's *keiretsu* network can be understood to specialize in specific phases of the auto product system rather than in specific components such as electronic parts, bodies, transmissions and so on. Denso, a manufacturer of electronic parts, is a firm which strives to learn at the whole system level by focusing on a particular system phase, viewing the product system as an 'electronic system', while Toyota Shatai (a manufacturer of car bodies) focuses on another particular system phase as a 'system for comfortable driving'. In fact, body manufacturers in the *keiretsu* network such as Kantō Jidōsha and Toyota Shatai initiated the development of Toyota's recent new cars in the field of RV (recreational vehicles). These cases suggest that even body manufacturing firms in the *keiretsu* network possess rich and wide knowledge at the product system level, not simply specializing in specific components (bodies) of the product system. The *keiretsu* system could be a mechanism to enhance the learning of know-what through co-habitation of some important system-perspectives that are differentiated across subcontracting firms, a mechanism based on stable, long-term relationships with subcontracting firms.

5 Bounded co-habitation and system evolution

System-based differentiation underlying the Japanese model of product innovation also suggests an alternative conceptualization of organizational integration. The conventional concept of cross-functional integration is required to commercialize a product by integrating functionally differentiated units into a whole product system. Therefore commercialization of a product is defined as the goal of an innovation project. However, given system-based differentiation, product commercialization does not necessarily mean the end of a project. The aim of system-based differentiation is to continuously deepen the organization's know-what of the product by incorporating its system-phase variety for the evolution of the whole product system in a desirable direction.

Functional differentiation provides a focusing device for an organization, which facilitates the learning of know-why within each functional discipline. Given functional differentiation, an organizational unit can deepen the disciplinary knowledge regarding a specific part of a product system through an iteration of problem-solving in a hierarchical fashion. An organization can secure know-how needed for creating interfaces and linkages of different functional knowledge through the accumulation of certain kinds of experience. However an organization can deepen know-what regarding 'what the product system should be' only by simultaneously possessing different system-perspectives focusing on different phases of the product system, creating interaction of those different perspectives on the product system.

One of the most effective ways to reach this condition for learning know-what is to push the different system-perspectives into a 'field' with limited time and scope, namely a product development project. The primary meaning of commercializing a product by setting a project in the Japanese firm in this process of *bounded co-habitation* consists of different perspectives on a product system. The essence of *integration* in the Japanese model is not like the jigsaw-puzzle-type of combining the parts defined around functional disciplines. The essence of integration under a system-based differentiation is characterized as the bounded co-habitation that forces different perspectives on a product system to interact with each other given a particular set of physical conditions.

The bounded co-habitation is an organizational mechanism of synchronizing different system-perspectives within a specific product development project, accelerating the learning of know-what of the product system to be developed. Bounded co-habitation enables an organization to identify and clarify the differences and trade-offs between differentiated system-perspectives, which consequently changes the understanding of system configuration within each perspective and occasionally incorporates new system-perspectives into the organization. Bounded co-habitation facilitates synchronization of differentiated system-perspectives within a project, which in turn encourages further amplification of phase variety of the product system as well as identification of some new system-perspectives. In this sense, bounded co-habitation provides a condition of learning know-what about the firm's future products. Thus system-based differentiation and bounded co-habitation are tied in a mutually enhancing relationship, while traditional concepts of functional differentiation and integration include trade-offs.

Hence, system-based differentiation and bounded co-habitation facilitate the iteration of product development projects, enabling a firm to evolve a whole product system by continuously improving its know-what of the product, which is labelled 'system evolution'. The conventional notion of integration capabilities focuses on the integrity of a particular product. In other words, cross-functional integration converges toward a better-balanced product system given a stable set of subsystems. However, the system evolution is not such a converging process of fine-tuning a specific product. Its essence lies in the continuous creation of new know-what of the product system through the interaction of differentiated system-perspectives on condition that the definitions of subsystems and their interdependencies are always uncertain.

Product development projects in Japanese firms are often observed to be seamlessly interlocked across product generations (IANSITI 1993). In Japanese firms, a project organization conducting the current product development often proceeds the development of the next generation of the product simultaneously. In other words, a 'project' is not physically distinctive, since it does not correspond to a specific product development. Such a Japanese type of project organization reflects the fact that it is not a mechanism of cross-functional integration for commercialization of a specific product but a vehicle of co-habitation of differentiated system-perspectives for continual system evolution.

A typical example of system evolution would be the miniaturization of products as seen in many consumer electronics products such as Sony's passport-sized video camera. Such innovation by miniaturizing a product system is neither based on changes within subsystems nor on changes of linkages of subsystems. Though it appears as an architectural innovation that changes linkages between given subsystems, the miniaturization of a product system can often be attributed to a totally new set of knowledge regarding 'what the system configuration is', that is, the way of decomposing the whole system into subsystems from the beginning. Such a new body of knowledge on system configuration directs a firm to develop new modularized components as well as high-density packaging technologies that are not included in the previous configuration of the product system. In short, miniaturization needs a *flexible categorization* of product subsystems in accordance with the accumulation of know-what through system-based differentiation and bounded co-habitation. The emerging technology, system LSI, is a typical example of flexible categorization, which drastically contributes to miniaturizing consumer electronic products. Since miniaturization is a process of system evolution, it can occasionally lead to product innovation encompassing a totally new system-perspective as seen in the case of the 'Walkman'.

6 Types of product systems and advantages of system-based differentiation

This paper has provided an alternative model of the Japanese firm's capabilities for product innovation, proposing the concepts of system-based differentiation and bounded co-habitation within the organization for innovation. As mentioned before, existing literature on innovation management has assumed that organizational capabilities of the Japanese firm can be regarded as integration capabilities to cope with product system complexity. However, the conceptual model proposed in this paper focuses on the third dimension of the product system, the variety of system phase, providing some different implications for advantages and disadvantages of the Japanese model.

Graph 2 classifies characteristics of product systems into four types along two dimensions, system complexity and system-phase variety. Existing literature based on the concepts of functional differentiation and cross-functional integration has assumed that the Japanese model is effective for products included in types 2 and 4 (e. g., automobile) while it cannot lead to competitiveness in low-system-complexity products included in types 1 and 3 (e. g., general chemicals and pharmaceuticals), since it has considered the vertical dimension only. However, such understanding of Japanese firms' capabilities raises several questions: Why are Japanese firms not competitive in the Aircraft industries regardless of their very high system complexity? Why are they quite competitive in innovations of electronic devices such as CCDs, LCDs, semiconductors and so forth though such product systems are less complicated than the assembled electronic products?

The degree of system-phase variety may be related to these tendencies of Japanese competitiveness. Pharmaceutical products are typical examples of product systems in type 1. Each pharmaceutical in general only has a limited range of use such as anti-cancer medicine. Hence, know-what or evaluation criteria of pharmaceutical products should be narrowly defined and clarified from the beginning, which reduces system-phase variety. If the strength of the Japanese model lies in its capability for coping with system-phase variety as emphasized in this paper, system-based differentiation would not be effective for innovations regarding these products.

Graph 2: Types of Product Systems

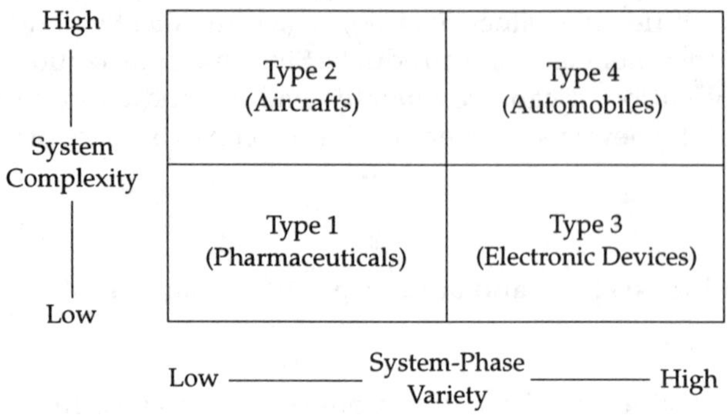

The weak competitive position of Japanese firms in the aircraft industry could be explained along the same logic focusing on the phase variety of the product system. Though characterized by high system complexity, the number of customers is small and evaluation criteria of the aircraft product system are relatively fixed and limited to a few dimensions: safety and efficiency come first. Thus the aircraft industry is assumed to be placed in type 2. Therefore, firms in the aircraft industry can pursue the logic of functional differentiation on a given specific phase of the product system since the phase variety has been virtually reduced just like in the case of pharmaceuticals. Such low phase variety of the aircraft system allows a firm to intensively and extensively use advanced information technologies as seen in the case of the Boeing 777, where technologies supporting the integration of development activities across functions and disciplines become available only after determining a specific phase of the product system.

Compared to this, the Japanese model is suitable regarding such products as automobiles and consumer electronics included in type 4 because these product systems encompass not only high system complexity but also high system-phase variety. In these industries, there are a number of customers as well as a variety of customer needs. Furthermore, there are a number of evaluation criteria for such product systems, each of which is quite unstable. Given these conditions of high system-phase variety, the Japanese firm can make the best of its organizational capabilities of system-based differentiation and bounded co-habitation to build competitive advantages of system evolution.

Japanese firms tend to possess strong competitive positions in innovations of electronic devices which are becoming more crucial in today's competitive environment. Nokia and Motorola have established dominant competitive positions in the world cellular phone industry. Looking at the electronic devices used in cellular phones, however, such as LCDs, ceramic filters, nickel-hydrogen batteries, frequency-controlling ICs and so forth, those developed and manufactured by Japanese firms account for 90% of all devices used in Nokia's cellular phone on a cost basis. Similarly, they account for almost 50% of the inside of Motorola's, although Motorola manufactures its own semiconductor devices. Electronic devices can be characterized by a high system-phase variety (type 3) because the criteria of evaluating their functionality vary depending on what product the device is used in. The know-what of the device can be defined only in the context of the final product in which they are used. Therefore, innovations in such electronic devices require a firm to continuously deepen not only the know-why and know-how within a particular device, but also the know-what of the device, paying attention simultaneously to different phases of the device corresponding to different applications. The principle of functional differentiation and integration tends to hinder this learning of know-what because it premises a stable system configuration that is fixed on a particular phase of the system.

The dichotomy of product innovation and process innovation is becoming meaningless in such device industries as LCDs and semiconductors. In these industries, the distinction between design and manufacturing functions are quite unclear and unstable throughout the innovation process. Under these conditions, it would be ineffective to differentiate organizational units on the basis of functional discipline and then integrate them into a whole product system. Instead, it is necessary to view the product as a multi-phase system from the beginning, simultaneously proceeding problem-solving and learning at different system phases by differentiating units on the basis of system perspective, and then synchronizing these system-level activities through bounded co-habitation. Thus electronic devices are typical examples of product systems with a high phase variety where system-based differentiation underlying the Japanese organizational capabilities becomes most effective.

On the other hand, the ongoing standardization of product systems in the PC industry represents the limits and weaknesses inherent in the Japanese approach of system-based differentiation. The PC industry in its early stage was included in type 4 just like other electronic products. However, the product system standards strategically established by Intel and Microsoft have essentially reduced system complexity and the system-phase variety of PCs. Components that determine a stable product system standard have the power of potentially unifying the various phases of a product system into a single one so that such components can maximize their functionality. In other words, PCs have been transformed from type 4 to type 1 by the standardization of the product system. In this case, organizational capabilities of the Japanese model to cope with system-phase variety may become meaningless, which explains the fact that Japanese firms are less competitive in the PC industry while they are leading innovators in more advanced computer industries such as mainframes and supercomputers.

Japanese firms are seen to be, by and large, weak in establishing industry standards. The Japanese capabilities based on system-based differentiation provide an explanation for this weakness. System-based differentiation leads to competitive advantages only under the condition of system-phase variety. However, the very effort of establishing standards may result in destroying the organizational capabilities of the Japanese firm since industry standards substantially reduce the phase variety of product systems, which is a dilemma included in the model of system-based differentiation.

As discussed above, any model has weaknesses as well as strengths. However, it will be very difficult, impossible even, for Japanese firms to switch to totally new capabilities by abandoning existing organizational capabilities, because organizational capabilities are by definition path-dependent and take a long time to develop. Hence it is important for researchers and practitioners to shape a clear understanding of the Japanese firm's organizational capabilities. The alternative conceptualization presented in this paper could open up a new 'system-perspective' for improving our understanding of the Japanese model of product innovation.

References

AOSHIMA, Y. (1997): *Impacts of the Use of CAD on the Process of New Product Development: A Case Study on the Development Project of the Boeing B777.* Working Paper, Institute of Innovation Research. Tōkyō: Hitotsubashi University.

CLARK, K. B. and T. FUJIMOTO (1991): *Product Development Performance: Strategy, Organization, and Management in the World Auto Industry.* Boston: Harvard Business School Press.

GARUD, R. (1996): On the Distinction between Know-how, Know-what and Know-why in Technological Systems. Paper Presented at the *Mitsubishi-IBM Conference on New Imperatives for Managing in Revolutionary Change.* Shizuoka, Japan, August 25–27, 1996.

HENDERSON, R. (1991): Breaking the Chains of Embedded Knowledge: Architectural Innovation as a Source of Competitive Advantage. In: *Design Management Journal* 2, No. 3, pp. 43–47.

HENDERSON, R. and K. CLARK (1990): Architectural Innovation: The Reconfiguration of Existing Product Technologies and the Failure of Established Firms. In: *Administrative Science Quarterly* 35, 1 (March), pp. 9–30.

IANSITI, M. (1993): *NEC*. Harvard Business School Case #9-693-095. Boston: Harvard Business School.

KUSUNOKI, K. (1995): Seihin kaihatsu no renzokusei to kyōsō yūi [Competitive Advantages of Continuous Product Development]. In: NONAKA, I. and A. NAGATA (eds.): *Nihongata inobēshon shisutemu* [The Japanese Systems of Innovation]. Tōkyō: Hakuto Shobō, pp. 281–350.

KUSUNOKI, K. and T. NUMAGAMI (1997): Intrafirm Transfers of Engineers in Japan. In: GOTŌ, A. and H. ODAGIRI (eds.): *Innovation in Japan*. New York/Oxford: Oxford University Press, pp. 173–203.

LAWRENCE, P. and J. LORSCH (1967): *Organization and Environments: Managing Differentiation and Integration*. Homewood, Ill.: Irwin.

NONAKA, I. and H. TAKEUCHI (1995): *The Knowledge-Creating Company*. New York/Oxford: Oxford University Press.

SIMON, H. A. (1969): *The Sciences of the Artificial*. Cambridge, Mass.: MIT Press.

VON HIPPEL, E. (1988): Task Partitioning: An Innovation Process Variable. In: *Research Policy* 19, pp. 407–418.

Commentary

System-Based Differentiation in Japanese Firms. Comments from a German Perspective

Axel V. WERDER

1 Introduction

Excellence in product innovation is one of the most important success factors in today's highly competitive markets. Japanese companies are usually regarded as being especially successful in managing the product innovation process. In his paper, Kusunoki presents a specific interpretation of how these firms organize product innovations. According to his conceptualization, the Japanese organization model is characterized by a 'system-based differentiation'. The purpose of the following remarks is to discuss his concept from a German point of view. The considerations are organized in the following way. First, the essence of Kusunoki's theory is briefly outlined (section 2). Subsequently, the reconceptualization of the Japanese model is analysed with regard to three questions: (1) In which sense is Kusunoki's explanation of the way Japanese firms organize innovations innovative itself? (3.1) (2) What are the strengths and the weaknesses of his concept (3.2). (3) Is a 'system-based differentiation'-kind of organizing product innovation promising for German companies? (3.3). The paper closes with a short conclusion and an outlook on further research questions (4).

2 The concept of system-based differentiation

Successful innovations are an essential ingredient of a company's competitive strength. Over the last ten years or so both management theory and practice have increasingly recognized the crucial role organization can play in fostering product innovations. Because Japanese companies are perceived worldwide to be especially innovative (at least in some industries), their special capabilities to organize the product innovation process have been intensively studied. The literature so far concludes that these capabilities lie in the ability of cross-functional integration. Cross-functional integration in this context means the coordination of interfaces between organizational units focused on specific functions like design, manufacturing and marketing (Kusunoki p. 365). Hence, a functional differentiation (or task partitioning respectively) of the product innovation process in Japanese companies is assumed.

According to Kusunoki, however, the mainstream-explanation of Japanese innovation successes by a cross-functional integration ability is misleading because it is based on a false assumption. He states that the organization of product innovation in Japanese firms does not really follow the principle of functional differentiation. Rather, "a totally different logic of differentiation" (p. 362) is actually underlying the task segmentation. The author labels this organization model a "system-based differentiation" (pp. 364). Consequently, in default of a functional differentiation, the strength of Japanese innovation management cannot consist in outstanding cross-functional integration capabilities.

A system-based differentiation refers to the 'phase variety' of each product. The concept of phase variety stresses that a product can be seen from a range of perspectives (p. 366). Depending on the particular perspective, different views of "what the product system is" (p. 363) emerge. In Kusunoki's example, a fax machine can for instance be viewed as a "business telecommunication tool" (as substitute for a telex machine), a "copier with a transmission function" (as substitute for a conventional copying machine) or as a "telephone with a memo pad" (a substitute for home-used telephones). Likewise, a watch can be interpreted as a device for indicating the time, as a piece of jewellery, as a possibility to express a specific life style (Swatch) and so on. Consequently, the respective perspective determines the way of thinking about the product's value for the customer. In other words, it reveals the evaluation criteria for the product (p. 364).

A system-based differentiation institutionalizes the concept of phase variety by establishing organizational units, which have a focus on different perspectives of the product's nature (in the sense explained) and not on different functions. Thus, for instance, in the automotive industry one organizational unit could be responsible for developing a new car generation from the perspective of seeing it as an "electronic system" while another unit could be responsible for viewing a car as a "system for comfortable driving" (p. 369, referring however to the inter-firm differentiation in Toyota's *keiretsu* network). Organizational units in a system-based differentiation model consequently are not only responsible for a single aspect of the whole product (as in the functional model). Rather, their responsibility is extended to the whole product, but limited to a special perspective. Thus, their responsibility can in short be called a "specialized-holistic" one, i. e., specialized on a particular perspective, but pursuing that perspective for the whole product (p. 366).

Differentiating the product innovation process on a system-basis especially fosters the understanding and learning about the use (fullness) of a product. Referring to a distinction between know-why, know-how and know-what as types of knowledge necessary for product innovation (GARUD 1996), a system-based differentiation supports primarily the creation of know-what. According to Kusunoki, this know-what is especially crucial for innovation successes (compared to the know-why of the functioning of a product's single subsystems and the know-how to combine the subsystems to the whole product). The reason why is that only rich know-what allows for radical innovations such as miniaturization (like in the case of Sony's Walkman or passport-sized video camera) which drastically changes the product system configuration (pp. 370).

In sum, the system-based differentiation of the product innovation process and the ability to coordinate the resulting different perspectives of the product in a sort of "bounded co-habitation" (pp. 369) lies at the core of the successful innovations found in Japanese firms. These organizational capabilities are especially important if products have a high phase-variety. Therefore, Japanese companies are primarily competitive in the corresponding industries such as automobiles and electronics (pp. 360).

3 Discussion of the concept

3.1 Is the concept of system-based differentiation new?

A system-based differentiation represents a specific mode of task segmentation. Each kind of task segmentation can be characterized by the applied principle or criterion respectively guiding the definition and demarcation of the task responsibilities of the single organizational units. For that reason, assessing the innovativeness of the system-based differentiation concept requires to answer the question whether this concept introduces a new segmentation criterion which has previously not played a significant role in organization theory and practice.

In Germany, four different kinds of relevant segmentation criteria have prevailed until now in companies and in the literature. These alternatives encompass the segmentation according to (1) functional aspects (R&D, manufacturing, marketing and so on), (2) product aspects (organizational units being responsible for product groups, single products or parts of a product), (3) customer aspects (age, gender, income, lifestyle etc.) and (4) regions (e. g., responsibilities for specific countries or continents). Taking these dominant segmentation principles into account, it is fair to say that with 'phase' or 'perspective' the concept of system-based differentiation introduces a fifth kind of differentiation criterion. In this regard, thus, the concept deserves without any doubt to be evaluated as being innovative. Since 'perspective' in the sense of 'specific nature of the product' is different from function, product, customer and region, a system-based differentiation contains the potential for a new focus of organizational units. Because of their (specialized) holistic orientation, system-based differentiated units are more strongly stimulated to engage in the whole product than are functional-oriented units. Furthermore, their engagement with the product should be more intensive compared to the one of customer- or region-oriented units since the product in question is just a part of the responsibilities of the latter two. Finally, a phase-orientation as conceptualized by Kusunoki must not be confused with a product-orientation (as it is found in the conventional multi-divisional M-form, see CHANDLER 1962: 324). As a consequence of the specialized (-holistic) focus, phase-oriented units concentrate on a specific purpose of the product. On the contrary, product-oriented units are responsible for the whole product without any specific perspective. In theory, thus, they are free to pursue every possible perspective of a product. In practice, however, this freedom is (too) seldom exploited. Rather, the lack of a special focus contains the risk of overlooking the phase variety of a product.

3.2 What are the strengths and weaknesses of a system-based differentiation?

Organization structures cannot be directly evaluated with respect to a company's goals such as profit or growth because the realization of such goals depends not only on organizational issues but also on a variety of other factors. Rather, structures have to be evaluated in the light of sub-goals which have a closer relation to organizational measures (SIMON ET AL. 1954: VI). For the purpose of assessing the efficiency of alternative ways of task segmentation, two sub-goals are especially important. These sub-goals are the resource efficiency and the coordination efficiency of an organization structure (FRESE & VON WERDER 1993: 24 pp.).

Resource efficiency generally expresses the extent to which the capital and human resources of a company are employed productively. In the context of innovation management, resource efficiency primarily means the scale of knowledge creation (with a given amount of resources), since knowledge—besides creativity—is an essential condition for successful innovation. *Coordination efficiency* measures the quality and cost of integrating interdependencies between organizational units. The sub-goal of coordination efficiency can be split up further into more concrete sub-goals because several kinds of interdependencies exist. The most relevant ones in practice are process interdependencies and program interdependencies.

Process interdependencies arise within the company and exist between units which succeed one another in the value chain. A typical example is the relation between the manufacturing unit and the sales unit, where the former delivers the manufactured products to the latter.

Program interdependencies, on the other hand, are of external nature in the sense that several units of the company address the same market (defined by customer or regional attributes) with different products. These products can be either substitutes or subsystems of a complex system. The first case exists for instance if the product programme of a company encompasses small as well as medium-sized cars which are offered to the customer by separate divisions of that company. Under these circumstances, the two divisions are programme-interdependent because the average customer will only buy a small *or* a medium-sized car. Unless these interdependencies are coordinated, the divisions will compete against each other. In the second case of the system selling, a coordination of the corresponding divisions is mandatory to a certain degree since the customer is interested in an integrated solution of his problem. Think for instance of establishing a complex communication network for a customer which is jointly carried out by the 'computer-division' and the 'telecommunication-division' of a company.

According to the distinction between process interdependencies and programme interdependencies, the sub-goal of coordination efficiency consequently can be divided into the two evaluation criteria of process efficiency and programme efficiency. *Process efficiency,* thus, deals with the quality and cost of coordinating process interdependencies, whereas *programme efficiency* measures the quality and cost of the coordination of programme interdependencies.

Employing the evaluation criteria introduced, the main strengths and weaknesses of a system-based differentiation are the following. The unique advantage of this organizational model is related to resource efficiency. As has been pointed out already, system-based differentiated units have the opportunity (and the duty) to continuously deepen their understanding of 'what the product is' and how—in this perspective—it can be improved. Therefore, this form of organizing product innovation is especially appropriate for an efficient creation of the know-what type of knowledge (this strength is also stressed by Kusunoki, p. 366, himself).

On the other hand, a system-based differentiation—like every organizational model—also has its own problems. They concern resource efficiency as well as coordination efficiency. As a logical consequence of fostering 'perspective-knowledge' (know-what), a system-based differentiation must be weaker in supporting the creation of knowledge about functions, customers or regions respectively compared to a functional, customer-oriented or regional segmentation. Thus, under the aspect of resource efficiency there is a trade-off between high(er) efficiency as far as perspective-knowledge is concerned and low(er) efficiency in terms of functional, customer-oriented respectively regional knowledge. Such trade-offs, however, are not a unique weakness of a system-based differentiation. Rather, they are an unalterable attribute of every uni-dimensional kind of segmentation. Therefore, the problem only lies in the weighting of the various kinds of knowledge. We will return to this point again later in greater detail.

Regarding coordination efficiency, a strictly (uni-dimensional) system-based differentiation establishes units merely with a focus on various perspectives of a single product. Consequently, such a structure has no built-in device (as opposed to a functional or a customer-oriented structure for example) for coordinating programme interdependencies between the product in question and other products of the firm. This default can be especially problematic in the case of system selling where solutions for complex customer problems require synchronized innovations of different product groups.

Furthermore, a system-based differentiation introduces additional interdependencies which can be classified as a sort of internal programme interdependencies. As a result of viewing a product in different ways and of striving for innovations from these different perspectives, system-based differentiated units are principally in the same position as divisions competing in the market against each other with substitutional products. If different perspectives on what the product could be (a watch as a time-indicator vs. a watch as a piece of jewellery) means different layouts and specifications of the product, at some point decisions have to be made about what the product should be (assuming a company is not willing or able to commercialize several perspectives). On the one hand, the (at least from a German point of view) 'natural' interest of each and every single unit to carry its specific perspective during this decision process can set free a lot of creativity. The units with the most convincing innovations will have the best chances to finally define what the product should be. This fostering of creativity and engagement in innovations is the good news—and of course very important since innovation management is striving for innovation. The bad news, on the other hand, is that the cost of this internal competition is comparatively high. Therefore, the efforts of the different units have to be coordinated to some degree.

Coordination is also necessary even if different perspectives do not require different layouts and specifications of the product. As far as developments in some units (e. g., in a unit viewing a car as an electronic system) are relevant for other units (e. g., a unit regarding a car as a system for comfortable driving), these process interdependencies between different perspectives have to be coordinated.

The short efficiency analysis carried out here, which is still quite rough, already reveals that besides its merits a system-based differentiation also has some shortcomings. In other words, this kind of segmentation does not meet all organizational challenges of resource and coordination efficiency either. Therefore, an evaluation of this model after all requires an assessment whether the strengths outweigh the weaknesses, whether the balance between pros and cons in other words is more favourable than the ones of alternative organization forms. This question cannot be answered in general. Rather, it depends on the company's competitive strategy. If a company has decided to compete by excellence in innovation and innovation can be derived mainly from viewing products in different perspectives, a system-based differentiation is obviously an effective (but also expensive) model. If, on the contrary, the pursued strategy emphasizes greater excellence in, for example, technology or customer-orientation,[1] alternative models may also be quite attractive.

---

[1] A point to consider is, for instance, that the average customer may not at all 'appreciate

3.3 Is the concept of system-based differentiation promising for German companies?

According to the preceding analysis, the appropriateness of a system-based differentiation depends on a company's competitive strategy. Whether this concept is promising for German firms, therefore, hinges on how strong companies in Germany emphasize (or should emphasize) the importance of know-what. Of course, this question cannot be answered definitely here. Rather, the influence of many factors (such as kind of market or industry, see also Kusunoki, p. 361) would have to be elaborated. Therefore, the following considerations can only have the status of a rough subjective assessment.

Nevertheless, despite lacking a more thorough analysis, it seems that the concept's basic idea of accentuating phase variety is very relevant to German companies. The importance of efforts for viewing products more often and intensively from different perspectives can hardly be overestimated. This does not mean, however, that buying the idea of phase variety must result in a strict (uni-dimensional) system-based differentiation. Rather than implying radical structural changes (like a transition from a functional segmentation or a matrix form to a purely perspective-oriented differentiation), the concept seems to suggest measures to change attitudes (within given structures). Because, for example, functional expertise also plays a vital role in product innovation, the creation of the corresponding knowledge should not be sacrificed too much.[2] In other words, know-what does not appear to be generally more important than know-why and know-how to justify 'perspective' as the dominant segmentation criterion for most (German) companies. Rather, a good compromise between the various aspects of resource efficiency and coordination efficiency could be in many companies to (maybe) add to the existing structure a (small) task force focused on elaborating different possible perspectives and—more importantly—to continuously call the attention of all (other) organizational units to the phase variety of each product—and of each task. To put it in a different way, the most crucial thing to do might be an education to 'think beyond the borders' of the own organizational unit and to always (try to) take interdependencies to other aspects of the product into account. In this sense, a functional unit for instance could also strive for learning and understanding more of the whole product.

excellence' in innovations if such excellence means, e.g., introducing 'new' car generations every year, thereby reducing the value of his recently purchased, but then already 'old' car.

[2] Current reorganization programmes such as lean management, business re-engineering and outsourcing, which are very popular in Germany (and throughout the western world), have already resulted in a painful loss of knowledge for some firms (see ARBEITSKREIS ORGANISATION 1996: 642).

4 Conclusion and further research questions

At the core of the concept of system-based differentiation lies the idea of the phase variety of each product. This idea can be understood both as an innovation philosophy and as an organizational principle. As an innovation philosophy, it represents the attitude to always be aware that a product can be seen in different perspectives. As an organizational principle, the concept introduces a new segmentation criterion for the task definition and demarcation of organizational units. Whilst the organization model has its specific strengths and weaknesses, following a philosophy of continuously paying attention to the phase variety of products while performing some sort of innovation-related tasks has its obvious merits.

The explanation of product innovation in Japanese firms presented by Kusunoki raises many interesting questions for further research of which a short selection shall be mentioned here briefly. The aim of Kusunoki's paper "... is to present an alternative conceptualization of the Japanese organizational capabilities" for product innovation (p. 358). To a certain degree, however, it remains unclear whether he really addresses organizational issues (in terms of task segmentation and so on) or rather the behaviour respectively attitude of the people fulfilling their tasks. It is well understood that tasks and responsibilities in Japanese firms are defined in a more vague fashion (as compared to German companies for example, see NONAKA & TAKEUCHI 1995: 78 pp.), and that structure influences behaviour. Nevertheless, it should be possible—and appears to be worthwhile—to distinguish between structure and behaviour and to study more thoroughly on the one hand which organization principles (especially segmentation criteria) are employed in Japanese innovation processes, and on the other hand, how people carry out their roles (defined by the specific organization structure). In-depth (case) studies of this kind may eventually even reveal that innovation processes in Japanese firms—in order to efficiently use resources—are quite conventionally organized, but carried out in a unique way. In particular, a variety-oriented attitude can be achieved, e. g., by flanking the basic (conventional) organization structure with specific measures such as job rotation, career path plans, and communication rules. Such findings would smoothly correspond to our distinction between paying attention to phase variety by means of an innovation philosophy and by an organizational principle.

A second interesting field of further research would be to continue clarifying the circumstances under which know-what is especially important. In this context, the measurement of phase variety as it has been proposed by Kusunoki (pp. 363) deserves more elaboration. For instance, according to Kusunoki, automobiles have a high phase variety and aircraft have a low one (pp. 371). He claims that many evaluation criteria (i. e., perspectives) exist for cars, whereas the criteria for aircraft are limited basically to safety and economies. However, aircraft, too, can be seen from a wide range of different perspectives. Examples are aircraft as transportation systems, as electronic systems, as environment-polluting systems, as navigating systems, as places for eating, relaxing, entertainment and so on.

As far as the concept of system-based differentiation serves as an organizational principle, the various perspectives provide the criterion for the segmentation of tasks. If the idea is to establish separate organizational units for each different perspective, another interesting question arises. In order to organize the product innovation process, the relevant different perspectives (guiding the task definition and demarcation of the units) must be known. Consequently, the concept has a good potential for supporting innovations within the boundaries of the already known perspectives. On the contrary, it has no specific feature for generating ideas about new perspectives previously not yet thought of. Thus, the relation (and the management) of innovations along known perspectives and innovations by innovative perspectives opens up another area of promising research.

References

ARBEITSKREIS ORGANISATION (1996): Organisation im Umbruch. (Was) kann man aus den bisherigen Erfahrungen lernen? [Organization in a State of Transition. (What) Can One Learn from Experience so far?]. In: *Schmalenbachs Zeitschrift für betriebswirtschaftliche Forschung* 48, 6, pp. 621–665.

CHANDLER, A. D. (1962): *Strategy and Structure. Chapters in the History of the Industrial Enterprise.* Cambridge/London: The M.I.T. Press.

FRESE, E. and A. V. WERDER (1993): Zentralbereiche – Organisatorische Formen und Effizienzbeurteilung [Central Staff Departments – Organizational Forms and Evaluation of Efficiency]. In: FRESE, E., A. V. WERDER and W. MALY (eds.): *Zentralbereiche* [Central Staff Departments]. Stuttgart: Schäffer-Poeschel, pp. 1–50.

GARUD, R. (1996): On the Distinction between Know-how, Know-what and Know-why in Technological Systems. Paper presented at the *Mitsubishi-IBM Conference on New Imperatives for Managing in Revolutionary Change,* Shizuoka, Japan, August 1996. Cited in Kusunoki, p. 364, of this volume.

NONAKA, I. and H. TAKEUCHI (1995): *The Knowledge-Creating Company. How Japanese Companies Create the Dynamics of Innovation.* New York/Oxford: Oxford University Press.

SIMON, H. A. ET AL. (1954): *Centralization vs. Decentralization in Organizing the Controller's Department.* New York: American Book – Stratford Press.

Change and Continuity:

On the Transformation of the Japanese Management System

XV Transformation of the Japanese Management System: A Contingency View

Takahiro FUJIMOTO

1 A brief overview of the contributions for this book

There have been a growing number of studies on the limits and strengths of so-called Japanese management practices in the wake of the Japanese economy's facing the post-*bubble* recession, a strong appreciation of the yen, pressures for regulatory reforms, as well as continued trade frictions in the first half of the 1990s. Some have argued that Japanese management practices have totally lost their internationally competitive advantages, while others insist that the strength of the Japanese-style management system, including those system elements adopted by non-Japanese firms, have basically remained intact in the 1990s. Some have declared a collapse of the Japanese-style system, whereas others emphasize its resilience. Some have prescribed that the Japanese firms need a fundamental overhaul for survival in the new global environment, while others insist that an incremental modification will suffice.

Such a variety of views on environmental changes and Japanese firms' adaptation are also found in the present book. Although most authors deal with the challenges and crises that the Japanese management system faces, some tend to emphasize continuity, whereas others stress discontinuity, and still others try to balance the two forces.

(1) Some of the chapters in this book are rather optimistic about the adaptive capabilities of certain Japanese management practices to environmental changes. For example, Yoshimura et al. indicate that the externalization of firms (*bunsha-ka*), typically found at such large Japanese business organizations like Matsushita, continues to be an effective pattern of inter-firm network management. They argue that the main reasons for such externalization include not only decentralization, risk reduction, capital gain or labour cost saving, but also an effective governance that facilitates the alertness and agility of the externalized units. Teramoto, Iwasaki and Takai, using their extensive data analysis, advocate a "re-management" of inter-organizational networks, or the strategic cooperation of group-member firms sharing a common vision, strategy and synergy. A case study is then presented: Yokogawa's "Global Group Management" comprising its increasingly independent group companies.

Molteni, through his case studies of a Fiat-Hitachi joint venture, Piaggio and Daihatsu joint venture, and TMI (Teijin) Europe, respectively, finds that international technology transfers from Japanese to European firms are more effective when the recipients are joint ventures under a Japanese majority ownership, and in the case of "greenfield" operations. Tachiki argues that Japanese companies are shifting their focus from an "export-oriented" strategy with closed corporate groupings to a "foreign direct investment oriented" approach seeking strategic alliances. He analyses regional headquarter (RHQ) organizations of Japanese firms in Asia-Pacific and identifies "economies of network."

Although their topics are considerably different, these authors seem to share the view that the Japanese practice of inter-organizational (but often intra-group or intra-firm) network management by large firms will remain effective, with some possible modifications undertaken. It should be noted that these studies deal mainly with the manufacturing sector for system products with rather integral architectures, in which Japanese manufacturers tended to be competitive partly through this management of rather closed networks of firms.

(2) Researchers on human resource management (HRM), and small or medium-sized firms, on the other hand, tend to balance continuity and discontinuity, or divergence and convergence, apparently reflecting the multifaceted nature of the changes in this field.

Nohara, for example, comparing Japanese and French hierarchical organizations in large companies, identifies an overlapping hierarchy of blue and white collar employees in Japan, in which both continuity and discontinuity are present. He then characterizes the adjustment of the Japanese HRM system in the post-*bubble* era as a combination of mechanical (peripheral) change, organic change (modification of the core), and structural change (fundamental changes of the core).

Ribault, using in-depth case studies of HRM systems in the Japanese retail sector, identifies a "hyperflexible integrated segmentation" of the labour force, integrating employees of different categories such as the core workers (*seishain*), *arubaito*, *pāto*, and external workers into a coherent organization. Whereas this HRM-organization policy in the retail sector significantly differs from the so-called 'Japanese management practice' that is based mainly on practices in large *manufacturing* firms—in that the retail sector heavily uses employees in peripheral categories—the system still seems to follow the conventional strength of Japanese organizations in terms of their internal organizational integration.

Dirks, on the other hand, focuses his attention on the recent increase in the use of employment transfers (or loaning) between firms such as *shukkō* (temporary transfer) and *tenseki* (irreversible one) in response to the post-*bubble* era. He defines this phenomenon as "quasi-internal" labour markets that include both sending and receiving firms (a corporate group, subcontracting network, etc.), and regards it as an effort towards a balance between flexibility and stability that are simultaneously required in the post-*bubble* era.

Susumu Watanabe argues that traditional subcontracting systems of dependent small and medium-sized firms, having evolved over the postwar period, contributed to the growth of the Japanese economy. As for the future, he assumes a balance-oriented view as well, predicting that the traditionally dependent subcontractors will be transformed into more independent entrepreneur-type firms, diversifying their partners while their relationships with primary parent firms will remain stable.

(3) There are other authors who emphasize the need for more structural adjustments which might be triggered by certain changes in the product architecture (i. e., fundamental schemes dividing a product into modules, allocating product functionality into such modules, and designing the interfaces across the modules) of the products in question.

Lecler, for example, predicts that the Japanese *keiretsu* system will be transformed into a more open network, as the products in question evolve into more open-architecture products with an industry-wide standardization of interfaces between modules. She observes that such open networks are already emerging in the Asian operations of Japanese automobile makers.

Kusunoki also pays attention to changes in product structures which may negatively affect the competitiveness of at least some of the Japanese firms. He argues that their traditional integration capabilities in product development may become obsolete when the products' system complexity and "system-phase variety" (equivocality of a product's concept) are reduced, as in the case of personal computers for example.

While some researchers express their concern about the impact of architectural changes that may render the Japanese manufacturing capabilities obsolete, others argue that there are certain types of industries in which the sheer capability of science and technology creates competitive advantages. This is a field in which Japan has not necessarily been competitive internationally. Hemmert, on the other hand, presents a stylized description of the Japanese R&D system (e. g., recruiting from colleges, training, three-layer labour system, production/R&D proximity, development focus, cross-functional integration and concurrency), which according to him contributes to firms' competitiveness. He asserts that this system has been able to adapt to environmental changes through rationalization (tightening belts), focus, and globalization.

(4) Researchers studying financial sectors and related issues, including main bank systems, corporate governance, and pension funds, seem to be advocating a more fundamental change of the Japanese practices.

Miyajima analyses the evolution of the Japanese main bank system (AOKI's framework) and firms' "contingent governance structure," in which control of the company is switched from insiders to the main bank when financial performance declines. Using statistical data, he demonstrates, by estimating the influence of financial performance on presidential turnover, that arm's length relations still existed in the 1950s, that the main bank system apparently then prevailed between the mid-1960s recession and the 1970s, and that the system may have been weakened over the 1990s. Shigeru Watanabe, on the other hand, looks at the history of corporate governance structures in postwar Japan from Agency Theory's point of view, and characterizes the observed pattern as a "quasi-LBO," in which over-lending by the Japanese firms and the main bank system resulted in the absorption of free-cash flows. He then argues that an internal governance system through ROE management needs to be established as corporate governance effectuated by the main bank system no longer works. Estienne studies the impact of deregulation in the field of pension funds. The traditional system that gave trust banks and insurance companies special status, as well as other strict regulations, will be abolished, and some (particularly large) Japanese firms are ready for taking up this opportunity. Such deregulation will also change the corporate pension governance structure.

To sum up, there seem to be different types and magnitudes of challenges and responses that Japanese firms in different sectors have been experiencing during the 1990s:

(1) *re-assuring* capabilities with minor modifications;
(2) *re-balancing* capabilities in changing environments;
(3) *re-aligning* capabilities to the changing product structures;
(4) *an overhaul* of capabilities responding to deregulation.

2 A contingency hypothesis on challenges and adaptation (incomplete)

Let me analyse the different nature of the "external shocks" and "internal evolution" presented in these chapters. After noting the variety of the works in this book, the basic idea for the following arguments is that adjustment strategies for Japanese management practices may vary between different sectors, although there may also be some driving forces common to all sectors.

To begin with, let us tentatively try to classify different types of shocks. The following matrix is a rough-cut typology of different cases of crises or challenges (graph 1).

The first three cases are of particular importance:

Case 1: Re-balancing in response to environmental changes:
Previously competitive export sectors; stable and integral architecture; typically auto industry

Basic requirements for competitive capabilities do not change much, although certain changes in both product and labour markets (e.g., low growth and demographic changes) may urge firms to re-balance their existing assets and capabilities. They need to strengthen their existing competencies, but also need to make sure not to 'overshoot'. Balanced performance for all stakeholders is a key.

Graph 1: Different types of external shocks

		product architectural changes: big	product architectural changes: small
traditional international competitiveness	high	case 2: Computer (re-aligning?)	case 1: Automobile (re-balancing?)
	low or unproven	case 3: Banking (overhaul?)	case 4: Agriculture

Case 2: Realigning to architectural changes

A product architectural change may make previously strong capabilities of Japanese firms obsolete: Drastic architectural changes toward a modular one, typically package software and PC industries.

The basics for winning the game do change in this case, thus previous capabilities may become obsolete. For example, *de facto* standards for inter-module interfaces may emerge over time—Japanese are not good at this type of the game.

The speed of these industries' evolution is often high. In this sense, Japanese firms have tended to be too slow regarding their executive decision making. Firms may also need to adopt some kind of 'Americanization strategy' as a move to open architecture strategy.

Case 3: Overhaul in response to deregulation and architectural changes

Typically a domestic sector that used to be protected and heavily regulated; lack of international competitiveness due to a lack of competitive pressures is common, a *big bang* may be imminent. De-regulation may reveal weaknesses of previously protected industries. As the power of the financial institutions may change, the corporate governance structure may need changes to protect competitiveness as well.

In sum, there seem to be different patterns in terms of such factors as international competitiveness, product architecture, and product-labour environments. In any case, we should not over-generalize the patterns of crisis and recovery of the Japanese firms in the 1990s.

3 Three modes of adaptation: equilibrium, revolution, or evolution

Let me now turn to the 'response' side. The responses of management systems to external environmental shocks may be interpreted in at least three different ways: instant adjustments, revolutionary changes, and evolutionary changes. There are three different perspectives behind these interpretations.

3.1 An equilibrium perspective

The first stance is the *equilibrium* perspective of the firm, which is a standard view in the neo-classical micro theory. According to this view, firms can adjust their resources and capabilities instantly to changes in market environments to reach an equilibrium, partly because of the assumption that firms' resources are malleable, and also because they make accurate decisions to maximize their profits or present value based on perfect information. As the surviving firms are always found to lie at the equilibrium point in the activity space, neither mis-adaptation nor over-adaptation exists in theory because of the given assumptions.

This perspective explains that the Japanese system of the 1980s did fit in well with the domestic environment of that period, and that the firms will modify their resources and capabilities smoothly as the situation changes toward the 21th century. This optimistic view may explain firms' behaviour in some of the Japanese industries where change is at most moderate. In many other industries, however, such optimism may not be an appropriate predictor of such adjustment.

3.2 A revolutionary paradigm change perspective

The second perspective is that of the *paradigm-change* view of the firm. This perspective sees the process of change as a discontinuous replacement or dethronement of the old system by a totally new one, rather than a continuous adaptation of the existing system to a new environment. What is assumed in this process of system transformation is *revolution* rather than evolution.

In this sense, the paradigm-change perspective finds its roots in Thomas KUHN's theory of scientific revolution (KUHN 1970) or even classical Marxist theories of economic system changes. What is common among such revolutionary views is the assumption that a stable system exists not because it has adapted itself to external environments but simply because it is internally consistent. Even where a gap between the system's capabilities and environmental requirements widens, the old system is unable to re-adapt itself to the new environments. Thus, systemic change occurs only in the form of a replacement of the old regime by a new one.

In this context, the problem of the so-called "Japanese management system" in the early 1990s might be interpreted as a situation in which the old paradigm based on continuous industrial growth, relatively closed product architectures and/or protected or regulated markets, has to be replaced by a completely new management paradigm for the post-growth era, and to undergo a transformation towards open product architectures, and/or open competition. This perspective predicts or advocates revolutionary changes.

3.3 An evolutionary capability-building perspective

The third perspective is the dynamic capability or evolutionary perspective. The capability-evolution perspective of firms and management systems (a dynamic version of the resource-capability view) has attracted the increasing attention of researchers in the social sciences over the recent years (PENROSE 1959, NELSON & WINTER 1982, DOSI 1982, NONAKA 1985, CHANDLER 1990, TEECE ET AL. 1992, BOYER & FREYSSENET 1997, FUJIMOTO 1998, etc.), although the origin of this line of research may be traced back to the work of Schumpeter. By capability (or competence) we mean a stable pattern of firms' productive resources (in PENROSE's sense) and their activities which create interfirm differences in organizational performance (competitiveness in particular) and are hard to imitate by competitors.

In this view, it is assumed that (i) in the long run, business firms are able to adapt their organizational capabilities to the competitive environments, but that (ii) in the short run, such adaptations tend to be incomplete due to the 'sticky' nature of the resource-capability, bounded rationality of firms, and so on. In this way, the resource-capability evolution perception disagrees with the notion that firms are totally unable to adapt their system to the environment (i. e., the revolutionary paradigm-change perspective), but it also disagrees with the assumption that firms can perfectly and continuously adapt their system to the environment (i. e., the equilibrium perspective). In this sense, the capability-evolution position is a middle-road view between these two extremes.

The resource-capability evolution view also emphasizes the notion that 'history matters.' When a firm re-adapts its productive resources and capabilities to the changing environment, it does so by retaining and utilizing most of the existing systems, adding new elements of functions and structures, subtracting what has become obsolete, and regaining thus overall balance. However, the firm's ability to move, accelerate, slow down, and re-direct within such evolutionary processes is limited, hence the pattern of its resource-capability at any one point in time is at least partially constrained by that of the previous period (or even the initial conditions). In other words, system responses to environmental changes, according to this perspective, tend to be 'awkward' in that delayed adaptations and over-adaptations are rules rather than exceptions at least in the short run.

This evolutionary perspective seems to fit particularly well with those industries in which the pace of technological change and/or industrial transformation is neither very high nor very low.

4 A case of the capability evolution: Toyota and the Japanese auto industry

Since it is not possible here to present concrete examples for all the three basic modes characterized above, let me discuss an example of a typical *Case 1* industry—the automobile sector. My solution here is that of a 're-balancing' approach, which I call *lean-on-balance* system.

4.1 Toward a Lean-on-Balance system: A prescription for the automobile industry

The postwar Japanese auto industry continued to grow for nearly 40 years since the early 1950s, when the Japanese domestic motor vehicle production was less than 100K units per year only. Its domestic production in units became the world's largest by the early 1980s, peaking in 1990 with about 13.5 million units. This was the year when the *International Motor Vehicle Program* praised the high competitiveness of leading Japanese car makers by referring to the concept of the "lean production system" (WOMACK ET AL. 1990).

The Japanese auto industry however began to face a series of problems in the first half of the 1990s: Labour shortage became a critical issue around 1991; the post-*bubble* recession negatively affected Japanese domestic sales and profitability in 1992; a loss of cost competitiveness arose due to the continued appreciation of the yen, Western 'reverse catch-up' and continued trade frictions mainly with the USA. Exports of Japanese motor vehicles decreased dramatically after 1993 (production overseas increased accordingly). Taken together, the Japanese auto industry has been experiencing a transition period from the era of continuous growth to an era of fluctuation in domestic production volume, which will also be the basic pattern of competitive environments for the Japanese auto industry into the next century.

As these 40 years of continuous growth ended, certain problems of the growth-oriented system surfaced in the early 1990s. First, unlike their tenacious pursuit of customer satisfaction, employee satisfaction related to the direct productive work (if not with regard to human resource management in general) had not been explicitly pursued by the Japanese auto makers, resulting in an insufficient attractiveness of work places (assembly lines in particular), an increase in employee turnover ratios, and difficulties in recruiting young people as permanent workers.

Second, although the production, development, and procurement systems of the Japanese auto firms have remained 'lean' (efficient, quick and flexible) in the 1990s, certain inefficient (or fat) factors have also surfaced as Japanese competitive advantages diminished: fat product designs, fat plant designs, fat distribution systems, and so on.

To sum up, the growth-oriented system that the Japanese auto industry had built up until the 1980s created certain problems of imbalance, including an imbalance between employee and customer satisfaction, between lean elements and fat elements coexisting in the total system, as well as an imbalance between the ability to handle inter-firm competition, cooperation and conflicts. These problems already potentially existed in the 1980s but had not surfaced because of this continued growth. They were finally revealed as the growth era ended. Thus, what firms now need will be a balance-oriented system that nevertheless manages to maintain the strengths of the so-called lean system of the 1980s, hence a trend "from the lean-on-growth system to the lean-on-balance system" (FUJIMOTO 1994, FUJIMOTO &TAKEISHI 1994).

4.2 An example: the 'Fat Product Design' syndrome

The 'fat design' problem and firms' efforts toward a 'lean product design' are one of the most important aspects to alleviate the fat-lean imbalance mentioned above. 'Fat design' refers to a problem that the Japanese auto makers faced in the late 1980s to the early 1990s, including excessive levels of product variety and model change frequency, as well as too many model-specific parts, over-quality, and over-specification of their products.

Many researchers and practitioners in the Japanese auto industry have regarded 'fat design' as the main cause of overload for product engineers and erosion of their cost competitiveness since the beginning of 1990s. Accordingly, design simplification, or 'lean design', has turned out to be the most effective means for cost reduction. The lean production system needs to be accompanied by 'lean product design'.

In fact, the Japanese firms of the mid 1990s seem to be moving in this direction. For example, a major part of the cost reduction at Toyota and other Japanese auto makers in 1993 to 1994 was based on design simplification, as opposed to a reduction of overhead, reduction of capital investment, or *kaizen* activities. Thus, by the mid 1990s, 'lean product design', or design simplification, has in fact become a main source of cost reduction for the Japanese auto makers struggling to regain their cost competitiveness.

However, there have already been some cases in which excessive simplification of new models apparently resulted in a loss of product integrity, lack of product differentiation, perceived deterioration of design quality, etc., leading to customer dissatisfaction and thus losses in market share, despite the products' competitive prices. This seems to indicate that lean designs actually involve a subtle balancing act, and that there is always a risk of overshooting into the opposite direction, i. e., over-simplification of product design.

What has made this challenge of design simplification more difficult to cope with has been, as pointed out before, the fact that consumers' expectations concerning product integrity (i. e., total product quality) and fundamental (not superficial) variety have not vanished, as the evolutionary view predicts. Once consumers experience a product of high product integrity and design quality, for example, they tend to set their reference points based on these products. Thus, while consumers' expectations regarding a product's price tend to fluctuate as their budget constraints change between booms and recessions, their expectations about total product quality tend to stay at this high level even after the boom period is over. In summary, one of the most powerful prescriptions for the Japanese auto makers to overcome their problems of the mid 1990s is 'lean design'.

4.3 Interpretation: An evolutionary view

Now, how can we interpret what has just been described—the fat design syndrome of the early 1990s? Without getting into details, we can apply the three basic perspectives discussed earlier and examine three different hypotheses: 'adaptation to the *bubble* environment', 'mis-adaptation to the post-growth environment,' and 'over-adaptation to variety and integrity.'

Table 1: Three hypotheses and perspectives on 'Fat Product Design'

Hypothesis	Perspective	Assumptions about the firm	Interpretation of the environment		
1 Adaptation to the *bubble* environment	Equilibrium	Firms can re-adapt resources/capabilities instantly/constantly	Late 1980s Mid 1990s	= =	abnormal (bubbly demand) back to normal
2 Mis-adaptation to the 'post-growth' environment	Paradigm-change (revolution)	Firms cannot re-adapt resources/capabilities; they can only replace them altogether	Late 1980s Early 1990s	= =	end of growth-proliferation era start of post-growth era (variety is no longer emphasized)
3 Over-adaptation to variety and integrity	Resource-capability (evolution)	Firms can re-adapt resources/capabilities, but only in the long run	Late 1980s Early 1990s	= =	variety and integrity emphasized still emphasized (customers' evolution continues)

While all these hypotheses seem to be able to tell at least part of the story in a complementary manner, my judgment is that the third 'over-adaptation' hypothesis is the most consistent with the above description (for further details, see FUJIMOTO 1997a).

For example, the most effective prescription to the 'fat design' problem seems to be neither a simple matter of 'going back to normal' as the 'adaptation to the *bubble*'-hypothesis would prescribe, nor 'changing everything', as the 'mis-adaptation to the post-growth'-hypothesis would propose. A more subtle balance was needed as the firms have had to simplify their product design without sacrificing the fundamental product differentiation and product integrity—the 'over-adaptation'-hypothesis based on an evolutionary perspective.

The 'over-adaptation'-hypothesis, just like the 'mis-adaptation'-hypothesis, analyses the 'fat design' syndrome as a long-term problem related to the limits of the growth-oriented system. Unlike the latter, however, the 'over-adaptation'-hypothesis does not reject all the capabilities of the 1980s as totally obsolete. Instead, it argues that the set of product development capabilities that the Japanese auto makers had accumulated up to the 1980s (e. g., variety expansion, frequent model changes, unique parts design, a high level of quality and flexibility, etc.) are still contributing to corporate competitive advantage in the 1990s because the market needs that emphasize fundamental product variety and integrity still continue to exist despite the end of the growth era. That is, whereas the 'mis-adaptation'-hypothesis emphasizes discontinuity between the 1980s and the 1990s, the 'over-adaptation'-hypothesis recognizes continuity in terms of variety, uncertainty, change, and sophistication of the customer needs (CLARK & FUJIMOTO 1991): While the era of growth has ended, the era of variety and integrity continues. The real problem has been, according to this view, that some firms had accumulated and utilized the very capabilities that contributed to their competitive advantages excessively, so that certain side effects surfaced.

Why does such *overshooting* happen? This hypothesis argues that there is a certain process by which those firms with relatively high dynamic capabilities tend to over-accumulate or over-use these organizational capabilities. Business firms compete not only on price over the short run but also by capability building in the long run. Under intense pressure of dynamic competition, a firm tends to accelerate its efforts to outperform its rivals in the race for capability building. The firm, however, knows in advance neither the level of its competitors' capabilities, nor the optimal level of the capabilities that the market calls for in the end. As a result, those firms which manage to outpace the others in this capability-building race also tend to suffer from side effects of over-adaptation. We will analyse this dynamic process of overshooting in further detail in the next section.

In summary, all of the three perspectives described above seem to be able to explain at least part of the 'fat design' phenomenon. The *bubble economy*, the post-growth transformation, and the overshooting—all appear to have influenced the 'fat design' syndrome. However, here we focus on the third interpretation, the 'over-adaptation'-hypothesis backed by the resource-capability evolution perspective.

The 'adaptation to the *bubble*'-hypothesis certainly explains part of the story, but it fails to distinguish between a long-term market evolution toward higher variety and sophistication of customer needs on the one hand, and a short-term deviation from the regular evolutionary path (i. e., a *bubble*) on the other hand, generally overlooking the former effect. As a result, this view tends to over-emphasize the negative impact of the *bubble* market, simply rejecting 'fat design' as something abnormal. The actual process described earlier appears to be more complicated and dynamic though. Hence, this interpretation cannot explain either why the tendency of the Japanese firms toward higher variety and frequent changes existed prior to the *bubble* era.

The 'mis-adaptation to the post-growth'-hypothesis is also persuasive in certain aspects, particularly in that it interprets the 'fat design' syndrome in a broader and long-term context of the 'limits of the growth-oriented system' in the post-growth era. The end of continuous growth was certainly an important factor that triggered this problem. The sharp dichotomy however between the growth and post-growth system that this interpretation argues for may be problematic. Such a black-or-white view may be too extreme and too simplistic to explain the complexity of the phenomenon in question. This view, for example, cannot explain why the Western auto firms are still trying to catch up with the Japanese firms in terms of both performance and capability even in the mid 1990s (CLARK & FUJIMOTO 1994, ELLISON ET AL. 1995, FUJIMOTO 1997b). This fact, discussed later on, indicates that most of the capabilities of the Japanese auto makers of the 1980s are still not obsolete in the arena of international competition, and that any hypothesis that the Japanese system of the 1980s has become totally invalid cannot be accepted.

Thus, the over-adaptation hypothesis seems to be most relevant for explaining the apparently complex process through which 'fat product' design emerged.

5 Evolutionary capability: A key for dynamic competition in the 'Case 1' industry?

If a pattern of industrial evolution follows 'case' or 'type 1' (e. g., the automobile), with stable and integral product architecture, international competition, and the Japanese firms thus having enjoyed competitiveness throughout the 1980s, what is the necessary competence that these companies need to possess in order to cope with the external shocks and crises in the 1990s and beyond? My argument is that a certain dynamic capability of capability-building, which I call *evolutionary capability,* is the key for survival and growth where the pattern of industrial evolution is emergent and multi-path (the following section is based on the discussion in FUJIMOTO 1998).

In recent years, I have explored evolutionary patterns of the manufacturing-development system of the Japanese auto makers, Toyota in particular (FUJIMOTO 1995, 1998). The present chapter can be regarded as an extension of this historical analysis, which was motivated by the following basic observations:

- Many of the capabilities were gradually acquired by the competing firms throughout the postwar period, particularly between the 1950s and 1970s. There were apparently no grand strategies regarding the sequence of capability acquisition. This was instead a long-term evolutionary process.
- Some aspects of the capabilities of the effective development-production systems could be found at all the Japanese manufacturers. Certain others of these aspects were found only with specific manufacturers known for their high competitive performance, typically Toyota. Still other aspects of the system were generic, or common for automobile mass-producers worldwide, in that they all had introduced some elements of the standard Fordist system directly or indirectly.

In order to analyse the evolutionary dynamics of this system, the author has classified patterns of systemic changes into several types (graph 2): (1) random trials (pure chance); (2) rational calculation (an organization deliberately chooses a new course of action that satisfies or maximizes its objective function by examining a feasible set of alternatives based on its understanding of environmental constraints and capability limits); (3) environmental constraints (an organization detects constraints imposed by objective or perceived environments, and voluntarily prohibits certain sets of actions); (4) entrepreneurial vision (a desirable set of activities is directly chosen by entrepreneurs within the organization based on their visions without much analysis of organizational capabilities and constraints); (5) knowledge transfer (a certain pattern is transferred from another organization, inside or outside of the industry, to the one in question).

Historical analyses of some major components of the system, based on the above framework, have revealed that the development-production capability of competitive Japanese auto makers gradually emerged as a result of complex interactions of entrepreneurial visions, historical imperatives, inter-firm and inter-industrial transfers of resources and practices, pure chance, as well as the firms' own evolutionary capability. These studies have clarified that the Toyota-style manufacturing system of the 1980s was formed not just by *ex ante* rational decision making by the founders-entrepreneurs of these companies, although the resulting system may have been *ex post* rational. Table 2 indicates the complexity of the dynamics in the selected cases. Some of the findings of the studies are summarized as follows (see FUJIMOTO 1998 for details):

Historical imperatives by forced growth and flexibility

Some of the region-specific imperatives that all the Japanese firms faced during the postwar era almost 'forced' them to make certain responses, some of which turned out to be contributing to the building-up of the competitive advantages of these firms. Many such responses were not recognized as competitive weapons when the firms first adopted them. Likewise, the imperative of forced flexibility in the given fragmented market also benefited the Japanese firms. This was partly due to the region-specific patterns of indus-

Graph 2: Generic paths of system emergence

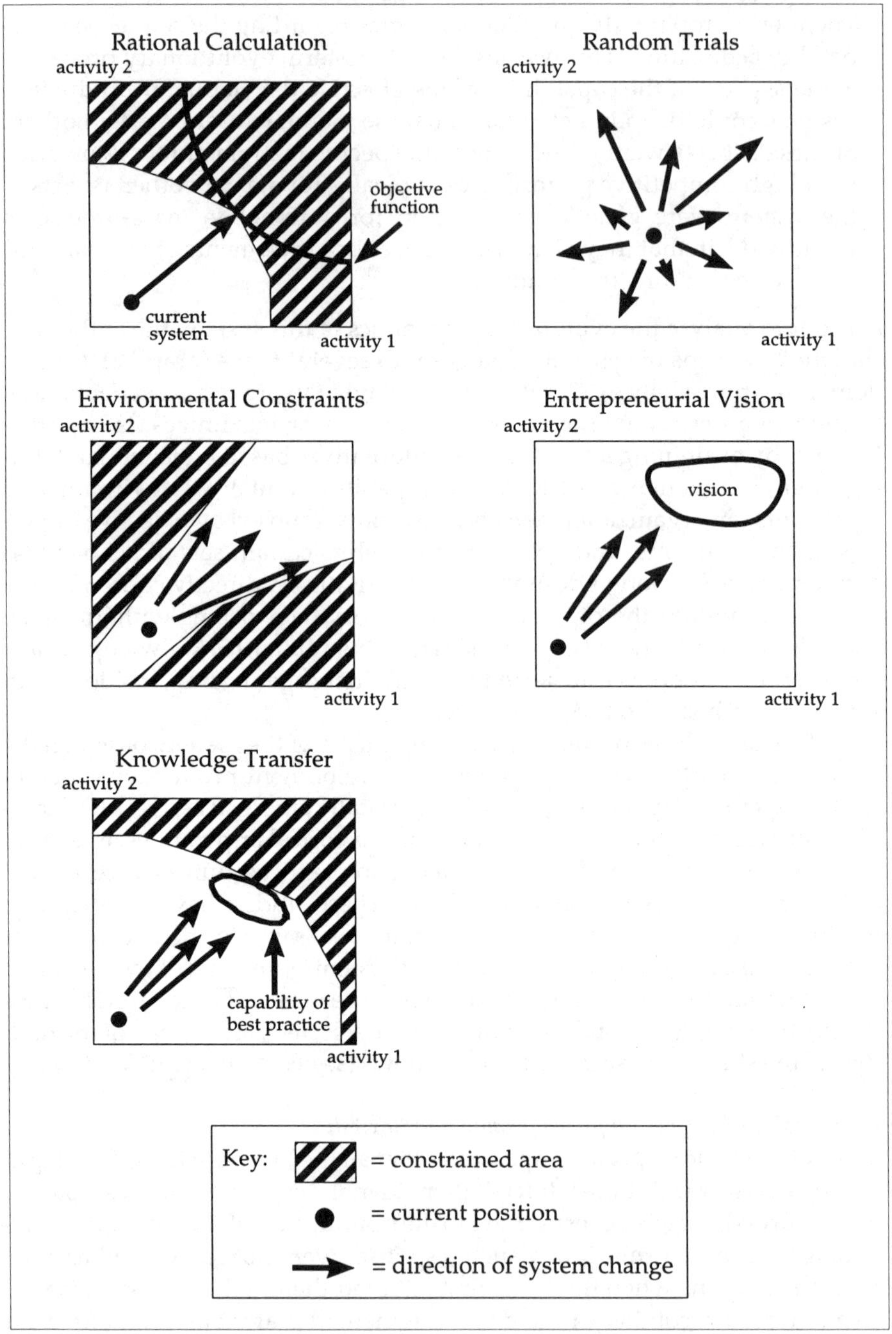

Source: FUJIMOTO (1995, 1998)

trial growth, i. e., a rapid production growth accompanied by swift product proliferation. The flexibility that firms acquired tended to be recognized as a necessary evil to cope with the fragmented market, rather than a measure for international competition, when the capabilities were first developed.

Benefits of historical imperatives by lack of technology
While an excessive use of high-tech automation equipment often became even an obstacle for productivity improvement, leading Japanese makers apparently avoided such problems. This may partly have been because they consciously rejected the temptation for over-specialization, but it also seems to have been a result of high technology being unavailable in the first place. To the extent that this was caused by certain region-specific technology gaps, this lack of technology may have brought about some unintended competitive benefits to firms of this region.

Knowledge transfer from Ford
Toyota's capability building was consistently motivated, since the 1930s, by perceived competitive pressures from the US mass producers, particularly Ford. Even with the strongly protected domestic market between the 1930s and 1950s, Toyota's consciousness of the imaginary competitive pressures persisted. Motivated partly by this consciousness concerning the international competition, Toyota adopted many elements of the Ford system and the American mass production system mostly indirectly, including moving conveyers, transfer machines, product and component designs, the Taylor system, supervisor training programmes, and statistical quality control. A pure dichotomy between the Ford system and the Toyota system as a 'post-Ford paradigm' is therefore misleading.

Transfer from other industries
Some of the linkages to other industries, which were technologically advanced in the past, may be firm-specific. For example, Toyota's inherent connection with the textile sector may have facilitated a knowledge transfer from there (particularly through Taiichi Ōno), contributing to its competitive advantages in production control techniques.

Unintended transfer
As in the case of engineers from the prewar aircraft industry, who were pushed into the auto sector as the former collapsed after the war, a knowledge transfer, which the receivers did not intend or induce, brought about a rapid development in automobile technologies and product development systems in postwar Japan.

Incomplete transfer
Although the Japanese auto firms tried to adopt many of the practices and techniques from the US mass producers (i. e., Ford system), some of these

transfers were incomplete due to the historical imperatives mentioned above and a lack of firms' absorption capacities. In this sense, the *kanban* system may be regarded as an incomplete version of the conveyer system, the U-shaped machine layout as an incomplete transfer machine, and *jidōka* as incomplete adaptive automation. The very incompleteness of these transfers may have facilitated their subsequent diffusion to the entire system. For example, the case of the *kanban* system may be regarded as a complete diffusion of an incomplete synchronization technology.

Self-fulfilling visions
Firm-specific entrepreneurial visions sometimes played an important role in building distinctive development-production capability. This was particularly the case when an apparently unrealistic vision, going against any common sense, triggered self-fulfilling efforts for achieving the bold objectives. Kiichirō Toyoda in the 1930s and 1940s played a pivotal role in this sense by advocating cost reduction without economies of scale, catch-up with Ford, and a just-in-time philosophy.

Ex-post dynamic capability
Even when none of the firms recognized the potential competitive advantage of the new system when first experimenting with it, some of them managed to create firm-specific competitive advantages by exercising post-trial capabilities: recognizing the potential competitive advantage of the new system, modifying it to exploit the given potential, institutionalizing and retaining it until the advantages were realized. For example, even though all the Japanese auto makers faced similar environmental pressures for adopting the black box parts system in the 1960s, only Toyota appears to have created a system that could fully exploit the potential advantages of this practice. Although all the Japanese auto makers accepted aircraft engineers after the war, Toyota was the only company that institutionalized the heavy-weight product manager system that had been prevalent in the aircraft industry. Thus, even when all the Japanese firms commonly faced certain historical imperatives that facilitated new practices, only some of them appear to have materialized this potential by employing firm-specific evolutionary capabilities.

In summary, an intertwined combination of the logic of system emergence, including historical imperatives, knowledge transfers, entrepreneurial vision and post-trial capabilities, appears capable of explaining why firm-specific, region-specific and universally adopted capabilities coexisted, as well as how they emerged within the effective product development and production systems in the Japanese auto industry of the 1980s. As for Toyota's firm-specific capabilities, this historical analysis has led the author to infer that Toyota's distinctive capabilities have included not only static ones, as documented in the existing literature, but also a dynamic one. Furthermore,

Table 2: Summary of evolution of selected production-development capabilities

	Just-in-Time	Multi Tasking with Product-Focus Layout	*Jidōka* and Flexible Equipment	*Kaizen* and TQC	Black Box Parts	Heavy-weight Product Manager
competitive effect (rationality)	creating pressure for productivity improvement throughput time inventory cost	productivity improvement	pressures for quality improvement flexibility	quality improvement productivity improvement	cost reduction by manufacturability development lead time and productivity	high product integrity development lead time and productivity
entrepreneurial vision	Kiichirō Toyoda, 1930s ("just-in-time" slogan) Taiichi Ōno, 1940s–50s (system building)	Kiichirō Toyoda, 1945 (a vision of rapid productivity catch-up without economy of scale)	Kiichirō Toyoda, 1931 (a vision of high productivity with small volume production)			
transfer from other industry	textile (bench marking of Nichibō) prewar aircraft production	textile: multi-machine operation in spinning (through Ōno)	textile: Sakichi Toyoda's automatic loom	TQC was established in other industries (e. g., process industry)	prewar locomotive or aircraft parts supplier	prewar aircraft industry (chief designer system) forced transfer (collapse of aircraft industry)
transfer from Ford system	the synchronization idea from Ford (invisible conveyer line) *Kanban* as "incomplete synchronization"	productivity bench force after the 1950 strikes modified Taylorism	adoption of Detroit-type automation where feasible U-shape layout as "incomplete transfer machine"	suggestion system from Ford Training-within-industry Statistical quality control		
imperative of forced growth with resource shortage		limit of permanent work force after the 1950 strikes "forced" productivity increase in the 1960s	shortage of investment fund: low cost automation had to be pursued	shortage of supervisors replacing craftsmen-foremen = needs for TWI	high production growth and model proliferation created pressures for subcontracting subassembly and design	
imperative of forced flexibility with small and fragmented market			"forced" flexibility of equipment due to small volume		product proliferation of the 1960s created pressures for subcontracting out design jobs	product proliferation with limited engineering resource created pressure for compact projects
imperative of shortage of technology	lack of computer production control technology in the 1950s and 60s		lack of adaptive control automation: *Jidōka* needs human intervention		lack of electric parts technology at Toyota in 1949 (separation of Nippon Densō)	
ex-post capability of the firm		flexible task assignment and flexible revision of work standards to better exploit opportunities of productivity increase		Toyota maintained momentum for TQC by creating organizations for diffusing it to suppliers	Toyota institutionalized a version of black box parts system that could better exploit competitive advantages	Only Toyota adopted heavy-weight product manager system from the aircraft industry as early as 1950s

the above analysis indicates that the company's dynamic capability has included not only a competence for performing *ex ante* rational problem solving in a linear manner (e. g., continuous improvements through Total Quality Management) but also a competence for managing ill-structured problem solving, emergent strategies, or the complex processes of system evolution. The author has labelled this latter ability the evolutionary capability, or *capability of capability building*.

My argument, based on the foregoing historical analysis, is that as long as the pattern of industrial evolution continues to be an emergent one in the above given sense, the evolutionary capability that companies such as Toyota have possessed for years may still continue to be the key for long-term success in the future.

6 Implication: A contingency view

Does the Japanese Management System need revolutionary change, evolutionary change, or just incremental adaptations toward the 21st century? The answer seems to depend on the nature of the industries in question in terms of *types of competition* (e. g., intra-architectural vs. inter-architectural, price vs. capability-building), *international competitiveness* for each type of competition (e. g., heavily regulated domestic sectors vs. internationally competent sectors), types of *product architecture* (e. g., open interface vs. closed interface), and so on. In some areas, a drastic re-alignment of firms' capability sets may be necessary; in other sectors, evolutionary adaptation to the new environments may be demanded.

Overall, the Japanese industry should be neither overly optimistic nor pessimistic. What is needed is a sector-by-sector contingency view, a long-term historical perspective, and a careful interpretation of the current dynamics.

References

BOYER, R. and M. FREYSSENET (1995): The Emergence of New Industrial Models. In: *Actes du GERPISA* (Université d'Evry-Val d'Essonne) 15, pp. 75–142.

CHANDLER, A. D. Jr. (1990): *Scale and Scope: The Dynamics of Industrial Competition*. Cambridge: Harvard University Press.

CLARK, K. B. and T. FUJIMOTO (1991): *Product Development Performance*. Boston: Harvard Business School Press.

CLARK, K. B. and T. FUJIMOTO (1994): The Product Development Imperative: Competing in the New Industrial Marathon. In: DUFFY, P. B. (ed.): *The Relevance of a Decade*. Boston: Harvard Business School Press, pp. 287–322.

DOSI, G. (1982): Technological Paradigms and Technological Trajectories. In: *Research Policy* 11, pp. 147–162.

ELLISON, D. J., K. B. CLARK, T. FUJIMOTO and Y. HYUN (1995): *Product Development Performance in the Auto Industry: 1990s Update*. Harvard Business School Working Paper 95–066.

FUJIMOTO, T. (1994): The Limits of Lean Production. In: *Politik und Gesellschaft* (Friedrich-Ebert-Stiftung, Germany), January, pp. 40–46.

FUJIMOTO, T. (1995): A Note on the Origin of the 'Black Box Parts' Practice in the Japanese Motor Vehicle Industry. In: SHIOMI, H. and K. WADA (eds.): *Fordism Transformed*. Oxford: Oxford University Press, pp. 184–216.

FUJIMOTO, T. (1997a): Capability Building and Over-Adaptation—A Case of 'Fat Design' in the Japanese Auto Industry. In: *Actes du GERPISA* (Université d'Evry-Val d'Essonne) 19, pp. 9–23.

FUJIMOTO, T. (1997b): The Dynamic Aspect of Product Development Capabilities: An International Comparison in the Automobile Industry. In: GOTŌ, A. and H. ODAGIRI (eds.): *Innovation in Japan*. Oxford: Oxford University Press, pp. 57–99.

FUJIMOTO, T. (1998): Reinterpreting the Resource-Capability View of the Firm: A Case of the Development-Production Systems of the Japanese Auto Makers. In: CHANDLER, A. D. ET AL. (eds.): *The Dynamic Firm*. Oxford: Oxford University Press, pp. 15–44.

FUJIMOTO, T. and A. TAKEISHI (1994): *Jidōsha sangyō 21-seiki e no shinario* [The Automobile Industry: A Scenario toward the 21st Century]. Tōkyō: Seisansei Shuppan.

KUHN, T. B. (1970): *Structure of Scientific Revolutions*. Chicago: University of Chicago Press.

NELSON, R. R. and S. G. WINTER (1982): *An Evolutionary Theory of Economic Change*. Cambridge, Mass.: Harvard University Press.

NONAKA, I. (1985): *Kigyō shinkaron* [The Theory of Corporate Evolution]. Tōkyō: Nihon Keizai Shinbunsha.

PENROSE, E. T. (1959): *The Theory of the Growth of the Firm*. Oxford: Basil Blackwell.

TEECE, D. J., G. PISANO and A. SHUEN (1992): *Dynamic Capabilities and Strategic Management*. University of California at Berkeley Working Paper.

WOMACK, J., D. T. JONES and D. ROOS (1990): *The Machine that Changed the World*. New York: Rawson Associates.

XVI Will Japanese and French "Exceptionalisms" Vanish? The Convergence Hypothesis Reconsidered

Robert BOYER

1 Rise and demise of the 'Japanese' management model: Myth and reality

One decade ago Japan was generally perceived as a model to be emulated both in terms of production methods (WOMACK, JONES and ROOS 1990) and labour management systems (KOIKE 1981, AOKI 1988, BROWN, REICH and STERN 1990). Economic performance was assumed to be closely related to lean production and the implementation of a high-skill, high-wage, high- productivity labour strategy. At the end of the 1980s, even Europe was expected to have recovered from its 'Eurosclerosis', due to the stimulus resulting from the completion of the Single Market.

Nowadays a rather different mood prevails. On one side, the seemingly endless boom in North America has brought about a lot of optimism about the future of the United States, which enjoys a very low unemployment rate and a revival of innovation in its high-tech sectors. On the other side, by contrast, Europe is facing slow and uncertain growth, and a lack of dynamism in terms of innovation and new products, consequently suffering from an unemployment rate unprecedented since the 1930s. The launching of the Euro has created some optimism only recently.

Japan is experiencing a similar episode: since the bursting of the financial *bubble*, the economy has not recovered and unemployment remains notably high (4.1 % in May 1998) for Japanese standards. Labour hoarding continues to be important, while profits and investments are still sluggish. This surprising change from the 1980s to the 1990s calls for some explanation.

- The crucial role of the macroeconomic context has to be taken into account (NOMURA 1997: 1–2). From a purely objective point of view, when the real exchange rate rises, eroding first price competitiveness and then competitiveness linked to quality, service and innovation, it becomes more and more difficult for the national management style—and more generally the domestic economic institutions—to cope with such a structural imbalance. In a sense, there always exists a strong tendency for the macroeconomic imbalance to push a given managerial system out of its zone of structural stability.

Graph 1: The role of macroeconomic evolution in the assessment of national institutions

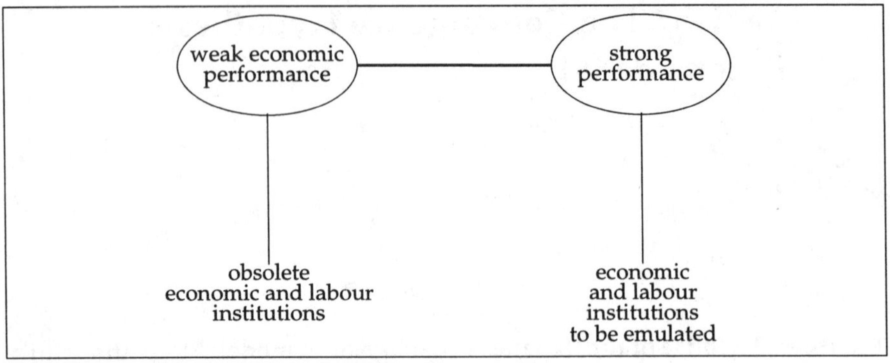

Graph 2: Convergence toward a market-led capitalism?

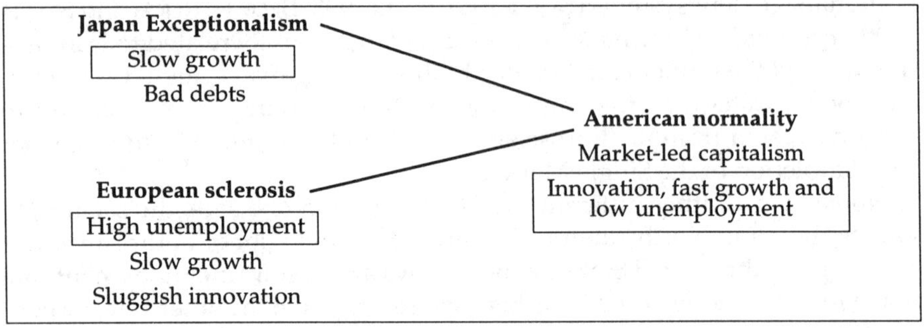

- However, the macroeconomic evolutions exert a more hidden influence on the legitimacy and perceived efficiency of domestic financial and economic institutions. When the economy is booming, any institution, however imperfect, appears relatively convenient, even efficient. On the contrary, when a severe recession sets in and a period of stagnation unfolds, firms, politicians, citizens, and unionists tend to reassess the relevance of domestic institutions. In such a case, they usually arrive at a negative assessment, since they are tempted to attribute to the functioning of existing institutions imbalances which initially took place in the international sphere or which are the results of distant structural changes. Paradoxically, many analysts do assume—at least implicitly—a kind of complementarity between macroeconomic performance and the efficiency of domestic institutions (graph 1).
- Both, the interpretations of the 1980s (rosy optimism about Japan) and the 1990s (gloomy pessimism about the future), finally share a common theoretical background. During the first period, analysts were convinced of the 'Japanization of the world' as they believed that the productive system of

Japan was overwhelmingly superior. A decade later, the same analysts or their followers forecast an 'Americanization' of the Japanese management style, since they are now convinced that the American market-led system is, after all, superior to any other. In both cases finally, the common hypothesis is that globalization implies not only the convergence of key macroeconomic variables, such as the rate of return on capital, but also of the institutional and organizational architecture (graph 2).

Therefore, the very same methods and features which used to be praised by foreign experts are now blamed as the cause for the long stagnation of growth, productivity and real wages (OECD 1995: 13, OECD 1997: 9). The common view now seems to be: the Japanese and European *exceptionalisms* are at the very origin of their poor macroeconomic performance. Consequently, national institutions should be reformed in order to converge towards the American-style organization and labour management (graph 2). This book does not follow this track. Quite to the contrary, while most authors recognize the structural transformations which are taking place in Japan, they do not conclude that the specificity of the Japanese labour institutions is necessarily over. Let us review and discuss the various arguments put forward by the authors.

2 Understanding the logic behind the Japanese wage-labour nexus

A basic interpretation of the obstacles to a Japanese recovery runs as follows: if true labour market adjustments were operating, a smooth and efficient reallocation of the work force into 'sunrise' sectors and newly created firms would be observed; thus the current difficulties originate from archaic and inefficient labour practices and management styles. The faster the convergence toward Anglo-American practices, the firmer the innovation and growth. According to this view, there exists a single-best way in the management of firms and labour institutions.

To verify this hypothesis one has to investigate if there really is no inherent logic at all behind the Japanese Human Resource Management (HRM) or, if there is one, why this logic is largely different from the North American or even European ones. Here France is taken as an example of a non-American wage-labour nexus.

In Japan, the key actor is the large company organizing a strong competition among wage earners, since their commitment and competence enhancement are crucial factors for promotion inside the internal labour market or, more exactly, along the career ladders (TACHIBANAKI 1996: 147, Nohara in this volume). Contrary to typical Fordism, blue and white collar workers receive similar types of labour contract, though carrying a more significant premium for length of service attributed to engineers and managers than to typical manual workers. This is a strong difference between France and Japan (Nohara). Within the large firm, internal mobility is the rule and external mobility the tool of last resort, when all other means have been exhausted over the course of a long and severe recession. Again by contrast, the number of workers is much more frequently varied in Fordist regimes, be it in the US or in France.

Similarly, each Japanese firm appears to have elaborated a highly idiosyncratic pay system, with an unequal weight given to cost of living adjustments, length of service, competence, profit sharing, etc., at least in the manufacturing sector though not necessarily for services such as the retailing sector (Ribault, in this volume). The full spectrum of practices can be labelled as *nenkō* (seniority)-based pay. In any case, these systems are in sharp opposition to the conventional Fordist collective agreements, which used to determine wages according to a precise hierarchy, more or less in relation with the level of education and the opposition between white and blue collar workers. France is an excellent example of such a configuration (table 1).

In this country, the State organizes both demand and supply as well as their interaction across a highly organized and institutionalized 'labour market'. In France, State regulations play a crucial role in the design and the cohesiveness of the industrial relations systems, whereas in Japan, the same impulse is provided by the large companies (AMABLE, BARRE and BOYER 1997: 203, 210, 214).

Furthermore, the Japanese system is characterized by a large and somehow functional *heterogeneity* of the wage-labour nexus (Ribault). This is an antidote to a recurring opposition in the analyses of the Japanese labour institutions:

- On one side some scholars (frequently foreign ones) overemphasize the role of the *keiretsu* and the large firms and tend to extrapolate this very specific labour contract to the whole labour force.
- On the other side, other experts point out that more than 70 %, nowadays even 80 %, of workers do not enjoy this status and that at the bottom of the hierarchy the labour conditions are rather different (lower wages, minimal welfare benefits, larger fluctuation in terms of work hours and income).

These two traits do belong to the same picture, since they define a complete and rather *coherent architecture*, through the differentiation and the ranking of a series of wage-labour contracts (EBIZUKA, UEMURA and ISOGAI 1997). Therefore, the "flexible rigidities" (DORE 1986) of the company-ist wage-labour nexus (YAMADA 1996) are complemented by the external and internal flexibility provided both by subcontractors in the manufacturing sectors and a subtle complementarity of part-time, small jobs of various kinds in the service sectors (Ribault).

Thus, it would be misleading to analyse the Japanese employment system as a mere, but drastic, imperfection of the American system for HRM, since the Japanese case displays a complete set of interdependent and coherent institutions, labour contracts, and incentives, promoting dynamic efficiency, as opposed to a conventional static efficiency, typical for the external flexibility prevailing in the Anglo-Saxon world (CAROLI 1995). The French configuration is an exception to the American model, as well, though still different from the Japanese one. Both, however, the French and the Japanese model have exhibited some efficiency and cohesiveness at least until the early 1990s.

Table 1: The wage-labour nexus in Japan and France compared: Strong structural differences

Components	Japan	France	Similarity	Dissimilarity
1. Work organization	Built upon competence enhancement via job mobility	Still strong job demarcation No career for blue collar workers		X
2. Social stratification within the firm	Similar career for blue and white collars	Clear dividing line between blue and white collars		X
3. Unions	Enterprise unions, but synchronized wage negotiations	National or sectorial unions, very weak at the firm level		X
4. Adjustments of hours/employment	• Hours are easily adapted • Significant internal and organized mobility	• Conventional or legal barriers to work time variations • External mobility, controlled or monitored by the Ministry of Labour		X X
5. Direct wage formation • individual • average	• *Nenkō*-based pay (length of service and experience) • High sensitivity to short-run disequilibria	• Workers are paid according to diploma, job classification and collective agreements • Moderate and sluggish response to short-run evolution		X X
6. Welfare	• Few universal benefits • Company centred welfare, large heterogeneity	• Large and highly institutionalized welfare system • Limited heterogeneity		X

Why do they differ so much? Basically because the contemporary employment systems are the outcome of a long industrial relations history and the co-evolution of social struggles, labour laws, economic specialization, and innovation systems. This strong differentiation of national trajectories is demonstrated by the short historical retrospect of the formation of unions in

Japan, and is confirmed by a larger international comparison (BOYER 1995: 548–549).

Each labour system displays both certain strengths and weaknesses and cannot evolve according to any universal criteria of economic efficiency. Instead, it is part of a larger institutional system, which needs to be but *viable* in the international competition, given the possible compensating factors associated to the real exchange rate, the credit regime, the innovation system, and so forth. This is a rather general result derived from institutional economics (NORTH 1990). However, this does not mean that a national system is bound to last forever: quite to the contrary, both in France and in Japan "the foundations of yesterday's success have become the source of today's impasse" (Nohara, p. 243).

3 Perceptions and challenges: Japan and France share some common features

The Japanese and French economies have been catching up to American international productivity levels following their distinct institutional forms, as recalled earlier for the wage-labour nexus (table 1). For abouta decade now, however, a comparable mutual *dissatisfaction* has emerged concerning the desirability and viability of the institutional architecture inherited from the second World War (table 2). So many changes have taken place in the political sphere, the financial system, international competition, technological paradigms, etc. that past capital-labour agreements and wage earner stratifications now appear obsolete to many managers, politicians, and civil servants.

It is important to recognize that these doubts about the viabilityof the Japanese employment system are, of course, internal: the question is how to cope with the unbalances inherited from—and exhibited by—the *bubble* years? However, external pressures are shaping the Japanese enterprise system (JES) as well. Will the JES be able to resist the structural transformations of its institutional forms, under pressure from current financial innovations and foreign competition?

Both in Japan and France, many doubts are expressed about the distinctiveness of the respective national institutions, and certain scholars forecast that the end of Japanese and French exceptionalism is a necessary condition for a recovery and the entering into a new growth era, propelled by information technologies and globalization. Similarly, public opinion seems to have lost any confidence in the ability of the authorities to monitor industrial and technological restructuring, which instead is to be left to market forces and private initiative.

These demands represent a major change with respect to the past distrust of the Japanese and French elites concerning the role of markets! Another source of change is brought about by financial deregulation and innovations: the Japanese (and to some extent French) banks have not yet totally resolved their bad-debt problems inherited from the speculation on real estate markets and the excessive risks taken in the new world of internationalized and deregulated finance (SAUTTER 1996, GEOFFRON & RUBINSTEIN 1996). The pressures directed at the recovery of profitability of banks (Japan) and industrial firms (France) are clearly exerting a negative influence upon the viability of past capital-labour contracts in both countries.

Table 2: The evolution during the 1990s: Clear similarities regarding structural shocks and representations

Sphere	Japan	France	Similarities	Disimilarities
General mood of public opinion	• Serious doubts about the "Japaneseness"	• Doubts about the legitimacy and efficiency of the French exceptionalism	X	
Power structure	• Loss of public trust for MITI and Ministry of Finance • More pressures from the US and Europe	• General doubts about the power and relevance of the politicians and civil servants • More European regulations	X	
Finance	• Large losses of the *jūsen* and banks after the bursting of the *bubble*	• Nationalized banks incur severe losses after the collapse of the housing *bubble*	X	
International trade	• Over-evaluation and then decline of the exchange rate with respect to the $	• Strong Franc linked to DM, thus an over-evaluation with respect to the $	X	
System of innovation	• The institutions which have promoted the catching-up process cannot cope with innovation at the technological frontier	• A State-led innovation regime is challenged by deregulation, European integration and globalization	X	
Conception of the labour market institutions	• Some companies are lured by the "American style" for HMR	• The job creating American machine is secretly and then openly admired	X	

The national policies and the evolution observed within the international system, both have resulted in a rather prolonged period of overvaluation of the yen and French franc with respect to the dollar. Thus, employment in the sectors exposed to international competition is being challenged in the mid-1990s, which is especially important in Japan, while the de-industrialization process in France already began in the early 1980s. Other structural changes are affecting the post-WWII Japanese and French employment systems as well: In each country, the very institutions which had promoted the rather impressive catching-up process (the so-called Japanese and French 'miracles') are now perceived to be barriers and disincentives to the re-deployment of firms toward the technological frontiers (AMABLE, BARRE and BOYER 1997: 307–312).

More precisely, the shift towards a productive paradigm centred upon new products, permanent innovation, and constant quality enhancement, in the context of over-capacity at the global level, challenges the past configuration of the wage-labour nexus both in Japan and in France. On one side, inhouse training and internal wage careers may not be sufficient any longer to nurture the talents required to invent new products and processes at the technological frontiers, a critique frequently directed at the Japanese configuration. On the other side, the overwhelming role of the State in basic and applied research, in the financing of innovation, in infrastructure development and even within the competitive manufacturing sector is traditionally blamed for explaining the delay of the French economy in mastering the technologies for the next century. In each case, the wage-labour nexus appears to be in need of a redefinition, either marginally or more structurally.

4 Just-in-time production in Japan, just-in-time employment in France?

Thus, in comparison with North America, Japan and France have been confronting similar shocks and challenges, though the reactions of their firms and wage earners have been rather dissimilar indeed (table 3). In both countries, a first response has been to reduce overtime and temporary contracts. As the recession has lingered on, however, the labour management tools applied have begun to differ greatly. Whereas in Japan, a significant internal labour mobility is being organized within the firm (for example, employee transfers from production to sales), within the *keiretsu* or towards certain subcontractors, in France compulsory redundancy is a major device in order to adapt employment to production. Paradoxically, *just-in-time employment* is much more frequent in France than just-in-time (JIT) production, in contrast to Japan where "the principle of JIT-production is not linked to JIT-employment" (NOMURA 1997: 13).

These diverging trajectories are reinforced by a labour deregulation enacted in France in 1986, which has abolished the need for the Ministry of Labour's consent prior to any worker lay-offs by firms. Conversely, with the long recession of the 1990s, the specific features of the Japanese wage-labour nexus have been strengthened: "The result of the post-*bubble* recession has been a return to Japanese normalcy and the traditional focus on regular male employees" (NOMURA 1997: 13). In France, over the last decade, the proportion of atypical labour contracts has increased; this development is in accordance with the modelling of segmented labour markets under conditions of increasing economic uncertainty. In Japan, however and quite on the contrary, these types of contracts have been reduced in order to preserve the core capital-labour compromise in the large firms, which have only marginally rationalized these agreements.

Table 3: Two patterns of labour management in hard times: Compulsory redundancy is the instrument of last resort in Japan, not in France.

Phase	Japan	France
I	1. Reduction of overtime is easy	1. Terminate contracts with limited duration
II	2. Terminate the contracts of temporary employees	2. Reduction of overtime, but limited by legal clauses and collective agreements
III	3. Reduction of hiring of new graduates 4. Temporary assignment to other business area or group company 5. Transfer to other business 6. Strengthen sales	3. Reduction of hiring of permanent workers, replaced by temporary workers 4. Temporary factory closure 5. Compulsory redundancy
IV	7. No overtime 8. Temporary factory closure 9. Restructuring	6. Possibly negotiation in order to reduce the number of redundant workers (wage concession, less working hours)
V	10. No recruiting 11. Voluntary redundancy 12. Introduction of other new business	7. Public subsidies in order to promote early retirement, hiring of long-term unemployed, youth training schemes
VI	13. Compulsory redundancy	

Source: Abstracted from various academic research papers and case studies

Another difference between the two countries relates to the issue of wage formation: with surprising speed Japanese real wages have been adjusted to the stagnating productivity (OECD 1995: 13, Boyer 1996a: 68), whereas in France real wages have continued to grow, though at a far slower rate than productivity increases. The wage-labour nexus, therefore, is facing opposite challenges.

- In Japan, profit rates have reached their lowest level since the 1950s, preventing the likelihood of a strong recovery, while open unemployment is kept rather low (even though it has risen to 4.1 % by May 1998), a fact which preserves a certain degree of morale and commitment among workers.
- To the contrary in France, the profit rate has recovered to pre-1973 levels, while investment is relatively low, given political and the 'European' un-

certainties and, more structurally, the lack of dynamism regarding private consumption, itself linked to a high level of unemployment (more than 12 % in early 1998).

The challenges to the post-WW II institutional architectures are therefore quite different: a questionable sustainability of continued low profitability in Japan vs. the issue of social acceptance of unemployment and labour market uncertainty in France.

There is no better evidence for the role of labour market institutions in the explanation of macroeconomic and social performance: similar shocks and structural transformations trigger rather distinct reactions by these labour institutions due to given historical path dependencies.

5 Relatively common challenges, continued divergent trajectories

The issue then becomes how to analyse the current configurations of labour market institutions in both countries? This is not an easy task for economists who are prone to diagnose any type of unemployment as the direct outcome of labour market imperfections. Hence, the standard assumption is that the faster deregulation and the stimulation of competition proceed, the sooner will the current problems be overcome. The authors of this book provide a different answer, and apparently a much more satisfactory one. First of all, a lot of flexibility within the large manufacturing companies can be observed, via transfers of employees (*shukkō*) and de-industrialization processes (*kūdōka*) (Dirks, in this volume), all the while some industrial districts suffer heavily during the present quasi-stagnation (NOMURA 1997).

Secondly, the retailing sector, an important part of private service industries, is far from rigid, since it combines a complete mosaic of labour contracts from *seishain* to *pāto* and *arubaito* of various kinds (Ribault, in this volume). It would be interesting to investigate further how this labour management has been coping with new demand trends, declining for department stores, but booming for convenient stores. The hunch here being, of course, that a lot of flexibility is provided by this large diversity of labour contracts.

Institutional economics definitely is in need of a *theory of institutional change*. In this respect, the distinction between "mechanical change" (absorption of external shocks without any change related to the core principles), "organic change" (i. e., an adaptation of previous rules and principles by, for example, extending them) and finally "structural change" (i. e., a response which modifies the core principles of corporate labour management) is especially important (Nohara). These analyses advance the very enlightening framework proposed, a decade ago, by Jean-Jacques Silvestre (GAZIER ET AL. 1998). In this regard, the respective evolutionary trends in Japan and France appear to be rather different, if not opposite (table 4):

Table 4: How transformed is the wage-labour nexus in Japan and France?

Components	Japan	France	Convergence/ Divergence
1. Work organization	• Most of the competencies are still manufactured in the firm	• Progressive erosion of job demarcations towards competence enhancement	Some convergence
2. Social stratification within the firms	• Creation of a parallel track for mid-career hirings	• The split between skilled and unskilled workers is still more acute	Divergence
3. Unions	• Decline in union density and power continues	• Continuous decline and division of unions	Convergence
4. Relation with subcontractors	• Significant tensions for smaller firms • Erosion of industrial districts	• Shift of employment from large to smaller firms • Few industrial districts	Criss-Crossing
5. Adjustment of hours/ employment	• Nearly all the tools for flexibility have been used • Finally employment has been adjusted • Few changes in the legal environment	• Many new forms of labour contracts have been created and used (including part-time) • Less State intervention concerning redundancies • Many changes in laws and regulations	Still very different patterns
6. Wage formation • individual	• Slow shift from *Nenkō*-based pay (length of service and experience) to ability-based pay • Annual salary for white collars is proposed	• Diploma are still important for getting a job • More profit sharing or firm-specific pay systems	Still different patterns
• average	• Few (or minor) changes	• No clear changes	Wage moderation but different mechanisms
7. Welfare	• Some extensions of the retirement schemes	• Rationalization and trimming down of the costs of welfare	Still very different systems

- In *Japan*, many of the post-WW II traits are still present today: competencies are mostly formed within the firm, mid-career changes are limited to a small fraction of professionals. Of course, innovations have taken place: parallel employment tracks have been created by some firms; ability-based pay is more an objective pursued by firms than an already existing reality; annual salary-systems only apply to certain groups of white collars; the bulk of social welfare is still provided by the firm, one reason for existing inequalities across sectors and firm sizes. Instead of the abrupt collapse of the system, as expected by foreign experts, one observes a range of adaptation measures and experiences at the margin of existing practices, adjusting the so-called 'life-time employment' and restricting it only to those employees for whom it is a rational strategy, given the firm-specificity of the human capital which is required for competitiveness. Thus, Japan experiences more of a period of *reforms and experiments* rather than a complete vanishing or breaking down of the former employment system.
- In *France*, as well, several reforms have been tried and implemented over a period of at least two decades. The labour system, however, continues to be permeated and strongly influenced by public interventions and regulations. The shift away from a labour contract based on tasks and jobs to one enhancing individual competence is far from completed, the more so, the more permanent the dividing line between manual and intellectual work, 'skilled' and 'unskilled' workers is. A large number of new labour contracts and public interventions have been designed (part-time jobs, youth employment schemes, programmes for the long-term unemployed, training and apprenticeship schemes, new links between universities and firms, etc.). However, to this day these activities have been unable to solve the unemployment problem: the share of new types of work contracts compared to total employment is steadily growing but unemployment remains very high. Similarly, profit sharing has been promoted by the 1986 law mentioned earlier, while its beneficial effects on employment creation have, in fact, been rather limited. Moreover, educational credentials continue to be a very important criteria in order to find a job. Last but not least, subsequent French government administrations have placed the control of welfare expenditures on the top of their agenda, while the fraction of income redistributed has been increasing continuously over the last two decades.

In summary, the 'Japanese-ness' and 'French-ness' of the wage-labour nexus remain clearly conspicuous even today, in spite of the many statements from large companies and government officials regarding the ostensible need to mimic and adopt the North American labour market institutions. No overwhelming and powerful convergence is observable to date.

6 An epochal change without any clear convergence: What future for Japanese labour management?

Our conclusion is not specific to a pair-wise comparison between France and Japan, as a multi-country comparison of the wage-labour nexus would deliver a similar and therefore more general conjecture. The widely held belief is that globalization is exerting a strong competitive pressure on economic systems with their different institutional architectures. Therefore, it is often assumed that most countries will sooner or later converge toward *the* one best way: lean production for work organization, external flexibility for labour markets, profit sharing (or, alternatively, competitive wage structures) for income formation, private welfare systems for health, retirement, schools and universities. Finally, even the life-style will converge toward a cosmopolitan if not American way of life.

Graph 3: No convergence of labour contracts and institutions towards the Anglo-American configuration

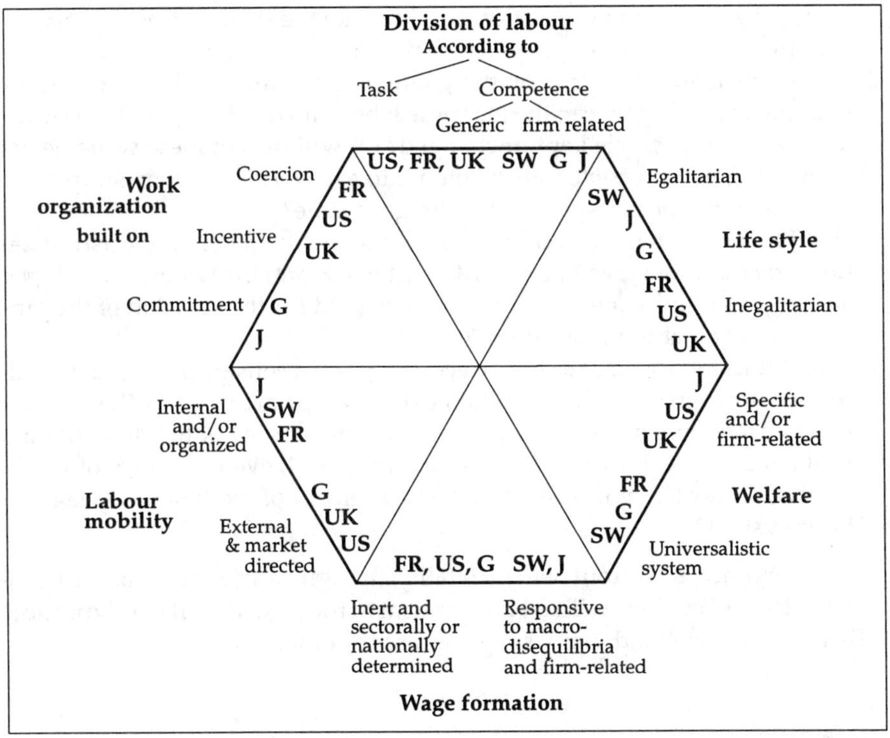

Notes: FR: France - G: Germany - J: Japan - UK: United Kingdom - US: United States - SW: Sweden

Source: BOYER (1996a: 56)

Compiling a series of international comparisons (BOYER 1995: 56), it is suggested that a large diversity of the various components of the wage-labour nexus continues to prevail in the 1990s (graph 3). According to their respective historical patterns of social struggle, economic specialization and political alliances, each country displays a highly idiosyncratic architecture of institutions governing the wage-labour nexus. Of course, with respect to most of this nexus' components, Japan appears to occupy a relatively extreme position along the entire spectrum of configurations. Provided that each of these configurations is associated with labour costs or product quality in line with foreign competition, these institutions can be reproduced and/or marginally transformed by piecemeal innovations and normal attrition of obsolete technologies and labour contracts (BOYER 1996b: 52).

In spite of the large given hysteresis, *various scenarios* are available to the Japanese labour management. Their likeliness will depend on the answers given to the following questions:

1. Provided the bad-debt problem can be resolved at last, the Japanese labour institutions may experience only *limited* transformations, along the trajectory followed after the first oil shock and *endaka* (yen appreciation). On the contrary, a protracted stagnation would make the structural *aggiornamiento* of the Japanese employment system more and more likely.
2. Given the aspirations held by the younger generation and the new international role of Japan, can the Japanese labour institutions and the prevailing management style kept unchanged? Or will the Japanese wage nexus be slowly but *irreversibly* transformed into a *totally new* system, simply because socially the old system is no longer viable?
3. Will Japanese foreign direct investment initiate the same de-industrialization process as observed previously for the UK and the US, and could *open and large* unemployment be the cost to be paid for the survival of the Japanese-ness of labour institutions?
4. Could the shift towards a service economy and a consumption-led growth induce a progressive *decay* of the post-WWII principles and the *re-emergence* of a more conventional wage-labour nexus? Is not the deregulation of the service sector (distribution, retailing) and, even more so, of the financial sector a major threat to the slow reform of the Japanese wage-labour system?

Convergence is far from being a fatality, though clearly the Japanese economy of the 21st century will not be identical to the post-WW II configuration. History lasts long, and many surprises are to come.

References

AMABLE, B., R. BARRE and R. BOYER (1997): *Les systèmes d'innovation à l'ère de la globalisation*. Paris: Economica.

AOKI, M. (1988): *Information, Incentives and Bargaining in the Japanese Economy.* Cambridge: Cambridge University Press.

BERGER, S. and R. DORE (1996): *National Diversity and Global Capitalism.* Ithaca: Cornell University Press.

BOYER, R. (1995): The Future of Unions: Is the Anglo-Saxon Model a Fatality, or Will Contrasting National Trajectories Persist? In: *British Journal of Industrial Relations* 33, 4, December, pp. 545–556.

BOYER, R. (1996a): *The Transformations of the Japanese Employment System and Post-Toyotism: What Lessons for Europe?* Mimeograph CEPREMAP, May.

BOYER, R. (1996b): The Convergence Hypothesis Revisited: Globalization but Still the Century of Nations. In: BERGER, S. and R. DORE (eds.): *National Diversity and Global Capitalism.* Ithaca: Cornell University Press, pp. 29–59.

BROWN, C., M. REICH and D. STERN (1990): Skills and Security in Evolving Employment Systems: Observations from Case Studies. Paper presented at the *Conference on Changing Occupational Skill Requirements: Gathering and Assessing the Evidence.* Brown University, 5–6 June, 1990.

CAROLI, E. (1995): Croissance et formation: le rōle de la politique éducative. In: *Economie et Prévision*, n° 116, 5, pp. 49–65.

DORE, R. (1986): *Flexible Rigidities.* London: The Athlone Press.

EBIZUKA, A., H. UEMURA and A. ISOGAI (1997): L'hypothèse de 'la relation hiérarchisée marché-firme' et l'économie japonaise de l'après guerre. In: *L'année de la Régulation 1997*, Vol. 1, Novembre. Paris: La Découverte, pp. 297–315.

GAREY, J., F. JANY-CATRICE and T. RIBAULT (1997): *France-Japon: L'emploi en détail. Essai de socio-économie comparative.* Rapport de Recherche Commissariat Général du Plan, MESR, IFRESI. Tōkyō: Maison Franco-Japonaise de Tokyo.

GAZIER, B., D. MARSDEN and J. J. SILVESTRE (1998): *Repenser l'économie du travail. De l'effet d'entreprise á l'effet societal.* Toulouse: Octares.

GEOFFRON, P. and M. RUBINSTEIN (1996): *La crise financière du modèle japonais.* Paris: Economica.

KOIKE, K. (1988): *Understanding Industrial Relations in Japan.* New York: Saint Martin Press.

MIYASHITA, K. and D. RUSSELL (1996): *Keiretsu: Inside the Hidden Japanese Conglomerates.* New York: MacGraw Hill.

NOMURA, M. (1997): Is Japanese Management Sustainable? Japanese Employment Practices in the 1990s. Paper presented at the conference *Between External Shocks and Internal Evolution: Towards a New Phase in Japanese Management Practices.* Maison Franco-Japonaise/German Institute for Japanese Studies, Tōkyō, October 30th–November 1st, 1997.

NORTH, D. (1990): *Institutions, Institutional Change and Economic Performance.* Cambridge: Cambridge University Press.

OECD (1995, 1996, 1997): *Perspectives de l'emploi.* Paris: OECD.

SAUTTER, Ch. (1996): *La France au miroir du Japon.* Paris: Editions Odile Jacob.

Tachibanaki, T. (1996): *Wage Determination and Distribution in Japan*. Oxford: Clarendon Press.

Womack, J. P., D. Jones and D. Roos (1990): *The Machine that Changed the World*. New York: MacMillan.

Yamada, T. (1996): Capitalisme japonais et compromis companie-iste face à la crise. Paper presented at the conference on *Capitalisme japonais et crise contemporaine: recherches recentes*. Paris, 16–18 December, 1996.

Yui, T. and K. Nakagawa (eds.) (1989): *Japanese Management In Historical Perspective*. Tōkyō: University of Tokyo Press.

The Authors

Robert Boyer is head of the CNRS research unit on 'Regulation, Human Resources and Economic Policies', economist at CEPREMAP, and lecturer at E.H.E.S.S. (Ecoles des Hautes Etudes en Sciences Sociales). His research areas concern economic history, macroeconomic modelling, and international labour market comparisons. He has published widely on these topics, among others *The Regulation School: A Critical Introduction* (Columbia University Press, New York, 1990), *The Search for Labour Market Flexibility* (Clarendon Press, Oxford, 1988) and *Contemporary Capitalism: The Embeddedness of Institutions* (ed., with Rogers Hollingsworth, Cambridge University Press, UK, 1997).

Daniel Dirks is head of the Economics Department and Vice-Director of the German Institute for Japanese Studies (DIJ) in Tōkyō. He received his Ph.D. at Witten/Herdecke University, Germany's first private university, where he also worked as lecturer before coming to Tōkyō in 1994. His research interests cover the restructuring activities of Japanese companies with a current emphasis on the human resource field.

Dieter Ernst is SSF research professor of international management at the Department of Industrial Economics and Strategy, Copenhagen Business School, and a senior research fellow at the Berkeley Roundtable on the International Economy (BRIE), University of California at Berkeley. Until 1992, he was a senior advisor at the OECD Development Centre (Paris). For over two decades, he has written about technology and international competition in various industries, and their implications for corporate organizations and strategies, as well as government policies.

Jean-François Estienne, a former fellow at the Maison Franco-Japonaise in Tōkyō, is an economist and demographer, specializing in finance, pension and life insurance systems. He is currently concluding a Ph.D. in economics on the future of pension systems in OECD countries with a focus on Japan. He has published a book (in French) on pensions and aging in Japan, and articles on Japan's demography, life insurance markets and pension systems.

Takahiro (Taka) Fujimoto has been an associate professor at Tokyo University's faculty of economics since 1990, and a senior research associate of Harvard Business School (HBS) since 1997. He graduated from Tokyo University and joined the Mitsubishi Research Institute as researcher and consultant in 1979. He was enrolled in the DBA course in Production and Operations Management at Harvard Business School between 1984 and 1989, where he wrote his doctoral thesis, *Organizations for Effective Product Development –The Case of the Global Automobile Industry.* He was a research associate at HBS in 1989–1990. His main publications in English include: *Product Development Performance: Strategy, Organization, and Management in the World Auto Industry* (1991), with Kim B. Clark; and *The Evolution of a Manufacturing System,* Oxford University Press (forthcoming), as well as numerous contributions to international journals and book editions.

Klaus Grefermann studied economics and technical science at the University of Hamburg, Germany, and Universitas Indonesia in Bogor, completing his Ph.D. in 1964. He has worked for several years as a consultant with a leading German company before becoming a senior research officer at the ifo Institute Munich. Since 1992, he has been the head of ifo's Industry Department. Holding leading positions in several industrial and research organizations, his main areas of research comprise corporate strategy, sector analyses, technical change, renewable natural resources, advertising and media, and economic forecasting.

Martin Hemmert is a research fellow with the German Research Association (DFG) at Essen University. He graduated in Business Administration at the University of Cologne in 1989 and received his doctoral degree from the same university in 1993. Previous positions have been those of research assistant at the Chair for Corporate Finance of the University of Cologne (1989–90), visiting researcher at the Institute of Business Research at Hitotsubashi University (1990–93), and research associate at the German Institute for Japanese Studies in Tōkyō (1993–98). His main fields of research are innovation management and industrial organization.

Jean-François Huchet is senior researcher at the French Research Centre on Contemporary China in Hong Kong since April 1997 after being senior researcher at the Maison Franco-Japonaise in Tōkyō from 1994 to 1997. He received his Ph.D. in Economics at Rennes University, France, where he also worked as lecturer in economics. He spent four years at Beijing University, P. R. of China, between 1987 and 1991 to complete his Ph.D. field research. His research interests cover the restructuring process of Chinese state enterprises, the structuration of Chinese corporate groups and the internationalization of Japanese firms

Marc Humbert is professor at the University of Rennes 1. He is director of the Research and Study Center on Enterprises, Technology, Institutions and Globalization (CERETIM).

Naoto Iwasaki is professor at the Faculty of Economics, Seijo University, Tōkyō. His major fields of interest are international management and business strategy. He is an expert in the areas of old established companies and human resource management in Japan. He has presented papers on both subjects at many international conferences.

Jacques Jaussaud is a senior lecturer in management at IAE, The University of Poitiers (France). His research interests lie in the areas of business strategy and human resource management (with a particular focus on Japan and Asian countries). He has published widely in these areas and is the editor of the French management journal, *Japon in Extenso.*

Tadao Kagono is professor of general management at the Graduate School of Business, Kōbe University. His principal areas of research include the cross-cultural comparison of management, organizational processes of strategy formulation and implementation, restructuring and transformation issues. He has published more than a dozen books including two in English, *Strategic vs. Evolutionary Management* (North Holland) and *How Japanese Companies Work* (Nihon Keizai Shinbun).

Ken Kusunoki is an associate professor at the Faculty of Commerce and the Institute of Innovation Research, Hitotsubashi University, Tōkyō. His current research interests lie in the organizational capabilities for technological innovation, especially in the electronics industries. His publications have appeared in many Japanese and international journals.

Yveline Lecler, doctor in social sciences (EHESS), is an associate professor at Lyon III University, and a senior research fellow at the Institute of East Asian Studies (Lyon II and III universities and CNRS). She has written numerous articles on Japanese SMEs, the subcontracting system, purchasing networks, and the globalization of the Japanese economy. In addition, she has published a book on industrial partnership in France and Japan.

Yannick Lung is professor of economics at the Université Montesquieu-Bordeaux IV (Research fields: Regional and Industrial Economics). He is co-director of the programme „Between Globalisation and Regionalisation: What Future for the Automobile Industry?" of the GERPISA-international network (Université d'Evry-Val d'Essonne & CRH-EHESS, Paris). He has published various books and papers on the automobile industry, and here particularly on the Japanese firms (internationalization strategies and management of product variety).

Hideaki Miyajima is professor at the School of Commerce, Waseda University, Tōkyō. He received an BA and M A in economics at Rikkyo University, Tōkyō, and from 1980–1985 worked at Tokyo University's Graduate School of Economics. Following a stay as research associate at the Institute of Social Sciences, Tokyo University (1985–87), he assumed his current position at Waseda University in 1995. He has published widely on issues of deregulation, corporate governance, and finance. Two major recent works are *Gendai Nihon Keizai* (Contemporary Japanese Economy), Yuhikaku, Tōkyō 1998 as co-author and *Competing Policies for Competitiveness; Business Government Relationships in the Golden Age of Capitalism.* Oxford University Press, forthcoming, as co-editor.

Corrado Molteni received a Doctor of Philosophy degree in Social Studies at Hitotsubashi University, Tōkyō, in 1986, following his Bachelor's degree in Economics and Business Administration at the Università Commerciale Luigi Bocconi, Milano (Italy), 1977. His current position is that of an affiliate professor of comparative economic systems and head of research at ISESAO – Institute of Economic and Social Studies for East Asia, Università Commerciale Luigi Bocconi, Milano.

Hiroatsu Nohara received his bachelor degree in economics in 1976 at Keiō University, Tōkyō, and his *Docteur en Economie* (3ème cycle) in 1981 at the Université d'Aix-Marseille II. Since 1984 he has been a research fellow at the CNRS (National Centre of Scientific Research) in France, and between 1994–1996 he was a visiting fellow at the Maison Franco-Japonaise in Tōkyō.

Thierry Ribault is researcher at the National Center for Scientific Research in Lille, France (CNRS). He received his Ph.D in economics at the University of Lille. He held a research position at the Maison Franco-Japonaise in Tōkyō from 1995 to 1997 in charge of an international comparative analysis of employment in retailing. His current interests deal with employment and human resources in the Japanese service sector.

Xavier Richet is professor of economics at the university of Marne la Vallee, France, where he is the head of GASI, a research centre specialized in conducting research on comparative economic systems, transition economies and new market economies. He presently works on the financial and industrial restructuring of firms in former Soviet-type economies and in China and Vietnam. He has published numerous books and articles on these issues.

Dennis S. Tachiki is a senior research fellow at the Center for Pacific Business Studies at the Sakura Institute of Research in Tōkyō. He has taught at the University of Minnesota, University of Michigan, and Sophia University. His current research areas cover the strategic management and technology transfer of Asian companies.

Tōru Takai is associate professor of international management at Obirin University, Tōkyō. He has been conducting research on international strategy and management, and the formation and implementation of strategic alliances. His current research interests focus on comparative studies of global companies in Japan and America.

Yoshiya Teramoto is professor of management and organizational behaviour at the Graduate School of Japan, Advanced Institute of Science and Technology. He has been researching on innovation and internalization within industrial networks. His publications on the topics of *network power, learning organizations, corporate governance,* etc. have appeared in various English and Japanese journals and books. He is currently investigating the dynamics of change in large Japanese corporations.

Diane-Gabrielle Tremblay is professor of economics and human resource management (HRM) as well as director of research at the Télé-université of Québec, Canada. She is also president of the Association of Political Economy, and member of the executive board of the Sociology of Work RC of the International Sociological Association. She has published numerous books and articles in the fields of labour economics, sociology of work, innovation, and Japanese vs. North American HRM and work organization.

Yasuhiro Ueno is associate professor of business policy at the Ōsaka Prefecture University. He studies diversification strategies and the role of headquarters of Japanese large corporations. He has published a book and articles including *The Performance Diversification among Japanese Large Corporations* (Ōsaka Prefecture University, in Japanese).

Shigeru Watanabe is a senior researcher at the Nomura Research Institute, and currently a visiting fellow at the Hoover Institution, Stanford University. On the subject of Japanese corporate finance, he has published *ROE Kakumei* (ROE Revolution), Tōyō Keizai Shinpōsha, Tōkyō, 1994). He has an MBA from the Graduate School of Business Administration, Harvard University.

Susumu Watanabe is professor of economics at Tokyo International University. Before assuming his current position in 1988, he worked at economic research units of the International Labour Office, Geneva, for 20 years. He has published numerous articles, mostly in English, on technology, labour and industrialization as well as on the Japanese economy. He is editor/author of *Microelectronics, Automation and Employment in the Automobile Industry* (John Wiley, 1987) and *Microelectronics and Third-World Industries* (Macmillan, 1993).

Axel v. Werder is a professor of business administration, especially organization theory and general management, at the faculty of economics and management, Technical University of Berlin, Germany. His current research interests concentrate on the argumentation rationality of management decisions, corporate governance, the development of generally accepted standards for top management, and concepts for the evaluation of organization structures.

Norihisa Yoshimura is assistant professor of business strategy at the faculty of economics, Wakayama University. He studies governance structures and the role of corporate headquarters of Japanese large corporations and has published several articles in this area.

Tsunehiko Yui is professor emer. at Meiji University's Department of Business Administration and an executive director of both the Business History Society of Japan and the Japan Business History Institute, as well as editorial advisor to *Business History* (U.K.). He received his Ph.D. in economics from the University of Tokyo and has been a guest professor at Harvard University, the London School of Economics and the University of Tokyo. He has published widely on Japanese economic and business history. His book *Development of Japanese Business* (in Japanese; English translation with J. Hirshmeier, 2nd. ed. 1981) was awarded the Yūshū Keizai Tosho Bunkashō (Excellence Award for Publications in Economics) in 1978 by the Nihon Keizai Shinbunsha.

Index